Fundamentals of Social Psychology

CANADIAN EDITION

Fundamentals of Social Psychology

CANADIAN EDITION

ELLIOT ARONSON
University of California, Santa Cruz

TIMOTHY D. WILSON
University of Virginia

ROBIN M. AKERT
Wellesley College

BEVERLEY FEHR
University of Winnipeg

Toronto

Library and Archives Canada Cataloguing in Publication

Fundamentals of social psychology / Elliot Aronson ... [et al.]. — Canadian ed.

Includes index.
ISBN 0-13-127584-4

1. Social psychology—Textbooks.   I. Aronson, Elliot

HM1033.F85 2006   302   C2005-903519-6

Copyright © 2006 Pearson Education Canada Inc., Toronto, Ontario.

Original edition entitled *Social Psychology* published by Pearson Education, Inc., Upper Saddle River, NJ. Copyright © 2005 by Pearson Education, Inc.

Pearson Prentice Hall. All rights reserved. This publication is protected by copyright and permission should be obtained from the publisher prior to any prohibited reproduction, storage in a retrieval system, or transmission in any form or by any means, electronic, mechanical, photocopying, recording, or likewise. For information regarding permission, write to the Permissions Department.

ISBN 0-13-127584-4

Vice President, Editorial Director: Michael J. Young
Senior Acquisitions Editor: Ky Pruesse
Signing Representative: Duncan MacKinnon
Executive Marketing Manager: Judith Allen
Developmental Editors: Lise Dupont, Suzanne Schaan
Production Editor: Kevin Leung
Copy Editor: Susan Broadhurst
Proofreader: Kathleen E. Richards
Production Coordinator: Peggy Brown
Permissions Research: Amanda McCormick
Photo Research: Lisa Brant
Composition: Joan M. Wilson
Art Director: Julia Hall
Cover and Interior Design: Miguel Acevedo
Cover Image: Getty Images/Taxi

1 2 3 4 5   10 09 08 07 06

Printed and bound in Canada.

To my grandchildren: Jacob, Jason, Ruth, Eliana, Natalie, Rachel, and Leo Aronson. My hope is that your wonderful capacity for empathy and compassion will help make the world a better place.

E.A.

To my family: Deirdre Smith, Christopher and Leigh Wilson.

T.D.W.

To my mentor, colleague, and friend, Dane Archer.

R.M.A.

To my family: Marvin, Genevieve, and Everett.

B.F.

Brief Contents

Preface   xvi

About the Authors   xxviii

CHAPTER 1   Introduction to Social Psychology   3

CHAPTER 2   Methodology: How Social Psychologists Do Research   21

CHAPTER 3   Social Cognition and Social Perception: How We Perceive and Think about the Social World   47

CHAPTER 4   Self-Knowledge and Self-Evaluation: Self-Understanding and the Need to Maintain Self-Esteem   83

CHAPTER 5   Attitudes and Attitude Change: Influencing Thoughts, Feelings, and Behaviour   119

CHAPTER 6   Conformity: Influencing Others   161

CHAPTER 7   Group Processes: Influence in Social Groups   195

CHAPTER 8   Interpersonal Attraction: From First Impressions to Close Relationships   229

CHAPTER 9   Prosocial Behaviour and Aggression: Helping and Harming Others   265

CHAPTER 10   Prejudice: Causes and Cures   309

Glossary   344

References   350

Credits   388

Name Index   393

Subject Index   407

Contents

Preface · xvi
About the Authors · xxviii

CHAPTER 1 Introduction to Social Psychology · 3

What Is Social Psychology? · 6
Social Psychology Compared to Sociology · 6
Social Psychology Compared to Personality Psychology · 7

The Power of Social Influence · 8

■ **FOCUS ON APPLICATIONS** The Fundamental Attribution Error: When We Blame the Victims of Violence · 9

■ **TRY IT!** Social Situations and Behaviour · 9

Underestimating the Power of Social Influence · 10
The Subjectivity of the Social Situation · 12

Social Psychology and Social Problems · 13

CHAPTER 2 Methodology: How Social Psychologists Do Research · 21

Social Psychology: An Empirical Science · 22

Formulating Hypotheses and Theories · 23

Descriptive Methods: Describing

Social Behaviour · 25
The Observational Method · 25

■ **FOCUS ON APPLICATIONS** Putting a Stop to Bullying: Can Social Psychological Research Help? · 25

The Correlational Method · 26

■ **TRY IT!** Correlation Does Not Equal Causation · 29

The Experimental Method: Answering Causal Questions · 30
Independent and Dependent Variables · 32
Internal Validity in Experiments · 32
External Validity in Experiments · 34

■ **FOCUS ON APPLICATIONS** When Experiments Mirror the Real World: Does Watching Violence on TV Actually Make You More Aggressive?   35

Ethical Issues in Social Psychology   37

CHAPTER 3   Social Cognition and Social Perception: How We Perceive and Think about the Social World   47

People as Everyday Theorists: Schemas and Their Influence   49

■ **FOCUS ON APPLICATIONS** Social Psychology in the Courtroom: Does It Matter How Lawyers Present Evidence?   50

Which Schemas Are Applied? Accessibility and Priming   51

Mental Strategies and Shortcuts: Heuristics   54
How Easily Does It Come to Mind? The Availability Heuristic   54
How Similar Is A to B? The Representativeness Heuristic   55
Taking Things at Face Value: The Anchoring and Adjustment Heuristic   56

■ **TRY IT!** Reasoning Quiz   58

Automatic versus Controlled Thinking   59

■ **FOCUS ON APPLICATIONS** Can Automatic Thinking Cost You Your Life?   61

Causal Attribution: Answering the "Why" Question   62
The Nature of the Attributional Process   62

■ **TRY IT!** Listen as People Make Attributions   63

■ **FOCUS ON APPLICATIONS** The Role of Attributions in Making the Adjustment to College or University   64

The Fundamental Attribution Error: People as Personality Psychologists   65
The Actor/Observer Difference   70
Self-serving Attributions   72

■ **TRY IT!** Self-serving Attributions in the Sports Pages   74

CHAPTER 4   Self-Knowledge and Self-Evaluation: Self-Understanding and the Need to Maintain Self-Esteem   83

The Nature of the Self   84
Cultural Differences in the Definition of Self   85

■ **TRY IT!** A Measure of Self-Concept Clarity   86

Gender Differences in the Definition of Self   88

■ **TRY IT!** A Measure of Relational Interdependence	89
Knowing Ourselves through Introspection	**90**
Focusing on the Self: Self-Awareness Theory	91
Knowing Ourselves through Observations of Our Own Behaviour	**93**
Inferring Who We Are from How We Behave: Self-Perception Theory	93
Knowing Ourselves through Self-Schemas	**94**
Knowing Ourselves through Social Interaction	**95**
Seeing Ourselves through the Eyes of Others: The Looking-glass Self	95
Knowing Ourselves by Comparing Ourselves to Others	97
The Need to Feel Good about Ourselves	**97**
Social Comparison Revisited	98
■ **FOCUS ON APPLICATIONS** Promoting Social Good through Social Comparison	99
Self-Discrepancy Theory	100
Self-Evaluation Maintenance Theory	102
■ **FOCUS ON APPLICATIONS** Distancing in the Family: A Way to Restore Self-Esteem?	104
Self-Affirmation Theory	105
■ **FOCUS ON APPLICATIONS** Using Our Close Relationships to Get a Self-Esteem Boost	106
Self-Evaluation: Biased or Accurate?	**108**
Self-Enhancement: Wanting to Feel Good about Ourselves, Regardless of the Facts	108
Self-Verification: Wanting to Know the Truth about Ourselves	109

CHAPTER 5 Attitudes and Attitude Change: Influencing Thoughts, Feelings, and Behaviour — 119

The Nature and Origin of Attitudes	**120**
Where Do Attitudes Come From?	120
■ **TRY IT!** Affective and Cognitive Bases of Attitudes	122
When Will Attitudes Predict Behaviour?	**123**
The Theory of Planned Behaviour: Implications for Safer Sex	126
Attitude Change	**127**
Persuasive Communications and Attitude Change	127
Fear and Attitude Change	131
Advertising and Attitude Change	133

How to Make People Resistant to Persuasion Attempts	137
Attitude Inoculation	137
■ **FOCUS ON APPLICATIONS** Using Social Psychology to Resist Peer Pressure	138
Changing Attitudes by Changing Our Behaviour: The Theory of Cognitive Dissonance	138
Decisions, Decisions, Decisions	140
■ **FOCUS ON APPLICATIONS** Can Dissonance Reduction Change Your Moral Standards?	141
■ **TRY IT!** Justifying Decisions	141
The Justification of Effort	142
■ **TRY IT!** Justifying Actions	144
The Psychology of Insufficient Justification	145
■ **FOCUS ON APPLICATIONS** Conserving Water	147
The Aftermath of Bad Deeds: How We Come to Hate Our Victims	149
Avoiding the Rationalization Trap	151
Learning from Our Mistakes	151
The Solar Temple Revisited	152

CHAPTER 6   Conformity: Influencing Others — 161

Conformity: When and Why	162
Informational Social Influence: The Need to Know What Is "Right"	163
When Will People Conform to Informational Social Influence?	165
■ **TRY IT!** Informational Social Influence and Emergencies	166
Normative Social Influence: The Need to Be Accepted	167
■ **FOCUS ON APPLICATIONS** Can Conformity Pressure Be Used to Increase Social Good? The Case of Littering	169
■ **TRY IT!** Unveiling Normative Social Influence by Breaking the Rules	169
Conformity and Social Approval: The Asch Line Judgment Studies	170
■ **FOCUS ON APPLICATIONS** How Do You Feel about Your Body?	172
When Will People Conform to Normative Social Influence?	173
Resisting Normative Social Influence	175
Minority Influence: When the Few Influence the Many	176
■ **FOCUS ON APPLICATIONS** Minority Influence in the Courtroom	176

Compliance: Requests to Change Your Behaviour	**177**
The Door-in-the-Face Technique	177
The Foot-in-the-Door Technique	179
Lowballing	180
Obedience to Authority	**181**
The Role of Normative Social Influence	183
The Role of Informational Social Influence	184

CHAPTER 7 Group Processes: Influence in Social Groups — 195

Definitions: What Is a Group?	**196**
Why Do People Join Groups?	197
The Composition and Function of Groups	197
How Groups Influence the Behaviour of Individuals	**199**
Social Facilitation: When the Presence of Others Energizes Us	199
■ **FOCUS ON APPLICATIONS** Performance in the Pool Hall: Does It Matter Whether Other People Are Watching You?	200
Social Loafing: When the Presence of Others Relaxes Us	202
Deindividuation: Getting Lost in the Crowd	205
■ **FOCUS ON APPLICATIONS** Sports and Aggression: Does What You Wear Change Who You Are?	207
Group Decisions: Are Two (or More) Heads Better than One?	**208**
Process Loss: When Group Interactions Inhibit Good Problem Solving	208
Group Polarization: Going to Extremes	211
■ **TRY IT!** Choice Dilemmas Questionnaire	212
Leadership in Groups	213
Conflict and Cooperation	**216**
Using Threats to Resolve Conflict	216
Negotiation and Bargaining	218

CHAPTER 8 Interpersonal Attraction: From First Impressions to Close Relationships — 229

Major Antecedents of Attraction	**231**
The Person Next Door: The Propinquity Effect	231

■ **FOCUS ON APPLICATIONS** Long-distance Propinquity: The Formation of Internet Relationships . . . 232
Similarity . . . 233
Reciprocal Liking . . . 234
The Effects of Physical Attractiveness on Liking . . . 235
Attraction and the Misattribution of Arousal . . . 238

Forming and Maintaining Close Relationships . . . **240**
What Is Love? . . . 240

■ **TRY IT!** The Passionate Love Scale . . . 241
The Role of Positive Illusions in Maintaining Relationships . . . 245
Why Do We Form and Maintain Relationships? . . . 245

■ **FOCUS ON APPLICATIONS** Youth and Beauty versus Status and Wealth: Gender Differences in Personal Ads . . . 246

■ **TRY IT!** What's Your Style? . . . 249

Ending Close Relationships . . . **254**
Why Relationships End . . . 254
The Experience of Breaking Up . . . 256

CHAPTER 9 Prosocial Behaviour and Aggression: Helping and Harming Others . . . 265

Basic Motives Underlying Prosocial Behaviour: Why Do People Help? . . . **267**
Evolutionary Psychology: Instincts and Genes . . . 267
Social Exchange: The Costs and Rewards of Helping . . . 268
Empathy and Altruism: The Pure Motive for Helping . . . 269

Personal Determinants of Prosocial Behaviour: Why Do Some People Help More than Others? . . . **273**
Gender Differences in Prosocial Behaviour . . . 273
The Effects of Mood on Prosocial Behaviour . . . 274

■ **TRY IT!** Mood and Helping Behaviour . . . 275

Situational Determinants of Prosocial Behaviour: When Will People Help? . . . **276**

■ **FOCUS ON APPLICATIONS** Are We Less Helpful When We're in a Hurry? . . . 277

How Can Helping Be Increased? . . . **282**
Instilling Helpfulness with Rewards and Models . . . 282

- **FOCUS ON APPLICATIONS** Does Reading This Chapter Make You a More Helpful Person? — 283

Aggression: Why We Hurt Other People — 284
What Is Aggression? — 284
Is Aggression Inborn or Is It Learned? — 284

Situational Causes of Aggression — 285
Imitation and Aggression — 286

- **FOCUS ON APPLICATIONS** Does Playing Violent Video Games Increase Aggression? — 288

Violent Pornography and Sexual Aggression — 288
Frustration as a Cause of Aggression — 290
Direct Provocation and Reciprocation — 291

- **TRY IT!** Insults and Aggression — 292

Alcohol — 292
Social Exclusion — 293
Aggressive Objects as a Cause of Aggression — 294
Gender Differences in Aggression — 294

- **TRY IT!** The Incidence of Violence in Intimate Relationships — 296

How to Reduce Aggression — 297
Does Punishing Aggression Reduce Aggressive Behaviour? — 297
Catharsis and Aggression — 298
What Are We Supposed to Do with Our Anger? — 299

CHAPTER 10 Prejudice: Causes and Cures — 309

Prejudice: The Ubiquitous Social Phenomenon — 310

- **TRY IT!** Multiculturalism: Is It Working? — 310

Prejudice, Stereotyping, and Discrimination Defined — 312
Prejudice: The Affective Component — 312
Stereotypes: The Cognitive Component — 312

- **TRY IT!** Stereotype Content: Where Does It Come From? — 313

Discrimination: The Behavioural Component — 314

- **FOCUS ON APPLICATIONS** Discrimination in the Housing Market: Can You Rent a Place if You Are Gay? — 314

What Causes Prejudice? — **314**
The Way We Think: Social Cognition — 315
What We Believe: Stereotypes — 318
The Way We Feel: Affect and Mood — 322

Effects of Stereotyping, Prejudice, and Discrimination — **324**

■ **FOCUS ON APPLICATIONS** "I'm Not as Good as You": When Targets of Prejudice Come to Despise Their Own Group — 324

Self-fulfilling Prophecies — 325
Self-blaming Attributions for Discrimination — 326
Stereotype Threat — 327

How Can Prejudice and Discrimination Be Reduced? — **329**
Learning Not to Hate — 329
Revising Stereotypical Beliefs — 330
The Contact Hypothesis — 331
Cooperation and Interdependence: The Jigsaw Classroom — 333

■ **TRY IT!** Jigsaw-Type Group Study — 335

Glossary — 344

References — 350

Credits — 388

Name Index — 393

Subject Index — 407

Preface

Fundamentals of Social Psychology, Canadian Edition, is an exciting new project. Building on our experience of writing a comprehensive text (*Social Psychology*, by Aronson, Wilson, Akert, and Fehr) and on the generous feedback that we have received on that text from students and professors alike, we have developed this alternative text.

Drawing on both classic and contemporary research, *Fundamentals of Social Psychology* combines a scientific approach and a focus on applications to cover the essential content. The excitement of social psychology is transmitted when students understand the whole context of the field: how theories inspire research; why research is performed as it is; how further research triggers new avenues of study. We have tried to convey our own fascination with the research process in a down-to-earth, meaningful way and have presented the results of the scientific process in terms of the everyday experience of the reader. However, we did not want to "water down" our presentation of the field. In a world where human behaviour can be endlessly surprising and where research results can be quite counterintuitive, it is important to prepare students by providing a firm foundation on which to build their understanding of this challenging discipline. An additional goal of this first Canadian edition of *Fundamentals of Social Psychology* is to capture the excitement of social psychology for students in Canada by presenting the field in a Canadian context.

Read on to learn more about the features, approach, and themes of the book.

COVERAGE OF CORE CONCEPTS

We set out to create a text that was considerably shorter than *Social Psychology*. How did we achieve that? By listening to what instructors and students said was important to them, we were able to streamline the coverage and focus on the core concepts of the discipline. This new book has only 10 chapters, compared to 13 in our comprehensive text. The topics of social cognition and social perception have been condensed into a single chapter, "Social Cognition and Social Perception: How We Perceive and Think About the Social World" (Chapter 3). The examination of self is now highlighted in a single chapter, "Self-Knowledge and Self-Evaluation: Self-Understanding and the Need to Maintain Self-Esteem" (Chapter 4). Chapter 9, "Prosocial Behaviour and Aggression: Helping and Harming Others," combines coverage of two sides of human behaviour. Throughout the rest of the chapters, we have focused on presenting the key ideas in an accessible way.

To accommodate the diverse ways in which instructors may choose to present topics, we have tried to create a sensible, yet flexible, organization. Each chapter of *Fundamentals of Social Psychology* is self-contained in terms of topics and concepts. Consequently, instructors can assign the chapters in any order they please; concepts are always explained in clear terms so that students won't need to have read earlier chapters in order to grasp the meanings of later ones. In whatever way you choose to arrange your course, we are confident that this text presents social psychology in a way that is sure to engage and fascinate students in Canada.

FEATURES

The key features of *Fundamentals of Social Psychology* are designed to engage students, help them learn, and encourage them to further explore topics of interest.

Chapter opening vignette. Each chapter opens with a real-life story that demonstrates key concepts covered in the chapter. These vignettes are referred to throughout the chapter, to bring the concepts to life.

Focus on Applications. These boxed features highlight social psychology studies that have been applied to real-world issues.

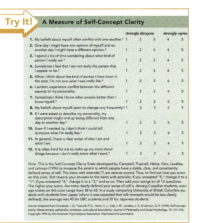

Try It! This feature provides students with the opportunity to apply the concepts they are learning to everyday life. Additional Try It! exercises are offered on the Companion Website for this text.

Thinking Critically. Found at the end of each major section within each chapter, these critical thinking questions encourage students to stop and consider the concepts covered.

Figures and tables. Throughout the text, figures and tables are used to illustrate and reinforce the concepts discussed.

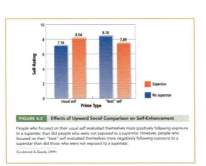

Live!Psych icons. Each Live!Psych icon in the margin indicates that an interactive simulation demonstrating the topic at hand can be found on the Companion Website.

Classic Research icons. Each Classic Research icon flags seminal research that has shaped the development of social psychology as a discipline of study.

Key terms and glossary. Key terms are shown in **boldface** where they first appear in the text, with a clear definition provided in the margin. Definitions are also gathered together in the Glossary at the end of the book.

> **Independent variable** the variable a researcher changes or varies to see if it has an effect on some other variable
>
> **Dependent variable** the variable a researcher measures to see if it is influenced by the independent variable; the researcher hypothesizes that the dependent variable will depend on the level of the independent variable

Quotations. Quotations from well-known authors in a variety of fields appear in the margin and provide added perspectives.

> Television has brought murder back into the home—where it belongs.
> —ALFRED HITCHCOCK, 1965

End-of-Chapter Study Aids

Summary. A brief summary at the end of each chapter highlights the key points in each section.

Key Terms and Key Online Search Terms. At the end of each chapter, a list of key terms offers an opportunity for quick review. The online search terms provide a tool for students to do further research on specific topics by searching for online resources.

Preface | xvii

If You Are Interested. This section provides suggestions for further reading.

Weblinks. A list of relevant websites offers yet another research tool.

Practice Quiz. A practice quiz at the end of each chapter uses multiple-choice, true/false, and fill-in-the-blank questions to test basic knowledge of the key concepts in the chapter. Students can also check their progress by visiting the Companion Website, where these quiz questions are incorporated into self-grading tests. Each test generates a Study Plan that shows students which specific sections of the chapter require further study to improve marks.

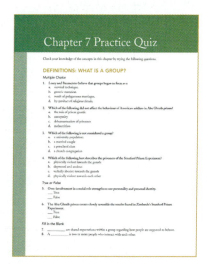

A STORYTELLING APPROACH

Social psychology is full of good stories, such as how the actions of people like Greg Baytalan—who cut short his vacation in Australia to assist in the grisly task of unloading the bodies of tsunami victims in Thailand—can be explained; how the Holocaust inspired investigations into obedience to authority and how this research helps us understand the recent abuse of Iraqi prisoners by American soldiers; and how reactions to the marriage of the Crown Prince of Japan to Masako Owada, a career diplomat, illustrate cultural differences in the self-concept. By placing research in a real-world context, we make the material more familiar, understandable, and memorable.

Opening Vignettes

Each chapter begins with a real-life vignette that epitomizes the concepts to come. We refer to this event at several points in the chapter to illustrate to students the relevance of the material they are learning. To show how the opening vignettes are tied to social psychological principles, here are a few examples:

- Chapter 5, "Attitudes and Attitude Change," begins with the intriguing story of the Solar Temple Cult. The leader of the cult, Luc Jouret, believed that the world was about to be destroyed by fire and that the only salvation was to take a "death voyage" by ritualized suicide to the star Sirius, where they would be reborn. Jouret set up headquarters in villages in Quebec and Switzerland. The people in Quebec who joined the cult were mainly respected professionals, including the mayor of Richelieu and his wife, people in upper management positions with Hydro-Québec, a civil servant, and a journalist. In 1994, 53 people, including the mayor of Richelieu and his wife, died in fires set in buildings owned by the cult. In all, 74 deaths linked to this cult have been documented.

    Why would respected, intelligent people willingly hand over their wealth and material possessions to a charismatic leader? How could they reach the point of handing over their very lives—and in some cases, even those of their children? Cognitive dissonance theory provides insight into what would otherwise seem to be utterly incomprehensible human behaviour. By the end of this chapter, students will see that these behaviours are not unfathomable, but rather are an extreme manifestation of a basic human tendency—the need to justify our actions.

- In Chapter 8, "Interpersonal Attraction," we draw students in by describing an incredible "love at first sight" experience in which Bradley Bird, a Winnipeg newspaper writer, fell in love with Nina, a woman from Georgia (near Russia), on a bus to Istanbul, Turkey. Despite their difficulty communicating in English, within hours they were intensely in love. They began to make plans for Nina to come to Canada. When Nina mentioned in a letter that Brad would need to travel to the Canadian Embassy in Turkey to plead her case, he dropped everything, including a teaching position that he had just secured, and booked a one-way ticket to Turkey and two tickets back to Canada. During this time, his attempts to reach Nina invariably failed. He finally managed to reach her sister who delivered the news that Nina had decided to return to her husband. Brad had never known there was a husband. Although one might have expected him to become extremely bitter, Brad maintains that he will always be thankful to Nina for giving him the happiest hours of his adult life.

    This vignette serves to raise two key questions that are addressed in Chapter 8: What exactly is love? And why are people so motivated to seek it—so motivated that they might even rearrange their lives after a chance meeting with a stranger?
- Chapter 10, "Prejudice," begins by introducing Mary Young, the Director of the Aboriginal Student Services Centre at the University of Winnipeg. Mary was raised in Bloodvein First Nation, an Ojibway community in northern Manitoba. Growing up, she thought of herself as Anishinabe and was comfortable with that identity. It wasn't until she moved to Winnipeg, at the age of 14, with the dream of being the first person from her community to graduate from high school, that she discovered that she was perceived as Indian. Moreover, she quickly learned that being labelled as an Indian made her the target of racism and prejudice. Mary had never expected to feel embarrassed about her cultural heritage and identity. However, hearing comments such as "the only good Indian is a dead Indian" filled her with shame and resentment that she was Native. Mary's story serves to illustrate prejudice against groups such as Canada's Native peoples and provides a hearth-wrenching glimpse into the effects of prejudice and discrimination on their targets.

"Mini" Stories in Each Chapter

Our storytelling approach is not limited to these opening vignettes. There are several "mini" stories woven into each chapter that illustrate specific concepts and make the material come alive. They each follow a similar format: First, we describe an example of a real-life phenomenon that is designed to pique students' interest. These stories are taken from current events (mainly Canadian), literature, and our own lives. Second, we describe an experiment that attempts to explain the phenomenon. This experiment is typically described in some detail, because we believe that students should not only learn the major theories in social psychology, but also understand and appreciate the methods used to test those theories. We often invite the students to pretend that they were participants in the experiment, to give them a better feel for what it was like and what was found. Here are a few examples of our "mini" stories (by thumbing through the book, you will come across many others):

- In Chapter 3, "Social Cognition and Social Perception," we introduce the idea of schemas and discuss research showing that people will distort evidence to make it schema-consistent. We illustrate this point with a humorous anecdote from Pamela Wallin about an experience she had covering a G-7 summit hosted by Canada. CTV had managed to secure interviews with the (then) British prime minister and the West German chancellor. Ms. Wallin excitedly asked viewers to stay tuned for interviews with Margaret Thatcher and Helmut Shit. She was mortified at her mispronunciation of his name and left the studio, fully expecting that her broadcasting career was over. To her amazement, the people she ran into commented that they thought for a moment that she had mispronounced the chancellor's name, but then realized that they hadn't had their coffee yet, or the vacuum cleaner was running, and so on. . . . In short, it was so inconsistent with Canadians' schemas that Pamela Wallin would make such a slip of the tongue on the air that they disbelieved their ears and concluded that she really had said "Schmidt."
- In Chapter 6, "Conformity," we discuss the classic Stanford Prison Experiment and show striking parallels between the results of that laboratory experiment and the real-world behaviour of American soldiers in charge of the Abu Ghraib prison in Iraq.

- In Chapter 7, "Group Processes," when introducing the concept of deindividuation, we offer the classic examples such as the My Lai incident in Vietnam. However, we also bring this concept closer to home by describing the brutal attack on a Toronto teen, Matti Baranovski, who was approached in a park by a group of youths wearing balaclavas, bandannas, and ski goggles to conceal their identities. The injuries that resulted from this attack were so severe that Matti Baranovski later died in hospital.

SOCIAL PSYCHOLOGICAL METHODS: ANOTHER GOOD STORY

It might seem that a storytelling approach would obscure the scientific basis of social psychology. Quite to the contrary, we believe that part of what makes the story so interesting is explaining to students how to test hypotheses scientifically. In recent years, the trend has been for textbooks to include only short sections on research methodology and to provide only brief descriptions of the findings of individual studies. In this book, we integrate the science and methodology of the field into our story in a variety of ways.

Separate Chapter on Methodology

Unlike virtually all other texts, particularly brief texts such as this one, we devote an entire chapter to methodology (Chapter 2). "But wait," you might say, "how can you maintain students' interest and attention with an entire chapter on such dry material?" The answer is by integrating this material into our storytelling approach. Even the "dry" topic of methodology can come alive by telling it like a story. We use the Kitty Genovese murder, and the research subsequently conducted to explain the non-intervention of bystanders, to illustrate the three major scientific methods (observational research, correlational research, and experimental research). Rather than a dry recitation of methodological principles, the scientific method unfolds like a story with a "hook" (What are the causes of real-world aggression?) and a moral (such interesting, real-world questions can be addressed scientifically). We have been pleased by the reactions to this chapter.

Detailed Descriptions of Individual Studies

We describe prototypical studies in more detail than most texts. We discuss how a study was set up, what the research participants perceived and did, how the research design derives from theoretical issues, and how the findings offer support for the initial hypotheses. As we mentioned earlier, we often ask readers to pretend that they were participants, to help them understand the study from the participants' point of view. Whenever pertinent, we've also included anecdotal information about how a study was done or came to be; these brief stories allow readers to see the hitherto hidden world of creating research. See, for example, the description of Aronson's jigsaw technique in Chapter 10 (pp. 333–335).

Emphasis on Classic, Modern, and Canadian Research

In emphasizing what is new, many texts have a tendency to ignore what is old. We have striven to strike a balance between current, up-to-date research findings and classic research in social psychology. Some older studies deserve their status as classics (for example, early work in dissonance, conformity, and attribution) and are important cornerstones of the discipline. These have been flagged with a "classic research" icon. For example, we present detailed descriptions of the Festinger and Carlsmith (1959) dissonance study (Chapter 5), the LaPiere (1934) study on attitude–behaviour inconsistency (Chapter 5), and the Asch (1956) conformity studies (Chapter 6). To illustrate for students how research on the classics has been updated, we follow a discussion of the classics with modern approaches to these same topics, such as research conducted at the University of British Columbia on the process of dissonance reduction in different cultures (Heine & Lehman, 1997a, in Chapter 4). We also place the issue of attitude–behaviour inconsistency in a modern context by including a section on the implications of attitude–behaviour inconsistency for safe sex (Chapter 5). In this section, we describe studies conducted at the University of Waterloo (MacDonald, Fong, Zanna & Martineau, 2000) and at McGill University (Hynie, Lydon, Cote, & Wiener, 1998), among others, that provide insight into why people report positive attitudes toward condoms, yet fail to use them. This way, students see the continuity and depth of the field, rather than viewing it only as a mass of studies published in the past few years.

As these examples illustrate, the inclusion of Canadian research is not gratuitous. We highlight how current Canadian research builds on classic contributions to social psychology (Canadian and non-Canadian alike) and showcase the role of Canadian research in moving the field forward. Perhaps most importantly, this coverage does not come at the expense of omitting other important classic and modern contributions made by non-Canadian researchers.

A CANADIAN CONTEXT

Canadian research and cultural examples are integrated throughout the text to provide a familiar context and comfortable learning environment for Canadian students. Here is just a partial listing of the rich Canadian content you will find woven into every chapter of *Fundamentals of Social Psychology*:

- Chapter 1, "Introduction to Social Psychology": The opening vignette contains stories taken from across the country that act as springboards for the social psychological investigation: Altruism is introduced with the story of Greg Baytalan, a B.C. man who gave up his vacation to unload the bodies of tsunami victims at a morgue in Thailand; David Tremblay and his hockey team's hazing rituals exemplify suffering and self-justification; and the tragic story of the Order of the Solar Temple cult points to a later discussion of our need to justify our actions.
- Chapter 2, "Methodology": In this chapter, we highlight a program of research by Debra Pepler and colleagues out of York University, who have developed unobtrusive observational methods for studying bullying in school playgrounds. The story of "Tillie the Rainmaker" illustrates that one cannot infer causation from correlations.
- Chapter 3, "Social Cognition and Social Perception": The opening vignette focuses on the story of Kevin Chappell, an Ottawa man who is unable to perceive objects due to a brain injury. This story is intended to illustrate the usefulness of schemas in navigating through the physical and social world and how difficult it would be to function without them. The chapter also contains the story of Nadia Hama, the B.C. woman who was suspected of dropping her baby off of the Capilano suspension bridge, to demonstrate attributions; cross-cultural research on Canadian and Japanese students by Heine and Lehman (1995), showing that unrealistic optimism may not be a universal phenomenon; and several studies on blaming the victim (Perrott, Miller, & Delaney, 1997, at Mount Saint Vincent University; Kristiansen & Giulietti, 1990, at Carleton University; Hafer, 2000a, b, at Brock University).
- Chapter 4, Self-Knowledge and Self-Evaluation: The Try It! box "A Measure of Self-Concept Clarity" is based on a scale developed by Campbell, Trapnell, Heine, Katz, Lavallee, and Lehman (1996) at the University of British Columbia. The chapter also includes studies by Baldwin and Holmes (1987) and Baldwin, Carrell & Lopez (1990) at the University of Waterloo on how priming significant relationships affects one's momentary sense of self, and studies by Lockwood and Kunda (1997, 1999, 2000) at the University of Toronto and the University of Waterloo looking at how we feel if we compare ourselves to someone who is better than we are. Cultural differences in self-evaluation are illustrated with studies by Heine (Heine, 2001) on self-enhancement in Canadian and Japanese students. We also include new research on close relationships as a self-affirmational resource by Sandra Murray and colleagues (Murray, Bellavia, Feeney, Holmes, & Rose, 2001).
- Chapter 5, "Attitudes and Attitude Change": This chapter features numerous studies on attitudes by Haddock and Zanna at the University of Waterloo and Esses at the University of Western Ontario (Esses, Haddock, & Zanna, 1993; Haddock & Zanna, 1994, 1998; Haddock, Zanna, & Esses, 1993, 1994). We also include a section on attitude–behaviour inconsistency as applied to condom use (MacDonald, Fong, Zanna, & Martineau, 2000; Maticka-Tyndale, Herold, & Mewhinney, 2001).
- Chapter 6, "Conformity": The opening vignette focuses on the need to conform, featuring the story of the vicious beating and murder of B.C. teenager Reena Virk. Also discussed is the case of a Canadian soldier who complained publicly about an out-of-date anthrax vaccine he was given during the Gulf War, and who was consequently silenced and assigned menial tasks as punishment for his nonconformity. The chapter also includes a recent study conducted by Tafarodi, Kang, and Milne (2002) at the University of Toronto, on the conformity pressures experienced by bicultural minority students.

- Chapter 7, "Group Processes": The opening vignette illustrates faulty group decision making with the story of allegedly unsafe vaccines given to Canadian military personnel. The chapter also includes the example of the murder of Toronto teen Matti Baranovski, in which some of his assailants wore disguises, illustrating deindividuation, and research by Vorauer and Claude (1998) on negotiations, showing that the assumption that our goals are obvious to everyone is not necessarily warranted. Finally, a major review paper by Kenneth Dion (University of Toronto) on group cohesion is featured in the If You Are Interested section.
- Chapter 8, "Interpersonal Attraction": Research conducted at various Canadian universities on how ordinary people define love is highlighted (Button & Collier, 1991; Fehr, 1988, 1993, 1994; Fehr & Russell, 1991). Another focus is research on the attachment theory perspective on close relationships, including studies on attachment and relationship satisfaction by Keelan, Dion, and Dion (1994) at the University of Toronto, and reactions to breakups (Sprecher, Felmlee, Metts, Fehr, & Vanni, 1998). In addition, the chapter addresses the conceptualization of avoidant attachment by Bartholomew (1990) and Bartholomew and Horowitz (1991); research by Baldwin and Fehr and colleagues on the instability of attachment styles and a reconceptualization of attachment styles as schemas (Baldwin & Fehr, 1995; Baldwin, Keelan, Fehr, Enns, & Koh-Rangarajoo, 1996); as well as new research on general versus relationship-specific attachment (Pierce & Lydon, 2001; Ross & Spinner, 2001). The chapter also features research by Murray and Holmes and colleagues at the University of Waterloo on the role of positive illusions in romantic relationships (Murray & Holmes, 1997, 1999; Murray, Holmes, & Griffin, 1996a, 1996b; Murray, Holmes, Dolderman, & Griffin, 2000).
- Chapter 9, "Prosocial Behaviour and Aggression": The opening vignette on altruism features some of the winners of the Year 2000 Canada Day People Who Make a Difference Awards. Also covered is a study by James McDonald and Stuart McKelvie (1992) at Bishop's University on embarrassment and prosocial behaviour. The latter part of the chapter highlights a number of studies by Pihl and colleagues at McGill University on alcohol and aggression (Hoaken & Pihl, 2000; Pihl & Peterson, 1995; Pihl, Young, Harden, Plotnick, Chamberlain, & Ervin, 1995) as well as research by Graham and colleagues on alcohol and aggression in various Ontario bars (Graham & Wells, 2001a, 2001b; Graham, West, & Wells, 2000; Wells, Graham, & West, 2000). The chapter features a study by Josephson (1987) showing that violent television programming increases aggression among those who are predisposed toward aggression. The chapter also includes research by Neil Malamuth and James Check (1981) on the effects of watching sexual violence in movies on men's attitudes toward violence against women.
- Chapter 10, "Prejudice": The Try It! exercise "Multiculturalism: Is It Working?" examines Canada's multiculturalism policy in light of research by Osbeck, Moghaddam, and Perreault (1997). The chapter discusses studies by Corenblum and colleagues, including Corenblum and Annis, (1993), in which Native children were more likely to want to play with a white child than a Native child, as well as more recent research examining Natives' attitudes toward white Canadians (Corenblum & Stephan, 2001). The chapter also includes research by Peter Grant (1992, 1993) finding that if a person's sense of social identity is threatened, that person might be especially likely to discriminate against an out-group; research by Sinclair and Kunda (2000) on the selective activation of social and gender stereotypes as a function of self-enhancement goals; research by Esses at the University of Western Ontario and Zanna at the University of Waterloo and their colleagues on emotions, cognitions, and behaviour as predictors of prejudice toward various ethnic groups (Esses & Zanna, 1995; Esses, Haddock, & Zanna, 1993; Haddock, Zanna, & Esses, 1993, 1994); and studies on self-blaming attributions for discrimination (Ruggiero & Taylor, 1997; Dion, 2001; Dion & Kawakami, 1996; Foster & Matheson, 1999; Quinn, Roese, Pennington, & Olson, 1999). The chapter also includes research conducted by Mark Schaller at the University of British Columbia on the origins of stereotype content (Schaller & Conway, 1999, 2001; Schaller & O'Brien, 1992; Schaller, Conway, & Tanchuk, 2002). An award-winning address by Kenneth Dion, University of Toronto, on the social psychology of prejudice appears in the If You Are Interested section.

INTEGRATED COVERAGE OF CULTURE AND GENDER

To understand behaviour in a social context, we must consider such influences as culture and gender. We look at these important topics in every chapter, as they apply to the topic at hand. In many places, we discuss the wonderful diversity of humankind, by presenting research on the differences between people of different cultures, races, or genders. We also discuss the commonalities people share, by illustrating the applicability of many phenomena across cultures, races, and genders. Here are examples:

- Chapter 1, "Introduction to Social Psychology": The issue of universality versus the cultural relativity of social psychological principles is introduced.
- Chapter 2, "Methodology": The issue of how to generalize the results of studies across different types of people is discussed in the section on external validity. In addition, we discuss issues involved in conducting cross-cultural research.
- Chapter 3, "Social Cognition and Social Perception": Culture is considered in several places, including the cultural determinants of schemas, implicit personality theories, and cultural differences in attribution processes. The chapter also describes how the gender of the victim influences victim-blaming attributions.
- Chapter 4, "Self-Knowledge and Self-Evaluation": A major focus of this chapter is cultural differences in definition and evaluation of the definition of self, featuring research by Heine, Lehman, Markus, Kitayama, and others. There also is a section on gender differences in the definition of the self.
- Chapter 5, "Attitudes and Attitude Change": This chapter includes a section on culture and the basis of attitudes. We also include an extensive discussion of cultural differences in dissonance and dissonance reduction. At the end of the chapter, we present research on effectiveness of different kinds of advertisements. In the context of a discussion of the effects of advertising, we consider ways in which the media can transmit cultural stereotypes about race and gender.
- Chapter 6, "Conformity": This chapter includes a discussion of the role of normative social influence in creating and maintaining cultural standards of beauty (see the second Focus on Applications box). We also discuss gender and cultural differences in conformity and a meta analysis by Bond and Smith (1996) comparing conformity on the Asch line task in 17 countries.
- Chapter 7, "Group Processes": We discuss research on gender and culture at several points in this chapter, including gender and cultural differences in social loafing.
- Chapter 8, "Interpersonal Attraction": The role of culture comes up at several points in this chapter, including sections on cultural standards of beauty. We also discuss cultural and gender differences in the effects of physical attractiveness on liking, conceptions of love, and reactions to the dissolution of relationships.
- Chapter 9, "Prosocial Behaviour and Aggression": In this chapter we include a section on gender differences in prosocial behaviour and a section on cultural differences in prosocial behaviour. We also include a major section on cultural differences in aggression, including a discussion of differences in homicide rates in different countries. We discuss research on gender differences in aggression and the effects of violent pornography on violence against women. A Try It! exercise focuses on gender differences in spousal violence.
- Chapter 10, "Prejudice": Issues about in-groups and out-groups and ways of reducing prejudice are central to this chapter. For example, we present research on stereotype threat, including American and Canadian studies on achievement in minority groups and men versus women. We also discuss recent research by Sinclair and Kunda (1999, 2000) on motivational factors underlying the activation of racial and gender stereotypes. In addition, a Try It! exercise prompts students to evaluate Canada's multiculturalism policy in light of social psychological findings.

THE EVOLUTIONARY APPROACH

In recent years, social psychologists have become increasingly interested in an evolutionary perspective on many aspects of social behaviour. Once again, our approach is to integrate this perspective into those parts of chapters where it is relevant, rather than devote a separate chapter to this topic. We present what we believe is a balanced approach, discussing evolutionary psychology as well as alternatives to it. Here are examples of places in which we discuss the evolutionary approach:

- Chapter 1, "Introduction to Social Psychology": We introduce the evolutionary perspective in this chapter.
- Chapter 7, "Group Processes": We discuss whether we have inherited the need to belong from our evolutionary past.
- Chapter 8, "Interpersonal Attraction": We present the evolutionary perspective on gender differences in romantic attraction and on why people fall in love.
- Chapter 9, "Prosocial Behaviour and Aggression": Evolutionary psychology is presented as one of the major theories of why humans engage in prosocial behaviour. We present evidence for and against this perspective and contrast it to other approaches, such as social exchange theory. We also include a section on whether aggression is inborn or learned, including a discussion of an evolutionary explanation of aggressive behaviour.
- Chapter 10, "Prejudice": We touch on the issue of whether there might be an evolutionary basis for prejudice.

SOCIAL PSYCHOLOGY: THE APPLIED SIDE

One of the best ways to capture students' interest is to point out the real-world significance of the material they are studying. From the vignette that opens each chapter and runs throughout it to the discussions of historical events, current affairs, and our own lives that are embedded in the story line, the narrative is highlighted by real, familiar examples. Applications are an integral part of social psychology, however, and deserve their own treatment. Therefore, in each chapter, we have included two or three Focus on Applications boxes in which we highlight social psychology studies that have been applied to real-world issues. For example, in Chapter 3, "Social Cognition and Social Perception," we present research showing that social psychological research on schemas is relevant to how juries process information presented by lawyers during trials. In Chapter 5, "Attitudes and Attitude Change," we show that the process of dissonance reduction can be used to encourage people to conserve water. In Chapter 8, "Interpersonal Attraction," we present analyses of "real-world" lonely hearts advertisements to see whether, as evolutionary theory would predict, women are likely to advertise their beauty and men their status and resources. We believe that these applied boxes will serve as a constant, vivid reminder of the applicability and relevance of social psychology to real-world situations.

Try It! Student Exercises

In each chapter, we feature a series of Try It! exercises, in which students are invited to apply the concepts they are learning to their everyday life. These exercises include detailed instructions about how to recreate social psychology experiments (for example, Baron's [1997] study on the relation between pleasant smells and helping in Chapter 9). Students also are encouraged to "get the feel" of social psychological research by completing measures such as Campbell and colleagues' (1996) self-concept clarity scale (Chapter 4) and the Passionate Love Scale (Chapter 8). Still others are quizzes that illustrate social psychological concepts, such as a Reasoning Quiz in Chapter 3. The format of, and the time frame required for, each of these exercises varies. You might want to flip through the book to look at other examples in more detail.

Try It! exercises are not only in the text itself, but built into the website as well. Students will find a new Try It! exercise for each chapter on the Companion Website. You can use Try It! exercises as class activities or as homework.

We believe that the Try It! exercises will generate a lot of interest in learning social psychological concepts by making them more memorable and engaging.

Live!Psych Web Simulations

The Live!Psych icons that you will notice in the margins of this text are designed to signal to readers that interactive audio and video simulations, dealing with the subject flagged in the text, are available on the Companion Website for this text. Use these online simulations anytime you'd like to reinforce concepts discussed in the text.

SUPPLEMENTS TO THE TEXT

A really good textbook should become part of the classroom experience, supporting and augmenting the instructor's vision for his or her class. *Fundamentals of Social Psychology* is accompanied by a number of supplements that will enrich both the instructor's presentation of social psychology and students' understanding of it.

Instructor's Supplements

Pearson Education Canada/CBC Video Library (ISBN 0-13-197855-1 [VHS]; 0-13-204394-7 [DVD]). Few will dispute that video is one of the most dynamic supplements you can use to enhance a class. The authors and editors of Pearson Education Canada have carefully selected videos on topics that complement *Fundamentals of Social Psychology* from popular CBC series such as *The National*, *The Health Show*, and *Undercurrents*. An excellent video guide found on the Instructor's Resource CD-ROM (see below) will help you integrate the videos into your lectures.

Instructor's Resource CD-ROM (ISBN 0-13-197851-9). This CD-ROM gathers the following instructor resources in one handy package. Some of these resources are also available for downloading from a password-protected section of our online catalogue at vig.pearsoned.ca. See your Pearson Education Canada sales representative for details.

- **Instructor's Manual.** The manual includes lecture ideas, teaching tips, suggested readings, chapter outlines, student projects and research assignments, Try It! exercises, critical thinking topics and discussion questions, and a media resource guide.
- **Test Item File.** Each question in this 2000-question test bank is referenced to text page number, topic, and skill level. It is available in both Microsoft Word and TestGen formats.
- **Pearson TestGen.** The Pearson TestGen is a special computerized version of the Test Item File that enables instructors to view and edit the existing questions, add questions, generate tests, and print the tests in a variety of formats. Powerful search and sort functions make it easy to locate questions and arrange them in any order desired. TestGen also enables instructors to administer tests on a local area network, have the tests graded electronically, and have the results prepared in electronic or printed reports.
- **PowerPoint Presentations.** These presentations cover the key concepts in each chapter.
- **Image Library.** Figures and tables from the text are provided in electronic format.
- **Video Guide.** The guide has a synopsis of each video, a list of the psychological principles it reinforces with respect to the text chapter, advance preparation, discussion questions, and in-class activities to help students focus on how concepts and theories apply to real-life situations.

Instructor Access Kit for Companion Website (ISBN 0-13-189054-9). Access to the Class Manager function gives instructors the ability to quickly and easily monitor student progress on quizzes and other activities in an online gradebook.

Pearson Advantage. For qualified adopters, Pearson Education is proud to introduce the Pearson Advantage. The Pearson Advantage is the first integrated Canadian service program committed to meeting the customization, training, and support needs for your course. Our commitments are made in writing and in consultation with faculty. Your local Pearson Education sales representative can provide you with more details on this service program.

Innovative Solutions Team. Pearson's Innovative Solutions Team works with faculty and campus course designers to ensure that Pearson technology products, assessment tools, and online course materials are tailored to meet your specific needs. This highly qualified team is dedicated to helping schools take full advantage of a wide range of educational technology by assisting in the integration of a variety of instructional materials and media formats.

Student Supplements

Companion Website (www.pearsoned.ca/aronson). Use the access code packaged with every new copy of this text to log on to the Companion Website for *Fundamentals of Social Psychology* and access the following resources:

- A self-grading pre-test and post-test for each chapter. As each test is completed, a study plan is generated to indicate which sections of the chapter require further study.
- Live!Psych interactive simulations that use audio and video components to reinforce key concepts. Icons in the margins of the text flag the topics covered in these simulations.
- An additional Try It! exercise for each chapter.
- Internet exercises
- Weblinks

Social Psychology Study Card (ISBN 0-13-204396-3). This laminated card provides an overview of the core concepts of social psychology for reference and study purposes.

Acknowledgments

Elliot Aronson is delighted to acknowledge the general contributions of his best friend (who also happens to be his wife), Vera Aronson. Vera, as usual, provided a great deal of inspiration for his ideas and acted as the sounding board for and supportive critic of many of his semiformed notions, helping to mould them into more sensible analyses. He would also like to thank his son, Joshua Aronson, a brilliant young social psychologist in his own right, for the many stimulating conversations that contributed mightily to the final version of this book.

Tim Wilson would like to thank his graduate mentor, Richard E. Nisbett, who nurtured his interest in the field and showed him the continuity between social psychological research and everyday life. He thanks his graduate students, Sara Algoe, David Centerbar, Elizabeth Dunn, Debby Kermer, Jaime Kurtz, and Anna MacIntosh, who helped keep him a well-balanced professor—a researcher as well as a teacher and author. He thanks his parents, Elizabeth and Geoffrey Wilson, for their overall support. Most of all, he thanks his wife, Deirdre Smith, and his children, Christopher and Leigh, for their love, patience, and understanding, even when the hour was late and the computer was still on.

Robin Akert would like to thank her students and colleagues at Wellesley College for their support and encouragement. In particular, she is beholden to Professors Jonathan Cheek and Patricia Berman, and to Kristen Fay, Alison Bibbins Ward, and Linda DuFresne. Their advice, feedback, and senses of humour were vastly appreciated. She also wishes to thank her students in social psychology. Their intelligence, perspicacity, dedication, and joie de vivre are her continuing sources of energy and motivation for this book. She is deeply grateful to her family, Michaela and Wayne Akert, and Linda and Jerry Wuichet; their inexhaustible enthusiasm and boundless support have sustained her on this project as on all the ones before it. Once again she thanks C. Issak for authorial inspiration. Finally, no words can express her gratitude and indebtedness to Dane Archer, mentor, colleague, and friend, who opened the world of social psychology to her and who has been her guide ever since.

Beverley Fehr would like to thank her colleagues at the University of Winnipeg and her social psychology colleagues at the University of Manitoba for their enthusiasm and support throughout this project. She is indebted to Lisa Sinclair, Wendy Josephson, and Marian Morry for their emotional and practical support, which included offering incisive feedback on individual chapters. Beverley would also like to express gratitude to her capable, highly skilled research assistants, Cheryl Harasymchuk, Joanne Vallely, and Lorissa Martens. On a more personal note, Beverley's dear friends Lydia Friesen Rempel and Lorrie Brubacher provided the unfailing emotional support and good cheer that have sustained her through many a project over the years. Beverley is also grateful to her husband, Marvin Giesbrecht, for his generosity and kindness in doing "more than his share" of domestic chores and the more mundane aspects of childcare so that she could focus on writing this book. Even though Beverley's children, Genevieve and Everett, are probably too young to realize it, their smiles and antics were an invaluable source of joy and energy. Finally, Beverley would like to thank the staff at Bread and Circuses Café, where much of her writing was done, for their warmth, friendliness, and the countless refills of coffee.

No book can be written and published without the help of a great many people working with the authors behind the scenes, and this book is no exception. Beverley would like to thank the people at Pearson Education Canada who worked with her on this text. She would like to express appreciation to Lise Dupont, Senior Developmental Editor, for her competence, good judgment, and unfailing patience. Lise has been an absolute pleasure to work with. Beverley would also like to thank Acquisitions Editor Ky Pruesse for his support and encouragement, Editorial Coordinator Söğüt Y. Güleç, Production Editor Kevin Leung, and Copy Editor Susan Broadhurst for their competence, conscientiousness, and good-natured patience in dealing with an author who constantly wanted to make "just one more little change."

Reviewers of Fundamentals of Social Psychology

The publishers and authors would like to thank the following reviewers whose feedback contributed to the development of this project:

Larry M. Anderson, Kwantlen University College
Michael T. Bradley, University of New Brunswick
Tanya M. Cassidy, University of Windsor
Matthew Cook, Red Deer College
Rory Coughlan, Trent University
Marinus Dieleman, Northern College
Alvin Gallay, Centennial College
Rosalie Hawrylko, Capilano College
Sara Pawson Herrington, Kwantlen University College
Christian Jordan, Wilfrid Laurier University
Connie Korpan, Grande Prairie Regional College
Diane LaChapelle, University of New Brunswick
Carrie Lavis, Niagara College
Paulo Matos, Algoma University College
Doug McCann, York University
Bev McLeod, Mount Royal College
Daniel Perlman, University of British Columbia
Stephen B. Perrott, Mount Saint Vincent University
Saba Safdar, University of Guelph
Lisa Sinclair, University of Winnipeg
Shelagh Skerry, Marianapolis College
Alwin Spence, John Abbott College
Murray Stainton, Trent University
Diane G. Symbaluk, Grant MacEwan College
Frank Winstan, Vanier College
Michael Wohl, Carleton University
Ted Wright, St. Francis Xavier University

About the Authors

Elliot Aronson

When I was a kid, we were the only Jewish family in a virulently anti-Semitic neighbourhood. I had to go to Hebrew school every day, late in the afternoon. Being the only youngster in my neighbourhood going to Hebrew school made me an easy target for some of the older neighbourhood toughs. On my way home from Hebrew school, after dark, I was frequently waylaid and roughed up by roving gangs shouting anti-Semitic epithets.

I have a vivid memory of sitting on a curb after one of these beatings, nursing a bloody nose or a split lip, feeling very sorry for myself and wondering how these kids could hate me so much when they didn't even know me. I thought about whether those kids were taught to hate Jews or whether, somehow, they were born that way. I wondered if their hatred could be changed—if they got to know me better, would they hate me less? I speculated about my own character. What would I have done if the shoe were on the other foot—that is, if I were bigger and stronger than they, would I be capable of beating them up for no good reason?

I didn't realize it at the time, of course, but eventually I discovered that these were profound questions. And some 30 years later, as an experimental social psychologist, I had the great good fortune to be in a position to answer some of those questions and to invent techniques to reduce the kind of prejudice that had claimed me as a victim.

Elliot Aronson is one of the most renowned social psychologists in the world. In 2002 he was chosen as one of the 100 most eminent psychologists of the twentieth century. He is currently Professor Emeritus at the University of California at Santa Cruz and Distinguished Visiting Professor at Stanford University.

Dr. Aronson is the only person in the 110-year history of the American Psychological Association to have received all three of its major awards: for distinguished writing, distinguished teaching, and distinguished research. Many other professional societies have honoured his research and teaching as well. These include the American Association for the Advancement of Science, which gave him its highest honour, the Distinguished Scientific Research award; the American Council for the Advancement and Support of Education, which named him Professor of the Year of 1989; the Society for the Psychological Study of Social Issues, which awarded him the Gordon Allport prize for his contributions to the reduction of prejudice among racial and ethnic groups. In 1992, he was named a Fellow of the American Academy of Arts and Sciences. He has served as President of the Western Psychological Association as well as President of the Society of Personality and Social Psychology.

Tim Wilson

One day, when I was eight, a couple of older kids rode up on their bikes to share some big news: They had discovered an abandoned house down a country road. "It's really neat," they said. "We broke a window and nobody cared!" My friend and I hopped onto our bikes to investigate. We had no trouble finding the house—there it was, sitting off by itself, with a big, jagged hole in a first-floor window. We got off our bikes and looked around. My friend found a baseball-sized rock lying on the ground and threw a perfect strike through another first-floor window. There was something exhilarating about the smash-and-tingle of shattering glass, especially when we knew there was nothing wrong with what we were doing. After all, the house was abandoned, wasn't it? We broke nearly every window in the house and then climbed through one of the first-floor windows to look around.

It was then that we realized something was terribly wrong. The house certainly did not look abandoned. There were pictures on the wall, nice furniture, books on shelves. We went home feeling frightened and confused. We soon learned that the house was the residence of an elderly couple who were away on vacation. Eventually my parents discovered what we had done and paid a substantial sum to repair the windows. For years, I pondered this incident: Why did I do such a terrible thing? Was I a bad kid? I didn't think so, and neither did my parents. How, then, could a good kid do such a bad thing? Even though the neighbourhood kids had said the house was abandoned, why couldn't my friend and I see the clear signs that someone lived there? How crucial was it that my friend was there and threw the first rock? Though I didn't know it at the time, these reflections touched on several classic social psychological issues, such as whether only bad people do bad things, whether the social situation can be powerful enough to make good people do bad things, and the way in which our expectations about an event can make it difficult to see it as it really is. Fortunately, my career as a vandal ended with this one incident. It did, however, mark the beginning of my fascination with basic questions about how people understand themselves and the social world—questions I continue to investigate to this day.

Tim Wilson did his undergraduate work at Williams College and Hampshire College and received his Ph.D. from the University of Michigan. Currently Sherrell J. Aston Professor of Psychology at the University of Virginia, he has published numerous articles in the areas of introspection, attitude change, self-knowledge, and affective forecasting, as well as the recent book Strangers to Ourselves: Discovering the Adaptive Unconscious (2002). *His research has received the support of the National Science Foundation and the National Institute for Mental Health. He has been associate editor of the* Journal of Personality and Social Psychology *and a member of the Social and Groups Processes Review Committee at the National Institute of Mental Health. He has been elected twice to the Executive Board of the Society for Experimental Social Psychology and is a Fellow in the American Psychological Society. Wilson has taught the Introduction to Social Psychology course at the University of Virginia for more than 20 years. He was recently awarded an All University Outstanding Teaching Award.*

Robin Akert

One fall day, when I was about 16, I was walking with a friend along the shore of the San Francisco Bay. Deep in conversation, I glanced over my shoulder and saw a sailboat capsize. I pointed it out to my friend, who took only a perfunctory interest and went on talking. However, I kept watching as we walked, and I realized that the two sailors were in the water, clinging to the capsized boat. Again I said something to my friend, who replied, "Oh, they'll get it upright, don't worry."

But I was worried. Was this an emergency? My friend didn't think so. And I was no sailor; I knew nothing about boats. But I kept thinking, "That water is really cold. They can't stay in that water too long." I remember feeling very confused and unsure. What should I do? Should I do anything? Did they really need help?

We were near a restaurant with a big window overlooking the bay, and I decided to go in and see if anyone had done anything about the boat. Lots of people were watching but not doing anything. This confused me too. Very meekly, I asked the bartender to call for some kind of help. He just shrugged. I went back to the window and watched the two small figures in the water. Why was everyone so unconcerned? Was I crazy?

Years later, I reflected on how hard it was for me to do what I did next: I demanded that the bartender let me use his phone. In those days before "911," it was lucky that I knew there was a Coast Guard station on the bay, and I asked the operator for the number. I was relieved to hear the Guardsman take my message very seriously.

It had been an emergency. I watched as the Coast Guard cutter sped across the bay and pulled the two sailors out of the water. Maybe I saved their lives that day. What really stuck with me over the years was how other people behaved and how it made me feel. The other bystanders seemed unconcerned and did nothing to help. Their reactions made me doubt myself and made it harder for me to decide to take action. When I later studied social psychology in college, I realized that on the shore of the San Francisco Bay that day, I had experienced the "bystander effect" fully: The presence of other, apparently unconcerned bystanders had made it difficult for me to decide whether the situation was an emergency and whether it was my responsibility to help.

Robin Akert graduated summa cum laude from the University of California at Santa Cruz, where she majored in psychology and sociology. She received her Ph.D. in experimental social psychology from Princeton University. She is currently a professor of psychology at Wellesley College, where she was awarded the Pinanski Prize for Excellence in Teaching early in her career. She publishes primarily in the area of nonverbal communication and recently received the AAUW American Fellowship in support of her research. She has taught the social psychology course at Wellesley College every semester for more than 20 years.

Beverley Fehr

I suspect that many social psychologists, like me, didn't start out with the intention of becoming social psychologists. I was attending university as a music major, taking psychology courses for interest. I enjoyed them, but kept experiencing a vague sense of disappointment—each course wasn't quite what I had thought psychology would be about. When I enrolled in a social psychology course one summer, I was delighted to have finally found a course that captured what I had been seeking. One day, as part of a class exercise, our professor handed out copies of Rubin's (1970) love and liking scale for us to complete with reference to a romantic partner and a friend. (This scale is still widely used in close relationships research today.) I was dating someone at the time about whom I cared deeply, although I had a feeling that he was not a particularly good choice as a long-term partner. I was astonished, upon scoring the scale, that the love score for this person was extremely high, but the liking score was distressingly low! Quite aside from the personal implications of this result, I was utterly fascinated that social psychologists could use the scientific method to gain insight into issues that are highly relevant to people's everyday lives. This and other experiences in that class prompted me to reconsider my career choice and I eventually changed my major to psychology. I suspect that this experience also played a role in my eventual decision to become a social psychologist who studies close relationships.

Beverley Fehr graduated with a B.A. (Hons.) from the University of Winnipeg, where she was awarded the Gold Medal for the highest standing in psychology. She received her M.A. (under the guidance of Jim Russell) and her Ph.D. (under the guidance of Dan Perlman) from the University of British Columbia. Her doctoral thesis on laypeople's conceptions of love and commitment won the Iowa/International Network for the Study of Personal Relationships Dissertation Prize. She has published numerous articles and book chapters on the topics of emotion and close relationships. Her book Friendship Processes *(1996) was awarded the 1997 Outstanding Academic Book Award by* Choice: Current Reviews for Academic Libraries. *Fehr's research is supported by grants from the Social Sciences and Humanities Research Council of Canada and the Fetzer Institute.*

The Pearson Education Canada

COMPANION WEBSITE

A Great Way to Learn and Instruct Online

The Pearson Education Canada Companion Website is easy to navigate and is organized to correspond to the chapters in this textbook. Whether you are a student in the classroom or a distance learner, you will discover helpful resources for in-depth study and research that empower you in your quest for greater knowledge and maximize your potential for success in the course.

[www.pearsoned.ca/aronson] Enter

PEC Companion Website

Fundamentals of Social Psychology, Canadian Edition, by Aronson, Wilson, Akert, and Fehr

Student Resources

The resources on this site provide students with tools for learning course material. The modules include the following:
- Learning Objectives
- Practice Tests
- Live!Psych Web Simulations
- Try It!
- Internet Exercises
- Weblinks

For the practice tests, students can send answers to the grader and receive instant feedback on their progress. As each test is completed, a study plan is generated to indicate which sections of the chapter require further study.

Use the access code packaged with this text to take advantage of these online resources to enhance your learning experience.

CHAPTER

1

Introduction to Social Psychology

Chapter Outline

WHAT IS SOCIAL PSYCHOLOGY?

Social Psychology Compared to Sociology

Social Psychology Compared to Personality Psychology

THE POWER OF SOCIAL INFLUENCE

Underestimating the Power of Social Influence

The Subjectivity of the Social Situation

SOCIAL PSYCHOLOGY AND SOCIAL PROBLEMS

The task of the psychologist is to try to understand and predict human behaviour. Different kinds of psychologists go about this in different ways, and in this book we will attempt to show you how social psychologists do it. Let's begin with a few examples of human behaviour. Some of these might seem important; others might seem trivial; one or two might seem frightening. To a social psychologist, all of them are interesting. Our hope is that by the time you finish reading this book, you will find all of these examples as fascinating as we do. As you read, try to think about how you would explain why each event unfolded as it did.

1. "Canadians amaze with their giving"; "Canadians open their wallets in record numbers." As this textbook is being written, headlines such as these appear daily in Canadian newspapers. Story after story documents the extent to which Canadians have been moved to assist the victims of the December 2004 tsunami disaster. These include benefit concerts, school

There has been an outpouring of aid to the victims of the tsunami earthquake.

bake sales, fundraising drives at sports events, and extended hours at the offices of relief organizations such as the Red Cross so that all donations can be accommodated. There are stories of families travelling long distances over icy roads so that their children could donate the contents of their piggy banks in the office of a relief organization. Two polls, released on January 14, 2005, reported that more than 50 percent of Canadians had donated money toward the tsunami relief effort—an unprecedented level of giving. Bruce Anderson, CEO of Decima Research, which conducted one of these polls, commented: "It's undoubtedly a reflection of our value system as a nation that so many people have felt moved to take action in response to this crisis" (Dugas, 2005).

One such person is Greg Baytalan, a 46-year-old health inspector from Kelowna, B.C. Baytalan was enjoying a vacation in Australia when he heard news of the tsunami and felt compelled to help. He flew to Thailand and began the gruesome task of unloading recovered bodies and carrying them to a morgue. This is an experience that Baytalan believes he will never be able to erase from his memory. In his words, "It was beyond horror" (Cheadle, 2005).

What would make a person such as Greg Baytalan give up his vacation to help complete strangers in a distant country, especially when doing so comes at such an enormous cost? Why have so many Canadians opened their hearts and their wallets to help the tsunami victims?

2. Sally was watching TV with a few friends. On the tube, Alberta Premier Ralph Klein was making an important policy speech. This was the first time Sally had listened carefully to one of Klein's substantive speeches. She was impressed by his homey, down-to-earth quality; she felt he was smart, honest, sincere, and compassionate. As soon as the speech was over, her friend Melinda said, "Boy, what a phony—I wouldn't trust that guy with my dirty laundry—I can't believe he's running our province. No wonder our health care has gone down the tubes!" The others quickly chimed in, voicing their agreement. Sally felt uncomfortable, and frankly was puzzled. Finally, she mumbled, "Yeah, I guess he did come off as a bit insincere."

What do you suppose was going on in Sally's mind? Did she actually come to see Premier Klein in a new light, or was she simply trying to "go along" in order to get along?

3. When David Tremblay, a former Quebec Nordiques prospect, joined the Pickering Panthers of the Ontario Hockey Association, he was blindfolded, shaved, and forced to sit in a hot liniment that badly burned his genitals. A few years later, he was hazed again when he received a hockey scholarship from an American university. That time, he was sick for days, suffering from alcohol

poisoning. How does he remember the teammates who inflicted this cruelty on him? Remarkably, with fondness . . . "They came by and checked on us when it was over . . . They didn't just beat the crap out of us and leave us" (O'Hara, 2000).

Why would David feel so happy to be part of a team that inflicted pain, embarrassment, and humiliation?

4. In the mid-1980s, Quebecers were introduced to the Order of the Solar Temple—a cult founded by Luc Jouret and his partner Joseph Di Mambro. Prominent citizens, including the highly respected mayor of Richelieu and his wife, joined the cult. They were taught that the only redemption from their sins was to experience death by fire, which would transport them to the star Sirius, where they would be reborn. Suicides were to take place during the spring or autumn equinox. The cult attracted worldwide attention in October 1994, when 53 cult members, including the mayor of Richelieu and his wife, died in a combined mass murder–suicide. An elaborate system of explosives set fire to the buildings they inhabited in Quebec and Switzerland. Nearly a year later, another 16 cult members, including several children, died in a remote village in France. So far, at least 74 members of this cult have died.

How can people agree to kill themselves and their own children? Were they crazy? Were they under some kind of hypnotic spell? How would you explain it?

We now have several questions about human social behaviour—questions we find fascinating. Why do people sometimes go to great lengths to help complete strangers, as Greg Baytalan did when he gave up his vacation to help carry the bodies of tsunami victims to a morgue? Why did Sally change her opinion about the sincerity of Premier Klein and bring it into line with her friends' opinion? Why did David Tremblay like being part of hockey teams that forced him to endure barbaric hazing rituals? And how could large numbers of people be induced to kill their own children and themselves in Quebec, Switzerland, and France? In this chapter, we will consider what these examples have in common and why they are of interest to us. We will also put forth some reasonable explanations based on social psychological research.

WHAT IS SOCIAL PSYCHOLOGY?

At the heart of social psychology is the phenomenon of social influence: We are all influenced by other people. When we think of social influence, the kinds of examples that readily come to mind are direct attempts at persuasion, whereby one person deliberately tries to change another person's behaviour. This is what happens in an advertising campaign when creative individuals employ sophisticated techniques to persuade us to buy a particular brand of toothpaste, or during an election campaign when similar techniques are used to get us to vote for a particular political candidate. Direct attempts at persuasion also occur when our friends try to get us to do something we don't really want to do ("Come on, have another beer—everyone is doing it") or when the schoolyard bully uses force or threats to get smaller kids to part with their lunch money or completed homework.

These direct social influence attempts form a major part of social psychology and will be discussed in our chapters on conformity, attitudes, and group processes. To the social psychologist, however, social influence is broader than attempts by one person to change another person's behaviour. For one thing, social influence extends beyond behaviour—it includes our thoughts and feelings, as well as our overt acts. In addition, social influence takes many forms other than deliberate attempts at persuasion. We are often influenced merely by the presence of other people. Moreover, even when we are not in the physical presence of other people, we are still influenced by them. Thus, in a sense we carry our mothers, fathers, friends, and teachers around with us, as we attempt to make decisions that would make them proud of us.

On a subtler level, each of us is immersed in a social and cultural context. Social psychologists are interested in studying how and why our thoughts, feelings, and behaviours are shaped by the entire social environment. Taking all these factors into account, we can define **social psychology** as the scientific study of the way in which people's thoughts, feelings, and behaviours are influenced by the real or imagined presence of other people (Allport, 1985).

Social Psychology Compared to Sociology

Social psychology's focus on social behaviour is shared by several other disciplines in the social sciences, most notably sociology. Both disciplines are concerned with the influence of social and societal factors on human behaviour. There are important differences, however. One major difference is the level of analysis. Social psychology is a branch of psychology, and as such is rooted in an interest in individual human beings, with an emphasis on the psychological processes going on in our hearts and minds. For the social psychologist, the level of analysis is the individual in the context of a social situation. For example, to understand why people intentionally hurt one another, the social psychologist focuses on the specific psychological processes that trigger aggression in specific situations. To what extent is aggression preceded by a state of frustration? If people are feeling frustrated, under what conditions will they vent their frustration with an overt, aggressive act? What factors might preclude an aggressive response by a frustrated individual? Aside from frustration, what other factors might cause aggression? We will address these questions in Chapter 9.

Sociology is more concerned with broad societal factors that influence events in a given society. Thus, the focus is on topics such as social class, social structure, and

---

Social psychology the scientific study of the way in which people's thoughts, feelings, and behaviours are influenced by the real or imagined presence of other people

social institutions. It goes without saying that because society is made up of collections of people, some overlap is bound to exist between the domains of sociology and social psychology. The major difference is this: Sociology, rather than focusing on the psychology of the individual, tends toward a more macro focus—that of society at large (see Table 1.1). Although sociologists, like social psychologists, are interested in aggressive behaviour, for example, sociologists are more likely to be concerned with why a particular society produces different levels and types of aggression in its members. Why, for example, is the murder rate in the United States so much higher than in Canada? Within Canada, why is the murder rate higher in some social classes than in others? How do changes in society relate to changes in aggressive behaviour?

Social Psychology Compared to Personality Psychology

Like social psychology, some other areas of psychology focus on studying individuals and the reasons they do what they do. Paramount among these is personality psychology. Let's discuss how social psychology and personality psychology differ in their approach and concerns (see also Table 1.1).

If you are like most people, when you read the examples presented at the beginning of this chapter and began to think about how those events might have come about, your first thoughts were about the strengths, weaknesses, flaws, and quirks of the personalities of the individuals involved. When people behave in interesting or unusual ways, it is natural to try to pinpoint what aspects of their personalities led them to respond as they did. Most of us explain these kinds of behaviours in terms of the personalities of the people involved. When we do so, we are behaving like personality psychologists who generally focus their attention on **individual differences**—the aspects of an individual's personality that make him or her different from other individuals. As we discuss next, social psychologists are convinced that to fully understand human behaviour, it is crucial to consider situational factors. Although social psychologists do not deny that people have different personalities, they believe that the situations in which people find themselves are often a much more powerful determinant of their behaviour than their personalities.

Individual differences the aspects of people's personalities that make them different from other people

Thinking Critically

Both personality psychologists and social psychologists focus on the individual, but they concentrate on different aspects of individual behaviour. How would you characterize the basic difference in the focus of these two disciplines?

TABLE 1.1	Social Psychology Compared to Related Disciplines
Sociology	Provides general laws and theories about societies, not individuals.
Social Psychology	Studies the psychological processes people have in common with one another that make them susceptible to social influence.
Personality Psychology	Studies the characteristics that make individuals unique and different from one another.

THE POWER OF SOCIAL INFLUENCE

When trying to convince people that their behaviour is greatly influenced by the social environment, the social psychologist is up against a formidable barrier: the inclination we all have for explaining people's behaviour in terms of their personalities. This barrier is known as the **fundamental attribution error**—the tendency to explain our own and other people's behaviour in terms of personality traits, thereby underestimating the power of social influence. For example, to explain why the people in the Solar Temple cult ended their own lives and those of their children, it seems natural to point to their personalities. Perhaps they were all "conformist types" or weak-willed; maybe they suffered from mental disorders. An understanding of personality psychology increases our understanding of human behaviour, but social psychologists are convinced that explaining behaviour primarily in terms of personality factors can be superficial because it leads to a serious underestimation of the role played by a powerful source of human behaviour: social influence. Remember that it was not just a handful of people who died in a ski resort in Quebec and in two villages in Switzerland—53 people died in October 1994, and almost a year later another 16 cult members died in a village in France. It is thought that, in all, 74 people lost their lives.

Sadly, this was not an isolated event. In the United States, in the late 1970s, 800 members of the Jonestown cult perished when they drank a deadly poison mixture. More recently, Uganda's Movement for the Restoration of the Ten Commandments of God claimed the lives of up to 1000 people, many of whom were children. While it is conceivable that all of these people were psychotic, that explanation is highly improbable. If we want a deeper, richer, more thorough explanation of these tragic events, we need

Fundamental attribution error the tendency to overestimate the extent to which people's behaviour is due to internal, dispositional factors (e.g., their personality) and to underestimate the role of situational factors

Why would reasonable persons blindly agree to hand themselves and their children over to a painful death? Though it may be easy to dismiss the followers of the Ugandan cult as extremely gullible or even crazy, such oversimplifications and denial of the power of social influence can lead us to blame the victims. Shown here are the primary leaders of Uganda's Movement for the Restoration of the Ten Commandments of God: (left to right) Ursala Kamuhangi, Cledonia Mwerinde, Joseph Kibweteere, and Dominic Kataribabo.

> **Try It!**
>
> ### Social Situations and Behaviour
>
> 1. Think about one of your friends or acquaintances whom you regard as a shy person. For a moment, try not to think about that person as "shy," but rather as someone who has difficulty relating to people in some situations but not in others.
> 2. Make a list of the social situations that you think are most likely to bring out your friend's "shy" behaviour.
> 3. Make a list of the social situations that might bring forth more outgoing behaviour on his or her part. (For example, if someone showed a real interest in one of your friend's favourite hobbies or topics of conversation, it might bring out behaviour that could be classified as charming or vivacious.)
> 4. Try to create a social environment in which this would be accomplished. Pay close attention to the effect it has on your friend's behaviour.

to understand what kind of power and influence the charismatic leaders of these cults possess, the nature of the impact of living in a closed society cut off from other points of view, and myriad other factors that might have contributed to the deaths. Thus, while reading this book, try to suspend judgment for a short time and consider the possibility that to understand why people do what they do, it is important to look closely at the nature of the social situation. Try It!, above, may help you do just that.

FOCUS ON APPLICATIONS

The Fundamental Attribution Error: When We Blame the Victims of Violence

The tendency to explain others' behaviour as due to internal rather than situational factors can lead to tragic consequences, including a tendency to blame those who are victimized or stigmatized for their plight. Even if people are made aware of the situational factors responsible for the plight of disadvantaged members of society (inadequate nutrition, disrupted family life), they may still see such individuals as responsible for their misfortunes. This tendency extends even to victims of violence. For example, women who are raped are often seen as having somehow "caused" the attack (Morry & Winkler, 2001), and battered wives are often seen as responsible for their abusive husbands' behaviour (Summers & Feldman, 1984). Research conducted at Carleton University (Kristiansen & Giulietti, 1990) and at Mount Saint Vincent University (Perrott, Miller, & Delaney, 1997) has shown that people justify blaming a victim of violence by assuming that the person must have done something to provoke the attack. The role that perceived provocation plays in judgments of blame was examined in a study by Kristiansen and Giulietti (1990). They asked participants to read the following scenario:

> Mrs. X explained that, as she was late coming home from work, she was preparing leftovers. Upon hearing this, Mr. X got upset and angry. He argued that, as she has a family to attend to, Mrs. X should ensure that she get home on time.

Some participants received the provocation version of this scenario. For these participants, the scenario went on to read:

> Mrs. X then became upset. She began to yell at Mr. X and as her anger heightened, she began to shout various obscenities at him, calling him a "nagging bastard."

All participants then read the same ending:

> Mrs. X then went into the kitchen to prepare dinner. Mr. X followed her. He grabbed her by the arm and slapped her, knocking her to the floor, and kicked her several times. He subsequently left the house.

In this study, participants who received the provocation information assigned more blame to the victim than those who did not receive this information. In conclusion, this tendency to see other people as responsible for their plight can result in tragic consequences, such as seeing the victims of abuse and violence as responsible for their suffering.

Underestimating the Power of Social Influence

When we underestimate the power of social influence, we experience feelings of false security and control. For example, when trying to explain why people do repugnant or bizarre things—such as the members of the Solar Temple cult's taking their own lives or killing their own children—it is tempting, and in a strange way comforting, to write off the victims as flawed human beings. Doing so helps the rest of us believe that it could never happen to us. However, by failing to appreciate fully the power of the situation, we tend to oversimplify complex situations; oversimplification decreases our understanding of the causes of a great deal of human behaviour. Among other things, this oversimplification can lead us to blame the victim in situations where the individual was overpowered by social forces too difficult for most of us to resist—as in the Solar Temple tragedy.

> The head monkey at Paris puts on a traveller's cap, and all the monkeys in America do the same.
>
> –HENRY DAVID THOREAU

Suppose these students were asked to play a game for money. Would they play cooperatively or competitively? Do you think their characters or the situation will be most likely to influence them?

Here is an example of the kind of oversimplification we are talking about: Imagine a situation in which people are playing a two-person game wherein each player must choose one of two strategies—they can play competitively, where they try to win as much money as possible and ensure that their partner loses as much as possible, or they can play cooperatively, where they try to ensure that both they and their partner win some money. We will discuss the details of this game in Chapter 7. For now, it is important to note that there are only two basic strategies people can use when playing the game—competitive or cooperative. Now think about some of your friends. How do you think they would play this game?

Few people find this question hard to answer; we all have a sense of the relative competitiveness of our friends. "Well," you might say, "I am certain that my friend Sam, who is a cutthroat business major, would play this game more competitively than my friend Anna, who is a really caring, loving person." That is, we think of our friends' personalities and answer accordingly. We usually do not think much about the nature of the social situation when making our predictions.

But how accurate are such predictions? Should we think about the social situation? To find out, Lee Ross and Steven Samuels (1993) conducted the following experiment. First, they chose a group of students at Stanford University who were considered by the resident assistants in their dorm to be either especially cooperative or especially competitive. The researchers did this by describing the game to the resident assistants and asking them to think of students in their dormitories who would be most likely to adopt the competitive or cooperative strategy. As expected, the resident assistants had no trouble thinking of students who fit each category.

Next, Ross and Samuels invited these students to play the game in a psychology experiment. There was one added twist: The researchers varied a seemingly minor aspect of the social situation—namely, what the game was called. They told half the participants that it was the Wall Street Game and half that it was the Community Game. Everything else about the game was identical. Thus, because people who were judged as either competitive or cooperative played the game under one of two names, the experiment resulted in four conditions.

Again, most of us go through life assuming that what really counts is an individual's personality—not something as trivial as what a game is called. Some people seem competitive by nature and would thus relish the opportunity to go head-to-head with a fellow student. Others seem much more cooperative and would thus achieve the most satisfaction by ensuring that no one lost too much money and no one's feelings were hurt. Right? Not so fast! As seen in Figure 1.1, even as trivial an aspect of the situation as the name of the game made a tremendous difference in how people behaved. When it was called the Wall Street Game, approximately two-thirds of the people responded competitively—regardless of their personalities—whereas when it was called the Community Game, only a third of the people responded competitively. The name of the game conveyed strong social norms about what kind of behaviour was appropriate in this situation and, as we will see throughout this book, social norms can shape people's behaviour in powerful ways.

This is not to say that personality differences do not exist or are unimportant. They do exist and frequently are of great importance. But we have learned that social and environmental situations are so powerful that they have dramatic effects on almost everyone. This is the domain of the social psychologist.

classic research

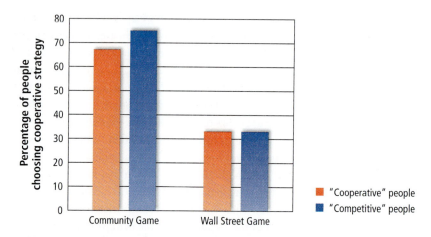

FIGURE 1.1 What Influences How Cooperative People Will Be—Their Personalities or the Nature of the Social Situation?

Ross and Samuels (1993) found that university students' personalities, as rated by the resident assistants in their dormitories, did not determine how cooperative or competitive they were in a laboratory game. The name of the game—whether it was called the Wall Street Game or the Community Game—did, however, make a tremendous difference. Such seemingly minor aspects of the social situation can have powerful effects on people's behaviour, overwhelming the differences in their personalities.

(Adapted from Ross & Samuels, 1993)

The Subjectivity of the Social Situation

We should note that other disciplines, such as anthropology and sociology, are also interested in how people are influenced by their social environments. Social psychology is distinct, however, primarily because it is concerned not so much with social situations in any objective sense, but rather with how people are influenced by their interpretations, or **construals**, of their social environments. To understand how people are influenced by their social world, social psychologists believe that it is more important to understand how they perceive, comprehend, and interpret the social world than it is to understand the objective properties of the social world itself (Lewin, 1943).

Such construals can be rather simple. Other construals might appear simple but are, in reality, remarkably complex. For example, suppose Maria gives Shawn a kiss on the cheek at the end of their first date. How will Shawn respond to the kiss? We would say that it depends on how he construes the situation: Does he interpret it as a first step—a sign of awakening romantic interest on Maria's part? Or does he see it as an aloof, sisterly expression—a signal that Maria wants to be friends but nothing more? Or does he see it as a sign that Maria is interested in him but wants things to go slowly in their developing relationship?

Were Shawn to misconstrue the situation, he might commit a serious blunder; he might turn his back on what could have been the love of his life—or he might express passion inappropriately. In either case, we believe that the best strategy for understanding Shawn's reaction would be to find a way to determine Shawn's construal of Maria's behaviour, rather than to dissect the objective nature of the kiss itself (its length, degree of pressure, etc.).

Construal the way in which people perceive, comprehend, and interpret the social world

This emphasis on construal has its roots in an approach called Gestalt psychology. Initially proposed as a theory of how people perceive the physical word, **Gestalt psychology** holds that we should study the subjective way in which an object appears in people's minds (the gestalt, or whole), rather than the way in which the objective, physical attributes of the object combine. For example, one way to try to understand how people perceive a painting would be to break it down into its individual elements—such as the exact amounts of primary colours applied to the different parts of the canvas, the types of brushstrokes used to apply the colours, and the different geometric shapes they form—and to attempt to determine how these elements are combined by the perceiver to form an overall image of the painting. According to Gestalt psychologists, however, it is impossible to understand the way in which an object is perceived simply by studying these building blocks of perception. The whole is different from the sum of its parts. One must focus on the phenomenology of the perceiver—that is, on how an object appears to people—instead of on the individual elements of the objective stimulus.

Gestalt psychology a school of psychology stressing the importance of studying the subjective way in which an object appears in people's minds, rather than the objective, physical attributes of the object

Thinking Critically

1. Why are most people prone to commit the fundamental attribution error?
2. What are some of the negative consequences of our tendency to underestimate the power of the social situation?

SOCIAL PSYCHOLOGY AND SOCIAL PROBLEMS

To summarize, social psychology can be defined as the scientific study of social influence. Social influence can best be understood by examining the subjective views people form about their environment. It might have occurred to you to ask why we want to understand social influence in the first place.

There are several answers to this question. The most basic is simple: We are curious. Social psychologists are fascinated by human social behaviour and want to understand it

Social psychologists investigate many kinds of relevant issues, such as whether watching violence on TV produces violent behaviour in children.

on the deepest possible level. In a sense, all of us are social psychologists. We all live in a social environment, and we all are more than mildly curious about such issues as how we become influenced, how we influence others, and why we fall in love with some people, dislike others, and are indifferent to still others.

Many social psychologists have another reason for studying the causes of social behaviour—namely, to contribute to the solution of social problems. From the beginnings of our young science, social psychologists have been keenly interested in such social problems as the reduction of hostility and prejudice, and the increase of altruism and generosity. Contemporary social psychologists have continued this tradition and have broadened the issues of concern to include such endeavours as inducing people to conserve natural resources such as water and energy (Dickerson et al., 1992), educating people to practise safer sex in order to reduce the spread of AIDS (Aronson, 1997a, 1998; Stone et al., 1994), understanding the relationship between viewing violence on television and the violent behaviour of television viewers (Eron et al., 1996; Josephson, 1987), developing effective negotiation strategies for the reduction of international conflict (Kelman, 1997), and helping people adjust to life changes such as entry to college or university or the death of a loved one (Harris, 1986). Throughout this book, we will examine many such examples of the applications of social psychology. Likewise, throughout this book we will discuss some of the underlying human motives and characteristics of the social situations that produce significant social behaviours, with the assumption that if we are interested in changing our own or other people's behaviour, we must first know something about these fundamental causes.

Thinking Critically

To what extent do situational factors contribute to the kinds of social problems that social psychologists are trying to solve? Can the power of the situation be used to promote social good?

Summary

People are constantly being influenced by others. **Social psychology** is defined as the scientific study of the way in which people's thoughts, feelings, and behaviours are influenced by the real or imagined presence of other people. Social influence is often powerful, usually outweighing and frequently overwhelming **individual differences** in people's personalities as determinants of behaviour. As a result, we must try to avoid making the **fundamental attribution error**—the tendency to explain our own and others' behaviour entirely in terms of personality traits, thus underestimating the power of social influence.

To appreciate the power of social influence, we must understand how people form **construals** of their social environments. We are not computer-like organisms who respond directly and mechanically to environmental stimuli; rather, we are complex human beings who perceive, think about, and sometimes distort information from our environment. Social psychologists' emphasis on the way in which people construe the social world has its roots in the tradition of **Gestalt psychology**.

Key Terms

Construal (p. 12)
Fundamental attribution error (p. 8)
Gestalt psychology (p. 13)
Individual differences (p. 7)
Social psychology (p. 6)

Key Online Search Terms

Social influence
Fundamental attribution error
Construal
Gestalt psychology

If You Are Interested

Aron, A., & Aron, E. (1992). *The heart of social psychology.* Lexington, MA: Lexington Books. A highly readable behind-the-scenes look at how eminent social psychologists view their discipline.

Dion, K. L. (2000). Canada. In A. E. Kazdin (Ed.), *Encyclopedia of psychology* (Vol. 2, pp. 5–12). Washington, DC: American Psychological Association & New York: Oxford University Press. In this brief article, University of Toronto social psychologist Kenneth Dion traces the history of psychology in Canada, covering such events as the birth of the Canadian Psychological Association, the establishment of research granting agencies, prominent research centres, and so on. In addition to providing an overview of the field, the author provides a trenchant analysis of the state of the field today. Issues such as the relation between researchers and practitioners are discussed.

Moghaddam, F. M., Taylor, D. M., & Wright, S. (1993). *Social psychology in cross-cultural perspective.* New York: W. H. Freeman. This book, written at McGill University, provides a fascinating look at the role of cultural factors in social psychology. The authors demonstrate that various phenomena that have been taken for granted in social psychology (e.g., cognitive dissonance, social influence) take a rather different form when examined outside the North American context.

Weblinks

www.cpa.ca
Canadian Psychological Association
The Canadian Psychological Association represents the interests of all aspects of psychology in Canada, and includes a section devoted to social psychology.

www.apa.org
American Psychological Association

www.apa.org/journals/psp.html
Journal of Personality and Social Psychology
This is the flagship journal for the field of social psychology. At this APA site, you can read the contents and abstracts of current issues of the journal.

www.spssi.org
The Society for the Psychological Study of Social Issues
This is the Web site for the Society for the Psychological Study of Social Issues (SPSSI). Traditionally, members of this society have been primarily social psychologists.

www.uiowa.edu/~grpproc/crisp/crisp.html
Current Research in Social Psychology
This site hosts a peer-reviewed electronic journal covering all aspects of social psychology.

www.socialpsychology.org
Social Psychology Network
Arguably the best online resource for social psychology, this page provides several links to topics related to social psychology, links to the home pages of social psychologists, and a search engine specifically for the information contained at the site.

Chapter 1 Practice Quiz

Check your knowledge of the concepts in this chapter by trying the following questions.

WHAT IS SOCIAL PSYCHOLOGY?

Multiple Choice

1. Social influence includes
   a. behaviour.
   b. thoughts and feelings.
   c. overt acts.
   d. all of the above.

2. All of the following are part of Allport's definition of social psychology except
   a. scientific study.
   b. thoughts, feelings, and behaviour.
   c. unconscious processes.
   d. the presence of other people.

3. Unlike sociology, analysis for social psychologists is at the _____ level.
   a. individual
   b. family
   c. tribal
   d. societal

4. If you believe that social behaviour is a function of individual differences, you are thinking like a/an
   a. sociologist.
   b. psychologist.
   c. personality psychologist.
   d. anthropologist.

True or False

5. Both social psychology and sociology examine how social influences impact human behaviour.
   ___ True
   ___ False

6. To understand aggression, social psychologists focus on societal factors such as poverty.
   ___ True
   ___ False

7. Social psychology shares no similarities with sociology.
   ___ True
   ___ False

8. Social influence includes behaviour, thoughts and feelings, and overt acts.
   ___ True
   ___ False

Fill in the Blank

9. _____ is what happens during an election when techniques are applied to convince us to vote for a particular candidate.

10. Unlike social psychologists, who focus on situational factors, personality psychologists tend to focus their attention on _____.

THE POWER OF SOCIAL INFLUENCE

Multiple Choice

11. When explaining behaviour, social psychologists believe that focusing on personality factors underestimates the role of
    a. mental disorders.
    b. unconscious processes.
    c. situational factors.
    d. internal factors.

12. Kristiansen and Guilietti (1990) found that participants who read that a perpetrator of violence had been provoked tended to assign
    a. more blame to the victim.
    b. more blame to the perpetrator.
    c. an equivalent amount of blame to the victim and the perpetrator.
    d. no blame to either the victim or the perpetrator.

13. Ross and Samuels (1993) found that there was greater competition when a game was labelled
    a. Wall Street Game.
    b. Board Game.
    c. Community Game.
    d. Attack Game.

14. According to social psychologists like Kurt Lewin, to understand how people are influenced by the social world, one must examine
    a. the objective reality of the social world.
    b. perceptions, comprehension, and interpretations.
    c. personality factors.
    d. all of the above

True or False

15. Ross and Samuels (1993) found that, in a laboratory game, personality factors were as important as the description of a game in people's choice of cooperative strategies.
    ___ True
    ___ False

16. We often fail to fully appreciate the power of the situation by instead developing complex explanations for the causes of social behaviour.
    ___ True
    ___ False

17. To blame victims of violence for their situation reflects the fundamental attribution error.
    ___ True
    ___ False

18. "The whole is greater than the sum of its parts" is a statement attributed to personality psychologists.
    ___ True
    ___ False

Fill in the Blank

19. _____ is the tendency to explain our own and other people's behaviour in terms of personality factors.

20. _____ is the way in which the social world is perceived, comprehended, and interpreted.

PERSONALIZED STUDY PLAN

Want to check your answers and access more study resources? Visit the Companion Website for *Fundamentals of Social Psychology* at **www.pearsoned.ca/aronson**, where you'll find the above questions incorporated in a pre-test and post-test for each chapter. These tests will be automatically graded online, allowing you to check your answers. A Study Plan, like the one below, groups the questions by section within the chapter and shows you which sections you need to focus on for further study.

Your Results for "Chapter 1, Pretest"

OVERALL SCORE: 60% of 10 questions

Group	Score	Proficient
What Is Social Psychology?	4 of 5	Yes
The Power of Social Influence	4 of 5	Yes

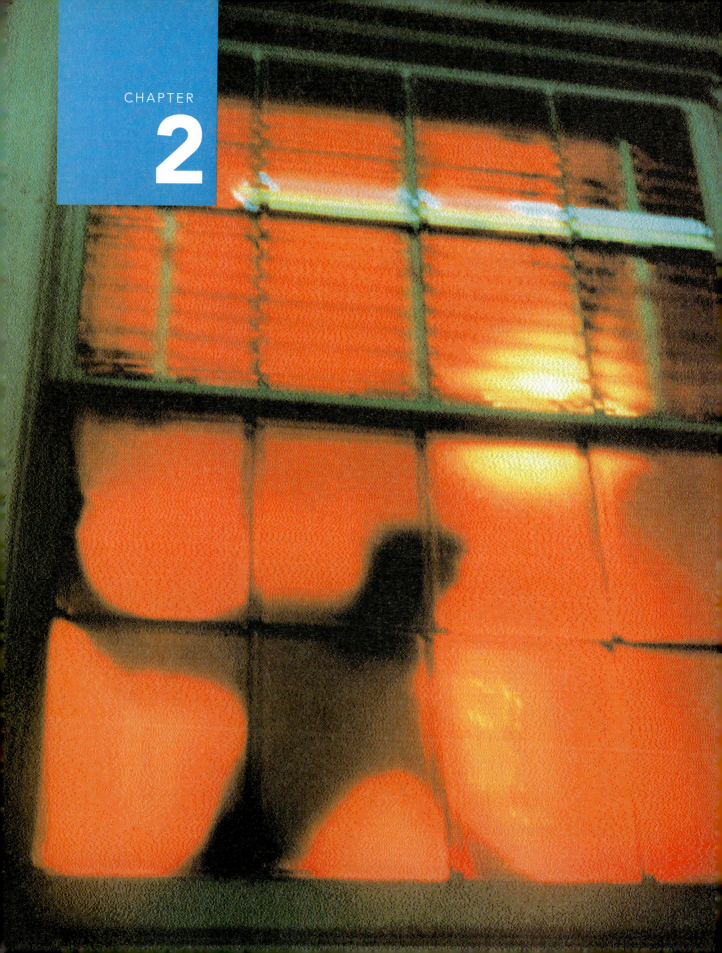

CHAPTER 2

Methodology: How Social Psychologists Do Research

Chapter Outline

SOCIAL PSYCHOLOGY: AN EMPIRICAL SCIENCE

FORMULATING HYPOTHESES AND THEORIES

DESCRIPTIVE METHODS: DESCRIBING SOCIAL BEHAVIOUR
The Observational Method
The Correlational Method

THE EXPERIMENTAL METHOD: ANSWERING CAUSAL QUESTIONS
Independent and Dependent Variables
Internal Validity in Experiments
External Validity in Experiments

ETHICAL ISSUES IN SOCIAL PSYCHOLOGY

As social psychologists, we are interested in finding ways of stopping violence when it occurs. If you happen to witness someone being attacked by another person you might not intervene directly, out of fear for your own safety. Most of us assume that we would help in some way, though, such as by calling the police. This very assumption was the reason people were so shocked by an incident that occurred in the early 1960s, in the Queensborough area of New York City. A woman named Kitty Genovese was attacked while walking to her car and brutally murdered in the alley of an apartment complex. The attack lasted 45 minutes. No fewer than 38 of the apartment residents admitted later that they had rushed to their windows after hearing Genovese's screams for help. However, not one of the bystanders attempted in any way to help her—none of them even telephoned the police.

As you might imagine, the Kitty Genovese murder received a great deal of publicity. Reporters, commentators, and pundits of all kinds came forward with their personal theories about why the bystanders had done nothing. The most popular explanation was that there is something dehumanizing about living in a metropolis that inevitably leads to apathy, indifference to human suffering, and lack of caring. The blame was laid on New York and New Yorkers; the general belief was that this kind of thing would not have happened in a small town, where people care about each other (Rosenthal, 1964). Was big-city life the cause of the bystanders' behaviour? Or was there some other explanation? Again, how can we find out?

This is the area where Kitty Genovese was attacked, in full view of her neighbours. Why didn't anyone call the police?

SOCIAL PSYCHOLOGY: AN EMPIRICAL SCIENCE

A fundamental principle of social psychology is that many social problems, such as the causes of and reactions to violence, can be studied empirically—meaning that we can answer questions about human social behaviour by conducting scientific research (Aronson, Wilson, & Brewer, 1998; Judd & McClelland, 1998; Kenny, Kashy, & Bolger, 1998). It is insufficient to rely on personal beliefs, folk wisdom, hope, or magazine polls when answering questions about human behaviour. Many personal observations are astute and accurate reflections of social reality, while others are far off the mark. Consider what folk wisdom has to say about the factors that influence how much we like other people. On the one hand, we know that "birds of a feather flock together," and with a little effort each of us could come up with many examples of liking and hanging around with people who share our backgrounds and interests. But on the other hand, folk wisdom *also* tells us that "opposites attract," and if we tried we could come up with examples of people with backgrounds and interests different from our own attracting us. Which is correct?

To answer this question, our observations must be translated into hypotheses that can be tested scientifically. And as for the question of whether opposites attract or whether similarity leads to attraction, stay tuned. We will discuss the research on this fascinating issue in Chapter 8.

Because we will describe the results of many empirical studies in this book, it is important to discuss how social psychological research is done. We begin with a warning: The results of some of the studies you encounter will seem obvious, because the topic of social psychology is something with which we are all intimately familiar—social behaviour and social influence. Note that this fact separates social psychology from other sciences. When you read about an experiment in particle physics, it is unlikely that the results will connect with your personal experiences and have a ring of familiarity. We don't know about you, but we have never thought, "Wow! That experiment on quarks was just like what happened to me while I was waiting for the bus yesterday," or "My grandmother always told me to watch out for quarks, positrons, and antimatter." When reading about the results of a study on helping behaviour or aggression, however, it is quite common to think, "Aw, come on, I could have predicted that. The same thing happened to me last Friday."

The thing to remember is that such findings appear obvious because most examples of human behaviour seem to make sense and to have been easily predictable—once we know their outcomes (Fischhoff, 1975; Hertwig, Gigerenzer, & Hoffrage, 1997; Nario & Branscombe, 1995). Hindsight is 20/20, as the saying goes. This phenomenon was illustrated in a study by Roese and Olson (1996). They asked students at the University of Western Ontario to read a story, based on First World War events, about a young British soldier who devised a plan to save a small village that was about to be invaded. In one condition, participants were told that the soldier managed to convince others in the military to accept his plan and the village was saved. When asked how predictable this outcome was, they felt it was obvious all along that the village would be saved. In another condition, participants were told that the soldier's plan was rejected and the village was destroyed. When asked how predictable this outcome was, these participants thought it was obvious that the village would be destroyed! As this study shows, the opposite finding of an experiment might seem just as obvious as the results that actually were obtained. The trick is to predict what will happen in an experiment *before* you know how it turned out. For example, if you give children a reward for something they already enjoy doing, will they subsequently like that activity more, the same, or less? When we ask our students that question, most of them reply that children will like an activity more if they are rewarded for doing so. However, social psychological experiments on this issue show that if people already enjoy doing something, giving them a reward for doing it will usually make them like it less (e.g., Lepper, 1995, 1996; Lepper, Greene, & Nisbett, 1973). Thus, findings that seem obvious in retrospect may not be easy to predict in advance.

Social psychology is an empirical science, with a well-developed set of methods to answer questions about social behaviour, such as the ones about violence with which we began this chapter. These methods are of three types: the observational method, the correlational method, and the experimental method. Any of these methods could be used to explore a specific research question; each is a powerful tool in some ways and a weak tool in others. Part of the creativity in conducting social psychological research involves choosing the right method, maximizing its strengths, and minimizing its weaknesses.

In this chapter, we will discuss these methods in detail. We, the authors of this book, are not primarily textbook writers—we are social scientists who have done a great deal of research in social psychology. As such, we will try to provide you with an understanding of both the joy and the difficulty of doing research. The joy comes in unravelling the clues to understanding interesting and important social behaviours, just as a sleuth gradually unmasks the culprit in a murder mystery. Each of us finds it exhilarating that we have the tools to provide answers to questions that philosophers have debated for centuries. At the same time, as seasoned researchers we have learned to temper this exhilaration with a heavy dose of humility, for the practical and ethical constraints involved in creating and conducting social psychological research are formidable.

Thinking Critically
Why do you think people feel that they "knew it all along" when they hear the findings of social psychology studies? How might this tendency be overcome?

FORMULATING HYPOTHESES AND THEORIES

There is lore in science that brilliant insights come all of a sudden, as when Archimedes shouted, "Eureka! I have found it!" when the solution to a problem flashed into his mind. Though such insights do sometimes occur suddenly, science is a cumulative process, and people often generate hypotheses from previous theories and research. We define a **theory** as an organized set of principles that can be used to explain observed phenomena.

Many studies stem from a researcher's dissatisfaction with existing theories and explanations. After reading other people's work, a researcher might believe that he or she has a better way of explaining people's behaviour (e.g., why they fail to help in an emergency). Social psychologists, like scientists in other disciplines, engage in a continual process of theory

Theory an organized set of principles that can be used to explain observed phenomena

> There is nothing so practical as a good theory.
>
> –KURT LEWIN, 1951

refinement: They develop a theory, test specific hypotheses derived from that theory, and based on the results revise the theory and formulate new hypotheses.

Theory is not the only way to derive a new hypothesis in social psychology. Researchers often observe a phenomenon in everyday life that they find curious and interesting. They then construct a theory about why this phenomenon occurs, and design a study to see if they are right.

Consider the murder of Kitty Genovese discussed earlier. As we saw, most people blamed her neighbours' failure to intervene on the apathy, indifference, and callousness that big-city life breeds. Two social psychologists who taught at universities in New York, however, had a different idea. Bibb Latané and John Darley got to talking one day about the Genovese murder. Here is how Latané describes it: "One evening after [a] downtown cocktail party, John Darley . . . came back with me to my 12th Street apartment for a drink. Our common complaint was the distressing tendency of acquaintances, on finding that we called ourselves social psychologists, to ask why New Yorkers were so apathetic" (Latané, 1987, p. 78). Instead of focusing on "what was wrong with New Yorkers," Latané and Darley thought it would be more interesting and more important to examine the social situation in which Genovese's neighbours found themselves: "We came up with the insight that perhaps what made the Genovese case so fascinating was itself what made it happen—namely, that not just one or two, but 38 people had watched and done nothing" (Latané, 1987, p. 78).

The researchers had the hunch that, paradoxically, the more people who witness an emergency, the less likely it is that any given individual will intervene. Genovese's neighbours might have assumed that someone else had called the police, a phenomenon Latané and Darley (1968) referred to as the *diffusion of responsibility*. Perhaps the bystanders would have been more likely to help had each thought he or she alone was witnessing the murder.

Once a researcher has a hypothesis, whether it comes from a theory, previous research, or observation of everyday life, how can he or she tell if it is true? How could Latané and Darley tell whether the number of eyewitnesses in fact affects people's likelihood of helping a victim? In science, idle speculation will not do; the researcher must collect data to test his or her hypothesis. Let's look at how the observational method, the correlational method, and the experimental method are used to explore research hypotheses such as Latané and Darley's. These methods are summarized in Table 2.1.

Thinking Critically

Do you think it is important to develop theories to explain human social behaviour? Why or why not?

TABLE 2.1	A Summary of Research Methods
Method	Questions Answered
1. Observational	Description: What is the nature of the phenomenon?
2. Correlational	Description: What is the relation between variable *X* and variable *Y*?
3. Experimental	Causality: Is variable *X* a cause of variable *Y*?

DESCRIPTIVE METHODS: DESCRIBING SOCIAL BEHAVIOUR

One goal of the social psychologist is to systematically describe human social behaviour. There are a number of tools, or methods, that are at the social psychologist's disposal in this enterprise. We will focus on two such methods: the observational method and the correlational method.

The Observational Method

As its name implies, the **observational method** is the technique whereby a researcher observes people and systematically records measurements of their behaviour. This method varies according to the degree to which the observer actively participates in the scene. At one extreme, the observer interacts with the people being observed, but does not try to alter the situation in any way. A classic example of this is Festinger and colleagues' infiltration of a doomsday cult (Festinger, Riecken, & Schacter, 1956). To be able to observe and interview members of the cult, these researchers joined the cult and pretended that they, too, believed the world was about to end. At the other end of the continuum, the observer neither participates nor intervenes in any way; instead, the observer is unobtrusive and tries to blend in with the scenery as much as possible. For example, Debra Pepler at York University and Wendy Craig at Queen's University have developed a particularly unobtrusive method for observing bullying behaviour in school settings (Atlas & Pepler, 1998; Craig & Pepler, 1997; Pepler & Craig, 1995). The children wear waist pouches that actually contain small microphones while a hidden video camera films their interactions. Thus, children can freely roam over relatively large areas (e.g., school playgrounds) while their behaviour is recorded. This combination of audio and visual technology allows the researchers to observe overt physical acts of aggression as well as subtler forms of bullying, such as indirect aggression and verbal threats or insults. (Subtle forms of bullying are especially difficult to detect when researchers rely on more traditional methods, such as standing outside a playground fence and making check marks whenever they notice particular behaviours.)

The waist-pouch microphone technology also addresses an age-old problem in observational research, namely that people change their behaviour when they are being observed. Bullies, for example, tend not to engage in bullying when adults are around (Craig & Pepler, 1997). Thus, an advantage of using unobtrusive measures, such as Pepler and Craig's, is that researchers can observe spontaneous, naturally occurring behaviour.

In all observational research—regardless of whether observers are on the spot or later analyze video- or audiotapes—it is important for the researchers to define clearly the behaviours of interest. For example, in Pepler and Craig's research an episode is classified as bullying only if there is a power imbalance between the individuals involved, if there is intent to harm on the part of the person doing the bullying, and if the victim shows distress (Atlas & Pepler, 1998; Craig & Pepler, 1997).

Observational method the technique whereby a researcher observes people and systematically records measurements of their behaviour

FOCUS ON APPLICATIONS

Putting a Stop to Bullying: Can Social Psychological Research Help?

Observational research can be used to address important social problems. For example, the research conducted on bullying by Debra Pepler and her colleagues led to the development

"So! How is everybody today?"
Copyright © *The New Yorker Collection* 2003 Mick Stevens from cartoonbank.com. All rights reserved.

of an anti-bullying intervention program that has been used in Toronto schools (Pepler et al., 1994). The program trains teachers and administrators to be vigilant about the problem of bullying and to make moderate and swift interventions. Although insufficient resources have hampered the researchers from fully implementing this program, there is evidence that this kind of intervention can be effective. A full-fledged program of this sort has been successfully used in Norway and Sweden, where researchers found that the incidence of bullying was reduced by as much as 50 percent among children in grades 4 to 7 (Olweus, 1996, 1997).

Operational definition the precise specification of how variables are measured or manipulated

The importance of clearly defining the behaviours of interest applies to all psychological research, not just observational studies. The term **operational definition** refers to the precise specification of how variables are measured or manipulated. Recall, for example, that a power imbalance is one criterion that Pepler and colleagues use to define bullying. Are you able to come up with an operational definition of this variable that would be useful in the context of observing playground interactions? Pepler and Craig operationally defined a power imbalance as a discrepancy, between the children involved, in terms of height and weight. In other words, in situations involving aggression on the playground, the researchers assumed that a bigger child was likely to be in a position of power relative to a smaller child.

If, on the other hand, the researchers were interested in observing bullying in a corporate boardroom, they presumably would specify a different operational definition of power imbalance—perhaps the discrepancy between the individuals' status in the corporation (manager versus secretary).

The Correlational Method

Often social scientists want to do more than document social behaviour—they want to understand relations between variables. For example, is there a relation between the amount of violence children see on television and their aggressiveness? To answer such questions, researchers frequently use a different approach: the correlational method.

The **correlational method** is a technique whereby two variables are systematically measured and the relation between them—how much you can predict one from the other—is assessed. For example, using the correlational method, researchers might be interested in testing the relation between children's aggressive behaviour and how much violent television they watch. Thus, the researchers would measure a child's level of aggression (perhaps at home, perhaps on the playground) as well as measure the amount of violent television programming watched by that child to see if there is any relation between these two variables.

Correlational method the technique whereby researchers systematically measure two or more variables, and assess the relation between them (i.e., how much one can be predicted from the other)

Researchers look at such relations by calculating a **correlation coefficient**, which is a statistic that assesses how well you can predict one variable based on another; for example, how well you can predict people's weight from their height. A positive correlation means that increases in the value of one variable are associated with increases in the value of the other variable. Height and weight are positively correlated; the taller people are, the more they tend to weigh. A negative correlation means that *increases* in the value of one variable are associated with *decreases* in the value of the other. For example, we might expect that as the number of classes skipped goes up, one's mark in the course goes down—the more classes skipped, the lower the final grade. It is also possible, of course, for two variables to be completely uncorrelated, so that a researcher cannot predict one variable from the other. For example, knowing someone's shoe size will not enable you to predict how many books that person owns.

Correlation coefficient a statistical technique that assesses how well you can predict one variable based on another; for example, how well you can predict people's weight from their height

Correlation coefficients are expressed as numbers that can range from −1.00 to +1.00. A positive or negative correlation of 1.00 means that two variables are perfectly correlated; thus, by knowing people's standing on one variable, the researcher can predict exactly where they stand on the other variable. In everyday life, of course, perfect correlations are rare. For example, one study found that the correlation between height and weight was +.47, in a sample of men ages 18 to 24 (Freedman et al., 1991). This means that, on average, the taller people were heavier than the shorter people, but there were exceptions. A correlation of −.47 would tell you that, on average, students who skip classes get lower grades, but once again there are exceptions. A correlation of zero means that two variables are not associated at all. The correlation between having positive attitudes toward condoms and actually using them is disturbingly close to zero—as low as +.23 in one sample of French-Canadian university students (Hébert et al., 1989). Thus, if you know that someone has positive attitudes toward using condoms, this information will not allow you to make a very accurate prediction about whether that person actually will use one the next time he or she has sex.

LIMITS OF THE CORRELATIONAL METHOD: CORRELATION DOES NOT EQUAL CAUSATION If a researcher finds that there is a correlation between two variables, it means that there are three possible relations between these variables. For example, researchers have found a correlation between the amount of violent television children watch and how aggressive they are (Eron, 1982). One explanation of this correlation is that watching TV violence causes kids to be more violent. It is equally probable, however, that the reverse is true: that kids who are violent to begin with are more likely to watch violent TV. Or there might be no causal relation between these two variables; instead, both TV watching and violent behaviour could be caused by a third variable, such as having neglectful parents who do not pay

Tillie Goren believes that she has the ability to end droughts because on several occasions when she has visited a drought-stricken area, it has started to rain. Is this a case of correlation or causation?

much attention to their kids. (In Chapter 9, we will present experimental evidence that supports the first causal relation.) When we use the correlational method, it is wrong to jump to the conclusion that one variable is causing the other to occur. A correlation suggests that a causal relationship *may* exist between variables, but it does not *prove* causation.

Unfortunately, one of the most common methodological errors in the social sciences is a researcher's forgetting this adage. Drawing causal conclusions from correlational data also frequently occurs in everyday life. Consider, for example, a column in the *Winnipeg Free Press* featuring Tillie the Rainmaker. It all began in 1986 when Tillie took a trip to Sacramento, California. As soon as she stepped off the plane, the skies poured with rain, ending a six-week drought. Until then, Tillie had seen herself as an average Jewish grandmother. But at that moment, she realized that she had special powers. Tillie claims to have ended many droughts and extinguished major forest fires since then. Winnipeg rabbi Alan Green is a strong supporter of Tillie and her work. "I can't prove scientifically that there is cause-and-effect," says Green. But he does believe that such things are possible. Besides, "It's a freely offered gift…There can be no harm" (Reynolds, 2000).

In a letter to the editor the next week, a psychology professor suggested that Tillie and her rabbi inferred causality from correlational events, when it may simply have been a coincidence that the rains started the moment Tillie stepped off the airplane ("Double deception," 2000). In some cases, inferring causality—believing that Tillie caused the rainfall through special powers—might be quite harmless, as Rabbi Green points out. However, it is not sound scientific practice, and the consequences can be quite serious, as demonstrated by a study of birth control methods and sexually transmitted diseases (STDs) in women (Rosenberg et al., 1992). These researchers examined the records of women who had visited a clinic for STDs, noting which method of birth control they used and whether they had STDs. Surprisingly, the researchers found that women who relied

Correlation Does Not Equal Causation

Try It!

It can be difficult to remember that correlation does not allow us to make causal inferences, especially when a correlation suggests a particularly compelling cause. It is easy to forget that there are alternative explanations for the obtained correlation; for example, other variables could be causing both of the observed variables to occur. For each of the following examples, think about why the correlation was found. Even if it seems obvious which variable was causing the other, are there alternative explanations?

Quiz

1. Recently, a politician extolled the virtues of the Boy and Girl Scouts organizations. In his salute to the Scouts, the politician mentioned that few teenagers convicted of street crimes had been members of the Scouts. In other words, he was positing a negative correlation between activity in Scouting and frequency of criminal behaviour. Why might this be?

2. A research study found that having a pet in childhood is correlated with a reduced likelihood of one's becoming a juvenile delinquent in adolescence. Why is this?

3. A recent study of soldiers stationed on army bases found that the number of tattoos a soldier has is correlated positively with his becoming involved in a motorcycle accident. Why?

4. Recently, it was reported that a correlation exists between people's tendency to eat breakfast in the morning and how long they live, such that people who skip breakfast die younger. Does eating Cheerios lead to a long life?

5. A few years ago, newspaper headlines announced, "Coffee suspected as a cause of heart attacks." Medical studies had found a correlation between the amount of coffee people drank and their likelihood of having a heart attack. Are there any alternative explanations?

6. A positive correlation exists between the viscosity of asphalt in city playgrounds and the crime rate. How can this be? When asphalt becomes viscous (softer), is some chemical released that drives potential criminals wild? When the crime rate goes up, do people flock to the playgrounds, so that the pounding of their feet increases the viscosity of the asphalt? What explains this correlation?

7. A news magazine recently reported that the more time fathers spend with their children, the less likely they are to sexually abuse them. Why might this be?

Answers

1. The politician ignored possible third variables that could cause both Scouts membership and crime, such as socioeconomic class. Traditionally, Scouting has been most popular in small towns and suburbs among middle-class youngsters; it has never been very attractive or even available to youths growing up in densely populated, urban, high-crime areas.

2. Families who can afford or are willing to have a pet might differ in any number of ways from families who neither can afford nor are willing to have one.

3. Did tattoos cause motorcycle accidents? Or, for that matter, did motorcycle accidents cause tattoos? The researchers suggested that a third (unmeasured) variable was in fact the cause of both: a tendency to take risks and to be involved in flamboyant personal displays led to tattooing one's body and to driving a motorcycle recklessly.

4. Not necessarily. People who do not eat breakfast might differ from people who do in any number of ways that influence longevity—for example, in how obese they are, in how hard-driving and high-strung they are, or even in how late they sleep in the morning.

5. Coffee drinkers may be more likely to engage in other behaviours that put them at risk, such as smoking cigarettes or not exercising regularly.

6. Both the viscosity of asphalt and the crime rate go up when the temperature is high—for example, on a hot summer day or night.

7. The news magazine concluded that spending time with one's child reduces the urge to engage in sexual abuse (Adler, 1997). But perhaps child abuse leads to less time with children, due to feelings of guilt or fear of being caught. Or perhaps there is a third variable, such as an antisocial personality, that contributes to parents abusing and spending less time with their child.

on condoms had significantly more STDs than women who used diaphragms or contraceptive sponges. This result was widely reported in the popular press, along with the conclusion that the use of diaphragms and sponges caused a lower incidence of disease. Some reporters urged women whose partners used condoms to switch to other methods.

Can you see the problem with this conclusion? The fact that the incidence of disease was correlated with the type of contraception women used is open to a number of causal interpretations. Perhaps the women who used sponges and diaphragms had sex with fewer partners. (In fact, condom users were more likely to have had sex with multiple partners in the previous month.) Perhaps the partners of women who relied on condoms were more likely to have STDs than the partners of women who used sponges and diaphragms. There is simply no way of knowing. Thus, the conclusion that any of the three types of birth control offered protection against STDs cannot be drawn from this correlational study.

Latané and Darley also might have used the correlational method to determine whether the number of bystanders is related to helping behaviour. They might have surveyed victims and bystanders of crimes and then correlated the total number of bystanders at each crime scene with the number of bystanders who helped or tried to help the victims. Let's say that a negative correlation was found in these data: The greater the number of bystanders, the less likely it was that any one of them intervened. Would this be evidence that the number of bystanders caused helping behaviour to occur or not? Unfortunately, no. Any number of unknown variables could be causing both the number of bystanders and the rate of helping to occur. For example, the seriousness of the emergency could be such a third variable, in that serious, frightening emergencies, as compared to minor mishaps, tend to draw a large number of bystanders and make people less likely to intervene. Other examples of the difficulty of inferring causality from correlational studies are shown in Try It! on page 29.

Thinking Critically

Suppose you read about a recent study that found a negative correlation between how mentally active older people are (how often they read the newspaper, play cards, do crossword puzzles, etc.) and how senile they are (how much memory loss they experience). The more mentally active the people are, the less senile they are. The researchers conclude that staying mentally active helps people avoid senility. Is this a valid conclusion? What are some other interpretations of the correlation found in the study?

THE EXPERIMENTAL METHOD: ANSWERING CAUSAL QUESTIONS

Experimental method the method by which the researcher randomly assigns participants to different conditions and ensures that these conditions are identical except for the independent variable (the one thought to have a causal effect on people's responses)

The only way to determine causal relations is with the **experimental method**, whereby the researcher systematically orchestrates the event so that people experience it in one way (they witness an emergency along with other bystanders) or another way (they witness the same emergency but are the sole bystanders). The experimental method is the method of choice in most social psychological research, because it allows the experimenter to make causal inferences. The observational method is extremely useful in helping us describe social behaviour; the correlational method is extremely useful in helping us understand what aspects of social behaviour are related. However, only a properly executed experiment allows us to make cause-and-effect statements. For this reason, the experimental method is the crown jewel of social psychological research design.

The experimental method always involves direct intervention on the part of the researcher. By carefully changing only one aspect of the situation (e.g., group size), the researcher can see whether this aspect is the cause of the behaviour in question (e.g., whether people help in an emergency). Sound simple? Actually, it isn't. Stop and think for a moment how you might stage such an experiment to test Latané and Darley's hypothesis about the effects of group size. A moment's reflection will reveal that some rather severe practical and ethical difficulties are involved. What kind of emergency should be used? Ideally (from a scientific perspective), it should be as true to the Genovese case as possible. Accordingly, you would want to stage a murder that passersby could witness. In one condition, you could stage the murder so that only a few onlookers were present; in another condition, you could stage it so that a great many onlookers were present.

Clearly, there are some glaring ethical problems with this scenario. No scientist in his or her right mind would stage a murder for unsuspecting bystanders. But how can we arrange a realistic situation that is upsetting enough to be similar to the Genovese case without it being too upsetting? In addition, how can we ensure that each bystander experiences the same emergency except for the variable whose effect we want to test—in this case, the number of bystanders?

Let's see how Latané and Darley (1968) dealt with these problems. Imagine you are a participant in their experiment. You arrive at the scheduled time and find yourself in a long corridor with doors to several small cubicles. An experimenter greets you and takes you into one of the cubicles, mentioning that five other students, seated in the other cubicles, will be participating with you. The experimenter leaves after giving you a pair of headphones with an attached microphone. You put on the headphones, and soon you hear the experimenter explaining to everyone that he is interested in learning about the kinds of personal problems college students experience. To ensure that people will discuss their problems openly, he explains, each participant will remain anonymous; each will stay in his or her separate room and communicate with the others only via the intercom system. Further, the experimenter says, he will not be listening to the discussion, so that people will feel freer to be open and honest. Finally, the experimenter asks that participants take turns presenting their problems, each speaking for two minutes, after which each person will comment on what the others said. To make sure this procedure is followed, he says, only one person's microphone will be turned on at a time.

The group discussion then begins. You listen as the first participant admits that he has found it difficult to adjust to college. With some embarrassment, he mentions that he sometimes has seizures, especially when under stress. When his two minutes are up, you hear the other four participants discuss their problems, after which it is your turn. When you have finished, it is the first person's turn to speak again. To your astonishment, after he makes a few further comments, he seems to begin to experience a seizure.

Stop and think for a moment: What would you have done in this situation? If you are like most of the participants in the actual study, you would have remained in your cubicle, listening to your fellow student having a seizure, and done nothing about it. Does this surprise you? Latané and Darley kept track of the number of people who left their cubicles to find the victim or the experimenter before the end of the victim's seizure. Only 31 percent of the participants sought help in this way. Fully 69 percent of the students remained in their cubicles and did nothing—just as Kitty Genovese's neighbours failed to offer her assistance in any way.

Does this finding prove that the failure to help was due to the number of people who witnessed the seizure? How do we know that it wasn't due to some other factor? Here is the major advantage of the experimental method. We know because Latané and Darley included two other conditions in their experiment. In these conditions, the procedure was identical to that described above, with one crucial difference: The size of the discussion group was smaller, meaning that fewer people were witnesses to the seizure. In one condition, the participants were told that there were three other people in the discussion group aside from themselves (the victim plus two others). In another condition, participants were told that there was only one other person in their discussion group (namely, the victim). In this latter condition, each participant believed that he or she was the only one who could hear the seizure. Did the size of the discussion group make a difference? As you'll see in a moment, it did.

Independent and Dependent Variables

Independent variable the variable a researcher changes or varies to see if it has an effect on some other variable

Dependent variable the variable a researcher measures to see if it is influenced by the independent variable; the researcher hypothesizes that the dependent variable will depend on the level of the independent variable

The number of people witnessing the emergency was the **independent variable** in the Latané and Darley study, which is the variable a researcher changes or varies to see if it has an effect on some other variable. The **dependent variable** is the variable a researcher measures to see if it is influenced by the independent variable; the researcher hypothesizes that the dependent variable will be influenced by the level of the independent variable. That is, the dependent variable is hypothesized to depend on the independent variable (see Figure 2.1). Latané and Darley found that their independent variable—the number of bystanders—did have an effect on the dependent variable—whether they tried to help. When the participants believed that four other people were witnesses to the seizure, only 31 percent offered assistance. When the participants believed that only two other people were aware of the seizure, the degree of helping behaviour increased to 62 percent of the participants. When the participants each believed that he or she was the only person listening to the seizure, nearly everyone helped (85 percent of the participants).

Internal Validity in Experiments

How can we be sure that the differences in helping behaviour across conditions in the Latané and Darley (1968) seizure study owed to the different numbers of bystanders who witnessed the emergency? Could this effect have been caused by some other aspect of the situation? Again, this is the beauty of the experimental method. We can be sure of the causal connection between the number of bystanders and helping because Latané and Darley made sure that everything about the situation was the same in the different conditions *except* the independent variable: the number of bystanders. Keeping everything the same but the independent variable is referred to as *internal validity* in an experiment (we'll provide a more formal definition of this term shortly). Latané and Darley were careful to maintain high internal validity by ensuring that everyone witnessed the same emergency. They prerecorded the supposed other participants and the victim, and played their voices over the intercom system.

The astute reader will have noticed, however, that there was a key difference between the conditions of the Latané and Darley experiment other than the number of bystanders: Different people participated in the different conditions. Maybe the observed differences in helping were due to characteristics of the participants rather than the independent variable. The people in the sole witness condition might have differed in any number of ways from their counterparts in the other conditions, making them more likely to help. Maybe

Independent Variable	Dependent Variable
The variable that is hypothesized to influence the dependent variable. Participants are treated identically except for this variable.	The response that is hypothesized to depend on the independent variable. All participants are measured on this variable.
Example: Darley and Latané (1968)	
The number of bystanders	How many subjects helped?
Participant + Victim	85%
Participant + Victim + Two others	62%
Participant + Victim + Four others	31%

FIGURE 2.1 Independent and Dependent Variables in Experimental Research

These results indicate that the number of bystanders strongly influences the rate of helping, but it does not mean that the size of the group is the only cause of people's decision to help. After all, when there were four bystanders, a third of the participants still helped; conversely, when each participant thought he or she was the only witness, some of them failed to help. Obviously, other factors influence helping behaviour—such as the bystanders' personalities and their prior experience with emergencies. Nonetheless, Latané and Darley succeeded in identifying one important determinant of whether people help: the number of bystanders present.

they were more likely to have had loving parents, to know something about epilepsy, or to have experience in helping in emergencies. Were any of these possibilities true, it would be difficult to conclude that the number of bystanders, rather than something about the participants' backgrounds, led to differences in helping.

Fortunately, there is a technique that allows experimenters to minimize differences among participants as the cause of the results: **random assignment to condition**. This is the process whereby all participants have an equal chance of taking part in any condition of an experiment; through random assignment, researchers can be relatively certain that differences in the participants' personalities or backgrounds are distributed evenly across conditions. Because Latané and Darley's participants were randomly assigned to the conditions of their experiment, it is very unlikely that the ones who knew the most about epilepsy all ended up in one condition. Knowledge about epilepsy should be randomly (roughly evenly) dispersed across the three experimental conditions. This powerful technique is the most important part of the experimental method.

To summarize, the key to a good experiment is to maintain high **internal validity**, which we can now define as making sure that the independent variable, and only the independent variable, influences the dependent variable. This is accomplished by controlling

Random assignment to condition the process whereby all participants have an equal chance of taking part in any condition of an experiment; through random assignment, researchers can be relatively certain that differences in the participants' personalities or backgrounds are distributed evenly across conditions

Internal validity ensuring that nothing other than the independent variable can affect the dependent variable; this is accomplished by controlling all extraneous variables and by randomly assigning people to different experimental conditions

all extraneous variables (other variables that could conceivably affect the independent variable) and by randomly assigning people to different experimental conditions (Campbell & Stanley, 1967). When internal validity is high, the experimenter is in a position to judge whether the independent variable causes the dependent variable. This is the hallmark of the experimental method that sets it apart from the observational and correlational methods: Only the experimental method can answer causal questions.

External Validity in Experiments

For all of the advantages of the experimental method, there are some drawbacks. By virtue of gaining enough experimental control over the situation to rule out the effects of extraneous variables, the situation can become somewhat artificial and removed from real life. For example, one could argue that Latané and Darley strayed far from the original inspiration for their study, the Kitty Genovese murder. What does witnessing a seizure while participating in a laboratory experiment in a college building have to do with a brutal murder in New York? How often in everyday life do we have discussions with other people through an intercom system? Did the fact that the participants knew they were in a psychology experiment influence their behaviour?

These are important questions that concern **external validity**, which is the extent to which the results of a study can be generalized to other situations and other people. Two kinds of generalizability are at issue: (a) the extent to which we can generalize from the situation constructed by an experimenter to real-life situations (generalizability across *situations*), and (b) the extent to which we can generalize from the people who participated in the experiment to people in general (generalizability across *people*).

GENERALIZABILITY ACROSS SITUATIONS A possible criticism of research in social psychology is that it is often conducted in artificial situations that cannot be generalized to real life. To address this problem, social psychologists attempt to increase the generalizability of their results by making their studies as realistic as possible. However, it is important to note that there are different ways in which an experiment can be realistic. By one definition—the similarity of an experimental situation to events that occur frequently in everyday life—it is clear that many experiments are decidedly unreal. In many experiments, people are placed in situations they would rarely, if ever, encounter in everyday life, such as occurred in Latané and Darley's group discussion of personal problems over an intercom system. We can refer to the extent to which an experiment is similar to real-life situations as the experiment's **mundane realism** (Aronson & Carlsmith, 1968).

It is more important to ensure that a study is high in **psychological realism**, which is the extent to which the psychological processes triggered in an experiment are similar to psychological processes that occur in everyday life (Aronson, Wilson, & Brewer, 1998). Even though Latané and Darley staged an emergency that in significant ways was unlike ones encountered in everyday life, was it psychologically similar to real-life emergencies? Were the same psychological processes triggered? Did the participants have the same types of perceptions and thoughts, make the same types of decisions, and choose the same types of behaviours that they would have in a real-life situation? If so, then the study is high in psychological realism and the results are generalizable to everyday life.

External validity the extent to which the results of a study can be generalized to other situations and to other people

Mundane realism the extent to which an experiment is similar to real-life situations

Psychological realism the extent to which the psychological processes triggered in an experiment are similar to psychological processes that occur in everyday life; psychological realism can be high in an experiment, even if mundane realism is low

| FOCUS ON APPLICATIONS |

When Experiments Mirror the Real World: Does Watching Violence on TV Actually Make You More Aggressive?

There is a trade-off between internal and external validity—that is, between (1) having enough control over the situation to ensure that no extraneous variables are influencing the results and (2) making sure that the results can be generalized to everyday life. The challenge is to devise an experiment that maximizes both.

Wendy Josephson's (1987) study on the relation between television violence and aggressive behaviour elegantly captures both internal validity and external validity. In this study, boys in grades 2 and 3 from 13 schools in Winnipeg watched either a violent or a nonviolent television show. Internal validity was achieved by controlling the television show the participants watched. For example, Josephson ensured that the violent and nonviolent shows were equivalent in terms of excitement, liking, and physiological arousal. This level of control ensured that any differences in subsequent behaviour between the two groups were due to differences in violent content, rather than to other variables that might be associated with violent programming, such as excitement. Internal validity was further enhanced by random assignment of participants to either the violent or the nonviolent condition.

External validity was maximized by having the participants play floor hockey in the school gymnasium (an activity typical for boys of this age) after they had finished viewing the television segment. (As you will see in Chapter 9, in social psychological research, aggression is often assessed in terms of the severity of electric shocks administered to another research participant—a procedure that may be high in internal validity, but that certainly lacks external validity.)

Observers who were unaware of whether the boys had seen the violent or nonviolent segment (a procedure known as keeping observers "blind" to the experiment's hypothesis) recorded instances of aggression. To make the observation as natural as possible, participants were told that the observers would be doing "play by plays" just as is done in "real" hockey games. The observers spoke into microphones, noted the number on a child's jersey, and recorded the kind of aggression that occurred. (One of the observers was Wendy Josephson's mother, who apparently had to swallow hard before recounting some of the instances of verbal aggression!)

The results of this study indicated that exposure to violent programming did, in fact, increase aggression, but only among boys who were predisposed to aggression.

Psychological realism is heightened if people find themselves engrossed in a real event. To accomplish this, it is often necessary to tell the participants a **cover story**—a false description of the study's purpose. You might have wondered why Latané and Darley told people that the purpose of the experiment was to study the personal problems of college students. It certainly would have been simpler to tell participants, "Look, we are interested in how people react to emergencies, so at some point during the study we are going to stage an accident, and then we'll see how you respond." We think you will agree, however, that such a procedure would be very low in psychological realism. In everyday life, we do not know when emergencies are going to occur and we do not have time to plan our

Cover story a description of the purpose of a study, given to participants, that is different from its true purpose; cover stories are used to maintain psychological realism

responses to them. Thus, the kinds of psychological processes triggered would differ widely from those of a real emergency, reducing the psychological realism of the study.

Further, as discussed earlier, people don't always know why they do what they do, or even what they will do until it happens. Thus, describing an experimental situation to participants and then asking them to respond normally will produce responses that are, at best, suspect. For example, after describing the Latané and Darley seizure experiment to our students, we often ask them to predict how they would respond, just as we asked you earlier. Invariably, most of our students think they would have helped the victim, even when they know that in the condition where the group size was six, most people did not help. Unfortunately, we cannot depend on people's predictions about what they would do in a hypothetical situation; we can only find out what people will really do when we construct a situation that triggers the same psychological processes as occur in the real world.

GENERALIZABILITY ACROSS PEOPLE One question we can ask about experiments such as Latané and Darley's is whether their findings are limited to college students, or whether we have learned something about human behaviour in general. We can be more confident that findings from experiments apply to people in general when research participants are selected randomly from the population at large. Thus, researchers try to select samples that are typical of the population on a number of characteristics important to a given research question (age, educational background, gender, religion). This process is known as **random selection**. Unfortunately, it is often impractical and expensive to select random samples for social psychology experiments. It is difficult enough to convince a random sample of people to agree to answer a few questions over the telephone as part of a political poll, and such polls can cost thousands of dollars to conduct. Imagine the difficulty Latané and Darley would have had convincing a random sample of Americans to board a plane to New York to take part in their study, not to mention the cost of such an endeavour.

Of course, concerns about practicality and expense are not good excuses for poor science. More importantly, given the goal of social psychology, it is unnecessary to select random samples for every experiment performed. As noted in Chapter 1, social psychologists attempt to identify basic psychological processes that make people susceptible to social influence. If we accept the premise that there are fundamental psychological processes shared by all people in all places, and that it is these processes that are being studied in social psychology experiments, then it becomes relatively unimportant to select participants from every corner of the earth. Many social psychologists assume that the processes they study—such as the diffusion of responsibility caused by the presence of others in an emergency—are basic components of human nature, common to New Yorkers, Nova Scotians, and Japanese alike.

Random selection a way of ensuring that a sample of people is representative of the population, by giving everyone in the population an equal chance of being selected for the sample

Thinking Critically

Suppose you wanted to investigate the question of whether playing violent video games makes teenagers more aggressive. Describe how you would use the observational, correlational, and experimental method to examine this question. What are the advantages and disadvantages of each technique?

ETHICAL ISSUES IN SOCIAL PSYCHOLOGY

Now that we have discussed the three major research methodologies in social psychology (observational, correlational, experimental), there are two remaining issues about research that we need to address. First, it is important to discuss ethical issues that arise in research in social psychology. Earlier, we mentioned that in order to maintain high psychological realism in experiments, researchers sometimes construct cover stories that mislead people about the true purpose of the study. Also, as we saw with the Latané and Darley study, people are sometimes put in situations that are upsetting. This illustrates that in their quest to create realistic, engaging situations, social psychologists frequently face an ethical dilemma. On the one hand, for obvious scientific reasons, we want our experiments to resemble the real world as much as possible and to be as sound and well controlled as we can make them. On the other hand, we want to avoid causing our participants undue and unnecessary stress, discomfort, or unpleasantness. These two goals often conflict as the researcher goes about the business of creating and conducting experiments.

Researchers are concerned about the health and welfare of the individuals participating in their experiments. Researchers are also in the process of discovering important information about human social behaviour—such as bystander intervention, prejudice, conformity, aggression, and obedience to authority. Many of these discoveries are bound to benefit society. Indeed, given the fact that social psychologists have developed powerful tools to investigate such issues scientifically, many scholars feel it would be immoral *not* to conduct these experiments. However, in order to gain insight into such critical issues, researchers must create vivid events that are involving for the participants. Some of these events, by their nature, are likely to produce a degree of discomfort for the participants. Thus, what is required for good science and what is required for ethical science can be contradictory. The dilemma cannot be resolved by making pious claims that no participant ever experiences any kind of discomfort in an experiment, or by insisting that all is fair in science and forging blindly ahead. Clearly, the problem calls for a middle ground.

The dilemma would be less problematic if researchers could obtain informed consent from their participants before participation. **Informed consent** is the procedure whereby the researcher explains the nature of the experiment to participants before it begins and asks for their consent to participate. If the experimenter fully describes to participants the kinds of experiences they are about to undergo and asks them if they are willing to participate, then the ethical dilemma is resolved. In many social psychology experiments, this sort of description is feasible—and where it is feasible, it is done. In other kinds of experiments, however, it is impossible. Suppose Latané and Darley had told their participants that a seizure was about to be staged, that it wouldn't be a real emergency, and that the hypothesis stated they should offer help. As we saw earlier, such a procedure would be bad science. In this kind of experiment, it's essential that the participant experience contrived events as if they were real; this is called a deception experiment. **Deception** in social psychological research involves misleading participants about the true purpose of a study or the events that transpire. (It is important to note that not all research in social psychology involves deception.)

Over the years, a number of guidelines have been developed to deal with these dilemmas about the ethics of experiments and to ensure that the dignity and safety of research participants are protected. For example, the Canadian Psychological Association has published a set of ethical principles that apply to psychology research and clinical

Informed consent the procedure whereby researchers explain the nature of the experiment to participants before it begins and obtain their consent to participate

Deception the procedure whereby participants are misled about the true purpose of a study or the events that will transpire

It is unlikely that an ethics committee would have approved this study.
© 1993 FarWorks Inc./Distributed by Universal Press Syndicate. All rights reserved.

practice; these guidelines are summarized in Figure 2.2. In addition, there is a set of ethics guidelines, the Tri-Council Policy Statement, that governs research conducted at Canadian universities. All psychology research is reviewed by a Research Ethics Board to ensure that the strict guidelines of the Tri-Council Policy are met. Any aspect of the experimental procedure that this committee judges to be stressful or upsetting must be changed or deleted before the study can be conducted.

In all research studies, participants must be told that they can withdraw at any time, for any reason, without fear of consequences for doing so. They also are assured of the anonymity and confidentiality of their responses.

When deception is used, the post-experimental interview, called the debriefing session, is crucial and must occur. **Debriefing** is the process of explaining to the participants, at the end of the experiment, the purpose of the study and exactly what transpired. If any participants experienced discomfort, the researchers attempt to undo and alleviate it. Finally, the debriefing session provides an opportunity to inform the participants about the goals and purpose of the research, thereby serving an important educational function. The best researchers question their participants carefully and listen to what they say, regardless of whether deception was used in the experiment. (For a detailed description of how debriefing interviews should be conducted, see Aronson, Ellsworth, Carlsmith, & Gonzales, 1990.)

In our experience, virtually all participants understand and appreciate the need for deception, as long as the time is taken in the post-experimental debriefing session to go over the purpose of the research and to explain why alternative procedures could not be used. Studies that have investigated the impact of participating in deception studies have consistently found that people do not object to the kinds of mild discomfort and

Debriefing the process of explaining to the participants, at the end of the experiment, the purpose of the study and exactly what transpired

> ### Ethical Principles of Psychologists in the Conduct of Research
>
> 1. **Respect for dignity of persons.** The central ethical principle underlying psychological research is respect for human dignity. This principle forms the foundation for the other principles that follow.
> 2. **Informed consent.** As much as possible, the researcher should describe the procedures to participants before they take part in a study, and document their agreement to take part in the study as it was described to them.
> 3. **Minimizing harm.** Psychologists must take steps to avoid harming their research participants.
> 4. **Freedom to withdraw.** Participants must be informed that they are free to withdraw from a study at any point, and that there will be no negative consequences for doing so.
> 5. **Privacy and confidentiality.** All information obtained from individual participants must be held in strict confidence.
> 6. **Use of deception.** Deception may be used only if there are no other viable means of testing a hypothesis, and only if a Research Ethics Board rules that it does not put participants at undue risk. After the study, participants must be provided with a full description and explanation of all procedures, in a post-experimental interview called the debriefing.

FIGURE 2.2 Procedures for the Protection of Participants in Psychological Research

Source: Adapted from *Canadian code of ethics for psychologists*, Canadian Psychological Association, 1991, and *Ethical principles of psychologists in the conduct of research*, American Psychological Association, 1992.

deceptions typically used in social psychological research (e.g., Christensen, 1988; Finney, 1987; Gerdes, 1979). For example, at the University of Manitoba, where attitudes toward deception research were assessed in 1970 and again, 20 years later, in 1990 (Sharpe, Adair, & Roese, 1992). At each time period, there was no evidence that students who had participated in deception studies felt negatively about their experience. In fact, participants who had been deceived were more likely to agree with arguments in favour of deception research than were those who had not experienced deception. And, importantly, those who had experienced deception did not show greater distrust of psychologists. Some studies have even found that people who participated in deception experiments said they had learned more and enjoyed the experiments more than did those who participated in non-deception experiments (Smith & Richardson, 1983). Latané and Darley (1970) reported that during their debriefing, the participants said that the deception was necessary and that they were willing to participate in similar studies in the future—even though they had experienced some stress and conflict during the study.

We do not mean to imply that all deception is beneficial. Nonetheless, if mild deception is used and time is spent after the study discussing the deception with participants and explaining why it was necessary, the evidence shows that people will not be adversely affected.

Thinking Critically

When do you think the use of deception is justified in social psychological research? When is it not?

Summary

The goal of social psychology is to answer questions about social behaviour scientifically. The principal research designs used are descriptive methods (observational and correlational) and experimental methods. Each has its strengths and weaknesses and is appropriate for certain research questions. Each method causes the researcher to make a different type of statement about his or her findings.

Descriptive methods allow a researcher to observe and describe a social phenomenon. **Observational methods** involve observing people and systematically recording measurements of their behaviour. The **correlational method** allows the researcher to determine if two or more variables are related—that is, whether one can be predicted from the other. The **correlation coefficient** is a statistical technique that reveals the extent to which one variable can be predicted from another. The major drawback of the correlational method is that it cannot determine causality. It is not possible to determine from a correlation whether A causes B, B causes A, or some other variable causes both A and B.

For this reason, the **experimental method** is the preferred design in social psychology; it alone allows the researcher to infer the presence of causality. In experiments, researchers vary the level of an **independent variable**, which is the one hypothesized to have a causal effect on behaviour. The **dependent variable** is the measured variable hypothesized to be caused or influenced by the independent variable. The researcher ensures that participants are treated identically except for the independent variable, and randomly assigns people to the experimental conditions. **Random assignment to condition**, the hallmark of true experimental design, minimizes the possibility that different types of people are unevenly distributed across conditions.

Experiments are designed to be as high as possible in **internal validity** (ensuring that nothing other than the independent variable is influencing the results) and in **external validity** (ensuring that the results can be generalized across people and situations). To increase generalizability across people, researchers try to select research participants who are representative of the population at large, a process known as **random selection**. **Mundane realism** reflects the extent to which the experimental setting is similar to real-life settings. **Psychological realism** reflects the extent to which the experiment involves psychological responses like those occurring in real life.

Finally, a major concern in social psychological research is the ethical treatment of participants. Canadian researchers carefully follow the Canadian Psychological Association's guidelines, which specify procedures such as obtaining **informed consent**, the participant's right to leave the study at any time, ensured anonymity and confidentiality, and **debriefing** following an experiment, particularly if **deception** (involving a **cover story** about the supposed purpose of the study) has been used.

Key Terms

Correlation coefficient   (page 27)
Correlational method   (page 27)
Cover story   (page 35)
Debriefing   (page 38)
Deception   (page 37)
Dependent variable   (page 32)
Experimental method   (page 30)
External validity   (page 34)
Independent variable   (page 32)
Informed consent   (page 37)
Internal validity   (page 33)
Mundane realism   (page 34)
Observational method   (page 25)
Operational definition   (page 26)
Psychological realism   (page 34)
Random assignment to condition   (page 33)
Random selection   (page 36)
Theory   (page 23)

Key Online Search Terms

Theory
Observational method
Correlational method
Correlation coefficient
Experimental method
Independent variable
Dependent variable
Internal validity
External validity

If You Are Interested

Aron, A., & Aron, E. N. (1990). *The heart of social psychology* (2nd ed.). Lexington, MA: Heath. A behind-the-scenes look at how social psychologists conduct research, based on interviews with leading researchers.

Aronson, E., Ellsworth, P., Carlsmith, J. M., & Gonzales, M. (1990). *Methods of research in social psychology* (2nd ed.). New York: Random House. An entertaining, thorough treatment of how to conduct social psychological research.

Weblinks

www.nova.edu/ssss/QR/web.html
Qualitative Research Web Sites
This is a good starting point to find out more about qualitative research methodology.

www.uwinnipeg.ca/~clark/research/cpaethics.html
Canadian Code of Ethics for Psychologists
This site contains the full text of the Canadian Psychological Association's code of ethics for psychologists.

http://psych.hanover.edu/research/exponnet.html
Psychological Research on the Net
This site includes some ongoing social psychological studies being conducted via the Internet.

www.socialresearchmethods.net/kb/index.htm
Research Methods Knowledge Base
This interesting online textbook is devoted to the topic of methods with a unique approach.

Chapter 2 Practice Quiz

Check your knowledge of the concepts in this chapter by trying the following questions.

SOCIAL PSYCHOLOGY: AN EMPIRICAL SCIENCE

Multiple Choice

1. From the perspective of social psychologists, human behaviour such as aggression is
    a. predictable.
    b. learned.
    c. caused by genetic factors.
    d. random.

2. Conducting empirically accurate social psychology research involves
    a. choosing the appropriate method.
    b. maximizing the method's strengths.
    c. minimizing the method's weaknesses.
    d. all of the above

True or False

3. Social psychology involves intimately familiar topics, and that separates social psychology from other sciences.
    ___ True
    ___ False

4. The key to a successful study involves making predictions after obtaining the results.
    ___ True
    ___ False

Fill in the Blank

5. Sayings such as "birds of a feather flock together" or "opposites attract" are examples of _____.
6. Observations must be translated into a hypothesis that is _____ testable.

DESCRIPTIVE METHODS: DESCRIBING SOCIAL BEHAVIOUR

Multiple Choice

7. A negative correlation means that
    a. as one variable increases, the other increases.
    b. both variables decrease sharply.
    c. neither variable is affected.
    d. as one variable increases, the other decreases.

8. One of the great disadvantages to the observational method is that
   a. the results cannot be re-examined.
   b. the variables are not defined.
   c. people may alter their behaviour when being watched.
   d. it is too expensive.

9. Which of the following correlations is the strongest?
   a. −.47
   b. −.23
   c. +.23

10. Operational definitions are key in
    a. observational studies.
    b. correlational studies.
    c. all psychological studies.
    d. correlational and observational studies only.

True or False

11. Use of the correlational method requires a causal relationship to exist between variables.
    ___ True
    ___ False

12. Once an operational definition has been made for a variable, it should remain constant across all studies.
    ___ True
    ___ False

Fill in the Blank

13. The technique in which a researcher observes people and records their behaviour is the _____.
14. _____ refers to the precise specification of how variables are measured or manipulated.

THE EXPERIMENTAL METHOD: ANSWERING CAUSAL QUESTIONS

Multiple Choice

15. In a study that uses the experimental method, the _____ is manipulated.
    a. dependent variable
    b. independent variable
    c. codependent variable
    d. confounding variable

16. The extent to which an experiment mirrors real-life situations is called
    a. mundane realism.
    b. real-life realism.
    c. psychological realism.
    d. experimenter realism.

17. Keeping everything but the independent variable the same in all conditions of an experiment
    a. is good ethical conduct.
    b. improves internal validity.
    c. is nearly impossible.
    d. is rarely practiced in social psychology.

18. In order to ensure that a sample of people is representative of the population of interest, _____ is used.
    a. representative sampling
    b. balanced-population sampling
    c. equitable sampling
    d. random sampling

True or False

19. Using random assignment maximizes the differences between participants in a research study.
    ___ True
    ___ False

20. The only way to determine a causal relationship is by using the experimental method.
    ___ True
    ___ False

Fill in the Blank

21. _____ is the extent to which the results of a study can be generalized to other situations or people.

22. The use of a _____ can heighten or maintain psychological realism.

ETHICAL ISSUES IN SOCIAL PSYCHOLOGY

Multiple Choice

23. Experiments that involve deception always include
    a. debriefing.
    b. discomfort.
    c. the absence of consent by participants.
    d. poor external validity.

24. Informed consent ensures
    a. deception will not be used.
    b. consent is implied but not confirmed.
    c. consent has been obtained from all participants.
    d. consent has been obtained from at least 85% of participants.

True or False

25. In experiments, conflict often occurs between maintaining mundane realism and proper ethical conduct.
    ___ True
    ___ False

26. Informed consent involves explaining the nature of the experiment immediately after it has concluded.
    ___ True
    ___ False

Fill in the Blank

27. _____ is the act of misleading research participants as to the true nature of the study.
28. _____ is the term for a researcher's efforts to alleviate any discomfort a participant may have experienced during the study.

PERSONALIZED STUDY PLAN

Want to check your answers and access more study resources? Visit the Companion Website for *Fundamentals of Social Psychology* at **www.pearsoned.ca/aronson**, where you'll find the above questions incorporated in a pre-test and post-test for each chapter. These tests will be automatically graded online, allowing you to check your answers. A Study Plan, like the one below, groups the questions by section within the chapter and shows you which sections you need to focus on for further study.

Your Results for "Chapter 2, Pre-test"

OVERALL SCORE: 71% of 14 questions

Group	Score	Proficient
Social Psychology: An Empirical Science	3 of 3	Yes
Descriptive Methods	2 of 4	No
The Experimental Method	3 of 4	Yes
Ethical Issues in Social Psychology	2 of 3	Yes

CHAPTER 3

Social Cognition and Social Perception: How We Perceive and Think about the Social World

Chapter Outline

PEOPLE AS EVERYDAY THEORISTS: SCHEMAS AND THEIR INFLUENCE
Which Schemas Are Applied? Accessibility and Priming

MENTAL STRATEGIES AND SHORTCUTS: HEURISTICS
How Easily Does It Come to Mind? The Availability Heuristic
How Similar Is A to B? The Representativeness Heuristic
Taking Things at Face Value: The Anchoring and Adjustment Heuristic

AUTOMATIC VERSUS CONTROLLED THINKING

CAUSAL ATTRIBUTION: ANSWERING THE "WHY" QUESTION
The Nature of the Attributional Process
The Fundamental Attribution Error: People as Personality Psychologists
The Actor/Observer Difference
Self-serving Attributions

Kevin Chappell was on his way to the top. It was 1988 and the 29-year-old with an IQ of 147 had just been accepted to medical school, had graduated at the top of his class from Trent University, and was working on a master's degree. He was also an avid soccer player and had played lead guitar in a rock and roll band. On January 30, 1988, he decided to go for a run after a hard day of studying. It was a dark, rainy evening and, as he crossed a street, he was hit by a car. From that moment, Chappell's life was changed immeasurably. He sustained severe brain damage, leaving him unable to recognize things. He could see objects, but didn't know what they were—a condition known as visual agnosia.

Psychologist Gordon Winocur, a specialist in memory at Trent University, met Chappell just after he had been diagnosed with visual agnosia. Chappell didn't touch the cup of coffee that Dr. Winocur had served him, which wasn't unusual for someone with this diagnosis. How can you drink a cup of coffee if you don't recognize what it is? However, one day Chappell happened to run into Winocur and greeted him by name. Dr. Winocur was stunned. How could someone who didn't recognize objects know who he was?

It became apparent that Chappell does recognize one thing—faces. He doesn't recognize arms, legs, or feet. He doesn't recognize faces that are upside down or sideways, but he does recognize faces that are upright (Scott, 2002). This ability probably makes him unique in the world. Dr. Winocur teamed up with two neuropsychologists, Morris Moscovitch from the University

Because of a brain injury, Kevin Chappell, shown here standing between his two sons, lives in a world of unidentifiable objects.

of Toronto and Marlene Behrmann from Carnegie Mellon University in Pittsburgh, to study Kevin Chappell formally. Their findings were published in the highly prestigious science journal *Nature* in 1992 (Behrmann, Winocur, & Moscovitch, 1992).

In order to recognize an object, we have to be able to perceive its parts, synthesize them, and match them to the representation of that object stored in our brains. According to Dr. Moscovitch, "Kevin seems to be fine at identifying the bits and pieces.... It's his ability to integrate the information rapidly and then match it to the internal representation that seems to be impaired" (Scott, 2002). A writer, interviewing Chappell, now age 44, shows him a pair of sunglasses. "It's brown with bits of silver and two horns," Chappell says. But what is it? Chappell has no idea. "I don't know what I see," he replies, "I have to guess" (Scott, 2002). It is hard to imagine what Kevin Chappell's world must be like. When we enter a classroom, for example, we do not see a bunch of objects that have platforms parallel to the floor connected to four legs with another flat surface at a right angle, which we then mentally assemble to figure out what they are. Instead of having to pause and think, "Let's see. Oh, yes, those are chairs," we quickly, unconsciously, and effortlessly categorize the objects as chairs. The fact that we do this automatically allows us to use our conscious minds for other, more important purposes ("What's going to be on the quiz today?" or "Should I strike up a conversation with that cute guy in the third row?"). Similarly, when we encounter people we know, the process of recognizing them requires little effort on our part, thereby allowing us to focus on our interaction with them.

In this chapter we will explore **social cognition** and **social perception**, areas of social psychology that focus on the way people think about themselves and the social world—how they select, interpret, remember, and use social information. As shall be seen in this chapter, we are able to make complex judgments about ourselves and others—including judgments about why people behave the way they do, or why we behave the way we do—at lightning speed. Of course, we also occasionally make mistakes, and sometimes these mistakes are costly. In this chapter we will examine how sophisticated we are as social thinkers, as well as the kinds of mistakes we are prone to make.

To understand how people think about the social world, we will first consider the procedures, rules, and strategies they use. It is often impossible to consider the overwhelming amount of information we have about the people around us. Consequently, individuals rely on a variety of mental shortcuts that serve them well. As we will see, people are quite practical, adopting different procedures and rules according to their goals and needs in a situation. We will also see that human reasoning is not perfect.

Social cognition how people think about themselves and the social world; more specifically, how people select, interpret, remember, and use social information to make judgments and decisions

Social perception the study of how we form impressions of and make inferences about other people

PEOPLE AS EVERYDAY THEORISTS: SCHEMAS AND THEIR INFLUENCE

We have knowledge about many things—objects, such as chairs and sunglasses; other people; ourselves; social roles (what a librarian or an engineer is like); and specific events (what usually happens when people eat a meal in a restaurant). **Schemas** are mental structures people use to organize their knowledge around themes or topics (Bartlett, 1932; Kunda, 1999; Markus, 1977; Taylor & Crocker, 1981). There are a number of different kinds of schemas. As already discussed, we have schemas of objects, such as chairs. However, social psychologists have tended to focus more on schemas pertaining to the social world. For example, our schema about car salespeople might be that they're smooth talkers, insincere, male, and knowledgeable about cars. Another important kind of schema is a self-schema—our knowledge of ourselves—what we are like as a person, our likes, our dislikes, and so on. Schemas profoundly affect the information we notice, think about, and remember, and ultimately, how we behave (Kerr & Stanfel, 1993; Trafimow & Schneider, 1994; Trafimow & Wyer, 1993; von Hippel et al., 1993). If you encounter a car salesperson who is sincere and honest, this information will be inconsistent with your schema, and under most circumstances you will forget it, ignore it, or fail to even notice it. Chances are you will treat this person the way you usually treat car salespeople. Thus, schemas act as filters, straining out information that is contradictory to or inconsistent with the prevailing theme (Fiske, 1993; Higgins & Bargh, 1987; Olson, Roese, & Zanna, 1996; Stangor & McMillan, 1992).

Sometimes, of course, a fact can be so inconsistent with a schema that we cannot ignore or forget it. If we encounter a car salesperson who fumbles for words, is honest, and is female, this person is such a glaring exception to our schema that she will stick in our minds—particularly if we spend time pondering how she could ever have ended up in car sales (Burgoon, 1993; Hastie, 1980; Stangor & McMillan, 1992). In most cases, however, we are likely to notice and interpret the behaviour of other people in ways that fit our preconceptions about them.

One of our authors, Beverley Fehr, recently heard a humorous story that illustrates this phenomenon at a fundraising breakfast for a counselling centre. Guest speaker Pamela Wallin described an incident that nearly cost her her broadcasting career—or so she thought. The setting was the G-7 economic summit in Quebec, and CTV had managed to arrange interviews with the British prime minister and the chancellor of West Germany. Wallin excitedly announced to viewers that they should stay tuned, because after the commercial break would be interviews with Margaret Thatcher and Helmut Shit. Convinced that she had just committed career suicide, Wallin left the studio. The first few people she ran into commented that for a moment they had thought she had mispronounced Chancellor Schmidt's name, but then realized that the vacuum cleaner had been on, or that they hadn't had their morning coffee yet, or…. In short, the fact that Wallin said "shit" on television was so inconsistent with people's schema of her that they convinced themselves they must have heard wrong—that she really must have said "Schmidt." Wallin was appointed as Canada's Consul General in 2002, which confirms that this incident had little, if any, negative impact on her career.

The power of schemas has been demonstrated in numerous laboratory studies. For example, participants in a study by Linda Carli (1999) read a story about a woman

> **Schemas** mental structures people use to organize their knowledge about the social world around themes or subjects; schemas affect the information we notice, think about, and remember

named Barbara and her relationship with a man named Jack. After dating for a while, Barbara and Jack went to a ski lodge for a weekend getaway. In one condition, the story ended with Jack proposing to Barbara; in the other condition, the story ended with Jack raping Barbara. Two weeks later, participants took a memory test in which they read several facts about Jack and Barbara and judged whether these facts had appeared in the story. In the marriage-proposal condition, people were likely to misremember details that were consistent with a proposal schema, such as "Jack wanted Barbara to meet his parents" and "Jack gave Barbara a dozen roses." Neither of these details had been in the story, but people in the proposal condition tended to think they were. Similarly, people in the rape condition were likely to misremember details that were consistent with a rape schema, such as "Jack liked to drink" and "Jack was unpopular with women."

As this study demonstrates, people don't remember exactly what occurred in a given setting as if their minds were a film camera recording precise images and sounds. Instead, they remember some information that was there (particularly information our schemas lead us to notice and pay attention to) and other information that was never there but that they have unknowingly added later (Darley & Akert, 1993; Markus & Zajonc, 1985). For example, if you ask people for the most famous line of dialogue in the classic Humphrey Bogart and Ingrid Bergman movie *Casablanca,* they will probably say, "Play it again, Sam." Similarly, if you ask them for one of the most famous lines from the original (1966–69) *Star Trek* television series, they will probably say, "Beam me up, Scotty."

Here is a piece of trivia that might surprise you: Both of these lines of dialogue are reconstructions—the characters in the movie and the television series never said them.

FOCUS ON APPLICATIONS

Social Psychology in the Courtroom: Does It Matter How Lawyers Present Evidence?

Our tendency to construct theories and schemas to interpret the world around us extends to many kinds of social situations, including the courtroom. According to Nancy Pennington and Reid Hastie (1990, 1992, 1993; Hastie & Pennington, 1991, 1995, 2000), jurors decide on a story that best explains all of the evidence, then try to fit this story to the possible verdicts they are allowed to render. If one of those verdicts fits well with their preferred story, they are likely to vote to convict on that charge. This has important implications for how lawyers present their cases. Lawyers typically present evidence in one of two ways. In the first, called the story order, they present evidence in the sequence that events occurred, corresponding as closely as possible to the story they want the jurors to believe. In the second, called the witness order, they present witnesses in the sequence they think will have the greatest impact, even if this means that events are described out of order. For example, a lawyer might save his or her best witness for last, so the trial ends on a dramatic, memorable note, even if this witness describes events that occurred early in the alleged crime.

If you were a lawyer, in which order would you present the evidence? You probably can guess which order Pennington and Hastie hypothesized would be most successful. If jurors are ultimately swayed by the story they think best explains the sequence of events, the best strategy should be to present the evidence in story order rather than witness order. To test their hypothesis, Pennington and Hastie (1988) asked mock jurors to listen to a simulated murder trial. The researchers varied the order in which the defence attorney and the prosecuting attorney presented their cases. In one condition both used the story order, while in another condition both used the witness order. In other conditions, one attorney used the story order while the other used the witness order.

The results provided clear and dramatic support for the story order strategy. When the prosecutor used the story order and the defence used the witness order, jurors were most likely to believe the prosecutor—78 percent voted to convict the defendant. When the prosecutor used the witness order and the defence used the story order, the tables were turned—only 31 percent voted to convict. Pennington and Hastie (1990) speculate that one reason the conviction rate in U.S. felony trials is so high—approximately 80 percent—is that in real trials prosecutors usually present evidence in story order, whereas defence attorneys usually use witness order. To those of our readers who are budding lawyers, remember this when you are preparing for your first trial!

Which Schemas Are Applied? Accessibility and Priming

The social world is full of ambiguous information that is open to interpretation. Imagine, for example, that you are riding on a city bus and a man gets on and sits beside you. You can't help but notice that he's acting a little strangely. He mutters incoherently to himself, stares at everyone on the bus, and repeatedly rubs his face with one hand. How would you make sense of his behaviour? You have several schemas you could use. What dictates your choice?

Your impression of the man on the bus can be affected by **accessibility**, defined as the extent to which schemas and concepts are at the forefront of our minds and therefore are likely to be used when we are making judgments about the social world (Higgins, 1996; Wyer & Srull, 1989). There are two kinds of accessibility: chronic and temporary. First, some schemas can be chronically accessible due to past experience (Chen & Andersen, 1999; Dijksterhuis & van Knippengerg, 1996; Higgins & Brendl, 1995; Rudman & Borgida, 1995). For example, if there is a history of alcoholism in your family, traits describing an alcoholic are likely to be very accessible to you, increasing the likelihood that this schema will come to mind when you are thinking about the behaviour of the man on the bus. If someone you know suffers from mental illness, however, then thoughts about how the mentally ill behave are more likely to be accessible than are thoughts about alcoholics, leading you to interpret the man's behaviour very differently.

Second, traits can also become temporarily accessible for more arbitrary reasons (Bargh, 1990, 1996; Higgins & Bargh, 1987). Whatever we happen to have been thinking or doing prior to a particular event can prime a schema, making it more accessible and thus more likely to be used to interpret that event. Suppose, for example, that right before the man on the bus sat down, you were reading Ken Kesey's *One Flew over the Cuckoo's Nest*, a novel about patients in a mental hospital. Given that thoughts about mental patients are accessible in your mind, you would probably assume that the man's strange behaviour was due to mental illness. If, on the other hand, thoughts about alcoholism were fresh in your mind—for example, you had just looked out the window and seen an alcoholic leaning against a building drinking a bottle of wine—you would probably assume that the man on the bus had had a few too many drinks (see Figure 3.1). These are examples of

Accessibility the extent to which schemas and concepts are at the forefront of people's minds and are therefore likely to be used when making judgments about the social world

FIGURE 3.1 How We Interpret an Ambiguous Situation: The Role of Accessibility and Priming

Priming the process by which recent experiences increase a schema's accessibility

priming, whereby a recent experience, such as reading Kesey's novel, increases the accessibility of certain kinds of information, such as traits describing the mentally ill, making it more likely that you will use these traits to interpret a new event—the behaviour of the man on the bus—even though this new event is completely unrelated to the one that originally primed the traits.

Tory Higgins, Stephen Rholes, and Carl Jones (1977) illustrated this priming effect in the following experiment. Research participants were told they would take part in two unrelated studies. The first was a perception study, in which they would be asked to identify different colours while at the same time memorizing a list of words. The second was a reading comprehension study, in which they would be asked to read a paragraph about someone named Donald and then give their impressions of him. This paragraph is shown in Figure 3.2. Take a moment to read it. What do you think of Donald?

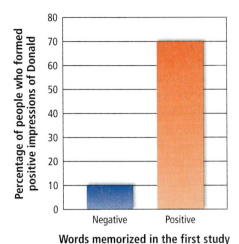

Description of Donald

Donald spent a great deal of time in his search of what he liked to call excitement. He had already climbed Mt. McKinley, shot the Colorado rapids in a kayak, driven in a demolition derby, and piloted a jet-powered boat—without knowing very much about boats. He had risked injury, and even death, a number of times. Now he was in search of new excitement. He was thinking, perhaps, he would do some skydiving or maybe cross the Atlantic in a sailboat. By the way he acted one could readily guess that Donald was well aware of his ability to do many things well. Other than business engagements, Donald's contacts with people were rather limited. He felt he didn't really need to rely on anyone. Once Donald made up his mind to do something it was as good as done no matter how long it might take or how difficult the going might be. Only rarely did he change his mind even when it might well have been better if he had.

FIGURE 3.2 Priming and Accessibility

People read the paragraph about Donald and formed an impression of him. In a prior study, some people had memorized words that could be used to interpret Donald in a negative way (reckless, conceited), while others had memorized words that could be used to interpret Donald in a positive way (adventurous, self-confident). As seen in the graph, those who had memorized the negative words formed a much more negative impression of Donald than did those who had memorized the positive words.

(Adapted from Higgins, Rholes, & Jones, 1977)

You might have noticed that many of Donald's actions are ambiguous and can be interpreted in either a positive or a negative manner. Take the fact that he piloted a boat without knowing much about it and wants to sail across the Atlantic Ocean. It is possible to put a positive spin on these acts, and decide that Donald has an admirable sense of adventure. It's just as easy, however, to put a negative spin on these acts, and assume that Donald is a rather reckless and foolhardy individual.

How did the participants interpret Donald's behaviour? Higgins and his colleagues (1977) found, as expected, that it depended on whether positive or negative traits were primed and accessible. In the first study, the researchers divided people into two groups and gave them diffcrent words to memorize. People who had first memorized the words *adventurous, self-confident, independent,* and *persistent* later formed positive impressions of Donald, viewing him as a likeable man who enjoyed new challenges. People who had first memorized *reckless, conceited, aloof,* and *stubborn* later formed negative impressions of Donald, viewing him as a stuck-up person who took needlessly dangerous chances.

To summarize, we have seen that the amount of information we face every day is so vast that we have to reduce it to a manageable size. In addition, much of this information is ambiguous or difficult to decipher. One way we deal with this "blooming, buzzing confusion," in William James' words, is to rely on schemas, which help us reduce the amount of information we need to take in and help us interpret ambiguous information. We turn now to other, more specific mental shortcuts that people use.

Thinking Critically

We use schemas to organize the overwhelming amount of information that we have to process, but this efficiency comes at a cost. What do you think are some of the greatest costs of using schemas?

MENTAL STRATEGIES AND SHORTCUTS: HEURISTICS

How did you decide which college or university to apply to? One strategy would be to investigate thoroughly each of the colleges and universities in Canada. You could read every catalogue from cover to cover, visit every campus, and interview as many faculty members, deans, and students as you could find. Getting tired yet? Such a strategy would, of course, be prohibitively time-consuming and costly. Instead of considering every college and university, most highschool students narrow down their choice to a small number of options and find out what they can about those schools.

This example is like many decisions and judgments we make in everyday life. When deciding which job to accept, what car to purchase, or whom to marry, we usually do not conduct a thorough search of every option ("Okay, it's time for me to get married; I think I'll consult the census lists of unmarried adults in my city and begin my interviews tomorrow"). Instead, we use mental strategies and shortcuts that make the decision easier, allowing us to get on with our lives without turning every decision into a major research project.

What kinds of shortcuts do people use? One, as we have already seen, is to use schemas to understand new situations. Rather than starting from scratch when examining our options, we often apply previous knowledge and schemas. We have many such schemas, about everything from colleges and universities (e.g., what community colleges versus universities are like) to other people. When making specific kinds of judgments and decisions, however, we do not always have a ready-made schema to apply. At other times, there are too many schemas that could apply, and it is not clear which one to use. What do we do?

At times like these, people often use mental shortcuts called **judgmental heuristics**. The word *heuristic* comes from the Greek word meaning "to discover"; in the field of social cognition, heuristics refers to the mental shortcuts people use to make judgments quickly and efficiently. Before discussing these heuristics, we should note that they do not guarantee people will make accurate inferences about the world. In fact, we will document many mental errors in this chapter. Reliance on heuristics also does not always lead to the best decision. For example, had you exhaustively studied every college and university in Canada, you might have found one you liked better than the one you are at now. However, the bottom line is that mental shortcuts are efficient, and usually lead to good decisions in a reasonable amount of time (Gigerenzer & Goldstein, 1996; Griffin, Gonzalez, & Varey, 2001; Nisbett & Ross, 1980).

How Easily Does It Come to Mind? The Availability Heuristic

Suppose you are sitting in a restaurant with several friends one night, when it becomes clear that the waiter made a mistake with one of the orders. Your friend Michael ordered the veggie burger with onion rings but instead got the veggie burger with fries. "Oh, well," he says, "I'll just eat the fries." This starts a discussion of whether he should have sent back his order, and some of your friends accuse Michael of being unassertive. He turns to you and asks, "Do you think I'm an unassertive person?" How would you answer this question?

One way, as we have seen, would be to call on a ready-made schema that provides the answer. If you know Michael well and have already formed a picture of how assertive he

> **Judgmental heuristics** mental shortcuts people use to make judgments quickly and efficiently

is, you could recite your answer easily and quickly: "Don't worry, Michael, if I had to deal with a used-car salesman, you'd be the first person I'd call." Suppose, though, that you've never really thought about how assertive Michael is and have to think about your answer. In these situations, we often rely on how easily different examples come to mind. If it is easy to think of times that Michael acted assertively ("that time he stopped someone from butting in line in front of him at the movies"), you will conclude that Michael is a fairly assertive guy. If it is easier to think of times that Michael acted unassertively ("that time he let a phone solicitor talk him into buying a Veg-O-Matic for $29.99"), you will conclude that he is fairly unassertive.

This mental rule of thumb is called the **availability heuristic**, which is basing a judgment on the ease with which you can bring something to mind (Dougherty, Gettys, & Ogden, 1999; Manis et al., 1993; Rothman & Hardin, 1997; Schwarz, 1998; Wänke, Schwarz, & Bless, 1995). When we speak of the availability heuristic, we are referring to a mental rule of thumb whereby people base a judgment on the ease with which they can bring something to mind. The first studies demonstrating the availability heuristic were conducted by Tversky and Kahneman (1973). In one of their studies, participants were presented with the names of famous and non-famous people. When asked to recall the names, participants were more likely to remember the famous ones, even though there were fewer famous than non-famous names on the list. Presumably, the famous names were more available in memory. Similar findings were obtained when this study was replicated with Canadian participants (McKelvie, 1995, 1997).

There are many situations in which the availability heuristic is a good strategy. If you can easily bring to mind several times when Michael stood up for his rights, he probably is an assertive person; if you can easily bring to mind several times when he was timid or meek, he probably is not an assertive person. The trouble with the availability heuristic is that sometimes what is easiest to bring to mind is not typical of the overall picture, leading to faulty conclusions.

Availability heuristic a mental rule of thumb whereby people base a judgment on the ease with which they can bring something to mind

How Similar Is A to B? The Representativeness Heuristic

People use another mental shortcut when trying to categorize something: They judge how similar it is to their idea of the typical case. Suppose, for example, that you attend a college in Alberta. One day you meet a student named Lyne in a lineup for one of the food outlets on campus. Lyne is fashionably dressed, orders a café au lait and a croissant, and from the way she pronounces "croissant," it's apparent she speaks French. Which province do you think Lyne is from? Because Lyne seems similar to many people's stereotype of a Quebecer, you might guess Quebec, or at least seriously entertain this possibility. If so, you would be using the **representativeness heuristic**, which is a mental shortcut whereby people classify something according to how similar it is to a typical case—such as how similar Lyne is to your conception of Quebecers (Dawes, 1998; Garb, 1996; Kahneman & Tversky, 1973; Lupfer & Layman, 1996; Thomsen & Borgida, 1996; Tversky & Kahneman, 1974).

Representativeness heuristic a mental shortcut whereby people classify something according to how similar it is to a typical case

Base rate information
information about the frequency of members of different categories in the population

Categorizing things according to representativeness is often a perfectly reasonable thing to do. If we did not use the representativeness heuristic, how else would we decide where Lyne comes from? Should we just randomly choose a province? Actually, there is another source of information we might use. If we knew nothing about Lyne, it would be wise to guess that she was from Alberta, because at Albertan colleges there are more in-province than out-of-province students. If we guessed Alberta, we would be using what is called **base rate information**, or information about the relative frequency of members of different categories in the population (e.g., the percentage of students at Albertan colleges who are from Alberta).

What do people do when they have both base rate information (knowing that there are more Albertans than Quebecers at a college) and contradictory information about the person in question (encountering Lyne, who dresses fashionably and likes café au lait and croissants)? To answer this question, Kahneman and Tversky (1973) devised the now-famous engineer-and-lawyer problem. Participants were told that they would read a description of a man randomly drawn from a population of 70 engineers and 30 lawyers (or, in another condition, 70 lawyers and 30 engineers). They then received a description of Jack, who possessed stereotypic engineering traits (conservative, careful, likes doing mathematical puzzles) and were asked what the chances were that he was an engineer (or a lawyer). Kahneman and Tversky found that participants based their estimates simply on whether the traits used to describe Jack fit their conception of lawyers or engineers, without taking into account base rate information (the number of lawyers or engineers in the population). Thus, participants were just as likely to assume Jack was an engineer when there were 30 engineers in the population as when there were 70, because in making their judgments they only focused on individuating information (Jack's qualities).

This study was replicated by Griffin and Buehler (1999) with students in Canada and Britain. They added some changes designed to increase the salience of base rate information. For example, they showed participants a clear bowl containing 70 white and 30 green balls as a vivid reminder of the number of engineers and lawyers in the population. However, even under these conditions, participants still failed to take base rates into account, and instead based their answers to questions about Jack's profession on information about Jack's traits.

We should note that although this is not a bad strategy if the information about the person is reliable, it can get us into trouble when the information is flimsy. Returning to our example of Lyne, given that the base rate of Quebecers attending universities in Alberta is low, you would need to have very good evidence that Lyne was a Quebecer before ignoring the base rate and guessing that she is one of the few exceptions. And given that it is not unusual to find people from Alberta who dress well, speak French, and enjoy café au lait and croissants, you would, in this instance, be wise not to ignore the base rate.

Taking Things at Face Value: The Anchoring and Adjustment Heuristic

Suppose you are trying to quit smoking and are sitting around with a group of friends who also smoke. "How likely am I to get cancer anyway?" you say, reaching for a cigarette. "I bet that not all that many people end up with lung cancer. In fact, of all the students at our college, I wonder how many will get cancer in their lifetimes?" One of your friends throws out a number: "I don't know," he says, "I'd guess maybe 2500." Would your friend's response influence your answer to the question? It would if you use the **anchoring and adjustment heuristic** (Tversky & Kahneman, 1974), a mental shortcut whereby people use a number or value as a starting point and then adjust their answer away from this anchor. You might begin by saying, "Hmm, 2500—that sounds high. I'd say it's a little lower than that—maybe around 2000." What if, on the other hand, your friend had estimated that only 100 students would get cancer? In that case, your response might be, "Hmm, 100—that sounds low. I think the number might be closer to 200."

Like all of the other mental shortcuts we have considered, the anchoring and adjustment heuristic is a good strategy under many circumstances. If you have no idea what the answer is, but your friend is a medical resident specializing in oncology, it is wise to stick pretty close to his answer. However, like the other heuristics, this one can get us into trouble. The problem with anchoring and adjustment is that people sometimes use completely arbitrary values as starting points and then stick too closely to these values. For example, Tim Wilson and colleagues (1996) asked university students to copy several words or numbers, supposedly as part of a study of handwriting analysis. In one condition, people copied several pages of numbers, all of which happened to be around 4500. In the other condition, people copied down words, such as *sofa*. Then, as part of what was supposedly an unrelated study, everyone was asked how many students at his or her university would get cancer in the next 40 years. Those who copied down numbers gave much higher estimates (average answer = 3145) than did those who copied down words (average answer = 1645). Similar anchoring effects have been found in many other studies (e.g., Allison & Beggan, 1994; Cadinu & Rothbart, 1996; Chapman & Bornstein, 1996; Czaczkes & Ganzach, 1996; Jacowitz & Kahneman, 1995; Slovic & Lichtenstein, 1971; Strack & Mussweiler, 1997).

The examples of anchoring and adjustment we have seen so far have concerned numerical judgments. This process, however, also occurs with many other kinds of judgments. When we form judgments about the world, we often allow our personal experiences and observations to anchor our impressions, even when we know our experiences are unusual (Gilovich, Medvec, & Savitsky, 2000). Suppose, for example, that you go to a popular restaurant that all your friends rave about. As luck would have it, the waiter is rude and your entrée is burned. You know your experience is atypical; after all, your friends have had great meals at this restaurant. Nonetheless, your experiences are likely to anchor your impression of the restaurant, making you reluctant to return.

To summarize, we have discussed two general types of strategies used by the social thinker: schemas and judgmental heuristics. Schemas are organized bodies of knowledge about people and situations that have a powerful effect on what information we notice, think about, and remember. When we make judgments about the social world, however, we do not always have a ready-made schema or we may not know which schema is most appropriate to use. In such cases, we rely instead on judgmental heuristics. The availability heuristic refers to judgments based on the ease with which something can be brought to mind. The representativeness heuristic helps us decide how similar one thing is to another; we use it to classify people or situations on the basis of their similarity to a typical case. When using this heuristic, we have a tendency to ignore base rate information—the probability that someone or something belongs in that classification. People also rely on the anchoring and adjustment heuristic, wherein an initial piece of information acts as an anchor, or a starting point, for subsequent judgments. Now that you have learned about some of the ways in which people reason, take the Try It! reasoning quiz on page 58.

Anchoring and adjustment heuristic a mental shortcut that involves using a number or value as a starting point, and then adjusting one's answer away from this anchor; people often do not adjust their answers sufficiently

Try It! Reasoning Quiz

Answer each of the following questions:

1. Consider the letter *R* in the English language. Do you think that this letter occurs more often as the first letter of words (e.g., *rope*) or more often as the third letter of words (e.g., *park*)?
   (a) the first letter
   (b) the third letter
   (c) about equally often as the first and third letter

2. Which of these do you think causes more fatalities in Canada?
   (a) accidental death
   (b) death from strokes
   (c) each causes about the same number of deaths

3. Suppose you flipped a fair coin six times. Which sequence is more likely to occur? (H = heads, T = tails)
   (a) HTTHTH
   (b) HHHTTT
   (c) both sequences are equally likely

4. After observing the sequence TTTTT, what is the probability that the next coin flip will be heads?
   (a) less than 0.5
   (b) 0.5
   (c) greater than 0.5

Answers

1. The correct answer is (b), the third letter. Tversky and Kahneman (1974) found that most people thought that the answer was (a), the first letter. Why do people make this mistake? Because, say Tversky and Kahneman, they find it easier to think of examples of words that begin with R. By using the availability heuristic, they assumed that the ease with which they could bring examples to mind meant that such words were more common.

2. The correct answer is (b). According to 1997 Statistics Canada information (Statistics Canada, 1997), deaths due to cerebrovascular disease (stroke is a major component) are nearly twice as likely as accidental deaths (16 051 cases versus 8226 cases). Slovic, Fischhoff, and Lichtenstein (1976) found that most people think that (a) is correct (accidental deaths). Why did people make this error? Again, it's the availability heuristic: Accidental deaths are more likely to be reported by the media, thus people find it easier to bring to mind examples of such deaths than they do deaths from strokes.

3. The correct answer is (c). Both outcomes are equally likely, given that the outcomes of coin flips are random events. Tversky and Kahneman (1974) argue that due to the representativeness heuristic, people expect a sequence of random events to "look" random. That is, they expect events to be representative of their conception of randomness. Thus, many people choose HTTHTH, because this sequence is more representative of people's idea of randomness than HHHTTT. In fact, the chance that either sequence will occur is 1 out of 26 times, or 1/64. As another illustration of this point, if you were to buy a lottery ticket with four numbers, would you rather have the number 6957 or 1111? Many people prefer the former number, because it seems more "random" and thus more likely to be picked. In fact, both numbers have a 1/1000 chance of being picked.

4. The correct answer is (b). Many people choose (c), because they think that after five tails in a row, heads is more likely "to even things out." This is called the gambler's fallacy, which is the belief that prior random events (five tails in a row) have an influence on subsequent random events. Assuming that the coin is fair, prior tosses have no influence on future ones. Tversky and Kahneman (1974) suggest that the gambler's fallacy is due in part to the representativeness heuristic: Five tails and one head seems more representative of a chance outcome than does six tails in a row.

> **Thinking Critically**
> Imagine highschool students trying to decide where to apply for college or university. Give examples of how students might use the availability, representativeness, and anchoring and adjustment heuristics when forming impressions of different colleges and universities and deciding where to apply.

AUTOMATIC VERSUS CONTROLLED THINKING

Think back to what it was like to learn a new skill, such as riding a bicycle or using in-line skates. The first time you rode a two-wheeler, you probably felt awkward and ungainly as you wobbled across the pavement, and you might have paid for your inexperience with a skinned elbow or knee. You were probably concentrating on what you were doing with your feet, knees, and hands, and it seemed as if you would never figure it out. Once you became an experienced rider, however, your actions became automatic, in the sense that you no longer had to think about what you were doing.

Just as our actions can become automatic, so too can the way we think (Bargh, 1994, 1996; Bargh & Ferguson, 2000; Ferguson & Bargh, 2004; Fitzsimons & Bargh, 2004; Wegner & Bargh, 1998). The more practice we have in thinking in a certain way, the more automatic that kind of thinking becomes, to the point where we can do it unconsciously, with no effort. **Automatic processing** can be defined as thinking that is nonconscious, unintentional, involuntary, and effortless. John Bargh and his colleagues (Ferguson & Bargh, 2004; Fitzsimons, & Bargh, 2004) are finding evidence that even rather complex behaviours can be triggered as a result of automatic processing. For example, in one study, participants who spent time looking for words such as "succeed", "master", and "achieve" on a word-search task later performed significantly better on a verbal task (supposedly as part of an unrelated experiment) than those who were not primed with achievement words (Bargh, Gollwitzer, Lee-Chai, Barndollar, & Trotschel, 2001). In another study by the same researchers, participants presented with words related to cooperation (i.e., "share", "cooperate") later behaved more cooperatively when playing a game with other participants (Bargh et al., 2001). Importantly, in studies such as these, participants were entirely unaware that their behaviour was influenced by the information to which they were previously exposed.

As with all of the strategies and properties of social cognition we have considered, however, efficiency comes with a cost. If we automatically categorize a thing or person incorrectly, we can get into trouble. For example, when Wendy Josephson was hired at the University of Winnipeg about 20 years ago, it was still relatively rare to find young women among the professoriate. (Most young women employed by the university were secretaries.) One day, as Wendy was waiting in the dean's office for a secretary to return, a senior male professor handed her some sheets of paper. He failed to notice her expression of puzzlement, and matter-of-factly asked her to please have them typed by Monday. He was extremely embarrassed when she pointed out that she was a professor, not a secretary. As this example suggests, we pigeonhole people quickly, such that our schemas based on race, gender, age, or physical attractiveness are invoked automatically (Devine, 1989a, 1989b; Fiske, 1989a). This is one reason stereotypes are so difficult to overcome—they often operate without our knowing it.

Clearly, not all thinking is automatic; like Rodin's statue of the thinker, sometimes we pause and think deeply about ourselves and the social world. This kind of thinking is called **controlled processing**, defined as thinking that is conscious, intentional, voluntary, and effortful. An example of controlled processing is the kind of conscious musing people often engage in: "I wonder what's for lunch today?" or "When will the authors get on with it and finish this chapter?" You can "turn on" or "turn off" this type of thinking at will, and you are fully aware of what you are thinking.

One purpose of controlled thinking is to provide checks and balances for automatic processing. Just as an airline captain can turn off the automatic pilot and take control of the plane when trouble occurs, so our controlled thinking takes over when unusual events occur. Unlike automatic processing, however, controlled thinking requires motivation

Automatic processing
thinking that is nonconscious, unintentional, involuntary, and effortless

Controlled processing
thinking that is conscious, intentional, voluntary, and effortful

and effort. We have to want to do it, and we have to have the time and energy to devote to it. Thus, when the stakes are low and we do not particularly care about the accuracy of a decision or judgment, we often let our automatic thinking do the job, without bothering to check or correct it.

According to Daniel Gilbert (1991, 1993, 1998a), people are programmed to automatically believe everything they hear and see. This automatic "seeing is believing" process is built into human beings, he suggests, because pretty much everything we hear and see is true. If we had to stop and deliberate about the truthfulness of everything we encountered, life would be difficult indeed ("Let's see, it looks like a car careening toward me down the street, but maybe it's really an illusion"... *CRASH!*). Occasionally, however, what we see or hear is not true; thus, we need a checks-and-balances system to be able to "unaccept" what we have initially believed. When we hear a political candidate say, "If elected, I will lower your taxes, balance the budget, reduce crime, and wash your car every Sunday afternoon," we initially believe what we hear, argues Gilbert (1991), but the "unacceptance" part of the process quickly kicks in, making us doubt the truth of what we've just heard ("Now wait just a minute..."). This process is depicted in Figure 3.3.

The interesting thing about this process is that the initial acceptance part occurs automatically, which, as we have seen, means that it occurs nonconsciously and without effort or intention. The assessment and unacceptance part of the process is the product of controlled processing, however, which means that people have to have the energy and motivation to do it. If people are preoccupied, tired, or unmotivated, the acceptance part of the process will operate unchecked, and this can lead to the acceptance of falsehoods. If we mindlessly watch television and do not think carefully about what is said, for example, we might mindlessly accept the outlandish claims being made in commercials (see Chapter 5).

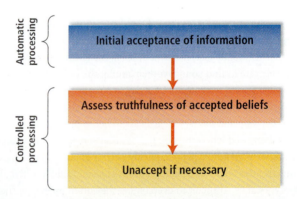

FIGURE 3.3 Gilbert's Theory of Automatic Believing

According to Gilbert (1991), people initially believe everything they hear and see. They then assess whether what they heard or saw is really true and "unaccept" it if necessary. The second and third parts of the process, in which people assess and unaccept information, take time and effort. If people are tired or preoccupied, these parts of the process are difficult to execute, increasing the likelihood that they will believe false information.

(Adapted from Gilbert, 1991)

Social Cognition and Social Perception | 61

Which man is holding a gun? According to Correll and colleagues (2002), if a man is black, even a nonthreatening object such as a cellphone is likely to be misinterpreted as a weapon.

FOCUS ON APPLICATIONS

Can Automatic Thinking Cost You Your Life?

The tendency to engage in automatic thinking can have serious, sometimes lethal, consequences. In February 1999, four New York police officers approached Amadou Diallo, a black immigrant to the United States, because he resembled sketches they had of a serial rapist. Diallo reached into his wallet, probably to show some identification. The officers assumed that Diallo was reaching for a gun and fired 41 shots, instantly killing him. If he had not been black, they might not have made the automatic association between race and weapons.

Consider, for example, a recent study conducted by Correll and colleagues (2002). People played a video game in which they saw photographs of young men in realistic settings, such as in a park, at a train station, and on a city sidewalk. Half of the men were African American and half were white. Half of the men in each group were holding a handgun and half were hold nonthreatening objects such as a cellphone, wallet, or camera. Participants were instructed to press a button labelled *shoot* if the man in the picture had a gun or a button labelled *don't shoot* if he did not. Like a real police officer, they had very little time to make up their minds (just over half a second). Participants won or lost points on each round of the game, modelled after the risks and benefits faced by officers in real life. Participants earned 5 points for not shooting someone who did not have a gun and 10 points for shooting someone who did have a gun. They lost 20 points if they shot someone who was not holding a gun and lost 40 points if they failed to shoot someone who was holding a gun (which, in real life, would be the most life-threatening situation for a police officer).

The results? Participants were especially likely to pull the trigger when the people in the pictures were black, whether or not these people were holding a gun. This "shooter bias" meant that people made relatively few errors when a black person was in fact holding a gun but also that they made the most errors, shooting an unarmed person, when a black person was not holding a gun. When the men in the picture were white, participants made about the same number of errors whether the men were armed or unarmed.

In the study by Correll and colleagues (2002), people had to respond so quickly that they had little time to control their responses or think about what they were doing. The errors they made were the result of automatic thinking that is rooted, perhaps, in the pervasive stereotypes about African Americans and violence.

Thinking Critically

Give examples of ways in which automatic thinking is beneficial to humans and ways in which it is harmful. If you could design the perfect human, would you change anything about the way that automatic and controlled thinking operate?

CAUSAL ATTRIBUTION: ANSWERING THE "WHY" QUESTION

At the beginning of this chapter, we defined social cognition as the study of how people select, interpret, and use information to make judgments about themselves and others. One of the most important judgments we make about ourselves and others concerns the causes of behaviour. In addition to trying to figure out what people are like, it is human nature to also want to know *why* they behave as they do. We also spend time thinking about the causes of our own behaviour. "Why did I snap at my sister last night?" you may wonder. "Am I too stressed out about school, or is she just an annoying person to have around?" How people go about answering the "why" question is the focus of **attribution theory**, the study of how we infer the causes of our own and other people's behaviour.

Attribution theory a description of the way in which people explain the causes of their own and other people's behaviour

The Nature of the Attributional Process

Fritz Heider (1958) is frequently referred to as the father of attribution theory. His influential book defined the field of social perception, and his legacy is still very much evident in current research (Gilbert, 1998a; Ross, 1998). Heider (1958) discussed what he called "naive" or "common sense" psychology. In his view, people were like amateur scientists, trying to understand other people's behaviour by piecing together information until they arrived at a reasonable explanation or cause.

Internal attribution the inference that a person is behaving in a certain way because of something about him or her, such as his or her attitude, character, or personality

External attribution the inference that a person is behaving in a certain way because of something about the situation he or she is in; the assumption is that most people would respond the same way in that situation

One of Heider's (1958) most valuable contributions is a simple dichotomy: We can make an **internal attribution**, deciding that the cause of the person's behaviour was something about her—her disposition, personality, attitudes, or character—an explanation that assigns the causality of her behaviour internally. Conversely, we can make an **external attribution**, deciding that the cause of a person's behaviour was something about the situation (see Try It! on page 63). This dichotomy was vividly illustrated in an incident that occurred in North Vancouver, British Columbia, on September 22, 1999. Nadia Hama made newspaper headlines when her 18-month-old daughter Kaya fell 47 metres from the Capilano Suspension Bridge. People in the media and on the street were quick to blame Hama and accuse her of intentionally throwing Kaya off the bridge. These accusations

Listen as People Make Attributions

Forming attributions is a major part of daily life (note the Rhona Raskin column on page 71). You can watch the attribution process in action, too. All it takes is a group of friends and an interesting topic to discuss. Perhaps one of your friends is telling you about something that happened to her that day, or perhaps your group is discussing another person whom everybody knows. As they talk, pay very close attention to what they say. They will be trying to figure out why the person being discussed did what she did or said what he said. In other words, they will be making attributions. Your job is to try to keep track of their comments and label the attributional strategies they are using.

In particular, do they make internal attributions, about a person's character or personality, or do they make situational attributions, about all of the other events and variables that make up a person's life? Do your friends seem to prefer one type of attribution over the other? If their interpretation is dispositional (internal), what happens when you suggest another possible interpretation, one that is situational? Do they agree or disagree with you? What kinds of information do they offer as "proof" that their attribution is right?

Observing people when they are making attributions in real conversations will show you just how common and powerful this type of thinking is when people are trying to understand each other.

mounted as it came to light that Kaya had Down's syndrome and that Hama had looked into placing her daughter for adoption. In short, Hama was portrayed as a bad mother who intentionally tried to kill her child.

Others agreed that Hama may have tried to kill her child, but made external attributions for her behaviour. They pointed to extremely high levels of stress in her life—the

According to Fritz Heider, we tend to see the causes of a person's behaviour as internal. So when a person asks us for money, we will most likely at first assume that he is at fault for being poor—perhaps lazy or drug addicted. If you knew the person's situation—that perhaps he has lost his job due to a plant closing—you might come up with a different, external attribution.

stress of raising a handicapped child, the stress of being embroiled in an ugly divorce, the stress of not receiving child-care payments from her estranged husband, and so on. Not surprisingly, Hama herself explained the situation in terms of external factors—stating that Kaya's fall had been accidental.

Whether we make internal or external attributions for someone's behaviour can have serious consequences. In Hama's case, those who made internal attributions concluded that she was a cold-hearted murderer. In contrast, those who made external attributions felt compassion, sympathy, and pity. Quite a difference! Most importantly, Nadia Hama's fate rested on the attributions made for Kaya's fall. In her case, police and Crown prosecutors did not find sufficient evidence to charge her with either attempted murder or criminal negligence causing bodily harm (D'Angelo, 2000); however, they did grant sole custody of Kaya and her brother to Kjeld Werbes, the father of both children and Hama's estranged husband.

FOCUS ON APPLICATIONS

The Role of Attributions in Making the Adjustment to College or University

Think back to when you first started attending your college or university. Was it a tough time? If you are like most students, the transition to post-secondary education had its rough spots. Believe it or not, how well students survive this transition depends, at least partly, on the kinds of attributions they make.

According to Tim Wilson and Patricia Linville (1982, 1985), many first-year students experience academic difficulties because of a damaging pattern of attributions. The difficulty is that first-year students do not realize how common such adjustment problems are and assume that their problems are due to personal inadequacies—in other words, they make an internal attribution instead of taking the situation into account.

Wilson and Linville tried to combat this pessimism by convincing first-year students who were concerned about their academic performance that the causes of poor performance are often temporary. In the treatment condition, students watched videotaped interviews of four senior students, each of whom mentioned that his or her grades had been poor or mediocre during the first year but had improved significantly since then. The students were also given statistics indicating that academic performance is often poor in the first year of college or university but improves thereafter.

The researchers hypothesized that this simple message would increase the students' motivation to try harder and remove needless worries about their abilities. In other words, the hope was that students would realize that their difficulties owed to external, situational factors, rather than attributing poor performance to internal factors. Judging by the students' future performance, this is just what happened. Compared to students in a control group who participated in the study but did not watch the videotaped interviews or see the statistics, students in the treatment condition improved their grades more in the following year and were less likely to drop out.

Similar results have been found in studies conducted in other countries, such as Canada and Belgium (Menec et al., 1994; Van Overwalle & De Metsenaere, 1990).

The Fundamental Attribution Error: People as Personality Psychologists

Another of Heider's (1958) important contributions was his observation that people generally prefer internal attributions over external ones. While either type of attribution is always possible, Heider (1958) noted that we tend to see the causes of a person's behaviour as residing in that person. We are perceptually focused on *people*—they are who we notice—while the *situation*, which is often hard to see and hard to describe, can be overlooked (Bargh, 1994; Carlston & Skowronski, 1994; Gilbert, 1998b; Newman & Uleman, 1993; Pittman & D'Agostino, 1985; Uleman & Moskowitz, 1994). When thinking this way, we are more like personality psychologists, who see behaviour as stemming from internal dispositions and traits, than social psychologists, who focus on the impact of social situations on behaviour. This bias toward being personality psychologists is so pervasive that social psychologist Lee Ross (1977) termed it the **fundamental attribution error** (Heider, 1958; Jones, 1990; Ross & Nisbett, 1991).

Fundamental attribution error the tendency to overestimate the extent to which people's behaviour is due to internal, dispositional factors, and to underestimate the role of situational factors

There have been many empirical demonstrations of the tendency to see people's behaviour as a reflection of their dispositions and beliefs, rather than as influenced by the situation (Allison et al., 1993; Miller, Ashton, & Mishal, 1990). In a classic demonstration of this effect, Edward Jones and Victor Harris (1967) asked university students to read a fellow student's essay that either supported or opposed Fidel Castro's rule in Cuba and then to guess how the author of the essay really felt about Castro (see Figure 3.4). In one condition, the researchers told the students that the author freely chose which position to take in the essay, thereby making it easy to guess how he or she really felt. If the author chose to write in favour of Castro, then clearly he or she must indeed be sympathetic to Castro. In another condition, however, the students learned that the author did not have any choice about which position to take—he or she had been assigned the position as a participant in

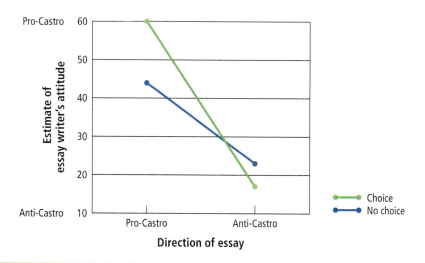

FIGURE 3.4 The Fundamental Attribution Error

Even when people knew that the author's choice of an essay topic was externally caused (in the no-choice condition), they assumed that what he or she wrote reflected how he or she really felt about Castro. That is, they made an internal attribution for the author's behaviour.

(Adapted from Jones & Harris, 1967)

a debate. Logically, if we know someone could not choose the topic, we should not assume the writer believes what he or she wrote. Yet the participants in this study, and in the dozens of others like it, assumed that the author really believed what he or she wrote, even when they knew he or she could not choose which position to take. As seen in Figure 3.4, people moderated their guesses a little bit—there was not as much difference in people's estimates of the author's attitude in the pro-Castro and anti-Castro conditions—but they still assumed that the content of the essay reflected the author's true feelings.

Why is the tendency to explain behaviour in terms of people's dispositions called the fundamental attribution error? It is not always wrong to make an internal attribution; clearly, people often do what they do because of the kind of people they are. However, there is ample evidence that social situations can have a strong impact on behaviour; indeed, the major lesson of social psychology is that these influences can be extremely powerful. The point of the fundamental attribution error is that people tend to underestimate these influences when explaining other people's behaviour. Even when a situational constraint on behaviour is obvious, as in the Jones and Harris (1967) experiment, people persist in making internal attributions (Lord et al., 1997; Newman, 1996; Ross, 1977; Ross, Amabile, & Steinmetz, 1977; Ross & Nisbett, 1991).

BLAMING THE VICTIM: AN UNFORTUNATE CONSEQUENCE OF THE FUNDAMENTAL ATTRIBUTION ERROR

The fundamental attribution error can lead to some tragic consequences, including a tendency to blame those who are victimized or stigmatized for their plights. Even if people are made aware of the situational factors responsible for the plight of disadvantaged members of our society (inadequate nutrition, disrupted family life), they may still see these individuals as responsible for their misfortune. For example, suppose a female student on your campus was the victim of a date rape by a male student. How do you think you and your friends would react? Would you wonder if she'd done something to trigger the rape? Was she acting suggestively earlier in the evening? Had she invited the man into her room?

Research by Elaine Walster (1966) and others has focused on such attributions (e.g., Burger, 1981; Lerner & Miller, 1978; Stormo, Lang, & Stritzke, 1997). In several experiments, they have found that the victims of crimes or accidents are often seen as causing their fates. For example, people tend to believe that rape victims are to blame for the rapes (Bell, Kuriloff, & Lottes, 1994; Burt, 1980; Lambert & Raichle, 2000). Sadly, such myths can make their way into the courtroom. Consider, for example, the 1998 case of *R. v. Ewanchuk*. The complainant in this case was a 17-year-old woman who was sexually assaulted by a man while he was interviewing her for a job. The man was 45-year-old Steve Ewanchuk, a contractor with a history of convictions for rape and sexual assault. At the time of this incident, he had been court-ordered not to hire any females under the age of 18 to work for him. The young woman testified in the Alberta Court of Queen's Bench that she did not consent to Ewanchuk's advances and, in fact, felt very afraid during the incident. The trial judge, however, held her responsible for not having communicated her fear, and ruled that consent had been implied. As a result, Ewanchuk was acquitted. The case then went to the Alberta Court of Appeal. One of the appeal judges commented that Ewanchuk's actions were "far less criminal than hormonal" and suggested that the 17-year-old should have taken actions to stop him by using "a well-chosen expletive, a slap in the face, or, if necessary, a well-directed knee" (*R. v. Ewanchuk*, 1998). Once again, Ewanchuk was acquitted. This decision was finally overturned by the Supreme Court of Canada in 1999, which ruled that there is no such thing as implied consent. One of the Supreme

Court judges, Justice L'Heureux-Dubé, wrote, "This case is not about consent, since none was given. It is about myths and stereotyping." These myths include the belief that a woman could resist the attack of a rapist if she really wanted to, that women deserve to be raped because of the way they dress, and so on. Despite the Supreme Court's ruling, concerns remain that women who are the victims of sexual assault will be further victimized by rape myths and victim blaming when they appear in the courtroom (L'Heureux-Dubé, 2001; Tang, 2000).

Similarly, battered wives are often seen as responsible for their abusive husbands' behaviour (Summers & Feldman, 1984). One way in which people justify blaming victims of violence is to assume that the victims must have done something to provoke the attack (Kristiansen & Giulietti, 1990; Perrott, Miller, & Delaney, 1997). These unfortunate consequences of the fundamental attribution extend to other kinds of situations as well, including blaming people for being lonely (Rotenberg, 1998) or overweight (Crandall et al., 2001), or for their health problems, such as heart disease and AIDS (Menec & Perry, 1998).

On a more positive note, you may be less vulnerable to making these kinds of attributions simply because you are taking this course! Guimond and Palmer (1996) studied the attributions of social science and commerce students at an Ontario university over a three-year period. The two groups of students made similar attributions for poverty and unemployment in their first year of university. However, by their third year, commerce students were more likely to make dispositional attributions—blaming the poor for their poverty and the unemployed for their unemployment, whereas social science students were more likely to make situational attributions. Similar results were obtained in a subsequent study comparing the attributions of social science and engineering students in a Canadian Armed Forces college (Guimond, 1999).

WHY DO PEOPLE COMMIT THE FUNDAMENTAL ATTRIBUTION ERROR? THE ROLE OF PERCEPTUAL SALIENCE AND CULTURE

Why do we commit the fundamental attribution error? One reason is that when we try to explain someone's behaviour, our focus of attention is usually on the person, not on the surrounding situation (Heider, 1958; Jones & Nisbett, 1972). In fact, as Daniel Gilbert and Patrick Malone (1995) have pointed out, the situational causes of another person's behaviour are practically invisible to us. If we don't know what happened to a person earlier in the day (she received an F on her midterm), we can't use that situational information to help us understand her current behaviour. Even when we know "her situation," we still don't know how she interprets it—for example, the F might not have upset her because she's planning to drop the course anyway. If we don't know the meaning of the situation for her, we cannot accurately judge its effects on her behaviour. Thus, information about the situational causes of behaviour is frequently unavailable to us or difficult to interpret accurately (Gilbert, 1998b; Gilbert & Malone, 1995).

What information does that leave us? Though the situation may be close to invisible, the individual is extremely prominent perceptually—*people* are what our eyes and ears notice. And as Heider (1958) pointed out, what we notice seems to be the reasonable and logical cause of the observed behaviour.

Several studies have confirmed the importance of perceptual salience—in particular, an elegant one by Shelley Taylor and Susan Fiske (1975). In this study, two male students engaged in a "get acquainted" conversation. (They were actually both accomplices of the experimenters and were following a specific script during their conversation.) At each session, six actual research participants also took part. They sat in assigned seats, surrounding the two conversationalists (see Figure 3.5). Two sat on each side of the actors; they had a clear, profile view of both individuals. Two sat behind each actor; these four participants could see the back of one actor's head and the face of the other. Thus, who was visually salient—that is, who the participants could see best—was cleverly manipulated in this study.

After the conversation, the research participants were asked questions about the two actors—for example, who had taken the lead in the conversation, and who had chosen the topics to be discussed. The person whom they could see best was the person they thought had the most impact on the conversation. Even though all participants heard the same conversation, those who were facing student A thought *he* had taken the lead and chosen the topics, whereas those who were facing student B thought *he* had taken the lead and chosen the topics. In comparison, those who could see both students equally well thought both were equally influential. **Perceptual salience**, or our visual point of view, helps explain why the fundamental attribution error is so widespread. We focus our attention more on people than on the surrounding situation because the situation is so hard to see or know; we underestimate (or even forget about) the influence of the situation when we are explaining human behaviour.

Recent research has suggested a second reason, in addition to perceptual salience, as to why the fundamental attribution error occurs: Western culture, which emphasizes individual freedom and autonomy, socializes us to prefer dispositional attributions over situational ones (Dix, 1993; Rholes, Newman, & Ruble, 1990). In comparison, collectivist (often Eastern) cultures emphasize group membership, interdependence, and conformity to group norms (Fletcher & Ward, 1988; Markus & Kitayama, 1991; Newman,

Perceptual salience
information that is the focus of people's attention; people tend to overestimate the causal role of perceptually salient information

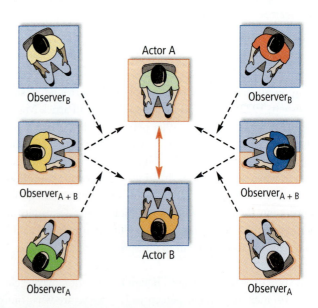

FIGURE 3.5 Manipulating Perceptual Salience

This is the seating arrangement for two actors and the six research participants in the Taylor and Fiske study. Participants rated each actor's impact on the conversation. Researchers found that people rated the actor they could see most clearly as having the largest role in the conversation.

(Adapted from Taylor and Fiske, 1975)

1991; Triandis, 1990; Zebrowitz-McArthur, 1988). These cultural values suggest that people would be socialized to prefer situational attributions over dispositional ones. As a result of this very different socialization, do people in collectivist cultures make fewer fundamental attribution errors than Westerners do?

To find out, Joan Miller (1984) asked people of two cultures—Hindus living in India and Americans living in the United States—to think of various examples of behaviours performed by their friends, and to explain why those behaviours occurred. Consistent with what we've said so far, the American participants preferred dispositional explanations for the behaviours. They were more likely to say that the causes of their friends' behaviours were the kinds of people they are, rather than the situation or context in which the behaviours occurred. In contrast, Hindu participants preferred situational explanations for their friends' behaviours (Miller, 1984).

The cultural explanation of the fundamental attribution error received further support from a clever study that compared newspaper articles in Chinese- and English-language newspapers. Michael Morris and Kaiping Peng (1994) targeted two similar crimes, both mass murders, one committed by a Chinese graduate student in Iowa, the other committed by a Caucasian postal worker in Michigan. The researchers coded all of the news articles about the two crimes that appeared in the *New York Times* and the *World Journal*, a Chinese-language U.S. newspaper. As you can see in Figure 3.6, journalists writing in English made significantly more dispositional attributions about both mass murderers than did journalists writing in Chinese. For example, English-language reporters described one murderer as a "darkly disturbed man" with a "sinister edge" to his personality. Chinese-language reporters, when describing the same murderer, emphasized more situational causes, such as "not getting along with his adviser" and his "isolation from the Chinese community."

In a study along the same lines, Chiu, Morris, Hong, and Menon (2000) asked members of the public in the United States and Hong Kong to read a scenario about patients who got sick because a pharmacy worker made an error while mixing medicines. As expected, Americans made more dispositional attributions (assigning responsibility to the

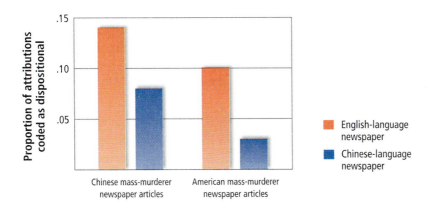

FIGURE 3.6 The Role of Culture in the Fundamental Attribution Error

Newspaper articles about two murderers, appearing in English- and Chinese-language newspapers, were coded for the types of attributions made. Journalists writing in English made significantly more dispositional attributions about both the Chinese and Anglo-American murderer than did journalists writing in Chinese.

(Adapted from Morris & Peng, 1994)

worker), whereas the Chinese were more likely to assign responsibility to the clinic (poor management, incompetent training of workers). This cultural difference was even more pronounced in a follow-up laboratory study when some participants answered the questions while performing another task. Presumably, under these conditions, participants engaged in automatic processing, with the result that American participants were especially likely to blame the worker and Chinese participants were especially likely to blame the clinic.

Thus, people in Western cultures appear to be more like personality psychologists, viewing behaviour in dispositional terms. When making attributions about others, the initial, automatic, and effortless attribution tends to be dispositional. Only if they are motivated to think more deeply will they come up with situational explanations (Lee, Hallahan, & Herzog, 1996; Webster, 1993). In contrast, people in Eastern cultures seem to be more like social psychologists, viewing behaviour in situational terms. Their initial, automatic, and effortless attribution tends to be situational, and again, only if they are motivated to engage in more cognitive work will they come up with possible dispositional attributions (Krull, 1993; Lee, Hallahan, & Herzog, 1996).

The Actor/Observer Difference

An interesting twist on the fundamental attribution error is that it does not apply to our attributions about ourselves to the same extent that it applies to our attributions about other people. While we tend to see others' behaviour as dispositionally caused (the fundamental attribution error), we are less likely to rely so extensively on dispositional attributions when we are explaining our own behaviour. Instead, we frequently make situational attributions about why we did what we did. Thus, an interesting attributional dilemma is created: The same action can trigger dispositional attributions in people observing the action and situational attributions in the person performing the action. This is called the **actor/observer difference** (Frank & Gilovich, 1989; Herzog, 1994; Johnson & Boyd, 1995; Jones & Nisbett, 1972; Robins, Spranca, & Mendelsohn, 1996). The letter to Rhona Raskin (page 71), is an interesting demonstration of the actor/observer difference. The writer is aware of the external forces affecting her life and shaping her behaviour. Raskin, however, will have none of it. She responds with a strong, internal attribution—the woman herself, not her situation, is the cause of her problems. As you might guess, the actor/observer difference can lead to some striking disagreements between people. Why, at times, do the attributions made by actors and observers diverge so sharply?

Actor/observer difference
the tendency to see other people's behaviour as dispositionally caused, while focusing more on the role of situational factors when explaining one's own behaviour

WHY DO PEOPLE SHOW THE ACTOR/OBSERVER DIFFERENCE? THE ROLE OF PERCEPTUAL SALIENCE AND INFORMATION AVAILABILITY Why do we show this tendency to give different explanations for our own behaviour than we do for the behaviour of others? One reason is our old friend perceptual salience (Jones & Nisbett, 1972). As we said earlier, just as we notice other people's behaviour more than their situation, so too do we notice our own situation more than our own behaviour. None of us is so egotistical or self-centred that we walk through life constantly holding up a full-length mirror to observe ourselves. We are looking outward; what is perceptually salient to us is other people, objects, and the events that unfold. We don't (and can't) pay as much attention to ourselves. Thus, when the actor and the observer think about what caused a given behaviour, they are swayed by the information that is most salient and noticeable to them: the actor for the observer, and the situation for the actor (Malle & Knobe, 1997; Nisbett & Ross, 1980; Ross & Nisbett, 1991).

The actor/observer difference occurs for another reason as well, having to do with information availability. Actors have more information about themselves than observers do (Greenwald & Banaji, 1989; Jones & Nisbett, 1972; Krueger, Ham, & Linford, 1996; Malle & Knobe, 1997). Actors know how they've behaved over the years; they know what happened to them that morning. They are far more aware than observers are of both the similarities and the differences in their behaviour across time and across situations. For example, if you are behaving in a quiet, shy fashion at a party, an observer is likely to make a dispositional attribution about you—"Gee, that person is quite an introvert." In fact, you may know that this is not your typical way of responding to a party setting. Perhaps you are shy only at parties where you don't know anyone, or you might be tired, or depressed by some recent bad news. Thus, it is not surprising that actors' self-attributions often reflect situational factors, because they know more about how their behaviour varies from one situation to the next than do most observers, who see them in limited contexts.

So far, our discussion of attributions has covered the role of perceptual salience, information availability, and culture. But what about a person's needs, desires, hopes, and fears—do these more emotional factors also create biases in our attributions? Are you motivated to see the world in certain ways because these views make you feel better, about both yourself and life in general? The answer is yes. Next, we will discuss some mental shortcuts that have a *motivational basis*; they are attributions that protect our self-esteem and our belief that the world is a safe and just place.

Dear Rhona:
I get harassing phone calls throughout the day from a woman whose boyfriend I know. Honestly, I was just friends with this guy, but since all this pestering started we've become sexually involved. I am not looking to steal him away from her—it's just great sex! It seems to work for him too. I suspect that he's never been the faithful type to begin with. I've asked her to stop bothering me but to no avail. Is this all destined to blow up into ugliness for me?
HARASSED

Dear H:
Your pleasure centre is wired to danger. It's my only explanation for a woman who'd even CONSIDER continuing to boink a guy who is so thoughtless that he not only cheats on his girlfriend, but also leaves a trail of crumbs to his co-conspirator. You act as though the girlfriend's behaviour is beyond belief. Really, it's yours that needs investigation. Yes, she is stalking you and there are restraining orders that can be put in place, but imagine all the effort that will take. And how predictably catty—two women fighting over a man. Oh right, you only care for the sensational part while the girlfriend wants the whole package. Go meditate on the concept of karma. Yours needs an overhaul.

The letter and its response depict actor/observer differences in attribution. The writer attributes her problems to the behaviour of the girlfriend of the man with whom she is having an affair, rather than to her own behaviour. Rhona Raskin, on the other hand, puts the blame squarely on the letter writer's shoulders and tells her to shape up.

Self-serving Attributions

Imagine that Alison goes to her chemistry class one day with some apprehension because she will find out how she did on the midterm. The professor gives Alison her exam. She turns it over and sees that she has received an A. What will Alison think is the reason for her great grade? It probably will come as no surprise that people tend to take personal credit for their successes but explain away their failures as due to external events that were beyond their control. Therefore, Alison is likely to think that her success was due to her—she's good at chemistry and just plain smart.

How can we explain this departure from the typical actor/observer pattern? The answer is that when people's self-esteem is threatened, they often make **self-serving attributions**. Simply put, these attributions refer to our tendency to take credit for our successes (by making internal attributions) but to blame others (or the situation) for our failures (Miller & Ross, 1975). Many studies have shown that people make internal attributions when they do well on a task but make external attributions when they do poorly (Davis & Stephan, 1980; Elig & Frieze, 1979; McAllister, 1996; Sedikides et al., 1998; Whitley & Frieze, 1985).

A particularly interesting arena for studying self-serving attributions is professional sports. Consider, for example, a headline that appeared in the sports section of the July 3,

Self-serving attributions explanations for one's successes that credit internal, dispositional factors and explanations for one's failures that blame external, situational factors

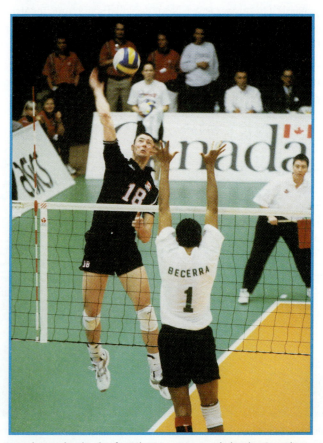

We can conjecture about what kinds of attributions were made by the Canadian men's volleyball team after its nine-game losing streak in 2000. The team is shown here in a match against Mexico.

2000, *Winnipeg Free Press*: "Injured Canadians tagged with ninth straight loss." The article describes yet another loss by Canada's men's volleyball team—this time in Argentina. How did the team explain this loss? One of the players, Jules Martens, offered this comment: "We get here and our major offensive players are injured; it's a different lineup again; it's a patch-work job...." The coach added, "People back at home don't understand the extreme conditions, that you rarely get a call (in a close situation), and in a rally point, that can swing a match." (The coach was referring to a call made by one of the officials that went against Canada.) Thus, both the players and the coach made self-serving attributions—blaming their loss on external factors, rather than on themselves.

Consider now another story in the same sports section. At the U.S. Senior Open golf tournament, Hale Irwin defeated Bruce Fleisher, who led after the first three rounds. How did Irwin account for his victory? "I did what I wanted to do early on.... I let Bruce know I'm there, and put pressure on him."

These examples are consistent with the findings of social psychological research on the attributions made by professional athletes and coaches for why their teams won or lost games. For example, Richard Lau and Dan Russell (1980) found that when explaining their victories, the athletes and coaches overwhelmingly pointed to aspects of their own teams or players; in fact, 80 percent of the attributions for wins were to such internal factors. Losses were more likely to be attributed to things external to one's own team.

Scott Roesch and James Amirkhan (1997) wondered whether a player's skill, experience, and type of sport (team sports versus solo sports such as tennis) affected the type of attribution he or she made about a sports outcome. The researchers found that less experienced athletes were more likely to make self-serving attributions than were experienced ones. Experienced athletes realize that losses sometimes are their fault and that wins are not always due to them. For example, after losing the 2002 CFL Western final against the Edmonton Eskimos, the Winnipeg Blue Bombers middle linebacker, Ryland Wickman, said, "I put the blame on my shoulders" (Tait, 2002). The Bombers all-star defensive tackle, Doug Brown, said, "I was embarrassed with my own performance.... It was a horrid performance, individually...that was probably the worst game I've ever played" (Tait, 2002). Roesch and Amirkhan (1997) also found that highly skilled athletes made more self-serving attributions than did those with less ability. The highly talented athlete believes that success is due to her prowess, while failure, an unusual (and upsetting) outcome, is due to teammates or other circumstances of the game. Finally, athletes in solo sports made more self-serving attributions than did those in team sports. Solo athletes know that winning or losing rests on their own shoulders.

As suggested in the Try It! box on the next page, it is interesting to examine sports pages for evidence that teams or players tend to take credit for their successes but blame external factors (injuries, poor officiating) for their losses.

The self-serving bias has a number of important implications that extend well beyond the world of sports. For example, it leads people to believe that their actions are rational and defensible, but that the actions of others are unreasonable and unjustified. This phenomenon was demonstrated by Sande and colleagues (1989), who found that American students attributed positive motives to their country for both positive actions (saving whales trapped in ice) and negative actions (building more nuclear-powered submarines). However, these same actions were attributed to negative, self-serving motives if participants were told they had been performed by the former Soviet Union.

> # Try It! Self-serving Attributions in the Sports Pages
>
> Do athletes and coaches tend to take credit for their wins but make excuses for their losses? Find out for yourself the next time you read the sports section of the newspaper or watch television interviews after a game. Analyze the sports figures' comments to see what kinds of attributions they make about the cause of their performance. Is the pattern a self-serving one?
>
> For example, after a win, does the athlete make internal attributions, such as "We won because of excellent teamwork; our defensive line really held today," or "My serve was totally on"? After a loss, does the athlete make external attributions, such as "All the injuries we've had this season have really hurt us" or "That line judge made every call against me"? According to the research, these self-serving attributions should occur more often than the opposite pattern—for example, where a winner says, "We won because the other team played so badly it was like they were dead" (external), or where a loser says, "I played terribly today. I stank" (internal).
>
> Finally, think about why people make self-serving attributions. For example, if a famous athlete such as Jarome Inginla attributes his team's loss to factors outside himself, do you think he is protecting his self-esteem, trying to look good in front of others, or making the most logical attribution he can given his experience (he's so talented, most team losses really aren't his fault!)?

Apparently one participant remarked that the only reason Soviets would save trapped whales was to slaughter and eat them later; another participant assumed that the whales must have been blocking Soviet shipping lanes! In contrast, Canadian students tended to attribute similar motives to American and Soviet actions.

Self-serving biases also tend to creep in whenever we work on tasks with others (Sande, Ellard, & Ross, 1986; Shestowsky, Wegener, & Fabrigar, 1998; Zanna & Sande, 1987). For example, in a classic study conducted at the University of Waterloo, Ross and Sicoly (1979) found that students working on a group project had very good memories when asked to recall their contributions to the project. However, their memories were considerably poorer when asked to recall the contributions of the other group members. Ross and Sicoly found that this tendency extends even to our closest relationships. In another study, they asked married couples living in student housing at the University of Waterloo to indicate the extent to which each spouse assumed responsibility for 20 different activities (cooking, deciding how money should be spent, resolving conflicts). Each person tended to overestimate his or her contribution, such that when the husband's and wife's estimates of responsibility were added, the total was greater than 100 percent!

CULTURE AND THE SELF-SERVING BIAS Recent research suggests that like the other attributional biases we have discussed, the self-serving bias has a strong cultural component. For example, traditional Chinese culture values modesty and harmony with others. Thus, Chinese students are expected to attribute their successes to other people (such as their parents or teachers) or to other aspects of the situation (such as the quality of their school), rather than to themselves (Bond, 1996; Leung, 1996). Indeed, in several experiments, researchers have found that Chinese participants take less credit for their successes than do American participants (Anderson, 1999; Lee & Seligman, 1997). Similarly, Heine and colleagues found that Asian students tend not to believe success feedback, but readily accept failure feedback, whereas Canadian students show just the opposite tendency (Heine, Takata, & Lehman, 2000).

DEFENSIVE ATTRIBUTIONS People also alter their attributions to deal with other kinds of threats to their self-esteem. One of the hardest things to understand in life is the occurrence of tragic events, such as rapes, terminal diseases, and fatal accidents. Even when they happen to strangers we have never met, they can be upsetting. They remind us that if such tragedies can happen to someone else, they can happen to us. Of all the kinds of self-knowledge that we have, the knowledge that we are mortal and that bad things can happen to us is perhaps the hardest to accept (Greenberg, Pyszczynski, & Solomon, 1986; Greening & Chandler, 1997). We thus take steps to deny this fact. One way we do so is by making **defensive attributions**, which are explanations for behaviour that defend us from feelings of vulnerability and mortality.

One form of defensive attribution is **unrealistic optimism**, wherein people believe that good things are *more* likely to happen to them than to others, and bad things are *less* likely to happen to them than to others (Harris, 1996; Heine & Lehman, 1995; Klein, 1996; Regan, Snyder, & Kassin, 1995; Weinstein & Klein, 1996). Suppose we asked you to estimate how likely it is that each of the following will happen to you, compared to how likely it is that they will happen to other students at your college or university—owning your own home, liking your postgraduate job, living past age 80, having a drinking problem, getting divorced, and being unable to have children. When Neil Weinstein (1980) asked students these and similar questions, he found that people were too optimistic. Virtually everyone thought that the good things were more likely to happen to them than to their peers and that the bad things were less likely to happen to them than to their peers.

Although unrealistic optimism may help us feel better in the short term, in the long term it can be a potentially fatal attribution error. For example, battered women have been found to be unrealistically optimistic about the personal risks they run when they return to live with their abusive partners. They estimate that their own risk is significantly lower than the risk of most battered women—even when the facts of their situation would suggest otherwise (Martin et al., 2000).

Another form of defensive attribution is the belief that bad things happen only to bad people. By clinging to this belief, we can convince ourselves that the world is a safe, orderly place. Melvin Lerner (1980) at the University of Waterloo has called this **belief in a just world**—the assumption that people get what they deserve and deserve what they get. By using this attributional bias, we do not have to acknowledge that there is randomness to life, that an accident or a criminal or unemployment may be waiting just around the corner for an innocent person. In an ingenious set of experiments, Carolyn Hafer (2000a, 2000b) at Brock University demonstrated that when people's belief in a just world was threatened by hearing about an attack on an innocent person, they tended to derogate the victim's character and to distance themselves from the victim. Presumably, by doing so they were able to convince themselves that bad things happen to bad people—and since they themselves were good, surely no misfortune would befall them.

? Thinking Critically

When we feel threatened, we sometimes resort to the defensive attribution of belief in a just world (bad things happen to other people because they made mistakes that we wouldn't make). Can this defensive attribution be applied to the tragic loss of thousands of lives on September 11, 2001? How does this affect people's anxiety about future terrorist attacks and the probability that they might themselves be harmed?

Defensive attributions explanations for behaviour that avoid feelings of vulnerability and mortality

Unrealistic optimism a form of defensive attribution wherein people think that good things are more likely to happen to them than to their peers and that bad things are less likely to happen to them than to their peers

> Skim milk masquerades as cream.
> —W. S. GILBERT,
> H.M.S. Pinafore

Belief in a just world a form of defensive attribution wherein people assume that bad things happen to bad people and that good things happen to good people

Summary

Social cognition is the study of how people select, interpret, and use information to make judgments and decisions. People have developed several strategies and rules to help them understand the social world. **Schemas** are cognitive structures that organize information around themes or subjects. Schemas have a powerful effect on the information we notice, think about, and remember. One determinant of the schema that people apply in a given situation is **accessibility**, the extent to which a schema is at the forefront of one's mind and therefore is likely to be used when making judgments about the social world. Schemas can become accessible through **priming**, the process by which recent experiences increase the likelihood that a particular schema, trait, or concept will be brought to mind.

In addition to schemas, we use **judgmental heuristics** to help us deal with the large amount of social information with which we are faced. Heuristics are rules of thumb people follow to make judgments quickly and efficiently. The **availability heuristic**, the ease with which we can think of something, has a strong effect on how we view the world. The **representativeness heuristic** helps us decide how similar one thing is to another; we use it to classify people or situations on the basis of their similarity to a typical case. We also have a tendency to ignore **base rate information**—the prior probability that something or someone belongs in that classification. People also rely on the **anchoring and adjustment heuristic**, wherein an initial piece of information acts as an anchor, or starting point, for subsequent thoughts on the topic. While all three heuristics are useful, they can also lead to incorrect conclusions.

An important kind of social thinking is **automatic processing**—thinking that is nonconscious, unintentional, involuntary, and effortless. Engaging in automatic processing is very efficient, freeing up cognitive resources for other purposes. However, this kind of thinking can lead to errors such as making faulty, snap judgments about others. Another kind of social thinking is **controlled processing**—thinking that is conscious, intentional, voluntary, and effortful—to counteract the negative effects of automatic processing. When people are unmotivated or preoccupied, however, controlled processing is difficult. In such cases, people are more likely to accept false information.

According to **attribution theory**, we are also motivated to determine why people do what they do, or why we ourselves behave in particular ways. In answering the "why" question, we can make an **internal attribution** (attribute the behaviour to the person) or an **external attribution** (attribute the behaviour to the situation). People also use various mental shortcuts when making attributions. One common shortcut is the **fundamental attribution error**, which is the tendency to overestimate the extent to which people do what they do because of internal, dispositional factors. A reason for this error is that a person's behaviour often has greater **perceptual salience** than the surrounding situation. Culture also plays a role: People from Western cultures are more likely to engage in the fundamental attribution error than are people from Eastern cultures. The **actor/observer difference** is a qualification of the fundamental attribution error: We are more likely to commit this error when explaining other people's behaviour than when explaining our own behaviour. The actor/observer effect occurs because perceptual salience and information availability differ for the actor and the observer.

People's attributions are also influenced by their personal needs. **Self-serving attributions** occur when people make internal attributions for their successes and external attributions for their failures. **Defensive attributions** help people avoid feelings of vulnerability or mortality. One type of defensive attribution is **unrealistic optimism** about the future, whereby we think that good things are more likely to happen to us than to other people, and that bad things are less likely to happen to us than to others. Another type of defensive attribution is the **belief in a just world**, whereby we believe that bad things happen to bad people and good things happen to good people.

Key Terms

Accessibility   (page 51)
Actor/observer difference   (page 70)
Anchoring and adjustment heuristic   (page 57)
Attribution theory   (page 62)
Automatic processing   (page 59)
Availability   (page 55)
Availability heuristic   (page 55)
Base rate information   (page 56)
Belief in a just world   (page 75)
Controlled processing   (page 59)
Defensive attributions   (page 75)
External attribution   (page 62)
Fundamental attribution error   (page 65)
Internal attribution   (page 62)
Judgmental heuristics   (page 54)

Perceptual salience (page 68)
Priming (page 52)
Representativeness heuristic (page 55)
Schemas (page 49)
Self-serving attributions (page 72)
Social cognition (page 48)
Social perception (page 48)
Unrealistic optimism (page 75)

Key Online Search Terms

Schema
Heuristics
Automatic versus controlled thinking
Internal versus external attribution
Defensive attributions

If You Are Interested

Gilovich, T. (1991). *How we know what isn't so: The fallibility of human reason in everyday life.* New York: Free Press. An entertaining overview of the many ways in which mental shortcuts can get us into trouble.

Gilovich, T., Griffin, D. W., & Kahneman, D. (Eds.). (2001). *The psychology of judgment: Heuristics and biases.* New York: Cambridge University Press. A state-of-the-art compilation of research on people's use of heuristics and other mental shortcuts assembled by a stellar cast of editors. Dale Griffin is now at the University of British Columbia. Daniel Kahneman, formerly at the University of British Columbia, received the Nobel Prize for Economic Science in October 2002 for his research on judgment and uncertainty.

Jones, E. E. (1990). *Interpersonal perception.* New York: Freeman. A review of social perception (with an emphasis on attribution theory) by one of the pioneers in the field.

Weblinks

www.psych.purdue.edu/~esmith/scarch.html
Social Cognition Paper Archive and Information Center
A recommended set of papers on social cognition research. This site provides abstracts of many social cognition papers as well as several links to topics related to social cognition.

www.mentalhelp.net/poc/view_doc.php?type=doc&&id=289&&cn=0&&clnt%3Dclnt00001&&
Being Human and the Illusory Correlation
From baseball announcers to stereotyping, this article discusses human inference and the illusory correlation.

www.as.wvu.edu/~sbb/comm221/chapters/attrib.htm
Attribution Theory
Attribution theory is thoroughly reviewed and discussed in the chapter provided at this site.

Chapter 3 Practice Quiz

Check your knowledge of the concepts in this chapter by trying the following questions.

PEOPLE AS EVERYDAY THEORISTS: SCHEMAS AND THEIR INFLUENCE

Multiple Choice

1. We are likely to attend to and interpret the behaviour of others in ways that
    a. fit our schemas about them.
    b. fit with our self-schema.
    c. run counter to our schemas.
    d. avoid the use of schematic thought.

2. Accessibility refers to the extent that schemas are
    a. used when judging the social world.
    b. at the forefront of our minds.
    c. both chronic and temporary.
    d. all of the above

True or False

3. Lawyers will alter the way that evidence is presented in a courtroom to adhere to the schemas of the jurors or the judge.
    ___ True
    ___ False

4. The use of schemas reduces both ambiguity and the amount of information we need to take in.
    ___ True
    ___ False

Fill in the Blank

5. _____ is a process where a recent experience increases a schema's accessibility.
6. _____ are mental structures people use to organize knowledge.

MENTAL STRATEGIES AND SHORTCUTS: HEURISTICS

Multiple Choice

7. _____ refers to mental shortcuts that people use to make judgments.
    a. Heretics
    b. Heuristics
    c. Speed judging
    d. Multi-judgmental processing

8. _____ is based on the ease with which something comes to mind.
    a. The representativeness heuristic
    b. The judgmental heuristic
    c. The accessibility heuristic
    d. The availability heuristic

True or False

9. The use of heuristics guarantees that people will make accurate inferences about the world.
    ___ True
    ___ False

10. Both schemas and heuristics are effective strategies for the social thinker.
    ___ True
    ___ False

Fill in the Blank

11. _____ refers to information about the frequency of members of different categories in the population.
12. The _____ heuristic involves using an initial piece of information as a starting point for further judgment.

AUTOMATIC VERSUS CONTROLLED THINKING

Multiple Choice

13. Which of the following does not describe automatic processing?
    a. nonconscious
    b. effortless
    c. intentional
    d. involuntary

14. Changing the stimuli that we see and hear daily is done through
    a. automatic processing.
    b. controlled processing.
    c. subconscious processing.
    d. interpersonal processing.

True or False

15. Automatic processing operates like a check and balance system for controlled processing.
    ___ True
    ___ False

16. Stereotypes are difficult to overcome and are often a function of automatic processing.
    ___ True
    ___ False

Fill in the Blank

17. Studies on the _____ link errors in automatic thinking with stereotypes about African Americans and violence.

18. _____ processing requires both motivation and effort.

CAUSAL ATTRIBUTION: ANSWERING THE "WHY" QUESTION

Multiple Choice

19. _____ is the study of how we explain our own as well as others' behaviour.
    a. Attribution theory
    b. Location theory
    c. Causality theory
    d. Schematic theory

20. When a/an _____ occurs, people tend to see their own behaviour as a reaction to situational factors.
    a. fundamental attribution error
    b. situational attribution error
    c. actor/observer bias
    d. personal-situational dilemma

21. Attributing one's behaviour to situational factors is a/an
    a. internal attribution.
    b. location attribution.
    c. pyramidal attribution.
    d. external attribution.

22. Self-serving attributions
    a. are frequent in professional sports.
    b. involve taking credit for success.
    c. involve blaming others for failure.
    d. all of the above

True or False

23. When people make the fundamental attribution error, they attribute behaviour to situational factors while overlooking personality traits.
    ___ True
    ___ False

24. Self-serving bias is more prevalent among veteran athletes.
    ___ True
    ___ False

Fill in the Blank

25. Both _____ and cultural factors influence the occurrence of the fundamental attribution error.
26. Unrealistic optimism and the belief in a just world are two examples of _____.

PERSONALIZED STUDY PLAN

Want to check your answers and access more study resources? Visit the Companion Website for *Fundamentals of Social Psychology* at **www.pearsoned.ca/aronson**, where you'll find the above questions incorporated in a pre-test and post-test for each chapter. These tests will be automatically graded online, allowing you to check your answers. A Study Plan, like the one below, groups the questions by section within the chapter and shows you which sections you need to focus on for further study.

Your Results for "Chapter 3, Pretest"

OVERALL SCORE: 69% of 13 questions

Group	Score	Proficient
People as Everyday Theorists	2 of 3	Yes
Mental Strategies and Shortcuts	3 of 3	Yes
Automatic versus Controlled Thinking	1 of 3	No
Causal Attribution	3 of 4	Yes

CHAPTER

4

Self-Knowledge and Self-Evaluation: Self-Understanding and the Need to Maintain Self-Esteem

Chapter Outline

THE NATURE OF THE SELF
Cultural Differences in the Definition of Self
Gender Differences in the Definition of Self

KNOWING OURSELVES THROUGH INTROSPECTION
Focusing on the Self: Self-Awareness Theory

KNOWING OURSELVES THROUGH OBSERVATIONS OF OUR OWN BEHAVIOUR
Inferring Who We Are from How We Behave: Self-Perception Theory

KNOWING OURSELVES THROUGH SELF-SCHEMAS

KNOWING OURSELVES THROUGH SOCIAL INTERACTION
Seeing Ourselves through the Eyes of Others: The Looking-glass Self
Knowing Ourselves by Comparing Ourselves to Others

THE NEED TO FEEL GOOD ABOUT OURSELVES
Social Comparison Revisited
Self-Discrepancy Theory
Self-Evaluation Maintenance Theory
Self-Affirmation Theory

SELF-EVALUATION: BIASED OR ACCURATE?
Self-Enhancement: Wanting to Feel Good about Ourselves, Regardless of the Facts
Self-Verification: Wanting to Know the Truth about Ourselves

In an episode of the television show *Friends*, Ross faces a dilemma. Rachel, whom he has pursued for years, has finally shown romantic interest in him, and they have shared their first kiss. The problem is that Ross is currently dating Julie, whom he also likes a great deal. What to do? Urged on by his friends Chandler and Joey, Ross makes a list of the things he likes and dislikes about each woman, to try to clarify his thoughts.

Ross was in good company in taking the "pluses and minuses" approach. More than two centuries ago, Benjamin Franklin gave this advice about how to make difficult choices:

> My way is to divide half a sheet of paper by a line into two columns, writing over the one Pro, and over the other Con. Then... I put down... short hints of the different motives.... When each is thus considered, separately and comparatively, and the whole lies before me, I think I can judge better, and am less likely to make a rash step. (quoted in Goodman, 1945, p. 746)

Not everyone, however, believes in listing pros and cons. Consider the Peruvian writer Mario Vargas Llosa's reaction to judging films at the Berlin film festival:

> I went to every screening with a fresh pack of notecards that I would dutifully cover with my impressions of each and every film. The result, of course, was that the movies ceased to be fun and turned into problems, a struggle against time, darkness and my own esthetic emotions, which these autopsies confused. I was so worried about evaluating every aspect of every film that my entire system of values went into shock, and I quickly realized that I could no longer easily tell what I liked or didn't or why. (Vargas Llosa, 1986, p. 23)

What is the best way to decipher one's feelings when facing a difficult choice? Is it best to make careful lists of pros and cons, as Franklin recommended, or to go with one's gut feelings, as Varga Llosa implied? More generally, what is the nature of the self, and how do people discover it? And once they have discovered it, how do they feel about it? As we shall see, the process by which we come to know ourselves, and how we evaluate this knowledge, is a fascinating one. These are the questions to which we turn.

THE NATURE OF THE SELF

Who are you? How did you come to be this person you call "myself"? One of the founders of psychology, William James (1842–1910), described the basic duality of our perception of self. First, the self is composed of our thoughts and beliefs about ourselves, or what James (1890) called the "known," or, more simply, the "me." Second, the self is also the active processor of information, the "knower," or the "I." In modern terms, we refer to the known aspect of the self as the **self-concept**, which is the contents of the self (our knowledge about who we are), and to the knower aspect as **self-awareness**, which is the act of thinking about ourselves. These two aspects of the self combine to create a coherent sense of identity. Your self is both a book (full of fascinating contents collected over time) and the reader of that book (who at any moment can access a specific chapter or add a new one). In this chapter we will first focus on these aspects of the self—the nature of the self-concept and how we come to know ourselves through self-awareness. Later in the chapter we will focus on self-esteem—whether we evaluate our self positively or negatively.

A good place to begin is with the question of whether we are the only species with a sense of self. Some fascinating studies by Gordon Gallup (1977, 1993, 1994; Gallup & Suarez, 1986) suggest that we are not alone in this regard. Gallup placed a mirror in an animal's cage until the animal became familiar with it. The animal was then briefly anesthetized and an odourless red dye was painted on its brow or ear (the "rouge test"). What happens when the animal wakes up and looks in the mirror? Chimpanzees and orangutans immediately touch the area of their heads that contains the red spot. Gorillas and many species of monkeys, on the other hand, do not seem to recognize that the image in the mirror is them. They rarely touch the red spot and, unlike chimps and orangutans, are no more likely to touch it when the mirror is present than when the mirror is absent. These studies indicate that chimps and orangutans have a rudimentary self-concept. They realize that the image in the mirror is them and not another ape, and recognize that they look different from the way they looked before (Gallup, 1997; Povinelli, 1993, 1994; Sedikides & Skowronski, 1997).

What about humans? When we are toddlers we seem to have a similar, rudimentary self-concept. Researchers have used a variation of the rouge test with humans and found that self-recognition develops at around two years of age (Povinelli, Landau, & Perilloux, 1996). Lewis and Brooks (1978), for example, found that 75 percent of 21- to 25-month-old infants touched their rouged noses, while only 25 percent of the 9- to 12-month-old infants did so.

As we grow older, this self-concept, of course, becomes more complex. Psychologists have studied how people's self-concept changes from childhood to adulthood, by asking people of different ages to answer the simple question "Who am I?" Typically, a child's self-concept is concrete, with references to clear-cut, easily observable characteristics such as age, sex, neighbourhood, and hobbies. In a study by Montemayor and Eisen (1977), for example, a nine-year-old answered the "Who am I?" question this way: "I have brown eyes. I have brown hair. I have brown eyebrows.... I'm a boy. I have an uncle that is almost seven feet tall." As we mature, we place less emphasis on physical characteristics and more emphasis on our psychological states (our thoughts and feelings), our traits or characteristics, and considerations of how other people judge us (Hart & Damon, 1986; Montemayor & Eisen, 1977; Sande, Goethals, & Radloff, 1988). Thus, we might define ourselves as an extro-

---

Self-concept the contents of the self; that is, our knowledge about who we are

Self-awareness the act of thinking about ourselves

Researchers have examined whether other species have a self-concept by seeing whether they recognize that an image in a mirror is themselves and not another member of their species. The same procedure has been used with humans, revealing that people develop a self-concept around the age of two.

vert, a cautious person, a spiritual person, an only child, a worrier, someone who is not very interested in politics, and so on.

Research conducted by Jennifer Campbell at the University of British Columbia suggests that some of us may have a clearer sense of self than others. Self-concept clarity is defined as the extent to which knowledge about the self is clearly or consistently defined (Campbell, 1990). Campbell and her colleagues have found that the extent to which one's knowledge of one's self is stable, and clearly and consistently defined, has important cognitive and emotional implications (Campbell & Fehr, 1990; Campbell, Assanand, & Di Paula, 2000).

For example, Campbell and colleagues (1996) found that people who were low in self-concept clarity were more likely to be neurotic and have low self-esteem, and were less likely to be aware of their internal states. They also tended to engage in chronic self-analysis and rumination—an involuntary, negative form of self-focus associated with threat or uncertainty ("Sometimes it's hard for me to shut off thoughts about myself"; Trapnell & Campbell, 1999). People low in self-concept clarity also were less likely to engage in positive forms of self-focus such as reflection ("I love exploring my 'inner self'"). (We will discuss rumination and reflection in greater detail later in this chapter.) Thus, not having a clear, confident sense of who you are can have negative effects on your thoughts and emotions. To find out where you stand in terms of self-concept clarity, see the Try It! box on page 86.

Cultural Differences in the Definition of Self

In June 1993, Masako Owada, a 29-year-old Japanese woman, married Crown Prince Naruhito of Japan. Masako was a very bright career diplomat in the foreign ministry, educated at Harvard and Oxford. She spoke five languages and was on the fast track to

Try It! A Measure of Self-Concept Clarity

	strongly disagree				strongly agree
1. My beliefs about myself often conflict with one another.*	1	2	3	4	5
2. One day I might have one opinion of myself and on another day I might have a different opinion.*	1	2	3	4	5
3. I spend a lot of time wondering about what kind of person I really am.*	1	2	3	4	5
4. Sometimes I feel that I am not really the person that I appear to be.*	1	2	3	4	5
5. When I think about the kind of person I have been in the past, I'm not sure what I was really like.*	1	2	3	4	5
6. I seldom experience conflict between the different aspects of my personality.	1	2	3	4	5
7. Sometimes I think I know other people better than I know myself.*	1	2	3	4	5
8. My beliefs about myself seem to change very frequently.*	1	2	3	4	5
9. If I were asked to describe my personality, my description might end up being different from one day to another day.*	1	2	3	4	5
10. Even if I wanted to, I don't think I could tell someone what I'm really like.*	1	2	3	4	5
11. In general, I have a clear sense of who I am and what I am.	1	2	3	4	5
12. It is often hard for me to make up my mind about things because I don't really know what I want.*	1	2	3	4	5

Note: This is the Self-Concept Clarity Scale developed by Campbell, Trapnell, Heine, Katz, Lavallee, and Lehman (1996) to measure the extent to which people have a stable, clear, and consistently defined sense of self. The items with asterisks (*) are reverse-scored. Thus, to find out how you score on this scale, first reverse your answers to the items with asterisks. If you answered "5," change it to a "1"; if you answered "4," change it to a "2," and so on. Then add your ratings on all 12 questions. The higher your score, the more clearly defined your sense of self is. Among Canadian students, average scores on this scale range from 38 to 43. In a study comparing University of British Columbia students with students from Japan (where it was expected that self-concepts would be less clearly defined), the average was 40 for UBC students and 35 for Japanese students.

Source: Adapted from Campbell, J. D., Trapnell, P. D., Heine, S. J., Katz, I. M., Lavallee, L. F., & Lehman, D. R. (1996). Self-concept clarity: Measurement, personality correlates, and cultural boundaries. *Journal of Personality and Social Psychology, 70,* 141–156. Copyright 1996 by the American Psychological Association. Reprinted with permission.

a prestigious diplomatic career. Her decision to marry the prince surprised some observers, because it meant she would have to give up her career. Indeed, she gave up any semblance of an independent life, becoming subservient to the prince and the rest of the royal family and spending much of her time participating in rigid royal ceremonies. Her primary role was to produce a male heir to the royal throne.

How do you feel about Masako's decision to marry the prince? Your answer may say something about the nature of your self-concept and the culture in which you grew up. As mentioned in Chapter 3, in many Western cultures people have an **independent view of the self**, which is a way of defining oneself in terms of one's own internal thoughts, feelings, and actions, and not in terms of the thoughts, feelings, and actions of others (Cross & Gore, 2003; Heine et al., 1999; Kitayama & Markus, 1994; Markus & Kitayama, 1991, 2001; Markus, Kitayama, & Heiman, 1996; Triandis, 1995). Westerners learn to define themselves as quite separate from other people and to value independence and uniqueness. Consequently, many Western observers were mystified by Masako's decision to marry the crown prince. They assumed she was coerced into the marriage by a backwards, sexist society that did not properly value her worth as an individual with an independent life of her own.

In contrast, many Asian and other non-Western cultures have an **interdependent view of the self**, which is a way of defining oneself in terms of one's relationships to other people and recognizing that one's behaviour is often determined by the thoughts, feelings, and actions of others. Connectedness and interdependence between people is valued, whereas independence and uniqueness are frowned upon. For example, when asked to complete sentences beginning with "I am...," people from Asian cultures are more likely to refer to social groups, such as one's family or religious group, than are people from Western cultures (Bochner, 1994; Triandis, 1989). To many Japanese and other Asians, Masako's decision to give up her career was not at all surprising, and was a positive, natural consequence of her view of herself as connected and obligated to others, such as her family and the royal family. What is viewed as positive and normal behaviour by one culture might be viewed very differently by another.

We do not mean to imply that every member of a Western culture has an independent view of the self and that every member of an Asian culture has an interdependent view of the self. Within cultures there are differences in the self-concept, and these differences are likely to increase as contact between cultures increases. It is interesting to note, for example, that Masako's decision to marry the prince was unpopular among at least some young Japanese women, who felt that her choice was not a positive sign of interdependence but a betrayal to the feminist cause in Japan (Sanger, 1993). Nonetheless, the differences between the Western and Eastern sense of self is real and has interesting consequences for communication between the cultures. Indeed, the differences in the sense of self are so fundamental that it is difficult for people with independent selves to appreciate what it is like to have an interdependent self, and vice versa. Western readers might find it difficult to appreciate the Asian sense of interdependence; similarly, many Japanese find it difficult to comprehend that North Americans could possibly know who they are, separate from the social groups to which they belong.

Consider again Jennifer Campbell's notion of self-concept clarity. It might already have occurred to you that self-concept clarity is probably a Western phenomenon, given that it is based on a premise that the self is a stable configuration of internal traits that govern behaviour across situations. One might expect, therefore, that the sense of self would be less clear in cultures in which the self is perceived as interdependent. To see whether

Independent view of the self defining oneself in terms of one's own internal thoughts, feelings, and actions, and not in terms of the thoughts, feelings, and actions of other people

Interdependent view of the self defining oneself in terms of one's relationships to other people; recognizing that one's behaviour is often determined by the thoughts, feelings, and actions of others

The squeaky wheel gets the grease.
—AMERICAN PROVERB

The nail that stands out gets pounded down.
—JAPANESE PROVERB

this is the case, Campbell and her colleagues (1996) administered the Self-Concept Clarity Scale to Canadian and Japanese students. Japanese participants did, in fact, have lower self-concept clarity than Canadians. Moreover, self-concept clarity was not as strongly linked to self-esteem for the Japanese as it was for the Canadians (Campbell et al., 1996).

Gender Differences in the Definition of Self

There is a stereotype that when women get together, they talk about interpersonal problems and relationships, whereas men talk about sports or politics—anything but their feelings. Research suggests that there is some truth to the stereotype (Fehr, 1996) and that it reflects a difference in women's and men's self-concept (Baumeister & Sommer, 1997; Cross, Bacon, & Morris, 2000; Cross & Madson, 1997; Gabriel & Gardner, 1999). Susan Cross and Laura Madson (1997) point out that starting in early childhood, girls are more likely to develop intimate friendships, cooperate with others, and focus their attention on social relationships. Boys are more likely to engage in competitive activities and focus on dominance over others (Maccoby, 1990). These differences persist into adulthood, such that men in North America are more likely to have an independent view of self, whereas women define themselves more in relation to other people. In other words, women have more *relational* interdependence (Brewer & Gardner, 1996). To see how much your self-concept is based on a sense of relational interdependence, answer the questions in the Try It! exercise, page 89.

When Harvard-educated Masako Owada abandoned her promising career to marry Crown Prince Naruhito of Japan and assumed the traditional roles required of her, many Western women questioned her decision. At issue for many were cultural differences relating to interdependence versus emphasis on independence of the self.

Research on the self conducted by a team consisting of David Watkins (University of Hong Kong), John Adair (University of Manitoba), and researchers from many other countries confirms this gender difference—at least in individualist cultures (Watkins, Adair, et al., 1998; Watkins, Akande, et al., 1998). These researchers have examined differences in self-concept by administering the sentence completion test ("I am...") to thousands of participants in as many as 15 different cultures. In these studies, gender differences in self-concepts typically are found only among individualist cultures (Canada, white South Africa, New Zealand). Specifically, the self-concepts of men are more likely to be independent ("I am honest"; "I am intelligent"), whereas the self-concepts of women are more likely to be relational/collectivist ("I am a mother"; "I am a sociable person"). In contrast, in collectivist cultures that emphasize interdependence (China, Ethiopia, black South Africa), women and men are equally likely to hold a relational/collectivist view of the self.

A Measure of Relational Interdependence

Instructions: Indicate the extent to which you agree or disagree with each of these statements.

	strongly disagree					strongly agree	
1. My close relationships are an important reflection of who I am.	1	2	3	4	5	6	7
2. When I feel close to someone, it often feels to me like that person is an important part of who I am.	1	2	3	4	5	6	7
3. I usually feel a strong sense of pride when someone close to me accomplishes something important.	1	2	3	4	5	6	7
4. I think one of the most important parts of who I am can be captured by looking at my close friends and understanding who they are.	1	2	3	4	5	6	7
5. When I think of myself, I often think of my close friends or family also.	1	2	3	4	5	6	7
6. If a person hurts someone close to me, I feel personally hurt as well.	1	2	3	4	5	6	7
7. In general, my close relationships are an important part of my self-image.	1	2	3	4	5	6	7
8. Overall, my close relationships have very little to do with how I feel about myself.	1	2	3	4	5	6	7
9. My close relationships are unimportant to my sense of what kind of person I am.	1	2	3	4	5	6	7
10. My sense of pride comes from knowing who I have as close friends.	1	2	3	4	5	6	7
11. When I establish a close friendship with someone, I usually develop a strong sense of identification with that person.	1	2	3	4	5	6	7

Note: To compute your score, first reverse the rating you gave to questions 8 and 9. That is, if you circled a 1, change it to a 7; if you circled a 2, change it to a 6; if you circled a 7, change it to a 1; and so on. Then total your answers to the 11 questions. High scores reflect more of a tendency to define yourself in terms of relational interdependence. Cross, Bacon, and Morris (2000) found that women tend to score higher than men; in eight samples of university students, women averaged 57.2 and men averaged 53.4.

Source: Adapted from Cross, Bacon, & Morris (2000).

This is not to say that men in individualist cultures are completely lacking in interdependence. Quite the contrary. According to recent research by Cross and Madson, interdependence is part of men's conception of self, but it is not the kind of relational interdependence shown by women. Rather, men tend to define themselves in terms of social groups, such as the sports teams to which they belong (Cross, Bacon, & Morris, 2000; Cross & Madson, 1997). This is known as *collective* interdependence (Gabriel & Gardner,

> There is one thing, and only one in the whole universe which we know more about than we could learn from external observation. That one thing is [ourselves]. We have, so to speak, inside information; we are in the know.
>
> —C. S. LEWIS, 1960

Introspection the process whereby people look inward and examine their own thoughts, feelings, and motives

1999). Shira Gabriel and Wendi Gardner (1999), for example, asked women and men to describe either a positive or a negative emotional event in their lives. Women tended to mention personal relationships, such as becoming engaged or the death of a family member. Men talked about events involving larger groups, such as the time they joined a fraternity or the time their sports team lost an important game.

Research on gender differences is controversial, and we should be clear about what researchers are saying here. First, Cross and Madson (1997) are not arguing that women in North America have the exact same sense of self as women and men in collectivist countries. Second, they acknowledge that men desire intimate relationships as much as women do. Moreover, as recent research is suggesting (Fehr and Broughton, 2001), even though there may be differences in how men and women in our culture define themselves, both sexes desire and value close intimate relationships.

The bottom line is that it is important not to overemphasize sex differences. As Kay Deaux and Marianne LaFrance (1998) point out, doing so stresses opposites rather than the vast overlap in the psychological makeup of women and men.

To summarize, interesting differences emerge across cultures and between women and men in how people define themselves. But how do people learn who they are in the first place? How did you discover those things that make you uniquely *you*? We will now discuss how people gain self-knowledge.

Thinking Critically
To what extent do you think who you are is determined by your gender? To what extent do you think who you are is determined by your culture?

KNOWING OURSELVES THROUGH INTROSPECTION

When we told you we were going to describe the sources of information you use to construct a self-concept, you might have thought, "Good grief! I don't need a social psychology textbook to tell me that! It's not exactly a surprise; I just think about myself. No big deal." In other words, you rely on **introspection**: You look inward and examine the "inside information" that you, and you alone, have about your thoughts, feelings, and motives—just as the quotation by C. S. Lewis suggests. And indeed, you do find some answers when you introspect. But there are two interesting things about introspection: First, people do not rely on this source of information as often as you might think—surprisingly, people spend very little time thinking about themselves. According to one study, only 8 percent of thoughts are about the self; most of the time we are thinking about work, other people, and our conversations with others (Csikszentmihalyi & Figurski, 1982). Second, even when people do introspect, the reasons for their feelings and behaviour can be hidden from conscious awareness (Wilson, 2002). As Nietzsche observed (see quotation on page 91), much of the self may be unknown. In short, self-scrutiny isn't all it's cracked up to be, and if this were our only source of knowledge about ourselves we would be in trouble.

Focusing on the Self: Self-Awareness Theory

As we just saw, we do not focus on ourselves very often. However, when we are thinking about ourselves, what happens? What are the consequences of turning the spotlight of consciousness on ourselves, instead of focusing our attention on the world around us?

According to **self-awareness theory**, when we focus our attention on ourselves, we evaluate and compare our current behaviour against our internal standards and values (Carver, 2003; Carver & Scheier, 1981; Duval & Silvia, 2002; Duval & Wicklund, 1972). In short, we become self-conscious, in the sense that we become objective, judgmental observers of ourselves. Let's say that you believe it is important for you to be honest with your friends. One day, while conversing with a friend, you lie to him. In the midst of this conversation, you catch sight of yourself in a large mirror. How do you think you will feel?

Shelley Duval and Robert Wicklund (1972) suggest that seeing yourself will make you aware of the disparity between your behaviour and your moral standards. If you can change your behaviour to match your internal guidelines (say something particularly nice to your friend or admit that you lied and ask for forgiveness), you will do so. If you feel you can't change your behaviour, then being in a state of self-awareness will be very uncomfortable, for you will be confronted with disagreeable feedback about yourself. In this situation, you will stop being self-aware as quickly as possible (by turning so that your back is to the mirror or by saying goodbye to your friend and leaving the room). Figure 4.1 illustrates this process—how self-awareness makes us conscious of our internal standards and directs our subsequent behaviour.

This dissatisfaction with ourselves can be painful. According to Sophia Moskalenko and Steven Heine (2002), we will often try to alleviate the pain of unpleasant realizations about the self. These researchers conducted a study in which some participants were told that they had done very poorly on a task that reflected their level of intelligence. Others were told that they had done well. The authors reasoned that the participants who were given the failure feedback would be highly motivated to escape self-awareness and, therefore, would be most likely to pay attention to a video that was on in the room. And that is exactly what happened.

Sometimes people go even further in their attempt to escape the self. Roy Baumeister (1991) has pointed out that such diverse activities as alcohol abuse, binge eating, sexual masochism, and suicide have one thing in common: All are effective ways of turning the internal spotlight away from oneself. Getting drunk, for example, is one way of avoiding negative thoughts about oneself (at least temporarily). Suicide, of course, is the ultimate way of ending self-scrutiny. The fact that people regularly engage in such behaviours, despite the risks, is an indication of how aversive self-focus can be (Hull, 1981; Hull & Young, 1983; Hull, Young, & Jouriles, 1986).

We hasten to add that self-awareness does not inevitably have negative effects. Self-focus can also be a way of keeping you out of trouble, by reminding you of your sense of right and wrong. For example, several studies have found that when people are self-aware (e.g., in front of a mirror), they are more likely to follow their moral standards, such as avoiding the temptation to cheat on a test (Beaman et al., 1979; Diener & Wallbom, 1976; Gibbons, 1978). And Baumeister (1991) points out that people also escape self-awareness through more positive means such as religious expression and spirituality.

> **Self-awareness theory** the idea that when people focus their attention on themselves, they evaluate and compare their behaviour to their internal standards and values

> We are unknown, we knowers, ourselves to ourselves; this has its own good reason. We have never searched for ourselves—how should it then come to pass, that we should ever find ourselves?
> —FRIEDRICH NIETZSCHE, 1918

> But as I looked into the mirror, I screamed, and my heart shuddered: for I saw not myself but the mocking, leering, face of a devil.
> —FRIEDRICH NIETZSCHE, Thus Spake Zarathustra

| FIGURE 4.1 | Self-Awareness Theory: The Consequences of Self-Focused Attention |

When people focus on themselves, they compare their behaviour to their internal standards.

(Adapted from Carver and Scheier, 1981)

Thus, self-awareness can have negative or positive effects. In those cases where self-awareness feels aversive, we can alleviate those bad feelings in either a constructive or a destructive manner.

Thinking Critically

Do you feel that we can gain an accurate sense of who we are through introspection? Why or why not?

"Steer clear of that group. They're all terribly self-aware."

The people on the couch look awfully smug; they must like what they see when they are self-aware.
Frascino © 1977 *The New Yorker* Collection. All rights reserved.

KNOWING OURSELVES THROUGH OBSERVATIONS OF OUR OWN BEHAVIOUR

If introspection has its limits, how else might we find out what sort of person we are and what our attitudes are? Well, if you aren't sure how you feel about something, there is another way you can find out: Observe your own behaviour. If you want to know whether you like country music, for example, you might think, "Well, I always listen to the country music station on my car radio," concluding that you like country tunes.

Inferring Who We Are from How We Behave: Self-Perception Theory

Do we actually answer the question of who we are by observing our own behaviour? As strange as it may sound, according to Daryl Bem (1972) such observations are an important source of self-knowledge.

Bem's (1972) **self-perception theory** argues that when our attitudes and feelings are uncertain or ambiguous, we infer these states by observing our behaviour and the situation in which it occurs. Let's consider each part of this theory. First, we infer our inner feelings from our behaviour only when we are not sure how we feel. If you've always known that you are a country music lover, then you do not need to observe your behaviour to figure this out (Andersen, 1984; Andersen & Ross, 1984). However, if you aren't sure how much you like country music, you are especially likely to use your behaviour as a guide to how you feel. This effect was demonstrated by Chaiken and

Self-perception theory the theory that when our attitudes and feelings are uncertain or ambiguous, we infer these states by observing our behaviour and the situation in which it occurs

Baldwin (1981) with University of Toronto students. First, the researchers assessed whether the participants had well-defined attitudes or poorly defined attitudes toward being an environmentalist. Then they asked participants to check off on a list which pro-ecology or anti-ecology actions they had performed ("I frequently leave on lights in rooms I'm not using") as a way of reminding them of their past behaviour. The researchers expected that being reminded of their past behaviour would influence only those participants whose attitudes were poorly defined. Indeed, participants with poorly defined environmental attitudes were strongly affected by these behavioural cues; those who were reminded of their pro-ecology behaviour subsequently reported that they held pro-environmental attitudes, whereas those who were reminded of their anti-ecology behaviour later reported more negative environmental attitudes. In contrast, being reminded of their past behaviour had little effect on the participants who already had clear (well-defined) attitudes on this issue.

Self-perception theory also claims that people evaluate whether their behaviour really reflects how they feel or whether the situation made them act in a certain way. If you freely choose to listen to the country radio station—no one makes you do it—you are especially likely to conclude that you listen to that station because you love country music. If it is your roommate and not you who always tunes in to the country station, you are unlikely to conclude that you listen to country music in your car because you love it.

> *I've always written poems…. I never know what I think until I read it in one of my poems.*
> —VIRGINIA HAMILTON ADAIR

Thinking Critically
When do you think people might be especially likely to rely on observations of their own behaviour to infer who they are? When do you think they might rely on other means (e.g., introspection)?

KNOWING OURSELVES THROUGH SELF-SCHEMAS

As we have seen, we can learn about ourselves in a variety of ways. What do we do with all of this information once we have it? Not surprisingly, we organize our self-knowledge in much the same way that we organize our knowledge about the external world—into schemas.

In Chapter 3, we noted that people use schemas—knowledge structures about a person, topic, or object—to understand the social world. It should come as no surprise that we form **self-schemas** as well, the organized knowledge structures about ourselves, based on our past experiences, that help us understand, explain, and predict our own behaviour (Andersen & Cyranowski, 1994; Cantor & Kihlstrom, 1987; Deaux, 1993; Malle & Horowitz, 1995; Markus, 1977; Markus & Nurius, 1986). Schemas also influence the kinds of experiences we remember. If being independent is part of your self-schema but being competitive is not, you will probably remember more times when you acted independently than competitively (Akert, 1993; Bahrick, Hall, & Berger, 1996; Markus, 1977; Thompson et al., 1996).

Finally, schemas also influence how we interpret new things that happen to us. Suppose, for example, that you lose a close tennis match to your best friend. How will you react? In part, the answer depends on the nature of your self-schemas. If you define yourself as competitive and athletic, you are likely to feel bad and want a rematch as soon as

Self-schemas organized knowledge structures about ourselves, based on our past experiences, that help us understand, explain, and predict our own behaviour

possible, whereas if you define yourself as cooperative and nurturing, losing the match won't be such a big deal.

Thinking Critically
Why do you think we organize information about ourselves in the form of a schema? What purpose might self-schemas serve?

KNOWING OURSELVES THROUGH SOCIAL INTERACTION

So far, we have seen that people learn about themselves through introspection and observations of their own behaviour, and that they organize this information into self-schemas. As important as these sources of self-knowledge are, there is still something missing. We are not solitary seekers of self-knowledge but social beings who often see ourselves through the eyes of other people. James (1890) stressed the importance of social relationships in our definition of self, noting that we can have different "selves" that develop in response to different social situations. For example, when one of our authors (Robin Akert) is at the stable, training her horse and chatting with other riders and stable hands, she presents a different aspect of herself than she does when she is at a psychology conference with her colleagues. Her "barn self" is more colloquial and she is less likely to talk about her latest research project. Not only is it true that we present ourselves differently to different people, but also we shape our self-definition according to how they view us. It's as if other people reflect their image of you back for you to see.

Seeing Ourselves through the Eyes of Others: The Looking-glass Self

The idea that we see ourselves through the eyes of other people—either present or imagined—and incorporate their views into our self-concept is called the **looking-glass self** (Cooley, 1902; Mead, 1934). Mark Baldwin and his colleagues have explored this idea in an ingenious set of experiments (Baldwin, 1992; Baldwin & Meunier, 1999; Baldwin & Sinclair, 1996). Imagine you were a participant in one of their studies. Think of an older member of your family. Try to form a vivid picture of this person in your mind. Imagine that this person is sitting beside you. Focus on the colour of the person's eyes or hair, and then focus on the sound of the person's voice. Imagine talking to this person.

Now imagine reading a story about a woman who engages in sexually permissive behaviour. How much do you think you would enjoy the story? This is the situation in which female students at the University of Waterloo found themselves (Baldwin & Holmes, 1987). Half of the participants were asked to visualize older family members as a way of priming a conservative internal audience. In other words, participants were induced to see themselves through the eyes of significant people in their lives—in this case, older members of their family. The other participants were asked to visualize friends from campus as a way of priming a permissive internal audience. They were then asked to participate in a supposedly unrelated study in which they would evaluate pieces of fiction. One of the stories, taken from *Cosmopolitan* magazine, described a woman's sexually permissive behaviour. The researchers found that women who had

Looking-glass self the idea that we see ourselves through the eyes of other people and incorporate their views into our self-concept

previously imagined older family members rated the story as less enjoyable than women who had imagined their university friends. Thus, participants' reactions to the story depended on whether they were seeing themselves through the eyes of their friends or their family members. There was one additional finding of note. Recall that earlier in this chapter we discussed research showing that when people are self-aware, they are more attuned to their beliefs and moral standards. Baldwin and Holmes also added a condition in which some participants were made to feel self-aware (by the presence of a mirror) while they were rating the passages. Their findings were even more pronounced among self-aware participants; thus, if you were imagining your grandmother or great-uncle Ted, and then saw yourself in a mirror while reading a sexual passage, you were even less likely to enjoy it!

The effects of an internal audience on our sense of self have been demonstrated in other domains as well. For example, in another study (Baldwin, Carrell, & Lopez, 1990) graduate students at the University of Michigan were asked to evaluate their recent research ideas. For some of the students, an evaluative authority figure was primed by subliminal exposure (flashing a slide so quickly that the participants weren't consciously aware of what had been shown) to the scowling face of their program director. Other students were exposed to an approving figure—the warm, friendly face of John Ellard, a postdoctoral student (now a social psychology professor at the University of Calgary). Students who were exposed to the face of their program director subsequently evaluated their research ideas more negatively than did those exposed to the face of John Ellard.

In a subsequent study, Baldwin and colleagues (1990) primed a sense of self as a Catholic among Catholic women at the University of Waterloo through subliminal exposure to a picture of Pope John Paul II looking disapproving (see photo below). Other participants (also Catholics) were exposed to the scowling face of a man who was unfamiliar to them (and therefore should not have had implications for their sense of self). All participants then read a sexually permissive passage. As expected, women exposed to the disapproving countenance of the Pope rated themselves more negatively than did women exposed to the disapproving face of an unfamiliar man. However, this effect was obtained only for women who defined themselves as practising Catholics. Presumably for these women, the Pope was an especially relevant internal audience.

The looking-glass self: In one study (Baldwin, Carrell, & Lopez, 1990), students were subliminally exposed either to a photo of the chair of their department, scowling, or to a photo of a postdoctoral student, smiling. Those exposed to their scowling chair subsequently rated their own research more negatively than did those exposed to the friendly postdoctoral student.

Thus, who we are is determined, at least in part, by the internal audience we have in mind. If we are reminded of a significant person in our lives who seems critical or disapproving, we will tend to see ourselves as possessing negative traits (e.g., immoral or incompetent). On the other hand, if we happen to have a supportive, approving internal audience in mind, we are more likely to view ourselves as having positive characteristics.

Knowing Ourselves by Comparing Ourselves to Others

We also come to know ourselves by comparison with other people (Brown, 1990; Collins, 1996; Kruglanski & Mayseless, 1990; McFarland & Miller, 1994; Niedenthal & Beike, 1997; Suls, Martin, & Wheeler, 2000; Wheeler, Martin, & Suls, 1997; Wood, 1989, 1996). Suppose, for example, we gave you a test that measured your social sensitivity, or how aware you are of other people's problems. The test involves reading excerpts from autobiographies and guessing the nature of the authors' personal problems, if any. After you've taken the test, we tell you that you achieved a score of 35. What have you learned about yourself? Not much, because you don't know what a score of 35 means. Is it a good score or a bad score? Suppose we told you that the test is scored on a scale from 0 to 50. Now what have you learned? A little more than you knew before, perhaps, but this is still pretty uninformative if you don't know how other people did on the test. If we told you that everyone else in your class scored between 0 and 20, you would probably say, "Wow—I really am an extremely sensitive person!" On the other hand, you might feel differently if we told you that everyone else scored between 45 and 50.

This example illustrates Leon Festinger's (1954) **social comparison theory**, which holds that people learn about their own abilities and attitudes by comparing themselves to other people. Not surprisingly, people find it most informative to compare themselves to others who are similar to them on important attributes or dimensions (Goethals & Darley, 1977; Miller, 1982; Wheeler, Koestner, & Driver, 1982; Zanna, Goethals, & Hill, 1975). For example, if you are wondering about your artistic ability, it will not be very informative to compare yourself to Picasso—one of the great artists of the twentieth century. It also will not be that informative to compare your artistic endeavours to the fingerpainting and scribbles of your four-year-old sister. It is better to compare yourself to the other people in your drawing class, if your goal is to assess your own abilities.

Social comparison theory the idea that we learn about our own abilities and attitudes by comparing ourselves to other people

Thinking Critically
Why is the study of the self an important topic in social psychology? How is the self-concept shaped by other people?

THE NEED TO FEEL GOOD ABOUT OURSELVES

As we have seen, we are motivated to understand ourselves. As we shall see next, we also have a need to feel good about ourselves. Sometimes these needs clash—we want accurate information about ourselves, even if that information is not necessarily flattering, but we also want to feel good about ourselves. Later, we discuss how we deal with these conflicting needs. But first, we discuss the need to maintain a positive self-evaluation.

Social Comparison Revisited

Earlier, we mentioned that one way we learn about our own attitudes and abilities is to compare them with those of other people. However, constructing an accurate image of ourselves is not the only reason that we engage in social comparison. We also use social comparison to boost our egos. Is it important to you to believe that you are a fabulous artist-in-the-making? Then compare yourself to your little sister—you have her beat! This use of **downward social comparison**—comparing yourself to people who are worse than you in a particular trait or ability—is a self-protective, self-enhancing strategy (Aspinwall & Taylor, 1993; Davison, Pennebaker, & Dickerson, 2000; Pyszczynski, Greenberg, & LaPrelle, 1985; Reis, Gerrard, & Gibbons, 1993; Wheeler & Kunitate, 1992; Wood & VanderZee, 1997).

Indeed, research shows that if you compare yourself to people who are less smart, less talented, or sicker than you are, you'll feel very good about yourself. For example, Joanne Wood, Shelley Taylor, and Rosemary Lichtman (1985) found evidence of downward comparison in interviews with cancer patients. The vast majority of patients spontaneously compared themselves to other cancer patients who were more ill than they were, presumably as a way of making themselves feel more optimistic about the course of their own conditions. More recently, Wood and her colleagues examined spontaneous social comparisons in everyday life by having students at the University of Waterloo keep track of times when they compared themselves to another person over a three-week period (Wood, Michela, & Giordano, 2000). An analysis of these diaries confirmed that people were most likely to spontaneously engage in downward social comparisons when they wanted to feel better about themselves.

How do we feel if we instead compare ourselves to someone who is better than we are—thus engaging in **upward social comparison**? According to Lockwood and Kunda (1997, 1999, 2000), the answer is, it depends. You might feel better or worse, depending on the sense of self that is activated (brought to mind) at the time. Imagine you were a participant in one of their studies. Think of a peak academic experience that made you especially proud. If you are like the math, biology, and computer science students at the University of Waterloo who participated in this study, you will have no trouble coming up with an answer (Lockwood & Kunda, 1999). Now imagine reading an article in your campus newspaper that describes a student, the same gender as you, who has had a stellar academic career. This person has won all kinds of awards, and university officials are raving about how truly outstanding this student is. How do you feel now? If you suddenly don't feel so good, you are not alone. Lockwood and Kunda found that when participants' "best self" had been activated, it was depressing for them to be exposed to a superstar. They tended not to feel very good about themselves, and their motivation to study hard took a dive.

What if, instead of describing your "best" self, you focused on your "usual" self? Other participants in this study did just that—they were simply asked to describe what they had done the day before. For these participants, reading about the superstar student was inspiring. They imagined that they, too, could achieve greatness, and as a result they felt very good about themselves—even better than participants who focused on their usual selves but did not read about the superstar. (These results are shown in Figure 4.2.)

Downward social comparison the process whereby we compare ourselves to people who are worse than we are in a particular trait or ability

> There is little satisfaction in the contemplation of heaven for oneself if one cannot simultaneously contemplate the horrors of hell for others.
>
> —P. D. JAMES,
> The Children of Men, *1992*

Upward social comparison the process whereby we compare ourselves to people who are better than we are in a particular trait or ability

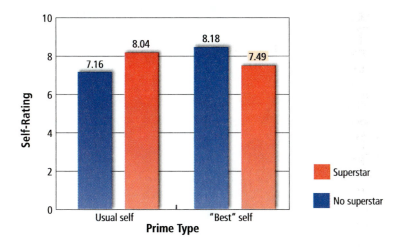

FIGURE 4.2 Effects of Upward Social Comparison on Self-Enhancement

People who focused on their usual self evaluated themselves more positively following exposure to a superstar than did people who were not exposed to a superstar. However, people who focused on their "best" self evaluated themselves more negatively following exposure to a superstar than did those who were not exposed to a superstar.

(Lockwood & Kunda, 1999)

FOCUS ON APPLICATIONS

Promoting Social Good through Social Comparison

We have seen that we can boost our self-esteem by comparing our performance to that of others. If others are doing more poorly than we are, that can make us feel better about ourselves (downward social comparison). If others are doing better than we are, that can motivate us to try harder to improve our own performance (upward social comparison). Might this basic human tendency to compare our performance to that of others be used to promote social good?

Consider a study conducted by Frans Siero and colleagues (1996) to try to get people to conserve energy in the workplace. At one unit of a factory in the Netherlands, employees were urged to engage in energy-saving behaviours. For example, announcements were placed in the company magazine asking people to close windows during cold weather and to turn off lights when leaving a room. In addition, employees got weekly feedback on their behaviour; graphs were posted that showed how much they had improved their energy-saving behaviours, such as how often they had turned off the lights. This intervention resulted in modest improvement. By the end of the program, for example, the number of times people left the lights on decreased by 27 percent.

Another unit of the factory took part in an identical program, with one difference. In addition to receiving weekly feedback on its own energy-saving actions, it received feedback about how the other unit was doing. The researchers hypothesized that this social comparison information would motivate people to do better than their colleagues in the other unit. They were right. By the end of the program, the number of times people left lights on had decreased by 61 percent. Engaging people's competitive spirit can have a large impact on their behaviour. Thus, our desire to perform well, relative to those around us, can not only give our self-esteem a boost but be good for the environment as well!

> "Of course you're going to be depressed if you keep comparing yourself with successful people."

This man has engaged in too much upward social comparison.
Hamilton © *The New Yorker Collection.* All rights reserved.

The researchers conclude that when we focus on our actual or usual self, exposure to outstanding others inspires us to generate higher hopes and aspirations for ourselves than we would have if we hadn't been exposed to the superstar. However, if we happen to be focusing on our best or ideal self, it can be depressing to realize that someone else has already surpassed our highest hopes and dreams.

In sum, we can feel good by comparing ourselves to those who are better than we are (upward social comparison), but only if we are focusing on our usual, ordinary self. Another route to feeling good is to engage in downward comparison and compare ourselves to those who are less fortunate. Doing so will make us look better by comparison.

Self-Discrepancy Theory

The work of E. Tory Higgins and his colleagues (Higgins, 1987, 1989, 1996, 1999; Higgins, Klein, & Strauman, 1987) is concerned with understanding how violations of personal standards influence how people feel about themselves. In particular, these researchers have taken a close look at the nature of the emotional distress that occurs when we perceive ourselves as not measuring up to our ideals and standards. **Self-discrepancy theory** posits that we become distressed when our sense of who we truly are—our actual self—is discrepant from our personal standards or desired self-conceptions. For Higgins and his colleagues, these standards are reflected most clearly in the various beliefs we hold about the type of person we aspire to be—our ideal self—and the type of person we believe we should be—our "ought" self. Comparing our actual self with our ideal and ought selves provides us with an important means of self-evaluation.

What happens when we become aware that we have failed to measure up to our own standards? Consider the predicament of Sarah, a first-year university student who has

Self-discrepancy theory the theory that we become distressed when our sense of who we truly are—our actual self—is discrepant from our personal standards or desired self-conceptions

always had very high academic standards. In terms of self-discrepancy theory, academic competence is a central component of her ideal self. In her first semester at a competitive, prestigious university, however, Sarah has discovered that those As are much harder to come by. As a matter of fact, in her introductory chemistry course—a prerequisite for her major—she barely managed to earn a C. Given this scenario, how is Sarah likely to experience this discrepancy between her ideal and actual selves?

To begin with, we might imagine that the threat to her self-concept as a high achiever would generate fairly strong levels of emotional discomfort—for example, disappointment in herself and perhaps an unaccustomed sense of uncertainty regarding her abilities. Self-discrepancy research supports this view. In a series of studies, Higgins and his colleagues (Higgins, 1989; Higgins et al., 1986) have found that when people are made mindful of a discrepancy between their actual and ideal selves, they tend to experience a pattern of feelings involving dejection, sadness, dissatisfaction, and other depression-related emotions.

On the other hand, what if Sarah had encountered a self-discrepancy involving her ought self—that is, not the ideal self she aspired to but the "should" self she felt obligated to uphold? Suppose that Sarah tried to achieve academic excellence mainly because her parents had always considered this standard highly important. How would Sarah experience this discrepancy between her actual and ought selves, in the face of a mediocre performance in her first semester at university? Research by Higgins and his colleagues indicates that, in this case, Sarah would be likely to experience fear, worry, tension, and other anxiety-related emotions.

How might Sarah attempt to cope with the negative feelings generated by either of these two forms of self-discrepancy? According to the theory, self-discrepancies not only produce emotional discomfort but also provoke strivings to minimize the gap between the actual and the ideal, or ought, selves. Thus, Sarah might convince herself that the grading was unfair, that her chemistry instructor was totally inept, or in some other way interpret her mediocre performance in the most positive light possible. A more beneficial approach might be to reassess her situation—concluding, perhaps, that maintaining her high academic standards might require greater effort than she has been accustomed to exerting in the past when her courses were less challenging.

SELF-DISCREPANCIES AND CULTURE In cultures that emphasize interdependence, self-criticism is valued because group members are expected to continually strive to improve themselves in order to function harmoniously with others (Heine et al., 1999). Heine and Lehman (1999) reasoned that this emphasis

Self-discrepancy theory posits that we are distressed when our sense of who we truly are does not match our desired self-conception. For this high-achieving student, finding out she's done poorly on a test would generate strong levels of emotional discomfort.

on self-criticism might lead people in Asian cultures to experience greater discrepancies between their ideal and actual selves than people in Western cultures. Indeed, when these researchers compared students at the University of British Columbia with students at Ritsumeikan University in Kyoto, Japan, they found that Japanese students viewed their actual selves as falling short of their ideal selves (particularly on traits they regarded as important) to a greater extent than did the Canadian students. However, interestingly, for Japanese students, discrepancies between their actual and ideal selves were not as depressing as they were for Canadian students. Heine and Lehman suggest that the Japanese participants might have been accustomed to thinking of their inadequacies as areas for improvement and therefore found it less upsetting that they weren't measuring up to their ideals.

Self-Evaluation Maintenance Theory

So far we have been focusing on situations in which our self-image is threatened by our own behaviour, such as failing to live up to our ideals. Abraham Tesser and his colleagues have explored how other people's behaviour can threaten our self-concept (Beach et al., 1996; Tesser, 1988; Tesser, Martin, & Mendolia, 1995).

Suppose you consider yourself to be a good cook—in fact, the best cook among all your friends and acquaintances. You love nothing better than playing with a recipe, adding your own creative touches, until, voilà—you have a delectable new creation. Then you move to another town, make new friends, and, alas, your favourite new friend turns out to be a superb cook, far better than you. How does that make you feel? We suspect that you might feel more than a little uneasy about the fact that your friend outdoes you in your area of expertise.

Now consider a slightly different scenario. Suppose your new best friend is not a superb cook, but a very talented artist. Are you likely to experience any discomfort in this situation? Undoubtedly not; in fact, you are likely to bask in the reflected glory of your friend's success. "Guess what?" you will probably tell everyone. "My new friend has sold some of her paintings in the most exclusive art galleries."

If being a good cook is an important aspect of her self-concept, and her best friend is a superb cook, she will try harder. Where *are* those capers?

The difference between these two cases is that in the first one, your friend is superior in an attribute that is important to you and may even be a central part of how you define yourself. We all have abilities and traits that we treasure—we are especially proud of being good cooks, talented artists, gifted musicians, or inventive scientists. Whatever our most treasured ability, if we encounter someone who is better at it than we are, there is likely to be trouble—trouble of the self-esteem variety. It is difficult to be proud of your ability to cook if your closest friend is a far better chef than you are.

This is the premise of Tesser's (1988) **self-evaluation maintenance theory**. One's self-concept can be threatened by another individual's behaviour; the level of the threat is determined by both the closeness of the other individual and the personal relevance of the behaviour. As seen in Figure 4.3, there is no problem if a close friend outperforms us on a task that is not relevant to us. In fact, we feel even better about ourselves. However, we feel bad when a close friend outperforms us on a task that is relevant to our self-definition. For example, Campbell, Fairey, and Fehr (1986) had students at the University of British Columbia participate in an experiment in which they performed two tests—one that supposedly assessed their social sensitivity, and another that supposedly assessed their aesthetic judgment. Some students participated in the experiment with a friend; others participated with a stranger. Later, the participants were given feedback indicating that they had done poorly on one of the tests—both they and their partners in the experiment got only 6 of the 12 questions correct. On the other test, their performance was better—they got 8 of the 12 questions correct and their partners got 11 correct. Which situation did participants prefer? Campbell and colleagues found that when the partners were close to them (their friends), participants preferred the test on which they and their friends received the same score—even though their performance was worse on that test (6 versus 8 questions correct).

> **Self-evaluation maintenance theory** the theory that one's self-concept can be threatened by another individual's behaviour and that the level of threat is determined by both the closeness of the other individual and the personal relevance of the behaviour

FIGURE 4.3 Self-Evaluation Maintenance Theory

On the other hand, when their partners were strangers, participants preferred the test on which they received a higher score—despite the fact that their partners outperformed them. This study illustrated that it is less threatening to our self-esteem to have performed poorly than to have a close friend trump our good performance.

RESTORING OUR SELF-ESTEEM If we are vastly outperformed by a friend in an area that matters to us, how do we go about dealing with this threat to our self-esteem? According to self-evaluation maintenance theory, we have three options. First, as shown in Figure 4.3, we can distance ourselves from the person who outperforms us, deciding that he is not such a close friend after all. Pleban and Tesser (1981) tested this possibility by having university students compete against other students, who are actually accomplices of the experimenter, on general knowledge questions. They rigged it so that in some conditions the questions were on topics that were highly relevant to people's self-definitions and the accomplices got many more of the questions correct. Just as predicted, this was the condition in which people distanced themselves the most from the accomplices, saying they would not want to work with them again.

An astute reader may have noticed that there appears to be a contradiction between the finding that we feel bad when a friend outperforms us and the findings of Lockwood and Kunda's (1997, 1999) research on upward social comparison (presented earlier in the chapter). Recall that they found that under some conditions, the outstanding behaviour of another person in a domain that is important to us can inspire us and make us feel good about ourselves. Can we resolve the issue of whether a friend's outstanding performance makes us feel good or bad? Lockwood and Kunda suggest that both can be true—the critical factor is whether we believe that our friend's success is attainable. If we think that we too can achieve such greatness, our friend's performance can be inspiring. However, if our friend's performance seems way out of our league, the effects on our self-evaluation will be negative—just as self-evaluation maintenance theory would predict.

FOCUS ON APPLICATIONS

Distancing in the Family: A Way to Restore Self-Esteem?

Sadly, the tendency to distance ourselves from others when our self-esteem is threatened is not limited to the laboratory; it occurs even in our closest relationships.

Tesser (1980) examined biographies of male scientists, noting how close these scientists were to their fathers. As the self-evaluation maintenance model would predict, when the scientists' fields of expertise were the same as their fathers', they had more distant and strained relationships with their fathers. Similarly, the greatest amount of friction between siblings was found to occur when the siblings were close in age and one sibling was significantly better on key dimensions, such as popularity or intelligence. Thus, when performance and relevance are high, it can be difficult to avoid conflicts with family members.

Consider how the novelist Norman Maclean (1983) describes his relationship with his brother in *A River Runs Through It*: "One of the earliest things brothers try to find out is how they differ from each other.... Undoubtedly, our differences would not have seemed so great if we had not been such a close family."

A second way to reduce such threats to our self-esteem is to change how relevant the task is to our self-definition. If our new friend is a far better cook than we are, we might lose interest in cooking, deciding that auto mechanics is really our thing. To test this prediction, Tesser and Paulhus (1983) gave people feedback about how well they and other students had done on a test of a newly discovered ability: cognitive-perceptual integration. When a participant learned that the other student was similar to him or her (high closeness) and had done better on the test, the participant was especially likely to say that this ability was not very important to him or her.

Finally, people can deal with self-esteem threats by changing the third component in the equation—their performance relative to the other person's. If our new best friend is a superb cook, we can try to make ourselves an even better cook. This won't work, however, if we are already performing to the best of our ability. If this is the case, we can take a more diabolic route, wherein we try to undermine our friend's performance so that it is not as good as ours. If our friend asks for a recipe, we might leave out a critical ingredient so that her salmon *en brioche* will be certain to flop. Indeed, Tesser and Smith (1980) found that when a task was self-relevant, people were more likely to help a stranger perform well than a close friend. In contrast, when the task was not self-relevant, they were more likely to help a friend than a stranger.

In sum, research on self-evaluation maintenance theory has shown that threats to our self-concept have fascinating implications for our interpersonal relationships. When we feel threatened, we are highly motivated to restore our self-esteem, even if that means distancing ourselves from someone who is close to us—or, if we are feeling really desperate for a self-esteem boost, even sabotaging their performance.

Self-Affirmation Theory

Another kind of threat to our self-esteem occurs when we behave in ways that are contrary to our attitudes. For example, if we smoke cigarettes, we will experience *cognitive dissonance*—a feeling of discomfort created when our attitudes are inconsistent with our behaviour. (We will discuss cognitive dissonance theory more fully in the next chapter.) We know that smoking is bad for us, and yet here we are doing it. In this situation, people are motivated to alleviate the discomfort, a process known as *dissonance reduction*. Thus, we might try to quit smoking or we might convince ourselves that smoking is not really bad for our health.

Sometimes, however, threats to our self-concept can be so strong and difficult to avoid that the normal means of reducing dissonance do not work. It can be difficult to stop smoking, as millions of people have discovered. It is also difficult to ignore all of the evidence indicating that smoking is bad for us and might even kill us. So what can we do? **Self-affirmation theory** suggests that people will reduce the impact of a dissonance-arousing threat to their self-concept by focusing on and affirming their competence in some dimension unrelated to the threat.

Research by Claude Steele and his colleagues (Aronson, Cohen, & Nail, 1998; Steele, 1988) shows how self-affirmation comes about. "Yes, it's true that I smoke," you might say, "but I am a great cook" (or a terrific poet, or a wonderful friend, or a promising scientist). Self-affirmation occurs when our self-esteem is threatened; if possible, we will attempt to restore our self-esteem by reminding ourselves of some irrelevant aspect of our self-concept that we cherish, as a way of feeling good about ourselves in spite of our stupid or immoral behaviour.

> The mind is a strange machine which can combine the materials offered to it in the most astonishing ways.
> —BERTRAND RUSSELL

Self-affirmation theory a theory suggesting that people will reduce the impact of a dissonance-arousing threat to their self-concept by focusing on and affirming their competence in some dimension unrelated to the threat

classic research

In a series of clever experiments, Steele and his colleagues demonstrated that if, prior to the onset of dissonance, you provide people with an opportunity for self-affirmation, they will often grab it (Steele, 1988; Steele & Liu, 1981). For example, Steele, Hoppe, and Gonzales (1986) asked students to rank-order 10 record albums, ostensibly as part of a marketing survey. As a reward, the students were then told that they could keep either their fifth- or sixth-ranked album. Ten minutes after making their choice, they were asked to rate the albums again. Participants spread apart their ratings of the record albums, rating the one they had chosen much higher than the one they had rejected. In this manner, they convinced themselves that they had made a smart decision.

However, Steele and his colleagues built an additional set of conditions into their experiment. Half of the students were science majors, and half were business majors. Half of the science majors and half of the business majors were asked to put on white lab coats while participating in the experiment. Why the lab coats? As you know, a lab coat is associated with science. Steele and his colleagues suspected that the lab coat would serve a "self-affirmation function" for the science majors but not for the business majors. The results supported their predictions. Whether or not they were wearing lab coats, business majors showed standard dissonance reduction. After their choice, they increased their evaluation of the chosen album and decreased their evaluation of the one they had rejected. Similarly, in the absence of lab coats, science majors reduced their dissonance in the same way. However, science majors who were wearing the lab coats resisted the temptation to distort their perceptions; the lab coats reminded these students that they were promising scientists and thereby short-circuited the need to reduce dissonance by changing their attitudes toward the albums. In effect, they said, "I might have made a dumb choice in record albums, but I can live with that because I have other things going for me; at least I'm a promising scientist!" A simplified version of these findings is presented in Figure 4.4.

FOCUS ON APPLICATIONS

Using Our Close Relationships to Get a Self-Esteem Boost

We have seen that people can deal with threats to their self-esteem by reminding themselves of the areas in which they are competent and performing well. Recent research by Sandra Murray, John Holmes, and their colleagues (Murray et al., 1998; Murray et al., 2001) suggests that people also use their close relationships as a self-affirmational resource.

These researchers conducted a series of studies with students at the University of Waterloo and at the State University of New York, Buffalo, who were in dating relationships. Some of the participants experienced threats to their self-concept. This was done, for example, by giving them false feedback indicating that they were not very intelligent. How did these participants restore their self-esteem? By exaggerating how much their partners appreciated and accepted them. In effect, these participants were saying, "I may not be that smart, but I have a wonderful partner who thinks I'm great!" Interestingly, people with high self-esteem were most likely to engage in this self-affirmational strategy. Thus, when we're feeling low, we can make ourselves feel better by simply reminding ourselves that there are people in our lives who think we're great!

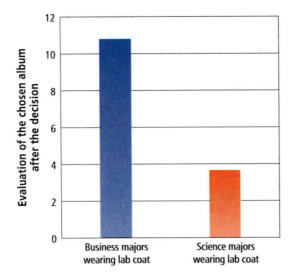

FIGURE 4.4 **Dissonance and Self-Affirmation**

People who were allowed the opportunity to affirm their values (science majors wearing lab coats) were able to avoid the pressure to reduce dissonance by increasing the attractiveness of the chosen albums.

(Adapted from Steele, Hoppe, & Gonzales, 1986)

SELF-AFFIRMATION AND CULTURE According to Heine and Lehman (1997a), the experience of dissonance may be unique to cultures in which the self is defined as independent. If the focus in a culture is on the individual, it becomes important for the individual to behave in ways that are consistent with his or her attitudes, because the person's behaviour is seen as diagnostic of what he or she is really like. On the other hand, if the self is defined in relation to others, as is the case in Asian cultures, behaviour is more likely to be tailored to the demands of the group. If an individual behaves in an attitude-inconsistent way, others are likely to invoke situational explanations. (You may recall from our discussion of the fundamental attribution error in Chapter 3 that people in Asian cultures do, in fact, make more situational attributions for others' behaviour than do those in Western cultures.) Based on this reasoning, Heine and Lehman hypothesized that people in Asian cultures should experience little dissonance when their attitudes and behaviours are inconsistent.

To test this idea, the researchers conducted a study similar to the one by Steele, Hoppe, and Gonzales (1986) just described. Students at the University of British Columbia and Japanese students visiting Vancouver signed up for a marketing research study. First, the researchers administered a bogus personality test. Then participants were asked to rate the desirability of 10 CDs. In the meantime, their personality tests supposedly had been scored. Some participants received positive personality feedback and others received negative feedback. (Participants in a control group did not receive any personality information.) Next, participants were given a choice between their fifth- and sixth-ranked CDs. After they made their selections, they were asked to rate all 10 CDs again.

Canadian participants in the control group showed classic dissonance reduction—they rated the chosen CD higher than they had previously and the rejected CD lower than they had previously. However, consistent with self-affirmation theory, Canadians who received positive personality feedback did not engage in dissonance reduction. In other words, because they had been reminded of what wonderful people they were, they did not feel a need to reduce dissonance by changing their ratings of the CDs. In contrast, those who received negative feedback were especially likely to engage in dissonance reduction.

And what about the Japanese participants? They did not show dissonance reduction in any of the conditions. Japanese students felt as bad as Canadian students did about the negative personality feedback and were more likely than Canadians to believe that it was accurate. However, they did not reduce dissonance by changing their ratings of the CDs, even under these circumstances.

Thinking Critically

To what extent do you think the way we feel about ourselves depends on the culture in which we were raised? Would you regard culture as one of the major determinants of self-esteem? What other factors play a role in determining self-evaluation?

SELF-EVALUATION: BIASED OR ACCURATE?

So far we have been operating on the assumption that people (at least in Western cultures) have a need to feel good about themselves. One way of feeling good about ourselves is to distort or exaggerate our positive qualities. We could even convince ourselves that we are better than most other people. Such positive illusions could certainly bolster our self-esteem. On the other hand, probably most of us don't want to live in a fantasy world in which we are fooling ourselves about the kind of person we are. In fact, we might even want other people to "tell it like it is" so that we develop an accurate picture of who we are. Thus, it seems we are caught between wanting to view ourselves in the most positive possible light and wanting an accurate assessment of what we are really like. Given these conflicting motives, do our self-evaluations tend to show a positivity bias, or do they tend to be accurate? Let's examine the evidence for each side of this issue.

Self-Enhancement: Wanting to Feel Good about Ourselves, Regardless of the Facts

Take a moment to answer the following questions: How attractive are you compared to the average student (of your gender) at your university? How adaptive are you compared to the average student? How well are you able to get along with others compared to the average student? Chances are, you see yourself as better than the average student with regard to at least some of these qualities, or perhaps even all of them. One way of boosting our self-esteem is to hold unrealistically positive views of ourselves, a tendency known as **self-enhancement**. "Well," you might be thinking, "in my case, it really isn't unrealistic to have a positive view of myself—I really am a great person." We don't doubt that you are a great person. The problem, however, is that most people have a tendency to think this way, and it really isn't possible for everyone to be better than most people, is it? This is why self-enhancement is defined as an unrealistically positive view of the self.

Research confirms that we really do tend to paint quite a flattering picture of ourselves. For example, when Heine and Lehman (1999) asked students at the University of

Self-enhancement a tendency to hold unrealistically positive views about ourselves

British Columbia the kinds of questions with which we began this section, they found that participants tended to view themselves as better than the average student. In research along the same lines, Jennifer Campbell (1986) found that students at the University of British Columbia showed a false uniqueness effect—they believed that many other students shared their weaknesses, but that they were unique in their strengths. Similarly, researchers at Simon Fraser University found that people tend to rate themselves as happier, more intelligent, more ethical, and even as having stronger emotional reactions than those around them (McFarland & Miller, 1990; Miller & McFarland, 1987).

Does engaging in this kind of unrealistic thinking actually make us feel better about ourselves? Apparently so. Research conducted at the University of British Columbia by Del Paulhus and colleagues has found that the more we distort reality to paint a flattering picture of ourselves, the higher our self-esteem is (Paulhus, 1998; Yik, Bond, & Paulhus, 1998).

SELF-ENHANCEMENT AND CULTURE As we have already discussed, self-enhancement appears to be largely a Western phenomenon. Unrealistically positive self views are not common in Eastern cultures. In fact, as mentioned earlier, in Asian cultures the tendency is to hold a negative view of oneself—a phenomenon known as self-effacement (Heine, 2001, 2004; Heine et al., 1999). This tendency to view the self negatively is established at a relatively young age. For example, Kwok (1995) compared self-evaluations of grade 4 students in Hong Kong and Canada. Students in Hong Kong, a culture that stresses self-effacement, rated themselves lower in scholastic competence, athletic competence, physical appearance, and overall self-worth than did students in Canada, a country that values self-enhancement. Interestingly, this was the case even though the Chinese students performed better than the Canadian students on standardized math tests.

Yik, Bond, and Paulhus (1998) found evidence of this cultural difference in a study in which they asked students at the University of British Columbia who were working on a group project to rate one another's personality traits. Canadian students showed classic self-enhancement—they rated themselves more positively than the other group members rated them. However, when students at the Chinese University of Hong Kong made similar ratings, the findings were opposite—Chinese students rated themselves more negatively than their peers rated them. Heine and Lehman (1997b) explored whether, in cultures that value interdependence, people might hold unrealistically positive views about the groups to which they belong, rather than about themselves as individuals. However, this was apparently not the case. Students in Japan rated students at their own university more negatively than students at a rival university and rated their own family as worse than the average family; Canadian students did just the opposite! Given findings such as these, you probably will not find it surprising that Asian university students score lower on measures of self-esteem than Canadian students do (Campbell et al., 1996; Endo, Heine, & Lehman, 2000; Heine & Lehman, 1997b; Heine & Renshaw, 2002; Sato & Cameron, 1999). A review of 70 studies on self-enhancement has led Steven Heine (2004) to conclude that East Asians simply don't do it!

Self-Verification: Wanting to Know the Truth about Ourselves

So far we have focused on research showing that, at least in North America, we are highly motivated to feel good about ourselves, to the point that we will happily distort reality to

Self-verification theory a theory suggesting that people have a need to seek confirmation of their self-concept, whether the self-concept is positive or negative; in some circumstances, this tendency can conflict with the desire to uphold a favourable view of oneself

maintain a highly positive self-concept. According to William Swann and his colleagues, we also are motivated to know the truth about ourselves—even if the truth hurts (Giesler, Josephs, & Swann, 1996; Swann, 1990, 1996; Swann & Hill, 1982; Swann & Pelham, 1988; Swann & Schroeder, 1995). Swann calls this **self-verification theory**, suggesting that people have a need to seek confirmation of their self-concept whether the self-concept is positive or negative. In some circumstances, this tendency can conflict with the desire to uphold a favourable view of oneself.

For example, consider Patrick, who has always thought of himself as a lousy writer with poor verbal skills. One day he is working on a term paper with a friend, who remarks that she thinks his paper is skilfully crafted, beautifully written, and superbly articulate. How will Patrick feel? He should feel pleased and gratified, we might predict, because the friend's praise gives Patrick's self-esteem a boost. On the other hand, Patrick's friend has given him feedback that challenges his long-standing view of himself as a poor writer, and he might be motivated to maintain this negative view. Why? For two reasons. First, according to self-verification theory, it is unsettling and confusing to have our views of ourselves disconfirmed; if we changed our self-concept every time we encountered someone with a different opinion of us, it would be impossible to maintain a coherent, consistent self-concept. Second, self-verification theory holds that it can be uncomfortable to interact with people who view us differently from the way we view ourselves. People who don't know us might have unrealistic expectations, and it would be embarrassing to have them discover that we are not as smart or as artistic or as creative as they think we are. Better to let them know our faults at the outset.

In short, when people with negative self-views receive positive feedback, opposing needs go head-to-head—the desire to feel good about themselves by believing the positive feedback (self-enhancement needs) versus the desire to maintain a consistent, coherent picture of themselves and avoid the embarrassment of being found out (self-verification needs). Which needs win out?

Several studies suggest that when the two motives are in conflict, our need to maintain a stable self-concept under certain conditions overpowers our compelling desire to view ourselves in a positive light (Aronson & Carlsmith, 1962; Brock et al., 1965; Marecek & Mettee, 1972; Swann, 1990). For example, Swann and his colleagues have found that people prefer to remain in close relationships with friends, roommates, and romantic partners whose evaluations of their abilities are consistent with their own (sometimes negative) self-evaluations (Swann, Hixon, & De La Ronde, 1992; Swann & Pelham, 1988). In other words, in a close relationship, most people find it better to be known than to be overrated.

We should point out, however, that recently Swann and colleagues (2002) have qualified this conclusion. Specifically, they suggest that whether we want to have accurate, rather than positive, feedback depends on two things—the dimension on which we are being evaluated and the nature of the relationship we have with the person doing the evaluating. For example, they found that when it comes to a quality such as physical attractiveness, we want dating partners to give us high marks—regardless of the facts. However, we want the truth when it comes to our other qualities. And if the person assessing our looks is a friend or a roommate, rather than a dating partner, it's honesty that counts. Similarly, if our artistic ability is being evaluated by our art instructor, or our athletic ability is being evaluated by our teammates, we prefer positivity over accuracy. However, if these people are evaluating our other qualities, the self-verification motive wins out.

Before leaving this topic, we should note that there are other limits to the need to self-verify. First, people generally strive to uphold their negative self-beliefs only when they are highly certain of those beliefs (Maracek & Mettee, 1972; Swann & Ely, 1984; Swann & Pelham, 1988). Thus, if Patrick had been less thoroughly convinced of his poor talents as a writer, he almost certainly would have been more receptive to his friend's praise. Second, if the consequences of being improperly evaluated are not too great—for example, if our contact with these individuals is rare so that it is unlikely they will discover we are not who we appear to be—then even people with negative views prefer positive feedback (Aronson, 1992). Finally, if people feel there is nothing they can do to improve their abilities, they generally prefer positive feedback to accurate feedback. Why remind ourselves that we are terrible if there is nothing we can do about it? If, however, people feel that a negative self-attribute can be changed with a little work, they prefer accurate feedback, because this information can help them figure out what they need to do to get better (Steele, Spencer, & Josephs, 1992).

Thinking Critically

1. How accurate do you think self-knowledge is? What are some ways in which people can make mistaken inferences about themselves?

2. Do you think people generally prefer feedback from others that boosts their self-esteem, or do you think people generally prefer accurate feedback? Might your answer depend on the culture in which you live?

Summary

In this chapter, we have explored how people come to know themselves. The **self-concept** refers to the contents of the self—namely our perception of our own thoughts, beliefs, and personality traits. People differ in the extent to which their sense of self is clearly defined. Those who are high in self-concept clarity are more likely to have high self-esteem.

There are, however, interesting cross-cultural and gender differences in the self-concept. In many Western cultures, people have an **independent view of the self**, whereby they define themselves mainly in terms of their own thoughts, feelings, and actions. In many Asian cultures, people have an **interdependent view of the self**, whereby they define themselves primarily in terms of their relationships with other people. In North America, women define themselves more in relation to other people and close intimate relationships than do men. This kind of interdependence is known as *relational* interdependence. Men are more likely to have an independent view of self. Men also show interdependence, but it takes a different form than in women. Specifically, men tend to focus on the groups to which they belong—a kind of interdependence known as *collective* interdependence.

There are four basic ways in which we come to know ourselves: through (1) **introspection**, (2) observations of our own behaviour, (3) self-schemas, and (4) social interaction. **Self-awareness** refers to the act of thinking about ourselves. Research on **self-awareness theory** has found that introspecting about ourselves can be unpleasant, because it focuses our attention on how we fall short of our internal standards. As a result, we may distract ourselves from these unpleasant feelings (e.g., by watching television). A benefit of self-focus is that it can make us more aware of our own feelings and traits.

Self-perception theory holds that we come to know ourselves through observations of our own behaviour, just as an outsider would. This occurs in particular when our internal states are unclear and there appears to be no external reason for our behaviour. People also organize information about themselves into **self-schemas**, which are knowledge structures about the self that help people understand, explain, and predict their own behaviour. Self-schemas also influence our memories—we are more likely to remember experiences that fit with our self-schemas.

Another way we come to know ourselves is through social interaction. According to the **looking-glass self**, our sense of who we are is based on others' perceptions of us. These perceptions become internalized and can influence our sense of self at any given time. We also know ourselves through comparison with others. **Social comparison theory** states that we will compare ourselves to others when we are unsure of our standing in some attribute and there is no objective criterion we can use. Typically, we choose to compare ourselves to similar others, for this is most diagnostic.

We also engage in social comparison to satisfy another basic human need, the need to maintain our self-esteem. **Downward social comparison**, comparing ourselves to those who are inferior in the relevant attribute, can make us feel better about ourselves—as long as we are confident that we are not vulnerable to their plight. **Upward social comparison**, comparing ourselves to those who are superior in the relevant attribute, can make us feel better about ourselves if we are focusing on our actual (usual) self, but it can make us feel worse about ourselves if we are focusing on our best or ideal self.

According to **self-discrepancy theory**, we will feel bad about ourselves when our actual self falls short of the self we feel we should be (our "ought" self) or the self we would like to be (our "ideal" self). Discrepancies between our actual and ideal selves produce feelings of dejection and depression, whereas discrepancies between our actual self and our ought self produce feelings of anxiety. **Self-evaluation maintenance theory** argues that we maintain our self-esteem by basking in the glory of a close other's accomplishments—as long as those accomplishments don't take place in a domain relevant to our self-definition. We feel threatened if a close other outperforms us in a relevant domain, and we seek to restore our self-esteem by distancing ourselves from the person, improving our performance, lowering the other person's performance, or reducing the relevance of the task. **Self-affirmation theory** argues that people deal with threats to their self-esteem by affirming themselves in some other area.

Research on **self-enhancement** suggests that the need to feel good about ourselves is so strong that we tend to hold unrealistically positive views of ourselves. In contrast, **self-verification theory** holds that we want accurate information about what we are like—even if it is not flattering. Generally, people opt for self-enhancement rather than self-verification. Finally, it is important to realize that self-enhancement is limited to individualistic (Western) cultures. In Asian countries, people are more likely to be self-critical, a phenomenon known as self-effacement.

Key Terms

Downward social comparison   (page 98)
Independent view of the self   (page 87)
Interdependent view of the self   (page 87)
Introspection   (page 90)
Looking-glass self   (page 95)
Self-affirmation theory   (page 105)
Self-awareness   (page 84)
Self-awareness theory   (page 91)
Self-concept   (page 84)
Self-discrepancy theory   (page 100)
Self-enhancement   (page 108)
Self-evaluation maintenance theory   (page 103)
Self-perception theory   (page 93)
Self-schemas   (page 94)
Self-verification theory   (page 110)
Social comparison theory   (page 97)
Upward social comparison   (page 98)

Key Online Search Terms

Self-concept
Self-awareness
Looking-glass self
Social comparison
Self-discrepancy
Self-evaluation maintenance
Self-enhancement versus self-verification

If You Are Interested

Baumeister, R. F. (1991). *Escaping the self: Alcoholism, spirituality, masochism, and other flights from the burden of selfhood.* New York: Basic Books. An intriguing look at the many different ways in which people try to escape too much self-focus.

Heine, S. J. (2003). Making sense of East Asian self-enhancement. *Journal of Cross-Cultured Psychology, 34,* 596–602. In this paper, University of British Columbia social psychologist Steven Heine, a leading researcher on culture and the self, describes the controversy over whether self-enhancement occurs in Asian cultures or whether it simply takes a different form. The author compares the results of 70 studies on the self-concepts of Asians and North Americans. He concludes that self-enhancement is alive and well in North America, but is largely absent in East Asian countries.

Proust, Marcel (1934). *Remembrance of things past.* This classic novel is full of insights about how people gain self-knowledge.

Tan, Amy (1989). *The joy luck club.* A poignant novel, also made into a feature film, about identity and growth within conflicting cultural contexts.

Weblinks

www.spsp.org
Society for Personality and Social Psychology
This is the division of the American Psychological Association that pertains to social psychology and personality.

http://college4.nytimes.com/guests/articles/2002/02/03/995523.xml
The Trouble with Self-Esteem
This New York Times article describes recent research suggesting that self-esteem also has a "down" side.

Chapter 4 Practice Quiz

Check your knowledge of the concepts in this chapter by trying the following questions.

THE NATURE OF THE SELF

Multiple Choice

1. The rouge test has demonstrated that self-recognition in humans develops
   a. at the age of two.
   b. at birth.
   c. throughout the lifespan.
   d. at puberty.

2. According to Campbell, self-concept clarity focuses on the _____ of self-knowledge.
   a. consistency
   b. randomness
   c. accuracy
   d. content

True or False

3. Women tend to desire and value close intimate relationships more than men do.
   ___ True
   ___ False

4. Self-concepts become less complex and more rigid as we age.
   ___ True
   ___ False

Fill in the Blank

5. Men tend to define their interdependence as more _____ than relational.
6. _____ is the act of thinking about ourselves.

KNOWING OURSELVES THROUGH INTROSPECTION

Multiple Choice

7. People rely on introspection:
   a. most of the time
   b. frequently
   c. rarely
   d. never

8. The act of becoming self-conscious is best described by
   a. self-awareness theory.
   b. self-consciousness theory.
   c. subconscious processing theory.
   d. sociobiology.

True or False

9. Duval and Wicklund state that behaviour and moral standards agree because of self-awareness.
   ___ True
   ___ False

10. Addictions, such as drugs and alcohol, lead to a deeper, more profound understanding of the self.
    ___ True
    ___ False

Fill in the Blank

11. People can escape their own _____ through positive means as well as negative means.
12. _____ means looking inward and describing our own thoughts and feelings.

KNOWING OURSELVES THROUGH SOCIAL INTERACTION

Multiple Choice

13. According to William James, we have
    a. one social self.
    b. different social "selves" across different situations.
    c. one genetically determined social self.
    d. no sense of self.

14. An approving internal audience causes us to see ourselves as
    a. immoral and incompetent.
    b. having both positive and negative characteristics.
    c. having neutral traits
    d. having positive characteristics.

True or False

15. According to research by Baldwin, an internal audience has little effect on our sense of self.
    ___ True
    ___ False

16. Comparing ourselves to others who are different is most informative.
    ___ True
    ___ False

Fill in the Blank

17. _____ holds that people learn about themselves through making comparisons to others.
18. Seeing ourselves through the eyes of others is our _____.

THE NEED TO FEEL GOOD ABOUT OURSELVES

Multiple Choice

19. Comparing yourself to someone who is better than you are is
    a. downward social comparison.
    b. outward social comparison.
    c. upward social comparison.
    d. parallel social comparison.

20. Behaving in ways that run counter to our attitudes causes
    a. cognitive dissonance.
    b. dissonance reduction.
    c. thought dysfunction.
    d. behavioural dysfunction.

True or False

21. People deal with threats to their self-esteem by reminding themselves of other areas in which they are less than competent.
    ___ True
    ___ False

22. According to self-discrepancy theory, we become distressed when we see ourselves as we truly are.
    ___ True
    ___ False

Fill in the Blank

23. _____ suggests people will reduce the impact of a threat to their self-concept by affirming their competence.
24. _____ involves comparing yourself to people who are worse than you in a trait or an ability.

SELF-EVALUATION: BIASED OR ACCURATE?

Multiple Choice

25. Wanting to feel good about ourselves regardless of the truth is
    a. predominant in Eastern cultures.
    b. predominant in Western cultures.
    c. unrelated to culture.
    d. reflecting a false uniqueness bias.

26. People prefer positive feedback about negative characteristics when
    a. they can do nothing to improve their abilities.
    b. the consequences of evaluation are great.
    c. they cannot self-verify.
    d. they have low self-esteem.

True or False

27. When it comes to physical attractiveness, we would rather have accurate than positive feedback from dating partners.
    ___ True
    ___ False

28. According to self-enhancement, we have a need for people to tell us the truth about ourselves.
    ___ True
    ___ False

Fill in the Blank

29. With regards to self-evaluation, _____ is one of the best ways to boost our self-esteem.
30. _____ states that we seek accurate feedback from others.

PERSONALIZED STUDY PLAN

Want to check your answers and access more study resources? Visit the Companion Website for *Fundamentals of Social Psychology* at **www.pearsoned.ca/aronson**, where you'll find the above questions incorporated in a pre-test and post-test for each chapter. These tests will be automatically graded online, allowing you to check your answers. A Study Plan, like the one below, groups the questions by section within the chapter and shows you which sections you need to focus on for further study.

Your Results for "Chapter 4, Pretest"

OVERALL SCORE: 76% of 17 questions

Group	Score	Proficient
The Nature of the Self	3 of 4	Yes
Knowing Ourselves through Introspection	3 of 3	Yes
Knowing Ourselves through Social Interaction	2 of 3	Yes
The Need to Feel Good about Ourselves	2 of 4	No
Self-Evaluation	3 of 3	Yes

CHAPTER

5

Attitudes and Attitude Change: Influencing Thoughts, Feelings, and Behaviour

Chapter Outline

THE NATURE AND ORIGIN OF ATTITUDES
Where Do Attitudes Come From?

WHEN WILL ATTITUDES PREDICT BEHAVIOUR?
The Theory of Planned Behaviour: Implications for Safer Sex

ATTITUDE CHANGE
Persuasive Communications and Attitude Change
Fear and Attitude Change
Advertising and Attitude Change

HOW TO MAKE PEOPLE RESISTANT TO PERSUASION ATTEMPTS
Attitude Inoculation

CHANGING ATTITUDES BY CHANGING OUR BEHAVIOUR: THE THEORY OF COGNITIVE DISSONANCE
Decisions, Decisions, Decisions
The Justification of Effort
The Psychology of Insufficient Justification
The Aftermath of Bad Deeds: How We Come to Hate Our Victims
Avoiding the Rationalization Trap
Learning from Our Mistakes

THE SOLAR TEMPLE REVISITED

March 1997. Quebec police were stunned when they learned that five people had committed suicide in St-Casimir, a village west of Quebec City. The people who died were members of the Solar Temple cult, discussed briefly in Chapter 1. The cult was lead by Luc Jouret and his right-hand man, Joseph Di Mambro. Those who joined the Solar Temple cult were mainly wealthy professionals, including the mayor of Richelieu, Quebec, and his wife; people in upper management positions at Hydro-Québec; a journalist; and a civil servant. Jouret was a charismatic spiritual leader with formidable powers of persuasion. A woman interviewed by *Maclean's* reported, "He asked all of us to empty our bank accounts" (Laver, 1994). She and her husband sold their property in Switzerland and handed over the proceeds—$300 000—to Jouret. Others followed suit. Most disturbing of all, Jouret convinced cult members that the world was about to be destroyed by fire, and that the only salvation was to take a "death voyage" by ritualized suicide to the star Sirius, where they would be reborn.

The cult attracted worldwide attention in October 1994, when buildings used by Jouret and his followers in a small village in Switzerland, and a chalet owned by Di Mambro in Morin Heights, Quebec, erupted in flames. Swiss firefighters discovered a chapel in which 22 cult members, cloaked in ceremonial robes, lay in a circle, with their faces looking up at a Christ-like figure resembling Jouret. In Morin Heights, police found the bodies of cult members clad in ceremonial robes and wearing red and gold medallions inscribed with the initials T. S. (*Temple Solaire*). At the end of the day, the death toll was 53 people, including several children. It is believed that both Jouret and Di Mambro died in the Swiss fires. So did the mayor of Richelieu, Quebec, and his wife (Laver, 1994).

Luc Jouret, leader of the Order of the Solar Temple cult, died in the 1994 mass murder–suicide along with 52 other members.

Sadly, the 1994 deaths did not put an end to the cult. Some of the remaining followers continued to take death voyages. However, by 1997, Quebec police believed that the Solar Temple cult had finally run its course. Apparently that was not the case. The five suicides in St- Casimir, Quebec, brought the total to 74 deaths in Canada and Europe over a five-year period.

How could intelligent, rational people be persuaded to hand over their money and, for some people, eventually even their lives to a charismatic leader? As we shall see in this chapter, people can be swayed by appeals to their fears, hopes, and desires. We shall also see that once people change their attitudes, a powerful process of self-justification sets in. We feel a strong need to justify our decisions, and in the process of doing so, become even more committed to our decision. But first, exactly what is an attitude, and how is it changed? These questions, which are some of the oldest in social psychology, are the subject of this chapter.

THE NATURE AND ORIGIN OF ATTITUDES

Attitude an evaluation of a person, object, or idea

Most social psychologists define an **attitude** as an evaluation of a person, object, or idea (Eagly & Chaiken, 1993, 1998; Olson & Zanna, 1993). Attitudes are evaluative in that they consist of a positive or negative reaction to something. People are not neutral observers of the world but constant evaluators of what they see. It would be very odd to hear someone say, "My feelings toward anchovies, snakes, chocolate cake, and my roommate are completely neutral." We can elaborate further on our definition of an attitude by stating more precisely what we mean by an "evaluation." Attitudes are made up of different components, or parts. Specifically, attitudes are made up of an affective component, consisting of your emotional reactions toward the attitude object (e.g., another person or a social issue); a cognitive component, consisting of your thoughts and beliefs about the attitude object; and a behavioural component, consisting of your actions or observable behaviour toward the attitude object.

For example, consider your attitude toward a particular model of car. First, there is your affective reaction, or the emotions and feelings the car triggers. These feelings might be a sense of excitement and aesthetic pleasure when you see the car, or feelings of anger and resentment (e.g., if you are a Canadian autoworker examining a new foreign-made model). Second, there is your cognitive reaction, or the beliefs you hold about the car's attributes. These might include your thoughts about the car's gas mileage, safety, steering and handling, and roominess. Third, there is your behavioural reaction, or how you act in regard to this type of car. For example, going to the dealership to test-drive the car and actually purchasing it are behaviours related to your attitude.

Where Do Attitudes Come From?

Social psychologists have focused primarily on the way that attitudes are created by people's cognitive, affective, and behavioural experiences. One important finding is that not all attitudes are created equally. Whereas attitudes have affective, cognitive, and behavioural components, any given attitude can be based more on one type of experience than another (Zanna & Rempel, 1988).

AFFECTIVELY BASED ATTITUDES An attitude based more on emotions and feelings than on an objective appraisal of pluses and minuses is called an **affectively based attitude** (Breckler & Wiggins, 1989; Zanna & Rempel, 1988). Sometimes we simply like a certain brand of car, regardless of whether it gets good gas mileage or whether it has 17 cup holders. Occasionally we even feel very positive about something—such as another person—in spite of having negative beliefs. As a guide to which attitudes are likely to be affectively based, consider the topics that etiquette manuals suggest should not be discussed at a dinner party: politics, sex, and religion. People seem to vote more with their hearts than their minds, for example, basing their decision to vote for a political candidate on how they feel about the person, rather than on a well-reasoned evaluation of policies (Abelson et al., 1982; Granberg & Brown, 1989).

COGNITIVELY BASED ATTITUDES Sometimes our attitudes are based primarily on a perusal of the relevant facts, such as the objective merits of an automobile. How many kilometres per litre of gas does it get? Does it have air conditioning? To the extent that a person's evaluation is based primarily on beliefs about the properties of an attitude object, we say it is a **cognitively based attitude**. The function of such an attitude is "object appraisal," meaning that we classify objects according to the rewards and punishments they can provide (Katz, 1960; Murray, Haddock, & Zanna, 1996; Smith, Bruner, & White, 1956). In other words, the purpose of this kind of attitude is to classify the pluses and minuses of an object so we can quickly tell whether it is worth our while to have anything to do with it. Consider your attitude toward a utilitarian object such as a vacuum cleaner. Your attitude is likely to be based on your beliefs about the objective merits of particular brands, such as how well they vacuum up dirt and how much they cost—not on how sexy they make you feel!

See Try It! on p. 122 for one way of measuring the bases of people's attitudes.

Affectively based attitude an attitude based primarily on people's feelings and emotions pertaining to the attitude object

Cognitively based attitude an attitude based primarily on a person's beliefs about the properties of an attitude object

> We never desire passionately what we desire through reason alone.
>
> —FRANÇOIS DE LA ROCHEFOUCAULD,
>
> Maxims, 1665

Attitudes toward abortion, the death penalty, and premarital sex are examples of affectively based attitudes.

Try It! Affective and Cognitive Bases of Attitudes

Fill out this questionnaire to see how psychologists measure the affective and cognitive components of attitudes.

1. Circle the number on each scale that best describes your feelings toward snakes:

hateful	−3	−2	−1	0	1	2	3	loving
sad	−3	−2	−1	0	1	2	3	delighted
annoyed	−3	−2	−1	0	1	2	3	happy
tense	−3	−2	−1	0	1	2	3	calm
bored	−3	−2	−1	0	1	2	3	excited
angry	−3	−2	−1	0	1	2	3	relaxed
disgusted	−3	−2	−1	0	1	2	3	accepting
sorrowful	−3	−2	−1	0	1	2	3	joyful

2. Circle the number on each scale that best describes the traits or characteristics of snakes:

useless	−3	−2	−1	0	1	2	3	useful
foolish	−3	−2	−1	0	1	2	3	wise
unsafe	−3	−2	−1	0	1	2	3	safe
harmful	−3	−2	−1	0	1	2	3	beneficial
worthless	−3	−2	−1	0	1	2	3	valuable
imperfect	−3	−2	−1	0	1	2	3	perfect
unhealthy	−3	−2	−1	0	1	2	3	wholesome

Instructions: Answer each of the above questions. Then, sum each of your responses to Question 1 and each of your responses to Question 2.

These scales were developed by Crites, Fabrigar, and Petty (1994) to measure the affective and cognitive components of attitudes. Question 1 measures the affective component of your attitude toward snakes; you were asked to rate your feelings on such scales as "hateful/loving." Question 2 measures the cognitive component of attitudes; you were asked to rate your beliefs about the characteristics of snakes on such scales as "worthless/valuable." Most people's attitudes toward snakes are more affectively than cognitively based. If this was true of you, your total score for Question 1 should depart more from zero (in a negative direction, for most people) than your total score for Question 2.

Now go back and fill out the scales again, but substitute "vacuum cleaners" for "snakes." Most people's attitudes toward a utilitarian object such as a vacuum cleaner are more cognitively than affectively based. If this was true of you, your total score for Question 2 should depart more from zero than your total score for Question 1.

Behaviourally based attitude an attitude based primarily on observations of how one behaves toward an attitude object

BEHAVIOURALLY BASED ATTITUDES Just as an attitude can be based primarily on cognition or affect, so too can it be based primarily on behaviour. A **behaviourally based attitude** is one based on observations of how you behave toward an attitude object. This may seem a little odd—how do we know how to behave if we don't already know how we feel? According to Daryl Bem's (1972) *self-perception theory* (discussed in Chapter 4), under certain circumstances people don't know how they feel until they see how they behave. For example, suppose you asked a friend how much she enjoys exercising. If she replies, "Well, I guess I like it, because I always seem to be going for a run or heading over to the gym to work out," we would say she has a behaviourally based attitude. Her attitude is based more on an observation of her own behaviour than on her cognitions or affect.

Thus, not all attitudes are created equally. They can be based on affect, cognition, or behaviour. Researchers at the University of Waterloo have conducted a series of studies to determine which attitudes are most likely to be based on affect, on cognition, or on behaviour (Esses, Haddock, & Zanna, 1993; Haddock & Zanna, 1994, 1998; Haddock, Zanna, & Esses, 1993, 1994). This program of research has revealed that when people hold negative attitudes toward a group (e.g., homosexuals, Pakistanis), those attitudes are likely to be based on cognition—specifically, the belief that members of that group threaten one's cherished values. When people hold positive attitudes toward a group (in this research, attitudes toward English Canadians, French Canadians, and Native Indians tended to be positive), those attitudes seem to be based on affect. These researchers also found that attitudes toward social issues such as capital punishment are more likely to be based on how we feel about the issue, rather than on what we think about it.

> How can I know what I think till I see what I say?
> —GRAHAM WALLAS,
> The Art of Thought, 1926

Thinking Critically
Why do you think negative attitudes are more likely to be based on cognition (thoughts), whereas positive attitudes are more likely to be based on affect (emotion)?

WHEN WILL ATTITUDES PREDICT BEHAVIOUR?

In the early 1930s, Richard LaPiere (1934) embarked on a sightseeing trip across the United States with a young Chinese couple. Because prejudice against Asians was commonplace among Americans at that time, he was apprehensive about how his Chinese friends would be treated. At each hotel, campground, and restaurant they entered, LaPiere worried that his friends would confront anti-Asian prejudice and that they would be refused service. Much to his surprise, this almost never happened. Of the 251 establishments he and his friends visited, only one refused to serve them.

After his trip, LaPiere wrote a letter to each establishment he and his friends had visited, asking if it would serve a Chinese visitor. Of the many establishments who replied, only one said it would. More than 90 percent said they definitely would not; the rest said they were undecided. People's attitudes—as expressed in their response to LaPiere's written inquiry—were in stark contrast to their actual behaviour toward LaPiere's Chinese friends.

LaPiere's study was not, of course, a controlled experiment. As LaPiere acknowledged, there are several reasons why his results may not show consistency between people's attitudes and behaviour. For example, he had no way of knowing whether the proprietors who answered his letter were the same people who had served him and his friends. Further, people's attitudes could have changed in the months that passed between the time they served the Chinese couple and the time they received the letter. Nonetheless, the lack of correspondence between people's attitudes and what they actually did was so striking that we might question the assumption that behaviour routinely follows from attitudes.

Theory of planned behaviour a theory that the best predictors of a person's planned, deliberate behaviours are the person's attitudes toward specific behaviours, subjective norms, and perceived behavioural control

Indeed, when Allan Wicker (1969) reviewed dozens of more methodologically sound studies, he reached the same conclusion: People's attitudes are poor predictors of their behaviour.

In subsequent research, social psychologists have discovered that under certain circumstances, attitudes actually can predict behaviours quite well (DeBono & Snyder, 1995; Fazio, 1990; Zanna & Fazio, 1982). According to Icek Ajzen and Martin Fishbein's **theory of planned behaviour** (Ajzen, 1985, 1996; Ajzen & Fishbein, 1980; Ajzen & Sexton, 1999; Fishbein & Ajzen, 1975), the best predictor of people's behaviour is their intention, which is in turn determined by three things: their attitudes toward the specific behaviour, their subjective norms, and their perceived behavioural control (see Figure 5.1). Let's consider each of these three in turn. First, specific attitudes. What is important here is not people's general attitude about something but their specific attitude toward the behaviour they are considering. According to the theory of planned behaviour, only specific attitudes toward the behaviour in question can be expected to predict that behaviour.

For example, in a study of married women's use of birth control pills, Andrew Davidson and James Jaccard (1979) asked a series of attitude questions, ranging from the general (the women's attitude toward birth control) to the specific (their attitude toward using birth control pills during the next two years; see Table 5.1). Two years later, the women were asked whether they had used birth control pills at any time since the last interview. As seen in Table 5.1, the women's general attitude toward birth control did not predict their use of birth control. This general attitude did not take into account other factors that could have influenced their decision, such as the women's concern about the long-term effects of the pill and their attitude toward other forms of birth control. The more specific the question was about the act of using birth control pills, the better this attitude predicted their actual behaviour.

This may be one reason LaPiere (1934) found in his study such inconsistency between people's attitudes and behaviours. His question to the proprietors—whether they would serve "members of the Chinese race"—was stated very generally. Had he asked a

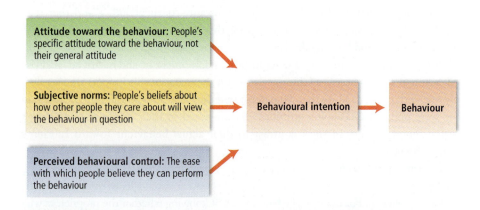

FIGURE 5.1 The Theory of Planned Behaviour

According to this theory, the best predictors of people's planned, deliberate behaviours are their behavioural intentions. The best predictors of their intentions are their attitudes toward the specific behaviour, their subjective norms, and their perceived control of the behaviour.

(Adapted from Ajzen, 1985)

TABLE 5.1	Specific Attitudes Are Better Predictors of Behaviour

Different groups of women were asked about their attitudes toward birth control. The more specific the question, the better it predicted their actual use of birth control. *Note:* If a correlation is close to 0, it means that there is no relationship between the two variables. The closer the correlation is to 1, the stronger the relationship between attitudes and behaviour.

Attitude Measure	Attitude–Behaviour Correlation
Attitude toward birth control	.08
Attitude toward birth control pills	.32
Attitude toward using birth control pills	.53
Attitude toward using birth control pills during the next two years	.57

(Adapted from Davidson & Jaccard, 1979)

> If actions are to yield all the results they are capable of, there must be a certain consistency between them and one's intentions.
>
> —FRANÇOIS DE LA ROCHEFOUCAULD,
>
> Maxims, 1665

much more specific question—such as whether they would serve an educated, well-dressed, well-to-do Chinese couple accompanied by a white American professor—they might have given an answer that was more in line with their behaviour.

In addition to measuring attitudes toward the behaviour, we also need to measure people's **subjective norms**—their beliefs about how those they care about will view the behaviour in question (see Figure 5.1). To predict someone's intentions, it can be as important to know these beliefs as to know his or her attitudes. For example, suppose we want to predict whether Kristen intends to go to a heavy metal concert, and we know that she has a negative attitude toward this behaviour—she can't stand heavy metal music. We would probably say she won't go. Suppose we also know, though, that Kristen's best friend, Malcolm, really wants her to go. Knowing this subjective norm—her belief about how a close friend views her behaviour—we might make a different prediction.

Finally, as seen in Figure 5.1, people's intentions are influenced by perceived behavioural control, which is the ease with which people believe they can perform the behaviour. If people think it is difficult to perform the behaviour, such as sticking to a gruelling exercise regimen, they will not form a strong intention to do so. If people think it is easy to perform the behaviour, such as remembering to buy milk on the way home from work, they are more likely to form a strong intention to do so.

A considerable amount of research supports the idea that asking people about these determinants of their intentions—attitudes toward specific behaviours, subjective norms, and perceived behavioural control—increases the ability to predict their behaviour. Most of this research has focused on behaviours related to health and exercise, such as smoking among Quebec highschool students (Hill et al., 1997); exercise among Alberta women and men receiving treatment for cancer (Courneya & Friedenreich, 1997, 1999); exercise, maintaining a low-fat diet, and smoking among Quebec men (Nguyen et al., 1996); participation in exercise classes for the elderly offered at the University of Western Ontario (Estabrooks & Carron, 1999); and competitive swimmers' adherence to intensive training in various clubs across Canada (Mummery & Wankel, 1999), to name a few. Following, we will focus on how the theory of planned behaviour applies to an important social issue, namely persuading people to engage in safer sex.

Subjective norms people's beliefs about how those they care about will view the behaviour in question

The Theory of Planned Behaviour: Implications for Safer Sex

There is one area in which people's attitudes are often inconsistent with their behaviour, even though the consequences can be fatal. The inconsistency takes the form of their having positive attitudes toward using condoms, expressing intentions to use condoms, but then failing to actually use them in sexual encounters (Hynie & Lydon, 1996). For example, in a study by Herold and Mewhinney (1993), nearly 100 percent of the patrons of various dating bars in southern Ontario agreed with statements such as "If I were to have sex with someone I just met, I would have no objections if my partner suggested that we use a condom." However, these favourable attitudes toward condom use did not translate into safe sex practices. Only 56 percent of the people at the bar who engaged in casual sex had used a condom in their most recent sexual encounter. Even more frightening, a mere 29 percent of the women and men who had engaged in casual sex in the past year reported that they had always used a condom.

Why would people with positive attitudes toward condom use risk their lives by not using them? The theory of planned behaviour can provide some clues. Perhaps subjective norms, perceived behavioural control, and behavioural intentions play a role. Can these variables help us understand why people so often fail to use condoms, despite having positive attitudes toward condom use? Let's take a look at some studies.

SUBJECTIVE NORMS People's beliefs about how others view the behaviour in question are an important determinant of their behaviour. Indeed, there is evidence that whether university students use condoms depends on the norms for sexual behaviour that operate among their friends (Winslow, Franzini, & Hwang, 1992). However, even if one's friends generally advocate condom use, certain situations may invoke a different norm. Importantly, our beliefs about how our sexual partner feels about condoms can exert a powerful influence on our behaviour. If we anticipate a negative reaction from our partner, we are less likely to end up using condoms (Hynie & Lydon, 1995). For example, some of the English- and French-speaking university students in Montreal who were interviewed by Maticka-Tyndale (1992) worried that if they suggested using a condom, their partner might not feel trusted. Thus, if people anticipate that their peer group, or more importantly their sexual partner, would not approve of condom use, they are more likely to engage in unprotected sex.

If people fear a negative reaction, they are less likely to raise the issue of condom use with a potential sexual partner.

PERCEIVED BEHAVIOURAL CONTROL If people think it is difficult to perform a behaviour, they will not form strong intentions to do so. What might be so difficult about using condoms? At first glance, it might seem like an easy thing to do. However, that is actually not the case. The first obstacle that some people face is discomfort or embarrassment about purchasing condoms. For example, a study conducted with sexually active students at the University of British Columbia found that those who were embarrassed about buying condoms bought them less often than did those who were not embarrassed (Dahl, Gorn, & Weinberg, 1998). Perhaps of greater importance, a series of studies conducted at McGill University suggests that people may not know how to broach the topic of condom use during a sexual encounter (Hynie et al., 1998; Hynie & Lydon, 1996). If you feel uncertain about how to approach the topic of condom use with your partner, you will be less likely to end up using condoms.

BEHAVIOURAL INTENTIONS People will not use condoms unless they intend to do so. What factors might affect people's intentions to use condoms? Researchers at the University of Waterloo (MacDonald, Zanna, & Fong, 1996; MacDonald et al., 2000) have found that for both women and men, alcohol intoxication is associated with lower intentions to use condoms—even among those who have positive attitudes toward condom use. MacDonald and colleagues explain that when people are intoxicated, their ability to process information is impaired, such that they are able to focus only on the most immediate aspects of the situation (short-term pleasure) rather than on the long-term consequences of their actions. These findings are alarming, given that alcohol is present in many of the settings in which people are likely to encounter cues that promote casual sex (bars, parties, "break loose" vacations; Maticka-Tyndale, Herold, & Mewhinney, 1998, 2001).

In summary, even the most positive attitudes toward condom use do not guarantee that people will practise safer sex. The theory of planned behaviour would suggest that other variables must be taken into account as well, including subjective norms, perceived behavioural control, and behavioural intentions.

Thinking Critically

Think about a behaviour you would like to change (starting an exercise program, drinking less coffee). Can you put the concepts of subjective norms, perceived behavioural control, and behavioural intentions to use in planning how you might go about changing this behaviour?

ATTITUDE CHANGE

As we have seen, attitudes do not necessarily translate into behaviour. However, this fact does not stop people from trying to change our attitudes, hoping that our behaviour will follow. For example, advertisers assume that changing people's attitudes toward products will result in increased sales, and politicians assume that positive feelings toward a candidate will result in a vote for that candidate on election day. But what is the best way to change people's attitudes? As we shall see next, this is a question that has fascinated social psychologists for decades. Here are some of their answers.

Persuasive Communications and Attitude Change

Suppose the Canadian Cancer Society has given you a five-figure budget to come up with an anti-smoking campaign that could be used nationwide. You have a lot of decisions ahead

Persuasive communication communication (e.g., a speech or television ad) advocating a particular side of an issue

> Of the modes of persuasion furnished by the spoken word there are three kinds. The first kind depends on the personal character of the speaker; the second on putting the audience into a certain frame of mind; the third on the proof, or apparent proof, provided by the words of the speech itself.
>
> —ARISTOTLE,
> Rhetoric

Yale Attitude Change Approach the study of the conditions under which people are most likely to change their attitudes in response to persuasive messages; researchers in this tradition focus on "who said what to whom"—that is, on the source of the communication, the nature of the communication, and the nature of the audience

of you. Should you pack your public service announcement with facts and figures? Or should you take a more emotional approach in your message, including frightening visual images of diseased lungs? Should you hire a famous movie star to deliver your message, or a Nobel Prize–winning medical researcher? Should you take a friendly tone and acknowledge that it is hard to quit smoking, or should you take a hard line and tell smokers to (as the Nike ads put it) "just do it"? You can see the point—it's not easy to figure out how to construct a truly **persuasive communication**, one that advocates a particular side of an issue.

Luckily, social psychologists have conducted many studies over the past 50 years on what makes a persuasive communication effective, beginning with Carl Hovland and his colleagues (Hovland, Janis, & Kelley, 1953). These researchers conducted many experiments on the conditions under which people are most likely to be influenced by persuasive communications. In essence, they studied "who says what to whom," looking at the *source of the communication* (how expert or attractive the speaker is); the *communication itself* (the quality of the arguments; whether the speaker presents both sides of the issue, whether fear is used); and the *nature of the audience* (which kinds of appeals work with hostile versus friendly audiences). Because these researchers were at Yale University, this approach to the study of persuasive communications is known as the **Yale Attitude Change Approach**.

To sell a product, it is effective to have a credible, trustworthy celebrity endorsement.

This approach yielded a great deal of useful information on how people change their attitudes in response to persuasive communications; some of this information is summarized in Figure 5.2.

Research inspired by the Yale Attitude Change Approach has been important in identifying the determinants of effective persuasion. However, it has not been clear which aspects of persuasive communications are most important—that is, when one factor should be emphasized over another. For example, let's return to that job you have with the Canadian Cancer Society—it wants to see your ad next month! If you were to read the many Yale Attitude Change studies, you would find much useful information about who should say what to whom in order to construct a persuasive communication. However, you might also find yourself saying, "Gee there's an awful lot of information here, and I'm not sure where I should place the most emphasis. Should I worry most about who delivers the ads? Or should I worry more about the content of the message itself?"

The Yale Attitude Change Approach

The effectiveness of persuasive communications depends on who says what to whom.

Who: The Source of the Communication
- Credible speakers (those with obvious expertise) persuade people more than speakers lacking in credibility (Hovland & Weiss, 1951; Petty, Wegener, & Fabrigar, 1997).
- Attractive speakers (whether due to physical or personality attributes) persuade people more than unattractive speakers do (Eagly & Chaiken, 1975; Petty, Wegener, & Fabrigar, 1997).

What: The Nature of the Communication
- People are more persuaded by messages that do not seem to be designed to influence them (Petty & Cacioppo, 1986; Walster & Festinger, 1962).
- Is it best to present a one-sided communication (one that presents only arguments favouring your position) or a two-sided communication (one that presents arguments for and against your position)? In general, two-sided messages work better, if you are sure to refute the arguments on the other side (Allen, 1991; Allen et al., 1990; Crowley & Hoyer, 1994; Lumsdaine & Janis, 1953).
- Is it best to give your speech before or after someone arguing for the other side? If the speeches are to be given back to back and there will be a delay before people have to make up their minds, it is best to go first. Under these conditions, there is likely to be a *primacy effect*, wherein people are more influenced by what they hear first. If there is a delay between the speeches and people will make up their minds immediately after hearing the second one, it is best to go last. Under these conditions, there is likely to be a *recency effect*, wherein people remember the second speech better than the first one (Haugtvedt & Wegener, 1994; Miller & Campbell, 1959).

To Whom: The Nature of the Audience
- An audience that is distracted during the persuasive communication often will be persuaded more than one that is not (Festinger & Maccoby, 1964; Petty & Cacioppo, 1986).
- People low in intelligence tend to be more easily influenced than people high in intelligence, and people with moderate self-esteem tend to be more easily influenced than people with low or high self-esteem (Rhodes & Wood, 1992).
- People are particularly susceptible to attitude change during the impressionable ages of 18 to 25. Beyond those ages, people's attitudes are more stable and resistant to change (Krosnick & Alwin, 1989; Sears, 1981).

FIGURE 5.2 The Yale Attitude Change Approach

THE CENTRAL AND PERIPHERAL ROUTES TO PERSUASION If you asked these questions, you would be in good company. Some well-known attitude researchers have wondered the same thing. When is it best to stress factors central to the communication—such as the strength of the arguments—and when is it best to stress factors peripheral to the logic of the arguments—such as the credibility or attractiveness of the person delivering the speech? This question has been answered by two influential theories of persuasive communication: Shelly Chaiken's **heuristic-systematic model of persuasion** (Chaiken, 1987; Chaiken, Liberman, & Eagly, 1989; Chaiken, Wood, & Eagly, 1996; Chen & Chaiken,

Heuristic-systematic model of persuasion the theory that there are two ways that persuasive communications can cause attitude change; people either process the merits of the arguments, known as systematic processing, or use mental shortcuts (heuristics), such as "Experts are always right," known as heuristic processing

Elaboration likelihood model the theory that there are two ways that persuasive communications can cause attitude change; the central route occurs when people are motivated and have the ability to pay attention to the arguments in the communication, and the peripheral route occurs when people do not pay attention to the arguments but are instead swayed by surface characteristics (e.g., who gave the speech)

1999), and Richard Petty and John Cacioppo's **elaboration likelihood model** (Petty & Cacioppo, 1986; Petty & Wegener, 1999). These theories specify when people will be influenced by what the speech says (the logic of the arguments) and when they will be influenced by more superficial characteristics (e.g., who gives the speech or how long it is).

Both theories state that under certain conditions people are motivated to pay attention to the facts in a communication. Thus they will be most persuaded when these facts are logically compelling. That is, sometimes people elaborate on what they hear, carefully thinking about and processing the content of the communication. Chaiken (1980) calls this *systematic processing*; Petty and Cacioppo (1986) call this the *central route to persuasion*. Under other conditions, people are not motivated to pay attention to the facts; instead, they notice only the surface characteristics of the message, such as how long it is and who is delivering it. Here, people will not be swayed by the logic of the arguments, because they are not paying close attention to what the communicator says. Instead, they are persuaded if the surface characteristics of the message—such as the fact that it is long or is delivered by an expert or an attractive communicator—make it seem like a reasonable one. Chaiken (1980) calls this *heuristic processing* because attitudes are based on simple rules or cognitive heuristics. (Recall from Chapter 3 that heuristics are defined as mental shortcuts people use to make judgments quickly and efficiently; in the context of attitudes, a heuristic can be viewed as a simple rule people use to decide what their attitude is, without having to spend a lot of time analyzing every little fact about the matter.) Petty and Cacioppo (1986) call this the *peripheral route to persuasion*, because people are swayed by things peripheral to the message itself.

What are the conditions under which people take the central versus the peripheral route to persuasion? The key, according to Petty, Cacioppo, and Chaiken, is whether people have the *motivation* and *ability* to pay attention to the facts. To the extent that people are truly interested in the topic and thus motivated to pay close attention to the arguments, they are more likely to take the central route. Similarly, if people have the ability to pay attention—for example, if nothing is distracting them—they will also take the central route (Chaiken, 1980; Fabrigar et al., 1998; Petty & Cacioppo, 1986; Petty & Wegener, 1999; see Figure 5.3).

Now that you know a persuasive communication can change people's attitudes in either of two ways—via the central or the peripheral routes—you may be wondering what difference it makes. Isn't the bottom line simply whether or not people change their attitudes? Should we care how they got to that point? If we are interested in creating long-lasting attitude change, we should care a lot. People who base their attitudes on a careful analysis of the arguments are more likely to maintain this attitude over time, more likely to behave consistently with this attitude, and are more resistant to counter-persuasion than people who base their attitudes on peripheral cues (Chaiken, 1980; Mackie, 1987; Petty, Haugvedt, & Smith, 1995; Petty & Wegener, 1998). For example, Perlini and Ward (2000) attempted to increase knowledge of AIDS among students attending high schools in Sault Ste. Marie by providing them with scripts describing characters who either had AIDS or were medical experts on AIDS. The purpose of these scripts was to educate the participants concerning how AIDS can be prevented, how it is contracted, and so on. The participants then acted out these various scripts in a role-play situation. Other participants received the same information about AIDS, but it was delivered via a lecture or videotape. The researchers reasoned that the active participation required by the role-play exercise

> The ability to kill or capture a man is a relatively simple task compared with changing his mind.
>
> —RICHARD COHEN, 1991

FIGURE 5.3 The Elaboration Likelihood Model Describes How People Change Their Attitudes When They Hear Persuasive Communications

would invoke the central route to persuasion. And, indeed, four weeks later, the role-play participants showed more positive attitudes toward AIDS prevention than did participants in the other groups. Those in the role-play condition also showed the greatest improvement in knowledge of AIDS prevention.

Fear and Attitude Change

So far our discussion of attitude change has focused on the kinds of persuasive messages that are likely to produce attitude change. Another approach to changing attitudes is to use fear. In fact, scaring people is one of the most common techniques for trying to change attitudes. When we asked you earlier how you would get people's attention when presenting your anti-smoking ad, it might have crossed your mind to use a **fear-arousing communication**, which is a persuasive message that attempts to change people's attitudes by arousing their fears. Public service ads often take this approach by trying to scare people into practising safer sex, wearing their seat belts, and staying away from drugs. In 2000, the

Fear-arousing communication a persuasive message that attempts to change people's attitudes by arousing their fears

Canadian government began to place frightening images on cigarette packages—larger and more graphic than those used anywhere else in the world. Europe may now follow Canada's lead. In October 2004, the European Union called for European governments to require that cigarette manufacturers display graphic images similar to those instituted by Canada.

Do such fear-arousing communications work? It turns out that fear can work, but only if a moderate amount of fear is created and if people believe that listening to the message will teach them how to reduce this fear (Petty, 1995; Rogers, 1983). Consider a study by Howard Leventhal and his colleagues (Leventhal, Watts, & Pagano, 1967), who showed a group of smokers a graphic film depicting lung cancer and gave the smokers pamphlets with specific instructions about how to quit smoking. These people reduced their smoking significantly more than did people who were shown only the film or only the pamphlet. Why? Seeing the film made people scared, and giving them the pamphlet reassured them that there was a way to reduce this fear—by following the instructions on how to quit. Seeing only the pamphlet didn't work very well, because little fear was motivating people to read it carefully. Seeing only the film didn't work very well either, because people were likely to tune out a message that raised fear but did not provide information about how to reduce it. This may explain why some attempts to frighten people into changing their attitudes and behaviour have not been very successful: They succeed in scaring people but do not provide specific recommendations for those people to follow (Becker & Josephs, 1988; DeJong & Winsten, 1989; Job, 1988; Soames, 1988).

Fear-arousing appeals will also fail if they are too strong, so that people feel very threatened. If people are scared to death, they will become defensive, will deny the importance of the threat, and will be unable to think rationally about the issue

This ad is clearly trying to scare people into changing their attitudes and behaviour. Do you think this ad works?

(Baron et al., 1992; Janis & Feshbach, 1953; Jepson & Chaiken, 1990; Liberman & Chaiken, 1992). According to Michael Conway at Concordia University and Laurette Dubé at McGill University (2002), humour can be an effective tool for reducing distress among people who find fear messages especially threatening. In a series of studies, they found that among those who were most threatened by fear messages, the use of humour resulted in greater attitude change and intentions to enact the desired behaviours (using sunscreen to avoid skin cancer and using condoms to avoid AIDS) than did nonhumorous messages.

So, if you have decided to arouse people's fear in your ad for the Canadian Cancer Society, keep these points in mind. First, try to create enough fear to motivate people to pay attention to your arguments but not so much fear that people will tune out or distort what you say. You may even want to throw in a bit of humour for the benefit of those who find fear-inducing messages especially distressing. Second, include some specific recommendations about how to stop smoking, so people will be reassured that paying close attention to your arguments will help them reduce their fear.

Advertising and Attitude Change

How many times, in a given day, does someone attempt to change your attitudes? Be sure to count every advertisement you see or hear, because advertising is nothing less than an attempt to change your attitude toward a consumer product, be it a brand of laundry detergent, a type of automobile, or a political candidate. Don't forget to include ads you get in the mail, calls from telemarketers, and signs you see on buses, as well as those ever-present television commercials. Even in our most private moments, we are not immune to advertisements, as witnessed by the proliferation of ads in washrooms—above the hand dryers and even inside washroom stalls. As if that weren't enough, advertisers are now trying to figure out how they can reach students during school hours! In the summer of 1999, Athena Educational Partners of Montreal offered Canadian schools a "deal." They would broadcast 12 minutes of Youth News Network newscasts in classrooms every day. The catch was that students would also be exposed to two minutes of commercials. In exchange, schools would receive televisions, VCRs, and even satellite dishes. This program has created a storm of controversy. So far, six provinces have banned Athena from broadcasting in their schools. However, Athena has not given up. Obviously, companies such as Athena are confident that the huge amounts of money they spend on advertising will pay off. But is this true? How effective are ads, anyway?

A curious thing about advertising is that most people think it works on everyone but themselves (Wilson & Brekke, 1994). A typical comment is "Sure, it influences most people, but not me. Seeing those ads for Scrubadub doesn't influence me at all." Contrary to such beliefs, substantial evidence indicates that advertising works; when a product is advertised, sales tend to increase (Ryan, 1991; Wells, 1997).

TAILORING ADVERTISEMENTS TO PEOPLE'S ATTITUDES Which types of ads work the best? Several studies have shown that it is best to fight fire with fire. If an attitude is cognitively based, try to change it with rational arguments; if it is affectively based, try to change it using emotion (Edwards, 1990; Edwards & von Hippel, 1995; Fabrigar & Petty, 1999; Shavitt, 1989; Snyder & DeBono, 1989). For example, in one study Sharon Shavitt (1990) gave people advertisements for different kinds of consumer products. Some of the items were ones Shavitt called utilitarian products, such as air

Advertisements for soft drinks tend to be emotion-based, trying to associate feelings of excitement, youth, and sexiness with a particular brand, as in this ad featuring Britney Spears. Rarely do ads for soft drinks say anything about the product, such as how its taste compares to that of its competitors.

conditioners and coffee. People's attitudes toward such products tend to be based on an appraisal of the utilitarian aspects of the products (how energy-efficient an air conditioner is), and thus are cognitively based. The other items were ones Shavitt called social identity products, such as perfume and greeting cards. People's attitudes toward these types of products are based more on their values and concerns about their social identity, and so are more affectively based.

As seen in Figure 5.4, people reacted most favourably to the ads that matched the type of attitude they had. If people's attitudes were cognitively based (toward air conditioners or coffee), the ads that focused on the utilitarian aspects of these products were most successful. If people's attitudes were more affectively based (toward perfume or greeting cards), the ads that focused on values and social identity concerns were most successful. Thus, if you ever get a job in advertising, the moral is to know what type of attitude most people have toward your product, and then tailor your advertising accordingly.

SUBLIMINAL ADVERTISING: A NEW FORM OF MIND CONTROL? We cannot leave the topic of advertising without discussing one of its most controversial topics—the use of **subliminal messages**, defined as words or pictures that, while not consciously perceived, supposedly influence people's judgments, attitudes, and behaviour. A majority of the public believes that these messages can unknowingly shape attitudes and behaviour (Zanot, Pincus, & Lamp, 1983). Given the near-hysterical claims that have been made about subliminal advertising, it is important to discuss whether it really works.

In the late 1950s, James Vicary supposedly flashed the messages "Drink Coca-Cola" and "Eat popcorn" during a movie and claimed that sales at the concession stand skyrocketed. According to some reports, Vicary made up these claims (Weir, 1984), but that

Subliminal messages words or pictures that are not consciously perceived but that supposedly influence people's judgments, attitudes, and behaviours

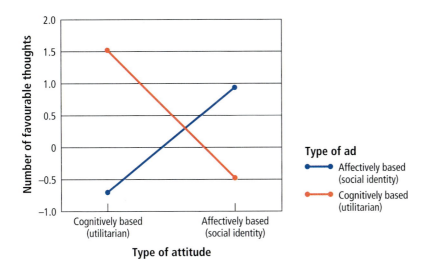

FIGURE 5.4 Effects of Affective and Cognitive Information on Affectively and Cognitively Based Attitudes

When people had cognitively based attitudes (toward air conditioners and coffee), cognitively based advertisements that stressed the utilitarian aspects of the products worked best. When people had more affectively based attitudes (toward perfume and greeting cards), affectively based advertisements that stressed values and social identity worked best. The higher the number, the more favourable the thoughts people listed about the products after reading the advertisements.

(Adapted from Shavitt, 1990)

was not the last attempt at subliminal persuasion. Wilson Bryan Key (1973, 1989), who has written several best-selling books on hidden persuasion techniques, maintains that advertisers routinely implant sexual messages in print advertisements, such as the word *sex* in the ice cubes of an ad for gin, and male and female genitalia in everything from pats of butter to the icing in an ad for cake mix. In addition, a large market has arisen for audiotapes containing subliminal messages to help people lose weight, stop smoking, improve their study habits, raise their self-esteem, and even shave a few strokes off their golf scores. In 1990, sales of subliminal self-help tapes were estimated to be $50 million (Krajick, 1990). Are subliminal messages effective? Do they really make us more likely to buy consumer products, or help us lose weight and stop smoking?

DEBUNKING THE CLAIMS ABOUT SUBLIMINAL ADVERTISING Simply stated, there is no evidence that the types of subliminal messages used in everyday life have any influence on people's behaviour. Hidden commands to eat popcorn do not cause people to line up at the movie concession stands in greater numbers than they would normally do, and the subliminal commands on self-help tapes do not (unfortunately!) help us quit smoking or lose a few pounds (Merikle, 1988; Moore, 1995; Pratkanis, 1992; Trappey, 1996). Anthony Greenwald and his colleagues (1991), for example, performed a careful test of the effectiveness of subliminal self-help tapes. Half of the participants listened to tapes that, according to the manufacturer, contained subliminal messages designed to improve memory ("My ability to remember and recall is increasing daily"), while the others listened to tapes that had subliminal messages designed to raise self-esteem ("I have high self-worth and high self-esteem"). The tapes had no effect on people's memory or self-esteem.

Interestingly, research participants in the Greenwald study *thought* the subliminal tapes were working, even though they were not. The researchers were a little devious, in that they correctly informed half of the participants about which tape they listened to, but misinformed the others (half of the people who got the memory tape were told it was designed to improve their memories, whereas the other half were told it was designed to improve their self-esteem). Those who thought they had listened to the memory tape believed their memories had improved, even if they had really heard the self-esteem tape. And people who thought they had listened to the self-esteem tape

There is no scientific evidence that implanting sexual images in advertising boosts sales of the product. The public is very aware of the technique, however—so much so that some advertisers have begun to poke fun at subliminal messages, right in their ads.

believed their self-esteem had improved, even if they had heard the memory tape. This finding explains why subliminal tapes are such a lucrative business. Even though the tapes don't work, people believe that they do.

EVIDENCE FOR SUBLIMINAL INFLUENCE IN THE LAB When we said that subliminal messages are ineffective, you may have noticed a qualification: They do not work when used in everyday life. There is some evidence for such effects in carefully controlled laboratory studies. As you may recall, in Chapter 4 we discussed research by Baldwin, Carrell, and Lopez (1990), who flashed slides of a scowling program director, a friendly postdoctoral student, or a disapproving-looking Pope so quickly that they were not consciously perceived. Nevertheless, these images did have the predicted effects on participants' self-evaluations. Several other researchers have found similar effects of pictures or words flashed at subliminal levels (e.g., Bargh & Pietromonaco, 1982; Bornstein & Pittman, 1992). However, all successful demonstrations of subliminal stimuli have been conducted under meticulous laboratory conditions that are difficult to reproduce in everyday life. Researchers have to ensure that the illumination of the room is just right, that people are seated just the right distance from a viewing screen, and that nothing else is occurring to distract them as the subliminal stimuli are flashed. Further, even in the laboratory there is no evidence that subliminal messages can get people to act counter to their wishes, values, or personalities, making them march off to the supermarket to buy products they don't want or vote for candidates they despise (Neuberg, 1988).

Ironically, the hoopla surrounding subliminal messages has obscured a significant fact about advertising: Ads are *more* powerful when we can consciously perceive them. As we have seen, there is ample evidence that the ads we encounter in everyday life and perceive consciously can have substantial effects on our behaviour—even though they do not contain subliminal messages. It is interesting that people fear subliminal advertising more than they do regular advertising, when regular advertising is so much more powerful (Wilson, Houston, & Meyers, 1998).

Thinking Critically

Think about some recent advertisements you have seen on television or in magazines. Can you think of examples of ads that targeted different kinds of attitudes? How did they do so? Do you think the ad campaigns will be successful, given the kinds of attitudes they are trying to change? Why or why not?

HOW TO MAKE PEOPLE RESISTANT TO PERSUASION ATTEMPTS

By now, you are no doubt getting nervous. With all of these clever methods to change your attitudes, are you ever safe from persuasive communications? Indeed you are, or at least you can be, if you use some strategies of your own. Here's how to ensure that all of those persuasive messages that bombard you don't turn you into a quivering mass of constantly changing opinion.

Attitude Inoculation

One approach is to get people to consider the arguments for and against their attitude before someone attacks it. The more people have thought about pro and con arguments beforehand, the better they can ward off attempts to change their minds using logical arguments. If people have not thought much about the issue—that is, if they formed their attitude via the peripheral route—they are particularly susceptible to an attack on that attitude using logical appeals.

William McGuire (1964) demonstrated this fact by using what he called **attitude inoculation**. This is the process of making people immune to attempts to change their attitudes by exposing them to small doses of arguments against their position. Having considered the arguments beforehand, people should thus be relatively immune to the effects of the communication—just as exposing them to a small amount of a virus can inoculate them against exposure to the full-blown viral disease.

In one study, for example, McGuire "inoculated" people by giving them brief weak arguments against various beliefs that most members of a society accept uncritically, such as the idea that we should brush our teeth after every meal. Two days later, people came back and read a much stronger attack on the truism, one that contained a series of logical arguments about why brushing your teeth too frequently is a bad idea. The people who had been inoculated against these arguments were much less likely to change their attitudes than were a control group who had not been. Why? Those inoculated with weak arguments had the opportunity to think about why these arguments were unfounded and were therefore in a better position to contradict the stronger attack they heard two days

> The chief effect of talk on any subject is to strengthen one's own opinions and, in fact, one never knows exactly what he does believe until he is warmed into conviction by the heat of the attack and defense.
>
> —CHARLES DUDLEY WARNER,
> Backlog Studies,
> 1873

Attitude inoculation the process of making people immune to attempts to change their attitudes by initially exposing them to small doses of the arguments against their position

later. The control group, never having considered why people should or should not brush their teeth frequently, was particularly susceptible to the strong communication arguing that they should not.

> **FOCUS ON APPLICATIONS**
>
> ## Using Social Psychology to Resist Peer Pressure
>
> Interestingly, the logic of McGuire's inoculation approach can be extended to real-world situations such as peer pressure. Consider Jake, a 13-year-old who is hanging out with some classmates, many of whom are smoking cigarettes. The classmates begin to make fun of Jake for not smoking, and dare him to take a puff. Many 13-year-olds, faced with such pressure, would cave in. But suppose we immunized Jake to such social pressures by exposing him to mild versions of them and showing him ways to combat these pressures. We might have him role-play a situation where a friend calls him a wimp for not smoking a cigarette, and teach him to respond by saying, "I'd be more of a wimp if I smoked it just to impress you." Would this help him resist the more powerful pressures exerted by his classmates?
>
> Several programs designed to prevent smoking among adolescents suggest that it would. For example, McAlister and his colleagues (1980) used a role-playing technique with grade 7 students, very much like the one described above. The researchers found that these students were significantly less likely to smoke three years after the study, compared to a control group that had not participated in the program. This result is encouraging and has been replicated in similar programs designed to reduce smoking (Chassin, Presson, & Sherman, 1990; Falck & Craig, 1988; Killen, 1985).

CHANGING ATTITUDES BY CHANGING OUR BEHAVIOUR: THE THEORY OF COGNITIVE DISSONANCE

We have been focusing on persuasion—those times when other people attempt to change our attitudes. But there is another route to attitude change that may surprise you. Sometimes we change our attitudes not because another person is trying to get us to do so, but rather because our own behaviour prompts us to do so. How does this happen? As we shall discuss next, this can happen when we behave in ways that are inconsistent with our attitudes. That realization produces discomfort. One way to alleviate the discomfort is to change our attitudes and bring them in line with our behaviour. Let's take a look at how this process works.

In our discussion of self-affirmation theory (Chapter 4), we introduced the idea of **cognitive dissonance**—the uncomfortable feeling we experience when our behaviour is at odds with our attitudes (or when we hold two conflicting attitudes). Leon Festinger (1957) was the first to investigate the precise workings of this powerful phenomenon, and elaborated his findings into what is arguably social psychology's most important and most provocative theory—the theory of cognitive dissonance. Cognitive dissonance most often occurs when we do something that conflicts with our attitudes (Aronson, 1968, 1969, 1992, 1998; Aronson et al., 1974; Harmon-Jones & Mills, 1998; Thibodeau & Aronson, 1992). Dissonance always produces discomfort and therefore motivates a person to try to reduce the discomfort, in much the same way that hunger and thirst produce discomfort that motivates a person to eat or drink. However, unlike satisfying hunger or thirst by eat-

Cognitive dissonance a feeling of discomfort caused by the realization that one's behaviour is inconsistent with one's attitudes or that one holds two conflicting attitudes

ing or drinking, the ways of reducing dissonance are not simple; rather, they often lead to fascinating changes in the way we think about the world and the way we behave.

How can we reduce dissonance? There are three basic ways:

- By changing our behaviour to bring it into line with the dissonant cognition
- By attempting to justify our behaviour through changing one of the dissonant cognitions
- By attempting to justify our behaviour by adding new cognitions (see Figure 5.5)

To illustrate, let's look at an example of absurd behaviour that millions of people engage in several times a day—smoking cigarettes. Suppose you are a smoker. Like most smokers, you are likely to experience dissonance because it is absurd to engage in behaviour that stands a good chance of producing a painful early death. How can you reduce this dissonance? The most direct way is to change your behaviour—to give up smoking. Your behaviour would then be consistent with your knowledge of the link between smoking and cancer. While many people have succeeded in doing just that, it's not easy—many have tried to quit and failed. What do these people do? It would be erroneous to assume that they simply swallow hard and prepare to die. They don't. Instead, they try to reduce their dissonance in a different way—namely, by convincing themselves that smoking isn't as bad as they thought.

Smokers can come up with pretty creative ways to justify their smoking; for example, some might try to convince themselves that the data linking cigarette smoking to

FIGURE 5.5 **How We Reduce Cognitive Dissonance**

cancer are inconclusive. Others will try to add new cognitions—for example, the erroneous belief that filters trap most of the harmful chemicals and thus reduce the threat of cancer. Some will add a cognition that allows them to focus on the vivid exception: "Look at old Sam Carouthers—he's 97 years old and he's been smoking a pack a day since he was 12. That proves it's not always bad for you." Still others will add the cognition that smoking is an extremely enjoyable activity, one for which it is worth risking cancer. Others may even succeed in convincing themselves that, all things considered, smoking is worthwhile because it relaxes them, reduces nervous tension, and so on.

This youngster may be thinking, "There's nothing wrong with putting on a little extra weight. After all, some professional football players weigh more than 300 pounds and earn millions of dollars a year. Pass the fries."

These justifications may sound silly to the nonsmoker. That is precisely our point. People experiencing dissonance will often go to extreme lengths to reduce it. We did not make up the examples of denial, distortion, and justification listed above; they are based on actual examples generated by people who have tried and failed to quit smoking. Similar justifications have been generated by people who try and fail to lose weight, who refuse to practise safer sex, or who receive unwelcome information about their health (Aronson, 1997b; Croyle & Jemmott, 1990; Goleman, 1982; Kassarjian & Cohen, 1965; Leishman, 1988). As we shall see, to escape from dissonance, people will engage in quite extraordinary rationalizing.

Decisions, Decisions, Decisions

Every time we make a decision—whether it is between two cars, two colleges, or two potential lovers—we experience dissonance. Why? Because the chosen alternative is seldom entirely positive, and the rejected alternative is seldom entirely negative. Let's pretend that you are trying to decide which of two attractive people to date: Chris, who is funny and playful, but a bit irresponsible; or Pat, who is interesting and smart, but not very spontaneous. You agonize over the decision but eventually decide to pursue a relationship with Pat. After you've made the decision, you will experience dissonance because despite Pat's good qualities, you did end up choosing to be with someone who is not very spontaneous. Dissonance also is created because you ended up turning down someone who is playful and fun. We call this **postdecision dissonance**.

Postdecision dissonance
dissonance that is inevitably aroused after a person makes a decision; such dissonance is typically reduced by enhancing the attractiveness of the chosen alternative and devaluing the rejected alternative

Cognitive dissonance theory predicts that in order to feel better about the decision, you will do some mental work to try to reduce the dissonance. What kind of work? You would convince yourself that Pat really was the right person for you and that Chris actually would have been a lousy choice. An early experiment by Jack Brehm (1956) illustrates this phenomenon. Brehm posed as a representative of a consumer testing service and asked women to rate the attractiveness and desirability of several kinds of appliances, such as toasters and electric coffee makers. Each woman was told that as a reward for having participated in the survey, she could have one of the appliances as a gift. She was given a choice between two of the products she had rated as being equally attractive. After she made her decision, her appliance was wrapped up and given to her. Twenty minutes later, each woman was asked to re-rate all of the products. Brehm found that after receiving the appliance of her choice, each woman rated its attractiveness somewhat higher than she had done the first time. Not only that, but all drastically lowered their rating of the appliances they might have chosen but had decided to reject.

In an interesting twist, Knox and Inkster (1968) intercepted people at the Exhibition Park Race Track in Vancouver who were on their way to place $2 bets and asked them how certain they were their horses would win. The investigators also intercepted other bettors just as they were leaving the $2 window, after having placed their bets, and asked them the same question. Almost invariably, people who had already placed their bets gave their horses a much better chance of winning than did those who had yet to place their bets. Since only a few minutes separated one group from another, nothing real had occurred to increase the probability of winning; the only thing that had changed was the finality of the decision—and thus the dissonance it produced.

To experience cognitive dissonance in action, see Try It! below.

Justifying Decisions

Talk to one or two friends or family members who are trying to decide between two alternatives—between two vehicles, two jobs, two items of clothing in a store, or even two relationship partners. Take note of the pluses and minuses that are mentioned for each alternative. Then, wait until the person has made his or her decision. Take note of the pluses and minuses mentioned for the option chosen and for the one rejected. Is the person even more positive later about the chosen alternative than he or she was before making the choice? Is the person also more negative about the rejected alternative than he or she was before making the choice? Cognitive dissonance theory predicts that the answer to each of these questions would be yes.

FOCUS ON APPLICATIONS

Can Dissonance Reduction Change Your Moral Standards?

Needless to say, life is made up of more than just decisions about cars, appliances, and racehorses. Our decisions often involve moral and ethical issues. The area of resolving moral dilemmas is a particularly interesting one in which to study dissonance. It turns out that dissonance reduction following a difficult moral decision can actually change our system of values.

This was illustrated by Judson Mills (1958) in an experiment he performed at an elementary school. Mills first measured the attitudes of grade 6 students toward cheating. He then had them participate in a competitive exam, offering prizes to the winners. The situation was arranged so it was almost impossible to win without cheating. Moreover, Mills made it easy for the children to cheat on the exam, and created the illusion that they could

Once an individual makes a final and irrevocable decision, he or she has a greater need to reduce dissonance. For example, at the racetrack, once we've placed our bet, our certainty is greater than it is immediately *before* we've placed our bet.

not be detected. Under these conditions, as one might expect, some of the students cheated and others did not. The next day, the students were again asked to indicate how they felt about cheating. Children who had cheated became more lenient toward cheating, and those who had resisted the temptation to cheat adopted a harsher attitude toward it.

Thus, through the process of reducing dissonance, the students experienced a change in their value systems. Subsequent research showed that these effects are quite long-lasting (Freedman, 1965).

The Justification of Effort

Suppose you expend a great deal of effort to get into a particular club, and it turns out to be a totally worthless organization, consisting of boring, pompous people engaged in trivial activities. You would feel pretty foolish, wouldn't you? Such a circumstance would produce a fair amount of dissonance; your cognition that you are a sensible adept human being is dissonant with your cognition that you worked hard to get into a worthless club. How would you reduce this dissonance? How would you justify your behaviour? You might start by finding a way to convince yourself that the club and the people in it are nicer, more interesting, and more worthwhile than they appeared to be at first glance. How can one turn boring people into interesting people and a trivial club into a worthwhile one? Easily. Activities and behaviours are open to a variety of interpretations; if we are motivated to see the best in people and things, we will tend to interpret these ambiguities in a positive manner. We call this the **justification of effort**—the tendency for individuals to increase their liking for something they have worked hard to attain.

Justification of effort the tendency for individuals to increase their liking for something they have worked hard to attain

In a now classic experiment, Elliot Aronson and Judson Mills (1959) explored the link between effort and dissonance reduction. In their experiment, university students

volunteered to join a group that would meet regularly to discuss various aspects of the psychology of sex. To be admitted to the group, they volunteered to go through a screening procedure. For one-third of the participants the procedure was an extremely effortful and unpleasant one, for one-third it was only very mildly unpleasant, and the final one-third were admitted to the group without undergoing any screening procedure.

Each participant was then allowed to listen in on a discussion being conducted by the members of the group they would be joining. Although they were led to believe that the discussion was a live, ongoing one, what they actually heard was a prerecorded tape. The taped discussion was arranged so it was as dull and bombastic as possible. After the discussion was over, each participant was asked to rate it in terms of how much he or she liked it, how interesting it was, how intelligent the participants were, and so forth. The major findings are shown in Figure 5.6.

Going through a lot of effort to become a soldier will increase the recruit's feelings of cohesiveness and pride in the corps.

The results supported the predictions. Participants who underwent little or no effort to get into the group did not enjoy the discussion very much. They were able to see it for what it was—a dull and boring waste of time. They regretted that they had agreed to participate. Participants who went through a severe initiation, however, succeeded in convincing themselves that the same discussion, while not as scintillating as they had hoped, was dotted with interesting and provocative tidbits, and therefore, in the main, was a worthwhile experience. In short, they justified their effortful initiation process by interpreting all the ambiguous aspects of the group discussion in the most positive manner possible.

It should be clear that we are not suggesting that most people enjoy effortful, unpleasant experiences—they do not. What we are asserting is that if a person agrees to go through a difficult or an unpleasant experience to attain some goal or object, that goal or object becomes more attractive (see Try It! on the next page).

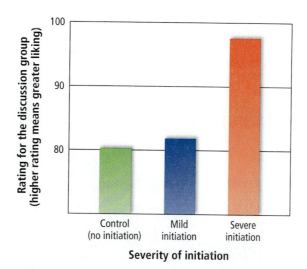

FIGURE 5.6 The Tougher the Initiation, the More We Like the Group

The more effort we put into gaining group membership, the more we like the group we have just joined.

(Adapted from Aronson & Mills, 1959)

As you know, it is not unusual for people in the military or on sports teams to be subjected to barbaric, cruel hazing rituals. On the face of it, one might expect that the victims of hazings would despise those who made them suffer. However, by now you are probably in a better position to understand the reactions of people such as Jean-François Caudron.

On the cover of the March 6, 2000, issue of *Maclean's* magazine, a headline reads, "A barbaric rite of passage: Hazing in university athletes." The article begins with the story of Jean-François Caudron from St-Hubert, Quebec, the recipient of a hockey scholarship from the University of Vermont. As a rookie, he would be subjected to a hazing that involved shaving his pubic hair, painting his toenails, and drinking warm beer until he vomited. Based on his experiences on Canadian hockey teams, Jean-François knew there was

Try It! Justifying Actions

Think about something that you have tackled in the past that required you to go to a lot of trouble or effort. Perhaps you waited for several hours in a long line to get tickets to a concert; perhaps you knowingly sat in your car through an incredible traffic jam because it was the only way you could visit a close friend.

1. Specifically, list the things you had to go through to attain your goal.
2. Do you think you might have tried to justify all that effort? Did you find yourself exaggerating the good things about the goal and minimizing any negative aspects of the goal? List some of the ways you might have exaggerated the value of the goal.
3. The next time you find yourself in that kind of situation, you might want to monitor your actions and cognitions carefully to see whether any self-justification is involved.

no escaping rookie night: "You knew about this night and you were nervous. You feel pressure that you have to do it." One might expect that Caudron would have nothing but bad memories about his hazing experiences. However, he describes it this way, "[O]nce it was over, I was so happy. I really felt part of the team" (O'Hara, 2000). If it weren't for cognitive dissonance theory, such a reaction would be very difficult to understand!

The Psychology of Insufficient Justification

Imagine that your best friend invites you to the first performance of a band that he has proudly put together. The vocalist is awful, the bass player shows little talent, and, as it turns out, your friend should have kept up with his saxophone lessons. Afterwards, your friend excitedly asks you how you enjoyed the band. How do you respond? You hesitate. Chances are you go through something like the following thought process: "Jeremy seems so happy and excited. Why should I hurt his feelings and possibly ruin our friendship?" So you tell Jeremy that the band was great. Do you experience much dissonance? We doubt it. There are a great many thoughts that are consonant with having told this lie, as outlined in your reasoning. In effect, your cognition that it is important not to cause pain to people you like provides ample **external justification** for having told a harmless lie.

COUNTER-ATTITUDINAL ADVOCACY What happens, on the other hand, if you say something you don't really believe and there is no ample external justification for doing so? That is, what if Jeremy sincerely needs to know your opinion of the band because he is thinking of quitting school to devote his life to music? If you still tell him the band is great, you will experience dissonance. When you can't find external justification for your behaviour, you will attempt to find **internal justification**—you will try to reduce dissonance by changing something about your attitudes or behaviour. How can you do this? You might begin by looking for positive aspects of the band—some evidence of creativity or potential that might be realized with a little more practice or a few new talented band members. If you look hard enough, you will probably find something. Within a short time, your attitude toward the band will have moved in the direction of the statement you made—and that is how saying becomes believing. This phenomenon is generally referred to as **counter-attitudinal advocacy**, a process that occurs when a person states an opinion or attitude that runs counter to his private belief or attitude. When

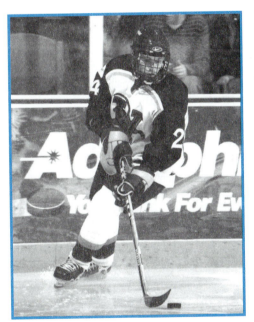

Our desire to maintain self-esteem can have surprising consequences. Social psychological research demonstrates that when people submit to a painful or embarrassing initiation in order to join a group, they need to justify the experience to avoid feeling foolish. One way they do that is to decide that the initiation was worth it because the group is so wonderful. Jean-François Caudron, pictured here, was subjected to severe initiations as a rookie, but remembers his teammates with fondness.

External justification a person's reason or explanation for dissonant behaviour that resides outside the individual (e.g., in order to receive a large reward or avoid a severe punishment)

Internal justification the reduction of dissonance by changing something about oneself (one's attitude or behaviour)

Counter-attitudinal advocacy the process that occurs when a person states an opinion or attitude that runs counter to his or her private belief or attitude

this is accomplished with a minimum of external justification, it results in a change in the individual's private attitude in the direction of the public statement.

This proposition was first tested in a groundbreaking experiment by Leon Festinger and J. Merrill Carlsmith (1959). In this experiment, university students were induced to spend an hour performing a series of excruciatingly boring and repetitive tasks. The experimenter then told them that the purpose of the study was to determine whether people would perform better if they had been informed in advance that the tasks were interesting. They were each informed that they had been randomly assigned to the control condition—that is, they had not been told anything in advance. However, the experimenter explained, the next participant, a young woman who was just arriving in the anteroom, was going to be in the experimental condition. The experimenter said that he needed to convince her that the task was going to be interesting and enjoyable. Since it was much more convincing if a fellow student rather than the experimenter delivered this message, would the participant do so? Thus, with this request the experimenter induced the participants to lie about the task to another student.

Half of the students were offered $20 to tell the lie (a large external justification), while the others were offered only $1 to tell it (a very small external justification). After the experiment was over, an interviewer asked the lie-tellers how much they had enjoyed the tasks they had performed earlier in the experiment. The results validated the hypothesis. Students who had been paid $20 for lying—that is, for saying that the tasks had been enjoyable—rated the activities as the dull and boring experiences they were. But those who had been paid only $1 for saying that the task was enjoyable rated the task as significantly more enjoyable. In other words, people who had received an abundance of external justification for lying told the lie but didn't believe it, whereas those who told the lie without a great deal of external justification succeeded in convincing themselves that what they said was closer to the truth.

USING COUNTER-ATTITUDINAL ADVOCACY FOR SOCIAL GOOD
Can the experiments on counter-attitudinal advocacy be used to tackle social problems? Would it be possible, for example, to get people to endorse a policy favouring a minority group and then see whether their attitudes become more favourable toward that group? Absolutely.

In an important set of experiments, Mike Leippe and Donna Eisenstadt (1994, 1998) demonstrated that laboratory experiments on counter-attitudinal advocacy could be applied directly to important societal problems—in this case, race relations and racial prejudice. They induced white students at an American university to write a counter-attitudinal essay publicly endorsing a controversial proposal at their university—to double the funds available for academic scholarships for African-American students. Because the total funds were limited, this meant cutting in half the scholarship funds available to white students. As you might imagine, this was a highly dissonant situation. How might they reduce dissonance? The best way would be to convince themselves that they really believed deeply in that policy. Moreover, dissonance theory would predict that their general attitude toward African Americans would become more favourable and much more supportive. And that is exactly what Leippe and Eisenstadt found.

Counter-attitudinal advocacy has also been applied to another important societal issue: the prevention of the spread of AIDS. As we discussed earlier in this chapter, although college and university students are aware of AIDS as a serious problem, a surprisingly small percentage use condoms every time they have sex. Is there anything that can be done about this? In the past several years, Elliot Aronson and colleagues (Aronson, Fried, & Stone, 1991; Stone et al., 1994) have had considerable success at convincing people to use condoms by employing a variation of the counter-attitudinal advocacy paradigm. They asked university students to compose a speech describing the dangers of AIDS and advocating the use of condoms every single time a person has sex. In one condition, the students merely composed the arguments. In another condition, the students composed the arguments and then recited them in front of a video camera, after being informed that the videotape would be played to an audience of highschool students. In addition, half of the students in each condition were made mindful of their own failure to use condoms by having them make a list of the circumstances in which they had found it particularly difficult, awkward, or impossible to use them.

Essentially, then, the participants in one condition—those who made a video for highschool students after having been made mindful of their own failure to use condoms—were in a state of high dissonance. This was caused by their being made aware of their own hypocrisy; they were fully aware of the fact that they were preaching behaviour to highschool students that they themselves were not practising. To reduce this dissonance, they would need to start practising what they were preaching. And that is exactly what Aronson and his colleagues found. Later, when the students were given the opportunity to purchase condoms very cheaply, those in the hypocrisy condition were the most likely to buy them. A follow-up telephone interview several months after the experiment demonstrated that the effects were long-lasting. People in the hypocrisy condition reported far greater use of condoms than did those in the control conditions.

FOCUS ON APPLICATIONS

Conserving Water

Several years ago, when California experienced severe water shortages, the administrators at one campus of the University of California realized that an enormous amount of water was being wasted by students using the university's athletic facilities. The administrators posted signs in the shower rooms of the gymnasiums exhorting students to conserve water by taking briefer, more efficient showers. The signs appealed to the students' consciences by urging them to take brief showers and to turn off the water while soaping up. The administrators were confident that the signs would be effective because the vast majority of students at this campus were ecology-minded and believed in preserving natural resources. However, systematic observation revealed that less than 15 percent of the students complied with the conservation message on the signs.

The administrators were puzzled—perhaps the majority of the students hadn't paid attention to the signs? After all, a sign on the wall is easy to ignore. So administrators made each sign more obtrusive, putting them on tripods at the entrances to the showers so the students had to walk around them. Though this increased compliance slightly (19 percent turned off the shower while soaping up), it apparently made a great many students angry. The signs were continually knocked over and kicked around, and a large percentage of students took inordinately *long* showers, apparently as a reaction against being told what to do. The signs were doing more harm than good, which puzzled the administrators even more. It was time to call in the social psychologists.

Elliot Aronson and his students (Dickerson et al., 1992) decided to apply the hypocrisy technique (used to increase condom purchases in a study just described; see Aronson, Fried, & Stone, 1991) to this new situation. The procedure involved intercepting female students who were on their way to the showers, introducing the experimental manipulations, and then having a research assistant casually follow them into the shower room and unobtrusively time their showers.

Research participants in one condition were asked to respond to a brief questionnaire about their water use, a task designed to make them mindful of how they sometimes wasted water while showering. In another condition, research participants made a public commitment, exhorting others to take steps to conserve water. Specifically, these participants were asked to sign their names to a public poster that read, "Take Shorter Showers. Turn Shower Off While Soaping Up. If I Can Do It, So Can YOU!" In the crucial condition—the "hypocrisy" condition—the participants did both; that is, they were made mindful of their own wasteful behaviour and indicated publicly (on the poster) that they were practising water conservation. In short, they were made aware that they were preaching behaviour they themselves were not practising.

Just as in the condom study described earlier, participants who were made to feel like hypocrites changed their behaviour so they could feel good about themselves. In this case, they took very brief showers. Indeed, the procedure was so effective that the average time students in this condition spent showering was reduced to 3.5 minutes. The hypocrisy procedure has also been found to increase other environmentally sound practices, such as recycling (Fried & Aronson, 1995).

INSUFFICIENT PUNISHMENT Another form of insufficient justification is insufficient punishment. Usually we think that if we really want to stop someone from behaving badly (trying to stop a bully from beating up little kids), we should dish out punishment—and make sure it is severe enough to have a deterrent effect. Right? Not so, according to dissonance theory. Dissonance theory would suggest just the opposite. Give the bully mild punishment. Then, when the bully stops beating up kids, dissonance is created. "I like beating up little kids, but I'm not doing it. Why?" This dissonance can be reduced by deciding "I guess I stopped because it's really not that much fun after all." In short, this is **insufficient punishment**. In contrast, if this bully had received severe punishment, he or she would have ample external justification for having stopped ("I'm not beating up kids because I'll be kicked out of school if a teacher sees me"). In this case, the behaviour may decrease, but probably only when a teacher is around. In other words, true attitude change hasn't taken place.

These speculations were put to the test by Elliot Aronson and J. Merrill Carlsmith (1963) in an experiment with preschoolers. In this study, the experimenter first asked each child to rate the attractiveness of several toys. He then pointed to a toy that the child considered to be among the most attractive, and told the child that he or she was not allowed to play with it. Half of the children were threatened with mild punishment (the experimenter said he would be annoyed) if they disobeyed; the other half were threatened with severe punishment (the experimenter said he would be very angry, would take the toys away, and would never come back again). The experimenter then left the room for several minutes to provide the children with the time and opportunity to play with the other toys and to resist the temptation of playing with the forbidden toy. None of the children played with the forbidden toy.

Insufficient punishment the dissonance aroused when individuals lack sufficient external justification for having resisted a desired activity or object, usually resulting in individuals' devaluing the forbidden activity or object

The experimenter then returned to the room and asked each child to rate how much he or she liked each of the toys. Initially, all of the children had wanted to play with the forbidden toy. During the temptation period, all of them had refrained from playing with it. Clearly, this disparity means that dissonance was aroused in the children. How did they respond? The children who had received a severe threat had ample justification for their restraint. They knew why they hadn't played with the attractive toy, and they thus had no reason to change their attitude about the toy. These children continued to rate the forbidden toy as highly desirable; indeed, some even found it more desirable than they had before the threat.

A parent can intervene to stop bullying after it takes place, but what might she do to make it less likely to happen in the future?

But what about the others? Lacking an abundance of external justification for refraining from playing with the toy, the children in the mild threat condition needed an internal justification to reduce their dissonance. They succeeded in convincing themselves that the reason they hadn't played with the toy was that they didn't really like it. They rated the forbidden toy as less attractive than they had at the beginning of the experiment. What we have here is a clear example of **self-justification** leading to self-persuasion in the behaviour of very young children. The implications for child rearing are fascinating.

Self-justification the tendency to justify one's actions in order to maintain one's self-esteem

The Aftermath of Bad Deeds: How We Come to Hate Our Victims

Imagine that you realize that your actions have hurt another person. How would you react? Would you be especially kind to that person in the future to make up for your transgression? Sadly, that is not what dissonance theory would predict. According to dissonance theory, in situations where we hurt someone, we come to dislike or hate that person as a way of justifying our cruelty. This phenomenon was demonstrated in an early experiment performed by Keith Davis and Edward E. Jones (1960). Participants watched a young man being interviewed, and then, on the basis of this observation, provided him with an analysis of his shortcomings as a human being. Specifically, the participants were told to tell the young man (a confederate) that they believed he was a shallow, untrustworthy, boring person. The participants succeeded in convincing themselves that they didn't like the victim of their cruelty—after the fact. In short, after saying things they knew were certain to hurt him, they convinced themselves that he deserved it. They found him less attractive than they had prior to saying the hurtful things to him.

classic research

Do people in real-world situations also use dissonance to justify cruel actions toward other human beings? Tragically, the answer appears to be yes. In March 1993, Canadian soldiers from the elite Canadian Airborne Regiment on a peacekeeping mission in Somalia captured 16-year-old Shidane Arone trying to sneak into their compound. He was tied up, savagely beaten, and tortured to death. A court martial later learned that one of the soldiers had beaten Shidane Arone with a wooden riot baton, a metal pipe, and his feet and fists. Others soldiers had joined in. According to newspaper reports, the young Somali boy's cries of "Canada, Canada, Canada" as he drifted in and out of consciousness could be heard across the compound. Canadians were shocked and deeply disturbed by this incident. Perhaps most shocking was that the soldiers posed for "trophy" photographs—in one photograph soldiers posed beside the unconscious Somali boy; in another photograph a soldier held the boy's head up by jamming a wooden baton into his bloody mouth; still others showed a soldier holding a gun to Shidane Arone's head. What was so chilling about these photographs was the broad smiles on the soldiers' faces. As James Travers, then editor of the *Ottawa Citizen* (one newspaper that published these photographs), commented, "They not only tortured, beat and killed him, but were obviously playing when they did this" (Boadle, 1994). How could anyone gleefully torture and murder a 16-year-old boy? By deciding that he deserved it. It may seem absurd to suggest that Canadian peacekeepers could convince themselves that an unarmed civilian boy deserved to be beaten to death for trying to enter their compound. However, as various inquiries into this tragedy revealed, some of the higher-ranking officers had issued orders to "abuse" any Somali intruders. This might have been all the justification they needed. In short, the soldiers might have convinced themselves that Shidane Arone deserved what he got.

Unfortunately, this was not an isolated event. As this textbook is being written, inquiries are being conducted into the behaviour of Americans in charge of the Abu Ghraib prison near Baghdad at which Iraqi prisoners were tortured and killed. The images of torture and humiliation bear a chilling resemblance to the photo of Shidane Arone shown here. One of the striking similarities across the horrific photos is the dehumanization of the victims—the prisoners are usually shown naked, with hoods over their faces, or crawling on all fours with leashes around their necks. Newspaper articles are filled with

When defenseless civilians such as the elderly, women, and children are targets of military violence, the soldiers committing the violence will be inclined to derogate or dehumanize their victims to reduce their own dissonance. Here, Master Corporal Clayton Matchee of the Canadian Airborne Regiment smiles and points at Somali teenager Shidane Arone, whom members of the regiment tortured and beat to death in 1993. This photo, taken by one of the soldiers, shows the dehumanization of the Somalians in the eyes of the soldiers.

the grisly details of the sadistic abuse that took place in this prison. People who inflict harm on those who cannot retaliate reduce dissonance by derogating their victims and deciding that the victims deserve their cruel treatment. Reducing dissonance in this way has sobering future consequences: It increases the likelihood that the atrocities people are willing to commit will become greater and greater through an endless chain of violence followed by self-justification (in the form of dehumanizing the victim), followed by greater violence and still more intense dehumanization. In this manner, unbelievable acts of human cruelty—such as the Nazi Final Solution that led to the murder of 6 million European Jews—can occur. Unfortunately, atrocities are not a thing of the past but occur in our lives today.

Avoiding the Rationalization Trap

The tendency to reduce dissonance by justifying our behaviour can lead us into an escalation of rationalizations that can be disastrous. We call this the **rationalization trap**: The potential is for dissonance reduction to produce a succession of self-justifications that ultimately results in a chain of stupid or irrational actions. The irony, of course, is that to avoid thinking of ourselves as stupid or immoral, we set the stage to increase our acts of stupidity or immorality.

Is there a way that people can be persuaded not to rationalize their behaviour when they make mistakes? It might be helpful to learn to tolerate dissonance long enough to examine the situation critically and dispassionately. We then stand a chance of breaking out of the cycle of action, followed by self-justification, followed by more intense action. For example, suppose Mary has acted unkindly toward a fellow student. To learn from that experience, she must be able to resist the need to derogate her victim. Ideally, it would be effective if she were able to stay with the dissonance long enough to say, "Okay, I blew it; I did a cruel thing. But that doesn't necessarily make me a cruel person. Let me think about why I did it."

We are well aware that this is easier said than done. However, a clue as to how such behaviour might come about is contained in some of the research on self-affirmation discussed previously (Steele, 1988). Suppose that immediately after Mary acted cruelly, but before she had an opportunity to derogate her victim, she was reminded of the fact that she had recently donated several units of blood to the Red Cross, or that she had recently received a high score on her physics exam. This self-affirmation would likely provide her with the ability to resist engaging in typical dissonance-reducing behaviour. In effect, Mary might be able to say, "It's true—I just did a cruel thing. But I am also capable of some really fine, intelligent, and generous behaviour."

Indeed, self-affirmation can serve as a cognitive buffer, protecting a person from caving in to temptation and committing a cruel or immoral act. This was demonstrated in an early experiment on cheating (Aronson & Mettee, 1968). In this experiment, university students were first given a personality test, and then given false feedback that was either positive (aimed at temporarily raising self-esteem) or negative (aimed at temporarily lowering self-esteem), or they received no information at all. Immediately afterwards, they played a game of cards in which, to win a large pot, they could easily cheat without being caught. The results were striking. Students in the high self-esteem condition were able to resist the temptation to cheat to a far greater extent than were the students in the other conditions. In short, a temporary boost in self-esteem served to inoculate these students against cheating, because the anticipation of doing something immoral was

Rationalization trap the potential for dissonance reduction to produce a succession of self-justifications that ultimately results in a chain of stupid or immoral actions

> Both salvation and punishment for man lie in the fact that, if he lives wrongly, he can befog himself so as not to see the misery of his position.
>
> —LEO TOLSTOY

more dissonant than it otherwise would have been. Thus, when they were put in a tempting situation, they were able to say to themselves, "Terrific people like me don't cheat." And they didn't (see also Spencer, Josephs, & Steele, 1993; Steele, Spencer, & Lynch, 1993). We find these results encouraging. They suggest a viable way of reversing the rationalization trap.

Thinking Critically

Suppose that you are the principal of a junior high school where bullying is a serious problem. How would you use "hypocrisy induction" to reduce bullying?

THE SOLAR TEMPLE REVISITED

At the beginning of this chapter, we raised a vital question regarding the followers of Luc Jouret and Joseph Di Mambro of the Solar Temple. How could intelligent people allow themselves to be led into what, to the overwhelming majority of us, is obviously senseless and tragic behaviour—resulting in mass suicide–murders? Needless to say, the situation is a complex one; there were many factors operating, including the charismatic persuasive power of each of these leaders, the existence of a great deal of social support for the views of the group (from other members of the group), and the relative isolation of each group from dissenting views, producing a closed system—a little like living in a roomful of mirrors.

In addition to these factors, we are convinced that one of the single most powerful forces common to all of these groups was the existence of a great deal of cognitive dissonance within the mind of each participant. You know from reading this chapter that when individuals make an important decision and invest heavily in that decision (in terms of time, effort, sacrifice, and commitment), the result is a strong need to justify those actions and that investment. The more they give up and the harder they work, the greater the need to convince themselves that their views are correct; indeed, they may even begin to feel sorry for those who do not share their beliefs. The members of the Solar Temple cult sacrificed a great deal for their beliefs: They abandoned their friends and families, relinquished their money and possessions, and, if female, subjected themselves to sexual exploitation. All of these sacrifices served to increase their commitment to the cult. Those of us who have studied the theory of cognitive dissonance were not surprised to learn that intelligent, respected, professional people could be persuaded that through death by fire they could escape the imminent apocalypse on earth and be reborn on the star Sirius. To begin to question these beliefs would have produced too much dissonance to bear. Although tragic and bizarre, the death voyages of the Solar Temple members are not unfathomable. They are simply an extreme manifestation of a process—cognitive dissonance—that we have seen in operation over and over again.

Thinking Critically

Now that you know about cognitive dissonance theory, is the behaviour of the Solar Temple cult members more understandable? Can we use this theory to try to persuade people not to join cults?

Summary

An **attitude** is a person's enduring evaluation of a person, object, or idea. All attitudes have affective, cognitive, and behavioural components. A **cognitively based attitude** is based mostly on people's beliefs about the properties of the attitude object. An **affectively based attitude** is based more on people's emotions and feelings. A **behaviourally based attitude** is based on people's actions toward the attitude object. Attitudes vary in terms of whether they are more likely to be based on affect, cognition, or behaviour.

When do people behave in line with their attitudes? According to the **theory of planned behaviour**, it is necessary to know people's attitudes toward the specific act in question, their **subjective norms** (their beliefs about how others view the behaviour in question), and whether they believe that it is easy or difficult to perform the behaviour (perceived behavioral control). Knowing these three things allows us to predict people's behavioural intentions, which are highly correlated with their actual behaviours.

The theory of planned behaviour is useful in understanding an area in which people's attitudes and behaviour are often inconsistent—namely, practising safer sex. Although people tend to express positive attitudes toward using condoms, they often fail to do so. One reason has to do with subjective norms—if people are in a situation where they believe their peers are not using condoms, or if they believe their partner would disapprove of condom use, they probably will not use them. Another reason is perceived behavioural control: If people find it embarrassing to buy condoms or to bring up the topic of condom use with their partner, it is unlikely that they will use condoms. Finally, condoms also will not be used if people's intentions to use them are undermined (e.g., due to excessive alcohol consumption).

The next part of the chapter focused on attitude change. One way attitudes change is when people receive a **persuasive communication**. According to the **Yale Attitude Change Approach**, the persuasiveness of a communication depends on aspects of the communicator, or source of the message; aspects of the message itself (e.g., its content); and aspects of the audience. The **heuristic-systematic model of persuasion** and the **elaboration likelihood model** specify when people are persuaded more by the strength of the arguments in the communication and when they are persuaded more by surface characteristics, such as the attractiveness of the speaker. People will take the *central route to persuasion* when they have both the ability and the motivation to pay close attention to the arguments. People will take the *peripheral route to persuasion* when they either do not want to or cannot pay close attention to the arguments. Under these conditions, they are persuaded by such peripheral cues as the attractiveness of the speaker or the length of the speech. Importantly, attitude change is longer-lasting and more resistant to attack when it occurs via the central route.

The effectiveness of persuasive communications also depends on the type of attitude people have. Appeals to emotion work best if the attitude is based on affect; appeals to utilitarian features work best if the attitude is based on cognition. Under controlled laboratory conditions, **subliminal messages** can have subtle effects on people's preferences, but there is no evidence that subliminal messages have been used successfully in real-world marketing campaigns.

It is possible to make people resistant to attacks on their attitudes. **Attitude inoculation** is the technique whereby people are exposed to small doses of arguments against their position, making it easier for them to refute these arguments when they hear them later.

In the latter half of the chapter we focused on another powerful determinant of attitude change: our own behaviour. According to **cognitive dissonance theory**, people experience discomfort (dissonance) whenever they behave in ways inconsistent with their attitudes or hold two conflicting attitudes. People reduce dissonance by either changing their behaviour or justifying their past behaviour. The resulting change in attitude stems from a process of self-persuasion.

Dissonance inevitably occurs after important decisions (**postdecision dissonance**) because the thought "I chose alternative X" is inconsistent with the thought "I might have been a lot better off with alternative Y." People reduce this dissonance by increasing their liking for the chosen alternative and decreasing their liking for the negative alternative. Dissonance also occurs after people choose to exert a lot of effort to attain something boring or onerous. A **justification of effort** occurs, whereby people increase their liking for what they have attained.

Another source of dissonance results when people commit foolish, immoral, or absurd acts for **insufficient punishment**. For example, when people say something against their attitudes (**counter-attitudinal advocacy**) for low **external justification**, they find an **internal justification** for their behaviour, coming to believe what they said. Similarly, if people avoid doing something desirable for insufficient punishment, they will come to believe that the activity wasn't that desirable after all.

Dissonance reduction also has sinister effects: If people find themselves acting cruelly toward someone for insufficient justification, they will derogate the victim, assuming he or she must have deserved it.

The problem with reducing dissonance in ways that make us feel better about ourselves (**self-justification**) is that it can result in a **rationalization trap**, whereby we set the stage for acts of increasing stupidity or immorality. As suggested by *self-affirmation theory*, we can avoid this trap by reminding ourselves that we are good and decent people, so we do not have to justify and rationalize every stupid or immoral act we perform.

Key Terms

Affectively based attitude   (page 121)
Attitude   (page 120)
Attitude inoculation   (page 137)
Behaviourally based attitude   (page 122)
Cognitive dissonance   (page 138)
Cognitively based attitude   (page 121)
Counter-attitudinal advocacy   (page 145)
Elaboration likelihood model   (page 130)
External justification   (page 145)
Fear-arousing communication   (page 131)
Heuristic-systematic model of persuasion   (page 129)
Insufficient punishment   (page 148)
Internal justification   (page 145)
Justification of effort   (page 142)
Persuasive communication   (page 128)
Postdecision dissonance   (page 140)
Rationalization trap   (page 151)
Self-justification   (page 149)
Subjective norms   (page 125)
Subliminal messages   (page 134)
Theory of planned behaviour   (page 124)
Yale Attitude Change Approach   (page 128)

Key Online Search Terms

Cognitively based attitude
Affectively based attitude
Behaviourally based attitude
Persuasive communication
Central route to persuasion
Peripheral route to persuasion
Attitude inoculation
Cognitive dissonance
Counter-attitudinal advocacy

If You Are Interested

Aronson, E. (1997). The theory of cognitive dissonance: The evolution and vicissitudes of an idea. In C. McGarty & S. A. Haslam (Eds.), *The message of social psychology: Perspectives on mind in society.* Oxford, England: Blackwell Publishers, Inc. A readable account, tracing the development and evolution of the theory in the context of general social psychology.

Eagly, A., & Chaiken, S. (1993). *The psychology of attitudes.* Fort Worth, TX: Harcourt Brace Jovanovich. An extremely thorough and insightful look at current social psychological research on attitudes.

Ivory, James (Director). (1993). *The remains of the day* [Film]. There are a great many films (available on video) that illustrate the workings of dissonance. Among the best is *The remains of the day,* adapted from Kazuo Ishiguru's classic novel. This stunning 1993 film explores self-justification from the perspective of a proper British butler, played by Sir Anthony Hopkins. Shying away from friendship and romance, the butler rationalizes his lonely lifestyle by reasserting his belief that such intimacy is improper for a man in his position, and is worth it because of the worthiness of his employer.

Olson, J. M., & Zanna, M. P. (1993). Attitudes and attitude change. *Annual Review of Psychology, 44,* 117–154. A comprehensive, incisive review of theory and research on attitudes and attitude change, written by two leading researchers in this area. James Olson is at the University of Western Ontario and Mark Zanna is at the University of Waterloo.

Weblinks

www.as.wvu.edu/~sbb/comm221/primer.htm
Primer of Practical Persuasion and Influence
An interesting and informative tutorial on influence from a communications perspective.

www.propagandacritic.com
Propaganda
This site discusses propaganda in detail and provides many examples of propaganda campaigns from the recent past.

www.adbusters.org/home
Adbusters
This magazine wants folks to get mad about corporate disinformation, injustices in the global economy, and any industry that pollutes our physical or mental commons.

http://fisher.osu.edu/marketing/scp
Society for Consumer Psychology
The Society represents the interests of behavioural scientists in the fields of psychology, marketing, advertising, communication, consumer behaviour, and other related areas.

www.colorado.edu/communication/meta-discourses/Theory/festinger.htm
Cognitive Dissonance Theory
This site provides several links related to cognitive dissonance theory.

Chapter 5 Practice Quiz

Check your knowledge of the concepts in this chapter by trying the following questions.

THE NATURE AND ORIGIN OF ATTITUDES

Multiple Choice

1. A(n) _____ is the evaluation of a person, an object, or an idea.
    a. attitude
    b. perception
    c. sensation
    d. belief

2. Attitudes toward social issues are mainly _____ based.
    a. affectively
    b. cognitively
    c. affectively and cognitively
    d. behaviourally

3. Of the following attitudes, which is most likely to be affectively based?
    a. politics
    b. religion
    c. capital punishment
    d. all of the above

True or False

4. The main function of cognitively based attitudes is object appraisal.
    ___ True
    ___ False

5. All attitudes are created equal.
    ___ True
    ___ False

Fill in the Blank

6. Attitudes contain affective, behavioural, and _____ components.
7. According to _____, people do not know how they feel until they see how they behave.

WHEN WILL ATTITUDES PREDICT BEHAVIOUR?

Multiple Choice

8. A famous study by LaPiere in the 1930s showed that
    a. our attitudes and our behaviours always match.
    b. our attitudes are not always consistent with our behaviours.
    c. our attitudes and behaviours are almost never related.
    d. prejudiced attitudes were infrequent in the 1930s.

9. According to the theory of planned behaviour, the best predictors of people's behaviour are their
    a. attitudes.
    b. values.
    c. religious beliefs.
    d. intentions.

10. Studies have shown that people will not use condoms unless they intended to do so. This is because of
    a. behavioural intentions.
    b. attitudinal intentions.
    c. lack of intelligence.
    d. lack of social skills.

11. In the theory of planned behaviour, which of the following is not a determinant of intentions?
    a. subjective norms
    b. morality
    c. attitudes toward specific behaviours
    d. perceived behavioural control

True or False

12. If a behaviour is difficult to perform, then a strong intention to do so will form.
    ___ True
    ___ False

13. Asking people about the determinants of their intentions increases the ability to predict their behaviour.
    ___ True
    ___ False

Fill in the Blank

14. The practice of _____ is an area where people's attitudes rarely match their behaviour.
15. _____ are people's beliefs about how those they care about will view their behaviour.

ATTITUDE CHANGE

Multiple Choice

16. Which of the following does not describe the Yale Attitude Change Approach?
    a. Look at the nature of communication.
    b. Look at the common attitudes of most Yale students.
    c. Look at the nature of the audience.
    d. Look at the source of the communication.

17. _____ is an example of a hidden persuasion technique.
    a. Unconscious persuasion
    b. Subliminal messaging
    c. Suppressed advertising
    d. Subtle persuasion

18. Subliminal messaging is _____ compared to regular advertising.
    a. less effective
    b. more effective
    c. equal in effectiveness
    d. more expensive

True or False

19. According to the heuristic-systematic model of persuasion, there is an infinite number of ways in which persuasive communication can change people's attitudes.
    ___ True
    ___ False

20. Fear-arousing communication theory states that fear can be persuasive if a high amount of fear can be stimulated.
    ___ True
    ___ False

Fill in the Blank

21. _____ and ability are key to determining whether people will take the central or peripheral route to persuasion.

22. _____ advocates a particular side of an issue.

CHANGING ATTITUDES BY CHANGING OUR BEHAVIOUR: THE THEORY OF COGNITIVE DISSONANCE

Multiple Choice

23. Knox and Inkster (1968) asked people betting on horses to judge how certain they were that their horse would win. They found that those questioned after making their bet were
    a. more uncertain than before betting.
    b. less confident than those who had yet to place a bet.
    c. more confident than those who had yet to place a bet.
    d. no different in their confidence from those who had yet to place a bet.

24. Which of the following will not reduce cognitive dissonance?
    a. denial of the dissonance
    b. changing behaviour
    c. changing a cognition
    d. adding consonant cognitions

25. Increasing one's liking for something one has worked hard for is termed
    a. overjustification effect.
    b. justification of effort.
    c. misattribution effect.
    d. attitude innoculation.

26. _____ looks at how dissonance reduction can lead to irrational actions.
    a. The self-justification effect
    b. Self-advocacy
    c. The dare-devil complex
    d. The rationalization trap

True or False

27. Counter-attitudinal advocacy occurs when a person's attitude runs counter to his friend's attitude.
    ___ True
    ___ False

28. External justification may occur as a means to avoid punishment or receive a reward.
    ___ True
    ___ False

Fill in the Blank

29. _____ occurs after a person has made a decision that she feels conflict over.
30. _____ occurs when there is a conflict between our attitudes and our behaviours.

PERSONALIZED STUDY PLAN

Want to check your answers and access more study resources? Visit the Companion Website for *Fundamentals of Social Psychology* at **www.pearsoned.ca/aronson**, where you'll find the above questions incorporated in a pre-test and post-test for each chapter. These tests will be automatically graded online, allowing you to check your answers. A Study Plan, like the one below, groups the questions by section within the chapter and shows you which sections you need to focus on for further study.

Your Results for "Chapter 5, Pretest"

OVERALL SCORE: 81% of 16 questions

Group	Score	Proficient
The Nature and Origin of Attitudes	4 of 4	Yes
When Will Attitudes Predict Behaviour?	3 of 4	Yes
Attitude Change	2 of 4	No
How to Make People Resistant to Attitude Change	4 of 4	Yes

CHAPTER

6

Conformity: Influencing Others

Chapter Outline

CONFORMITY: WHEN AND WHY

INFORMATIONAL SOCIAL INFLUENCE: THE NEED TO KNOW WHAT IS "RIGHT"

When Will People Conform to Informational Social Influence?

NORMATIVE SOCIAL INFLUENCE: THE NEED TO BE ACCEPTED

Conformity and Social Approval: The Asch Line Judgment Studies

When Will People Conform to Normative Social Influence?

Resisting Normative Social Influence

MINORITY INFLUENCE: WHEN THE FEW INFLUENCE THE MANY

COMPLIANCE: REQUESTS TO CHANGE YOUR BEHAVIOUR

The Door-in-the-Face Technique

The Foot-in-the-Door Technique

Lowballing

OBEDIENCE TO AUTHORITY

The Role of Normative Social Influence

The Role of Informational Social Influence

The judgment issued by the Honourable Mr. Justice Macaulay on May 10, 1999, begins with the following statement: "Reena Virk died on November 14, 1997 after a vicious beating" (*Her Majesty the Queen* v. *Warren Paul Glowatski*, 1999). Justice Macaulay presided over the trial of Warren Glowatski, who was charged with second-degree murder in Virk's death. The transcript documents the events that led up to the tragic death of this 14-year-old girl. During an exchange with Virk, a fellow student extinguished a lit cigarette on her forehead. Friends of this student joined in and began beating Virk. One girl testified that she had grabbed a lighter and tried to set Virk's hair on fire; others began punching and kicking Virk in the head and face. According to a pathologist's report, Virk's head injuries alone were severe enough to be life-threatening. She also suffered massive internal injuries. The pathologist considered these injuries comparable to crush injuries that would result from being run over by a car. The unconscious Virk was dragged by Kelly Ellard and Warren Glowatski to the Gorge waterway, not far from downtown Victoria. According to some reports, Ellard smoked a cigarette as she stood with one foot on Virk's head, holding it underwater. Glowatski and, eventually, Ellard were charged with second-degree murder. (Six other girls involved in the beating were given sentences ranging from a 60-day conditional sentence to one year in jail.)

Reena Virk, a B.C. teenager, was first savagely beaten by her schoolmates and then drowned by two other teenagers. She died on November 14, 1997.

Glowtaski appealed his conviction, but it was upheld by the Appeal Court. Ellard was tried three times. Her most recent trial resulted in a conviction of second-degree murder.

Canadians were horrified by Reena Virk's death. How could ordinary highschool students in Victoria, B.C., engage in such brutal, savage acts against a defenceless 14-year-old? Why did some students join in and escalate the attacks on Virk? Why did other students stand by and do nothing, rather than attempt to stop this tragedy?

Sadly, as we shall see, the need to conform to a group probably played a role in Virk's murder. People feel tremendous pressure to go along with others—we want to be accepted, to belong. Perhaps more important, we do not want to risk paying the price for going against the group—even when our failure to act may cost another person's life. Under what conditions and for what reasons are we likely to fall under the influence of others? This is the key question to be addressed in this chapter.

CONFORMITY: WHEN AND WHY

Conformity a change in behaviour due to the real or imagined influence of other people

> Do as most do, and [people] will speak well of thee.
> —THOMAS FULLER

> It were not best that we should all think alike; it is difference of opinion that makes horse races.
> —MARK TWAIN

Think for a moment about the word **conformity**, which we can define as a change in behaviour due to the real or imagined influence of others (Kiesler & Kiesler, 1969). Which of the quotations that appear in the margin beside this paragraph do you find more appealing? Which one best describes your immediate reaction to the word *conformity*?

We wouldn't be surprised if you preferred the Mark Twain quotation. North American culture stresses the importance of not conforming (Hofstede, 1986; Markus, Kitayama, & Heiman, 1996). This is part of being in an individualistic culture—one that emphasizes being independent, thinking for yourself, and standing up for yourself. We want to be perceived as people who make up our own minds—not as spineless, weak conformists, not as puppets but as players. As a result, we may maintain the belief that our behaviour is not influenced by others, even when reality suggests otherwise.

People do conform—sometimes in extreme and surprising ways, as suggested by the deaths of 74 Solar Temple cult members (discussed in Chapter 5). But, you might argue, this is an unusual case; surely most people do not conform to this extent. Perhaps the followers of Luc Jouret and Joseph Di Mambro were disturbed people who were somehow predisposed to do what charismatic leaders told them to do. There is, however, another more chilling possibility. Maybe most of us would have acted the same way, had we been exposed to the same long-standing conformity pressures. According to this view, almost anyone would have conformed had he or she been put in these same extreme situations.

If this statement is true, we should be able to find other situations in which people, put under strong social pressures, conform to surprising degrees. Unfortunately, we do not have to look very far to find such instances. We opened this chapter with the deeply disturbing story of Reena Virk, who died at the hands of a group of highschool students. Once one of the students began attacking Virk, others went along. In Chapter 5, we described the chilling story of Shidane Arone, who was tortured to death by Canadian peacekeepers in Somalia. In that situation as well, one soldier began beating the boy and others joined in. And, of course, the Holocaust provides countless horrific examples of conformity at its worst.

The examples we have seen so far are all cases of "bad" conformity: Human beings lost their lives as a result of people's going along with others. However, conformity is not simply "good" or "bad" in and of itself. Rather than labelling conformity as good or bad, the social psychologist is interested in *why* people conform. Knowing why and when people are influenced by others will help us understand whether a given act of conformity in our own lives is wise or foolish.

Thinking Critically

What are some of the negative consequences of conformity? Can you think of situations in which conformity might have positive effects?

INFORMATIONAL SOCIAL INFLUENCE: THE NEED TO KNOW WHAT IS "RIGHT"

How should you address your psychology professor—as Dr. Berman, Professor Berman, Ms. Berman, or Patricia? How should you vote on a proposal to increase your tuition in order to increase student services? Is the scream you just heard coming from a person joking with friends or from the victim of a mugging? In these and many other everyday situations, we feel uncertain about what to think or how to act. We simply don't know enough to make a good or accurate choice. One of the important things we receive from interacting with other people is information. Asking others what they think or watching what they do helps us reach a definition of the situation (Kelley, 1955; Thomas, 1928). When we subsequently act like everyone else, we are conforming, but not because we are weak spineless individuals with no self-reliance. Instead, the influence of other people leads us to conform because we see them as a source of information to guide our behaviour. This is called **informational social influence** (Cialdini, 1993; Cialdini, Kallgren, & Reno, 1991; Cialdini & Trost, 1998; Deutsch & Gerard, 1955).

As an illustration of how other people can be a source of information, imagine you are a participant in the following experiment by Muzafer Sherif (1936). In the first phase of the study, you are seated alone in a dark room and asked to focus your attention on a dot of light 5 metres away. The experimenter asks you to estimate in centimetres how far the light moves. You stare earnestly at the light, and yes, it moves a little. You say, "About 5 centimetres," though it is not easy to tell exactly. The light disappears and then comes back; you are asked to judge again. The light seems to move a little more, and you say, "10 centimetres." After several of these trials, the light seems to move about the same amount each time—about 5 to 10 centimetres.

Now, the interesting thing about this task is that the light was not actually moving at all. It looked as if it was moving because of a visual illusion called the autokinetic effect. If you stare at a bright light in a uniformly dark environment (e.g., a star on a dark night), the light will appear to waver. This occurs because you have no stable reference point to anchor the position of the light. The distance that the light appears to move varies from person to person but becomes consistent for each person over time. In Sherif's (1936) experiment, the participants all arrived at their own stable estimates during the first phase of the study, but these estimates differed from person to person. Some people thought the

Informational social influence conforming because we believe that others' interpretation of an ambiguous situation is more correct than ours and will help us choose an appropriate course of action

light was moving only 2.5 centimetres or so, whereas others thought it was moving as much as 25 centimetres.

Sherif chose to use the autokinetic effect because he wanted a situation that would be ambiguous—where the correct definition of the situation would be unclear to his participants. In the second phase of the experiment, a few days later, the participants were paired with two other people, each of whom had had the same prior experience alone with the light. Now the situation became a truly social one, as all three made their judgments out loud. Remember, the autokinetic effect is experienced differently by different people; some see a lot of movement, some not much at all. After hearing their partners give judgments that were different from their own, what did people do?

Over the course of several trials, people reached a common estimate, and each member of the group conformed to that estimate. These results indicate that people were using each other as a source of information, coming to believe that the group estimate was the correct one (see Figure 6.1).

An important feature of informational social influence is that it can lead to **private acceptance**, whereby people conform to the behaviour of others because they genuinely believe that these other people are correct. It might seem equally plausible that people publicly conformed to the group but privately maintained the belief that the light was moving only a small amount. For example, maybe someone privately believed that the light was moving 25 centimetres, but announced that it had moved 7.5 centimetres (the group estimate) to avoid looking silly or foolish. This would be a case of **public compliance**, where a person conforms publicly without necessarily believing in what the group is saying or doing. Sherif cast doubt on this interpretation, however, by asking people to judge the lights once more by themselves, after participating in groups. Even though they no longer had

Private acceptance conforming to other people's behaviour out of a genuine belief that what they are doing or saying is right

Public compliance conforming to other people's behaviour publicly, without necessarily believing in what they are doing or saying

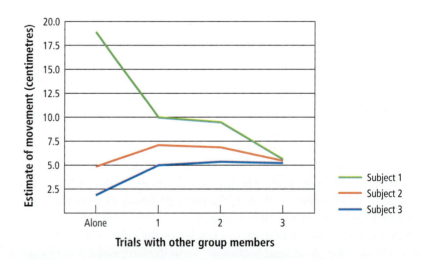

FIGURE 6.1 One Group's Judgments in Sherif's (1936) Autokinetic Studies

People estimated how far a point of light appeared to move in a dark room. When they saw the light by themselves, their estimates varied widely. When they were brought together in groups and heard other people announce their estimates, they conformed to the group's estimate of how much the light moved.

(Adapted from Sherif, 1936)

to worry about looking silly in front of other participants, they continued to give the answer the group had given earlier. These results suggest that people were relying on each other to define reality and came to privately accept the group estimate.

In everyday life, of course, we are rarely asked to judge how much a stationary light is moving. However, there are many everyday situations in which we rely on other people to help us define what is going on. For example, you might be feeling quite calm about your upcoming midterm until you run into a group of acquaintances from class, all of whom are extremely tense and stressed-out about the exam. After talking with them, you feel a little disturbed, too—are you being too complacent about this test? "Maybe they're right," you think. Like the research participants in Sherif's experiment, you may find yourself relying on other people to help you reach a definition of the situation: "Maybe I'm being way too calm about this midterm.... I'd better study some more tonight."

When Will People Conform to Informational Social Influence?

What kinds of situations are most likely to produce conformity because of informational social influence? We will discuss three: ambiguous situations, crises, and situations in which an expert is present.

WHEN THE SITUATION IS AMBIGUOUS You may have had the experience of hearing a fire alarm in a building. What did you do? If you are like most people, you turned to the people around you to determine whether the situation was an emergency. If other people seemed unconcerned and weren't making moves to leave the building, you probably decided that there wasn't a need to evacuate. On the other hand, if other people started rushing toward the emergency exit doors, your behaviour would probably be quite different. When you are unsure of the correct response, the appropriate behaviour, or the right idea, you will be most open to influence from others. The more uncertain you are, the more you will rely on others (Baron, Vandello, & Brunsman, 1996; Tesser, Campbell, & Mickler, 1983).

WHEN THE SITUATION IS A CRISIS When the situation is a crisis, we usually do not have time to stop and think about exactly which course of action we should take. We need to act, and act now. If we feel scared and panicky, and are uncertain what to do, it is only natural for us to see how other people are responding—and to do likewise. Unfortunately, the people we imitate may also feel scared and panicky, and not behave rationally.

Luc Jouret, a leader of the Solar Temple cult, apparently was convinced that the world was coming to an end and managed to persuade his followers that this was true. Needless to say, this constituted a crisis for those who accepted this belief, and they turned to him for guidance. Sadly, they believed him when he said that death by fire was the correct course of action so they could be reborn on the star Sirius. Such instances of mind control or "brainwashing" can actually be extreme cases of informational social influence. When people believe that they are in a crisis situation, they are more likely to succumb to these forms of influence.

WHEN OTHER PEOPLE ARE EXPERTS Typically, the more expertise or knowledge a person has, the more valuable he or she will be as a guide in an ambiguous or crisis situation (Allison, 1992; Bickman, 1974; Cialdini & Trost, 1998). For example, a passenger who sees smoke coming out of an airplane engine will probably look around for the flight attendants to check their reaction; they have more expertise than the vacationer in the next seat. However, there can be situations in which even experts can make mistakes, and in those cases conformity can be costly.

How can we tell in which cases other people are a good source of information and in which cases we should resist other people's definition of a situation? First, it is important to consider carefully whether other people's reactions to a situation are any more legitimate than your own. Do the actions of other people or experts seem sensible? If you behave the way they do, will it go against your common sense, or against your internal moral compass that tells you what is right and wrong? Finally, it is also important to remind ourselves that it is possible to resist illegitimate or inaccurate informational social influence. Some Solar Temple cult members refused to take their own lives, and not every student on the scene participated in the fatal attack on Reena Virk. The Try It! below focuses on how informational social influence works in daily life. It is important to understand how social informational influence operates in our day-to-day lives so that we are in a better position to know when it is and is not useful.

Try It! Informational Social Influence and Emergencies

One of the most interesting examples of informational social influence in action is the behaviour of bystanders in emergencies. An emergency is by definition a crisis situation. In many respects, it is an ambiguous situation as well. Sometimes there are "experts" present, but sometimes there aren't. In an emergency, the bystander is thinking, "What's happening? Is help needed? What should I do? What's everybody else doing?"

As you'll recall from the story told by Robin Akert on page xxviii, trying to decide if an emergency is really happening and if your help is really needed can be very difficult. Bystanders often rely on informational social influence to help them figure out what to do. Other people's behaviour is a source of important information in an unusual situation; unfortunately, as we saw in Akert's story, if other people are acting as if nothing is wrong, you could be misled by their behaviour and also interpret the situation as a non-emergency. In that case, informational social influence has backfired.

To explore informational social influence, gather some stories about people's reactions to emergencies when they were bystanders (not victims). Think about your own experiences, and ask your friends to tell you about emergencies they have been in. As you recollect your own experience, or talk to your friends about their experiences, note how informational social influence played a role:

1. How did you (and your friends) decide that an emergency was really occurring? Did you glance at other passersby and watch their responses? Did you talk to other people to help you figure out what was going on?

2. Once you decided it was an emergency, how did you decide what to do? Did you do what other people were doing; did you show (or tell) them what to do?

3. Were there any experts present, people who knew more about the situation or how to offer assistance? Did you do what the experts told you to do? If you were in the role of expert (or were at least knowledgeable) at the scene of the emergency, did people follow your lead?

The issues raised by these questions are all examples of informational social influence in action.

> **Thinking Critically**
> Which of the factors discussed do you think best explain the conditions under which people are most likely to succumb to informational social influence? What strategies might be most effective in helping people resist informational social influence?

NORMATIVE SOCIAL INFLUENCE: THE NEED TO BE ACCEPTED

In many cities in Canada, teens flock to all-night raves where they buy drugs such as ecstasy from strangers. Between 2 and 3 a.m., emergency departments in hospitals have come to expect teens who are experiencing "bad trips" from having taken the drug. A Toronto Public Health report published in 2000 documented that in the previous two years, there were 13 ecstasy-related deaths in Ontario alone (the report notes that statistics from other Canadian cities are not widely available; Research Group on Drug Use, Toronto Public Health, 2000). Despite this, a Canada-wide survey of drug use among students in grades 7 to 12 categorizes ecstasy as a drug that increased in use during the 1990s and is currently at a "stable, but elevated" level of use (Centre for Addiction and Mental Health, Ontario Student Drug Use Survey, 2003).

Why do some young people continue to engage in such risky behaviour? Why does anyone follow the group's lead when the resulting behaviour is less than sensible and may even be dangerous? We doubt that these teenagers risk their lives due to informational conformity—it is difficult to argue that a teenager at a rave would say, "Gee, I don't know what to do. A stranger wants to sell me drugs that might kill me. I guess it must be a good idea; I see other people doing it." This example tells us that there is another reason why we conform, aside from the need for information: We also conform so we will be liked and accepted by other people. This is known as **normative social influence**.

Conformity for normative reasons occurs in situations where we go along with others, not because we are using them as a source of information but rather because we don't want to attract attention, be made fun of, get into trouble, or be rejected. Groups have certain expectations about how group members should behave, and members in good standing conform to these rules, or **social norms**. Members who do not are perceived as different, difficult, and eventually deviant. Deviant members can be ridiculed, punished, or even rejected by other group members (Kruglanski & Webster, 1991; Levine, 1989; Miller & Anderson, 1979; Schachter, 1951). Stanley Schachter (1951) demonstrated how the group responds to an individual who ignores their normative influence. He asked groups of university students to read and discuss a case history of "Johnny Rocco," a juvenile delinquent. Most of the students took a middle-of-the-road position about the case, believing that Rocco should receive a judicious mixture of love and discipline. Unbeknownst to the participants, however, Schachter had planted an accomplice in the group, who was instructed to disagree with the group's recommendations. He consistently argued that Rocco should receive the harshest amount of punishment, regardless of what the other group members argued.

Normative social influence the influence of other people that leads us to conform in order to be liked and accepted by them; this type of conformity results in public compliance with the group's beliefs and behaviours, but not necessarily with private acceptance of the group's beliefs and behaviours

Social norms the implicit or explicit rules a group has for the acceptable behaviours, values, and beliefs of its members

Krista Piche paid a high price for not conforming to the military code of silence after being sexually assaulted by a petty officer. She filed a complaint, despite being advised by a medical warrant officer not to do so. Military brass responded by forcing her to work alongside the man who had assaulted her and repeatedly denied her requests for a transfer. Although a career with the military had been her lifelong dream, these consequences of nonconformity made her life so unbearable that she eventually left the military.

How was the deviant treated? He received the most comments and questions from the real participants throughout the discussion, until near the end, when communication with him dropped sharply. The group had tried to convince the deviant to agree with them; when it appeared that wouldn't work, they ignored him. In addition, they punished the deviant. After the discussion, they were asked to nominate one group member who should be eliminated from further discussions if the size of the group had to be reduced. They nominated the deviant. They were also asked to assign group members to various tasks in future discussions. You guessed it—they assigned the unimportant or boring jobs, such as taking notes, to the deviant.

Are the findings of Schacter's 1951 study relevant today? Consider the case of Master Seaman Biden, a military police officer with 20 years of service in the Canadian Forces. He was injected with the anthrax vaccine during the Gulf War and subsequently experienced medical problems. When he learned that the vaccine was out of date and that the Michigan manufacturer of the drug had been charged by the U.S. government for numerous health violations, he wrote a letter to his Member of Parliament. Subsequently, Biden received a scathing letter from his commanding officer because members of the military are expected not to voice complaints publicly. He was ordered to stop talking to the media and was ostracized at work. Biden told an *Ottawa Citizen* reporter that he was assigned menial jobs that were usually done by junior privates: "He cleaned rifles while junior officers sat idle, sipping coffee" (Blanchfield, 2000). The parallels between Biden's experience and the way in which participants in Schacter's 1951 study treated a deviant group member are striking!

How do people react when even minor social norms are violated? Find out for yourself by completing the following Try It! exercise.

Try It!

Unveiling Normative Social Influence by Breaking the Rules

Every day, you talk to a lot of people—friends, professors, co-workers, and strangers, too. When you have a conversation (whether long or short), you follow certain interaction "rules" that operate in North American culture. These rules for conversation include nonverbal forms of behaviour that we consider "normal" as well as "polite." You can find out how powerful these norms are by breaking them and noting how people respond to you; their response is normative social influence in action.

For example, when in conversation, we stand a certain distance from each other—not too far and not too close. About two-thirds of a metre to a metre is typical in our culture. In addition, we maintain a good amount of eye contact when we are listening to the other person; in comparison, when we're talking, we look away from the person more often.

What happens if you break these normative rules? For example, have a conversation with a friend and stand either too close or too far away (30 centimetres or 2 metres). Have a typical, normal conversation with your friend, changing only the spacing you normally use with this person. Note how he or she responds. If you're too close, your friend will probably back away; if you continue to keep the distance small, he or she may act uncomfortable and even terminate your conversation sooner than usual. If you're too far away, your friend will probably come closer; if you back up, he or she may think you are in a strange mood. In either case, your friend's response will probably include the following: looking at you a lot, having a puzzled look on his or her face, acting uncomfortable or confused, talking less than normal or ending the conversation, and so on.

You have acted in a non-normative way, and your conversational partner is, first, trying to figure out what is going on and, second, responding so as to get you to stop acting oddly. From this one brief exercise, you will get an idea of what would happen if you behaved "oddly" all the time—people would try to make you change, and then they would probably start avoiding or ignoring you.

When you're done, please "debrief" your friend, telling him or her about the exercise, so that your behaviour is understood. Let your friend see what it's like to alter interpersonal distance by talking to you too close or too far away.

FOCUS ON APPLICATIONS

Can Conformity Pressure Be Used to Increase Social Good? The Case of Littering

Compared to other environmental problems, littering may not appear to be all that serious. Most people seem to think it isn't a big deal to leave a paper cup at the side of the road instead of putting it in a garbage can. Unfortunately, those paper cups add up and the cost of cleanup to taxpayers is increasing. Aside from the cost, the material people discard is polluting water systems and endangering wildlife. How can we get people to do the right thing when they have those empty paper cups in hand?

One approach is to remind people of the social norms against littering. Reno, Cialdini, and Kallgren (1993) conducted a field experiment to investigate the power of social norms. As people left a local library and approached their cars in the parking lot, an accomplice walked by them, picked up a fast-food bag that had been discarded on the ground, and put the bag in the trash. In a control condition, no bag was on the ground, and the accomplice simply walked by the library patrons. When the patrons got to their cars, they each found a pamphlet on their windshields. The question was: How many patrons would litter by throwing the pamphlet on the ground?

Reno and colleagues hypothesized that seeing the accomplice pick up the fast-food bag would be a vivid reminder of the social norm that littering is bad and other people disapprove of it, and hence would lower the patron's own inclination to litter. They were right. In this condition, only 7 percent of the patrons tossed the pamphlet on the ground, compared to 37 percent in the control condition. Thus, although conformity often has negative effects, one can also put conformity to good use.

Conformity and Social Approval: The Asch Line Judgment Studies

You probably don't find it too surprising that people sometimes conform in order to be liked and accepted by others. After all, if the group is important to us and it is a matter of wearing the right kind of clothing or using the right "cool" words, why not go along? But surely we won't conform when we are certain of the correct way of behaving and the pressures are coming from a group that we don't care all that much about. Or will we? To find out, Solomon Asch (1951, 1956) conducted a series of classic studies exploring the parameters of normative social influence. Asch initiated this program of research because he believed that there are limits to how much people will conform. Naturally, people conformed in the Sherif studies, he reasoned, given that the situation was highly ambiguous—trying to guess how much a light was moving. Asch believed, however, that when a situation was completely unambiguous, people would act like rational, objective problem-solvers. When the group said or did something that contradicted an obvious truth, surely people would reject social pressures and decide for themselves what was going on.

To test his hypothesis, Asch conducted the following study. Had you been a participant, you would have been told that this was an experiment on perceptual judgment and that you would be taking part with seven other students. Here's the scenario. The experimenter shows everyone two cards, one with a single line, the other with three lines labelled 1, 2, and 3. He asks each of you to judge and then announce aloud which of the three lines on the second card is closest in length to the line on the first card (see Figure 6.2).

It is crystal clear that the correct answer is the second line. Not surprisingly, each participant says, "Line 2." Your turn comes next to last, and of course you say, "Line 2," as well. The last participant concurs. The experimenter then presents a new set of cards and asks the group to again make their judgments and announce them out loud. Again, the answer is obvious, and everyone gives the correct answer. At this point, you are probably thinking to yourself, "What a boring experiment! How many times will we have to judge these silly lines? I wonder what's for dinner tonight."

As your mind starts to wander, something surprising happens. The experimenter presents a third set of lines, and again the answer is obvious—line 3 is clearly the closest in length to the target line. But the first participant announces that the correct answer is line 1! "Geez, this guy must be so bored that he fell asleep," you think. Then the second person announces that he also believes that line 1 is the correct answer. The third, fourth, fifth,

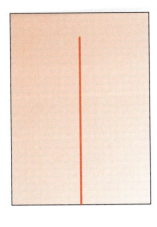
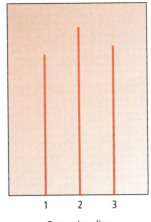

Standard line   Comparison lines

FIGURE 6.2   The Judgment Task in Asch's Line Studies

In a study of normative social influence, participants judged which of the three comparison lines on the right was closest in length to the standard line on the left. The correct answer was obvious (as it is here). However, members of the group (actually confederates) said the wrong answer out loud. Now the participant was in a dilemma: Should he say the right answer and go against the whole group, or should he conform to the members' behaviour and give the obviously wrong answer?

(Adapted from Asch, 1956)

and sixth participants concur; then it is your turn to judge. By now startled, you are probably looking at the lines very closely to see whether you missed something. But no, line 3 is clearly the correct answer. What will you do? Will you bravely blurt out, "Line 3," or will you go along with the group and give the obviously incorrect answer, "Line 1"?

As you can see, Asch set up a situation to determine whether people would conform even when the right answer was cut and dried. The other participants were actually accomplices of the experimenter, instructed to give the wrong answer on 12 of the 18 trials. Contrary to what Asch thought would happen, a surprising amount of conformity occurred: 66 percent of the participants conformed on at least one trial. On average, people conformed on about one-third of the 12 trials on which the accomplices gave the incorrect answer.

Why did people conform so much of the time? The fear of being the lone dissenter can be very strong, causing people to conform, at least occasionally. One participant, for example, had this to say about why he conformed: "Here was a group; they had a definite idea; my idea disagreed; I didn't want particularly to make a fool of myself.... I felt I was definitely right ... [but] they might think I was peculiar" (Asch, 1955). In other words, people know that what they are doing is wrong but go along anyway so as not to feel peculiar or look like fools. These reasons illustrate an important fact about normative pressures: In contrast to informational social influence, normative pressures usually result in public compliance without private acceptance—that is, people go along with the group even if they do not believe in what they are doing or think it is wrong (Cialdini, Kallgren, & Reno, 1991; Cialdini, Reno, & Kallgren, 1990; Cialdini & Trost, 1998; Deutsch & Gerard, 1955; Sorrels & Kelley, 1984).

> It isn't difficult to keep alive, friends—just don't make trouble—or if you must make trouble, make the sort of trouble that's expected.
> —ROBERT BOLT,
> A Man for All Seasons

Participants in an Asch line study. The real participant is seated in the middle. He is surrounded by the experimenter's accomplices, who have just given the wrong answer on the line task.

What is especially surprising about Asch's results is that people were concerned about looking foolish in front of complete strangers. It is not as if the participants were in danger of being ostracized by a group that was important to them. Nor was there any risk of open punishment or disapproval for failing to conform, or of losing the esteem of people they really cared about, such as friends and family members. Yet decades of research indicate that conformity for normative reasons can occur simply because we do not want to risk social disapproval, even from complete strangers we will never see again (Crutchfield, 1955; Tanford & Penrod, 1984). As Moscovici (1985) comments, the Asch studies are "one of the most dramatic illustrations of conformity, of blindly going along with the group, even when the individual realizes that by doing so he turns his back on reality and truth."

FOCUS ON APPLICATIONS

How Do You Feel about Your Body?

Conforming for normative reasons can have extremely negative consequences in our everyday lives. Take, for example, the pressure that women in our society feel to conform to the ideal of thinness. In fact, the ideal of thinness currently portrayed in the media and in women's magazines is considered dangerous by Canadian and World Health Organization officials (Spitzer, Henderson, & Zivian, 1999). The fact that the ideals are getting thinner at a time when average young women in Canada and the United States are getting heavier means that women are receiving a strong message that their bodies do not conform to cultural standards of beauty.

As a result, girls and women are attempting to create the ideal body through dieting, and, more disturbingly, through eating disorders such as anorexia nervosa and bulimia (Gimlin, 1994; Jackson, 1993; Morry & Staska, 2001). It is estimated that 200 000 to 300 000 Canadian women aged 13 to 40 currently have anorexia nervosa, and that twice

Cultural standards for women's bodies change rapidly. Whereas today's female models and movie stars tend to be lean and muscle-toned, the female icons of the 1940s and 1950s, such as Marilyn Monroe, were curvaceous, heavier, and less muscular.

> No woman can be too slim or too rich.
>
> —WALLIS SIMPSON, DUCHESS OF WINDSOR

as many have bulimia. These illnesses are fatal for 10 to 15 percent of those affected (Support, Concern and Resources for Eating Disorders, 2002). Thus, the sociocultural pressure for thinness operating on women is a potentially fatal form of normative social influence.

What about men? Are they immune from this form of social influence? Apparently not. The ideal body type for males is much more muscular now than in the past (Petrie et al., 1996; Pope et al., 1999). And, apparently, men are feeling pressure to conform. There is mounting evidence that men, especially those who read fitness magazines (which, of course, portray very muscular bodies), are engaging in dangerous behaviour such as crash diets and anabolic steroid use (Morry & Staska, 2001; Spitzberg & Rhea, 1999). Thus, beware the insidious effects that normative influence can have in your life.

When Will People Conform to Normative Social Influence?

Although conformity is commonplace, we are not lemmings who always do what everyone else is doing. Exactly when are people most likely to conform to normative pressures?

The answer to this question is provided by Bibb Latané's (1981) **social impact theory**. According to this theory, the likelihood that you will respond to social influence from other people depends on three variables: (a) strength, referring to how important the group of people is to you; (b) immediacy, referring to how close the group is to you in space and time during the influence attempt; and (c) number, referring to how many people are in the group.

Social impact theory predicts that conformity will increase as strength and immediacy increase. Clearly, the more important a group is to us, and the more we are in its presence, the more likely we will be to conform to its normative pressures. In other words, normative pressures are much stronger when they come from people whose friendship, love, and respect we cherish, because there is a large cost to losing this love and respect. Thus, groups to which we are highly attracted and with which we strongly identify will exert more

Social impact theory the theory that conforming to social influence depends on the strength, immediacy, and number of other people in a group

normative influence on us than groups to which we have little or no attachment (Abrams et al., 1990; Clark & Maass, 1988; Hogg, 1992; Nowak, Szamrej, & Latané, 1990). This phenomenon was examined in a recent fascinating study by Tafarodi, Kang, and Milne (2002). These researchers reasoned that members of bicultural visible-minority groups (people who are second-generation Canadians or who came to Canada as young children) might feel that they are not fully accepted as members of the majority group because of their physical distinctiveness. As a result, such people might be especially motivated to conform to the majority group in terms of dress, speech, or behaviour. This hypothesis was tested among Chinese women (who were either born in Canada or had come to Canada as young children) attending the University of Toronto. The women were asked to participate in a study on aesthetic judgment and were told they would be required to rate how much they liked various pieces of art (presented on a computer screen). The computer "happened" to display various sets of ratings of each painting, including those supposedly given by Chinese Canadians and European Canadians. Half of the participants completed their ratings in view of a mirror (intended to remind them of their visible-minority status); the other half completed the ratings without a mirror. Tafarodi and colleagues reasoned that participants who were reminded of their distinctive appearance (relative to the majority group) would be most likely to conform to the ratings of the majority (European Canadians). And that is exactly what happened. Thus, when we are attracted to a group and are reminded that we don't quite fit in, we will be especially motivated to conform.

Finally, recall that according to social impact theory, the variable of group size (number of people in the group) also has an effect on conformity. It turns out that as the size of the group increases, each additional person has less of an influencing effect—going from 3 to 4 people makes more of a difference than going from 53 to 54 people. It is like the law of diminishing returns in economics, where increasing one's total wealth by $1 seems much greater if we have only $1 to start with than if we have $1000. Asch's (1955) initial research and that of later researchers has established that although conformity pressures generally increase as the size of the majority increases (Bond & Smith, 1996), conformity pressures peak once the majority reaches about 4 or 5 in number (Gerard, Wilhelmy, & Conolley, 1968; McGuire, 1968; Rosenberg, 1961)—just as social impact theory suggests.

THE ROLE OF CULTURE IN CONFORMITY In North America, we use the expression "The squeaky wheel gets the grease." In Japan, you would be more likely to hear "The nail that stands out gets pounded down" (Markus & Kitayama, 1991). Is it the case, as these quotations suggest, that the society in which one is raised affects the frequency of normative social influence? Perhaps not surprisingly, the answer is yes. Rod Bond and Peter Smith (1996) conducted a meta-analysis of 133 Asch line judgment studies conducted in 17 countries. Participants in collectivist cultures showed higher rates of conformity on the line task than did participants in individualist cultures. In fact, in individualist countries, including Canada (Lalancette & Standing, 1990), the rate of conformity in Asch-type studies has been declining. In contrast, in collectivist cultures conformity is a valued trait, not a negative one as in North America. Because emphasis is on the group and not the individual, people in such cultures value normative social influence because it promotes harmony and supportive relationships in the group (Guisinger & Blatt, 1994; Kim et al., 1994; Markus, Kitayama, & Heiman, 1996).

Resisting Normative Social Influence

Whereas normative social influence is often useful and appropriate, there are times when it is not. What can we do to resist inappropriate normative social influence? Fortunately, there are some strategies that work.

STOP AND THINK The best way to prevent ourselves from following the wrong social norm is to become more aware of what we are doing. If we stop and think carefully about whether the norm that seems to be operating is really the right one to follow, we will be more likely to recognize the times when it is not. Although this may sound overly simple, when we are facing conformity pressure, often our tendency is to mindlessly follow norms rather than stop and assess whether what we're doing is right. Being aware of normative influence and how it works can protect us from mindlessly going along with the crowd.

If you can get a few allies to agree with you, it's easier to buck the majority and believe some rather strange things. Ernst Zundel, a German Holocaust denier who was deported from Canada to Germany in 2005 for propagating hate, tries through his books and Web site to convince people that the Holocaust never happened, despite the massive amount of documented evidence to the contrary.

THE IMPORTANCE OF AN ALLY If you are in a situation in which you don't want to go along with the crowd but you fear the repercussions if you don't, try to find another person (or better yet, a group) who thinks the way you do. The importance of having an ally was demonstrated by Asch (1955). In a variation of his conformity experiment, he had six of the seven confederates give the wrong answer, while one confederate gave the right answer on every trial. Now the participant was not alone. Having even one ally dramatically helped him or her resist normative pressures. People conformed on an average of only 6 percent of the trials in this study, compared to 32 percent in the version where all confederates gave the wrong answer. Several other studies have found that observing another person resist normative social influence emboldens the individual to do the same (Allen & Levine, 1969; Morris & Miller, 1975; Nemeth & Chiles, 1988).

Thinking Critically

1. Groups of friends have their own social norms—expectations for how group members should think and act. Can you identify some of the social norms in your friendship group? What happens when one of your friends breaks a group norm? How does the group respond to the deviant?
2. To what extent do you think normative conformity affects your body image? Do you think you are immune from such pressures, or do you think they have affected how you feel about your appearance, now or when you were younger?

MINORITY INFLUENCE: WHEN THE FEW INFLUENCE THE MANY

We shouldn't end our discussion of social influence by leaving the impression that the individual never has an effect on the group. As Serge Moscovici (1985, 1994) says, if groups really did succeed in silencing nonconformists, rejecting deviants, and persuading everyone to go along with the majority point of view, then how could change ever be introduced into the system? We would all be like robots, marching along with everyone else in monotonous synchrony, never able to adapt to changing reality.

Instead, Moscovici (1985, 1994) argues, the individual, or the minority of group members, can influence the behaviour or beliefs of the majority. This is called **minority influence**. The key is consistency. People with minority views must express the same view over time, and different members of the minority must agree with each other. If a person in the minority wavers between two different viewpoints or if two individuals express different minority views, the majority will dismiss them as people who have peculiar and groundless opinions. If, however, the minority expresses a consistent, unwavering view, the majority is likely to take notice and may even adopt the minority view (Moscovici & Nemeth, 1974).

Before leaving this topic, we should note that minorities exert their influence on the group via informational social influence. (People in the minority can rarely influence others through normative means—the majority has little concern for how the minority views them.) The minority introduces new unexpected information to the group and causes the group to examine the issues more carefully. Such careful examination may cause the majority to realize that the minority view has merit, leading the group to adopt all or part of the minority's view (Wood et al., 1994).

Minority influence the case where a minority of group members influences the behaviour or beliefs of the majority

> Never let anyone keep you contained, and never let anyone keep your voice silent.
> —ADAM CLAYTON POWELL

FOCUS ON APPLICATIONS

Minority Influence in the Courtroom

In the classic movie *12 Angry Men*, a jury has just finished listening to the evidence in a murder case and all of the jurors except one vote to convict the defendant. However, over the next 90 minutes, the lone holdout, played by Henry Fonda, persuades his peers that there is reason to doubt that the young Hispanic defendant is guilty. At first, the other jurors pressure Fonda to change his mind (using techniques of normative and informational conformity), but in the end, reason triumphs and the other jurors come to see that Fonda is right. As entertaining as this movie is, research indicates that it does not reflect the reality of most jury deliberations (Ellsworth & Mauro, 1998; MacCoun, 1989).

Harry Kalven Jr. and Hans Zeisel (1966) interviewed members of more than 200 juries in actual criminal trials. In the vast majority of the cases (97 percent), the jury's final decision was the same as the one favoured by a majority of the jurors on the initial vote. The majority opinion usually carries the day, bringing dissenting jurors into line. And what happens if a dissenting juror does not succumb to pressure to go along with the majority opinion?

We have already discussed research showing that dissenters eventually may be rejected by the group (Schachter, 1951). Juries are no exception. Consider, for example, the case of Thomas Sophonow, a Vancouver man who was wrongfully convicted of the murder of Barbara Stoppel. In the third Sophonow trial, jurors were unable to reach a unanimous verdict after five long days of deliberation—apparently because one juror refused to go along with the rest of the group. In a startling move, the judge dismissed this juror because she supposedly had claimed to possess "psychic powers and special gifts." (The juror who was removed maintains that she said no such thing.) Once the problematic juror was removed, it took little time for the remaining 11 members to render a guilty verdict.

If jury deliberation is stacked toward the initial, majority opinion, why not just abandon the deliberation process, letting the jury's initial vote determine a defendant's guilt or innocence? For two reasons, this would not be a good idea. First, forcing juries to reach a unanimous verdict makes them consider the evidence more carefully, rather than simply assuming that their initial impressions of the case are correct (Hastie, Penrod, & Pennington, 1983). Second, even if minorities seldom succeed in persuading the majority to change their minds about guilt or innocence, minorities often do change people's minds about the degree of guilt. In criminal trials, juries usually have some discretion about the type of guilty verdict they can reach. Pennington and Hastie (1990) found that people on a jury who have a minority point of view often convince the majority to change their minds about the specific verdict to render. Thus, while a minority is unlikely to convince a majority to change its verdict from first-degree murder to not guilty, it might well convince the majority to change the verdict to second-degree murder.

Thinking Critically
Can you think of situations in which a minority managed to sway the opinions of the majority? What strategies for doing so seem most effective?

COMPLIANCE: REQUESTS TO CHANGE YOUR BEHAVIOUR

We can hardly make it through a day without a request from someone asking us to do something we would rather not do, be it a letter from a charity asking for money, a telephone call (invariably during dinner) from someone selling time-share vacation property, or a friend wanting to borrow $25. Social psychologists have studied when and why people are likely to conform to these kinds of requests. It turns out that there are several effective strategies for eliciting **compliance**—that is, a change in our behaviour due to a direct request from another person.

Compliance a change in behaviour due to a direct request from another person

The Door-in-the-Face Technique

Suppose you have agreed to go door to door and ask people to donate money to the Canadian Heart Association. Here is a good way to get people to give. First, ask people to donate a large amount of money, with the full expectation that they will refuse. When someone answers the door, you might say, "Hello, I'm asking for donations to the Canadian Heart Association. Do you think you could donate $500?" Once people refuse, you immediately retreat to a more reasonable request: "Well, okay, but do you think you could donate $5?" This approach is called the **door-in-the-face technique**, because the first request is purposefully so large that people will want to slam the door shut. Several studies show that it works well in getting people to agree to the second, more reasonable request

Door-in-the-face technique a technique to get people to comply with a request, whereby people are presented first with a large request, which they are expected to refuse, and then with a smaller, more reasonable request, to which it is hoped they will acquiesce

(Cialdini & Trost, 1998; Patch, Hoang, & Stahelski, 1997; Reeves et al., 1991; Wang, Brownstein, & Katzev, 1989).

For example, Robert Cialdini and colleagues (1975) decided to see whether they could get students to volunteer to chaperone problem adolescents on a two-hour trip to the zoo. When they approached students on a university campus, only 17 percent agreed to this request. In another condition, before asking people to go on the zoo trip, the experimenter made a very large request. The students were asked if they would be willing to work as unpaid counsellors at a juvenile detention centre. The experimenter went on to explain that the position would require two hours of their time per week and that they would have to make a commitment for a minimum of two years. Not surprisingly, no one agreed to such a large request. When students refused, the experimenter said, "Well, we also have another program you might be interested in," and went on to ask if they would chaperone the zoo trip. These students were three times more likely to agree to go on the zoo trip than were the students asked this smaller request alone (see Figure 6.3).

Why does the door-in-the-face technique work? The answer lies in the **reciprocity norm**, which says that if people do something nice for us, we should reciprocate by doing something nice for them (Cialdini, Green, & Rusch, 1992; Cialdini & Trost, 1998; Uehara, 1995; Whatley et al., 1999). Salespeople and charities often capitalize on this tendency for people to follow the reciprocity norm mindlessly. They give us a small gift, such as greeting cards, personalized address labels, or free food to taste in the grocery store. Their plan is to make us feel obligated to reciprocate by buying their product or giving money to their cause (Church, 1993; James & Bolstein, 1992). To illustrate how strong the reciprocity norm is—and how mindlessly people follow it—one researcher chose some

Reciprocity norm a social norm stating that receiving anything positive from another person requires you to reciprocate (or behave similarly) in response

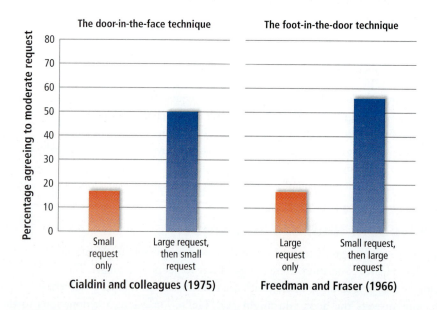

FIGURE 6.3 Two Ways to Increase Compliance with a Request

Both the door-in-the-face technique and the foot-in-the-door technique increase compliance to a moderate request. Which technique is likely to lead to the most long-term compliance, whereby people agree to repeated moderate requests? See the text for the answer.

(Adapted from Cialdini et al., 1975; Freedman & Fraser, 1966)

names at random out of the telephone book and sent each person a Christmas card, signed with his name (Kunz & Woolcott, 1976). Most people sent a card back to him, even though he was a complete stranger!

In the case of the door-in-the-face technique, the reciprocity norm is invoked when the person backs down from an extreme request to a smaller one. This puts pressure on us to reciprocate by moderating our position too—from an outright "no" to a "well, okay, I guess so." We feel as if the requester is doing us a favour by changing his or her position, trying to meet us halfway; because of the reciprocity norm, we then feel obligated to return the favour and appear reasonable, too.

The Foot-in-the-Door Technique

Imagine that you are participating in a study in order to fulfil your Introductory Psychology research requirement. At the end of the study, the experimenter asks if you would mind spending 5 or 10 minutes rating some materials for her next study. You agree to help her out. Then, she makes another request: Would you volunteer to spend a few extra hours participating in research—over and above the hours required for your research requirement—so that some graduate students can complete their studies?

This is a situation in which some University of Western Ontario students found themselves (Gorassini & Olson, 1995). They were participants in a study on the **foot-in-the-door technique**, a compliance technique in which people are presented first with a small request, to which they are expected to acquiesce, followed by a larger request, to which it is hoped they will also acquiesce. The expression *foot-in-the-door* comes from salespeople who discovered that they were more likely to make a sale if they could get the customer to agree to an initial, smaller request, such as letting them into the house to display their products. This technique is thus the opposite of the door-in-the-face method. Does this technique work?

In a classic study, Jonathan Freedman and Scott Fraser (1966) tested whether homeowners would agree to put up a large obtrusive sign in their front yards that said "Drive Carefully." When someone came to their door and asked the homeowners to do this, only 17 percent agreed. But what if they had agreed earlier to a smaller request? The researchers first asked a different group of homeowners to sign a petition indicating that they were in favour of safe driving. Just about everyone agreed to this innocuous request. Two weeks later, a different individual approached these homeowners and asked them to put the sign in their front yard. Though the sign was just as big and obtrusive to these people as to those in the control group, who had not been contacted earlier, they were more than three times more likely to agree to put it in their front yards.

Interestingly, it works for a very different reason than does the door-in-the-face technique. Instead of invoking a reciprocity norm, it triggers a change in self-perception. By agreeing to the small request, people come to view themselves as the kind of people who help others. Once this self-image is in place, it makes people more likely to agree to the second, larger request, even when it comes later. Thus, if you are collecting money for the Canadian Heart Association and want your neighbours to donate on a long-term basis, first ask them for a small amount, such as 50 cents or $1. If they agree, they will come to view themselves as the kind of people who give to this worthy cause, increasing the likelihood that future donations will be forthcoming (Burger, 1999; Cialdini, 1993; Cialdini, Trost, & Newsom, 1995; Dillard, 1991; Dolin & Booth-Butterfield, 1995).

Foot-in-the-door technique a technique to get people to comply with a request, whereby people are presented first with a small request, to which they are expected to acquiesce, followed by a larger request, to which it is hoped they will also acquiesce

We have shown that both the door-in-the-face and the foot-in-the-door techniques are effective at eliciting compliance. But when you are going door to door campaigning for the Canadian Heart Association, obviously you cannot use both of these techniques. Which should you choose? The answer is: "It depends." If you are soliciting a one-time donation, it probably doesn't matter. But, if you are hoping to create long-term change (create a neighbourhood in which people regularly contribute to good causes), you should go for the foot-in-the-door technique. The change in self-perception that accompanies having agreed to a small request seems to be relatively long-lasting, thereby increasing the chances of future compliance.

Lowballing

Lowballing an unscrupulous strategy whereby a salesperson induces a customer to agree to purchase a product at a very low cost, then subsequently raises the price; frequently, the customer will still make the purchase at the inflated price

Another technique for inducing compliance is called **lowballing** (Cialdini et al., 1978; Weyant, 1996). Robert Cialdini, a distinguished social psychologist, temporarily joined the sales force of an automobile dealership to observe this technique closely. Here's how it works: You enter an automobile showroom, intent on buying a particular car. Having already priced it at several dealerships, you know you can purchase it for about $22 000. You are approached by a personable, middle-aged man, who tells you he can sell you one for $20 000. Excited by the bargain, you agree to the deal and, at the salesperson's request, write out a cheque for the down payment.

You rub your hands in glee as you imagine yourself driving home in your shiny new bargain. But alas, 10 minutes later the salesperson returns, looking forlorn. He tells you that in his zeal to give you a good deal, he made an error in calculation and the sales manager caught it. The price of the car actually comes to $22 499. You are disappointed. Moreover, you are pretty sure you can get it a bit cheaper elsewhere. The decision to buy is not irrevocable. Yet, as research by Cialdini and colleagues (1978) suggests, far more people will go ahead with the deal than if the original asking price had been $22 499, even though the reason for purchasing the car from this particular dealer—the bargain price—no longer exists. Why?

There are at least three reasons that lowballing works. First, while the customer's decision to buy is certainly reversible, a commitment of sorts does exist, due to the act of signing a cheque for a down payment. This creates the illusion of irrevocability, even though, if the car buyer really thought about it, he or she would quickly realize it is a nonbinding contract. However, in the razzle-dazzle world of high-pressure sales, even temporary illusion can have powerful consequences. Second, this commitment triggered the anticipation of an exciting event: driving away with a new car. To thwart the anticipated event (by not going ahead with the deal) would produce disappointment. Third, although the final price is substantially higher than the customer thought it would be, it is probably only slightly higher than the price at another dealership. Under these circumstances, the customer in effect says, "Oh, what the heck. I'm already here, I've already filled out the forms, I've already written out the cheque—why wait?" And off he or she goes, in a shiny new car.

Thinking Critically

Think about the people at your school, and identify some aspect of their behaviour that you would like to change. How would you go about doing it using the three compliance techniques discussed in this chapter?

OBEDIENCE TO AUTHORITY

The kinds of compliance we have just discussed can be annoying; a skilful salesperson, for example, can make us buy something we don't really need. Rarely, however, do such instances of everyday compliance have life-or-death consequences. Yet, unfortunately, another kind of social influence can be extremely serious and even tragic—**obedience**, or conformity in response to the commands of an authority figure, to hurt or kill a fellow human being. Consider the My Lai massacre in Vietnam. On the morning of March 16, 1968, in the midst of the Vietnam War, a company of American soldiers boarded helicopters that would take them to the village of My Lai. One of the helicopter pilots radioed that he saw Vietcong soldiers below, and so the American soldiers jumped off the helicopters with rifles firing. They soon realized the pilot was wrong: There were no enemy soldiers. Instead, the soldiers found several villagers—all women, children, and elderly men—cooking their breakfast over small fires. Inexplicably, the leader of the platoon, Lieutenant William Calley, ordered one of the soldiers to kill the villagers. Other soldiers began firing, and the carnage spread. The Americans rounded up and systematically murdered all the villagers of My Lai. They shoved women and children into a ravine and shot them; they threw hand grenades into huts filled with cowering villagers. Though no one knows the exact number of deaths, the estimates range from 450 to 500 people (Hersch, 1970; Time, 1969).

Why did the soldiers obey Lieutenant Calley's order to kill innocent villagers? We suspect that all of the reasons people conform combined to produce this atrocity. The behaviour of the other soldiers made the killing seem like the right thing to do (informational influence); the soldiers wanted to avoid rejection and ridicule from their peers (normative influence); and the soldiers followed the obedience to authority social norm

Obedience conformity in response to the commands of an authority figure

> We all have the capacity for love and evil—to be Mother Teresa, to be Hitler or Saddam Hussein. It's the situation that brings that out.
>
> —PHILIP ZIMBARDO

Under strong social pressure, individuals will conform to the group, even when this means doing something immoral. During the Iraq war, American soldiers such as Lynndie England abused and tortured Iraqis in the Abu Ghraib prison. Why did the soldiers commit this atrocity? As you read this chapter, you will see how the social influence pressures of conformity and obedience can cause decent people to commit indecent acts.

too readily, without questioning or taking personal responsibility for what they were doing (mindless conformity). It was the power of these conformity pressures, not personality defects in the American soldiers, that led to the tragedy. This makes the incident all the more frightening because it implies that similar incidents can occur with any group of soldiers if similar conformity pressures are present. The atrocities committed by American soldiers in the Abu Ghraib prison in Iraq serve as a chilling reminder of this. These are not isolated examples. The twentieth century was marked by repeated atrocities and genocides—in Germany, Ukraine, Rwanda, Cambodia, Bosnia, Afghanistan, among other countries.

How can we be sure that it was social influence and not the work of evil people that produced these atrocities? The way to find out is to study social pressure in the laboratory under controlled conditions. We could take a sample of ordinary citizens, subject them to various kinds of social influence, and see to what extent they will conform and obey. Can an experimenter influence ordinary people to commit immoral acts, such as inflicting severe pain on an innocent bystander? Stanley Milgram (1963, 1974, 1976) decided to find out, in what has become the most famous series of studies in social psychology.

Imagine you were a participant in one of Milgram's studies. You answer an ad in the paper asking for participants in a study on memory and learning. When you arrive at the laboratory, you meet another participant, a 47-year-old, somewhat overweight, pleasant-looking fellow. The experimenter explains that one of you will play the role of a teacher and the other that of a learner. You draw a slip of paper out of a hat and discover that you will be the teacher. It turns out that your job is to teach the other participant a list of word pairs (blue–box, nice–day) and then test him on the list. The experimenter instructs you to deliver an electric shock to the learner whenever he makes a mistake, because the purpose of the study is to examine the effects of punishment on learning.

You watch as the other participant—the learner—is strapped into a chair in an adjacent room and electrodes are attached to his arm. You are seated in front of a shock generator whose 30 switches deliver varying levels of shock in 15-volt increments, from 15 to 450 volts. There are labels accompanying these switches, from "Slight Shock," to "Danger: Severe Shock," to an ominous "XXX" beside the highest levels (see the photos on the next page). The experimenter tells you that the first time the learner makes a mistake, you should give him a shock of 15 volts—the smallest amount—and then increase the amount by 15 volts for each subsequent mistake he makes. So that you will know what the shocks feel like, the experimenter gives you a sample shock of 45 volts, which is rather painful.

You read the list of word pairs to the learner and then begin the testing phase. Everything begins smoothly, as the learner gets the first few answers right. Then he gets some wrong and, as instructed, you deliver the shocks. At this point, you are probably becoming concerned about the number and severity of the shocks you will have to give. When you get to the 75-volt level, the learner, whom you can hear over an intercom, emits a painful "Ugh!" Perhaps you pause and ask the experimenter what you should do. "Please continue," he responds. As the learner continues to make mistakes, you deliver a few more shocks. The learner protests, shouting, "Ugh! That's all! Get me out of here!" You look at the experimenter with grave concern. He tells you, "It is absolutely essential that you continue." What would you do? How many people do you think would continue

Left: The shock generator used in the Milgram experiments. Right: The learner (an accomplice of the experimenter) is strapped into the chair and electrodes are attached to his arm. (Adapted from Milgram, 1974)

to obey the experimenter and increase the level of shock until they had delivered the maximum amount—450 volts?

When this question was posed to psychology majors at Yale University, they estimated that only about 1 percent of the population would go to this extreme. A sample of middle-class adults and a panel of psychiatrists made similar predictions. However, from our discussion of conformity thus far, you are probably not as optimistic. While no one would have believed that such travesties as the Holocaust or, more recently, the abuse of Iraqi prisoners in Abu Ghraib prison could have occurred, they did. Like the people who committed these horrific acts, most of Milgram's participants succumbed to the pressure of an authority figure. The average maximum amount of shock delivered was 360 volts, and 62.5 percent of the participants delivered the 450-volt shock—the maximum amount. A full 80 percent of the participants continued giving the shocks even after the learner, who earlier had mentioned that he had a heart condition, screamed, "Let me out of here! Let me out of here! My heart's bothering me. Let me out of here!... Get me out of here! I've had enough. I won't be in the experiment any more" (Milgram, 1974). (Note that the learner was an accomplice of the experimenter and did not actually receive any shocks.)

Why did so many research participants (who ranged in age from their twenties to their fifties and included blue-collar, white-collar, and professional workers) conform to the wishes of the experimenter, to the point that they (at least in their own minds) were inflicting great pain on another human being? Why were the students, middle-class adults, and psychiatrists so wrong in their predictions about what people would do? Each of the reasons that explain why people conform combined in a dangerous way, causing Milgram's participants to obey. Let's take a close look at how this worked in the Milgram experiments.

The Role of Normative Social Influence

First, it is clear that normative pressures made it difficult for people to refuse to continue. As we have seen, if someone really wants us to do something, it can be difficult to say no. This is particularly true when the person is in a position of authority over us. Milgram's participants probably believed that if they refused to continue, the experimenter would be disappointed, hurt, or maybe even angry—all of which put pressure on them to continue. It is important to note that this study, unlike the Asch study, was set up so the experimenter actively attempted to get people to conform, giving such stern commands as "It is absolutely essential that you continue." When an authority figure is so insistent that we

> When you think of the long and gloomy history of man, you will find more hideous crimes have been committed in the name of obedience than in the name of rebellion.
>
> —C. P. SNOW,
> Either-Or

obey, it is difficult to say no (Blass, 1993, 1996; Hamilton, Sanders, & McKearney, 1995; Miller, 1986).

The fact that normative pressures were present in the Milgram experiments is clear from a variation of the study he conducted. This time there were three teachers, two of whom were confederates of the experimenter. One confederate was instructed to read the list of word pairs; the other was instructed to tell the learner whether his response was correct. The (real) participant's job was to deliver the shocks, increasing their severity with each error, as in the original experiment. At 150 volts, when the learner gave his first vehement protest, the first confederate refused to continue despite the experimenter's command that he do so. At 210 volts, the second confederate refused to continue. The result? Seeing their peers disobey made it much easier for the actual participant to disobey as well. In this experiment, only 10 percent of the participants gave the maximum level of shock (see Figure 6.4). This result is similar to Asch's finding that people did not conform nearly as much when one accomplice bucked the majority and consistently gave the correct answer.

The Role of Informational Social Influence

Despite the power of the normative pressures in Milgram's original study, they are not the sole reason people complied. The experimenter was authoritative and insistent, but he did not point a gun at participants and tell them to "conform or else." The participants were free to get up and leave any time they wanted to. Why didn't they, especially when the experimenter was a stranger they had never met before and probably would never see again?

As we saw earlier, when people are in a confusing situation and unsure of what they should do, they use other people to reach a definition of the situation. Informational social influence is especially powerful when the situation is ambiguous, when it is a crisis, and when the other people in the situation have some expertise. The situation faced by Milgram's participants was clearly confusing, unfamiliar, and upsetting. It all seemed straightforward enough when the experimenter explained it to them, but then it turned into something else altogether. The learner cried out in pain, but the experimenter told the participant that while the shocks were painful they did not cause any permanent tissue damage. The participant didn't want to hurt anyone, but he or she had agreed to be in the study and to follow directions. When in such a state of conflict, it was only natural for the participants to use an expert—the experimenter—to help them decide what they should do (Darley, 1995; Krakow & Blass, 1995; Meeus & Raaijmakers, 1995).

Another version of the experiment that Milgram performed supports the idea that informational influence was operative. This version was identical to the original one except for two critical changes. First, the experimenter never said which shock levels were to be given, leaving this decision up to the teacher (the real participant). Second, the situation was arranged so the experimenter was "unexpectedly" called away from the experiment. The participant was instructed to carry on, and another "teacher"—actually a confederate who was supposedly there to record how long it took the learner to respond—said that he had just thought of a good system: How about if they increased the level of shock each time the learner made a mistake? He insisted that the real participant follow this procedure.

Note that in this situation, the expertise of the person giving the commands has been removed. And in this situation, people were much less likely to use the non-expert as a source of information about how they should respond. As seen in Figure 6.4, in this ver-

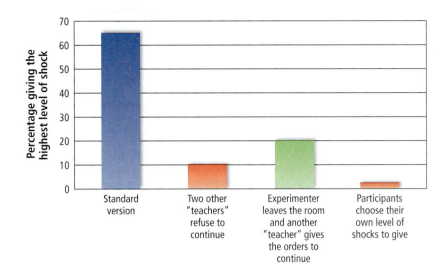

FIGURE 6.4 The Results of Different Versions of the Milgram Experiment

Obedience is highest in the standard version, where the participant is ordered to deliver increasing levels of shock to another person (left panel). Obedience drops when other participants model disobedience or when the authority figure is not present (two middle panels). Finally, when no orders are given to increase the shocks, almost no participants do so (right panel). The contrast in behaviour between the far-left and far-right panels indicates just how powerful the social norm of obedience is.

(Adapted from Milgram, 1974)

sion compliance dropped from 65 percent giving the maximum amount of shock to only 20 percent. (The fact that 20 percent still complied suggests that some people were so uncertain about what to do that they used even a non-expert as a guide.)

An additional variation conducted by Milgram underscores the importance of authority figures as experts in eliciting such conformity and obedience. In this variation, two experimenters gave the real participants their orders. At 150 volts, when the learner first cried out that he wanted to stop, the two experimenters began to disagree about whether they should continue the study. At this point, 100 percent of the participant–teachers stopped responding. Note that nothing the victim ever did caused all of the participants to stop obeying; however, when the authorities' definition of the situation became unclear, the participants broke out of their conforming role.

These studies demonstrate that social pressures can combine in insidious ways to make humane people act in an inhumane manner. According to Philip Zimbardo (quoted in Dittman, 2004), a well-known social psychologist and former president of the American Psychological Association, the findings of Milgram's obedience studies provide insight into the horrific mistreatment and deaths of prisoners in Iraq's Abu Ghraib prison. Zimbardo argues that many of the conditions that promoted inflicting pain on the learner in the Milgram experiments applied to the Iraq situation: The American soldiers were in an unfamiliar, ambiguous situation in which the rules kept changing. The soldiers feared repercussions if they did not comply with orders from authority figures to torture or kill. In most cases, the abuse began gradually, and then escalated to more extreme forms. The soldiers did not feel personally responsible for their behaviour, and so on. In short, the conditions that were found to produce evil in the Milgram experiments, conducted more than 30 years ago, were reproduced in the Abu Ghraib prison. And in this real-world context, the results were even more tragic. Sadly, the words of Stanley Milgram (1976) still apply to the kinds of atrocities, such as the treatment of the Iraqi prisoners, we are witnessing today:

> Even [Adolf] Eichmann was sickened when he toured the concentration camps, but in order to participate in mass murder he had only to sit at a desk and shuffle papers. At the same time the man in the camp who actually dropped Cyclon-B into the gas chambers is able to justify his behaviour on the grounds that he is only following orders from above. Thus there is fragmentation of the total human act; no one man decides to carry out the evil act and is confronted with its consequences. The person who assumes full responsibility for the act has evaporated. Perhaps this is the most common characteristic of socially organized evil in modern society.

Thinking Critically

Why are people so obedient to authority figures, even when they are being ordered to commit heinous acts? Which explanation presented in this chapter do you believe best answers the "why" question?

Summary

In this chapter, we focus on **conformity**, or how people change their behaviour due to the real (or imagined) influence of others. We found that there are two main reasons people conform: informational and normative social influences.

Informational social influence occurs when people look to the behaviour of others as an important source of information and use it to choose appropriate courses of action for themselves. This reaction typically occurs in *ambiguous*, *confusing*, or *crisis* situations, where the definition of the situation is unclear. *Experts* are powerful sources of influence, since they typically have the most information about appropriate responses.

Normative social influence occurs for a different reason. We change our behaviour to match that of others not because they seem to know better what is going on, but because we want to remain a member of the group, continue to gain the advantages of group membership, and avoid the pain of ridicule and rejection. We conform to the group's **social norms**—implicit or explicit rules for acceptable behaviours, values, and attitudes. Normative social influence can occur even in unambiguous situations; people will conform to others for normative reasons even if they know that what they are doing is wrong. Normative social influence is apparent in societal messages about the ideal body image for women and men, thereby contributing to feelings of dissatisfaction with one's body and negative behaviours such as eating disorders and steroid use.

Whereas informational social influence usually results in **private acceptance**, wherein people genuinely believe in what other people are doing or saying, normative social influence usually results in **public compliance** but not private acceptance of other people's ideas and behaviours.

Social impact theory specifies when normative social influence is most likely to occur, by referring to the *strength*, *immediacy*, and *number* of the group members. We are more likely to conform when the group is one we care about, when the group members are unanimous in their thoughts or behaviours, and when the group size is three or more.

Minority influence, whereby a minority of group members influences the beliefs and behaviour of the majority, can occur under certain conditions. To influence a majority, minority group members must present their views consistently. Minorities influence majorities via informational social influence.

Another form of social influence is **compliance**—conforming in response to requests from others. An effective compliance technique is the **door-in-the-face technique**, where a requester starts out with a big request in order to get people to agree to a second, smaller request. This technique works because of the **reciprocity norm**; when the requester retreats from the larger to the smaller request, it puts pressure on people to reciprocate by agreeing to the smaller request. The **foot-in-the-door technique** is also effective; here the requester starts out with a very small request to get people to agree to a larger request. Another effective compliance technique is **lowballing**, in which a person makes a commitment to an attractive offer. The deal is then changed so the offer is no longer as attractive. Nevertheless, the person tends to go along with this much less attractive deal.

One of the most insidious forms of social influence is **obedience**—conforming to the commands of an authority figure. In Milgram's classic study of obedience, informational and normative pressures combined to cause chilling levels of obedience, to the point that a majority of participants administered what they thought were near-lethal shocks to a fellow human being. Unfortunately, the conditions that produced such extreme antisocial behaviour in Milgram's laboratory have been present in real-life tragedies, such as the Holocaust and the treatment of Iraqi prisoners in Abu Ghraib.

Key Terms

Compliance   (page 177)
Conformity   (page 162)
Door-in-the-face technique   (page 177)
Foot-in-the-door technique   (page 179)
Informational social influence   (page 163)
Lowballing   (page 180)
Minority influence   (page 176)
Normative social influence   (page 167)
Obedience   (page 181)
Private acceptance   (page 164)
Public compliance   (page 164)
Reciprocity norm   (page 178)
Social impact theory   (page 173)
Social norms   (page 167)

Key Online Search Terms

Informational social influence
Normative social influence
Private acceptance
Public compliance
Door-in-the-face technique
Foot-in-the-door technique
Lowballing
Obedience to authority

If You Are Interested

Cialdini, R. B. (1993). *Influence: Science and practice* (3rd ed.). New York: HarperCollins. An extremely readable and entertaining account of research on conformity, with applications to everyday life.

Lumet, Sydney (Director). (1957). *12 angry men* [Film]. A gripping account of jury deliberations, this film stars Henry Fonda as the lone dissenter on a jury, desperately trying to convince his peers that their judgment of guilty in a murder case is wrong.

Milgram, S. (1974). *Obedience to authority: An experimental view*. New York: Harper & Row. A detailed description of the most famous studies in social psychology: those in which people were induced to deliver what they believed were lethal shocks to a fellow human being. Thirty years after it was published, Milgram's book remains a poignant and insightful account of obedience to authority.

Zanna, M. P., Olson, J. M., & Herman, C. P. (1987). *Social influence: The Ontario Symposium* (Vol. 5). Hillsdale, NJ: Lawrence Erlbaum. A collection of papers by prominent social psychologists, presented at the University of Waterloo as part of the 1984 Ontario Symposium series. The chapters in Part II of this volume, Compliance and Conformity, are especially relevant to this chapter.

Weblinks

www.ex.ac.uk/~PWebley/psy1002/asch.html
The Asch Effect
This site provides a brief discussion and summary of follow-up research on the Asch conformity studies.

www.science.wayne.edu/~wpoff/cor/grp/influenc.html
Influence
This site provides a concise but thorough overview of social psychological principles and research on influence.

Chapter 6 Practice Quiz

Check your knowledge of the concepts in this chapter by trying the following questions.

INFORMATIONAL SOCIAL INFLUENCE: THE NEED TO KNOW WHAT IS "RIGHT"

Multiple Choice

1. Sherif's (1936) autokinetic studies looked at
    a. private acceptance.
    b. public compliance.
    c. groupthink.
    d. ambiguity.

2. What was ironic about Sherif's autokinetic study was that
    a. the light moved far less than was perceived by participants.
    b. the light moved far more than was perceived by participants.
    c. the light actually did not move at all.
    d. the light was irrelevant to the experiment; noise was the critical factor.

3. In the Sherif autokinetic study, the number of trials with other group members required for the estimate of movement to converge was
    a. one.
    b. two.
    c. three.
    d. zero; individual and group estimates were always the same.

4. People are more likely to conform when
    a. situations are clear-cut.
    b. there is a crisis.
    c. an expert is absent.
    d. all of the above

True or False

5. We conform to others because we are weak and unable to stand up for what we believe.
    ___ True
    ___ False

6. Brainwashing is an extreme case of informational social influence.
    ___ True
    ___ False

Fill in the Blank

7. _____ is when people conform to others' behaviour because they believe it to be correct.
8. Believing that others are a source of information to guide our behaviour is _____.

NORMATIVE SOCIAL INFLUENCE: THE NEED TO BE ACCEPTED

Multiple Choice

9. Social impact theory depends on which of the following?
    a. how important the group is
    b. how close the group is in space and time
    c. how many are in the group
    d. all of the above

10. In a classic 1951 study, Schachter asked groups of students to read and discuss a case history of a juvenile delinquent. A confederate of the experimenter argued the juvenile delinquent should receive the harshest amount of punishment. The group members' reaction to the confederate was
    a. to change their opinions to be consistent with the confederate.
    b. to change their opinions but also to isolate the confederate.
    c. to ignore the confederate and punish him for being deviant.
    d. to assign to the confederate the important tasks for future discussions.

11. People conformed in the Asch studies because they feared
    a. the experimenter.
    b. being seen as part of the group.
    c. being seen as different from other group members.
    d. being accused of not understanding the experimental task.

12. Tafarodi and colleagues (2002) reminded minority participants of their distinctive appearance before completing a rating task by
    a. flashing their minority membership on a computer screen.
    b. having the ratings done in front of a mirror.
    c. asking participants to invite a friend from their minority group to take part.
    d. having participants announce their minority group membership to others.

True or False

13. The best way to prevent conformity from social influence is to find an ally.
    ___ True
    ___ False

14. Men who read fitness magazines are more likely to engage in dangerous behaviours such as steroid use.
    ___ True
    ___ False

Fill in the Blank

15. _____ study is an example of normative social influence.
16. _____ are rules made by a group regarding good behaviour, values, and beliefs.

COMPLIANCE: REQUESTS TO CHANGE YOUR BEHAVIOUR

Multiple Choice

17. _____ is a change in behaviour due to another's request.
    a. Compliance
    b. Conformity
    c. Social decency
    d. Social confusion

18. Which of the following is not a compliance technique?
    a. lowballing
    b. the door-in-the-foot technique
    c. the door-in-the-face technique
    d. the foot-in-the-door technique

19. If a friend asked you to loan her $1000 and, if you refused, then asked for $50, this would be an example of
    a. lowballing.
    b. the door-in-the-foot technique.
    c. the door-in-the-face technique.
    d. the foot-in-the-door technique.

True or False

20. The foot-in-the-door technique operates on the reciprocity norm.
    ___ True
    ___ False

21. Lowballing will not work when selling a car if the price of the car is much higher than at another dealership.
    ___ True
    ___ False

22. If you are soliciting for this donation and future donations, you should use the foot-in-the-door technique over the door-in-the-face technique.
    ___ True
    ___ False

Fill in the Blank

23. _____ presents people with a smaller request in order to get them to agree to a larger request.
24. _____ is a social norm operating on a principle similar to the golden rule.

OBEDIENCE TO AUTHORITY

Multiple Choice

25. _____ caused the people in Milgram's experiment to conform.
    a. Normative social influence alone
    b. Informational social influence alone
    c. A combination of normative and information social influence
    d. Personality factors

26. Seeing a confederate refuse to continue in the Milgram study despite the experimenter's instructions is an example of
    a. normative social influence.
    b. informational social influence.
    c. the role of personality factor.
    d. all of the above

True or False

27. The Milgram study has little to say about obedience in the 21st century.
    ___ True
    ___ False

28. Milgram's experiment has not been found to be applicable to obedience situations today.
    ___ True
    ___ False

Fill in the Blank

29. _____ involves responding to an authority figure.
30. An important variable in the Milgram experiment was the presence of an _____ .

PERSONALIZED STUDY PLAN

Want to check your answers and access more study resources? Visit the Companion Website for *Fundamentals of Social Psychology* at **www.pearsoned.ca/aronson**, where you'll find the above questions incorporated in a pre-test and post-test for each chapter. These tests will be automatically graded online, allowing you to check your answers. A Study Plan, like the one below, groups the questions by section within the chapter and shows you which sections you need to focus on for further study.

Your Results for "Chapter 6, Pretest"

OVERALL SCORE: 74% of 19 questions

Group	Score	Proficient
Informational Social Influence	3 of 4	Yes
Normative Social Influence	5 of 6	Yes
Compliance	3 of 5	No
Obedience to Authority	3 of 4	Yes

CHAPTER

7

Group Processes: Influence in Social Groups

Chapter Outline

DEFINITIONS: WHAT IS A GROUP?
Why Do People Join Groups?
The Composition and Function of Groups

HOW GROUPS INFLUENCE THE BEHAVIOUR OF INDIVIDUALS
Social Facilitation: When the Presence of Others Energizes Us
Social Loafing: When the Presence of Others Relaxes Us
Deindividuation: Getting Lost in the Crowd

GROUP DECISIONS: ARE TWO (OR MORE) HEADS BETTER THAN ONE?
Process Loss: When Group Interactions Inhibit Good Problem Solving
Group Polarization: Going to Extremes
Leadership in Groups

CONFLICT AND COOPERATION
Using Threats to Resolve Conflict
Negotiation and Bargaining

In 1998, Canadian military officials made a decision to vaccinate Canadian soldiers against anthrax, a deadly biological weapon, before being deployed to the Gulf War. One soldier who had served in the military for 26 years, Sergeant Michael Kipling, refused to be vaccinated. He had serious concerns about health risks associated with the drug. For his disobedience, Kipling was court-martialled.

During the court martial, several facts came to light. One was that the anthrax vaccine was not licensed for use in Canada, and therefore Health Canada had recommended that the military seek informed consent from soldiers before administering the drug. Another was that the military's legal advisers had made a similar recommendation. However, Canada's highest military commanders decided to ignore the advice of both Health Canada and their own lawyers and imposed the vaccine on soldiers without their consent.

Louise Richard before and after her tour of duty in the Gulf War. She believes that the anthrax vaccine is responsible for her mysterious illnesses.

One consequence of this decision is the debate that rages over whether medical symptoms experienced by half of the 4500 Canadians involved in the Gulf War are the result of the anthrax vaccine. Louise Richard, for example, was a healthy, athletic military nurse when she left for the Gulf in 1991. Now she is too ill to work. She suffers from fatigue, depression, memory loss, gastrointestinal problems, and excessive bleeding. She also has lost all of her hair and has started to lose her teeth. Military officials blame such symptoms on stress and possible exposure to chemical warfare. People like Michael Kipling and Louise Richard believe that the anthrax vaccine is to blame.

There was yet another, very serious, consequence of the military's decision to impose the vaccine on soldiers. According to Canada's chief military judge, Colonel Guy Brais, who presided over Michael Kipling's court martial, this decision violated the human rights of soldiers. In his decision, Judge Brais agreed with the defence that the vaccine Kipling had been ordered to take could have been unsafe, and that his common law and Charter rights were therefore violated. In his words, "The government... could never be justified to impose inoculation of soldiers with unsafe and dangerous vaccines" (Edmonds, 2000).

Why would military officials ignore the advice of Health Canada and their own lawyers and impose a potentially unsafe vaccine on Canadian soldiers? Surely Canada's top military commanders wouldn't be prepared to place Canadian soldiers at risk? And surely they wouldn't want to administer a possibly dangerous substance without obtaining informed consent from the soldiers? Or would they? In this chapter, we will focus on how people interact in groups, and how groups can end up making decisions that have tragic consequences.

DEFINITIONS: WHAT IS A GROUP?

Group a collection of two or more people who interact with each other and are interdependent, in the sense that their needs and goals cause them to rely on each other

Six students sitting around a table in the library are not a group. But if they meet to study for their social psychology test together, they are. A **group** is defined as a collection of two or more people who interact with each other and are interdependent, in the sense that their needs and goals cause them to rely on one another (Cartwright & Zander, 1968; Lewin, 1948). Thus, groups are more than a bunch of people who happen to be occupying the same space. Rather, groups are people who have assembled together for a common purpose, such as citizens meeting to solve a community problem, or people who have gathered to blow off steam at a party.

Stop for a moment to think of the number of groups to which you belong. Don't forget to include your family, campus groups, community groups (such as churches or synagogues), sports teams, and more temporary groups (such as your classmates in a small seminar). All of these count as groups because you interact with the other group members and you are interdependent, in the sense that you influence them and they influence you.

Why Do People Join Groups?

Why do people join groups? Forming relationships with other people fulfills a number of basic human needs. So basic, in fact, that there may be an innate need to belong to social groups. Roy Baumeister and Mark Leary (1995) argue that in our evolutionary past there was a substantial survival advantage to establishing bonds with other people. People who bonded together were better able to hunt for and grow food, find mates, and care for children. Consequently, the need to belong has become innate and is present in all societies. Consistent with this view, people in all cultures are motivated to form relationships with other people and to resist the dissolution of these relationships (Gardner, Pickett, & Brewer, 2000; Manstead, 1997).

Groups have a number of other benefits. As we saw in Chapter 6, other people can be an important source of information, helping us resolve ambiguity about the social world. Groups become an important part of our identity as well, helping us define who we are—witness the number of times people wear clothing with the name of their group (volleyball team, the name of their school) emblazoned on it.

The Composition and Function of Groups

The groups to which you belong probably vary in size from two or three members to several dozen members. Most social groups, however, range in size from two to six members (Desportes & Lemaine, 1998; Levine & Moreland, 1998). This is due in part to our definition of social groups as involving interaction between members. If groups become too large, you cannot interact with all of the members; for example, the college or university you attend is not a social group, because you are unlikely to meet and interact with every student there.

Another important feature of groups is that the members tend to be alike in age, sex, beliefs, and opinions (George, 1990; Levine & Moreland, 1998; Magaro & Ashbrook, 1985). The reason for this is twofold: First, groups tend to attract people who are similar to one another to begin with. Second, group members also become more similar to one another over time (Moreland, 1987).

SOCIAL ROLES Most groups also have well-defined **social roles**, which are shared expectations about how particular people are supposed to behave. Whereas norms specify how all group members should behave, roles specify how people who occupy certain positions in the group should behave. A boss and an employee in a business occupy different roles and are expected to act in different ways in that setting. Like social norms, roles can be very helpful, because people know what to expect from each other. When members of a group follow a set of clearly defined roles, they tend to be satisfied and perform well (Barley & Bechky, 1994; Bastien & Hostager, 1988).

There are, however, two potential costs to social roles. First, people can get so "into" a role that their personal identities and personalities are lost. Suppose, for example, that you agreed to take part in a two-week psychology experiment in which you were randomly assigned to play the role of either a prison guard or a prisoner in a simulated prison. You might think that the role you were assigned to play would not be very important; after all, everyone knows it is only an experiment and that people are just pretending to be guards or prisoners. Philip Zimbardo and his colleagues, however, had a different hypothesis. They believed that social roles can be so powerful that they "take over" our personal identities, and we become the role we are playing. In one of the most famous studies in social

Social roles shared expectations in a group about how particular people are supposed to behave

classic research

psychology, Zimbardo and colleagues built a mock prison in the basement of the psychology department at Stanford University and paid students to play the role of guard or prisoner (Haney, Banks, & Zimbardo, 1973). The role students played was determined by the flip of a coin. The guards were outfitted with a uniform of khaki shirts and pants, a whistle, a police nightstick, and reflecting sunglasses; the prisoners were outfitted with a loose-fitting smock with an identification number stamped on it, rubber sandals, a cap made from a nylon stocking, and a locked chain attached to one ankle.

The researchers planned to observe the students for two weeks, to see whether they began to act like real prison guards and prisoners. As it turned out, the students quickly assumed these roles—so much so that the researchers had to end the experiment after only six days. Many of the guards became quite abusive, thinking of creative ways of verbally harassing and humiliating the "prisoners." The prisoners became passive, helpless, and withdrawn. Some prisoners, in fact, became so anxious and depressed that they had to be released from the study earlier than others. Remember, everyone knew they were in a psychology experiment and that the "prison" was only make-believe. However, people got "into" their roles so much that their personal identities and sense of decency somehow were lost.

In Chapter 6, we referred to Philip Zimbardo's observation that many of the factors that contributed to the high levels of obedience in the classic Milgram study also were present in the recent abuse of Iraqi prisoners in Abu Ghraib prison. Zimbardo also believes that the same psychological processes that operated in his "mock" prison, set up in a university basement more than 30 years ago, were present in Abu Ghraib—the role of prison guard, the anonymity, and the dehumanization of the prisoners all contributed to the tragic loss of decency among the Americans in charge of the prison (Dittman, 2004).

Philip Zimbardo and his colleagues randomly assigned students to play the role of prisoner or guard in a mock prison. The students assumed these roles all too well. Those playing the role of guard became quite aggressive, whereas those playing the role of prisoner became passive, helpless, and withdrawn. People got "into" their roles so much that their personal identities and sense of decency somehow were lost.

The second potential drawback of social roles is that there is a cost to acting inconsistently with the expectations associated with them. The next time you report to your job, try telling your boss that you are going to decide what she should do that day. Role expectations are especially problematic when they are arbitrary or unfair. All societies, for example, have expectations about how people who occupy the roles of women and men should behave. As we discuss in Chapter 10, these role expectations can constrain the way people behave and result in negative attitudes toward people who decide to act inconsistently with the role they are expected to play.

Thinking Critically

Think of several groups you belong to. Do these groups meet the definition of a group presented in the text? What kinds of benefits do you receive from being a member of these groups?

HOW GROUPS INFLUENCE THE BEHAVIOUR OF INDIVIDUALS

Do you act differently when other people are around? Simply being in the presence of other people can have a variety of effects on our behaviour. We will begin by looking at how a group affects your performance on something with which you are very familiar: taking a test in a class.

Social Facilitation: When the Presence of Others Energizes Us

It is time for the final exam in your psychology class. You have spent countless hours studying the material, and you feel ready. When you arrive, you see that the exam is scheduled in a tiny, packed room. You squeeze into an empty desk, elbow to elbow with your classmates. The professor arrives and says that if any students are bothered by the close quarters, they can take the test by themselves in one of several smaller rooms down the hall. What should you do?

The question is whether the mere presence of others will affect your performance (Geen, 1989; Guerin, 1993; Kent, 1994; Sanna, 1992). The mere presence of other people can take one of two forms: (a) performing a task with others who are doing the same thing you are, or (b) performing a task in front of an audience that is not doing anything except observing you. The point is that in either case, you are not interacting with these other people—they're just present in the same room, constituting a nonsocial group. Does their presence make a difference? If you take your exam in the crowded room, will you feel nervous and have trouble recalling the material? Or will the presence of classmates motivate you to do even better than if you took the test alone?

To answer this question, we need to talk about insects—cockroaches, in fact. Believe it or not, a classic study using cockroaches as research participants suggests an answer to the question of how you should take your psychology test. Zajonc, Heingartner, and Herman (1969) built a contraption to see how cockroaches' behaviour was influenced by the presence of their peers. The researchers placed a bright light (which cockroaches dislike) at the end of a runway and timed how long it took a roach to escape the light by running to the other end, where it could scurry into a darkened box. As it happened, the individual cockroaches performed the task faster when they were in the presence of other roaches than when they were by themselves.

Now, we would not give advice, based on one study that used cockroaches, on how you should take your psychology test. But the story does not end here. There have been dozens of studies on the effects of the mere presence of other people, involving human beings as well as other species such as ants and birds (e.g., Bond & Titus, 1983; Guerin, 1986; Rajecki, Kidd, & Ivins, 1976; Zajonc & Sales, 1966). There is a remarkable consistency to the findings of these studies. As long as the task is a relatively simple, well-learned one—as escaping a light is for cockroaches—the mere presence of others improves performance. For example, in one of the first social psychology experiments ever done, Norman Triplett (1898) asked children to wind up fishing line on a reel, either by themselves or in the presence of other children. They did so faster when in the presence of other children.

SIMPLE VERSUS DIFFICULT TASKS Before concluding that you should stay in the crowded classroom to take your exam, we need to consider another issue: What happens when we give people a more difficult task to do and place them in the presence of others? To find out, Zajonc and colleagues (1969) included another condition in the cockroach experiment. This time, the cockroaches had to solve a maze that had several runways, only one of which led to the darkened box. When working on this more difficult task, the opposite pattern of results occurred: The roaches took longer to solve it when other roaches were present than when they were alone. Many other studies have also found that people and animals do worse in the presence of others when the task is difficult (e.g., Bond & Titus, 1983; Geen, 1989).

> Mere social contact begets...a stimulation of the animal spirit that heightens the efficiency of each individual workman.
> —KARL MARX,
> Das Kapital, 1867

FOCUS ON APPLICATIONS

Performance in the Pool Hall: Does It Matter Whether Other People Are Watching You?

Suppose that you decide to stop at a local pool hall and shoot a few racks. Will you perform better or worse if people are watching you wield your pool cue? As we have seen, it should depend on whether shooting pool is a simple or complex task for you. This is what James Michaels and colleagues (1982) found in a field study conducted in the pool hall of a university student union. A team of four students observed several different players from a distance, until they found ones who were experienced (defined as those who made at least two-thirds of their shots) or novices (defined as those who made no more than one-third of their shots). They then casually approached the table and watched people play.

Imagine that you are one of the players. There you are, shooting a little pool, when suddenly you notice four strangers standing around watching you. What will happen to your performance? The prediction made by social facilitation theory is clear. If you have played so much pool that you would feel comfortable challenging Cliff Thorburn or Minnesota Fats, the arousal caused by the presence of others should improve your game. If you are a novice and feel as if you are all thumbs, the arousal caused by the presence of others should make your game go to pieces. This is exactly what Michaels and colleagues (1982) found. The novices made significantly fewer of their shots when they were observed, whereas the experts made significantly more of their shots.

AROUSAL AND THE DOMINANT RESPONSE In an influential article published in 1965, Robert Zajonc offered an elegant theoretical explanation for why the presence of others facilitates a well-learned or dominant response but inhibits a less practised or new response. His argument has two steps. First, the presence of others increases physiological arousal (our bodies become more energized), and second, when such arousal exists, it is easier to do something that is simple (called the dominant response) but harder to do something complex or learn something new. Consider, for example, something that is second nature to you, such as riding a bicycle or writing your name. Arousal, caused by the presence of other people watching you, should make it even easier to perform these well-learned behaviours. But let's say you have to do something more complex, such as learning a new sport or working on a difficult math problem. Now arousal will lead you to feel flustered and do less well than if you were alone. This phenomenon became known as **social facilitation**, which is the tendency for people to do better on simple tasks and worse on complex tasks when they are in the presence of others and their individual performance can be evaluated.

WHY THE PRESENCE OF OTHERS CAUSES AROUSAL Why does the presence of others lead to arousal? Researchers have developed three theories to explain the role of arousal in social facilitation. Other people cause us to become particularly alert and vigilant; they make us apprehensive about how we're being evaluated; and they distract us from the task at hand.

The first explanation suggests that the presence of other people makes us more alert. When we are by ourselves reading a book, we don't have to pay attention to anything but the book; we don't have to worry that the lamp will ask us a question. When someone else is in the room, however, we have to be alert to the possibility that he or she will do something that requires us to respond. Because people are less predictable than lamps, we are

Social facilitation the tendency for people to do better on simple tasks and worse on complex tasks when they are in the presence of others and their individual performance can be evaluated

Research on social facilitation finds that people do better at a well-learned task when in the presence of others than when they are alone. Actors, like these cast members of London's Globe Theatre, who know their lines well, should perform better when the theatre is full than when it is empty.

in a state of greater alertness in their presence. This alertness, or vigilance, causes mild arousal. The beauty of this explanation (which is the one preferred by Robert Zajonc [1980]) is that it explains both the animal and the human studies. A solitary cockroach need not worry about what the cockroach in the next room is doing. However, it needs to be alert when in the presence of another member of its species—and the same goes for human beings.

The second explanation focuses on the fact that people are not cockroaches and are often concerned about how others are evaluating them. When other people can see how you are doing, the stakes are raised: You feel as if the other people are evaluating you and you will feel embarrassed if you do poorly and pleased if you do well. This concern about being judged, called *evaluation apprehension,* can cause mild arousal. According to this view, then, it is not the mere presence of others, but the presence of others who are evaluating us that causes arousal and subsequent social facilitation (Blascovich et al., 1999; Bond, Atoum, & VanLeeuwen, 1996; Cottrell, 1968).

The third explanation centres on how distracting other people can be (Baron, 1986; Huguet et al., 1999; Sanders, 1983). It is similar to Robert Zajonc's (1980) notion that we need to be alert when in the presence of others, except that it focuses on the idea that any source of distraction—be it the presence of other people or noise from the party going on in the apartment upstairs—will put us in a state of conflict, because it is difficult to concentrate on what we are doing. Trying to pay attention to two things at once produces arousal, as anyone knows who has ever tried to read the newspaper while a two-year-old clamours for attention. Consistent with this interpretation, Robert Baron (1986) found that nonsocial sources of distraction, such as a flashing light, cause the same kinds of social facilitation effects as does the presence of other people.

We have summarized research on social facilitation in the top half of Figure 7.1. (We will discuss the bottom half of the figure in a moment.) This figure illustrates that there is more than one reason that the presence of other people is arousing. The consequences of this arousal, however, are the same. When an individual is around other people, that individual does better on tasks that are simple and well learned, but worse on tasks that are complex and require them to learn something new.

We can now conclude that you should take your psychology exam in the presence of your classmates, assuming you know the material well, so that it is relatively simple for you to recall it. The arousal produced by being elbow to elbow with your classmates should improve your performance. We can also conclude, however, that when you study for an exam—that is, when you learn new material—you should do so by yourself, and not in the presence of others. In this situation, the arousal caused by others will make it more difficult to concentrate on the new material.

Social Loafing: When the Presence of Others Relaxes Us

When you take your psychology exam, your individual efforts will be evaluated (you will be graded on the test). Often when you are in the presence of others, however, your efforts cannot be distinguished from those of the people around you. Such is the case when you clap after a concert (no one can tell how loudly you are clapping) or when you play an instrument in a band (your instrument blends in with the others).

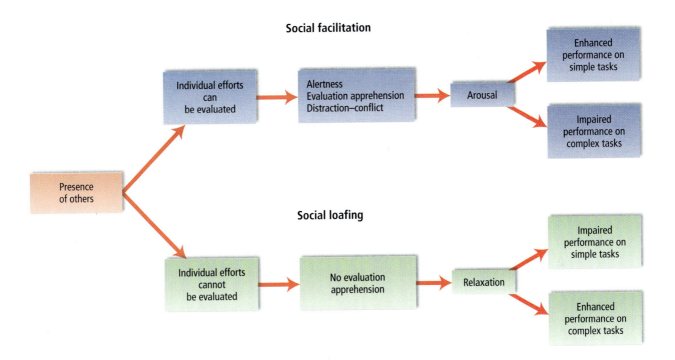

FIGURE 7.1 Social Facilitation and Social Loafing

The presence of others can lead to social facilitation or social loafing. The important variables that distinguish the two are evaluation, arousal, and the complexity of the task.

(Adapted from Cottrell et al., 1968)

These situations are just the opposite of the kinds of social facilitation settings we have just considered. In social facilitation, the presence of others puts the spotlight on you, making you aroused. However, if being with other people means we can merge into a group, becoming less noticeable than when we are alone, we should become relaxed. Will this relaxation produced by becoming lost in the crowd lead to better or worse performance? Once again, the answer depends on whether we are working on a simple or a complex task.

Let's first consider simple tasks, such as trying to pull as hard as we can on a rope. The question of how working with others would influence performance on such a task was first studied in the 1880s by a French agricultural engineer, Max Ringelmann (1913). He found that when a group of men pulled on a rope, each individual exerted less effort than when he did it alone. A hundred years later, social psychologists Bibb Latané, Kipling Williams, and Stephen Harkins (1979) called this **social loafing**, which is the tendency for people to do worse on simple tasks but better on complex tasks when they are in the presence of others and their individual performance cannot be evaluated. "Many hands make light work," as the proverb says, and social loafing in groups has since been found for a variety of simple tasks, such as clapping your hands, cheering loudly, and thinking of as many uses for an object as you can (Hoeksema–van Orden, Gaillard, & Buunk, 1998; Karau & Williams, 1995; Shepperd, 1995; Williams, Harkins, & Latané, 1981).

Social loafing the tendency for people to do worse on simple tasks but better on complex tasks when they are in the presence of others and their individual performance cannot be evaluated

> Which of us... is to do the hard and dirty work for the rest—and for what pay?
>
> —JOHN RUSKIN

Pulling on a rope or cheering loudly is a pretty simple task. What happens on complex tasks when our performance is lost in the crowd? Recall that when our performance in a group cannot be identified, we become more relaxed. Recall also this chapter's earlier discussion of the effects of arousal on performance: Arousal enhances performance on simple tasks but impairs performance on complex tasks. By the same reasoning, becoming relaxed should impair performance on simple tasks—as we have just seen—but improve performance on complex tasks. The idea is that when people are not worried about being evaluated, they are more relaxed and should thus be less likely to "tense up" on a difficult task, and do it better as a result (see bottom panel of Figure 7.1).

To test this idea, Jeffrey Jackson and Kipling Williams (1985) asked participants to work on mazes that appeared on a computer screen. The mazes were either simple or complex. Another participant worked on identical mazes on another computer in the same room. The researchers either said they would evaluate each person's individual performance (causing evaluation apprehension) or stated that a computer would average the two participants' scores and no one would ever know how well any one person performed (reducing evaluation apprehension). The results were just as predicted. When people thought their score was being averaged with another person's, they were more relaxed, and this relaxation led to better performance (less time) on the difficult mazes (see the right side of Figure 7.2) but worse performance (more time) on the easy mazes (see the left side of Figure 7.2).

GENDER AND CULTURAL DIFFERENCES IN SOCIAL LOAFING: WHO SLACKS OFF THE MOST? Marie and Hans are working with several classmates on a class project, and no one can assess their individual contributions. Who is more likely to slack off and let the others do most of the work—Hans or Marie? If you said Hans, you are probably

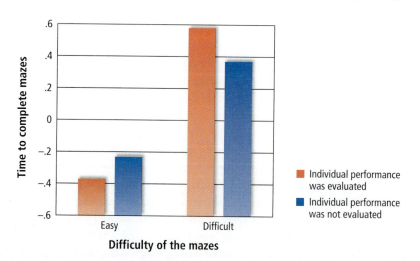

FIGURE 7.2   Social Loafing

When students worked on easy mazes, those who thought their individual performance would not be evaluated did worse (they took more time to complete them, as seen on the left side of the graph). When students worked on difficult mazes, those who thought their individual performance would not be evaluated did better (they took less time to complete them, as seen on the right side of the graph).

(Adapted from Jackson & Williams, 1985)

right. Karau and Williams (1993) reviewed more than 150 studies of social loafing and found that the tendency to loaf is stronger in men than in women. Why? Women tend to focus on the collective, caring more about the welfare of others in groups. Men are more likely to be individualistic, focusing more on their own performance and less on the group (Cross & Madson, 1997; Eagly, 1987; Wood, 1987). This different emphasis on collectivism versus individualism, as you may recall from Chapter 4, also exists across cultures. Many Asian societies stress collectivism, whereas many Western societies stress individualism. Consequently, there are also cultural differences in social loafing. Karau and Williams (1993) found that the tendency to loaf is stronger in Western cultures than in Asian cultures. It is important not to exaggerate these differences; there is evidence that women and men and members of Asian and Western cultures engage in social loafing when in groups (e.g., Chang & Chen, 1995). Nonetheless, social loafing is stronger in men and members of Western cultures.

To summarize, you need to know two things to predict whether the presence of others will help or hinder your performance—whether your individual efforts can be evaluated and whether the task is simple or complex. If your performance can be evaluated, the presence of others will make you alert and aroused. This will lead to social facilitation effects, where people do better on simple tasks but worse on complex tasks (see top of Figure 7.1 on page 203). If your efforts cannot be evaluated (you are one cog in a machine), you are likely to become more relaxed. This leads to social loafing effects, where people do worse on simple tasks but better on complex tasks (see bottom of Figure 7.1).

These findings have numerous implications for the way in which groups should be organized. If you are a manager who wants your employees to work on a relatively simple problem, a little evaluation apprehension is not such a bad thing—it should improve performance. You shouldn't place your employees in groups where their individual performance cannot be observed, because social loafing (lowered performance on simple tasks) is likely to result. On the other hand, if you want your employees to work on a difficult, complex task, then lowering their evaluation apprehension—by placing them in groups in which their individual performance cannot be observed—is likely to result in better performance.

Deindividuation: Getting Lost in the Crowd

So far, we have discussed the ways in which a group affects how hard people work and how successfully they learn new things. However, being in a group can also cause **deindividuation**, which is the loosening of normal constraints on behaviour when people are in a crowd, leading to an increase in impulsive and deviant acts (Lea, Spears, & de Groot, 2001). In other words, getting lost in a crowd can lead to an unleashing of behaviours that we would never dream of doing by ourselves. Throughout history, there have been many examples of groups of people committing horrendous acts that no individual would do on his or her own. In previous chapters, we discussed the chilling murder of a young Somalian boy at the hands of Canadian peacekeepers. We also described the abuse of Iraqi prisoners at the hands of American soldiers in Abu Ghraib prison. In Europe, mobs of soccer fans sometimes attack and bludgeon each other. The list of atrocities goes on and on. The United States has a shameful history of whites—often cloaked in the anonymity of white robes—lynching African Americans.

Brian Mullen (1986) content-analyzed newspaper accounts of 60 lynchings committed in the United States between 1899 and 1946, and discovered an interesting fact: The more

Deindividuation the loosening of normal constraints on behaviour when people are in a group, leading to an increase in impulsive and deviant acts

> If you can keep your head when all about you are losing theirs…
>
> —RUDYARD KIPLING, "If", 1909

When people can lose their identity in a group, they are more likely to commit impulsive and deviant acts. Matti Baranovski, a Toronto teen, was brutally beaten to death in November 1999 by a group of youths wearing balaclavas, masks, goggles, and other disguises. Here, his grieving mother lays a wreath on the casket at his funeral.

people there were in the mob, the greater the savagery and viciousness with which they killed their victims. Robert Watson (1973) studied 24 cultures and found that warriors who hid their identities before going to battle—for example, by using face and body paint—were significantly more likely to kill, torture, and mutilate captive prisoners than warriors who did not hide their identities.

Sadly, we do not have to go back in history to see examples of the deadly combination of anonymity and being in a group. On November 14, 1999, 15-year-old Matti Baranovski and his friends were approached in a Toronto park by a group of youths looking for a fight. One of the youths wore ski goggles; another covered the lower half of his face with a blue bandanna. Still others wore masks or balaclavas to disguise themselves. The youths approached Matti's friends, took their cigarettes, and searched their wallets for money. When Matti questioned what they were doing, they turned on him, viciously punching and kicking him in the head and body. The last kick in the face broke his neck, and Matti died from these injuries.

In trying to understand how such violence can occur, some analysts pointed to the fact that the attackers were in a group and that they were wearing disguises. As noted in one newspaper story, "Disguises tend to make those wearing them capable of far more terrible acts of violence than would normally occur" (Simmie, 1999).

Exactly what is it about deindividuation that leads to impulsive (and often violent) acts? Research by Steven Prentice-Dunn and Ronald Rogers (1989) and Ed Diener (1980) points to two factors. First, the presence of others (or the wearing of uniforms and disguises) makes people feel less accountable for their actions, because it reduces the likelihood that any individual will be singled out and blamed (Zimbardo, 1970).

FOCUS ON APPLICATIONS

Sports and Aggression: Does What You Wear Change Who You Are?

It is not uncommon to be asked to wear uniforms that make us look like everyone else in the vicinity, an arrangement that might make us feel less accountable for our actions and hence more aggressive. Does wearing a uniform, as when you are on a sports team, increase aggressiveness? Several studies suggest that it does. Rehm, Steinleitner, and Lilli (1987) randomly assigned grade 5 students in German schools to various five-person teams, then watched the teams play handball against each other. All of the members of one team wore orange shirts and all of the members of the other team wore their normal street clothes. The children who wore the orange shirts (and were thus harder to tell apart) played the game significantly more aggressively than did the children who wore their everyday clothing (and were thus easier to identify).

Even the colour of a uniform can make a difference. Mark Frank and Thomas Gilovich (1988) noted that in virtually all cultures, the colour black is associated with evil and death. They examined penalty records and recorded the colour of uniforms worn by teams in the National Hockey League and the National Football League from 1970 to 1986. Interestingly, teams that wore black uniforms ranked near the top of their leagues in terms of penalties. Moreover, if a team switched to a non-black uniform, there was an immediate decrease in the number of penalties. These researchers also conducted an experiment in which participants played a game wearing either white or black uniforms. Those who wore black uniforms showed greater aggressiveness than did those who wore white uniforms.

As this is being written, the big story in sports is that former Colorado Avalanche player Steve Moore has filed a civil lawsuit against Todd Bertuzzi of the Vancouver Canucks. Bertuzzi assaulted Moore during a hockey game in March 2004. Moore suffered a broken neck and other injuries. The game took place in Vancouver, which means that Bertuzzi was wearing the dark-coloured uniform that Canucks players use during home games. Might Bertuzzi's assault have been less severe if the game had been played in Colorado, where he would have being wearing the "away" white uniform? Although we can't be sure, the research we have been discussing does raise that possibility. Thus, something as seemingly superficial as whether we are wearing a uniform while playing our favourite sport—as well as the colour of that uniform—can affect our level of aggressiveness.

Second, the presence of others lowers self-awareness, thereby shifting people's attention away from their moral standards. As discussed in Chapter 4, it is difficult to focus inward on ourselves and outward on the world around us at the same time; thus, at any given point we vary as to how self-aware we are (Carver & Scheier, 1981; Duval & Wicklund, 1972). One consequence of focusing on ourselves is that we are reminded of our moral standards, making us less likely to behave in some deviant or antisocial manner

("I believe that hurting other people is wrong; I'm not going to torture this prisoner—even if the other soldiers are doing so"). If we are focusing on our environment, however, self-awareness will be low and we will be more likely to forget our moral standards and act impulsively.

Thinking Critically
Think of times that you experienced deindividuation when in a group. How did this influence you?

GROUP DECISIONS: ARE TWO (OR MORE) HEADS BETTER THAN ONE?

We have just seen that the presence of other people influences individual behaviour in a number of interesting ways. We turn now to one of the major functions of groups: to make decisions. In the Canadian judicial system, many verdicts are determined by groups of individuals (juries), rather than single individuals. The Supreme Court is made up of nine justices—not one single, sage member of the judiciary. Similarly, government and corporate decisions are often made by groups of people who meet to discuss the issues, and all Canadian prime ministers have a Cabinet and the Privy Council to advise them.

Is it true that two (or more) heads are better than one? Most of us assume that the answer to this question is yes. A lone individual may be subject to all sorts of whims and biases, whereas several people together can exchange ideas, catch each other's errors, and reach better decisions. We have all taken part in group decisions in which we listened to someone else and thought to ourselves, "Hmm, that's a really good point—I would never have thought of that." In general, groups will do better than individuals if they rely on the person with the most expertise (Davis & Harless, 1996) and are stimulated by each other's comments.

Sometimes, though, two heads are not better than one. Several factors, as we will see, can cause groups to actually make worse decisions than individuals.

Process Loss: When Group Interactions Inhibit Good Problem Solving

One problem is that a group will do well only if the most talented member can convince the others that she or he is right—which is not always easy, given that many of us find it extremely difficult to admit that we are wrong (Henry, 1995; Laughlin, 1980; Maier & Solem, 1952). You undoubtedly know what it's like to try to convince a group to follow your idea, be faced with opposition and disbelief, and then have to sit there and watch the group make the wrong decision. Ivan Steiner (1972) called this phenomenon **process loss**, defined as any aspect of group interaction that inhibits good problem solving. Process loss can occur for a number of reasons. Groups might not try hard enough to find out who the most competent member is and instead rely on somebody who really doesn't know what he or she is talking about. The most competent member might find it difficult to disagree with everyone else in the group (recall our discussion of normative conformity pressures in Chapter 6). Other causes of process loss involve communication problems within the

> Nor is the people['s] judgement always true:
> The most may err as grossly as the few.
>
> —JOHN DRYDEN,
> Absalom and Achitophel, 1682

Process loss any aspect of group interaction that inhibits good problem solving

group—in some groups, people don't listen to each other; in others, one person is allowed to dominate the discussion while the others tune out (Watson et al., 1998).

FAILURE TO SHARE UNIQUE INFORMATION Another example of process loss is the tendency for groups to focus on what its members already know in common, failing to discuss information that some members have but others do not. Consider a medical team trying to decide on the course of treatment of a person with abdominal pain. Some members of the team may have unique information not known by the other members. For example, the doctor who first examined the patient in the emergency room may be the only one who knows that the patient had mussels for dinner that night, whereas one of the attending physicians may be the only one to have seen the results of a blood test showing that the patient has an abnormally high white blood cell count. Obviously, to make the most informed decision, the group needs to pool all of the information and use it to decide on the best course of treatment.

As obvious as this is, there is a funny thing about groups: They tend to focus on the information they share and ignore unique information known only to some members of the group. In one study, for example, participants met in groups of four to discuss which candidate for student body president was the most qualified (Stasser & Titus, 1985). In the shared information condition, each participant was given the same packet of information to read; all participants in this condition learned that candidate A had eight positive qualities and four negative qualities, making him superior to the other candidates. Not surprisingly, when this group met to discuss the candidates, almost all of the members chose candidate A.

In the unshared information condition, everyone learned that candidate A had four negative qualities. But each person was only given information about two positive qualities. And—here's the catch—the two positive qualities cited in each person's packet were unique, different from those listed in other participants' packets. If the participants had shared the information in their packets, they would have learned that candidate A had a total of eight positive qualities and four negative qualities—just as people in the shared information condition knew. However, most of the groups in the unshared information condition never realized that candidate A had more good than bad qualities, because they focused on the information they shared rather than on the information they did not share. As a result, few of these groups chose candidate A.

Fortunately, the tendency for groups to fail to share important information known to only some of the members can be overcome. An effective approach is to assign different group members to specific areas of expertise so they know that they alone are responsible for certain types of information. The "expert" is then more likely to bring up the information that only he or she possesses and the rest of the group is more likely to pay attention to it. Thus, it is important that group members learn who is responsible for what kinds of information and take the time to discuss these unshared data (Stewart & Stasser, 1995; Stasser, 2000).

GROUPTHINK: MANY HEADS, ONE MIND In most studies on group problem solving, people who have never met before are asked to work on tasks that are unfamiliar and sometimes trivial. Do groups make better decisions if their members are used to working with each other and if they are dealing with important, real-world problems? Our opening example of the Canadian military's decision to administer the anthrax vaccine suggests not. Let's see why.

Groupthink a kind of thinking in which maintaining group cohesiveness and solidarity is more important than considering the facts in a realistic manner

Group cohesiveness qualities of a group that bind members together and promote liking between members

Using real-world events, Irving Janis (1972, 1982) developed an influential theory of group decision making that he called **groupthink**, defined as a kind of thinking in which maintaining group cohesiveness and solidarity is more important than considering the facts in a realistic manner. **Group cohesiveness** refers to qualities of a group that bind members together and promote liking among them (Dion, 2000; Hogg, 1993; Prentice, Miller, & Lightdale, 1994). The more cohesive a group is, the more its members are likely to stay in the group, take part in group activities, and try to recruit like-minded members (Levine & Moreland, 1998; Sprink & Carron, 1994). This can be a good thing. However, as we shall see, one drawback of group cohesiveness is that the group members' concern with maintaining good relations can get in the way of finding good solutions to a problem.

Group cohesiveness is not the only factor that can contribute to poor decision making. According to Janis's theory, groupthink is most likely to occur when the group is also isolated from contrary opinions and ruled by a directive leader who makes his or her wishes known. When these preconditions of groupthink are met, several symptoms appear; these are outlined in Figure 7.3. The group begins to feel it is invulnerable and can do no wrong. People do not voice contrary views (they exercise self-censorship) because they are afraid of ruining the high morale, or *esprit de corps*, of the group, or because they are afraid of being criticized by others. If anyone does voice a contrary viewpoint, the rest of the group is quick to criticize that person, pressuring him or her to conform to the majority view. This creates an illusion of invulnerability, in which it looks as though everyone agrees. Groups also appoint

Antecedents of groupthink	Symptoms of groupthink	Defective decision making
The group is highly cohesive: The group is valued and attractive, and people very much want to be members. **Group isolation:** The group is isolated, protected from hearing alternative viewpoints. **A directive leader:** The leader controls the discussion and makes his or her wishes known. **High stress:** The members perceive threats to the group. **Poor decision-making procedures:** No standard methods to consider alternative viewpoints.	**Illusion of invulnerability:** The group feels it is invincible and can do no wrong. **Belief in the moral correctness of the group:** "God is on our side." **Stereotyped views of out-group:** Opposing sides are viewed in a simplistic, stereotyped manner. **Self-censorship:** People decide themselves not to voice contrary opinions so as not to "rock the boat." **Direct pressure on dissenters to conform:** If people do voice contrary opinions, they are pressured by others to conform to the majority. **Illusion of unanimity:** An illusion is created that everyone agrees, for example, by not calling on people known to disagree. **Mindguards:** Group members protect the leader from contrary viewpoints.	Incomplete survey of alternatives Failure to examine risks of the favoured alternative Poor information search Failure to develop contingency plans

FIGURE 7.3 **Groupthink: Antecedents, Symptoms, and Consequences**

Under some conditions, maintaining group cohesiveness and solidarity is more important to a group than considering the facts in a realistic manner (see antecedents). When this happens, certain symptoms of groupthink occur, such as the illusion of invulnerability (see symptoms). These symptoms lead to defective decision making.

(Adapted from Janis, 1982)

"mindguards"—group members who ensure that the leader is shielded from information that might cause him or her to question the correctness of the group's decision.

The perilous state of groupthink causes people to implement an inferior decision-making process (see Figure 7.3). The group does not consider the full range of alternatives, does not develop contingency plans, and does not adequately consider the risks of its preferred choice. Groupthink may well have been behind the decision of the military leaders to go ahead with the anthrax vaccine despite the fact that Health Canada had not approved it and military lawyers had advised against it. Can you think of other decisions that were plagued by groupthink? One example is the fateful decision by NASA to go ahead with the February 2003 launch of the space shuttle *Challenger*, despite the objections of engineers who said that the freezing temperatures presented a severe danger to the rubber O-ring seals (the ones that eventually failed during the launch, causing the rocket to explode and kill all on board).

The decision to launch the space shuttle *Challenger*, which tragically exploded due to defective O-ring seals, appears to have been the result of groupthink on the part of NASA officials, who disregarded engineers' concerns about the quality of the seals.

Since Janis proposed his theory, it has been put to the test by a number of researchers. Some studies have found that group cohesiveness by itself does not increase groupthink (Adlag & Fuller, 1993; Mohamed & Wiebe, 1996; Tetlock et al., 1992). However, group cohesiveness does increase groupthink when it is accompanied by the other risk factors identified by Janis, such as the presence of a directive leader or high stress (see Figure 7.3; Esser, 1998; Hogg & Hains, 1998; Mullen et al., 1994; Schafer & Crichlow, 1996; Turner et al., 1992).

How can groupthink be avoided? A wise leader can take several steps to ensure that his or her group is immune to this style of decision making. The leader should not take a directive role, but should remain impartial. He or she should invite outside opinions from people who are not members of the group and who are thus less concerned with maintaining group cohesiveness. He or she should divide the group into subgroups that first meet separately and then meet together to discuss their different recommendations. The leader might also take a secret ballot or ask group members to write down their opinions anonymously; doing so would ensure that people give their true opinions, uncensored by a fear of recrimination from the group (Flowers, 1977; McCauley, 1989; Zimbardo & Andersen, 1993). Obviously, highly directive authoritarian leaders might not welcome feedback from group members that contradict the leader's view. However, leaders who are truly concerned about avoiding faulty decisions can benefit from taking these steps.

Group Polarization: Going to Extremes

Maybe you are willing to grant that groups sometimes make poor decisions. Surely, though, groups will usually make less risky decisions than a lone individual will—one individual might be willing to bet the ranch on a risky proposition, but if others help make the decision they will interject reason and moderation. Or will they? The question of whether groups or individuals make riskier decisions has been examined in numerous studies. Participants are typically given the Choice Dilemmas Questionnaire (CDQ), a series of stories that present a dilemma for the main character and ask the reader to choose how much probability of success there would have to be before the reader would recommend the risky alternative (Kogan & Wallach, 1964). An example of a CDQ item about a chess player appears next in Try It! People choose their answers alone and then meet in a group to discuss the options, arriving at a unanimous group decision for each dilemma.

Many of the initial studies found, surprisingly, that groups make riskier decisions than individuals do. For example, when deciding alone, people said the chess player should make the risky gambit only if there was at least a 30 percent chance of success. But after discussing the problem with others in a group, people said the chess player should go for it even if there was only a 10 percent chance of success (Wallach, Kogan, & Bem, 1962). Findings such as these became known as the *risky shift*. Yet with more research, it became clear that such shifts were not the full story. It turns out that groups tend to make decisions that are more extreme in the same direction as the individual's initial predispositions, which happened to be risky in the case of the chess problem. What happens if

Try It! Choice Dilemmas Questionnaire

You will need four or five friends to complete this exercise. First, copy the questionnaire in the table below and give it to each of your friends to complete by themselves, without talking to each other. Do not tell your friends that they will be discussing the questionnaire with the others. Then bring everyone together and ask them to discuss the dilemma and arrive at a unanimous decision. They should try to reach a consensus so that every member of the group agrees at least partially with the final decision. Finally, compare people's initial decisions (made alone) with the group decision. Who made the riskier decisions on average: people deciding by themselves or the group?

As discussed in the text, groups tend to make riskier decisions than individuals on problems such as these. In one study, for example, individuals recommended that the chess player make the risky move only if there was at least a 30 percent chance of success. After discussing the problem with others in a group, however, they recommended that the chess player make the move even if there was only a 10 percent chance of success. Did you find the same thing? Why or why not? If the group did make a riskier decision, was it due more to the persuasive arguments interpretation discussed in the text, the social comparison interpretation, or both? (Adapted from Wallach, Kogan, & Bem, 1962)

The Choice Dilemmas Questionnaire

A low-ranked participant in a national chess tournament, playing an early match against a highly favoured opponent, has the choice of attempting or not attempting a deceptive but risky manoeuvre that might lead to quick victory if it is successful or almost certain defeat if it fails. Please indicate the lowest probability of success that you would accept before recommending that the chess player play the risky move.

_____ 1 chance in 10 of succeeding
_____ 3 chances in 10 of succeeding
_____ 5 chances in 10 of succeeding
_____ 7 chances in 10 of succeeding
_____ 9 chances in 10 of succeeding
_____ I would not recommend taking the chance

people are initially inclined to be conservative? In cases such as these, groups tend to make even more conservative decisions than individuals do.

Consider this problem: Domenic, a young married man with two children, has a secure but low-paying job and no savings. Someone gives him a tip about a stock that will triple in value if the company's new product is successful but that will plummet if the new product fails. Should Domenic sell his life insurance policy and invest in the company? Most people recommend a safe course of action here: Domenic should buy the stock only if the new product is certain to succeed. When they talk it over in a group, they become even more conservative, deciding that the new product would have to have a nearly 100 percent chance of success before they would recommend that Domenic buy stock in the company.

The finding that groups make more extreme decisions in the direction of people's initial inclinations—toward greater risk if the members' initial tendency is to be risky and toward greater caution if the members' initial tendency is to be cautious—has become known as **group polarization** (Brown, 1965; Friedkin, 1999; Myers & Arenson, 1972; Teger & Pruitt, 1967). Group polarization occurs for two main reasons. According to the *persuasive arguments* interpretation, all individuals bring to the group a set of arguments—some of which other individuals have not considered—supporting their initial recommendation. For example, one person might stress that cashing in the life insurance policy is an unfair risk to Domenic's children, should he die prematurely. Another person might not have considered this possibility; thus, she becomes more conservative as well. The result is that group members end up with a greater number of arguments in support of their position than they initially started out with. A series of studies by Eugene Burnstein and Amiram Vinokur (1977) supports this interpretation of group polarization, whereby each member presents arguments that other members had not considered (Burnstein & Sentis, 1981).

According to the *social comparison* interpretation, when people discuss an issue in a group they first check how everyone else feels. What does the group value—being risky or being cautious? In order to be liked, many people then take a position that is similar to everyone else's but a little more extreme. In this way, the individual supports the group's values and also presents himself or herself in a positive light—a person in the vanguard, an impressive thinker. Both the persuasive arguments and the social comparison interpretations of group polarization have received support (Blascovich, Ginsburg, & Veach, 1975; Brown, 1986; Burnstein & Sentis, 1981; Isenberg, 1986; Zuber, Crott, & Werner, 1992).

Leadership in Groups

A critical question we have not yet considered is the role of the leader in group decision making. The question of what makes a great leader has intrigued psychologists, historians, and political scientists for some time (Bass, 1990, 1997; Billsberry, 1996; Burns, 1978; Chemers, 2000; Fiedler, 1967; Hollander, 1985; Klenke, 1996; Simonton, 1987). According to the **great person theory**, certain key personality traits make a person a good leader. However, despite countless attempts, researchers have not found strong associations between personality and leadership. For example, Bradley and colleagues (2002) followed Canadian Forces officer candidates over a five-year period and found little relation between personality variables and leadership ability. Only one trait emerged as particularly useful in predicting who would make a good leader, and that was dominance. The

Group polarization the tendency for groups to make decisions that are more extreme than the initial inclinations of their members

Great person theory the theory that certain key personality traits make a person a good leader, regardless of the nature of the situation facing the leader

> Leadership cannot really be taught. It can only be learned.
> —HAROLD GENEEN, 1984

Contingency theory of leadership the theory that leadership effectiveness depends both on how task-oriented or relationship-oriented the leader is and on the amount of control and influence the leader has over the group

Task-oriented leader a leader who is concerned more with getting the job done than with the feelings of and relationships between the workers

Relationship-oriented leader a leader who is concerned primarily with the feelings of and relationships between the workers

authors note that dominance may be a particularly important trait for leaders in a military setting. But what about in other settings? Do you think that the manager of a daycare, for example, would have to be dominant to be an effective leader?

As you undoubtedly know by now, one of the most important tenets of social psychology is that, to understand social behaviour, it is not enough to consider personality traits alone—we must take the social situation into account as well. Thus, being good social psychologists, we should consider both the nature of the leader and the situation in which the leading takes place. This view of leadership states that it is not enough to be a great person; you have to be the right person at the right time in the right situation.

LEADERSHIP: THE RIGHT PERSON IN THE RIGHT SITUATION Several theories of leadership focus on characteristics of the leader, his or her followers, and the situation (e.g., Dienesch & Liden, 1986; Hollander, 1958; House, 1971). The best-known theory of this type is Fred Fiedler's (1967, 1978) **contingency theory of leadership**. According to Fiedler, there are two kinds of leaders: those who are task-oriented and those who are relationship-oriented. The **task-oriented leader** is concerned more with getting the job done than with the feelings of and relationships between the workers. The **relationship-oriented leader** is concerned primarily with the feelings of and relationships between the workers.

The crux of Fiedler's contingency theory is that neither type of leader is *always* more effective than the other; it depends on the nature of the situation—specifically, on the amount of control and influence a leader has over the group. In "high-control" work situations, the leader has excellent interpersonal relationships with subordinates, his or her position in the company is clearly perceived as powerful, and the work to be done by the group is structured and well defined. In "low-control" work situations, the opposite holds—the leader has poor relationships with subordinates and the work to be done is not clearly defined.

As seen in Figure 7.4, task-oriented leaders are most effective in situations that are either very high or very low in control. When situational control is very high, people are happy, everything is running smoothly, and there is no need to worry about people's feelings

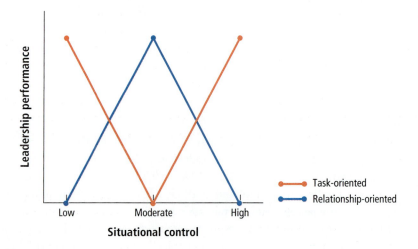

FIGURE 7.4 Fiedler's Contingency Theory of Leadership

According to Fiedler, task-oriented leaders perform best when situational control is high or low, whereas relationship-oriented leaders perform best when situational control is moderate.

and relationships. The leader who pays attention only to the task will get the most accomplished. When situational control is very low, the task-oriented leader is best at taking charge and imposing some order on a confusing, ill-defined work environment. Relationship-oriented leaders, however, are most effective in situations that are moderate in control. Under these conditions, the wheels are turning fairly smoothly but some attention to the squeakiness caused by poor relationships and hurt feelings is needed. The leader who can soothe such feelings will be most successful.

Fiedler's contingency theory has been tested with numerous groups of leaders, including business managers, college administrators, military commanders, and postmasters. These studies have generally been supportive, conforming well to the pattern shown in Figure 7.4 (Chemers, 2000; Peters, Hartke, & Pohlmann, 1985; Schriesheim, Tepper, & Tetrault, 1994; Strube & Garcia, 1981).

GENDER AND LEADERSHIP An old adage says that because of sex discrimination, a woman has to be "twice as good as a man" in order to advance. Unfortunately, there do seem to be differences in the ways that female and male leaders are evaluated (Biernat et al., 1998). If a woman's style of leadership is stereotypically "masculine" (autocratic, "bossy," and task-oriented), she is evaluated more negatively than are men who have the same style (Eagly, Makhijani, & Klonsky, 1992). This is especially true if men are doing the evaluating (Butler & Geis, 1990). In other words, many men are uncomfortable with women who use the leadership techniques that men typically use.

Even though more and more women are entering the workforce, stereotypes about the leadership styles of women and men abound. Women are thought to care more about the feelings of their co-workers, to be more interpersonally skilled than men, and thus to be more relationship-oriented. Men are often characterized as assertive, controlling, and dominant (Deaux & LaFrance, 1998; Klenke, 1996). Is there any truth to these stereotypes?

To find out, Alice Eagly and her colleagues examined hundreds of studies to answer questions about the leadership styles of women versus men (Carli & Eagly, 1999; Eagly & Karau, 2002; Eagly, Karau, & Makhijani, 1995). The bad news is that there are two forms of prejudice against women. First, if women behave consistent with the stereotype (relationship-oriented, focused on workers' feelings), they are often perceived as having less leadership potential. On the other hand, if they behave in a way that is consistent with the stereotypical male leadership style (assertive, controlling), they are perceived negatively for not "acting like a woman should." These two kinds of prejudice might help explain why there is a shortage of women in leadership roles in our country. The one bit of good news is that there is now a growing recognition that effective leaders must be able to act in both stereotypical female (warm, nurturant) and stereotypical male (assertive, dominant) ways (Eagly & Karau, 2002).

Thinking Critically
Would you prefer to work with a task-oriented leader or a relationship-oriented leader? Does your response depend on the situation (whether the organization is running smoothly)? Does your response depend on your gender?

CONFLICT AND COOPERATION

We have just examined how people work together to make decisions; in these situations, group members have a common goal. Often, however, people have incompatible goals, placing them in conflict. This can be true of two individuals, such as romantic partners who disagree about who should clean the kitchen, or two groups, such as a labour union and company management who disagree over wages and working conditions. It can also be true of two nations, as in the case of the long-standing conflict between Israel and its Arab neighbours, or between the Serbians, Croatians, and Muslims in the former Yugoslavia. The nature of conflict, and how it can be resolved, has been the topic of a great deal of social psychological research (Allison, Beggan, & Midgley, 1996; De Dreu, Harinck, & Van Vianen, 1999; Deutsch, 1973; Levine & Thompson, 1996; Pruitt, 1998; Thibaut & Kelley, 1959).

Sometimes negotiations fail and armed conflict results, as in the United States' invasion of Iraq. Other times conflicts can be resolved peacefully. Social psychologists have performed experiments to test ways in which conflict resolution is most likely to occur.

Using Threats to Resolve Conflict

When caught in a conflict, many of us are tempted to use threats to get the other party to cave in to our wishes, believing that we should "walk softly and carry a big stick." Parents commonly use threats to get their children to behave, and teachers often threaten their students with demerits or a visit to the principal.

A classic series of studies by Morton Deutsch and Robert Krauss (1960, 1962) indicates that threats are not an effective means of reducing conflict. These researchers developed a game in which two participants imagined they were in charge of trucking companies named Acme and Bolt. The goal of each company was to transport merchandise as quickly as possible to a destination. The participants were paid 60 cents for each "trip," but had 1 cent subtracted for every second it took them to make the trip. The most direct route for each company was over a one-lane road on which only one truck could travel at a time. This placed the two companies in direct conflict, as seen in Figure 7.5. If Acme and Bolt both tried to take the one-lane road, neither truck could pass and both would lose money. Each company could take an alternative route, but this was much longer, guaranteeing they would lose at least 10 cents on each trial. The game lasted until each side had made 20 trips.

How did the participants respond to this dilemma? After a while, most of them worked out a solution that allowed both trucks to make a modest amount of money. They took turns waiting until the other person crossed the one-lane road, then would take that

Group Processes | 217

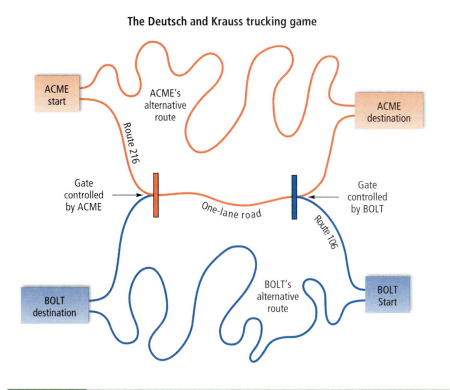

FIGURE 7.5 The Trucking Game

Participants play the role of the head of either Acme or Bolt Trucking Company. To earn money, they have to drive their trucks from the starting point to their destination as quickly as possible. The quickest route is the one-lane road, but both trucks cannot travel on this road at the same time. In some versions of the studies, participants were given gates that they used to block the other's progress on the one-lane road.

(Adapted from Deutsch & Krauss, 1960)

> My own belief is that Russian and Chinese behavior is as much influenced by suspicion of our intentions as ours is by suspicion of theirs. This would mean that we have great influence over their behavior—that, by treating them as hostile, we assure their hostility.
>
> —J. WILLIAM FULBRIGHT

route as well. In a later version of the study, the researchers gave Acme a gate that could be lowered over the one-lane road, thereby blocking Bolt from using that route (unilateral threat condition). You might think that using force—the gate—would increase Acme's profits, because all Acme had to do was threaten Bolt, telling it to stay off the one-lane road or else. In fact, quite the opposite happened. When one side had the gate, both participants lost more than when neither side had the gate—as seen in Figure 7.6. This figure shows the total amount earned or lost by both sides. (Acme won slightly more than Bolt when it had the gate but won substantially more when neither side had a gate.) Bolt did not like to be threatened, and often retaliated by parking its truck on the one-lane road, blocking the other truck's progress. Meanwhile, the seconds ticked away and both sides lost money.

What would happen if the situation were more equitable, with both sides having gates? Surely they would learn to cooperate very quickly, recognizing the stalemate that would ensue if both used their gates. To the contrary, as you can see in Figure 7.6, both sides lost more money in the bilateral threat condition than in any of the other conditions. The

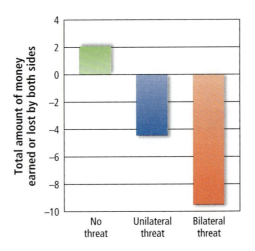

FIGURE 7.6 Results of the Trucking Game Studies

When threats were introduced by giving one (unilateral threat condition) or both sides (bilateral threat condition) a gate, both sides lost more money.

(Adapted from Deutsch & Krauss, 1962)

owners of the trucking companies both threatened to use their gates, and did so with great frequency. Once Acme used the gate to block Bolt, Bolt retaliated and blocked Acme the next time its truck came down the road—producing a stalemate that was not in either of their interests.

How might cooperation be increased in this kind of situation? Krauss and Deutsch reasoned that it might be helpful if the two sides communicated in an open, constructive manner. Thus, in another variation of their trucking study, they instructed each side to communicate, telling them to work out a solution that was fair to both parties—one they would be willing to accept if they were in the other person's shoes. Under these conditions, verbal communication increased the amount of money both sides won, because it fostered trust instead of adding fuel to the competitive fires (Deutsch, 1973, 1990; Krauss & Deutsch, 1966; Pruitt, 1998; Voissem & Sistrunk, 1971).

Negotiation and Bargaining

In the trucking game, there were only a couple of ways to get the truck to its destination. In contrast, in everyday life people often have many more options. It is therefore particularly important that people learn to communicate when dealing with real-world conflict. By talking, bargaining, and negotiating, people can arrive at agreements that are satisfactory to both sides. **Negotiation** is defined as a form of communication between opposing sides in a conflict, in which offers and counteroffers are made and a solution occurs only when both parties agree (Bazerman & Neale, 1992; De Dreu, Weingart, & Kwon, 2000; Pruitt, 1998). How successful are people at negotiating mutually beneficial solutions?

One limit to successful negotiation is that people often assume they are locked in a conflict in which only one party can come out ahead. They don't realize that, as in the conflicts we have reviewed, solutions favourable to both parties are available. Consider a labour union and a company negotiating a new contract. The company has proposed a 2 percent

Negotiation a form of communication between opposing sides in a conflict, in which offers and counteroffers are made and a solution occurs only when both parties agree

salary increase and no additional vacation days, whereas the union has proposed a 6 percent salary increase and 6 additional vacation days. After protracted negotiations, the two sides decide to compromise on both issues, agreeing to a 4 percent salary increase and 3 additional vacation days. Sounds fair, doesn't it?

The problem with such compromises is they assume that both issues (in this case, the salary increase and additional vacation days) are equally important to both parties, and often that is not true. Suppose that the labour union cared much more about increasing salaries than getting additional vacation days, whereas the company cared much more about minimizing vacation days than keeping salaries in check. In this case, a better solution for both sides would be to trade off issues, such that the union would get the 6 percent salary increase (which it cared about the most) in return for no increase in vacation days (which the company cared about the most). This type of compromise is called an **integrative solution**, defined as a solution to a conflict whereby the parties make trade-offs on issues according to their different interests; each side concedes the most on issues that are unimportant to it but that are important to the other side.

It might seem that such integrative solutions would be relatively easy to achieve. After all, the two parties simply have to sit down and figure out which issues are most important to each. However, we often find it difficult to identify integrative solutions (Hoffman et al., 1999; Thompson, 1997; Thompson & Hrebec, 1996). One barrier is a tendency for us to assume that what is important to us is obvious to everyone—including our opponent. Vorauer and Claude (1998) demonstrated that this assumption is not necessarily warranted. In their study, students at the University of Manitoba participated in negotiation sessions. When later questioned, negotiators assumed that it was obvious what their goals had been during the interaction. However, outside observers were no better than chance at identifying the negotiators' goals.

Integrative solution a solution to a conflict whereby the parties make trade-offs on issues according to their different interests; each side concedes the most on issues that are unimportant to it but that are important to the other side

> Yet, there remains another wall. This wall constitutes a psychological barrier between us,... [a] barrier of distorted and eroded interpretation of every event and statement.... I ask, why don't we stretch out our hands with faith and sincerity so that together we might destroy this barrier?
>
> —FORMER EGYPTIAN PRESIDENT ANWAR AL-SADAT, SPEAKING BEFORE THE ISRAELI KNESSET, 1977

If the right strategies are used, negotiation can lead to successful resolution of conflict. Here, Toby Anderson (left), chief negotiator for the Labrador Inuit Association, signs the documents of the Labrador Inuit Land Claims on May 10, 1999. Bob Warren (centre), chief negotiator for Newfoundland Labrador, and Jim MacKenzie (right), chief negotiator for the Government of Canada, look on.

If uninvolved, outside observers are unable to tell what is important to us; chances are that those with whom we are engaged in conflict will be even less able to do so. Indeed, there is ample evidence that when negotiators are in the heat of battle and care deeply about the outcome, they tend to distrust the other side, making it more difficult to realize that there is common ground beneficial to both parties (O'Connor & Carnevale, 1997; Ross & Ward, 1995, 1996; Thompson, 1995). This is one reason why people often use neutral mediators to solve labour disputes, legal battles, and divorce proceedings: Mediators are often in a better position to recognize that there are mutually agreeable solutions to a conflict (Carnevale, 1986; Emery & Wyer, 1987; Kressel & Pruitt, 1989; Ross & LaCroix, 1996).

The bottom line? When you are negotiating with someone, it is important to keep in mind that integrative solutions are often available. Try to gain the other side's trust and communicate your own interests in an open manner. Remember that the way you construe the situation is not necessarily the same as the way the other party construes the situation. You may well discover that the other side communicates its interests more freely as a result, increasing the likelihood that you will find a solution beneficial to both parties.

Thinking Critically

Suppose that you are the leader of a country that is in conflict with a neighbouring country over where the border should be and who should have access to valuable natural resources near the border. Based on the research discussed in this chapter, discuss several ways in which you might try to resolve this conflict peacefully.

Summary

A **group** consists of two or more people who interact with each other and are interdependent, in the sense that their needs and goals cause them to influence each other. Groups have well-defined **social roles**, shared expectations about how group members are expected to behave. The roles that people assume in groups, and the expectations that come with those roles, are powerful determinants of people's feelings and behaviour in groups. Groups can influence the behaviour of individuals in a number of other ways. For example, when people's individual efforts on a task can be evaluated, the mere presence of others leads to **social facilitation**: Their performance is enhanced on simple tasks but impaired on complex tasks. When their individual efforts cannot be evaluated, the mere presence of others leads to **social loafing**: Performance is impaired on simple tasks but enhanced on complex tasks. Finally, the mere presence of others can lead to **deindividuation**, which is the loosening of normal constraints on behaviour when people are in groups, leading to an increase in impulsive and deviant acts.

One of the major functions of groups is to make decisions. Are groups better or worse than individuals at making decisions? It turns out that groups make better decisions than individuals if they are good at pooling ideas and listening to the expert members of the group. Often, however, **process loss** occurs, whereby the most expert individual is unable to sway the rest of the group. Further, groups often focus on the information they have in common and fail to share unique information. This latter problem can be avoided if the group knows that individual members have been assigned to specific areas of expertise.

Tightly knit, cohesive groups are also prone to **groupthink**, a phenomenon in which maintaining **group cohesiveness** and solidarity is more important than considering the facts in a realistic manner. **Group polarization** indicates that groups are also prone to make more extreme decisions in the direction toward which its members were initially leaning; these group decisions can be more risky or more cautious, depending on the group members' initial inclinations.

Leaders usually play crucial roles in group decisions. There is little support for the **great person theory**, which argues that good leadership is purely a matter of having the right personality traits. Leadership effectiveness is a function of both the kind of person a leader is and the nature of the situation. Research on Fiedler's **contingency theory of leadership** has found that leadership performance depends both on whether a group has a **task-oriented leader** or a **relationship-oriented leader** and on whether the work environment is high or low in situational control. Women tend to lead more democratically than men, although women are able to adopt a "masculine" leadership style when the job requires it.

Often groups have incompatible goals, which places them in conflict with each other. Creating trust through open communication is crucial in solving this kind of conflict. In **negotiation**, it is important to look for an **integrative solution**, whereby each side concedes the most on issues that are unimportant to it but important to its adversary.

Key Terms

Contingency theory of leadership   (page 214)
Deindividuation   (page 205)
Great person theory   (page 213)
Group   (page 196)
Group cohesiveness   (page 210)
Group polarization   (page 213)
Groupthink   (page 210)
Integrative solution   (page 219)
Negotiation   (page 218)
Process loss   (page 208)
Relationship-oriented leader   (page 214)
Social facilitation   (page 201)
Social loafing   (page 203)
Social roles   (page 197)
Task-oriented leader   (page 214)

Key Online Search Terms

Social facilitation
Social loafing
Deindividuation
Process loss
Groupthink
Group polarization
Contingency theory of leadership
Integrative solution

If You Are Interested

Dion, K. L. (2000). Group cohesion: From "field of forces" to multidimensional construct. *Group Dynamics: Theory, Research and Practice, 4:* 7–26. A comprehensive review of theorizing and research on group cohesiveness written by a prominent University of Toronto social psychologist. The review ends with the author's assessment of which approaches to studying group cohesiveness hold the greatest promise for understanding this important concept.

Janis, I. (1982). *Groupthink: Psychological studies of policy decisions and fiascoes* (2nd ed.). Boston: Houghton Mifflin. Janis argues persuasively that many important policy decisions, from U.S. President Kennedy's decision to invade Cuba to the escalation of the Vietnam war, were flawed by groupthink, wherein maintaining group cohesiveness and solidarity was more important than considering the facts in a realistic manner.

Kasdan, Lawrence (Director). (1983). *The big chill* [Film]. Seven college housemates meet again at the funeral of a close friend who has committed suicide. A poignant and often funny look at group dynamics.

Weblinks

www.vcu.edu/hasweb/group/gdynamic.htm
Group Dynamics
This site provides links to various articles, activities, journals, and associations dealing with group dynamics.

www.trinity.edu/~mkearl/socpsy-8.html
Collective Behavior and the Social Psychologies of Social Institutions
This site examines the influence of larger societal influences on social behaviour. For example, the site includes a survey examining whether people attributed their attitudes on various issues to personal experience, friends/family, media, religion, and so on. The results indicate that people attribute many of their attitudes to societal influences such as media and religion.

www.asanet.org/sectioncbsm/
Collective Behavior and Social Movements
This is the home page of the Collective Behavior and Social Movements section of the American Sociological Association. The purpose of this section is to foster the study of emergent and extra-institutional social forms and behaviour, particularly crowds and social movements.

http://physinfo.ulb.ac.be/cit_courseware/research/theories2.htm
Groupthink
This site provides a summary of groupthink and includes advice on groupthink prevention.

Chapter 7 Practice Quiz

Check your knowledge of the concepts in this chapter by trying the following questions.

DEFINITIONS: WHAT IS A GROUP?

Multiple Choice

1. Leary and Baumeister believe that groups began to form as a
    a. survival technique.
    b. genetic mutation.
    c. result of polygamous marriages.
    d. by-product of religious rituals.

2. Which of the following did not affect the behaviour of American soldiers in Abu Ghraib prison?
    a. the role of prison guards
    b. anonymity
    c. dehumanization of prisoners
    d. malnutrition

3. Which of the following is not considered a group?
    a. a university population
    b. a married couple
    c. a preschool class
    d. a church congregation

4. Which of the following best describes the prisoners of the Stanford Prison Experiment?
    a. physically violent towards the guards
    b. depressed and anxious
    c. verbally abusive towards the guards
    d. physically violent towards each other

True or False

5. Over-involvement in a social role strengthens our personality and personal identity.
    ___ True
    ___ False

6. The Abu Ghraib prison events closely resemble the results found in Zimbardo's Stanford Prison Experiment.
    ___ True
    ___ False

Fill in the Blank

7. _____ are shared expectations within a group regarding how people are supposed to behave.
8. A _____ is two or more people who interact with each other.

HOW GROUPS INFLUENCE THE BEHAVIOUR OF INDIVIDUALS

Multiple Choice

9. A possible explanation for Todd Bertuzzi's assault on Steve Moore during an NHL game has been attributed to
    a. the colour of Bertuzzi's jersey.
    b. a neurological disorder.
    c. the colour of Moore's jersey.
    d. social loafing.

10. The tragic beating of Matti Baranovski by a group of masked teens is an example of
    a. social loafing.
    b. social facilitation.
    c. hypersocial activity.
    d. deindividuation.

11. Deindividuation often produces acts of violence because
    a. the presence of others lowers self-awareness.
    b. the presence of others makes people feel more accountable for their actions.
    c. the presence of others impairs catharsis.
    d. all of the above

12. When working in groups, women tend to _____ less than men as a result of being more _____.
    a. social loaf; concerned for the group's welfare
    b. social loaf; concerned with their own performance
    c. contribute; stubborn
    d. contribute; concerned with their own performance

True or False

13. When a task is very difficult, the mere presence of others improves our performance.
    ___ True
    ___ False

14. Focussing on our environment rather than on ourselves increases the chances we will act impulsively.
    ___ True
    ___ False

Fill in the Blank

15. _____ leads to an increase in impulsive and deviant acts.
16. _____ is the tendency to do worse on simple tasks when individual performance cannot be evaluated.

GROUP DECISIONS: ARE TWO (OR MORE) HEADS BETTER THAN ONE?

Multiple Choice

17. Which of the following best describes groupthink?
    a. thinking used to maintain group cohesiveness
    b. thinking used to maintain group solidarity
    c. thinking that outweighs realistic considerations
    d. all of the above

18. Which of the following is not a reason for group polarization?
    a. persuasive arguments
    b. social comparison
    c. social advancement
    d. all of the above

19. According to the _____, certain personality traits make a person a good leader.
    a. great person theory
    b. multi-dimensional leadership inventory
    c. personality-leadership questionnaire
    d. theory of social hierarchy

20. Which of the following is a type of group leader?
    a. task-oriented
    b. task-deviant
    c. relationship-deviant
    d. task-relationship

True or False

21. The consistency theory of personality is the best theory for describing leadership effectiveness.
    ___ True
    ___ False

22. Male leaders are thought of as more assertive and controlling than females.
    ___ True
    ___ False

Fill in the Blank

23. _____ includes the qualities that bind a group together.
24. _____ is any aspect of group interaction that inhibits good problem solving.

CONFLICT AND COOPERATION

Multiple Choice

25. One type of conflict is _____, where each side concedes and there are trade-offs.
    a. integrative solutions
    b. interpretive solutions
    c. equity solutions
    d. equilateral compromising

26. According to the trucking game developed by Deutsch and Krauss, people respond
    a. negatively to negotiations.
    b. negatively to bilateral threats.
    c. negatively to cooperation.
    d. all of the above

True or False

27. People in conflict usually believe both sides will be satisfied through negotiation.
    ___ True
    ___ False

28. Integrative solutions are easy to obtain once the two sides in conflict begin negotiations.
    ___ True
    ___ False

Fill in the Blank

29. _____ involves a series of offers and counter-offers between two conflicting groups.
30. _____ are often in the best position to recognize the mutually agreeable solutions to a conflict.

PERSONALIZED STUDY PLAN

Want to check your answers and access more study resources? Visit the Companion Website for *Fundamentals of Social Psychology* at **www.pearsoned.ca/aronson**, where you'll find the above questions incorporated in a pre-test and post-test for each chapter. These tests will be automatically graded online, allowing you to check your answers. A Study Plan, like the one below, groups the questions by section within the chapter and shows you which sections you need to focus on for further study.

Your Results for "Chapter 7, Pretest"

OVERALL SCORE: 73% of 15 questions

Group	Score	Proficient
Definitions: What Is a Group?	4 of 4	Yes
How Groups Influence the Behaviour of Individuals	3 of 4	Yes
Group Decisions	3 of 4	Yes
Conflict and Cooperation	1 of 3	No

CHAPTER

8

Interpersonal Attraction: From First Impressions to Close Relationships

Chapter Outline

MAJOR ANTECEDENTS OF ATTRACTION
The Person Next Door: The Propinquity Effect
Similarity
Reciprocal Liking
The Effects of Physical Attractiveness on Liking
Attraction and the Misattribution of Arousal

FORMING AND MAINTAINING CLOSE RELATIONSHIPS
What Is Love?
The Role of Positive Illusions in Maintaining Relationships
Why Do We Form and Maintain Relationships?

ENDING CLOSE RELATIONSHIPS
Why Relationships End
The Experience of Breaking Up

"Then I met Nina..." These four words changed a man's life. A few years ago, Bradley Bird, a Canadian newspaper writer in his early forties, was on a trip, covering a series of sad, dark events—the experiences of Chechen refugees and conflict in Kosovo and Kurdish Turkey. As he wearily boarded a bus in Georgia (near Russia), bracing himself for the 20-hour ride to northeast Turkey for one last story, a woman took the seat beside him. She was a tall, attractive, raven-haired woman in her thirties. Bradley recalls, "I looked at her... and was pleased to see a face as lovely as I'd ever beheld, with dark mysterious eyes, a perfect nose, and full red lips" (Bird, 2001). The woman's name was Nina. To Bradley's surprise, he found himself asking her whether there was a man in her life. She answered no. He surprised himself still more by saying, "You need me, and I need you." Because she said she spoke only a little English, he repeated it to make sure she understood. She smiled and they gazed into each other's eyes. It was midnight and the driver turned off the interior lights. Her arm brushed against his in the darkness. "The sensation

A trip to Istanbul proved to be a heartbreaker for writer Bradley Bird.

was incredible," Bradley exclaims, "electric, and I couldn't stop myself, I gave her arm a gentle squeeze." Nina reciprocated.

At first they tried to hide their feelings from the other passengers, but by 12 hours into the ride, they were unable to contain their joy. Bradley informed the driver that his plans had changed and he would now stay on the bus an additional 13 hours so he could have more time with Nina. The driver and passengers began to celebrate with them. An older, heavy man brought out a bottle of vodka to mark the occasion. Bradley began to make plans for Nina to come to Canada. When he returned home, he mailed her the documents she would need to get a visa. It was May. Nina wrote back, assuring Bradley of her desire to be with him. She also told him he would have to return to Turkey and plead her case to the Canadian Embassy there. By this time, it was August, and Bradley had accepted a teaching position. What to do now? The answer was clear. Bradley promptly quit his job and booked a flight to Turkey and two return tickets to Canada. He had trouble reaching Nina, but finally managed to track down her sister in Bulgaria and asked her to let Nina know that he was coming. "Oh, Bradley," she said, "Nina is back with her husband. Her daughter insisted on it." With those words, Bradley's dream of a life with Nina was shattered. But Bradley Bird isn't bitter. This is how he sums up the experience: "I will always be grateful to Nina for giving me 33 of the happiest hours of my adult life" (Bird, 2001).

As Bradley Bird's experience illustrates, the need to love and be loved is one of the most basic, fundamental human needs. Despite all of the warning signs—the fact that he had just met this woman and knew nothing about her, the fact that he wasn't able to reach her once he had solidified the plans to go get her—Bradley just couldn't help himself. He fell in love with the mysterious Nina, and it changed his life. He gave up the job he had just landed and put all of his energies into bringing Nina to Canada. And this man in his forties, who had experienced other relationships (he was once married), describes the bus ride with Nina as the happiest 33 hours of his adult life!

What, exactly, is love, and why are we so motivated to seek it—even when it comes at a high cost? This is one of the basic questions we will address in this chapter. We will discuss the antecedents of attraction, from the initial liking of two people meeting for the first time, to the love that develops in close relationships. We will also discuss the processes whereby relationships end. As we consider this research, you may want to think about how you can put these social psychological findings to good use in your own life—although we can't guarantee that a thorough reading of this chapter will save you from completely rearranging your life because of a chance meeting with a gorgeous mysterious stranger on a bus.

MAJOR ANTECEDENTS OF ATTRACTION

As Ellen Berscheid (1985; Berscheid & Reis, 1998) has noted, we human beings, the most social of social animals, have survived as a species largely because of our ability to know whether another creature or human being is good or bad for us. "Matters of interpersonal attraction are quite literally of life and death importance, not just to the individual but to all of humankind" (Berscheid, 1985). What factors cause one person to be attracted to another? Let's find out.

The Person Next Door: The Propinquity Effect

There are approximately 5 billion people in the world. In your lifetime, however, you will have the opportunity to meet and interact with only a minuscule percentage of that population. Thus, it will not surprise you to learn that one of the simplest determinants of interpersonal attraction is proximity—sometimes called *propinquity*. The people who, by chance, you see and interact with most often are most likely to become your friends and lovers (Berscheid & Reis, 1998; Fehr, 1996; Newcomb, 1961; Segal, 1974). This includes people in your city, your neighbourhood, and on your street. Now, this might seem obvious. However, the striking thing about proximity and attraction, or the **propinquity effect**, as social psychologists call it, is that it works on a micro level.

For example, consider a classic study conducted in a housing complex for married students at MIT, conducted by Leon Festinger, Stanley Schachter, and Kurt Back (1950). The residents had been assigned to their apartments at random, as vacancies opened up, and nearly all of them were strangers when they moved in. The researchers asked the residents to name their three closest friends in the housing project. Just as the propinquity effect would predict, 65 percent of the residents mentioned people who lived in the same building, even though the other buildings were not far away. Even more striking was the pattern of friendships within a building. The researchers found that 41 percent of next-door neighbours indicated they were close friends, 22 percent of those who lived two doors apart did so, and only 10 percent of those who lived on opposite ends of the hall did so.

The propinquity effect works because of familiarity, or the **mere exposure effect**: The more exposure we have to a stimulus, the more apt we are to like it. We see certain people a lot, and the more familiar they become, the more friendship blooms. Of course, if the person in question is an obnoxious jerk, then, not surprisingly, the more exposure you have to him or her, the greater your dislike (Swap, 1977). However, in the absence of such negative qualities, familiarity breeds attraction and liking (Bornstein, 1989; Bornstein & D'Agostino, 1992; Griffin & Sparks, 1990; Moreland & Zajonc, 1982; Zajonc, 1968).

A good example of the propinquity and mere exposure effects is your classroom. All semester long, you see the same people. Does this increase your liking for them? Richard Moreland and Scott Beach (1992) tested this hypothesis by planting female research confederates in a large university classroom. The women did not interact with the professor or the other students; they simply walked in and sat quietly in the first row, where everyone could see them. The confederates differed in how many classes they attended, from 15 meetings down to the control condition of zero. At the end of the semester, the students in the class were shown slides of the women, whom they rated on several measures of liking and attractiveness. It turns out that mere exposure had a definite effect on liking. Even though they had never interacted, the students liked the women more, the more often they had seen them in class.

> Contrary to popular belief, I do not believe that friends are necessarily the people you like best; they are merely the people who got there first.
>
> —SIR PETER USTINOV,
> *Dear Me,*
> *1977*

Propinquity effect the finding that the more we see and interact with people, the more likely they are to become our friends

Mere exposure effect the finding that the more exposure we have to a stimulus, the more apt we are to like it

Close friendships are often formed in college and university, in part because of propinquity.

In summary, we are most likely to form relationships with the people around us. By crossing paths with the same person, we start to become familiar with him or her, and—voilà!—the seeds of friendship (or perhaps even romance) have been sown.

> FOCUS ON APPLICATIONS

Long-distance Propinquity: The Formation of Internet Relationships

Computer-mediated communication offers a new twist on the propinquity effect. Even if someone is thousands of kilometres away, you can meet that person in a chat room or through e-mail. How are computer-based relationships different from the ones formed in everyday life? Do computer relationships survive when they move from the computer screen to face-to-face interactions? Researchers are beginning to explore these questions (Fehr, 1996; Lea & Spears, 1995; Walther, Anderson, & Park, 1994).

Meeting people online poses inherent problems due to the medium itself. First, people may exaggerate or even lie about themselves in an e-mail, and the recipient has no way to detect dishonesty. Second, the flurry of e-mails between two people tends to create a high level of emotional intimacy—sometimes too quickly. With no real information about the person (such as you'd get from a face-to-face interaction), you may create an idealized image that quickly dies upon meeting him or her.

On the other hand, recent laboratory experiments have shown that people report being more comfortable revealing their "true" self to a partner over the Internet compared to a face-to-face interaction (Bargh, McKenna, & Fitzsimons, 2002; McKenna, Green, & Gleason, 2002). Interestingly, McKenna and colleagues (2002) found that participants also tended to report more liking for an Internet partner than a partner they met in person—even when (unbeknownst to the participants) it was actually the same person! Perhaps most important, research is showing that relationships formed over the Internet are highly similar to relationships developed face to face in terms of quality and depth (Bargh & McKenna, 2004). A recent two-year follow-up of romantic relationships originally formed over the Internet found that breakup rates were similar to those generally reported for relationships formed "in person" (McKenna, Green, & Gleason, 2002). Although there is still much to be learned about Internet relationships, the data suggest that, thanks to computers, propinquity may soon no longer be a prerequisite for the formation of romantic relationships.

Similarity

Though propinquity does affect friendship choices, it is also the case that we don't become good friends with everyone who is near us in physical space. What about the match between our interests, background, attitudes, and values and those of the other person? Are we more attracted to people who are like us (the concept of **similarity**), or are we more attracted to people who are our opposites (the concept of **complementarity**)? Folk wisdom may suggest that "opposites attract," but research evidence proves that it is similarity, not complementarity, that draws people together (Berscheid & Reis, 1998).

For example, dozens of tightly controlled experiments have shown that if all you know about a person (whom you've never met) is his or her opinions on several issues, the more similar those opinions are to yours, the more you will like him or her (Byrne & Nelson, 1965). And what happens when you do meet? In a classic study, Theodore Newcomb (1961) randomly assigned male students at the University of Michigan to be roommates in a particular dormitory at the start of the school year. Would similarity predict friendship formation? The answer was yes. Men became friends with those who were demographically similar (e.g., shared a rural background), as well as with those who were similar in attitudes and values (e.g., were also engineering majors or also held liberal political views).

Similarity attraction to people who are like us

Complementarity attraction to people who are opposite to us

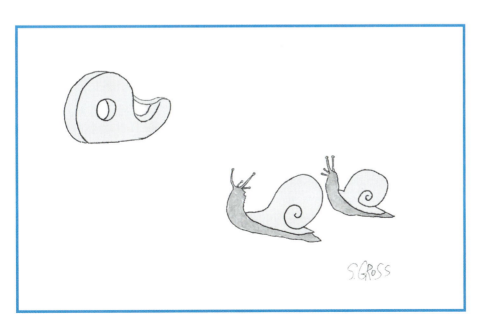

"I don't care if she is a tape dispenser. I love her."
Copyright © *The New Yorker Collection* 1998 Sam Gross from cartoonbank.com. All rights reserved.

Since Newcomb conducted this research, dozens of studies have demonstrated that similarity in terms of attitudes and values is an important predictor of attraction in both friendships and romantic relationships (Fehr, 1996). Similarity in other domains matters as well. For example, we are more likely to be attracted to someone who enjoys the same kinds of leisure activities as we do (Jamieson, Lydon, & Zanna, 1987; Werner & Parmelee, 1979). We also are attracted to people who are similar to us in terms of interpersonal style and communication skills (Burleson & Samter, 1996).

Why is similarity so important in attraction? There are several possibilities. First, we tend to think that people who are similar to us will be inclined to like us. Given this reasonable assumption, we take the first steps and initiate a relationship (Berscheid, 1985; Condon & Crano, 1988). Second, people who are similar provide us with important social validation for our characteristics and beliefs—that is, they provide us with the feeling that we are right (Byrne & Clore, 1970). Finally, according to the rewards-of-interaction explanation, if a person feels the same way we do on important issues, we assume it would be enjoyable to spend time with him or her. As you may have experienced, it is not very pleasant to interact with someone who disagrees with you on everything (Berscheid & Hatfield, 1978; Burleson, 1994). Thus, the desire to be liked and validated and to have enjoyable interactions all play a role in increasing our attraction to a like-minded person and diminishing the attractiveness of someone who is dissimilar (Byrne, Clore, & Smeaton, 1986; Cate & Lloyd, 1992; Dryer & Horowitz, 1997; Fehr, 1996; Holtz, 1997).

Reciprocal Liking

Most of us like to be liked. Not surprisingly, **reciprocal liking**—liking someone who likes us in return—is one of the prime determinants of interpersonal attraction. Liking is so powerful that it can even make up for the absence of similarity. For example, in one experiment, when a young woman expressed interest in male research participants simply by maintaining eye contact, leaning toward them, and listening attentively, the men expressed great liking for her despite the fact that they knew she disagreed with them on important issues (Gold, Ryckman, & Mosley, 1984). Other research confirms that a crucial determinant of whether we will like someone is the extent to which we believe that person likes us (Berscheid & Walster, 1978; Condon & Crano, 1988; Kenny, 1994; Kubitscheck & Hallinan, 1998; Secord & Backman, 1964).

Interestingly, reciprocal liking can come about because of a self-fulfilling prophecy, as demonstrated in an experiment by Rebecca Curtis and Kim Miller (1986). University students who did not know one another took part in the study in pairs. The researchers led some students to believe that they were liked by the students with whom they would be paired. Other students were led to believe that they were disliked by their partners for the study. The pairs of students were then given an opportunity to have a conversation. Just as predicted, those individuals who thought they were liked behaved in more likeable ways with their partners; they disclosed more about themselves, disagreed less about the topic under discussion, and generally behaved in a warmer, more pleasant manner than did those individuals who thought they were disliked. As a result, their partners ended up liking them—more so than did the partners of students who believed they were disliked (see Figure 8.1).

Before we leave this topic, we should note that reciprocal liking effects can only occur if you like yourself in the first place. People with negative self-concepts tend to be skep-

---

Reciprocal liking when you like someone and that person also likes you

> Life is to be fortified by many friendships. To love, and to be loved, is the greatest happiness of existence.
> —SYDNEY SMITH, 1855

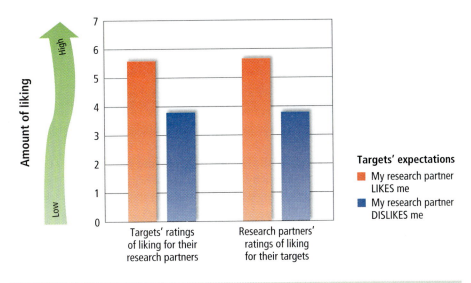

FIGURE 8.1 Liking and Being Liked

Research participants were given false feedback that their research partners either did or did not like them. They liked their partners more if they had been told beforehand that their partners liked them (see left side of figure), and their partners responded in kind (see right side of figure). Beliefs did indeed create reality.

(Adapted from Curtis & Miller, 1986)

tical that others actually do like them and therefore do not necessarily reciprocate liking (Swann, Stein-Seroussi, & McNulty, 1992). Thus, if people think of themselves as not being worth much or even as unlikeable, another person's friendly behaviour toward them will seem unwarranted, and they may not respond, setting in motion a self-fulfilling prophecy (Murray et al., 1998).

The Effects of Physical Attractiveness on Liking

Propinquity, similarity, and reciprocal liking are not the only determinants of whom we will come to like. We also are affected by people's looks—their physical attractiveness. How important is physical appearance to our first impressions of people? A classic study by Walster (Hatfield) and her colleagues revealed a surprising answer (Walster [Hatfield] et al., 1966). These researchers matched 752 incoming students at the University of Minnesota for a blind date at a dance during orientation week. The students had previously taken a battery of personality and aptitude tests; however, the researchers paired them at random. On the night of the dance, the couples spent a few hours together dancing and chatting. They then evaluated their dates and indicated whether they would like to date those people again. Of the many possible characteristics that could have determined whether they liked each other—such as their partners' intelligence, independence, sensitivity, or sincerity—the overriding determinant was physical attractiveness. What's more, there was no great difference between men and women on this score. (Note that other research has shown that although both sexes value attractiveness, men generally place more emphasis on looks than women do. Later, when we discuss evolutionary theories of love, we will consider some reasons for this gender difference.)

The findings of Walster (Hatfield) and colleagues, and subsequent replications (including a study among gay men that also showed that physical attractiveness was the best predictor of liking; Sergios & Cody, 1985), raise a perplexing issue: When people are asked about the qualities they desire in a dating partner or a mate, neither women nor men place physical attractiveness at the top of the list (Buss & Barnes, 1986). Yet when it comes to people's actual behaviour (what people do, rather than what they say), appearance seems to be the only thing that matters—at least in first-impression situations. Are people unaware of the importance they place on looks, or are they simply unwilling to admit that they so highly value such a superficial characteristic?

To find out, Hadjistavropoulos and Genest (1994) designed a clever study. They presented female students at the University of Saskatchewan with photographs of men varying in physical attractiveness, along with descriptions of their (supposed) personality traits. Participants were asked to rate the men in terms of their desirability as dating partners. The researchers found that attractive men received higher ratings than unattractive men. Moreover, attractiveness was the best predictor of desirability—more so than personality information. So far, this sounds just like the other studies we have been describing. But here's the interesting twist: Some of the participants were connected to an impressive-looking apparatus that they were told was a highly accurate lie detector. The researchers reasoned that if people aren't aware of the emphasis they place on looks, lie detector participants should give the same responses as participants who were not connected to a lie detector. If, on the other hand, people are aware that they base their evaluations of people on looks but feel they shouldn't admit it, then those who are attached to a lie detector should be more likely to "confess" to this than those who are not. And that is exactly what happened. These findings suggest that we are aware of the value we place on looks—but as long as we can get away with it, we won't admit it.

WHAT IS ATTRACTIVE? Bombarded as we are with media depictions of attractiveness, it is not surprising to learn that we share a set of criteria for defining beauty (Fink & Penton-Voak, 2002; Tseëlon, 1995). Look at the photographs on page 237 of models and actors who are considered attractive in Western culture. Can you describe the facial characteristics that have earned them this label? Michael Cunningham (1986) designed a creative study to determine these standards of beauty. He asked male university students to rate the attractiveness of 50 photographs of women, taken from a college yearbook and from an international beauty pageant program. Cunningham then carefully measured the relative size of the facial features in each photograph. He found that high attractiveness ratings were given to faces with large eyes, a small nose, a small chin, prominent cheekbones and narrow cheeks, high eyebrows, large pupils, and a big smile. Cunningham and his colleagues also examined women's ratings of male beauty in the same manner. They found that higher attractiveness ratings of men were associated with large eyes, prominent cheekbones, a large chin, and a big smile (Cunningham, Barbee, & Pike, 1990).

CULTURAL STANDARDS OF BEAUTY Are people's perceptions of what is beautiful or handsome similar across cultures? According to a recent review of this literature by University of Toronto social psychologist Karen Dion (2002), the answer is a surprising yes (see also Berscheid & Reis, 1998; Cunningham et al., 1995; Jones & Hill, 1993; Langlois et al., 2000; McArthur & Berry, 1987; Rhodes et al., 2001). Though racial and ethnic groups do vary in specific facial features, people from disparate cultures agree with each other on what is physically attractive in the human face.

Research has found that we share some standards of beauty. In females, large eyes, prominent cheekbones and narrow cheeks, high eyebrows, and a small chin are associated with beauty; in males, large eyes, prominent cheekbones, and a large chin are rated as most beautiful. Today's popular models and film stars—such as Brad Pitt, Michelle Pfeiffer, Denzel Washington, Naomi Campbell, Benjamin Bratt, and Lucy Liu—fit these criteria.

ASSUMPTIONS ABOUT ATTRACTIVE PEOPLE Most people assume that physical attractiveness is highly correlated with other desirable traits. Karen Dion, Ellen Berscheid, and Elaine Walster (Hatfield) (1972) have referred to this as the "what is beautiful is good" stereotype (Ashmore, Solomon, & Longo, 1996; Brigham, 1980; Hatfield & Sprecher, 1986a). Most research on the "what is beautiful is good" stereotype has been conducted with young people—usually university students. Perlini, Bertolissi, and Lind (1999) replicated the original Dion, Berscheid, and Walster study, with a twist. They showed photographs of attractive and unattractive younger and older women to first-year university students and senior citizens living in Sault Ste. Marie, Ontario. The researchers found that participants attributed more positive qualities to attractive women—regardless of their age. There was, however, one exception. Older men attributed more positive qualities to attractive young women than to attractive older women. Thus, it appears that the "what is beautiful is good" stereotype applies to older people as well. The exception is older men, for whom the stereotype seems to be "what is beautiful *and younger* is good"—at least with regard to their perceptions of women.

Luckily for those of us who do not look like supermodels, the stereotype is relatively narrow, affecting people's judgments about an individual only in specific areas. Reviews of this literature conducted by Alice Eagly and her colleagues (1991) and by Alan Feingold (1992a) have revealed that physical attractiveness has the largest effect on both men's and women's attributions when they are making judgments about social competence: The beautiful are thought to be more sociable, extroverted, and popular than the less attractive. They are also seen as more sexual, more happy, and more assertive.

> Beauty is a greater recommendation than any letter of introduction.
>
> —ARISTOTLE, FOURTH CENTURY BC

As you might expect, there appears to be a kernel of truth in the "what is beautiful is good" stereotype. The reason is that beautiful people, from a young age, receive a great deal of social attention that helps them develop good social skills (which, in turn, may lead to other positive outcomes, such as interpersonal and occupational success; Berscheid & Reis, 1998; Feingold, 1992a). Not surprisingly, the way we treat people affects how they behave and, ultimately, how they perceive themselves.

Can a "regular" person be made to act like a "beautiful" one through the self-fulfilling prophecy? Mark Snyder, Elizabeth Decker Tanke, and Ellen Berscheid (1977) decided to find out. They gave male university students a packet of information about another research participant, including her photograph. The photograph was of either an attractive woman or an unattractive woman. The purpose of the photograph was to invoke the men's stereotype that "what is beautiful is good"—that the woman would be more warm, likeable, poised, and fun to talk to if she was physically attractive than if she was unattractive. The men then had a telephone conversation with a woman, who they were told was the woman in the photograph. (They actually spoke with another woman.) The important question is this: Did the men's beliefs create reality? Yes. The men who thought they were talking to an attractive woman responded to her in a warmer, more sociable manner than did the men who thought they were talking to an unattractive woman. Not only that, but the men's behaviour influenced how the women themselves responded. When observers later listened to a tape recording of the women's half of the conversation, they rated the women whose male partners thought they were physically attractive as more attractive, confident, animated, and warm than the women whose male partners thought they were unattractive. In short, if a man thought he was talking to an attractive woman, he spoke to her in a way that brought out her best and most sparkling qualities.

This study was later replicated with the roles switched. Andersen and Bem (1981) showed female participants a photograph of an attractive or unattractive man; the women then had a phone conversation with him. The men on the other end of the line were unaware of the women's belief about them. Just as in the Snyder, Tanke, and Berscheid (1977) study, the women acted on their stereotype of beauty, and the unknowing men responded accordingly.

Attraction and the Misattribution of Arousal

Imagine that you go to see a scary movie with an extremely attractive date. As you are sitting there, you notice that your heart is thumping and you are a little short of breath. Is this because you are wildly attracted to your date, or because the movie is terrifying you? It is unlikely that you could say, "Fifty-seven percent of my arousal is due to the fact that my date is gorgeous, 32 percent is due to the scary movie, and 11 percent is due to indigestion from all the popcorn I ate." Because of this difficulty in pinpointing the precise causes of our arousal, we sometimes form mistaken emotions. You might think that most of your arousal is a sign of attraction to your date, when in fact a lot of it is due to the movie (or maybe even indigestion).

In recent years, many studies have demonstrated the occurrence of such **misattribution of arousal**, whereby people make mistaken inferences about what is causing them to feel the way they do (Ross & Olson, 1981; Savitsky et al., 1998; Schachter, 1977; Storms & Nisbett, 1970; Valins, 1966; Zillmann, 1978). Consider, for example, an intriguing field experiment by Donald Dutton and Arthur Aron (1974). Imagine you are one of the participants (all of whom were men). You are one of many people visiting the Capilano

Misattribution of arousal the process whereby people make mistaken inferences about what is causing them to feel the way they do

Canyon in scenic North Vancouver. Spanning the canyon is a narrow, 137-metre suspension bridge made of wooden planks attached to wire cables. You decide to walk across it. When you get a little way across, the bridge starts to sway from side to side. You feel as though you are about to tumble over the edge and you reach for the handrails, but they are so low that it feels even more likely that you will topple over. Then you make the mistake of looking down. You see nothing but a sheer 70-metre drop to rocks and rapids below. You become more than a little aroused—your heart is thumping, you breathe rapidly, and you begin to perspire. At this point, an attractive young woman approaches you and asks whether you could fill out a questionnaire for her, as part of a psychology project on the effects of scenic attractions on people's creativity. You decide to help her out. After you complete the questionnaire, the woman thanks you and says she would be happy to explain her study in more detail. She tears off a corner of the questionnaire, writes down her name and phone number. How attracted do you think you would be to this woman? Would you phone her and ask her out?

When people are aroused, in this case due to crossing a scary bridge, they often misattribute this arousal to the wrong source—such as attraction to the person they are with.

Think about this for a moment, and now imagine that the same woman approaches you under different circumstances. You decide to take a leisurely stroll farther up the Capilano River. You notice a wide sturdy bridge made of heavy cedar planks. The bridge has high handrails, even though it is situated only 3 metres above a shallow rivulet that runs into the main river. You are peaceably admiring the scenery when the woman asks you to fill out her questionnaire. How attracted do you feel toward her now? Dutton and Aron's prediction is clear: If you are on the high, scary bridge, you will be considerably aroused and will mistakenly think some of this arousal is the result of attraction to the beautiful woman. This is exactly what happened in the actual experiment. Half of the men (50 percent) who were approached on the high suspension bridge telephoned the woman later, whereas relatively few of the men (12.5 percent) who were approached on the low, sturdy bridge called her. (As you probably have guessed, the woman was a confederate—someone hired by the researchers—and she approached only men who were not accompanied by a woman.)

In summary, we have discussed four major determinants of attraction: propinquity, similarity, reciprocal liking, and physical attractiveness. After getting to this point in the chapter, you should be in a pretty good position to make a favourable first impression the next time you meet someone. Suppose you want Claudia to like you. You should hang around her (preferably on high scary bridges) so you become familiar, emphasize your similarity to her, and find ways of showing that you like her. It also wouldn't hurt to look your best. But what if you want to do more than make a good impression? What if you want to have a close friendship or a romantic relationship? Stay tuned.

 Thinking Critically
Think about a friendship or romantic relationship you had that has ended. Next, think about how your relationship started. To what extent did propinquity, similarity, reciprocal liking, and physical attractiveness bring the two of you together?

> Love is something so divine,
> Description would but make it less;
> 'Tis what I feel, but can't define,
> 'Tis what I know, but can't express.
>
> —BEILBY PORTEUS

FORMING AND MAINTAINING CLOSE RELATIONSHIPS

Social psychologists face a daunting task when trying to measure such complex feelings as love and passion. Trying to understand how people develop and sustain relationships is no easy task, either. However, as we will see, important strides have been made toward our understanding of close relationships.

What Is Love?

In the opening of this chapter, we described Bradley Bird's falling-in-love experience. But what, exactly, is love? For centuries, philosophers, poets, and novelists have grappled with this question. More recently, social psychologists have attempted to provide a scientific answer.

COMPANIONATE VERSUS PASSIONATE LOVE If you have ever been in love, think back to how you felt about your sweetheart when you first got to know him or her. You probably felt a combination of giddiness, longing, joy, and anxiety—the kinds of feelings that Bradley Bird experienced when he met Nina. Now think about how you feel toward your mother, or your brother, or a very close friend. You might also use the word *love* to describe how you feel about these important people in your life, but in this case the feelings are probably quite different from the feelings you have for your sweetheart. Ellen Berscheid and Elaine Walster (Hatfield) (1974; Berscheid & Walster [Hatfield], 1978) attempted to capture this distinction when they proposed that there are two major kinds

Gwyneth Paltrow and Joseph Fiennes exemplify the early stages of passionate love in this scene from *Shakespeare in Love*.

of love: companionate love and passionate love. **Companionate love** is defined as the feelings of intimacy and affection we feel toward someone with whom our lives are deeply intertwined. People can experience companionate love in nonsexual relationships, such as close friendships or familial relationships, or in sexual relationships, where they experience feelings of intimacy but not a great deal of heat and passion.

Passionate love involves an intense longing for another person. When things are going well—the other person loves us, too—we feel great fulfilment and ecstasy. When things are not going well, we feel great sadness and despair. This kind of love is characterized by obsessive thoughts about the loved one, as well as heightened physiological arousal wherein we actually feel shortness of breath and a thumping heart when we are in the loved one's presence (Regan, 1998; Regan & Berscheid, 1999).

Elaine Hatfield and Susan Sprecher (1986b) developed a questionnaire to measure passionate love. Passionate love, as measured by this scale, consists of strong uncontrollable thoughts; intense feelings; and overt acts toward the target of one's affection. Find out if you are experiencing (or have experienced) passionate love, by filling out the questionnaire in the following Try It!

Companionate love the feelings of intimacy and affection we feel for another person about whom we care deeply

Passionate love the feelings of intense longing, accompanied by physiological arousal, we feel for another person; when our love is reciprocated, we feel great fulfillment and ecstasy, but when it is not, we feel sadness and despair

The Passionate Love Scale

These items ask you to describe how you feel when you are passionately in love. Think of the person you love most passionately right now. If you are not in love right now, think of the last person you loved passionately. If you have never been in love, think of the person whom you came closest to caring for in that way. Choose your answer by remembering how you felt at the time when your feelings were the most intense.

For each of the 15 items, choose the number between 1 and 9 that most accurately describes your feelings. The answer scale ranges from 1, "not at all true," to 9, "definitely true." Write the number you choose next to each item.

```
     1        2        3        4        5        6        7        8        9
Not at all true                   Moderately true                   Definitely true
```

1. I would feel deep despair if _____ left me.
2. Sometimes I feel I can't control my thoughts; they are obsessively on _____.
3. I feel happy when I am doing something to make _____ happy.
4. I would rather be with _____ than anyone else.
5. I'd get jealous if I thought _____ were falling in love with someone else.
6. I yearn to know all about _____.
7. I want _____—physically, emotionally, and mentally.
8. I have an endless appetite for affection from _____.
9. For me, _____ is the perfect romantic partner.
10. I sense my body responding when _____ touches me.
11. _____ always seems to be on my mind.
12. I want _____ to know me—my thoughts, my fears, and my hopes.
13. I eagerly look for signs indicating _____'s desire for me.
14. I possess a powerful attraction for _____.
15. I get extremely depressed when things don't go right in my relationship with _____.

Scoring: Add up your scores for the 15 items. The total score can range from a minimum of 15 to a maximum of 135. The higher your score, the more your feelings for the person reflect passionate love; the items to which you gave a particularly high score reflect those components of passionate love that you experience most strongly.

Source: Adapted from Hatfield and Sprecher (1986b).

Triangular theory of love the idea that different kinds of love comprise varying degrees of three components: intimacy, passion, and commitment

TRIANGULAR THEORY OF LOVE Other researchers are not satisfied with a simple dichotomy of two kinds of love. Robert Sternberg (1986, 1988, 1997; Sternberg & Beall, 1991), for example, presents a **triangular theory of love**, which depicts love as comprising three basic components: intimacy, passion, and commitment.

Intimacy refers to feelings of being close to and bonded with a partner. Passion refers to the "hot" parts of a relationship—feelings of arousal and sexual attraction. Commitment consists of two decisions—the short-term one to love your partner and the long-term one to maintain that love and stay with your partner. These three ingredients—intimacy, passion, and commitment—can be combined in varying degrees to form different kinds of love (see Figure 8.2). Love can consist of one component alone or of any combination of these three parts. For example, you may feel a great deal of passion or physical attraction (infatuation love) but not know the person well enough to experience intimacy and not be ready to make any kind of commitment. As the relationship develops, it might blossom into romantic love, characterized by passion and intimacy, and maybe even consummate love—the blending of all three components. Sternberg uses the term *companionate love* in the same way we explained earlier, to describe love characterized by intimacy and commitment but not passion (Aron & Westbay, 1996; Hassebrauck & Buhl, 1996; Lemieux & Hale, 1999).

ORDINARY PEOPLE'S DEFINITION OF LOVE So far we have been discussing social psychologists' answers to the question "What is love?" Beverley Fehr (1988, 1994; Fehr & Russell, 1991) has been interested in how ordinary people define love. This is an important issue because the way in which people define love can determine how they act in their close relationships (deciding whether they are truly "in love," or whether they are experiencing the kind of love that leads to commitment, or whether they are no longer in

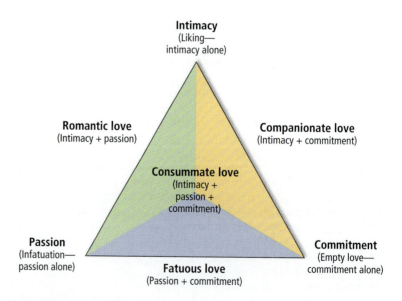

FIGURE 8.2 The Triangle of Love

According to the triangular theory of love, there are seven different forms of love, each made up of varying degrees of intimacy, passion, and commitment.

(Adapted from Sternberg, 1988)

love and should leave). In an initial set of studies, Fehr (1988) asked students at the University of British Columbia to list the features or characteristics of the concept of love. The definitions of love that were generated included both companionate features (warmth, intimacy, caring) and passionate features (heart rate increases, sexual attraction, thinking about the other person all the time). Other participants were then shown these features and asked to rate which were most prototypical, or important. As shown in Table 8.1, contrary to the stereotype that university students would view love only in passionate terms, Fehr found that companionate love was seen as capturing the meaning of love, more so than passionate love. Moreover, participants reported that they relied on the level of companionate love, rather than the level of passionate love, when deciding whether a relationship was progressing or deteriorating.

These studies have been replicated by researchers on the east coast of Canada (Button & Collier, 1991) and on the west coast of the United States (Aron & Westbay, 1996; Luby & Aron, 1990). Participants in these studies have shown remarkable agreement on the features of love. The companionate features of love are especially likely to be mentioned, and also consistently receive the highest importance ratings. These findings suggest that, at least within North America, people tend to agree on the meaning of love (Fehr, 1993).

GENDER AND LOVE Who is all mushy and romantic when it comes to love? Who is practical and solid? If you are like many people, you will answer "women" to the first question and "men" to the second. But think back to our opening story of Bradley Bird and you may come up with a different answer—one that is more consistent with the results of social psychological research. Indeed, when social psychologists began to conduct research on this question, they found that men fall in love more quickly than women and are more likely to endorse romantic beliefs such as "True love lasts forever" (Rubin, Peplau, & Hill, 1981; Sprecher & Metts, 1989). Men are also more likely than women to report having experienced love at first sight—as Bradley Bird can attest. In contrast, women hold a more

TABLE 8.1 Ratings of Features of Love

Highest Ratings		Lowest Ratings	
Trust	7.50	Think about the other all the time	4.45
Caring	7.28	Energy	4.28
Honesty	7.17	Heart rate increases	4.26
Friendship	7.08	Euphoria	4.12
Respect	7.01	Gazing at the other	4.10
Concern for the other's well-being	7.00	See only the other's good qualities	3.45
Loyalty	7.00	Butterflies in stomach	3.41
Commitment	6.91	Uncertainty	2.88
Accept other the way s/he is	6.82	Dependency	2.81
Supportiveness	6.78	Scary	2.28

Note: Ratings were made on a scale where 1 = extremely poor feature of love, and 8 = extremely good feature of love.

The features of love to which students at the University of British Columbia assigned the highest ratings portray companionate love; the features that received the lowest ratings portray passionate love.

Source: Fehr, 1988.

practical, friendship-based orientation to love (essentially, a companionate view of love). One of the first studies to report this finding was conducted by Kenneth Dion and Karen Dion (1973) at the University of Toronto. This gender difference continues to be found, even among culturally diverse participants (Dion & Dion, 1993; we will discuss this research in greater detail in the next section on Culture and Love).

CULTURE AND LOVE Though love is certainly a human emotion experienced everywhere on the planet, culture does play a role in how people label their experiences and in what they expect in close relationships.

Throughout this book we have noted that Western and Eastern cultures vary in important ways, with Western cultures emphasizing that the individual is autonomous, self-sufficient, and defined in terms of his or her personal qualities. Eastern cultures, in contrast, tend to be collectivistic, emphasizing the individual's loyalty to the group and defining him or her through membership in the group (Heine et al., 1999; Hofstede, 1984; Hui & Triandis, 1986; Markus, Kitayama, & Heiman, 1996; Triandis, 1995). Do these cultural differences translate into different definitions of love?

According to Karen Dion and Kenneth Dion (1993, 1996, 2001a), romantic love has less value in collectivist societies than in individualist societies. In individualist societies, romantic love is a heady, highly personal experience; one immerses oneself in the new partner and often virtually ignores friends and family for a while. The decision as to who to become involved with or marry is for the most part a personal one. In comparison, in collectivist cultures the individual in love must take into account the wishes of family and other group members; in fact, marriages are often by arrangement, with the respective families matching up the bride and groom (Fiske et al., 1998; Levine et al., 1995).

Dion and Dion (1993) assessed views of love among a heterogeneous sample of University of Toronto students. Their research participants fell into three groups by ethnocultural background: Asian (Chinese, Korean, Vietnamese, Indian, and Pakistani), Anglo-Celtic (English, Irish, and Scottish), and European (Scandinavian, Spanish, German, and Polish). The researchers found that the Asian students were more likely than

Although people all over the world experience love, how "love" is defined varies across cultures.

Anglo-Celtic or European students to identify with a companionable, friendship-based romantic love, a "style of love that would not disrupt a complex network of existing family relationships." Thus, love can vary in definition and behaviour in different societies. We all love, but we do not necessarily all love in the same way—or at least we don't describe it in the same way.

The Role of Positive Illusions in Maintaining Relationships

Even if we have the most loving, committed relationship imaginable, there are times when we will experience doubts about our choice of partner and question whether ours really is a good relationship. What makes people "hang in there" when the going gets tough? Recent research conducted at the University of Waterloo suggests that we maintain our relationships by indulging in **positive illusions**—that is, fantasies in which we convince ourselves that we have the most wonderful partner and the most wonderful relationship in the world, regardless of the facts. This process of idealization has been explored in several studies by Sandra Murray, John Holmes, and their colleagues.

Do we actually hold idealistic, rather than realistic, views of our partner? The answer to this question is yes (Murray et al., 2000; Murray, Holmes, and Griffin, 1996a). For example, Murray, Holmes, and Griffin (1996a) asked dating and married couples to rate their own attributes, their partners' attributes, and attributes of an ideal partner. Take, for example, the case of Lucia and Mario. If Lucia's perception of Mario is accurate (based on reality), the way in which she rates him (in terms of intelligence, humour, and consideration) should be very similar to how Mario rates himself on these attributes. If, however, Lucia holds an idealistic view of Mario, she should rate him more positively than he rates himself. And that is exactly what these researchers found. In fact, participants' ratings of their partners closely resembled their ratings of an ideal partner.

Is it actually beneficial to see our partners in idealistic ways? Wouldn't relationships be better off if we perceived our partners as they really are? Apparently not. In fact, it would seem that the rosier the glasses through which we view our partners, the better. Murray and Holmes have consistently found that the more that people idealize their partners (and the more that their partners idealize them), the greater their satisfaction with the relationship (Murray et al., 2000; Murray & Holmes, 1997, 1999; Murray, Holmes, & Griffin, 1996a). Moreover, doing so has survival value; relationships in which partners idealize one another are those most likely to endure (Murray, Holmes, & Griffin, 1996b). Perhaps most astonishing, Murray and colleagues have found that, over time, people begin to live up to the idealized images their partners have of them. Stated differently, individuals who idealize their partners ultimately create the partners they wish for! Thus, in the world of close relationships, dreams can actually come true!

Positive illusions idealization of our romantic relationships and partners in order to maintain the relationship

Why Do We Form and Maintain Relationships?

We began this chapter with a crucial question: Why are people so highly motivated to seek loving relationships? If you were to ask a group of social psychologists this question, you would probably get a number of answers, depending on each psychologist's theoretical persuasion. Chances are that you would hear the following: It's all about survival (evolutionary theories); it's all about your mother (attachment theories); and it's all about cashing in on the benefits of a close relationship (social exchange theories). Probably each of these theories tells part of the story. As you read about them, you may wish to think about which theory seems to explain best your motivation for seeking love.

EVOLUTIONARY EXPLANATIONS When asked the question "Why do I love thee? Let me count the ways," evolutionary theorists give some rather startling answers. The basic tenet of evolutionary biology is that an animal's "fitness" is measured by its reproductive success—that is, its ability to pass on its genes to the next generation. Reproductive success is not just part of the game; it *is* the game. Has human behaviour evolved in specific ways to maximize reproductive success? Evolutionary psychologists say yes; they argue that males and females have very different agendas because of their differing roles in producing offspring.

For females, reproduction is costly in terms of time, energy, and effort, and this means they must consider carefully when and with whom to reproduce. In comparison, reproduction has few costs for males. The **evolutionary approach** to love argues that reproductive success for the two sexes translates into two very different behaviour patterns. Male animals would do best to pursue frequent pairings with many females, and female animals would do best to pair infrequently and only with carefully chosen males (Berkow, 1989; Symons, 1979).

Now, what does this have to do with falling in love? David Buss and colleagues (Buss, 1985, 1988a, 1996; Buss & Schmitt, 1993) state that the evolutionary approach explains the different strategies of men and women in romantic relationships. A female, facing high reproductive costs, will look for a male who can supply the resources and support she needs to bear a child. A male will look for a female who appears capable of reproducing successfully. More specifically, men will respond to the physical appearance of women, since age and health denote reproductive fitness; women will respond to the economic and career achievements of men, since these variables represent resources they and their offspring will need (Buss, 1988b). The Bradley Bird and Nina relationship described at the beginning of this chapter would seem to fit this profile. He was swept off of his feet by her beauty; she may have been attracted to him because of the better life he could offer her.

Several studies have tested these predictions and found support for them. For example, Buss and colleagues (Buss, 1989; Buss et al., 1990) asked more than 9000 adults in 37 countries (including various regions of Canada) how important and desirable various characteristics were in choosing a marriage partner. In general, women valued ambition, industriousness, and good earning capacity in a potential mate more than men did. Men valued physical attractiveness in a mate more than women did, a finding echoed in other research discussed earlier (Buss & Barnes, 1986; Buss & Schmitt, 1993; Hatfield & Sprecher, 1995; Lundy, Tan, & Cunningham, 1998; Regan & Berscheid, 1997). We should point out, however, that in these studies the top characteristics on both women's and men's lists are the same, and they include honesty, trustworthiness, and a pleasant personality.

Evolutionary approach an approach derived from evolutionary biology that states that men and women are attracted to different characteristics in each other (men are attracted by women's appearance; women are attracted by men's resources) because this maximizes their reproductive success

> Men seek to propagate widely, whereas women seek to propagate wisely.
>
> —ROBERT HINDE

FOCUS ON APPLICATIONS

Youth and Beauty versus Status and Wealth: Gender Differences in Personal Ads

"Attractive, blond, blue-eyed 22-year-old seeks wealthy older man...." "Successful, well-to-do man in his forties seeks attractive, slim, younger woman...." Sound familiar? According to evolutionary theory, men value physical attractiveness in a mate whereas women value status and resources. To see whether this theory applies to real-world mate selection, several researchers have analyzed the content of personal ads placed in newspapers and on the Internet (Bereczkei et al., 1997; Deaux & Hanna, 1984; Koestner & Wheeler, 1988; Rajecki, Bledsoe, & Rasmussen, 1991).

Just as the theory would predict, women are more likely to advertise their beauty than are men. Men are more likely to advertise their wealth. Moreover, some studies have found that women who say they are physically attractive are more likely to get replies to their ads, whereas men are most likely to get replies when they advertise their resources (e.g., Baize & Schroeder, 1995). Rajecki, Bledsoe, and Rasmussen (1991) found that an even more important variable affecting reply rates was age—in their study, relatively younger women and older men were most likely to receive responses to their ads. Given that youth in women signifies reproductive capability and age in men signifies resources, this finding, too, can be explained from an evolutionary point of view. Thus, when we're feeling lonely and are hoping to meet that "special someone," not just anyone will do—whom we choose may be driven by an evolutionary agenda.

It may have occurred to you that the data we have been discussing could be explained in other ways. Indeed, the evolutionary approach to love has attracted its share of criticism and generated considerable controversy (Bradshaw, Bubier, & Sullivan, 1994; McKelvie & McLellan, 1993, 1994). Some social psychologists argue that the theory is untestable: It is so flexible that it can be used to explain anything (Sternberg & Beall, 1991). Others argue that men value physical attractiveness and youth in a partner simply because they have been conditioned to do so by decades of advertising and media images (Hatfield & Rapson, 1993). Still other researchers note that, around the world, women have less power, status, wealth, and other resources than men do. If women need to rely on men to achieve economic security, then they must consider this characteristic when choosing a mate. In comparison, men are free to choose a woman using more frivolous criteria such as good looks (Rosenblatt, 1974). Interestingly, the more economic power women have in a given culture, the more likely they are to value physical attractiveness in a man (Gangestad, 1993). As you can see, when discussing human mate preference it is difficult to disentangle "nature" (inborn preferences) from "nurture" (cultural norms and gender roles). The evolutionary approach is an interesting, exciting, and controversial theory. Further theorizing and research are required before we will fully understand the extent to which human love follows a biological imperative.

ATTACHMENT STYLES AND INTIMATE RELATIONSHIPS The evolutionary approach takes the long view—how people act today is based on behaviour patterns that evolved from our species' hominid past. Another theory of love, attachment theory, also focuses on the past, but on the more recent past, stating that our behaviour in adult relationships is based on our experiences as infants with our parents or caregivers. This approach draws on the groundbreaking work of John Bowlby (1969, 1973, 1980) and Mary Ainsworth (Ainsworth et al., 1978) on how infants form bonds to their primary caregivers (usually their mothers). The theory of **attachment styles** states that the kinds of bonds we form early in life influence the kinds of relationships we form as adults.

Mary Ainsworth and her colleagues (1978) identified three types of relationships between infants and their mothers. Infants with a **secure attachment style** typically have caregivers who are responsive to their needs and who show positive emotions when interacting

> In my very own self, I am part of my family.
>
> —D. H. LAWRENCE

Attachment styles the expectations people develop about relationships with others, based on the relationship they had with their primary caregiver when they were infants

Secure attachment style an attachment style characterized by trust, a lack of concern with being abandoned, and the view that one is worthy and well liked

Avoidant attachment style an attachment style characterized by a suppression of attachment needs, because attempts to be intimate have been rebuffed; people with this style find it difficult to develop intimate relationships

Anxious/ambivalent attachment style an attachment style characterized by a concern that others will not reciprocate one's desire for intimacy, resulting in higher-than-average levels of anxiety

with them. These infants trust their caregivers, are not worried about being abandoned, and come to view themselves as worthy and loved. Infants with an **avoidant attachment style** typically have caregivers who are aloof and distant, rebuffing the infant's attempts to establish intimacy. These infants desire to be close to their caregivers but learn to suppress this need, as if they know that attempts to be intimate will be rejected. People with this style find it difficult to become close to other people. Infants with an **anxious/ambivalent attachment style** typically have caregivers who are inconsistent and overbearing in their affection. These infants are unusually anxious, because they can never predict when and how their caregivers will respond to their needs. People with this style desperately seek closeness to others, but experience mixed, conflicted feelings even when they are in loving relationships.

The key assumption of attachment theory is that the particular attachment style we learn as infants and young children typically stays with us throughout life and generalizes to all of our relationships with other people (Collins & Sroufe, 1999; Fury, Carlson, & Sroufe, 1997; Hartup & Laursen, 1999). In a groundbreaking study, Cindy Hazan and Philip Shaver (1987) asked adults to choose one of three descriptions according to how they typically feel in romantic relationships. The descriptions were designed to capture the three kinds of attachment styles we described above. The researchers also asked people questions about their current and past relationships. The results of this study were consistent with an attachment theory perspective. Securely attached adults reported that they easily become close to other people, readily trust others, and have satisfying romantic relationships. People with an avoidant style reported that they are uncomfortable becoming close to others, find it hard to trust others, and have less satisfying romantic relationships. People with an anxious/ambivalent style also tended to have less satisfying relationships but of a different type: They are likely to be obsessive and preoccupied with their relationships, fearing that their partners do not want to be as intimate or close as they desire.

Several other studies have reported similar findings (Collins & Read, 1990; Feeney & Noller, 1990; Hazan & Shaver, 1994a, 1994b; Kirkpatrick & Davis, 1994; Morgan & Shaver, 1999; Simpson, 1990; Simpson, Rholes, & Phillips, 1996; see Reis & Patrick, 1996, for a review). For example, at the University of Toronto, Keelan, Dion, and Dion (1994) found that people who were securely attached maintained high levels of satisfaction, commitment, and trust in their romantic relationships over the four-month period of the study, whereas those who were insecurely attached (avoidants and anxious/ambivalents) showed decreases in satisfaction, commitment, and trust over time.

In an important conceptual development, Kim Bartholomew, a social psychologist at Simon Fraser University, proposed that there are actually two kinds of avoidant attachment (Bartholomew, 1990; Bartholomew & Horowitz, 1991). People with a **fearful avoidant style** consciously desire intimate relationships,

Attachment theory predicts that the attachment style we learn as infants stays with us throughout life and generalizes to our relationships with other people.

Fearful avoidant style a type of avoidant attachment in which close relationships are avoided due to mistrust and fears of being hurt

but avoid them because they are afraid to trust others and worry that they will be hurt if they allow themselves to become too close to another person. People with a **dismissive avoidant style** claim that they do not need close relationships, but rather prefer to be independent and self-sufficient. Bartholomew developed a scale to assess secure attachment, preoccupied attachment (similar to anxious/ambivalent attachment discussed earlier), and these two avoidant types (Bartholomew & Horowitz, 1991). This scale appears in the following Try It! Many studies have confirmed this four-category model. For example, people with a fearful avoidant style have a negative view of themselves and of other people, whereas people with a dismissive avoidant style have a positive view of themselves, but a negative view of others (Bartholomew & Horowitz, 1991). People with a fearful style also report greater distress when a romantic relationship ends than do those with a dismissive style (Sprecher et al., 1998). What's your style? See the following Try It!

Dismissive avoidant style a type of avoidant attachment in which the person is self-sufficient and claims not to need close relationships

MULTIPLE ATTACHMENT REPRESENTATIONS Please reread the attachment descriptions in the following Try It! For each description, try to think of a relationship (with a romantic partner, friend, or parent) in which you felt that way. When students at the University of Winnipeg were asked to do so, most of them were able to think of relationships that matched each style (Baldwin et al., 1996). Indeed, researchers are now beginning to acknowledge that rather than possessing one single attachment style that applies to all of our relationships, we can have different kinds of attachment to different people in our lives. For example, Ross and Spinner (2001) recently asked students at the University of New Brunswick and adults from the community to fill out the Bartholomew

What's Your Style?

Which description below best captures your approach to relationships?

Secure style	47%	It is relatively easy for me to become emotionally close to others. I am comfortable depending on others and having others depend on me. I don't worry about being alone or having others not accept me.
Preoccupied (Anxious) style	14%	I want to be completely emotionally intimate with others, but I often find that others are reluctant to get as close as I would like. I am uncomfortable being without close relationships, but I sometimes worry that others don't value me as much as I value them.
Dismissing Avoidant style	18%	I am comfortable without close emotional relationships. It is very important for me to feel independent and self-sufficient, and I prefer not to depend on others or have them depend on me.
Fearful Avoidant style	21%	I am somewhat uncomfortable getting close to others. I want emotionally close relationships, but I find it difficult to trust others completely or to depend on them. I sometimes worry that I will be hurt if I allow myself to become too close to others.

Note: The percentages in each category are based on a sample of Introductory Psychology students.

Source: Adapted from Bartholomew & Horowitz, 1991.

and Horowitz (1991) scale for four specific relationships (mother, father, friend). The researchers found that relationship-specific attachment ratings can be quite different from people's reports of their general attachment style. As the authors explain, "Knowing, for example, that an individual is securely attached to his or her mother tells us relatively little about whether that individual is also securely attached in other relationships" (Ross & Spinner, 2001).

A similar conclusion was reached by McGill University researchers Tamarha Pierce and John Lydon (2001). In a series of studies, they found that people's overall attachment style is correlated with, but distinct from, their attachment in specific relationships (mother, father, best friend, and romantic partner). Interestingly, these researchers found that, over time, attachment to specific partners changed in the direction of global, overall attachment, rather than vice versa. In other words, if you are generally secure, your attachment in specific relationships will tend to become secure, whereas the attachment you experience in any particular relationship is less likely to change your overall style.

Findings such as these have led researchers such as Mark Baldwin and Beverley Fehr (1995; Baldwin et al., 1996) to suggest that attachment styles might best be conceptualized as schemas, rather than as stable personality traits. (As you will recall from Chapter 3, schemas are mental structures that people use to organize information—in this case, relational information.) Based on our experiences in relationships, we associate certain kinds of relational information with particular people. From this perspective, although our relationship with our mother is likely to remain important, it's not the only relationship for which we have a schema. Further, as we discussed in Chapter 3, once we have formed schemas, they are resistant to change—but not impossible to change. In the context of attachment theory, this is good news, because it implies that people can learn new and healthier ways of relating to others than they experienced in infancy (Kirkpatrick & Hazan, 1994; Kojetin, 1993). Thus, even if we did not experience secure attachment to our mothers, we are not doomed to a lifetime of unhappy relationships.

SOCIAL EXCHANGE THEORIES Social exchange and equity theories are based on the simple notion that relationships operate on an economic model of costs and benefits, much the way that the marketplace operates (Blau, 1964; Homans, 1961; Kelley & Thibaut, 1978; Thibaut & Kelley, 1959). **Social exchange theory** states that how people feel about their relationships will depend on their perception of the rewards they receive from the relationship and their perception of the costs they incur, as well as their perception of what kind of relationship they deserve and the probability that they could have a better relationship with someone else. In other words, we buy the best relationship we can get, one that gives us the most value for our emotional dollar. The basic concepts of social exchange theory are reward, cost, outcome, comparison level, and comparison level for alternatives (Thibaut & Kelley, 1959).

Rewards are the positive, gratifying aspects of the relationship that make it worthwhile and reinforcing. They include the positive personal characteristics and behaviour of our relationship partner (similarity, attractiveness, sense of humour) and our ability to acquire external resources by virtue of knowing this person (gaining access to money, status, activities, or other interesting people; Lott & Lott, 1974). Costs are, obviously, the other side of the coin, and all relationships have some costs attached to them (putting up with those annoying habits and characteristics of the other person). The outcome of the relationship is based on a calculation of the **reward/cost ratio**—you can think of it as a

Social exchange theory the theory holding that how people feel about a relationship depends on their perceptions of the rewards and costs of the relationship, the kind of relationship they deserve, and their chances of having a better relationship with someone else

Reward/cost ratio in social exchange theory, the notion that there is a balance between the rewards that come from a relationship and the personal cost of maintaining the relationship. If the ratio is not favourable, the result is dissatisfaction with the relationship

mathematical formula in which outcome equals rewards minus costs. (If you come up with a negative number, your relationship is not in good shape.)

How satisfied you are with your relationship depends on another variable—your **comparison level**, or what you expect the outcome of your relationship to be in terms of costs and rewards (Kelley & Thibaut, 1978; Thibaut & Kelley, 1959). Over time, you have amassed a long history of relationships with other people, and this history has led you to have certain expectations as to what your current and future relationships should be like. Some people have a high comparison level, expecting to receive many rewards and few costs in their relationships. If a given relationship doesn't match this expected comparison level, they will be unhappy and unsatisfied. In contrast, people who have a low comparison level would be happy in the same relationship, because they expect relationships to be difficult and costly.

Finally, your satisfaction with a relationship also depends on your perception of the likelihood that you could replace it with a better one—or your **comparison level for alternatives**. There are a lot of people out there. Could a relationship with a different person (or even being alone) give you a better outcome, or greater rewards for fewer costs, than your current relationship? People who have a high comparison level for alternatives, perhaps because they believe the world is full of fabulous people dying to meet them or because they are not afraid to be on their own, are more likely to get out of a relationship. People with a low comparison level for alternatives will be more likely to stay in a costly relationship because, to them, what they have is not great but is better than what they think they could find elsewhere.

Social exchange theory has received a great deal of empirical support; friends and romantic couples do pay attention to the costs and rewards in their relationships, and these affect how people feel about a relationship. There also is evidence that people are more likely to end a relationship when they perceive that attractive alternatives are available (Attridge & Berscheid, 1994; Bui, Peplau, & Hill, 1996; Drigotas, Safstrom, & Gentilia, 1999; Rusbult, 1983; Rusbult & Van Lange, 1996; South & Lloyd, 1995).

Rewards, costs, and alternatives do not tell the whole story, however. As you may have observed, many people do not leave their partners, even when they are dissatisfied and their alternatives look bright. Caryl Rusbult and her colleagues would agree; they say we need to consider at least one additional factor to understand close relationships: a person's level of investment in the relationship (Kelley, 1983; Rusbult, 1980, 1983, 1991; Rusbult, Martz, & Agnew, 1998). In her **investment model** of close relationships, Rusbult defines investments as anything people have put into a relationship that will be lost if they leave it. Examples include tangible things, such as financial resources and possessions (e.g., a house), as well as intangible things, such as the emotional welfare of one's children, or time and emotional energy spent building the relationship. As seen in Figure 8.3, the greater the investment individuals have in a relationship, the less likely they are to leave, even if satisfaction is low and alternatives are available. In short, to predict whether people will stay in an intimate relationship, we need to know (a) how satisfied they are with the relationship (that is, the level of rewards minus costs), (b) whether they believe that attractive alternatives are available, and (c) the extent of their investment in the relationship.

This model has been supported in studies of dating and married couples, lesbian and gay couples, for close friends, and for residents of the United States, the Netherlands, and Taiwan (Kurdek, 1992; Lin & Rusbult, 1995; Rusbult, 1991; Rusbult & Buunk, 1993). The model also has been used to explain why women stay in abusive relationships (Rusbult & Martz, 1995).

> Love is often nothing but a favorable exchange between two people who get the most of what they can expect, considering their value on the personality market.
>
> —ERICH FROMM,
> The Sane Society,
> 1955

Comparison level people's expectations about the level of rewards and costs they deserve in a relationship

Comparison level for alternatives people's expectations about the level of rewards and punishments they would receive in an alternative relationship

Investment model the theory holding that people's commitment to a relationship depends on their satisfaction with the relationship in terms of rewards, costs, and comparison level; their comparison level for alternatives; and how much they have invested in the relationship that would be lost by leaving it

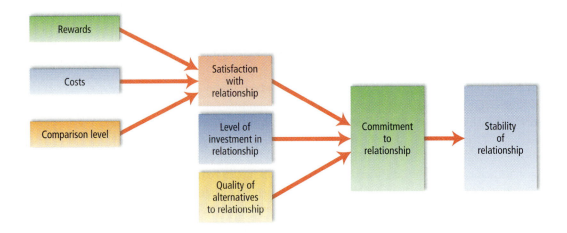

FIGURE 8.3 The Investment Model of Commitment

People's commitment to a relationship depends on three variables: how satisfied they are (rewards minus costs), how much they feel they have invested in the relationship, and whether they have good alternatives to this relationship. These commitment variables in turn predict how stable the relationship will be. For example, a woman who feels that the costs exceed the rewards in her relationship would have low satisfaction. If she also felt she had little invested in the relationship, and a very attractive person was expressing interest in her, she would have a low level of commitment. The end result is low stability; most likely, she will break up with her current partner.

(Adapted from Rusbult, 1983)

Thus, when it comes to long-term relationships, commitment is based on more than just the amount of rewards and punishments doled out (the level of satisfaction); it also depends on the quality of alternatives available and how heavily the individual has invested in the current relationship.

EQUITY THEORY Some researchers have criticized social exchange theory for ignoring an essential variable in relationships—the notion of fairness. Proponents of **equity theory** argue that people are not simply out to get the most rewards for the least cost; they are also concerned about equity in their relationships, wherein the rewards and costs they experience and the contributions they make to the relationship are comparable to the rewards, costs, and contributions of the other person (Homans, 1961; Walster, Walster, & Berscheid, 1978). These theorists describe equitable relationships as the most happy and stable type. In comparison, inequitable relationships result in one person feeling overbenefited (getting a lot of rewards, incurring few costs, devoting little time or energy to the relationship) or underbenefited (getting few rewards, incurring a lot of costs, devoting a lot of time and energy to the relationship).

According to equity theory, both underbenefited and overbenefited partners should feel uneasy about this state of affairs, and both should be motivated to restore equity to the relationship. This makes sense for the underbenefited person (who wants to continue feeling miserable?), but why should the overbenefited individual want to give up what social exchange theory indicates is a cushy deal—many rewards for little cost and little work? Hatfield and Walster (1978) argue that equity is all about fairness; people will eventually

Equity theory the theory holding that people are happiest with relationships in which the rewards and costs that a person experiences and the contributions that he or she makes to the relationship are roughly equal to the rewards, costs, and contributions of the other person

feel uncomfortable or even guilty if they get more than they deserve in a relationship. However, let's face facts—being overbenefited just doesn't feel as bad as being underbenefited, as several studies have shown (Buunk & Prins, 1998; Hatfield et al., 1982; Sprecher, 1998; Sprecher & Schwartz, 1994; Traupmann et al., 1981).

EXCHANGE VERSUS COMMUNAL RELATIONSHIPS Before leaving this topic, we want to mention one last criticism of social exchange theories. Margaret Clark and Judson Mills do not deny that **exchange relationships** exist. However, they suggest that concern about exchange and fairness are limited to our relationships with strangers and acquaintances. In contrast, our interactions with close friends, family members, and romantic partners are governed less by an equity norm and more by a desire to help each other in times of need (Clark, 1984, 1986; Clark & Mills, 1979, 1993; Clark & Pataki, 1995; Mills & Clark, 1982, 1994). In these **communal relationships**, people give in response to the other's needs, regardless of whether they are repaid. A good example of a communal relationship is parenting. As a friend of ours recently put it, "You spend years catering to your child's every need—changing diapers, sitting up with her in the middle of the night when she is throwing up, coaching her soccer team—knowing full well that sooner or later, she will reach an age when she will prefer to spend her time with anyone but you!"

Clark and her colleagues have conducted numerous studies that show that we are much more concerned with tit-for-tat exchange in relationships that are not close, and much more likely to give in response to the needs of those to whom we are close (Clark, 1984; Clark & Mills, 1979; Clark & Waddell, 1985; Williamson & Clark, 1989, 1992). Does this mean that people in communal relationships are completely unconcerned with equity? No. As we saw earlier, people do feel distressed if they believe that their intimate relationships are inequitable. However, equity takes on a somewhat different form in communal relationships than it does in less intimate ones. In communal relationships, the partners are more relaxed about what constitutes equity at any given time; they believe that things will eventually balance out and that a rough kind of equity will be achieved over time. If this is not the case—if they come to feel that there is a chronic imbalance—the relationship will be in trouble and eventually may end.

Exchange relationships
relationships governed by the need for equity (for a comparable ratio of rewards and costs)

Communal relationships
relationships in which people's primary concern is being responsive to the other person's needs

> The friendships which last are those wherein each friend respects the other's dignity to the point of not really wanting anything from him.
>
> —CYRIL CONNOLLY

Close relationships can have either exchange or communal properties. Family relationships are typically communal; acquaintanceships are typically based on exchange, though they can become communal if they grow into friendships.

In summary, social psychologists have come up with a number of answers to the important question, "Why do we love?" According to evolutionary theories, we love in order to increase our chances of reproduction, thereby ensuring the survival of our species. According to attachment theory, we learned lessons about how worthy we are of love from our primary caregiver and those lessons determine whether we seek loving relationships, as well as the quality of those relationships. Finally, according to social exchange theories, we love because of the benefits we receive from relationship partners.

Thinking Critically

1. Think about which attachment styles best describe you and a former friend or partner. Did you have matching or dissimilar styles? Do you think a difference in your attachment styles played a role in the ending of your relationship?

2. According to the investment model, satisfaction, investment, and alternatives predict whether people will stay together or break up. How would you describe yourself and your friend or partner in terms of these three variables? Was one of you more invested than the other? What about your respective comparison levels of alternatives?

ENDING CLOSE RELATIONSHIPS

As you may have experienced, some relationships are more likely to resemble nightmares, rather than dreams, come true. In Canada, just over one-third of marriages end in divorce (Statistics Canada, 1999a). The dissolution of other kinds of relationships is not publicly recorded. However, in longitudinal studies of dating relationships, a typical finding is that half of couples break up within a few years, with gay and lesbian relationships showing some of the highest rates of dissolution (Sprecher, 1994; Sprecher & Fehr, 1998). And even though people tend not to break up with friends formally, the loss of friendships is a common experience (Fehr, 1996). After several years of studying what love is and how it blooms, social psychologists are now beginning to explore the end of the story—how it dies.

Why Relationships End

As you might expect, the reasons that relationships end are complex and multifaceted. Moreover, different kinds of relationships end for different reasons. For example, common reasons given for the dissolution of marriage are financial difficulties, unemployment, alcoholism, sexual infidelity, low religiosity, and premarital pregnancy (Sprecher & Fehr, 1998; White, 1990). Not all of these reasons would apply to dating relationships or friendships. However, there also are some important commonalities across relationships.

One place to look for clues is among the predictors of attraction. If the factors that caused you to be attracted to someone are no longer present, the relationship is likely to be in trouble. For example, at the beginning of this chapter we identified similarity as an important predictor of attraction. As you might expect, if spouses, friends, or dating partners become dissimilar, the relationship is vulnerable to dissolution (Fehr, 1996; Sprecher & Fehr, 1998). Statements such as "We grew apart" or "We seemed to be going in different directions" reflect the role of dissimilarity in the breakup of relationships. In a fascinating study, Diane Felmlee (1995) asked 300 university students to focus on a romantic relationship that had ended and to list the qualities that had first attracted them to the person and the characteristics they ended up disliking most about the person. Felmlee found that

Relationships can end for many reasons. For example, in "fatal attractions," the very qualities that once attracted you ("He's so mature and wise") can become the very reason you break up ("He's too old").

30 percent of these breakups were examples of "fatal attractions." The qualities that were initially so attractive ("He's so unusual and different," "She's so exciting and unpredictable") became the very reasons why the relationship ended ("He and I have nothing in common," "I can never count on her"). "Fatal attractions" were most likely to occur for qualities in which the partners were dissimilar.

The theories of attraction discussed earlier also shed light on the issue of why relationships end. For example, as mentioned earlier, social exchange theorists find that relationships are likely to end when rewards are low and costs are high (in other words, when the relationship is low in satisfaction), when attractive alternatives are available to one or both partners, and when the partners have invested little in the relationship (Rusbult, 1983; Rusbult, Martz, & Agnew, 1998). Equity also plays a role in the ending of relationships. People are likely to end relationships that they feel are inequitable—particularly if they are feeling underbenefited.

Finally, there is another reason that relationships end—a reason few of us are willing to admit—and that is sheer boredom. According to Aron and Aron (1986, 1997), as another person becomes familiar to us, there is less that is new and exciting for us to discover about him or her. Marriage or cohabiting relationships may be especially susceptible to boredom. The day-to-day routine of living together may lead people to feel that they are in a rut and are missing out on excitement and passion (Baumeister & Bratslavsky, 1999; Fincham & Bradbury, 1993). John La Gaipa, who has conducted extensive research on friendship at the University of Windsor, maintains that friendships also dissolve because of boredom, but that this is not a socially acceptable basis for terminating a friendship. Thus, when asked why a friendship ended, we are likely to mention reasons such as disloyalty or betrayals of trust (La Gaipa, 1982). We suspect that people who terminate a marriage would be especially likely to offer such reasons—even if the culprit was sheer boredom.

> Love is like war; easy to begin but very hard to stop.
> —H. L. MENCKEN

The Experience of Breaking Up

As the words of a 1970s hit put it, "They say that breaking up is hard to do...." Indeed, the breakup of a relationship is one of life's more painful experiences. What, exactly, determines just how painful a breakup is going to be? To find out, Sprecher and colleagues (1998) examined a number of predictors of distress following the breakup of a romantic relationship. First of all, they found that the pain is greatest for the person who is being rejected. Other researchers also have found—and you may have experienced this—that the person who does the breaking up usually experiences less heartbreak than the person who is "dumped" (Akert, 1998; Helgeson, 1994; Lloyd & Cate, 1985). In addition, as you might expect based on our earlier discussion of social exchange theory, Sprecher and colleagues found that the higher a person's level of satisfaction and commitment, the greater the distress when the relationship ended. If you are happy in a relationship and want it to last forever, it can be heartbreaking to discover that your partner wants out. Also consistent with social exchange theory, participants experienced less distress if they were interested in alternative relationships. The opposite was true if their former partners had attractive alternatives available to them—then, needless to say, participants felt greater distress.

The good news is that the participants reported that they felt significantly less distress currently than they had immediately after the breakup. Thus, if by some unfortunate circumstance your heart has been broken, take comfort in the fact that time really does heal wounds.

Thinking Critically

If you have ever experienced the breakup of a romantic relationship, think back to why you believe your relationship ended. Do your reasons match the findings of the research reported in this section? Are there additional predictors of breakups that researchers should be looking at?

Summary

In the first part of this chapter, we discussed the variables that cause initial attraction between two people. One such variable is physical proximity, or the **propinquity effect**. People you come into contact with the most are most likely to become your friends and lovers. Why? An answer is found in the **mere exposure effect**—the more familiar something or someone becomes, the greater our liking. **Similarity** between people, whether in attitudes, values, or activity preferences, is another powerful cause of attraction and liking. How people behave toward us is also of importance. In general, we like others who behave as if they like us. This is known as **reciprocal liking**. Though most people are reluctant to admit it, *physical attractiveness* also plays an important role in liking. Physical attractiveness of the face has a cross-cultural component; people from different cultures tend to agree on what is beautiful. The "what is beautiful is good" stereotype indicates that people assume that physical attractiveness is associated with other desirable traits. Finally, attraction can also occur due to **misattribution of arousal**—mistakenly assuming that feelings of physiological arousal from some other source are caused by the presence of an attractive person in our environment.

In the second part of this chapter, we examined the causes of attraction (or love) in close relationships. Social psychologists have offered several definitions of love. One important distinction is between **companionate love**—feelings of intimacy and affection for those with whom our lives are intertwined—and **passionate love**—feelings of intense longing and arousal. Ordinary people's definition of love includes both companionate and passionate components, although the companionate aspect is seen as the true meaning of love. The **triangular theory of love** distinguishes among three components of love: intimacy, passion, and commitment.

Though love is universal, there are gender and cultural differences in the definition and experience of love. Men hold a more romantic, passionate view of love than do women. People who live in individualist cultures are more likely to emphasize passionate love than are people who live in collectivist cultures, where companionate love is valued.

One way in which we maintain our relationships, once they are formed, is by holding **positive illusions**. The more we idealize our partner, the greater our satisfaction with a relationship and the more likely the relationship will endure.

A number of theories have been proposed to explain *why* human beings are so motivated to seek love. The **evolutionary approach** to love states that men and women are attracted to different characteristics in each other because this maximizes reproductive success. This view maintains that when choosing a marriage partner, women care more about men's resources and men care more about women's appearances.

The *theory of attachment* points to people's past relationships, specifically with their primary caregiver, as a significant determinant of the quality of their close relationships as adults. Infants can be classified as having one of three types of attachment relationships: **secure, anxious/ambivalent**, and **avoidant**. The avoidant style can be further divided into **dismissive avoidant** and **fearful avoidant**. People who report having been securely attached as infants have the most intimate and satisfying relationships. Recent research suggests that people have different attachment patterns in different relationships. Thus, **attachment styles** may be best thought of as schemas, rather than as stable personality traits.

Social exchange theory argues that how people feel about their relationships depends on their assessment of the **rewards and costs** of the relationship. To determine whether people will stay in a relationship, we also need to know their **comparison level**—the outcomes they have come to expect in relationships—and their **comparison level for alternatives**—their expectations about how happy they would be in other relationships or alone. According to the **investment model**, to predict whether a relationship will last, we need to know not only each person's satisfaction and comparison level for alternatives, but also how much has been invested in the relationship.

There are exceptions to the rule of social exchange. **Equity theory** states that we are happiest when relationships are fair—when what we contribute is comparable to what our partner contributes. According to Clark and Mills, **exchange relationships** are limited to our relationships with strangers and acquaintances. Long-term intimate relationships are usually **communal relationships**, in which people are less concerned with an immediate accounting of who is contributing what and are more concerned with helping their partners when they are in need.

Unfortunately, intimate relationships end. There are a number of reasons why, including dissimilarity between the partners. Relationships also end when costs are greater than rewards (when the relationship is no longer satisfying), when attractive alternatives are available, and when investments are low. While the experience of breaking up is never pleasant, variables such as whether or not we were responsible for the breakup affect the amount of distress we experience.

Key Terms

Anxious/ambivalent attachment style   (page 248)
Attachment styles   (page 247)
Avoidant attachment style   (page 248)
Communal relationships   (page 253)
Companionate love   (page 241)
Comparison level   (page 251)
Comparison level for alternatives   (page 251)
Complementarity   (page 233)
Dismissive avoidant style   (page 249)
Equity theory   (page 252)
Evolutionary approach   (page 246)
Exchange relationships   (page 253)
Fearful avoidant style   (page 248)
Investment model   (page 251)
Mere exposure effect   (page 231)
Misattribution of arousal   (page 238)
Passionate love   (page 241)
Positive illusions   (page 245)
Propinquity effect   (page 231)
Reciprocal liking   (page 234)
Reward/cost ratio   (page 250)
Secure attachment style   (page 247)
Similarity   (page 233)
Social exchange theory   (page 250)
Triangular theory of love   (page 242)

Key Online Search Terms

Propinquity effect
Similarity
Reciprocal liking
Companionate love
Passionate love
Attachment styles
Comparison level
Comparison level for alternatives
Investments
Equity
Exchange versus communal relationships
Commitment calibration hypothesis
Positive illusions

If You Are Interested

Brehm, S. S., Miller, R. S., Perlman, D., & Campbell, S. M. (2002). *Intimate relationships* (3rd ed.). New York: McGraw-Hill. A comprehensive, readable overview of the entire field of interpersonal attraction, from first impressions to intimate relationships. One of the authors, Daniel Perlman, is at the University of British Columbia.

Dion, K. K., & Dion, K. L. (2001). Gender and relationships. In R. K. Unger (Ed.), *Handbook of the psychology of women and gender*. New York: John Wiley and Sons (pp. 256–271). This chapter, written by two prominent social psychologists at the University of Toronto, presents a state-of-the-art review and analysis of gender differences in close relationships. In the first section, the authors discuss how major theories of close relationships (many of which are discussed in this chapter) explain gender differences. The second section examines research on gender differences and focuses on topics such as romanticism, long-distance relationships, and cross-sex friendships. The final section deals with gender, culture, and relationships.

Fehr, B. (1996). *Friendship processes*. Thousand Oaks, CA: Sage. A University of Winnipeg social psychologist documents the life course of friendships: how they are formed, maintained, and terminated. Theories of friendship and gender differences in friendship are discussed as well.

Goodwin, R. (1999). *Personal relationships across cultures*. New York: Routledge. An engaging analysis of relationship processes in different cultures. In addition to topics discussed in this chapter (e.g., love, attraction), the author examines phenomena such as arranged marriages, the role of family networks in mate selection, and so on.

Weblinks

www.iarr.org
International Association for Relationship Research
An organization of researchers who focus on friendships and love relationships. Includes reviews of recent journal articles, links to researchers, and contents of recent conventions.

www.psychology.sunysb.edu/attachment
Attachment Theory and Research
This is a comprehensive site on developmental research on attachment theory.

www.personalityonline.com/tests/engine.html?testid=4
The Love Type Test
This "love test" assesses your feelings toward your partner in terms of Sternberg's triangualr theory of love.

Chapter 8 Practice Quiz

Check your knowledge of the concepts in this chapter by trying the following questions.

MAJOR ANTECEDENTS OF ATTRACTION

Multiple Choice

1. The propinquity effect works as a result of
    a. deprivation anxiety.
    b. similarity.
    c. mere exposure.
    d. age and gender.

2. The recent increase in people meeting online has challenged the
    a. statistical variance approach.
    b. population effect principle.
    c. theory of social isolation.
    d. propinquity effect.

3. Which concept best describes the saying "birds of a feather flock together"?
    a. similarity
    b. opposites attract
    c. incongruency
    d. equity

4. Snyder, Tanke, and Berscheid (1977) found that males provided with a photo of an attractive female and then asked to speak to ostensibly the same female on the phone
    a. were too nervous to communicate effectively.
    b. were more sociable to the female, but the female was unaffected.
    c. were more sociable to the female, and the female was more attractive.
    d. were less sociable to the female.

5. Dutton and Aron found that men approached by an attractive female on a swaying bridge attributed their arousal to the
    a. woman.
    b. height.
    c. task of calling her later.
    d. psychological questionnaire.

6. _____ is a prime determinant of interpersonal attraction.
    a. Anger
    b. Reciprocal liking
    c. Dissimilarity
    d. Social loafing

True or False

7. The propinquity effect works on the micro level.
   ___ True
   ___ False

8. In first impression situations, physical attractiveness plays a small role in shaping whether or not we are attracted to others.
   ___ True
   ___ False

Fill in the Blank

9. _____ results from mistaken inferences about what causes people to feel the way they do.
10. _____ attraction is most likely for people opposite to ourselves.

FORMING AND MAINTAINING CLOSE RELATIONSHIPS

Multiple Choice

11. According to Berscheid and Walster, the two kinds of love are
    a. companionate and passionate.
    b. compassionate and passionate.
    c. compassionate and companionate.
    d. passionate and platonic.

12. _____ is not a component of the triangular theory of love.
    a. Intimacy
    b. Passion
    c. Commitment
    d. Secrecy

13. Which of the following is an attachment style?
    a. dismissive avoidant
    b. avoidant
    c. anxious/ambivalent
    d. all of the above

14. _____ are relationships governed by the need for equity.
    a. Exchange relationships
    b. Equity relationships
    c. Long-term relationships
    d. Dual-income earner relationships

True or False

15. The evolutionary approach is useful in social psychology in examining our culturally subjective experiences.
    ___ True
    ___ False

16. According to Dion and Dion, collectivist societies value romantic love more than individualistic societies.
    ___ True
    ___ False

17. "I would feel despair if _____ left me" is one item from a companionate love scale.
    ___ True
    ___ False

18. Surveying university students, Fehr found that companionate love captures best the meaning of love.
    ___ True
    ___ False

19. Murray, Holmes, and Griffin found that for both dating and married couples, it is better to see partners not as they are but rather as similar to an ideal partner.
    ___ True
    ___ False

20. The theory of attachment styles states that our adult relationships are influenced by the bonds we formed as adolescents.
    ___ True
    ___ False

Fill in the Blank

21. _____ involve the belief that we have the most wonderful partner and the most wonderful relationship.

22. An unbalanced _____ can result in dissatisfaction with a relationship.

ENDING CLOSE RELATIONSHIPS

Multiple Choice

23. In Canada, over one-third of marriages
    a. involve teenagers.
    b. end in divorce.
    c. end in separation.
    d. include adopted children.

24. _____ couples show higher rates of dissolution than _____ couples.
    a. Homosexual; heterosexual
    b. Heterosexual; homosexual
    c. Married; common-law
    d. Engaged; married

25. When asked why a friendship has ended, the most common response is
    a. dissimilarity.
    b. boredom.
    c. disloyalty.
    d. that attractive alternatives are available.

26. The good news about relationship breakups is that
    a. it is very easy to find another partner.
    b. less distress is felt after some time has past.
    c. most relationship breakups cause little or no distress.
    d. there is no distress if the relationship is seen as having been satisfactory.

True or False

27. Most marriages dissolve for the same reasons.
    ___ True
    ___ False

28. Boredom is one of the reasons that romantic relationships end.
    ___ True
    ___ False

Fill in the Blank

29. A relationship is in trouble when the factors that caused the _____ are no longer present.
30. The person who does the breaking up will feel less heartbroken than the person being _____.

PERSONALIZED STUDY PLAN

Want to check your answers and access more study resources? Visit the Companion Website for *Fundamentals of Social Psychology* at **www.pearsoned.ca/aronson**, where you'll find the above questions incorporated in a pre-test and post-test for each chapter. These tests will be automatically graded online, allowing you to check your answers. A Study Plan, like the one below, groups the questions by section within the chapter and shows you which sections you need to focus on for further study.

Your Results for "Chapter 8, Pretest"

OVERALL SCORE: 73% of 15 questions

Group	Score	Proficient
Major Antecedents of Attraction	3 of 5	No
Forming and Maintaining Close Relationships	5 of 6	Yes
Ending Close Relationships	3 of 4	Yes

CHAPTER

9

Prosocial Behaviour and Aggression: Helping and Harming Others

Chapter Outline

BASIC MOTIVES UNDERLYING PROSOCIAL BEHAVIOUR: WHY DO PEOPLE HELP?

Evolutionary Psychology: Instincts and Genes

Social Exchange: The Costs and Rewards of Helping

Empathy and Altruism: The Pure Motive for Helping

PERSONAL DETERMINANTS OF PROSOCIAL BEHAVIOUR: WHY DO SOME PEOPLE HELP MORE THAN OTHERS?

Gender Differences in Prosocial Behaviour

The Effects of Mood on Prosocial Behaviour

SITUATIONAL DETERMINANTS OF PROSOCIAL BEHAVIOUR: WHEN WILL PEOPLE HELP?

HOW CAN HELPING BE INCREASED?

Instilling Helpfulness with Rewards and Models

AGGRESSION: WHY WE HURT OTHER PEOPLE

What Is Aggression?

Is Aggression Inborn or Is It Learned?

SITUATIONAL CAUSES OF AGGRESSION

Imitation and Aggression

Violent Pornography and Sexual Aggression

Frustration as a Cause of Aggression

Consider the following story:

January 20, 2000. As Montrealers were making their way to work, they passed a man lying on the sidewalk, arms outstretched, crying and begging for help. It was −41 degrees Celsius. The man was Gino Laplante. He was 38 years old and suffered from psychiatric problems. Because he was lying in the middle of the sidewalk, people had to walk around him to avoid stepping on him. Anne Lavictoire was one of those people. However, unlike the others, she decided to go back to see if she could help. She discovered that Laplante's hands were already frozen. She called for an ambulance and tried to keep him warm. It took 15 or 20 minutes for the ambulance to arrive. By then, it was too late: Gino Laplante had frozen to death on a sidewalk in Montreal on a cold Thursday morning.

Based on this event, what is your view of human nature? Are human beings capable of such cruel, callous actions as passing by a man who is freezing to death? Can people ever be counted on to be kind and compassionate to those around them?

Now consider the following stories:

Jake Rupert, a reporter for the *Ottawa Citizen*, was moved to tears as he watched the 400-metre snowshoe final at the Canadian Special Olympics 2000 Winter Games. There were only 50 metres remaining when the front runner fell down. As he struggled to get up, 20-year-old John Rokosh and another athlete caught up to him. They stopped, helped him up, and then the three of them finished the race. Rokosh came in third. What was his response when a reporter asked him why he didn't just keep going? "Because that wouldn't be fair, silly" (Sinclair, 2000).

A 13-year-old Winnipeg boy, Rocky Flett, was on his way to a grocery store in February 2000 when he heard the cries of young children coming from a house. He could smell smoke. Rocky rushed into the house and rescued three children. An adult in the house had collapsed on the stairs from smoke inhalation. Rocky ran to a neighbour's house and got help rescuing the adult. When asked why he ran into a burning building three times, Rocky's response was "I didn't stop to think. I just did it."

Direct Provocation and Reciprocation

Alcohol

Social Exclusion

Aggressive Objects as a Cause of Aggression

Gender Differences in Aggression

HOW TO REDUCE AGGRESSION

Does Punishing Aggression Reduce Aggressive Behaviour?

Catharsis and Aggression

What Are We Supposed to Do with Our Anger?

 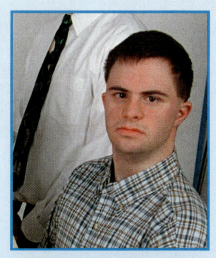

Rocky Flett (left) and John Rokosh (right) are two of many people who exhibit prosocial behaviour. What makes some people help others even at considerable cost to themselves?

John Rokosh and Rocky Flett were two of the six winners of the Year 2000 Canada Day People Who Make a Difference Awards sponsored by the *Winnipeg Free Press*.

Based on these stories, what is your view of human nature now? Are human beings inclined to respond when they see another person in need? Can people be counted on to help?

Why is it that people sometimes perform acts of great self-sacrifice and heroism, whereas at other times they act in such uncaring, heartless ways? These are the basic questions to be addressed in this chapter. First, let's take a look at the positive side of human nature—those times when people can be counted on to help others. In the latter half of the chapter, we will examine the more negative side of human nature—those times when people hurt, rather than help, one another.

BASIC MOTIVES UNDERLYING PROSOCIAL BEHAVIOUR: WHY DO PEOPLE HELP?

We begin this chapter by considering the major determinants of **prosocial behaviour**, which we define as any act performed with the goal of benefiting another person. We will be particularly concerned with prosocial behaviour motivated by **altruism**, which is the desire to help another person even if it involves a cost to the helper. Someone might act in a prosocial manner out of self-interest—he or she hopes to get something in return. Altruism is helping purely out of the desire to benefit someone else, with no benefit (and often a cost) to oneself. John Rokosh stopped to help an athlete with whom he was competing, thereby forfeiting his chances of coming in first. Rocky Flett risked his life by rescuing three children and an adult from a burning house.

We will begin by considering the basic origins of prosocial behaviour and altruism: Why do people help others? Few questions have intrigued observers of the human condition as much as this one. Is the willingness to help a basic impulse with genetic roots? Is it something that must be taught and nurtured in childhood? Is there a pure motive for helping, such that people are willing to aid their fellow human beings even when they have nothing to gain? Or are people willing to help only when there is something in it for them? Let's see how psychologists have addressed these centuries-old questions.

Evolutionary Psychology: Instincts and Genes

According to Charles Darwin's (1859) theory of evolution, natural selection favours genes that promote the survival of the individual. Any gene that furthers our survival and increases the probability that we will produce offspring is likely to be passed on from generation to generation. Several psychologists have pursued these ideas, spawning the field of evolutionary psychology, which, as you may recall from previous chapters, is the attempt to explain social behaviour in terms of genetic factors that have evolved over time according to the principles of natural selection (Buss, 1996, 1999; Buss & Kenrick, 1998; Ketelaar & Ellis, 2000; Simpson & Kenrick, 1997; Wright, 1994). Darwin realized early on that a potential problem exists with evolutionary theory. How can it explain altruism? If people's overriding goal is to ensure their own survival, why would they ever help others at a cost to themselves? One way in which evolutionary psychologists have attempted to resolve this dilemma is to introduce the notion of **kin selection**, the idea that behaviours that help a genetic relative are favoured by natural selection (Hamilton, 1964; Meyer, 1999). People can increase the chances that their genes will be passed along not only by having their own children, but also by ensuring that their genetic relatives survive and have children. Because a person's blood relatives share some of his or her genes, the more that person ensures his or her survival, the greater the chance that his or her genes will flourish in future generations.

One problem with this explanation of prosocial behaviour, however, is that it has difficulty explaining why complete strangers sometimes help each other, even when there is no reason for them to assume that they share some of the same genes. For example, it seems absurd to say that 13-year-old Rocky Flett somehow calculated how genetically

---

Prosocial behaviour any act performed with the goal of benefiting another person

Altruism the desire to help another person even if involves a cost to the helper

> Altruism based on kin selection is the enemy of civilization. If human beings are to a large extent guided to favor their own relatives and tribe, only a limited amount of global harmony is possible.
>
> —E. O. WILSON, 1978

Kin selection the idea that behaviour that helps a genetic relative is favoured by natural selection

Norm of reciprocity the expectation that helping others will increase the likelihood that they will help us in the future

similar the occupants of the burning house were to him before deciding to save their lives. To explain such cases of altruism, evolutionary psychologists also point to the **norm of reciprocity**, which is the expectation that helping others will increase the likelihood that they will help us in the future. The idea is that as human beings were evolving, a group of completely selfish individuals, each living in his or her own cave, would have found it more difficult to survive than a group whose members had learned to cooperate with one another. Those who were most likely to survive, the argument goes, were people who developed an understanding with their neighbours about reciprocity: "I will help you now, with the agreement that when I need help, you will return the favour." Because of its survival value, such a norm of reciprocity may have become genetically based (Baron, 1997; Cosmides & Tooby, 1992; de Waal, 1996; Shackelford & Buss, 1996; Simon, 1990; Trivers, 1971).

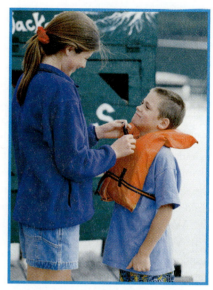

According to evolutionary psychology, prosocial behaviour occurs in part because of kin selection, such as this young woman helping her little brother.

As we saw in earlier chapters, evolutionary theory has had its critics. The application of this theory to prosocial behaviour is no exception. How, for example, can evolutionary theory explain why complete strangers sometimes help each other, even when there is no reason to assume they share genes or that the favour will ever be returned? It seems absurd to say that the heroes of September 11, 2001, who lost their lives saving others from the World Trade Center in New York, somehow calculated how genetically similar they were to those in need before they decided to help. We turn now to other possible motives behind prosocial behaviour that do not necessarily originate in people's genes.

Social Exchange: The Costs and Rewards of Helping

Though some social psychologists disagree with evolutionary approaches to prosocial behaviour, they do agree that altruistic behaviour can be based on self-interest. In fact, a theory in social psychology—social exchange theory—argues that much of what we do stems from the desire to maximize our rewards and minimize our costs (Homans, 1961; Lawler & Thye, 1999; Thibaut & Kelley, 1959; see Chapter 8 for a more in-depth description of social exchange theory). When it comes to helping, social exchange theory would argue that people help only when the benefits outweigh the costs. Thus, true altruism, in which people help even when doing so is costly, does not exist, according to this theory.

What might be the benefits of helping? There are actually a number of them. For example, considerable evidence indicates that people are aroused and disturbed when they see another person suffer, and that they help at least in part to relieve their own distress (Dovidio, 1984; Dovidio et al., 1991). Thus, it is rewarding to have our distress alleviated. By helping others, we can also gain such rewards as social approval from others and increased feelings of self-worth. Finally, helping someone is an investment in the future, the social exchange being that, someday, someone will help you when you need it. If this sounds a bit far-fetched or even naive, think about how deeply this idea permeates our society on both a secular and a religious level. Being a good person and treating others with compassion (and receiving such treatment in return) are the hallmark of a civilized society, part of what early philosophers called "the social contract." Few of us would want to live in a "dog-eat-dog" world; we need to believe that kindness will be reciprocated, at least some of the time.

If you are like many of our students, you may be experiencing discomfort over this view of helping behaviour, finding it a rather cynical portrayal of human nature. Is true altruism, motivated only by the desire to help someone else, really such a mythical act? Must we trace all prosocial behaviour to the self-interest of the helper? You may be relieved to learn that according to some social psychologists, people do have hearts of gold and sometimes help only for the sake of helping—as we shall see now.

Empathy and Altruism: The Pure Motive for Helping

C. Daniel Batson (1991) is the strongest proponent of the idea that people often help purely out of the goodness of their hearts. Batson acknowledges that people sometimes help others for selfish reasons. However, he argues that people's motives also are sometimes purely altruistic, in that their only goal is to help the other person, even if doing so involves some cost. Pure altruism is likely to come into play, he maintains,

> Let him who neglects to raise the fallen, fear lest, when he falls, no one will stretch out his hand to lift him up.
>
> —SAADI,
> The Orchard,
> 1257

> I once saw a man out of courtesy help a lame dog over a stile, and [the dog] for requital bit his fingers.
>
> —WILLIAM CHILLINGWORTH

Helping behaviour is common in virtually all species of animals. Sometimes, helping behaviour even crosses species lines. In August 1996, a three-year-old boy fell into a pit containing seven gorillas at the Brookfield, Illinois, zoo. Binti, a seven-year-old gorilla, immediately picked up the boy. After cradling him in her arms, she placed the boy near a door where zookeepers could get to him. Why did she help? Evolutionary psychologists would argue that prosocial behaviour is selected for and thus becomes part of the genetic makeup of members of many species. Social exchange theorists would argue that Binti had been rewarded for helping in the past. In fact, because she had been rejected by her mother, she had received training in parenting skills from zookeepers and had been rewarded for caring for a doll (Bils & Singer, 1996).

Empathy the ability to experience events and emotions (e.g., joy and sadness) the way another person experiences them

Empathy-altruism hypothesis the idea that when we feel empathy for a person, we will attempt to help him or her purely for altruistic reasons, regardless of what we have to gain

when we feel **empathy** for the person in need of help, defined as the ability to put ourselves in the shoes of another person, experiencing events and emotions the way that person experiences them. Suppose, for example, that you are at the grocery store and see a man holding a baby and a bag full of diapers, toys, and rattles. As the man reaches for a box of Cheerios, he loses his grip on the bag and its contents spill on the floor. Will you stop and help him pick up his things? According to Batson, it depends first on whether you feel empathy for him. If you do, you will help, regardless of what you have to gain. Your goal will be to relieve the other person's distress, not to gain something for yourself. This is the crux of Batson's **empathy-altruism hypothesis**.

What if you do not feel empathy? If, for whatever reason, you do not share the man's distress, then, Batson says, social exchange concerns come into play. What's in it for you? If there is something to be gained, such as obtaining approval from the man or from onlookers, you will help the man pick up his things. If you will not profit from helping, you will go on your way without stopping. Batson's empathy-altruism hypothesis is summarized in Figure 9.1.

FIGURE 9.1 Batson's (1991) Empathy-Altruism Theory

Batson and colleagues have devised a series of clever experiments to unravel people's motives (e.g., Batson, 2002; Batson et al., 2002; Batson & Powell, 2003). Imagine you were one of the participants (an Introductory Psychology student) in a study by Miho Toi and Daniel Batson (1982). You are asked to evaluate some tapes of new programs for your school's radio station. There are many different pilot tapes for this program, and you are told that only one person will be listening to each tape. The one you hear is an interview with a student named Carol Marcy. She describes a bad automobile accident and explains that because she is still in a wheelchair, it has been very difficult to keep up with her course work. Carol goes on to mention that she will have to drop her Introductory Psychology class unless she can find a student from whom she can borrow lecture notes.

After you listen to the tape, the experimenter hands you a note from one of Carol's professors, saying that he was wondering whether the student who listened to Carol's tape would be willing to meet with her and share his or her Introductory Psychology lecture notes.

As you have no doubt gathered, the point of the study was to look at the conditions under which people agreed to help Carol. Toi and Batson (1982) pitted two motives against each other: self-interest and empathy. First, they varied how much empathy people felt toward Carol. In the high-empathy condition, people were told to try to imagine how Carol felt about what had happened to her and how it had changed her life. In the low-empathy condition, people were told to try to be objective and to not be concerned with how Carol felt. These instructions had the expected effect on people's feelings: Those in the high-empathy condition reported feeling more empathy with Carol than did people in the low-empathy condition.

Second, Toi and Batson varied how costly it would be *not* to help Carol. In one condition, participants learned that Carol would start coming back to class the following week and happened to be in the same Introductory Psychology section as they were; thus, they would see her every time they went to class. This was the high-cost condition, because it would be unpleasant to refuse to help Carol and then run into her on a weekly basis. In the low-cost condition, people learned that Carol would be studying at home and would not be coming to class; thus, they would never have to face her in her wheelchair and feel guilty about not helping her out.

When deciding whether to help Carol, did people take into account the costs involved? According to the empathy-altruism hypothesis, people should have been

> It is one of the beautiful compensations of this life that no one can sincerely try to help another without helping himself.
>
> —CHARLES DUDLEY WARNER, 1873

Calvin seems to be an advocate of social exchange theory.

motivated by genuine altruistic concern, and should have helped regardless of the costs—if empathy was high (see Figure 9.1 on page 270). As you can see in the right side of Figure 9.2, this prediction was confirmed. In the high-empathy condition, about as many people agreed to help when they thought they would see Carol in class as when they thought they would not see her in class. This suggests that people had Carol's interests in mind, not their own. In the low-empathy condition, however, many more people agreed to help when they thought they would see Carol in class than when they thought they would not see her in class (see the left side of Figure 9.2). This suggests that when empathy was low, social exchange concerns came into play, in that people based their decision to help on the costs and benefits to themselves. They helped when it was in their interests to do so (when they would see Carol in her wheelchair and feel guilty for not helping) but not otherwise (when they thought they would never see her again).

The Toi and Batson (1982) study and others (Batson, 1998; Piliavin & Charng, 1990) suggest that when we feel empathy for another person, our motives do seem to be pure, causing us to help even when we have nothing to gain by doing so.

In summary, we have discussed three basic motives underlying prosocial behaviour: the idea that helping is an instinctive reaction to promote the welfare of those genetically similar to us (evolutionary psychology); that the rewards of helping often outweigh the costs, making it in people's self-interest to help (social exchange theory); and that, under some conditions, powerful feelings of empathy and compassion for the victim prompt selfless giving (the empathy-altruism hypothesis). Each of these approaches has supporters and critics.

Thinking Critically

Why do people help others at a cost to themselves? Compare the major theories that explain altruistic behavior.

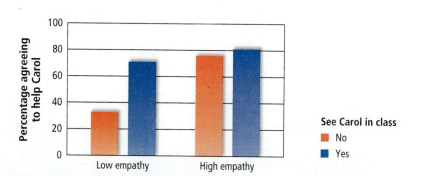

FIGURE 9.2 Altruism versus Self-interest

Under what conditions did people agree to help Carol with the work she missed in her Introductory Psychology class? When empathy was high, people helped regardless of the costs and rewards (regardless of whether they would encounter her in their psychology class). When empathy was low, people were more concerned with the rewards and costs for them—they helped only if they would encounter Carol in their psychology class and thus feel guilty about not helping.

(Adapted from Toi & Batson, 1982)

PERSONAL DETERMINANTS OF PROSOCIAL BEHAVIOUR: WHY DO SOME PEOPLE HELP MORE THAN OTHERS?

Are some people more willing to extend help than others? Although psychologists have searched for evidence of an altruistic personality—a type of person who is willing to help at any cost in any situation—they have come up empty-handed. Studies of both children and adults indicate that people with high scores on personality tests of altruism are not much more likely to help than those with lower scores (Batson, 1998; Magoo & Khanna, 1991; Piliavin & Charng, 1990). But yet it does seem as though some people are more helpful than others, doesn't it? It turns out that there are some personal factors that are strongly linked to helping. First, it matters whether you are male or female. Second, it matters whether you are in a good or bad mood.

> Both men and women belie their nature when they are not kind.
>
> —GAMALIEL BAILEY

Gender Differences in Prosocial Behaviour

Consider two scenarios. In one, someone performs a dramatic heroic act, such as storming the cockpit of United Flight 93 to fight the terrorists who are heading toward Washington, DC. In the other, someone is involved in a long-term helping relationship, such as assisting a disabled neighbour with household chores. Who is most likely to help in the first situation, and who is most likely to help in the second?

According to a review of more than 170 studies by Alice Eagly and Maureen Crowley (1986; Eagly, 1987), the answer is males in the first situation and females in the second situation. In Western cultures, part of the male sex role is to be chivalrous and heroic, whereas part of the female sex role is to be nurturant and caring, valuing close long-term relationships. As a result, we might expect men to help more in situations that call for brief brave and heroic acts, and women to help more in long-term relationships that

Whereas men are more likely to perform chivalrous and heroic acts, women are more likely to be helpful in long-term relationships that involve greater commitment.

involve less danger but more commitment, such as volunteering at a nursing home. For example, an analysis of volunteering among Canadians (ages 15 to 65+) found that women were more likely than men to engage in both formal and informal volunteering (Ekos Research Associates and Canadian Policy Research Networks, 1999).

The Effects of Mood on Prosocial Behaviour

Sometimes we feel up and sometimes we feel down; believe it or not, these transitory emotional states are a key determinant of prosocial behaviour. Alice Isen and Paul Levin (1972) explored the effect of good moods on prosocial behaviour in shopping malls in San Francisco and Philadelphia. They boosted the mood of shoppers in a simple way—namely, by leaving a dime in the coin-return slot of a pay telephone at the mall and waiting for someone to find it. As the lucky shoppers left the phone with their newly found dime, an assistant of Isen and Levine purposefully dropped a folder a few feet in front of the shopper, to see whether the shopper would stop and help him pick up his papers. It turned out that finding the dime had a dramatic effect on helping. Only 4 percent of the people who did not find a dime helped the man pick up his papers. In comparison, 84 percent of the people who found a dime helped.

Researchers have found this "feel good, do good" effect in diverse situations, and have shown that people are more likely to help others when they are in a good mood for a number of reasons, including doing well on a test, receiving a gift, thinking happy thoughts, and listening to pleasant music. And when people are in a good mood, they are more helpful in many ways—as long as doing so will prolong their good mood—including contributing money to charity, helping someone find a lost contact lens, tutoring another student, donating blood, and helping co-workers on the job (Carlson, Charlin, & Miller, 1988; George & Brief, 1992; Isen, 1999; Salovey, Mayer, & Rosenhan, 1991). See Try It! on page 275 for a way of doing your own test of the "feel good, do good" hypothesis.

What is it about being in a good mood that makes people more altruistic? Social psychologists have come up with three explanations. First, when we are in a good mood, we tend to see the good side of other people. A victim who might normally seem clumsy or annoying will, when we are feeling cheerful, seem like a decent, needy person who is worthy of our help (Carlson, Charlin, & Miller, 1988; Forgas & Bower, 1987). Second, if we see someone in need of help, then being a Good Samaritan will prolong our good mood. In comparison, not helping when we know we should is a surefire "downer," deflating our good mood (Clark & Isen, 1982; Isen, 1987; Williamson & Clark, 1989). Finally, good moods increase the amount of attention we pay to ourselves, and this factor in turn makes us more likely to behave according to our values and ideals. Because most of us value altruism and because good moods increase our attention to this value, this is another reason why good moods increase helping behaviour (Berkowitz, 1987; Carlson, Charlin, & Miller, 1988; Salovey & Rodin, 1985).

Suppose you just had a fight with a friend or just found out you did poorly on a test and were feeling sad. Given that feeling happy leads to greater helping, it might seem that feeling sad would decrease helping. Surprisingly, sadness can also lead to an increase in helping, at least under certain conditions (Carlson & Miller, 1987; Salovey, Mayer, & Rosenham, 1991). When people are sad, they are motivated to engage in activities that make them feel better (Wegener & Petty, 1994). The idea that people help in order to alleviate their own sadness and distress is called the **negative-state relief hypothesis**, developed by Robert Cialdini (Cialdini, Darby, & Vincent, 1973; Cialdini & Fultz, 1990; Cialdini

Negative-state relief hypothesis the idea that people help in order to alleviate their own sadness and distress

Try It! Mood and Helping Behaviour

Think back to the last time you smelled the delicious aroma of fresh-baked chocolate chip cookies. Did it put you in a good mood? Robert Baron (1997) predicted that people would be in better moods when they are around pleasant fragrances, and that this improved mood would make them more helpful. Consistent with his prediction, shoppers were more likely to help a stranger (by giving change for a dollar) when they were approached in locations with pleasant smells than when they were approached in locations with neutral smells.

See if you can replicate this effect at a shopping mall in your area. Pick locations in the mall that have pleasant aromas or neutral aromas. For his pleasant aroma conditions, Baron (1997) used locations near a cookie store, a bakery, and a gourmet coffee café. The areas with neutral smells should be as identical as possible in all other respects; for example, Baron (1997) picked locations that were similar in the volume of pedestrians, lighting, and proximity to mall exits, such as areas outside clothing stores.

At each location, approach an individual who is alone. Take out a loonie and ask the passerby for change. If the person stops and gives you change, count it as helping. If he or she ignores you or says he or she does not have any change, count it as not helping. Did you replicate Baron's (1997) results? He found that 57 percent of people helped in the locations with pleasant aromas, whereas only 19 percent of people helped in the locations with neutral aromas.

Note: Before conducting this study you might want to seek the permission of the mall manager. The manager of the mall in which Baron (1997) conducted his study requested that the researchers approach only persons of the same gender as themselves, because of a concern that cross-gender requests for change would be perceived as "pick-up" attempts. You might want to follow this procedure as well.

et al., 1987). It is an example of the social exchange theory approach to helping that we discussed earlier. People help someone else with the goal of helping themselves—namely, to relieve their own sadness and distress. For example, if we are feeling down, we are more likely to donate money to a charity. The warm glow of helping the charity lifts us out of the doldrums (Cialdini, Darby, & Vincent, 1973).

It is also the case that when people have done something that has made them feel guilty, helping another person balances things out, reducing their guilty feelings (Baumeister, Stillwell, & Heatherton, 1994; Estrada-Hollenbeck & Heatherton, 1998). For example, Mary Harris and her colleagues (1975) found that churchgoers were more likely to donate money to charities before attending confession than afterwards, presumably because confessing to a priest reduced their guilt.

Thus, whether or not people help depends on their gender and the kind of mood they are in. However, gender and mood do not tell the whole story. As you might expect, social psychologists also emphasize the importance of situational factors. Indeed, there is compelling evidence that we are more likely to help in some situations than others. What might those situations be? Stay tuned.

> If you want others to be happy, practice compassion. If you want to be happy, practice compassion.
>
> —THE DALAI LAMA

? Thinking Critically

What factors will influence whether someone will intervene in an emergency, such as helping a person who slips and breaks an ankle on a patch of ice? What factors will determine whether someone will help on a more long-term basis, such as volunteering at a homeless shelter?

SITUATIONAL DETERMINANTS OF PROSOCIAL BEHAVIOUR: WHEN WILL PEOPLE HELP?

Remember Kitty Genovese, the young woman who was murdered in New York while her neighbours turned deaf ears to her cries for help? In trying to explain this tragedy, some analysts suggested that perhaps New York was to blame. Perhaps Kitty Genovese's neighbours were so overloaded with urban stimulation that they dismissed Genovese's cries as one small addition to the surrounding din. This seems unlikely, though, given that similar cases have been reported in small towns (Hsu, 1995). Bibb Latané and John Darley (1970) are two social psychologists who taught at universities in New York at the time of the Genovese murder. As we discussed in Chapter 2, they too were unconvinced that the stresses and stimulation of urban life were responsible for the failure to help. They ultimately developed a step-by-step description of how bystanders decide whether to intervene in an emergency (see Figure 9.3), and concluded that the decision to intervene is actually highly complex. Let's begin with the first step: whether people notice that someone needs help.

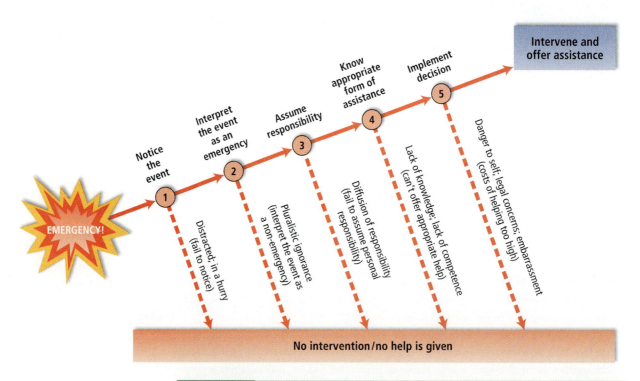

FIGURE 9.3 Bystander Intervention Decision Tree: Five Steps to Helping in an Emergency

Latané and Darley (1970) showed that people go through five decision-making steps before they help someone in an emergency. If bystanders fail to take any one of the five steps, they will not help. Each step, as well as the possible reasons why people decide not to intervene, is outlined above.

(Adapted from Latané & Darley, 1970)

NOTICING AN EVENT Sometimes it is clear that an emergency has occurred, as in the seizure experiment where it was obvious that the other student was in danger. Other times, however, it is not as clear. If you are late for an appointment and are hurrying down a crowded street, you might not notice that someone has collapsed in the doorway of a nearby building. Obviously, if people don't notice that an emergency has occurred, they will not intervene and offer to help.

FOCUS ON APPLICATIONS

Are We Less Helpful When We're in a Hurry?

What determines whether people notice an emergency? John Darley and Daniel Batson (1973) demonstrated that something as seemingly trivial as how much of a hurry people are in can make more of a difference than what kind of people they are. These researchers conducted a study that mirrored the parable of the Good Samaritan, wherein many passersby failed to stop to help a man lying unconscious on the side of the road. The research participants were people we might think would be extremely altruistic—seminary students preparing to devote their lives to the ministry. The students were asked to walk to another building, where they would be recorded while making a brief speech. Some were told that they were late and should hurry to keep their appointment. Others were told that there was no rush, because the assistant in the other building was a few minutes behind schedule. As they walked to the other building, each of the students passed a man who was slumped in a doorway. The man (an accomplice of the experimenters) coughed and groaned as each student walked by. Did the seminary students stop and offer to help him? If they were not in a hurry, most of them (63 percent) did. If they were hurrying to keep their appointment, however, very few of them (10 percent) did. Many of the students who were in a hurry did not even notice the man.

It is perhaps unsurprising that when people are in a rush, they pay less attention to what's going on around them, making them less likely to help someone in need. What is surprising is that such a seemingly trivial matter as how much of a hurry we are in can overpower the kind of people we are. Darley and Batson (1973) tested the seminary students on a variety of personality measures that assessed how religious they were. They also varied the topic of the speech. Specifically, some students were asked to speak on the parable of the Good Samaritan—surely seminary students speaking on this topic would be especially likely to stop and help a man slumped in a doorway, given the similarity of this incident to the parable. However, if the students were in a hurry, they were unlikely to help, even if they were very religious individuals about to give a speech about the Good Samaritan. We should note that Darley and Batson did find one variable that made a difference—namely, whether the students saw religion as a quest (an open-minded search for truth) or a set of traditions. Those who viewed religion as a quest were no more likely to stop, but those who did stop were more responsive to the man's needs than those who viewed religion as a set of traditions.

INTERPRETING THE EVENT AS AN EMERGENCY Just because people notice someone slumped in a doorway does not mean they will help. The next determinant of helping is whether the bystander interprets the event as an emergency—in other words, as a

Pluralistic ignorance the phenomenon whereby bystanders assume that nothing is wrong in an emergency because no one else looks concerned

situation in which help is needed (see Figure 9.3). Often we are uncertain about what's going on, such as whether the smoke we see is a sign of a fire. One of the first things we do in such situations is look around to see how other people are responding. If other people look up, shrug, and go about their business, we are likely to assume that there is nothing to worry about. There is a danger in doing so, however, because it results in a state of **pluralistic ignorance**, the phenomenon whereby bystanders assume that nothing is wrong in an emergency because no one else looks concerned.

Pluralistic ignorance was demonstrated in another classic experiment by Latané and Darley (1970). Imagine that you have agreed to take part in a study of people's attitudes toward the problems of urban life, and you arrive at the appointed time. A sign instructs you to fill out a questionnaire while you are waiting for the study to begin. You take a copy of the questionnaire, sit down, and work on it for a few minutes. Then something odd happens: White smoke starts coming into the room through a small vent in the wall. Before long, the room is so filled with smoke that you can barely see the questionnaire. What will you do?

In fact, there was no real danger—the experimenters were pumping smoke into the room to see how people would respond to this potential emergency. Not surprisingly, when people were by themselves, most of them took action. Within two minutes, 50 percent of the participants left the room and found the experimenter down the hall, reporting that there was a potential fire in the building; by six minutes, 75 percent of the participants left the room to alert the experimenter. But what would happen if people were not alone? It would seem that the larger the group, the greater the likelihood that someone would report the smoke.

To find out whether more bystanders would increase the chances of helping, Latané and Darley (1970) included a condition in which three participants took part at the same time. Surprisingly, in only 12 percent of the three-person groups did someone report the

Emergency situations can be confusing. Does this man need help? Have the bystanders failed to notice him, or has the behaviour of the others led each of them to interpret the situation as a non-emergency—an example of pluralistic ignorance?

smoke within two minutes, and in only 38 percent of the groups did someone report the smoke within six minutes. In the remaining groups, the participants sat there filling out questionnaires even when they had to wave away smoke with their hands to see what they were writing. What went wrong?

Because it was not clear that the smoke constituted an emergency, the participants used each other as a source of information. Indeed, it is in ambiguous situations, such as seeing smoke coming from a vent, that people in groups will be in a state of pluralistic ignorance, convincing each other that nothing is wrong (Clark & Word, 1972; Solomon, Solomon, & Stone, 1978).

ASSUMING RESPONSIBILITY In trying to understand the Kitty Genovese murder, Latané and Darley (1970) focused on the fact that many people heard her cries. Paradoxically, they thought, it might be that the greater the number of bystanders who observe an emergency, the less likely it is that any one of them will help.

How can this be? Surely the more people who witness an emergency, the greater one's chances of receiving help. In a series of now classic experiments, Latané and Darley (1970) found that just the opposite is true. In terms of receiving help, there is no safety in numbers. Think back to the seizure experiment we discussed in Chapter 2 (Darley & Latané, 1968). In this study, people sat in individual cubicles, participating in a group discussion of university life (over an intercom system) with students in other cubicles. One of the other students suddenly had a seizure. There was actually only one real participant in the study. The other "participants," including the one who had the seizure, were prerecorded voices. The point of the study was to see whether the real participant tried to help the seizure victim, by trying to find him or by summoning the experimenter, or whether, like Kitty Genovese's neighbours, he or she simply sat there and did nothing.

Kitty Genovese and the alley in which she was murdered. Ironically, Genovese would probably be alive today had *fewer* people heard her desperate cries for help.

As Darley and Latané anticipated, the answer depended on how many people the participant thought were witnessing the emergency. When people believed they were the only ones listening to the student have the seizure, most of them (85 percent) helped within 60 seconds. By two-and-a-half minutes, 100 percent of the people who thought they were the only bystander had offered assistance (see Figure 9.4). In comparison, when the research participants believed there was one other student listening, fewer people helped. As you can see in Figure 9.4, as the number of bystanders increased, the probability of helping decreased. Dozens of other studies, conducted both in the laboratory and in the field, have found the same thing. The greater the number of bystanders who witness an emergency, the less likely any one of them is to help the victim—a phenomenon called the **bystander effect**.

Why is it that people are less likely to help when other bystanders are present?

If we are the only bystander present, we realize that if we don't help, nobody will. However, when there are many witnesses, a **diffusion of responsibility** occurs, whereby each bystander's sense of responsibility to help decreases as the number of witnesses increases. Because other people are present, no individual bystander feels a strong sense that it is his or her personal responsibility to take action. Each person (falsely) assumes that he or she does not have to help, because surely someone else will do so. Most likely, Kitty Genovese's

Bystander effect the finding that the greater the number of bystanders who witness an emergency, the less likely it is that any one of them will help

Diffusion of responsibility each bystander's sense of responsibility to help decreases as the number of witnesses increases

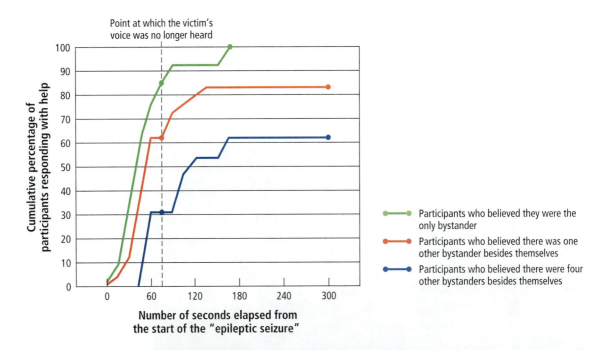

FIGURE 9.4 Bystander Intervention: The Presence of Bystanders Reduces Helping

When people believed that they were the only one witnessing a student having a seizure—when they were the lone bystander—most of them helped him immediately, and all did so within a few minutes. When they believed that someone else was listening as well—that there were two bystanders—they were less likely to help and did so more slowly. And when they believed that four others were listening—that there were five bystanders—they were even less likely to help.

(Adapted from Darley & Latané, 1968)

neighbours assumed that there was no need to call the police because someone else would already have made the call. The sad irony of Genovese's murder is that she probably would be alive today had *fewer* people heard her cries for help.

There is a clear take-home message here: If you are in an accident, for example, and need help, do not yell out, "Will someone help me?" Single out one person—"Hey, you in the blue shirt and sunglasses, would you please call 911?"—and you will probably receive help more quickly.

KNOWING HOW TO HELP Even if a person has made it this far in the helping sequence—noticing an event has occurred, interpreting it as an emergency, and taking responsibility—an additional condition must still be met: The person must decide what form of help is appropriate. Suppose, for example, that on a hot summer day you see a woman collapse in the street and you decide she is gravely ill. No one else seems to be helping, so you decide it is up to you. But what should you do? Has the woman had a heart attack? Or is she suffering from heat stroke? Should you call an ambulance, administer CPR, or try to get her out of the sun? If people don't know what form of assistance to provide, obviously they will be unable to help.

DECIDING TO IMPLEMENT THE HELP Finally, even if you know exactly what kind of help is appropriate, there are reasons why you might decide not to intervene. For one thing, you might not be qualified to deliver the right kind of help. It may be clear, for instance, that the woman has had a heart attack and is in desperate need of CPR, but if you don't know how to administer CPR you'll be unable to help her. Or you might be afraid of making a fool of yourself. It can be embarrassing to intervene, only to discover that a situation actually wasn't an emergency. Even some forms of helping might be embarrassing. For example, in South Africa, Edwards (1975) conducted a study in which a female confederate "accidentally" dropped either her purse or a box of tampons while walking down a street. Nearly everyone (95 percent) who saw the woman drop her purse returned it. In comparison, 59 percent of bystanders returned the tampons. One potential helper was about to return the tampons, but quickly dropped the box when he realized what it contained! This study was replicated in Canada by James McDonald and Stuart McKelvie (1992) at Bishop's University. In their study, a male confederate dropped either a mitten or a box of condoms while walking through a shopping mall. Nearly half (47 percent) of the people who saw him drop the mitten retrieved it. As for the condoms? Only 17 percent of bystanders returned them. One man "helped" by kicking the condoms along the floor of the mall until they caught up with the confederate! Thus, costs such as potential embarrassment can make people less likely to help.

In sum, five steps must be taken before people will intervene in an emergency. They have to notice the event, interpret it as an emergency, decide it is their responsibility to help, know how to help, and decide to act. If people fail to take any one of these steps, they will not intervene. Given how difficult it can be to take all five steps, it is not surprising that incidents such as the Kitty Genovese murder can occur.

Thinking Critically

Think about an emergency situation—one you witnessed or perhaps heard about in the media—in which bystanders failed to provide help to a person in need. At which stages of the Latané and Darley model did the helping process break down for the various bystanders? Now think about an emergency situation in which help was provided. Did the helper navigate through all five steps of this model?

> When death, the great reconciler, has come, it is never our tenderness that we repent of, but our severity.
>
> —GEORGE ELIOT (MARIAN EVANS),
> Adam Bede, 1859

HOW CAN HELPING BE INCREASED?

Most religions stress some version of the Golden Rule, urging us to do unto others as we would have others do unto us. There are many saintly people in the world who succeed in following this rule, devoting their lives to the welfare of others. We would all be better off, however, if prosocial behaviour was more common than it is. How can we get people, when faced with an emergency, to act more like Mother Teresa and less like Kitty Genovese's neighbours?

Instilling Helpfulness with Rewards and Models

One answer is to cultivate helping behaviour early on. Several studies suggest that prosocial behaviour in children increases when parents and others reward such behaviours with praise, smiles, and hugs (Fischer, 1963; Grusec, 1991). Of course, we don't want children to help just so they can receive rewards—we want them to internalize helpful behaviour. One way of accomplishing this is to tell children, after they have helped, that they did so because they are kind and helpful people. Such comments encourage children to perceive themselves as altruistic people, so they will help in future situations even when no rewards are forthcoming (Grusec et al., 1979). The same is true for adults: Believing that we are helping someone in order to get a reward diminishes our view of ourselves as altruistic, selfless people (Batson et al., 1978; Uranowitz, 1975).

Another way for parents to increase prosocial behaviour in their children is to behave prosocially themselves. Children who observe their parents helping others (e.g., volunteering to help the homeless) learn that helping others is a valued act. Interviews with people who have gone to great lengths to help others—such as Christians who helped Jews escape from Nazi Germany during the Second World War—indicate that their parents were also dedicated helpers (London, 1970; Rosenhan, 1970). Of course children also imitate adults other than their parents. Indeed, there is evidence that teachers, relatives, and even television characters can serve as models for children (Rushton, 1975).

Adult approval serves as a powerful reward for children when they behave prosocially.

Children are good imitators and learn prosocial behaviour from observing other people (e.g., their parents) behaving prosocially.

FOCUS ON APPLICATIONS

Does Reading This Chapter Make You a More Helpful Person?

As we have seen, there are many barriers to helping. Can these be overcome so that we will be more likely to reach out to another in times of need? Believe it or not, there is evidence that simply being aware of the barriers to helping can increase the chances that we will offer help in real-world emergency situations.

A number of years ago at Cornell University, several students intervened to prevent another student from committing suicide. As is often the case with emergencies, the situation was a very confusing one, and at first the bystanders were not sure what was happening or what they should do. The student who led the intervention said she was reminded of a lecture she had heard on bystander intervention in her Introductory Psychology class a few days earlier and had realized that if she didn't act, no one might (Savistky, 1998).

Consider also a more recent incident at Vassar College, where some students looked outside their dormitory and saw a student being attacked by a mugger. Like Kitty Genovese's neighbours, most of them did nothing, probably because they assumed that someone else had already called the police. One of the students, however, immediately called campus police because she was struck by how similar the situation was to the studies on bystander intervention she had read about in her Social Psychology course—even though she had taken the course more than a year earlier (Coats, 1998).

Indeed, research has confirmed that having people listen to a lecture on Latané and Darley's (1970) bystander intervention research actually makes them more likely to intervene in an emergency situation—even if that situation arises well after the lecture took place (Beaman et al., 1978). Thus, simply being aware of the barriers to prosocial behaviour makes it more likely that you can overcome them and reach out to others.

> **Thinking Critically**
> How do you think prosocial behaviour can be increased most effectively in children? What about adults?

AGGRESSION: WHY WE HURT OTHER PEOPLE

So far we have focused on prosocial behaviour—those times when people help others. However, sadly, there is another side to human behaviour as well. In the rest of this chapter, we will focus on aggression—those times when people hurt, rather than help, each other. We begin with the fundamental question "What is aggression?" and then move on to another fundamental question "What causes it?" Are human beings instinctively aggressive? Can situational factors cause "normal people" to commit violence? Can aggression be prevented or reduced? These are social psychological questions of the utmost importance. Needless to say, we don't have all the answers. By the time you reach the end of this chapter, however, we hope you will have gained some insight into the issues. But first, let's be sure we know what we mean by the term.

What Is Aggression?

Social psychologists define **aggression** as intentional behaviour aimed at causing either physical or psychological pain. It is not to be confused with assertiveness—even though people often loosely refer to others as "aggressive" if they stand up for their rights, write letters to the editor complaining about real or imagined injustices, or display a great deal of ambition. Our definition is clear: Aggression is an intentional action aimed at doing harm or causing pain. The action might be physical or verbal; it might succeed in its goal or not. It is still aggression. Thus, if someone throws a beer bottle at your head, and you duck so the bottle misses, the throwing was still an aggressive act. The important thing is the intention. By the same token, if a car driver unintentionally runs you down while you're attempting to cross the street, that is not an act of aggression, even though the damage would be far greater than that caused by a flying beer bottle.

Is Aggression Inborn or Is It Learned?

Scientists, philosophers, and other serious thinkers are not in complete agreement about whether aggression is an inborn instinctive phenomenon or is learned (Baron & Richardson, 1994; Berkowitz, 1993; Geen, 1998).

According to Lore and Schultz (1993), the universality of aggression among vertebrates strongly suggests that aggressiveness has evolved and has been maintained because it has survival value. However, it is also the case that nearly all organisms also have evolved strong inhibitory mechanisms that enable them to suppress aggression when it is in their best interests to do so. Social psychologists are in general agreement with the interpretation of the animal research offered by Lore and Schultz. Indeed, there is a lot of support for the view, taken by most social psychologists, that for humankind, innate patterns of

---

Aggression intentional behaviour aimed at causing either physical or psychological pain

Man's inhumanity to man Makes countless thousands mourn.

—ROBERT BURNS, "MAN WAS MADE TO MOURN"

Is this kind of aggression "only natural"?

behaviour are infinitely modifiable and flexible. Consider, for example, how widely human cultures vary in their degree of aggressiveness. European history, when condensed, consists of one major war after another; in contrast, the Lepchas of Sikkim, the Pygmies of Central Africa, and the Arapesh of New Guinea live in apparent peace and harmony—with acts of aggression being extremely rare (Baron & Richardson, 1994).

Evidence of cross-cultural variability in violence also comes from a study by Archer and McDaniel (1995), in which teenagers from 11 countries were asked to read stories involving conflict among people. The participants were asked to describe how they thought the characters in the stories would resolve the issue. Their responses were coded for the presence of violence (threatening another person with a weapon, use of physical coercion, injury or death of another person). Teenagers in New Zealand produced the most violent responses. The United States ranked fourth and Canada ranked seventh. Koreans generated the least violent responses to these stories.

Taking findings such as these into account, we would conclude that although an instinctual component of aggression is almost certainly present in human beings, aggression is not caused entirely by instinct or biology. More importantly, from a social psychological perspective there are clear examples of situational and social events that can produce aggressive behaviour. We turn to these next.

Thinking Critically
Is it important to know whether aggressiveness in humans is inborn? Why or why not?

SITUATIONAL CAUSES OF AGGRESSION

As social psychologists, we are particularly interested in the kinds of situational factors that produce aggressive behaviour. As we will see, certain situations are conducive to aggression—so conducive that even the most docile, laid-back person among us might resort to aggressive behaviour. What might some of these situations be?

Imitation and Aggression

A major cause of aggression has its roots in social learning. Children frequently learn to solve conflicts aggressively by imitating adults and their peers, especially when they see that the aggression is rewarded. For example, in high-contact sports (football and hockey) the more aggressive players frequently achieve the greatest fame (and the highest salaries) and the more aggressive teams win more games. For instance, in one study it was found that among hockey players, those most frequently sent to the penalty box for overly aggressive play tended to be the ones who scored the most goals (McCarthy & Kelly, 1978). What lessons are children learning from observing aggression among athletes and other adults?

In a classic series of experiments, Albert Bandura and his associates (1961, 1963) demonstrated the power of **social learning theory**—a theory holding that we learn social behaviour (e.g., aggression) by observing others and imitating them. The basic procedure in the Bandura experiments was to have an adult knock around a plastic air-filled "Bobo" doll (the kind that bounces back after it's been knocked down). The adult would smack the doll around with the palm of his or her hand, strike it with a mallet, kick it, and yell aggressive things at it. Children were then allowed to play with the doll. In these experiments, the children imitated the aggressive models and treated the doll in an abusive manner. Children in a control condition, who did not see the aggressive adult in action, almost never unleashed any aggression against the hapless doll. Moreover, the children who watched the aggressive adult used identical actions and identical aggressive words to those of the adult. In addition, many went beyond mere imitation—they also engaged in novel forms of aggressive behaviour.

The classic experiments by Albert Bandura and his colleagues make it clear that observing other people behaving aggressively can increase the aggressive behaviour of the viewer. Where are people likely to witness aggressive actions? As you might have guessed, television is a culprit. According to some estimates, more than half of all TV programs portray violence—often by heroes who "get away" with violence or are even rewarded for it

Social learning theory the theory that we learn social behaviour (e.g., aggression) by observing others and imitating them

> Children have never been very good at listening to their elders, but they have never failed to imitate them.
> —JAMES BALDWIN,
> Nobody Knows My Name

It is clear from the studies of Bandura, Ross, and Ross (1961, 1963) that children learn aggressive behaviour through imitation and modelling.

(Cantor et al., 2001; Seppa, 1997). This raises an important question: Does watching violence on TV make people more violent? Let's take a close look at the data.

A number of long-term studies indicate that the more violence individuals watch on TV as children, the more violence they exhibit years later as teenagers and young adults. For example, in an impressive longitudinal program of research, Eron and Huesmann and their colleagues (Eron, 1982, 1987; Eron et al., 1996; Huesmann, 1982; Huesmann & Miller, 1994) assessed the television viewing habits of nearly 900 eight-year-old children. The researchers found a small but significant correlation between the amount of violent TV watched and the children's aggressiveness, as rated by their teachers and classmates. More striking was the finding that the impact of watching violent television accumulated over time. Ten years later, when the original research participants were 18 years of age, the correlation between television violence and aggression was stronger than it had been at age 8! Although these are powerful data, they do not definitively prove that watching a lot of violence on TV causes children to become violent teenagers. To demonstrate conclusively that watching violence on TV actually causes violent behaviour, the relationship must be shown experimentally.

Because this is an issue of great importance to society, it has been well researched. The overwhelming thrust of the experimental evidence demonstrates that watching violence does indeed increase the frequency of aggressive behaviour in children (for reviews of the literature, see Cantor et al., 2001; Eron et al., 1996; Geen, 1994, 1998; Huesmann & Miller, 1994; Hughes & Hasbrouck, 1996; Wood, Wong, & Chachere, 1991). Here is an example of the kind of experiments on which this conclusion is based. In an experiment conducted by Wendy Josephson (1987), nearly 400 boys from various Winnipeg schools were shown either a violent police film or an exciting but nonviolent film about bike racing. Later, the boys played a game of floor hockey. The highest level of aggression during the hockey game was shown by boys who were rated by their teachers as generally high in aggression and who had seen the violent film. These boys hit others with their sticks, threw elbows, and yelled aggressive things at their opponents—more so than boys who had seen the violent film but were rated as nonaggressive by their teacher, and more so than boys who had seen the nonviolent film.

Why does media violence affect viewers' aggression? There are four distinct reasons:

1. *"If they can do it, so can I."* When people watch characters on TV expressing violence, it might simply weaken their previously learned inhibitions against violent behaviour.

2. *"Oh, so that's how you do it!"* When people watch characters on TV expressing violence, it might trigger imitation, providing them with ideas as to how they might go about it.

3. *"I think it must be aggressive feelings that I'm experiencing."* Watching violence makes feelings of anger more easily available and makes an aggressive response more likely simply through priming. Thus, exposing children to an endless supply of violence on TV, in films, and in video games makes it more likely that aggression will come to mind as a response to situations (Signorielli, Gerbner, & Morgan, 1995).

4. *"Ho-hum, another brutal beating—what's on the other channel?"* Watching a lot of violence seems to reduce both our sense of horror about violence and our sympathy for the victims, thereby making it easier for us to live with violence and perhaps easier for us to act aggressively.

> Television has brought murder back into the home—where it belongs.
>
> —ALFRED HITCHCOCK, 1965

Media violence may serve to give kids already prone to aggression permission to be aggressive. It also may make children not prone to aggression more aggressive.

FOCUS ON APPLICATIONS

Does Playing Violent Video Games Increase Aggression?

The April 20, 1999, Columbine High School killings raised the disturbing question of whether violent entertainment, such as violent video games, can contribute to aggression. Apparently Eric Harris and Dylan Klebold enjoyed playing a bloody, extremely violent video game licensed by the U.S. military to train soldiers how to kill. For a class project, Harris and Klebold produced a videotape that was an eerie rendition of the killings they subsequently carried out. Their videotape, modelled after the video game, featured the two of them wearing trench coats, carrying guns, and killing school athletes.

Recent research by Craig Anderson and his colleagues (Anderson & Dill, 2000; Bartholomew & Anderson, 2002) confirms that playing violent video games actually produces violent behaviour. This does not mean that all people, or even a sizable proportion, will necessarily engage in real-world violence through watching violence in the media. However, the fact that some people are influenced—and that the results can be tragic—cannot be denied.

Violent Pornography and Sexual Aggression

If viewing aggression in films and on television contributes to aggressiveness, doesn't it follow that viewing pornographic material could increase the incidence of sexual aggression? Many people think so. For example, Lavoie, Robitaille, and Hébert (2000) conducted discussion groups with youths who frequented a teen drop-in centre in Quebec City. Both males and females perceived pornography as a cause of sexual violence in relationships.

Research confirms these perceptions. For example, Sommers and Check (1987) found that women living in shelters or attending counselling groups for battered women in the Toronto area reported much greater consumption of pornographic material by their partners than did a comparison group of women who were not battered. (The battered women experienced higher levels of verbal aggression, physical aggression, and sexual aggression from their partners than did the control group.) In addition, 39 percent of the battered women (versus 3 percent of the control group) answered "yes" to the question "Has your partner ever upset you by trying to get you to do what he'd seen in pornographic pictures, movies, or books?" Similarly, in Lavoie and colleagues' study of Quebec City teenagers, participants reported that it was not uncommon for them or their partners to imitate acts of sexual violence observed in pornographic movies or magazines.

The findings from carefully controlled laboratory studies show that exposure to violent pornography promotes greater acceptance of sexual violence toward women (Dean & Malamuth, 1997; Donnerstein, 1980; Donnerstein & Berkowitz, 1981; Donnerstein & Linz, 1994; Malamuth, 1981, 1986; Malamuth et al., 1995; Malamuth & Brière, 1986). For example, Neil Malamuth and James Check (1981) asked students at the University of Manitoba to watch a movie shown at a campus theatre, supposedly as part of a study on the evaluation of movies. The participants saw either a movie that contained sexual violence against women or a nonviolent movie that portrayed a positive, caring relationship. Several days later, the students were asked to complete a Sexual Attitudes Survey in their psychology class. The researchers found that male students who had viewed the movie containing sexual violence were more accepting of violence against women than were those who had seen the nonviolent movie.

In a similar study (Malamuth, 1981), male students at the University of Manitoba viewed one of two erotic films. One version portrayed two mutually consenting adults engaged in lovemaking; the other version portrayed a rape incident. After viewing the film, the men were asked to engage in sexual fantasy. Those men who had watched the rape version of the film created more violent sexual fantasies than did those who had watched the mutual consent version. Other studies have found that prolonged exposure to depictions of sexual violence against women (so-called slasher films) makes viewers more accepting of this kind of violence and less sympathetic toward the victims (Linz, Donnerstein, & Penrod, 1984, 1988; Zillmann & Bryant, 1984).

We have seen that exposure to sexual violence is associated with greater acceptance of violence toward women and with more violent fantasies. But do laboratory studies show that men who view violent pornography actually behave aggressively toward women? Sadly, the answer is yes. In one experiment (Donnerstein & Berkowitz, 1981), male participants were angered by a female accomplice. They were then shown one of three films—an aggressive-erotic one involving rape, a purely erotic one without violence, or a film depicting nonerotic violence against women. After viewing one of these films, the men took part in a supposedly unrelated experiment that involved teaching the female accomplice by means of administering electric shocks to her whenever she gave incorrect answers. They were also allowed to choose whatever level of shock they wished to use. (Needless to say, as with other experiments using this procedure, no shocks were actually received.) The men who had earlier seen the violent pornographic film subsequently administered the most intense shocks; those who had seen the erotic nonviolent film administered the lowest level of shocks. There is also evidence showing that those who view violent pornographic films will administer more intense shocks to a female confederate than to a male confederate (Donnerstein, 1980).

Unfortunately, these are not isolated findings. Researchers at the Canadian National Foundation for Family Research and Education recently conducted a meta-analysis of 46 American and Canadian studies on the effects of pornography. They reached the following conclusion:

Exposure to pornographic material puts one at increased risk for developing sexually deviant tendencies, committing sexual offences, experiencing difficulties in one's intimate relationships, and accepting the rape myth (Paolucci-Oddone, Genius, & Violato, 2000).

This is a deeply disturbing conclusion given that violence is a prevalent theme in pornographic materials—materials that have now become widely available because of the Internet. For example, an analysis of adults-only fiction paperback books found that almost one-third of all sex episodes involved the use of force (physical, mental, or blackmail) by a male to make a female engage in unwanted sex (Smith, 1976).

Frustration as a Cause of Aggression

Imagine that your friend Alain is driving you to the airport so you can take a plane home for the Christmas holidays. Alain is starting out a bit later than you feel comfortable with, but when you mention it he accuses you of being overly anxious and assures you that you will arrive there with time to spare. Halfway to your destination, Alain's car grinds to a halt in bumper-to-bumper traffic. You glare at Alain. He smiles lamely and says, "How was I supposed to know there would be so much traffic?" Should he be prepared to duck?

Frustration-aggression theory the theory that frustration—the perception that you are being prevented from obtaining a goal—will increase the probability of an aggressive response

As the above scenario suggests, frustration is a major cause of aggression. Frustration occurs when a person is thwarted on the way to an expected goal or gratification. All of us have experienced some degree of frustration from time to time; indeed, it's unlikely we can get through a week without experiencing it. According to **frustration-aggression theory**, people's perception that they are being prevented from obtaining a goal will increase the probability of an aggressive response (Dollard et al., 1939). As we shall see in a moment, this is not meant to imply that frustration always leads to aggression—but it frequently does. In a classic experiment by Barker, Dembo, and Lewin (1941), young children were shown a roomful of attractive toys that were kept out of their reach. The children stood outside a wire screen looking at the toys—fully expecting to play with them because they had been allowed to earlier—but were unable to reach them. After a painfully long wait, the children were finally allowed to play with the toys. In a control condition, a different group of children was allowed to play with the toys directly, without first being frustrated. This second group of children played joyfully with the toys. However, the frustrated group, when finally given access to the toys, was extremely destructive: These children tended to smash the toys, throw them against the wall, and step on them.

Subsequent research has clarified that frustration does not always produce aggression. Rather, it seems to produce anger or annoyance and a readiness to aggress if other things about the situation are conducive to aggressive behaviour (Berkowitz, 1978, 1988, 1989, 1993; Gustafson, 1989). For example, the size and strength of the person responsible for your frustration—as well as that person's ability to retaliate—will influence whether you react with aggression. It is undoubtedly easier to slam the phone down on a persistent telemarketer than to take out your anger against your frustrator if he turns out to be a defensive lineman for the Edmonton Eskimos and is staring you in the face.

Feelings of frustration can occur when we are blocked or delayed as we strive to reach a goal. For example, being stuck in a traffic jam can elicit aggressive responses, ranging from pointless honking to fistfights or even shootings.

Direct Provocation and Reciprocation

Another cause of aggression stems from the urge to reciprocate after being provoked by aggressive behaviour from another person. While the Christian plea to "turn the other cheek" is wonderful advice, it does not appear to be the typical reaction of most human beings. This has been illustrated in countless experiments in and out of the laboratory. Typical of this line of research is an experiment by Robert Baron (1988), in which participants prepared an advertisement for a new product; their ad was then evaluated and criticized by an accomplice of the experimenter. In one condition, the criticism, while strong, was done in a gentle and considerate manner ("I think there's a lot of room for improvement"); in the other condition, the criticism was given in an insulting manner ("I don't think you could be original if you tried"). When provided with an opportunity to retaliate, subjects who were treated harshly were far more likely to do so than were those in the "gentle" condition.

It is important to point out that, when provoked, people do not always reciprocate. One determinant of reciprocation is the intentionality of the provocation; if we are convinced it was unintentional, most of us will not reciprocate (Kremer & Stephens, 1983; VanOostrom & Horvarth, 1997). Similarly, if there are mitigating circumstances, and we are aware of them, counter-aggression will not occur. For example, if we find out that the classmate who was rude to us just received an unfair grade on a chemistry exam, we are less likely to seek retaliation (Johnson & Rule, 1986). To identify the conditions under which you are most likely to resist the urge to reciprocate, answer the questions in Try It! on the next page.

> ## Try It! Insults and Aggression
>
> Think about the last time you were insulted.
> - Who insulted you?
> - What were the circumstances?
> - Did you take it personally or not?
> - How did you respond?
>
> How does your behaviour relate to the material you have just finished reading?

Alcohol

As most socially active university students know, alcohol tends to lower inhibitions against committing behaviour frowned on by society, including acts of aggression (Desmond, 1987; Taylor & Leonard, 1983). A series of studies conducted in various bars and nightclubs in London, Ontario, confirms that the greater the consumption of alcoholic beverages, the greater the likelihood of aggressive behaviour (Graham & Wells, 2001a, 2001b; Graham, West, & Wells, 2000; see also White, 1997; Yudko et al., 1997). Intoxication also has been implicated as a factor in cases of air rage, crime (statistics reveal that more than half of the individuals who have committed violent crimes were drinking heavily at the time; Murdoch, Pihl, & Ross, 1990; Pihl & Peterson, 1995), and with family violence (Holtzworth-Munroe et al., 1997). In fact, according to data gathered by Statistics Canada (2000), if a spouse drinks heavily, the rate of marital violence is six times higher than if a spouse drinks moderately or not at all. Not only is violence more likely to occur when alcohol is involved, but it also tends to be more severe than when alcohol is not involved (Johnson, 2001; Wekerle & Wall, 2002; Wells, Graham, & West, 2000).

Is there any evidence that alcohol also increases aggression in a direct manner? In other words, can we be sure that alcohol is a direct cause of aggression? Obviously, it is not ethical to administer large amounts of alcohol to research participants and then observe whether they behave violently toward their loved ones. However, researchers have administered alcohol to people to see if they behave more aggressively in laboratory situations. These studies show that when individuals ingest enough alcohol to make them legally drunk, they tend to respond more violently to provocations than do those who have ingested little or no alcohol. For example, research conducted with students at McGill University has found that intoxicated men (women are generally not participants in alcohol studies because of the chance that a woman might be pregnant and not know it) who are provoked administer stronger shocks to a fictitious opponent than participants who are not intoxicated (Hoaken & Pihl, 2000; Pihl et al., 1995). To give one last example, University of Waterloo researchers (MacDonald, Zanna, & Holmes, 2000) found that men who were intoxicated described a conflict with their dating partners or spouses in more negative terms and perceived their partners more negatively compared to those who had consumed little or no alcohol.

In short, it appears that whenever people are intoxicated, the stage is set for aggression. This does not mean that people who have ingested alcohol necessarily go around picking fights. However, alcohol consumption does increase the likelihood of aggressive behaviour.

Social Exclusion

It is becoming an all-too-common theme: A high-school student shows up at school one day with a gun and goes on a killing rampage. Analyses of these tragedies often paint a picture of the killers as socially isolated individuals who experienced rejection from their peers. They then deal with the pain of rejection by mounting a lethal attack on those whose acceptance they craved most.

"Oh, that wasn't me talking. It was the alcohol talking."
© *The New Yorker Collection*, 1975, Dana Fradon. From cartoonbank.com. All rights reserved

Is there validity to these kinds of analyses? Does social exclusion actually lead to aggressive behaviour? Jean Twenge and colleagues (2001) decided to find out. Imagine you are a participant in one of their studies. You arrive at a laboratory along with four or five other students. First, you spend 15 minutes chatting as part of a getting-acquainted exercise. Then, you are informed that the actual experiment involves working in groups on a task. You and the other students are asked to "name the two people (out of those you met today) you would most like to work with." You eagerly write down the names of the two people you enjoyed most during the getting-acquainted discussion. The experimenter then collects the names and tells you she will be back shortly to announce the group assignments.

November 20, 2000. Students from Lester B. Pearson High School in Calgary sob after a 17-year-old student was stabbed to death at school.

To your horror, when she returns she says, "I hate to tell you this, but no one chose you as someone they wanted to work with." How do you react?

If you are like the actual participants in this study, you react with aggression. The rest of the experiment was set up so participants were given an opportunity to deliver loud bursts of white noise to a confederate who insulted them. Those participants who had been rejected earlier were much more aggressive toward the confederate (gave longer and louder bursts of noise) than those who were told they had been accepted by the group. Quite remarkably, the experience of being excluded from a group of strangers in a laboratory provoked considerable levels of aggression in this study (and other similar studies conducted by these researchers; Twenge et al., 2001). It is perhaps little wonder that those who experience the sting of rejection from classmates on a daily basis end up reacting with extreme aggression.

Aggressive Objects as a Cause of Aggression

Aggressive stimulus an object that is associated with aggressive response (e.g., a gun) and whose mere presence can increase the probability of aggression

Is it conceivable that the mere presence of an **aggressive stimulus**—an object associated with aggressive responses (e.g., a gun) might increase the probability of aggression? In a classic experiment by Leonard Berkowitz and Anthony LePage (1967), university students were made angry. Some of them were made angry in a room in which a gun was left lying around (ostensibly from a previous experiment), and others were made angry in a room in which a neutral object (a badminton racket) was substituted for the gun. Participants were then given the opportunity to administer electric shocks to a fellow student. Those individuals who had been made angry in the presence of the gun administered more intense electric shocks than did those made angry in the presence of the badminton racket.

These findings, replicated in the United States and Europe (Frodi, 1975; Turner & Leyens, 1992; Turner & Simons, 1974; Turner et al., 1977), are provocative, and point to a conclusion opposite to a familiar slogan often used by opponents of gun control: "Guns don't kill; people do." Guns *do* kill. Consider Seattle, Washington, and Vancouver, British Columbia. They are twin cities in a lot of ways; they have similar climates, populations, economies, general crime rates, and rates of physical assault. They differ, however, in two respects: (a) Vancouver severely restricts handgun ownership, while Seattle does not, and (b) the murder rate in Seattle is more than twice as high as that in Vancouver (Sloan et al., 1988). Is the one the cause of the other? We cannot be sure. However, the laboratory experiments discussed above strongly suggest that the ubiquitous presence of that aggressive stimulus in the United States might be a factor. This speculation receives additional support from Dane Archer and Rosemary Gartner (1984), who, in a cross-national study of violence, found that the homicide rate in countries all over the world is highly correlated with the availability of handguns. Britain, for example, where handguns are banned, has one-quarter the population of the United States and one-sixteenth as many homicides.

Gender Differences in Aggression

Who is more likely to be aggressive? Males or females? If you guessed the former, you're correct—or, at least, mostly correct. Many studies have shown that men are generally more aggressive than women. But—and this is important—the size of this gender difference varies, depending on the situation. For example, an analysis of 64 separate experiments revealed that although men are generally more aggressive than women, this difference becomes much smaller when women and men are provoked (Bettencourt & Miller, 1996). In fact, a recent study conducted at McGill University found that women were just as aggressive as men when subjected to strong provocation (Hoaken & Pihl, 2000). Which gender is most aggressive also depends on the kind of aggression we are talking about. Most research has focused on physical aggression and, here, boys and men generally are more aggressive. However, research with children shows that boys and girls tend to be equally verbally aggressive. If one focuses on indirect or covert aggression (social exclusion, alienation), girls show higher levels than boys (e.g., Pepler & Craig, 2005).

Why are women more likely to be the victims of severe spousal aggression?

In discussing gender differences, we must also consider additional situational factors, such as the target of aggression. It is well established that men's aggression is generally directed at other men (friends or strangers). Men's aggression is also more likely to take place in bars or other public places, more likely to involve alcohol consumption, and tends to have less emotional impact. Women's aggression, on the other hand, is much more likely to be directed at a romantic partner, is less likely to involve alcohol, and tends to have a highly negative emotional impact (Graham & Wells, 2001a, 2001b). It might surprise you to learn that women are more likely to report physical aggression toward a romantic partner than are men. This gender difference was confirmed in a recent analysis of well over 100 studies (Archer, 2000; for examples of other Canadian studies that have found this gender difference, see Kwong, Bartholomew, & Dutton, 1999; Sharpe & Taylor, 1999). However, once again, we hasten to add some "buts." First, physical aggression is most likely to be reported among younger women in dating relationships. Second, women's physical aggression does less damage than men's physical aggression; women are much more likely to suffer serious injuries at the hands of their male partners than the other way around. In fact, women are at far greater risk of being murdered by their partners than are men. To learn more about gender differences in physical aggression in the context of close relationships, see Try It! on page 296.

Thus, which gender is most aggressive depends on a variety of situational factors. This suggests that women's and men's behaviour can also be modified, or changed, by situational or social factors. Indeed, as we shall see next, social psychologists are convinced that aggressive behaviour can be changed.

Thinking Critically
Does exposure to violence in the media make people more violent?

Try It! The Incidence of Violence in Intimate Relationships

Violence in intimate relationships is usually assessed using the Conflict Tactics scale (or variations of it), in which people report whether their partners have used any of the following types of violence:

- threatened to hit
- threw something
- pushed, grabbed, or shoved
- slapped
- kicked, bit, or hit
- hit with something
- beat
- choked
- used or threatened to use a gun or knife
- sexual assault

To see how knowledgeable you are about the incidence of spousal violence (including in common-law relationships) in Canada, answer the following questions:

1. Which of these kinds of violence do you think is most common in marriages?
2. Which of these kinds of violence is more likely to be experienced by women?
3. Which of these kinds of violence is more likely to be experienced by men?

Answers

Note: The percentages we report below are based on Statistics Canada (1999b) information gathered on 26 000 Canadians. Respondents were asked whether violence with current partners occurred in the past five years. In cases where a marriage had ended in the past five years, respondents reported on violence that had occurred with their former spouses. The rates of violence reported for these marriages that had ended were considerably higher than the rates of violence reported for marriages that were currently intact.

1. The most prevalent kinds of spousal violence are "threatened to hit" (54 percent of those who reported violence from a spouse), "pushed, grabbed, or shoved" (52 percent), and "slapped" (41 percent).

2. Women were most likely to report being pushed, grabbed, or shoved (72 percent of women versus 34 percent of men). They were also much more likely than men to report the more severe forms of violence. For example, they were much more likely than men to report being beaten (13 percent versus 4 percent), choked (10 percent versus zero percent), or sexually assaulted by their spouses (8 percent versus zero percent).

3. Men were most likely to report that their spouses had thrown something at them (54 percent of men versus 35 percent of women). They also were twice as likely as women to report being kicked, bitten, or hit (41 percent versus 19 percent), and were more likely to report that they had been slapped (51 percent versus 30 percent).

HOW TO REDUCE AGGRESSION

Throughout history, beleaguered parents have attempted to curb the aggressive behaviour of their children. One of the prime techniques is punishment. After all, as the old saying goes, "Spare the rod and spoil the child." How well does punishment work? Let's consider the data.

Does Punishing Aggression Reduce Aggressive Behaviour?

Punishment is a complex event, especially as it relates to aggression. On the one hand, you might guess that punishing any behaviour, including aggression, would reduce its frequency. On the other hand, because severe punishment itself usually takes the form of an aggressive act, the punishers are actually modelling aggressive behaviour for the person whose aggressive behaviour they are trying to stamp out, and might induce that person to imitate the action. This seems to be true—for children. As we saw in Chapter 5, several experiments with preschoolers have demonstrated that the threat of relatively severe punishment for committing a transgression has little impact on diminishing the attractiveness of the transgression. On the other hand, the threat of mild punishment—of a degree just powerful enough to get the child to cease the undesired activity temporarily—can induce the child to try to justify his or her restraint and thereby produce a diminution in the attractiveness of the action (Aronson & Carlsmith, 1963; Freedman, 1965). Dan Olweus (1994, 1995a, 1995b, 1995c, 1996, 1997) has applied these ideas in the Norwegian and Swedish school systems in hopes of curbing bullying. Olweus was able to reduce the occurrence of bullying behaviour among grades 4 through 7 students by as much as 50 percent, by training teachers and administrators to be vigilant to the problem and to make moderate and swift interventions. The intervention strategy was effective both immediately and over the long haul. (As mentioned in Chapter 2, unfortunately, the results were not quite as positive when the Norwegian intervention program was adapted for use in Toronto schools, in part because a more modest version of the program was instituted [Pepler et al., 1994].) Overall, this research indicates that children, who have not yet formed their values, are more apt to develop distaste for aggression if the punishment for aggressive actions is swift and not severe enough to make it unnecessary for the children to justify their restraint.

What about adults? A study by the National Academy of Sciences (see Berkowitz, 1993) demonstrated that consistency and

Schoolyard bullying, derision, and taunting make life miserable for a sizable proportion of children in most countries.

certainty of punishment were far more effective deterrents of violent behaviour than was severe punishment. The fact that mild punishment, consistently meted out, can be quite effective in reducing adults' violent behaviour was demonstrated in a simple but powerful field experiment on reducing domestic violence conducted by the Minneapolis Police Department (Cohn, 1987; Sherman & Berk, 1984). In this experiment, police officers were randomly assigned to one of three conditions. In the first condition, they performed brief, on-the-spot counselling when called to intervene in a domestic violence situation; in the second condition, they asked the perpetrator to leave the scene for eight hours; in the third condition, they arrested the perpetrator. Police reports were then carefully monitored over the next six months. The results indicated that during those months, 19 percent of the perpetrators given counselling and 24 percent of those asked to leave the premises repeated their aggressive actions, whereas only 10 percent of those placed under arrest (and made to spend a night or two in jail) repeated their actions. These data show that when law enforcement officers demonstrate that they are taking the offence seriously by hauling the perpetrator off to jail, domestic violence is diminished. The findings led the Minneapolis Police Department to revamp its policies regarding the arrest of perpetrators of domestic violence, a move that has attracted considerable attention.

Closer to home, in 1990 Manitoba instituted a Family Violence Court to deal specifically with family violence cases, and in 1997 Ontario established similar courts. These specialized courts are part of an overall response to family violence that includes a zero-tolerance policy for arrest and early intervention in domestic abuse situations. Although one might argue whether arrest constitutes "mild" punishment, the message being sent from these courts is that family violence is a crime with immediate consequences. Although it is too early to tell whether this approach will have long-term benefits, it is encouraging that the rate of spousal assault has declined since these courts were established (Statistics Canada, 2000).

Catharsis and Aggression

"Get it out of your system" has been common advice for a great many years. So, if you are feeling angry (the belief goes), don't try to ignore it, but instead yell, scream, curse, throw some crockery at the wall—and then you'll be rid of it and it won't fester and grow into something truly uncontrollable. This common belief, held even among some professional psychologists, is based on an oversimplification of the psychoanalytic notion of **catharsis** (see Dollard et al., 1939; Freud, 1933). Freud believed that unless people were allowed to express their aggression in relatively harmless ways, the aggressive energy would be dammed up, and pressure would build and eventually explode into acts of extreme violence or manifest itself as symptoms of mental illness. Alas, Freud's view was misinterpreted and advice columnists began encouraging people to blow off steam when angry. This was supposed to make them feel better and reduce the likelihood that they would engage in subsequent acts of destructive violence. But does this square with the data?

Consider a recent study by Bushman, Baumeister, and Stack (1999). They asked university students to read an article, supposedly published in *Science*, titled "Research Shows That Hitting Inanimate Objects Is an Effective Way to Vent Anger." In the article, a Harvard psychologist claimed that people who vent their anger by hitting a punching bag subsequently behave less aggressively toward others. Other participants read the same article, except that the word "Effective" was changed to "Ineffective" in the title, and

Catharsis the notion that "blowing off steam"—by performing an aggressive act, watching others engage in aggressive behaviour, or engaging in a fantasy of aggression—relieves built-up aggressive energies and hence reduces the likelihood of further aggressive behaviour

the article stated that venting one's anger did *not* reduce aggression. In the next part of the experiment, the participants were insulted by a confederate. Some participants were given a chance to vent their anger by hitting a punching bag; other participants were not. Later, all participants were given an opportunity to deliver bursts of noise either to the person who insulted them or to a different person. It turned out that the most aggressive participants (those who delivered the longest and loudest blasts of noise) were those who had read the pro-catharsis message and had hit the punching bag. Moreover, they were equally aggressive, regardless of whether the target was the person who had angered them or an innocent person. Thus, it appears that venting anger actually increases anger, rather than reduces it.

Similar conclusions have been reached in studies that have examined whether participating in aggressive sports has a cathartic effect, or whether simply watching aggressive sports might be an effective way to blow off steam (Arms, Russell, & Sandilands, 1979; Branscombe & Wann, 1992; Goldstein & Arms, 1971; Patterson, 1974; Russell, 1983). These studies have consistently found that playing or watching aggressive sports does not decrease people's aggressive feelings—if anything, it increases them.

What Are We Supposed to Do with Our Anger?

Surely Sigmund Freud was not totally wrong when he suggested that stifled anger might be harmful to the individual. Indeed, recent research suggests that stifling powerful emotions can lead to physical illness (Pennebaker, 1990). However, if it is harmful to keep our feelings bottled up and harmful to express them, what are we supposed to do with them? This dilemma isn't as difficult as it might seem.

TRAINING IN COMMUNICATION AND PROBLEM-SOLVING SKILLS As we indicated earlier, there is nothing wrong with anger; it is part of being human. What causes the problem is the expression of anger in violent ways. Thus, one way to reduce violence is to teach people how to communicate anger or criticism in constructive ways, how to negotiate and compromise when conflicts arise, how to be more sensitive to the needs and desires of others, and so on. When feelings of anger are expressed in a clear, open, nonpunitive manner, the result can be greater mutual understanding and a strengthening of the relationship.

It almost seems too simple. Yet we have found such behaviour to be a reasonable option that will have more beneficial effects than, on the one hand, shouting, name-calling, and throwing crockery or, on the other hand, suffering in silence as you grin and bear it (Aronson, 1999).

There is evidence to back up our claims.

Fans watching aggressive sports do not become less aggressive—contrary to the idea of catharsis.

> Something of vengeance I had tasted for the first time; an aromatic wine it seemed, on swallowing, warm and racy; its after-flavour, metallic and corroding, gave me a sensation as if I had been poisoned.
>
> —CHARLOTTE BRONTË,
> Jane Eyre,
> 1847

> I was angry with my friend;
> I told my wrath, my wrath did end.
>
> —WILLIAM BLAKE

For example, in a classic experiment by Joel Davitz (1952), children were allowed to play in groups of four. Some of these groups were taught constructive ways to relate to each other and were rewarded for such behaviour; others were not so instructed but were rewarded for aggressive or competitive behaviour. Next, the youngsters were deliberately frustrated. This was accomplished by building up the expectation that they would be shown a series of entertaining movies and be allowed to have fun. The experimenter began to show a movie and to hand out candy bars, but then he abruptly terminated the movie at the point of highest interest and took the candy bars away. Now the children were allowed to play freely. As you have learned, this was a setup for the occurrence of aggressive behaviour. However, those children who had been trained for constructive behaviour displayed far more constructive activity and far less aggressive behaviour than did those in the other group. A great many elementary and secondary schools are now specifically training students to employ these nonaggressive strategies for resolving conflict (Eargle, Guerra, & Tolan, 1994; Educators for Social Responsibility, 2001; Ester, 1995).

DEFUSING ANGER THROUGH APOLOGY Suppose you are scheduled to be at your friend's house at 7:30 p.m. in order to drive her to a concert scheduled to start at 8:00. The concert is an exciting one for her—it involves one of her favourite soloists—and she has been looking forward to it for several weeks. You rush out of your house with just barely enough time to get there, but after driving for a few minutes you discover that you have a flat tire. By the time you change the tire and get to her house, you are already 20 minutes late for the concert. Imagine her response if you (a) casually walk in, grin at her, and say, "Oh well, it probably wouldn't have been an interesting concert anyway. Lighten up; it's not such a big deal. Where's your sense of humour?" or (b) run in with a sad and anguished look on your face, show her your greasy and dirty hands, tell her you left your house in time to make it but unaccountably got this flat tire, apologize sincerely and profusely, and vow to find a way to make it up to her.

Our guess is that your friend would be prone toward aggression in the first instance but not in the second. This guess is supported by a host of experiments (Baron, 1988, 1990; Ohbuchi & Sato, 1994; Weiner et al., 1987). Typical of these experiments is one by Ohbuchi, Kameda, and Agarie (1989) in which university students performed poorly on a complex task because of errors made by the experimenter's assistant while presenting the materials. In three conditions, the assistant (a) apologized publicly, (b) apologized privately, or (c) did not apologize at all. In a fourth condition, the senior experimenter removed the harm by indicating that he surmised there was an administrative blunder and therefore did not hold the students responsible for their poor performance. The results were clear: The students liked the assistant better and showed far less tendency to aggress against him if he apologized than if he didn't apologize, even if the harm was subsequently removed by the experimenter. Moreover, whether the apology was public or private made little difference; any apology—sincerely given, and in which the perpetrator took full responsibility—proved to be an effective way to reduce aggression. Thus, another way to reduce aggression is for the individual who caused the frustration to take responsibility for the action, apologize for it, and indicate that it is unlikely to happen again.

THE MODELLING OF NONAGGRESSIVE BEHAVIOUR Earlier in the chapter, when discussing prosocial behaviour, we argued that helpfulness can be instilled in children by exposing them to positive models—people who are behaving in prosocial ways. Similarly, when nonaggressive behaviour is modelled, children are likely to follow suit. In a series of experiments, children were first allowed to witness the behaviour of youngsters who behaved nonaggressively when provoked; when the children were subsequently placed in a situation in which they themselves were provoked, they showed a much lower frequency of aggressive responses than did children who were not exposed to the nonaggressive models (Baron, 1972; Donnerstein & Donnerstein, 1976; Vidyasagar & Mishra, 1993). In short, children learn what they see. If they are exposed to helpful, nonaggressive role models, that is the behaviour they will imitate.

Thinking Critically
Everyone who has gone to school knows that schoolyard bullying is a pervasive problem. How might bullying be reduced?

Mahatma Gandhi was effective in bringing about the independence of India from the British Empire, using and modelling nonviolent resistance. Being nonviolent in the face of violence is difficult, but effective.

> Man must evolve for all human conflict a method which rejects revenge, aggression, and retaliation.
>
> —MARTIN LUTHER KING JR., NOBEL PRIZE ACCEPTANCE SPEECH, 1964

Summary

For centuries people have debated the determinants of **prosocial behaviour**—that is, acts performed with the goal of benefiting another person. People have been particularly intrigued with the causes of **altruism**, which is the desire to help another person even if it involves cost to the helper. According to the evolutionary psychology explanation, prosocial behaviour has genetic roots because people further the survival of their genes by helping genetic relatives (**kin selection**). In addition, there is a survival advantage to following the **norm of reciprocity**, whereby people help strangers in the hope that they will receive help when they need it.

Social exchange theory views helping behaviour as a weighing of rewards and costs: helping in situations where the rewards for helping are greater than the costs. Rewards include recognition, praise, and the relief of personal distress. Neither of these theories sees helping behaviour as a form of altruism; self-gain is always involved. In contrast, the **empathy-altruism hypothesis** suggests that people do sometimes behave in truly altruistic ways, namely when they experience **empathy** for those in need.

Prosocial behaviour is multidetermined, and both personal and situational factors can override or facilitate basic motives to help. Personal determinants include gender and mood. Though one sex is not more altruistic than the other, the ways in which men and women help often differ, with men more likely to help in heroic chivalrous ways and women more likely to help in nurturant ways that involve a long-term commitment. Interestingly, being in either a good or a bad mood—compared to being in a neutral mood—can increase helping. Good moods increase helping for several reasons, including the fact that they allow us to see the good side of other people, making us more willing to help them. Bad moods can also increase helping. According to the **negative-state relief hypothesis**, helping someone makes us feel good, lifting us out of the doldrums.

Situational factors are an important determinant of whether people will help. According to Latané and Darley's model of bystander intervention, a potential helper must make five decisions before providing help: (1) notice the event, (2) interpret the event as an emergency (here **pluralistic ignorance** can occur, whereby everyone assumes nothing is wrong, because no one else looks concerned). According to the **bystander effect**, the greater the number of people who witness an emergency, the less likely it is that one of them will help. The reason is that there is a **diffusion of responsibility** created. People therefore have to (3) accept personal responsibility for helping, before they can progress to the final steps of the helping process: (4) know how to help, and, finally, (5) implement the help.

How can helping be increased? One way is for parents to reward their children for helping. Children also are more likely to be helpful when they observe adults engaging in helpful behaviours. Research has also indicated that teaching people about the determinants of prosocial behaviour makes them more aware of why they sometimes don't help, with the happy result that they help more in the future.

In the latter half of the chapter we shift our focus from helping others to hurting others. We define **aggression** as intentional behaviour aimed at doing harm or causing physical or psychological pain to another person. Because aggressiveness has had survival value, most contemporary social psychologists accept the proposition that it is part of our evolutionary heritage. At the same time, we know that human beings have developed exquisite mechanisms for controlling their aggressive impulses and that human behaviour is flexible and adaptable to changes in the environment. Thus, whether aggression is actually expressed depends on a complex interplay between our biological propensities and the social situations in which we find ourselves.

There are many situational causes of aggression. Aggression can be produced through the imitation of aggressive models, either in face-to-face situations or by viewing violence in films or on TV. The possible effects of viewing violence in the media are of particular interest to social psychologists because of the pervasiveness of violent programming. Violence in the media has been shown to lead to greater aggressiveness in children and in adults. These findings extend to the viewing of violent pornography, which has been shown to increase the acceptance and perpetration of sexual violence. The **frustration-aggression theory** states that the experience of frustration can increase the probability of an aggressive response. However, frustration alone does not automatically lead to aggression; it is more likely to produce aggression if one is thwarted on the way to a goal in a manner that is either illegitimate or unexpected. Aggression can also be produced by direct provocation or social exclusion—the experience of being rejected by one's social group. Finally, the mere presence of an **aggressive stimulus**—or an object associated with aggressive responses, such as a gun—can result in increased aggression.

Research on gender differences shows that, generally, men are more physically aggressive than are women. However, a number of situational factors (e.g., the target of aggression) influence the size and direction of this difference.

Aggression can be reduced in a number of ways. Punishing aggressive behaviour in order to reduce it is tricky; punishment can be effective if it is not too severe and if it follows closely on the heels of the aggressive act. However, severe or delayed punishment is not an effective way to reduce aggression. There is no evidence that committing an aggressive action or watching others behave aggressively—the notion of **catharsis**—reduces aggression. It is much more likely that committing or witnessing aggression will trigger further acts of aggression. The most effective approaches include training people in the use of communication skills so that they are able to discuss the reasons for anger and hostility, apologizing, and exposing people to nonaggressive role models.

Key Terms

Aggression   (page 284)
Aggressive stimulus   (page 294)
Altruism   (page 267)
Bystander effect   (page 280)
Catharsis   (page 298)
Diffusion of responsibility   (page 280)
Empathy   (page 270)
Empathy-altruism hypothesis   (page 270)
Frustration-aggression theory   (page 290)
Kin selection   (page 267)
Negative-state relief hypothesis   (page 274)
Norm of reciprocity   (page 268)
Pluralistic ignorance   (page 278)
Prosocial behaviour   (page 267)
Social learning theory   (page 286)

Key Online Search Terms

Altruism
Empathy
Bystander effect
Frustration
Provocation
Social exclusion
Catharsis

If You Are Interested

Aronson, E. (2000). *Nobody left to hate: Teaching compassion after Columbine.* New York: Worth/Freeman. A discussion of the causes of school violence and some suggestions for remedies.

Baron, R. A., & Richardson, D. R. (1994). *Human aggression.* New York: Plenum. A penetrating analysis of the social psychology of aggression.

Clark, M. S. (1991). *Prosocial behavior: Review of personality and social psychology* (Vol. 12). Newbury Park, CA: Sage. A resource containing chapters by top researchers in the field of prosocial behaviour, many of whom were cited in this chapter. Topics include the development of altruism, the debate about whether people are ever truly altruistic or are always concerned with their self-interest, the effects of mood on helping, and the consequences of helping.

Pepler, D. J., & Craig, W. M. (2005). Aggressive girls on troubled trajectories: A developmental perspective. In D. J. Pepler, K. C. Madsen, C. Webster, & K. S. Levene (Eds.), The development and treatment of girlhood aggression (pp. 3–28) Mahwah, NJ: Lawrence Erlbaum. This state-of-the-art compendium on the nature and treatment of girls' aggression features chapters by a number of Canadian researchers, including Debra Pepler (York University and the Hospital for Sick Children), Wendy Craig (Queen's University), Raymond Baillargeon, Richard Tremblay (both at the Université de Montréal), and J. Douglas Willms (University of New Brunswick), to name a few. A broad, informative overview of a long-neglected but important topic.

Tavris, C. (1989). *Anger: The misunderstood emotion.* New York: Touchstone/Simon & Schuster. An interesting and well-written analysis of anger.

Weblinks

www.volunteer.ca
Volunteerism Canada
This site provides information on volunteerism in Canada.

www.giraffe.org
The Giraffe Heroes Project
This site is about an organization that promotes prosocial behaviour, and it provides a wealth of educational information.

www.apa.org/pubinfo/altruism.html
What Makes Kids Care?
This article from the APA site discusses how to teach gentleness and caring to children.

www.media-awareness.ca/english/issues/violence/index.cfm
Media Violence
This section of the Media Awareness Network site presents Canadian perspectives on the media violence debate and brings together a wide range of background information, contacts, and resources.

www.hc-sc.gc.ca/hppb/familyviolence
National Clearinghouse on Family Violence
The National Clearinghouse on Family Violence is a national resource centre for Canadians seeking information about violence within the family and looking for new resources being used to address it.

www.drdriving.org
Dr. Driving's Road Rage and Aggressive Driving Prevention
This site, developed by a social psychologist, provides many links to articles on road rage and aggressive driving.

Chapter 9 Practice Quiz

Check your knowledge of the concepts in this chapter by trying the following questions.

BASIC MOTIVES UNDERLYING PROSOCIAL BEHAVIOUR: WHY DO PEOPLE HELP?

Multiple Choice

1. Kinship selection is the idea that behaviour that helps a genetic relative is favoured by
   a. birth order.
   b. natural selection.
   c. its cultural context.
   d. we interfamilial relations.

2. Which of the following is not considered a benefit of helping?
   a. it relieves our own stress
   b. we gain social approval
   c. it ensures someone will help us when we need it
   d. we make money

True or False

3. Social exchange theory argues that we act in order to minimize the rewards we receive.
   ___ True
   ___ False

Fill in the Blank

4. _____ is the ability to experience things the way others do.
5. _____ is any act performed with the goal of helping another.

PERSONAL DETERMINANTS OF PROSOCIAL BEHAVIOUR: WHY DO SOME PEOPLE HELP MORE THAN OTHERS?

Multiple Choice

6. Two factors that your textbook identifies as affecting helping are
   a. gender and mood.
   b. gender and age.
   c. age and race.
   d. mood and religion.

7. People who show high levels of altruism _____ those with low levels.
   a. help less than
   b. help the same as
   c. help more than
   d. give better help than

True or False

8. People are more likely to help others when they are upset and need to boost their self-esteem.
   ___ True
   ___ False

9. Women are more likely to engage in both formal and informal acts of volunteering.
   ___ True
   ___ False

Fill in the Blank

10. _____ is the idea that people help to alleviate their own distress or sadness.

SITUATIONAL DETERMINANTS OF PROSOCIAL BEHAVIOUR: WHEN WILL PEOPLE HELP?

Multiple Choice

11. _____ occurs when bystanders assume nothing is wrong because others do not seem concerned.
    a. Bystander ignorance
    b. Bystander incompetence
    c. Pluralistic ignorance
    d. Social loafing

12. According to _____, each bystander's sense of responsibility is _____.
    a. diffusion of ambiguity; decreased
    b. diffusion of responsibility; increased
    c. diffusion of responsibility; decreased
    d. the bystander effect; increased

True or False

13. In order to obtain help, it is best to address bystanders as individuals and single them out.
    ___ True
    ___ False

Fill in the Blank

14. There are _____ steps people must take prior to intervening in an emergency.

15. _____ shows that the more bystanders present during an emergency, the less likely anyone is to help.

AGGRESSION: WHY WE HURT OTHER PEOPLE

Multiple Choice

16. A study by Archer and McDaniel found teenagers in _____ tend to be the most aggressive.
    a. the United States
    b. the Caribbean
    c. Korea
    d. New Zealand

17. Aggression is thought to be
    a. innate.
    b. an instinctive phenomenon.
    c. learned.
    d. all of the above

True or False

18. All cultures exhibit similar levels and types of aggression.
    ___ True
    ___ False

19. Most academics agree that aggression is innate.
    ___ True
    ___ False

Fill in the Blank

20. Acts of aggression can be both physical and _____.

SITUATIONAL CAUSES OF AGGRESSION

Multiple Choice

21. Pornography that is violent towards women
    a. increases the chances of aggressive actions in men.
    b. decreases the chances of aggressive attitudes in men.
    c. surprisingly has no effect on aggression.
    d. increases the chances of aggressive actions in women.

22. Anderson and colleagues found that playing violent video games
    a. decreases aggressive behaviour.
    b. increases aggressive behaviour.
    c. has no effect on aggressive behaviour.
    d. increases altruistic behaviour.

True or False

23. Women are more verbally aggressive than men.
    ___ True
    ___ False

Fill in the Blank

24. _____ states that being prevented from attaining a goal can lead to aggression.
25. The _____ theory states that aggression is learned through observation.

HOW TO REDUCE AGGRESSION

Multiple Choice

26. _____ is an effective way to reduce aggression.
    a. Communication
    b. Catharsis
    c. Repression
    d. Denial

27. The notion of catharsis can be attributed to
    a. Skinner.
    b. Allport.
    c. Freud.
    d. Anderson.

True or False

28. Aggression can be reduced when the person causing the aggression takes responsibility.
    ___ True
    ___ False

29. Severe punishments are better deterrents to aggression than mild punishments.
    ___ True
    ___ False

Fill in the Blank

30. _____ is the idea that aggressive acts relieve built-up tension.

PERSONALIZED STUDY PLAN

Want to check your answers and access more study resources? Visit the Companion Website for *Fundamentals of Social Psychology* at **www.pearsoned.ca/aronson**, where you'll find the above questions incorporated in a pre-test and post-test for each chapter. These tests will be automatically graded online, allowing you to check your answers. A Study Plan, like the one below, groups the questions by section within the chapter and shows you which sections you need to focus on for further study.

Your Results for "Chapter 9, Pretest"

OVERALL SCORE: 76% of 21 questions

Group	Score	Proficient
Basic Motives Underlying Prosocial Behaviour	3 of 4	Yes
Personal Determinants of Prosocial Behaviour	3 of 3	Yes
Situational Determinants of Prosocial Behaviour	2 of 4	No
Aggression	2 of 3	Yes
Situational Causes of Aggression	3 of 4	Yes
How to Reduce Aggression	3 of 3	Yes

CHAPTER

10

afraid

I heard
"The Only Good Indian
Is a Dead Indian"
I never heard that on
The reserve
I was fine before I
Came to the city
What is wrong with me
Now?
I have no answer
All I know is that
I am afraid of making
A mistake
I am afraid if I succeed
It will not make any
Difference.
There was a time
Laughing at myself
Came easily
Now all I feel is
Shame
I am afraid to open
My mouth
I know that I am not dead
Does this mean
I am no good?
I must be no good
Because I feel ugly
I hate being Indian
Why was I born on the
Reserve anyway?
There is nothing I can do
To change that
I can't change who I am
I'm afraid I am
Not prepared to die
Just yet
So I have to try
Harder
"To Be a Good Indian."

Mary Young

Prejudice: Causes and Cures

Chapter Outline

PREJUDICE: THE UBIQUITOUS SOCIAL PHENOMENON

PREJUDICE, STEREOTYPING, AND DISCRIMINATION DEFINED
Prejudice: The Affective Component
Stereotypes: The Cognitive Component
Discrimination: The Behavioural Component

WHAT CAUSES PREJUDICE?
The Way We Think: Social Cognition
What We Believe: Stereotypes
The Way We Feel: Affect and Mood

EFFECTS OF STEREOTYPING, PREJUDICE, AND DISCRIMINATION
Self-fulfilling Prophecies
Self-blaming Attributions for Discrimination
Stereotype Threat

HOW CAN PREJUDICE AND DISCRIMINATION BE REDUCED?
Learning Not to Hate
Revising Stereotypical Beliefs
The Contact Hypothesis
Cooperation and Interdependence: The Jigsaw Classroom

Meet Mary Young, Director of the Aboriginal Student Services Centre at the University of Winnipeg. Mary grew up in Bloodvein First Nation, an Ojibway community in northern Manitoba. When she was growing up, Mary understood that she was a treaty Indian according to the Indian Act, but being an Indian was not part of her identity. She thought of herself as Anishinabe, and she was comfortable with that identity. At the age of 14, she moved to Winnipeg with the dream of being the first person from Bloodvein to graduate from high school. With that move came the startling discovery that the other students thought of her as Indian. Moreover, *Indian* was not a neutral term—it was saturated with negative connotations. Mary learned quickly that being labelled as "Indian" meant that she was less acceptable, less deserving, and less worthy than the white students attending her high school.

Mary comments, "When I left home at the age of fourteen...my goal was to finish high school. I never expected that I would have difficulty with my identity, my cultural background, nor did I think I was going to allow myself to feel ashamed of my family, including my own shame of being an 'Indian.'" In reflecting on this life-shattering experience, Mary wrote the poem that appears on the first page of this chapter.

Of all the social behaviours we discuss in this book, prejudice is perhaps the most widespread and certainly among the most dangerous. Prejudice touches nearly everyone's life. We are all victims or potential victims of stereotyping and discrimination, for no other reason than our membership

Mary Young felt the impact of racism in her life when she moved from her First Nations community to Winnipeg to attend high school.

in an identifiable group—whether it be ethnic, religious, gender, national origin, sexual orientation, obesity, or disability. However, some people are more strongly victimized than others. People who are members of visible minorities report the greatest degree of prejudice and discrimination, and if they are of a minority status in more than one way, they are especially likely to be discriminated against. For example, black immigrants to Canada experience more prejudice and discrimination than do white immigrants, and this experience is compounded for a black person who is Muslim or is female (Dion, 2001; Dion & Dion, 2001b). Similarly, researchers at York University found that women of colour feel that both gender and racial stereotypes are applied to them (Patterson, Cameron, & Lalonde, 1996).

PREJUDICE: THE UBIQUITOUS SOCIAL PHENOMENON

Racial and ethnic identity is a major focal point for prejudice. Canada, for example, views itself as a country that embraces multiculturalism, a country that appreciates the diversity that different racial and ethnic groups contribute to its social fabric. However, all you have to do is ask Canadians about their attitudes toward Aboriginals, Pakistanis, East Asians, or Sikhs, and it quickly becomes apparent that diversity is not always celebrated, or even tolerated (Esses & Gardner, 1996; Pruegger & Rogers, 1993). (The Try It! box raises some interesting issues about the merits of multiculturalism.) In fact, groups such as these are common targets of prejudice. Even particular subgroups of white Canadians are subjected to prejudice, as witnessed by the long-standing popularity of "Newfie" jokes, the tensions between anglophones and francophones in Quebec, and "centre of the universe" comments about Torontonians.

Try It! Multiculturalism: Is It Working?

In a country such as the United States, members of different nationalities or ethnic groups are expected to assimilate to the majority. The image is one of a "melting pot," as opposed to the image of the "cultural mosaic" often used to describe Canada. In Canada, cultural groups are encouraged to maintain their values and customs while participating in Canadian society. (Canada formally passed a Multiculturalism Act in 1987.) Slogans such as "celebrating differences" reflect our country's multicultural orientation. Recently, some social psychologists have begun to question the merits of this approach. As you may recall from Chapter 8, similarity is one of the best predictors of attraction and liking. Might it actually be counterproductive for intercultural relations to emphasize differences between groups? Consider the results of a study of English Canadians, French Canadians, Jews, Indians, Algerians, and Greeks living in Montreal. The researchers found that the more similar the respondents perceived a group to be to their own group, the greater their willingness to associate with members of that group (Osbeck, Moghaddam, and Perreault, 1997).

These findings raise some intriguing questions (which you may want to discuss with a friend):

1. What are the implications of these findings for Canada's policy of multiculturalism?
2. Is it actually possible to "celebrate differences"?
3. Are there ways in which basic similarities between groups could be highlighted, while allowing for an appreciation of differences?

Other aspects of your identity also leave you vulnerable to prejudice—for example, your gender, your sexual orientation, and your religion. Even your profession or hobbies can lead to your being stereotyped. We are all familiar with the "dumb jock" and "computer nerd" stereotypes. Some people have negative attitudes about blue-collar workers; others about "MBA types." The point is that none of us emerges completely unscathed from the effects of prejudice; it is a problem of and for all humankind.

Granted, many manifestations of prejudice are less frequent and less flagrant than they used to be. As the norm swings toward tolerance for certain out-groups, many people simply become more careful—outwardly acting unprejudiced, but inwardly maintaining their prejudiced views. This phenomenon is called **modern prejudice** (Dovidio & Gaertner, 1996; Gaertner & Dovidio, 1986; McConahay, 1986). One consequence of modern prejudice is that social psychologists have had to devise subtler ways of measuring it. For example, the Modern Racism Scale is a subtle, indirect measure of racial prejudice (McConahay, 1986). It turns out that people who are reluctant to express blatant prejudice nevertheless are quite willing to agree with statements such as, "Minorities are getting too demanding in their push for special rights." Research conducted in Canada, the United States, and Europe has shown that those who score high on modern prejudice scales are more likely to show signs of prejudice when it is "safe" to do so or when it is assessed in subtle ways (Kawakami, Dion, & Dovidio, 1998; Lepore & Brown, 1997). For example, research has shown that those who score high on explicit measures of prejudice argue that immigrants should be sent back home. Those who score high on modern racism scales do not advocate this view, but instead show their prejudice in more covert, socially acceptable ways (refusing to support actions that will improve immigrants' rights and quality of life; Pettigrew, 1998). Parallel to the issue of racism, people who are opposed to equality for women may be reluctant to say so directly, but they seem to find it acceptable to express disagreement with social policies aimed at increasing equality between men and women. At the University of Ottawa, Francine Tougas and her colleagues (1995) have developed a scale—the Neosexism Scale—to assess sexist attitudes in a subtler manner. Recently, researchers have attempted to measure prejudice through automatic processing, in other words, at a more unconscious level rather than having participants directly report on their attitudes. One popular technique is the Implicit Association Test which is intended to assess implicit attitudes toward various targets, social groups, or even the self (Greenwald, McGhee, & Schwartz, 1998; Dasgupta & Greenwald, 2001; Greenwald, Nosek & Banaji, 2003). It has been most commonly used to assess attitudes toward stereotyped groups. Imagine you are a participant in one of Greenwald's studies. You are seated at a computer screen and various first names are being flashed. If the name is typical for blacks, you press a key on your left as quickly as possible; if the name is typical for whites, you press a key on your right. The computer records your reaction time. The task then changes: You are now told that you will be seeing various words. If the word is a pleasant word, you are to press the key on your left; if the word is unpleasant, press the key on your right. Eventually, the two tasks are combined so that you are using the same key to respond to a black name and a pleasant word, for example. The idea is that if you are prejudiced, it will take you longer to respond when black names are associated with pleasant words than when white names are associated with pleasant words. The association of white names with positive qualities is assumed to be an automatic one and, therefore, you are able to respond quickly. Note, that you are not directly being asked whether you feel positively about blacks or whites, but rather that your attitudes are being inferred from how quickly you associate positive or negative qualities with particular groups. Thus, these techniques are useful because they "get around" the tendency for people not to admit to being prejudiced on self-report scales.

Thus, although people may be less likely to blatantly express prejudice toward particular groups than they were in the past, prejudice remains widespread. During the past half-century, social psychologists have contributed greatly to our understanding of the psychological processes underlying prejudice and have begun to identify and demonstrate some possible solutions. What is prejudice? How does it come about? How can it be reduced?

Modern prejudice outwardly acting unprejudiced while inwardly maintaining prejudice

We all decry prejudice, yet all are prejudiced.
—HERBERT SPENCER, 1873

Thinking Critically
Do you think that prejudice is less common now than it used to be, or has it simply become less socially acceptable to express blatant prejudice?

PREJUDICE, STEREOTYPING, AND DISCRIMINATION DEFINED

Prejudice is an attitude toward a group of people. Attitudes, as discussed in Chapter 5, are made up of three components: an affective or emotional component, representing the type of emotion linked with the attitude (anger, warmth); a cognitive component, involving the beliefs or thoughts (cognitions) that make up the attitude; and a behavioural component, relating to one's actions—people don't simply hold attitudes; they often act on them as well.

Prejudice: The Affective Component

Although prejudice can involve either positive or negative affect (Wright & Taylor, 2003), social psychologists (and people in general) reserve the word *prejudice* for use only when it refers to negative attitudes about others. Indeed, most social psychological research on prejudice has focused on negative attitudes toward particular groups. Thus, we will define **prejudice** as a hostile or negative attitude toward people in a distinguishable group, based solely on their membership in that group. For example, when we say that an individual is prejudiced against Aboriginals, we mean that he or she feels hostility or dislike toward Aboriginal people as a whole.

Prejudice a hostile or negative attitude toward a distinguishable group of people, based solely on their membership in that group

Stereotypes: The Cognitive Component

Close your eyes for a moment and imagine the appearance and characteristics of the following people: a cheerleader, a Pakistani cabdriver, a Jewish doctor, a black musician. Our guess is that this task was not difficult. We all walk around with images of various "types" of people in our heads. The distinguished journalist Walter Lippmann (1922), who was the first to introduce the term *stereotype*, described the distinction between the world out there and stereotypes—"the little pictures we carry around inside our heads." Within a given culture, these pictures tend to be remarkably similar. For example, we would be surprised if your image of the cheerleader was anything but bouncy, full of pep, pretty, nonintellectual, and (of course!) female. We would also be surprised if the Jewish doctor or the Pakistani cabdriver in your head were female—or if the black musician was playing classical music.

It goes without saying that there are male cheerleaders, female doctors, and black classical musicians. Deep down, we know that cabdrivers come in every size, shape, race, and gender. However, we tend to categorize according to what we regard as normative within a culture. In this sense, one can think of a stereotype as a particular kind of schema (see Chapter 3). Stereotyping, however, goes a step beyond simple categorization. A **stereotype** is a generalization about a group of people in which identical characteristics are assigned to virtually all members of the group, regardless of actual variation among the members. Once formed, stereotypes are resistant to change on the basis of new information.

Stereotype a generalization about a group of people in which identical characteristics are assigned to virtually all members of the group, regardless of actual variation among the members

It is important to point out that stereotyping does not necessarily lead to negative actions toward other groups. Stereotyping is merely a way in which we simplify how we look at the world—and we all do it to some extent. For example, Gordon Allport (1954) described stereotyping as "the law of least effort." According to Allport, the world is simply too complicated for us to have a highly differentiated attitude about everything. Instead, we maximize our cognitive time and energy by developing elegant accurate attitudes about some topics, while relying on simple sketchy beliefs for others. (This should remind you of the discussion of schemas in Chapter 3.) Given our limited information-processing capacity, it is reasonable for us to take shortcuts and adopt certain rules of thumb in our attempt to understand other people (Fiske, 1989b; Fiske & Depret, 1996; Taylor, 1981; Taylor & Falcone, 1982). To the extent that the resulting stereotype is based on experience and is at all accurate, it can be an adaptive shorthand way of dealing with complex events. On the other hand, if the stereotype blinds us to individual differences within a class of people, it is maladaptive, unfair, and can lead to discrimination. For one insight into where stereotypes might come from, see Try It! below.

Stereotype Content: Where Does It Come From?

Try It!

Have you ever wondered where stereotypes come from? Who decides whether positive or negative characteristics apply to a given group? And who decides which particular positive or negative characteristics apply? These are questions that have been addressed in a program of research conducted at the University of British Columbia by Mark Schaller and his colleagues (Schaller & Conway, 1999, 2001; Schaller, Conway, & Tanchuk, 2002; Schaller & O'Brien, 1992). According to these researchers, the traits or characteristics of a group that other people are most likely to talk about are the traits that become part of the stereotype of that group. Moreover, the more these traits are talked about, the more likely it is they will remain part of that group's stereotype over time. In short, it is the traits that have the highest communicability, or "gossip" value, that will become part of the stereotype of a particular group. You may wish to test this hypothesis yourself or with a group of friends. First, list the traits or characteristics you would be most likely to mention if you were talking about the following groups:

- White Canadians (more specifically, white Canadians living in Vancouver)
- Chinese
- East Indian
- First Nations

Now, check whether any of the traits you (or your friends) mentioned are part of the following stereotypes of these groups (as identified by a multicultural group of students at the University of British Columbia; Schaller, Conway, & Tanchuk, 2002):

- White Canadians: athletic, individualistic, pleasure-loving, straightforward, sportsmanlike
- Chinese: ambitious, loyal to family ties, intelligent, efficient, conservative
- East Indian: very religious, tradition-loving, aggressive, loyal to family ties, physically dirty
- First Nations: poor, physically dirty, lazy, tradition-loving, superstitious

Schaller and colleagues' research suggests that the traits you and others would be most likely to mention would be traits that are part of the stereotype of that group. These researchers also found that positive traits are more likely to become part of the stereotype of the largest groups in a society (in Vancouver, white Canadians, followed by Chinese people), whereas negative traits were more likely to become part of the stereotype of smaller groups (First Nations people). To make matters even worse, they found that negative traits were more likely than positive traits to persist over time. In other words, once a negative trait becomes part of a stereotype of a group, it becomes very difficult to shed it.

Schaller and colleagues conclude that, "In a sense, traits are like viruses: Those that are more highly communicable are more likely to infect the stereotypic beliefs of a population and are less likely to be gotten rid of" (Schaller, Conway, & Tanchuk, 2002).

Discrimination: The Behavioural Component

This brings us to the final component of prejudice—the action component. Stereotypic beliefs often result in unfair treatment. We call this **discrimination**, defined as unjustified negative or harmful action toward the members of a group, simply because of their membership in that group. If you are an elementary school math teacher and you have the stereotypic belief that girls are hopeless at math, you might spend less time in the classroom coaching a girl than you would a boy. If you are a police officer and you have the stereotypic belief that blacks are more violent than whites, this might affect your behaviour toward a specific black man you are trying to arrest. As we shall see in this chapter, the effects of discrimination are insidious and widespread.

Discrimination unjustified negative or harmful action toward a member of a group, simply because of his or her membership in that group

Is this roughly the stereotypical image that comes to mind when you are asked to imagine a Pakistani cab driver?

FOCUS ON APPLICATIONS

Discrimination in the Housing Market: Can You Rent a Place if You Are Gay?

Stewart Page examined discriminatory behaviour toward gays and lesbians by landlords in two cities in Ontario (London and Windsor) and in Detroit, Michigan. In one study, a caller inquiring about accommodation that had been advertised in a local paper identified himself or herself as homosexual ("I guess it's only fair to tell you that I'm a gay person [or lesbian]") or did not mention his or her sexual orientation (Page, 1998). Landlords were more likely to claim that the accommodation was unavailable when the caller identified himself or herself as gay or lesbian than when no mention was made of his or her sexual orientation. In a subsequent study, Page (1999) found that landlords were five times more likely to say that the accommodation was unavailable when the caller mentioned that she or he had AIDS. Thus, discrimination has wide-ranging effects in our society, including whether you are denied housing.

 Thinking Critically

Is stereotyping an inevitable by-product of our tendency to organize information into schemas? Do you think stereotypes, once formed, can be changed?

WHAT CAUSES PREJUDICE?

What makes people prejudiced? Is it "natural" or "unnatural"? Evolutionary psychologists have suggested, as noted in Chapter 9, that animals have a strong tendency to favour genetically similar others and to shy away from, or even aggress against, genetically dissimilar

organisms, even if the latter have never done them any harm (Buss & Kenrick, 1998; Rushton, 1989; Trivers, 1985). Thus, prejudice might be built in—an essential part of our biological survival mechanism inducing us to favour our own family, tribe, or race, and to express hostility toward outsiders. On the other hand, it is conceivable that, as humans, we are different from the lower animals; perhaps our natural inclination is to be friendly, open, and cooperative. If this were the case, then prejudice would not come naturally. Rather, the culture (parents, community, media) might, intentionally or unintentionally, instruct us to assign negative qualities and attributes to people who are different from us.

No one knows for sure whether prejudice is a vital and necessary part of our biological makeup. However, most social psychologists would agree that the specifics of prejudice must be learned. As we shall see next, prejudice is a by-product of the way we process social information—the way we think. It is also a by-product of what we think—our beliefs—as well as our feelings toward particular groups. Thus, prejudice seems to involve our heads and our hearts.

> Prejudices are the props of civilization.
> —ANDRÉ GIDE, 1939

The Way We Think: Social Cognition

Our first explanation for what causes prejudice is that it is the inevitable by-product of the way we process and organize information. As discussed in Chapter 3, we tend to categorize and group information together, to form schemas and to use these to interpret new or unusual information, and to depend on what are often faulty memory processes. The same holds true when the information we are organizing and simplifying is information about groups of people. Specifically, information consistent with our schemas about these groups will be given more attention, will be rehearsed (or recalled) more often, and therefore will be remembered better than information that is not consistent with these notions (Bodenhausen, 1988; Bodenhausen & Lichtenstein, 1987; Dovidio, Evans, & Tyler, 1986; Wyer, 1988).

We also tend to "fill in the blanks" with schema-consistent information. In a study by Kunda, Sinclair, and Griffin (1997), students at the University of Waterloo were told that Michael was either a salesperson or an actor, and that his friends described him as very extroverted. They were then asked, "What kinds of behaviours do you suppose they have in mind when they describe him this way?" The researchers found that when told that Michael was a salesperson, participants generated pushy descriptions ("loud speaking," "monopolized conversation"), whereas when Michael was described as an actor, they generated descriptions such as "life of the party" and "not afraid of the spotlight." In other words, given a stereotype label, we fill in the blanks with all kinds of stereotype-consistent information.

As you may recall from Chapter 3, schemas also are highly resistant to change—even in the face of contradictory evidence. Not surprisingly, this tendency also applies to our schemas of our groups. Indeed, it appears that we have a remarkable ability to explain away disconfirming evidence and thereby maintain our stereotypes, as illustrated by the following 1951 cartoon. While 10 Mexicans are seen in the background working hard, the cartoon focuses on the stereotypical image in the foreground. The cartoon's message is that the lazy individual is the true exemplar of his ethnic group. No matter how many others refute the stereotype, the cartoon is implying, it is still true. (Note that half a century ago, not only was this message considered acceptable, but the cartoon was chosen as one of the best of the year.)

> I will look at any additional evidence to confirm the opinion to which I have already come.
>
> —LORD MOLSON, BRITISH POLITICIAN

Research confirms that we are quite good at dismissing evidence that might disconfirm our stereotypes. In a study by William Ickes and his colleagues (1982), male university students were led to expect that the person with whom they would be interacting was either friendly or extremely unfriendly. During the interaction, the person behaved in a friendly manner. How was his behaviour interpreted? Those who expected him to be unfriendly interpreted his friendly behaviour as phony—as a temporary, fake response to their own nice behaviour. They were convinced that underneath it all, he really was an unfriendly guy. Thus, even behaviour that completely contradicts the stereotype of a group can be reinterpreted in ways that leave our stereotypes intact.

SOCIAL CATEGORIZATION: US VERSUS THEM

The first step in prejudice is the creation of groups—putting some people in one group based on certain characteristics and others in a different group based on their different characteristics. This kind of categorization is the underlying theme of human social cognition (Brewer & Brown, 1998; Rosch & Lloyd, 1978; Taylor, 1981). However, this simple cognitive process has profound implications because the process of classifying people into groups is rarely a neutral one. According to social identity theory (Tajfel, 1982a, 1982b; Turner et al., 1987), other people are seen as either belonging to our group (known as the *in-group*) or to a different group (known as the *out-group*). And, it probably comes as no surprise that we tend to evaluate people in the in-group more positively than those in the out-group. For example, when researchers at Queen's University assessed the attitudes of more than 3000 Canadians toward 14 different ethnic groups, the results were clear—people assigned the most favourable ratings to their own ethnic group (Kalin & Berry, 1996). In contrast, outgroups are often seen as possessing negative traits and are often disliked. Lalonde, Moghaddam, and Taylor (1987) found evidence of this among fans at home games of the McGill hockey team. The fans rated the opposing teams higher in negative characteristics such as arrogance and aggressiveness than they did their own team. In fact, as each game progressed, the ratings of the two teams increasingly diverged.

This cartoon depicts a common stereotype of the Mexican as lazy. Note how your eye focuses on the one sleeping person but tends to ignore the 10 hardworking people. Without intending to, the cartoonist is showing us how powerfully distorting a stereotype can be.
Alain ® 1951 *The New Yorker: 25th Annual Album,* Harper & Bros

This tendency to favour the in-group while denigrating the out-group is so pervasive that people show this bias even under the most minimal conditions. Such effects have been demonstrated by British social psychologist Henri Tajfel and his colleagues, who have created entities they refer to as minimal groups (Tajfel, 1982a, 1982b; Tajfel & Billig, 1974; Tajfel & Turner, 1979). In these experiments, complete strangers are formed into groups using the most trivial criteria imaginable. For example, in one experiment participants watched a coin toss that randomly assigned them to either group *X* or group *W*. The striking thing about the Tajfel research is that despite the fact that the participants were strangers prior to the experiment and didn't interact with one another during it, they behaved as if those who shared the same meaningless label were their dear friends or close kin. They liked the members of their own group better; they rated the members of their in-group as more likely than out-group members to have pleasant personalities and to have done better work. Most striking, the participants allocated more money and other rewards to those who shared their label, and did so in a rather hostile, cutthroat manner—that is, when given a clear choice, they preferred to give themselves only $2 if it meant giving the out-group person $1, rather than give themselves $3 if that meant the out-group member received $4 (Brewer, 1979; Hogg & Abrams, 1988; Mullen, Brown, & Smith, 1992; Oakes & Turner, 1980; Reichl, 1997).

Why do we show this tendency to favour the in-group and discriminate against the out-group even when group membership is based on something as trivial as the toss of a coin? There is a two-part answer to this question. The first part is that belonging to a group gives us a social identity—a sense of belonging (Corenblum & Stephan, 2001; Gagnon & Bourhis, 1996; Grant, 1992, 1993; Guimond, 2000). The second part is that having a social identity, in turn, contributes to feelings of self-esteem (Lemyre & Smith, 1985; Meindl & Lerner, 1984). Thus, by perceiving members of our group as possessing positive qualities and members of out-groups as possessing negative qualities, we can boost our own group and our identification with it. And that makes us feel good.

OUT-GROUP HOMOGENEITY There is another consequence of social categorization: the perception of **out-group homogeneity** (Linville, Fischer, & Salovey, 1989; Quattrone, 1986). In-group members tend to perceive those in the out-group as more similar to each other (homogeneous) than they really are, as well as more homogeneous than the in-group members. In short, "they" are all alike. George Quattrone and Edward E. Jones (1980) studied this phenomenon using rival universities: Princeton and Rutgers. The rivalry between these universities is based on athletics, academics, and even class-consciousness, with Princeton being private and Rutgers public. Male research participants at the two schools watched videotaped scenes in which three different young men were asked to make a decision—for example, in one videotape an experimenter asked a man whether he wanted to listen to rock music or classical music while he participated in an experiment on auditory perception. The participants were told that the man was either a Princeton or a Rutgers student; thus, for some of them the

Out-group homogeneity the perception that those in the out-group are more similar (homogeneous) to each other than they really are, as well as more similar than the members of the in-group

Wearing our school colours is a way of demonstrating that we are members of the in-group.

student in the videotape was an in-group member, and for others he was an out-group member. The participants' job was to predict what the man in the videotape would choose. After they saw the man make his choice (rock or classical music), they were asked to predict what percentage of male students at that institution would make the same choice.

Did the predictions vary according to the in-group or out-group status of the target men? As you can see in Figure 10.1, the results support the out-group homogeneity hypothesis: When the target person was an out-group member, the participants believed his choice was more predictive of what his peers would choose than when he was an in-group member (a student at their own school). In other words, if you know something about one out-group member, you are more likely to feel you know something about all of them. Similar results have been found in a wide variety of experiments in the United States, Europe, Australia, and Canada (Duck, Hogg, & Terry, 1995; Hartstone & Augoustinos, 1995; Judd & Park, 1988; Ostrom & Sedikides, 1992). For example, Hilton, Potvin, and Sachdev (1989) assessed the perceptions that francophone landlords in Montreal held of French Quebecers, English Quebecers, Italians, Asians, and Haitians. And, indeed, members of each out-group were perceived as more homogeneous than members of their own group (French Quebecers).

What We Believe: Stereotypes

If we have a negative stereotype of a group, we will show prejudice toward members of that group. Right? Although that is often the case, it's actually not that simple. The relation between stereotyping and prejudice is a highly complex one. One of the complexities is that our stereotypes are not activated in every situation. As we will see, whether our stereotypes are turned "on" or "off" has important implications for prejudice. It is also the case

FIGURE 10.1 Judgments about In-Group and Out-Group Members

After watching the target person make a choice between two alternatives, participants were asked to estimate what percentage of students at their school (in-group) and their rival school (out-group) would make the same choice. An out-group homogeneity bias was found: Students' estimates for out-group members were higher (greater similarity) than for in-group members.

(Adapted from Quattrone & Jones, 1980)

that our attitudes toward members of another group are determined not only by our stereotype of that group, but also by our perception of that group's stereotype of *us*.

THE ACTIVATION OF STEREOTYPES

Imagine this scenario: You are a member of a group, judging another person's performance. Someone in your group makes an ugly stereotypical comment about the individual. Will the comment affect your judgment of the performance? "No," you are probably thinking, "I'd disregard it completely." But would you be able to do so? Is it possible that the comment would trigger in your mind all the other negative stereotypes and beliefs about people in that group and affect your judgment about this particular individual—even if you neither believe the stereotype nor consider yourself prejudiced against this group?

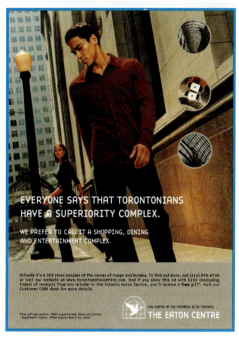

No one can escape being stereotyped. Do you agree or disagree with this notion of Toronto?

Greenberg and Pyszczynski (1985) conducted a study in which participants watched a debate between a black person and a white person. When a confederate made a racist comment about the black debater, participants rated the black debater's performance lower than when no racist remark was made. In other words, this derogatory comment activated other negative stereotypical beliefs about blacks, so that the participants who heard it rated the same performance as less skilled than did those who had not heard the racist remark.

Similar results were obtained by Henderson-King and Nisbett (1996), who showed that all it took was one negative action by one African American (actually a confederate of the experimenters) to activate the negative stereotypes against blacks and to discourage the participants from wanting to interact with a different African American. These findings suggest that stereotypes in most of us lurk just beneath the surface. It doesn't require much to activate the stereotype, and once activated it can have dire consequences for how a particular member of that out-group is perceived and treated.

How does this activation process work? Patricia Devine and her colleagues (Devine, 1989a, 1989b; Zuwerink et al., 1996) have done some fascinating research on how stereotypical beliefs affect cognitive processing. Devine differentiates between automatic processing of information and controlled processing of information. An automatic process is one over which we have no control. For example, even if you score very low on a prejudice scale, you are certainly familiar with certain stereotypes that exist in the culture, such as "Native Canadians are lazy," "Jews are money-hungry," or "Homosexual men are effeminate." These stereotypes are automatically triggered under certain conditions—they just pop into one's mind. However, for people who are not deeply prejudiced, their controlled processes can suppress or override these stereotypes. For example, such a person can say to himself or herself, "Hey, that stereotype isn't fair and it isn't right—Jews are no more money-hungry than non-Jews. Ignore the stereotype about this person's ethnicity." What Devine's theory suggests, therefore, is a two-step model of cognitive processing. The automatic processing brings up information—in this case, stereotypes—but the controlled (or conscious) processing can refute or ignore it.

Although we may often activate stereotypes, recent work has shown there are conditions under which we do not automatically do so (Devine, 2003; Quinn, Macrae, & Bodenhausen, 2003). One determining factor is a motivational one, namely whether it is in our self-interest to bring to mind the stereotype of a certain group. How might this work? Consider Michael, a university student, who receives a negative evaluation on a term paper he wrote for a course taught by a black professor. Michael's stereotype of blacks is that they are not very competent. How might Michael repair the damage to his self-esteem caused by receiving a low grade? Based on our discussion so far, you can probably answer this question. Michael can activate his stereotype of blacks as incompetent. This allows him to dismiss the criticism of his work as stemming from an incompetent source, with the result that he will not feel as bad about his negative evaluation.

Now consider Chris, a classmate of Michael's. He also subscribes to a stereotype of blacks as incompetent. However, unlike Michael, Chris received a very positive evaluation of his term paper. Chris is eager to accept the professor's praise and enjoy the boost in self-esteem it produces. On the other hand, it is difficult to feel good about praise that comes from a person who has been stereotyped as incompetent. How can Chris resolve this dilemma? According to a recent, groundbreaking program of research by Lisa Sinclair at the University of Winnipeg and Ziva Kunda at the University of Waterloo, Chris might inhibit (literally push out of his mind) his stereotype of blacks. This would allow him to revel in the praise he received.

In a series of studies, Sinclair and Kunda have shown that we not only selectively activate stereotypes, but also can inhibit, or push out of minds, our stereotypes in the service of self-enhancement. For example, in one study (Sinclair & Kunda, 1999) male students (none of whom was black) were asked to participate in research on managers' evaluations of employees' interpersonal skills. The participants answered questions that supposedly assessed their interpersonal skills, and then received an evaluation (via videotape) from either a white manager or a black manager (both managers were confederates). Half of the participants received a positive evaluation from the manager ("I was very impressed with this person, I think he has really good interpersonal skills"), while the others received a negative evaluation ("I was not very impressed with this person").

Sinclair and Kunda predicted that participants who received negative feedback from the black manager would activate their (negative) stereotype of blacks. In contrast, participants who were praised by the black manager were expected to inhibit the black stereotype. How could the researchers tell whether participants activated or inhibited their stereotype of blacks? In the next phase of the experiment, the students were asked if they would participate in a supposedly unrelated study on word completions. The word fragments presented could be completed to form either racial or nonracial words. For example, _ _ A C K could be completed as BLACK or as any number of nonracial words (e.g., SNACK); C R _ _ _ could be completed as CRIME or as a nonracial word such as CREEK. The researchers reasoned that participants who activated their stereotype of blacks would be most likely to use racial word completions, while those who inhibited their stereotype of blacks would show the fewest racial word completions.

The results are shown in Figure 10.2. In interpreting these findings, you may wish to think of the participants who were evaluated by a white manager as the control group. These participants give us a sense of how many racial word completions came to mind for participants who were not motivated to activate or inhibit their stereotype of blacks. As you can see in the figure, participants who received negative feedback from a black manager generated more racial words than did those who received negative feedback from a white manager. This is evidence of stereotype activation. In contrast, those who were praised by the black manager pushed the stereotype of blacks right out of their minds—they came up with even fewer racial word completions than did participants who were praised by a white manager. This is evidence of stereotype inhibition. Finally, as you might expect, participants who were criticized by the black manager rated his skill at evaluating them lower than did participants who were praised by a black manager. (White managers who gave negative feedback also were rated as less skilled than white managers who gave positive feedback, but this difference was not nearly as pronounced as it was for black managers.)

In other research, Sinclair and Kunda (2000) demonstrated that similar processes operate when people stereotype women. For example, in one study they asked students at the University of Waterloo to evaluate their course instructors and to indicate the grade they received in each course. Students rated their female instructors as less competent than male professors when they received a low grade in the course—but not when they received a high grade. The researchers sum up this phenomenon as "She's fine if she praised me but incompetent if she criticized me." In contrast, the ratings of male professors did not depend as much on the grades that students received from them.

In short, this research suggests that if we can salvage our self-esteem by activating negative stereotypes about a group, we will do so. However, if a negative stereotype will interfere with a self-esteem boost (when we are praised by a member of a stereotyped group), we simply push that stereotype out of our minds.

META-STEREOTYPES Recently, Jacquie Vorauer and her colleagues (Vorauer, 2003; Vorauer et al., 2000; Vorauer & Kumhyr, 2001) have raised the intriguing possibility that

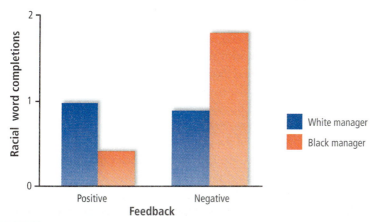

FIGURE 10.2 Number of Racial Completions as a Function of Feedback Favourability and Manager Race

(Sinclair & Kunda, 1999)

Meta-stereotype a person's beliefs regarding the stereotype that out-group members hold about their own group

our level of prejudice depends not solely on whether our stereotype of a particular group is positive or negative, but also on whether we think members of that group have a positive or negative stereotype of us. These researchers have introduced the term **meta-stereotype** to refer to a person's beliefs regarding the stereotype that out-group members hold about their own group. In a series of studies conducted at the University of Manitoba, Vorauer and her colleagues have shown that white students believe that Native Canadians perceive white Canadians as prejudiced, unfair, selfish, arrogant, wealthy, materialistic, phony, and so on (Vorauer, Main, & O'Connell, 1998).

What are the implications of this meta-stereotype? Vorauer and colleagues found that when white students expected to interact with an Aboriginal person, those who thought that they personally would be perceived in terms of the meta-stereotype anticipated that the interaction would be unpleasant (Vorauer, Main, & O'Connell, 1998). These participants also expressed the greatest amount of prejudice. Perhaps most striking, the participants' beliefs about whether an Aboriginal person would stereotype them predicted their attitudes and reactions more strongly than did their own stereotypes of Aboriginals. In other words, the way in which participants expected to be perceived by the other person was the most important determinant of their reactions.

The Way We Feel: Affect and Mood

So far, we have focused on the cognitive aspect of prejudice—namely, the stereotypes we hold of different groups. As we have seen, under certain conditions stereotyping is indeed related to prejudice. However, as Esses, Haddock, and Zanna (1993) point out, "there is more to prejudice than merely the attribution of stereotypes to groups." Their research suggests that the emotions elicited by a particular group are important in determining our level of prejudice—perhaps even more important than our stereotypes. Before discussing some of their studies, we should note that these researchers suggest that prejudice is also a product of our perception that a particular group promotes or hinders values that we cherish (symbolic beliefs) and a product of our experiences with members of the group (behaviour) (Maio, Esses, & Bell, 1994). As we will see, of all these predictors of prejudice (emotion, stereotypes, symbolic beliefs, and behaviour), the results generally are strongest for emotion.

For example, Haddock, Zanna, and Esses (1993, 1994) assessed University of Waterloo students' attitudes toward four ethnic groups (English Canadians, French Canadians, Native Canadians, and Pakistanis) as well as homosexuals. To find out what best predicted these attitudes, the researchers asked the participants to describe the emotions they experienced when thinking about members of each group, their stereotypic beliefs (characteristics you would use to describe the group), and their symbolic beliefs (the values that you believe members of the group promote or hinder). Behaviour was assessed by asking participants to describe the frequency of contact and the quality of their most recent experiences with members of these groups.

Which of these variables best predicted attitudes (prejudice)? It turns out that all of these variables were related to attitudes. However, overall, the strongest relations were found for emotion. There was some variation, though, depending on the group being rated. Specifically, emotion was the best predictor of attitudes (prejudice) for the groups toward which participants expressed the lowest levels of prejudice (English Canadians and Native Canadians). Thus, for these groups, knowing how someone feels about members of the group would allow you to predict his or her level of prejudice with the greatest accuracy. Symbolic beliefs best predicted attitudes (prejudice) toward the groups against which participants expressed the highest levels of prejudice (Pakistanis and homosexuals). Thus, for these groups, prejudice would be predicted most accurately by asking whether the group threatens important beliefs or values. (As this textbook is being written, the debate over the proposed same-sex marriage legislation is heated and intense, on both sides. It seems quite clear that people's reactions to this issue are determined by their core beliefs and value systems.) Finally, stereotypes did not strongly predict attitudes toward any of these groups when emotions, symbolic beliefs, and behaviour were taken into account.

Recent research by Corenblum and Stephan (2001) suggests that emotion is also a strong predictor of the prejudice that minority groups feel toward majority groups. In this study, white Canadians and Native Canadians were asked about their stereotypes, symbolic beliefs (agreement with statements such as "Natives and white Canadians have many incompatible values"), and emotions—specifically, anxiety about interacting with out-group members. All of these variables, but especially emotion, predicted the level of prejudice that white Canadians felt toward Native Canadians as well as the level of prejudice that Native Canadians felt toward white Canadians. Thus, the more threatened and anxious people expect to feel while interacting with members of another group, the greater their prejudice toward that group—regardless of whether their group is in a majority or minority position.

It is important to point out that even though we have been speaking of predictors of prejudice, the research we have been discussing does not actually tell us whether negative emotions *cause* people to be prejudiced toward certain groups, or whether prejudice produces nasty feelings in people. How might we disentangle this? One way would be to change people's emotions and see if that has an effect on their attitudes. Esses and Zanna (1995) did just that. In a series of experiments, they induced either a positive, neutral, or negative mood in their participants. The moods were created in a variety of ways—by having participants listen to music that was supposed to produce certain

Recent research has suggested that mood affects prejudice; people in a good mood feel more favourably toward other racial or ethnic groups.

moods; by having them describe events in their lives that made them feel extremely happy, unhappy, or neutral; or simply by having them read positive, negative, or neutral statements into a tape recorder. Regardless of how the mood was created, participants in a bad mood described various ethnic groups in more negative terms than did those who were in a good mood or a neutral mood.

We want to be clear on the point that these researchers are making. They are not saying that stereotyping never produces prejudice. Indeed, earlier in this chapter we presented evidence to the contrary. However, this program of research does suggest that an even stronger determinant of prejudice is how we feel about a group.

Thinking Critically

What role does cognition (thinking) play in producing prejudice? What role does emotion play? Is prejudice most likely to be the result of our thoughts or our feelings toward particular groups?

EFFECTS OF STEREOTYPING, PREJUDICE, AND DISCRIMINATION

Simple dislike of a group can lead to extreme hatred, to thinking of its members as less than human, and to behaviour such as torture, murder, and genocide. However, even when murder or genocide is not the culmination of prejudiced beliefs, the targets of prejudice will suffer in less dramatic ways. We will now focus, in some detail, on the ways in which prejudice and discrimination can affect their targets.

FOCUS ON APPLICATIONS

"I'm Not as Good as You": When Targets of Prejudice Come to Despise Their Own Group

In a classic experiment conducted in the United States in the late 1940s, social psychologists Kenneth Clark and Mamie Clark (1947) demonstrated that African-American children—some of them only three years old—were already convinced that it was not particularly desirable to be black. In this experiment, the children were offered a choice between playing with a white doll or a black doll. The great majority of them rejected the black doll, feeling that the white doll was prettier and generally superior.

You may be thinking, "But that was more than 50 years ago and it took place in the United States. Surely these findings are no longer relevant, and surely they wouldn't apply to Canada!" As it turns out, all you have to do is substitute "Aboriginal" for "African American" to get similar results. Corenblum and Annis (1993) presented white and Native children attending schools in Brandon, Manitoba, with drawings of white and Native boys and girls. When asked which child they would like to play with, Native children were slightly more likely to choose a white child than a Native child. (White children overwhelmingly chose the white child.) Native children also attributed more positive qualities (friendliness) to a white child than to a Native child. Conversely, they attributed more negative qualities to a Native child (is bad, gets into fights) than to a white child. Thus, members of disadvantaged groups may internalize prejudice and stereotyping and come to view their group as inferior.

Self-fulfilling Prophecies

All other things being equal, if you believe that Amy is stupid and treat her accordingly, chances are that she will not say a lot of clever things in your presence. This is the well-known **self-fulfilling prophecy**. How does this come about? If you believe that Amy is stupid, you probably will not ask her interesting questions and you will not listen intently while she is talking; indeed, you might even look out the window or yawn. You behave this way because of a simple expectation: Why waste energy paying attention to Amy if she is unlikely to say anything smart or interesting? This is bound to have an important impact on Amy's behaviour, for if the people she is talking to aren't paying much attention, she will feel uneasy and will probably clam up and not come out with all the poetry and wisdom within her. This in turn serves to confirm the belief you had about her in the first place. The circle is closed; the self-fulfilling prophecy is complete.

The relevance of this phenomenon to stereotyping and discrimination was elegantly demonstrated in an experiment by Carl Word, Mark Zanna, and Joel Cooper (1974). They asked white university undergraduates to interview several job applicants; some of the applicants were whites, and others were African Americans. Unwittingly, the students displayed discomfort and lack of interest when interviewing African-American applicants. For example, they sat farther away, tended to stammer when talking, and terminated the interview far sooner than when they were interviewing white applicants. Can you guess how this behaviour might have affected the African-American applicants? To find out, the researchers, in a second experiment, systematically varied the behaviour of the interviewers (actually confederates) so it coincided with the way the real interviewers had treated the African-American or white interviewees in the first experiment. However, in the second experiment, all of the interviewees were white. The researchers videotaped the proceedings and had the applicants rated by independent judges. They found that those applicants who were interviewed the way African Americans had been interviewed in the first experiment were judged to be far more nervous and far less effective than those who were interviewed the way whites had been interviewed in the first experiment. In sum, these experiments demonstrate clearly that when African Americans are interviewed by whites, they are unintentionally placed at a disadvantage and are likely to perform less well than their white counterparts (see Figure 10.3).

On a societal level, the insidiousness of the self-fulfilling prophecy goes even further. Suppose there is a general belief that a particular group is irredeemably stupid, uneducable, and fit only for menial jobs. Why waste educational resources on them? Hence, they are given inadequate schooling. Thirty years later, what do you find? An entire group that with few exceptions is fit only for menial jobs. "See? I was right all the time," says the bigot. "How fortunate that we didn't waste our precious educational resources on such people!" The self-fulfilling prophecy strikes again.

If a child of colour believes that white dolls are more desirable than black dolls, what stereotypes has she internalized?

Self-fulfilling prophecy the case whereby people (a) have an expectation about what another person is like, which (b) influences how they act toward that person, which (c) causes that person to behave in a way consistent with people's original expectations

A little black girl yearns for the blue eyes of a little white girl, and the horror at the heart of her yearning is exceeded only by the evil of fulfillment.

—TONI MORRISON,
The Bluest Eye

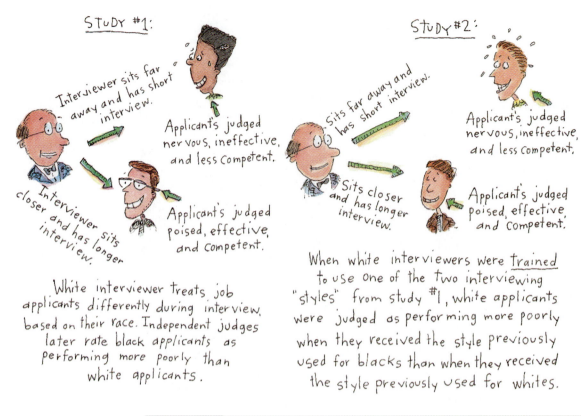

FIGURE 10.3 An Experiment Demonstrating Self-fulfilling Prophecies

Self-blaming Attributions for Discrimination

Can you explain the following paradox? Numerous studies have found that members of disadvantaged groups often report that their group is discriminated against, but that they personally have not been the target of discrimination (Dion & Kawakami, 1996; Taylor et al., 1990; Taylor, Ruggiero, & Louis, 1996). For example, in research conducted at Carleton University (Foster & Matheson, 1999) and at the University of Western Ontario (Quinn et al., 1999), women reported greater group than personal discrimination in terms of pay equity, career opportunities, and sexual harassment. In Toronto, the Housing New Canadians Project examined experiences of discrimination among immigrant groups and found evidence of the personal-group discrimination discrepancy among Jamaicans and Somalis (Dion, 2001). In other words, members of these groups claimed that their group overall has encountered greater housing discrimination than they personally have experienced. These effects are widespread and tend to be most pronounced among members of visible minorities.

How can we explain these findings? According to a program of research by Karen Ruggiero and Donald Taylor (1995, 1997; Taylor, Ruggiero, & Louis, 1996), individuals tend to minimize the discrimination they experience and instead blame themselves. In one of their first studies (Ruggiero & Taylor, 1995), female students from various faculties at McGill University took a test that would supposedly predict how successful they would be in their future careers. Moreover, they were told that anyone who performed well on the test would have a chance to win $50. After taking the test, the women learned that it would be graded by a group of male evaluators, and that either 100 percent, 75 percent, 50 percent, 25 percent, or 0 percent of the evaluators were known to discriminate against women. All of the participants received a mark of F on the test. They were then asked why they got such a low mark. Was it the quality of their answers? Was it the result of discrimination? Not surprisingly, participants who were told that 100 percent of the male evaluators were known to discriminate against women chalked up their low mark to discrimination. However, if there was any room for ambiguity at all, the women attributed their low grade to themselves (the quality of their answers) and not to discrimination. Remarkably, women who were told that there was a 75 percent chance they had been discriminated against blamed themselves as much as those who were told there was a 25 percent chance of discrimination. Ruggiero and Taylor (1997) obtained similar results in a study focusing on racial discrimination. Participants were East Asian and black (West Indian) students at McGill University who were told that white evaluators would be grading their test. Once again, participants attributed failure on the test to discrimination only when it was 100 percent certain. In all other conditions, participants blamed themselves for their poor performance.

These findings are extremely disturbing, because in real-world situations one can rarely be 100 percent certain that one has been discriminated against. The results of this research suggest that, in most cases, victims of discrimination will blame themselves instead. Sadly, as Ruggiero and Taylor point out, this pattern may set up a vicious cycle. If minority group members blame themselves for negative outcomes, majority group members are able to justify their ongoing discrimination.

Before leaving this topic, we should also note that there is another view—some researchers have found evidence that rather than minimizing discrimination, members of disadvantaged groups may become hypervigilant for signs of discrimination (Major, Quinton, & McCoy, 2002). According to Crocker and Major (1989), it is less damaging to our self-esteem if we blame negative outcomes, such as a poor mark on a test, on prejudice or discrimination, rather than our own shortcomings. Which view is correct? Do targets of prejudice and discrimination tend to minimize their poor treatment and blame themselves, or are they "on the alert" for signs of discrimination (so that they can preserve their self-esteem by attributing negative outcomes to prejudice)? Although this is an area of lively debate, Wright and Taylor (2003) suggest that the targets of prejudice and discrimination probably do both—whether they minimize or are hypervigilant to signs of discrimination may depend on a number of situational and motivational factors. For example, if a close friend tells a derogatory joke about your ethnic or religious group, you may minimize his or her behaviour to maintain your relationship. You might react quite differently if your professor were to tell the same joke, particularly if you haven't been doing very well in the course.

Stereotype Threat

Claude Steele and Joshua Aronson (Aronson, Quinn, & Spencer, 1998; Steele, 1997; Steele & Aronson, 1995a, 1995b) wondered whether the lower academic performance that has been observed among African-American students in the United States might be attributable to a phenomenon they termed **stereotype threat**. Specifically, when African-American students find themselves in highly evaluative educational situations, most

Stereotype threat the apprehension experienced by members of a minority group that they might behave in a manner that confirms an existing cultural stereotype tend to experience apprehension about confirming the existing negative cultural stereotype of "intellectual inferiority." In effect, they are saying, "If I perform poorly on this test, it will reflect poorly on me and on my race." This extra burden of apprehension in turn interferes with their ability to perform well in these situations. For example, in one of their experiments, Steele and Aronson administered a difficult verbal test, the GRE, individually to African-American and white students at Stanford University. Half of the students of each race were led to believe that the investigator was interested in measuring their intellectual ability; the other half were led to believe that the investigator was merely trying to develop the test itself—and, because the test was not yet valid or reliable, they were assured that their performance would mean nothing in terms of their actual ability.

The results confirmed the researchers' speculations. White students performed equally well regardless of whether they believed the test was being used as a diagnostic tool. The African-American students who believed the test was non-diagnostic of their abilities performed as well as white students; in contrast, the African-American students who were led to believe that the test was measuring their abilities performed less well than white students. In subsequent experiments in the same series, Steele and Aronson also found that if race is made more salient, the decrement in performance among African Americans is even more pronounced.

The phenomenon of stereotype threat applies to gender as well. As you know, a common stereotype of women is that, compared to men, they are not very good at math. In an experiment by Spencer, Steele, and Quinn (1999), when women were led to believe that men generally performed better on a particular test, they did not perform as well as men; however, in another condition, when women were led to believe that the same test did not generally show gender differences, they performed as well as men. These effects were replicated in Canada by Walsh, Hickey, and Duffy (1999). Male and female university students in Newfoundland were told that they would be taking a math test. The researchers mentioned that on Part A of the test, men typically scored higher than women, and that the purpose of Part B was

What message is this female student getting about the competence of women? How likely is it that she will want to demonstrate her competence in the future?
© 1992 Gary Hallgren

to compare the performance of Canadian students with American students. (These instructions were reversed for other students, such that they were told that Part A was a comparison with American students, and that on Part B men usually outperformed women.) Women scored lower than men only on the part of the test where they expected to be outperformed by men. They did as well as men on the part they believed was a comparison of the performance of Canadian and American university students.

Subsequent research has shown that stereotype threat does not occur every time members of disadvantaged groups are in a performance situation. For example, stereotype threat is less likely to occur if the task is easy, or if it is not particularly important to the person to perform well in that domain (Wright & Taylor, 2003). However, there are unfortunately many everyday situations in which members of disadvantaged groups do fear that they will let their group down if they don't perform well. Sadly, this extra stress and pressure can actually make these fears of poor performance come true.

Thinking Critically
What are some of the factors that might cause differences in test performance between members of dominant (majority) groups and members of minority groups?

HOW CAN PREJUDICE AND DISCRIMINATION BE REDUCED?

Sometimes subtle, sometimes brutally overt—prejudice is indeed ubiquitous. Does this mean that prejudice is an essential aspect of human social interaction and will therefore always be with us? We social psychologists do not take such a pessimistic view. We tend to agree with Henry David Thoreau, who said, "It is never too late to give up our prejudices." People can change. But how? We now focus on a few strategies for eliminating, or at least reducing, this noxious aspect of human social behaviour.

Learning Not to Hate

It is obvious that parents and teachers play a crucial role in teaching children to treat others in a nondiscriminatory manner. The important role that teachers can play was illustrated by the life-altering lesson in prejudice that Jane Elliot (1977), a teacher in Riceville, Iowa, taught her grade 3 class. Elliot was concerned that her young students were leading too sheltered a life. The children all lived in rural Iowa, they were all white, and they were all Christian. Elliot felt it was important to give them some direct experience about what stereotyping and discrimination felt like, from both sides. To achieve this end, Elliot divided her class by eye colour. She told her students that blue-eyed people were superior to brown-eyed people—smarter, nicer, more trustworthy, and so on. The brown-eyed youngsters were required to wear special cloth collars around their necks so they would be instantly recognizable as a member of the inferior group. She gave special privileges to the blue-eyed youngsters; for example, they got to play longer at recess, could have second helpings at the cafeteria, and were praised in the classroom. How did the children respond?

In a matter of hours, Elliot succeeded in creating a microcosm of a prejudiced society in her classroom. Just a few hours before the experiment began, the children had been a cooperative, cohesive group; once the seeds of divisiveness were planted, there was trouble.

> Our minds thus grow in spots; and like grease spots, the spots spread. But we let them spread as little as possible; we keep unaltered as much of our old knowledge, as many of our old prejudices and beliefs, as we can.
>
> —WILLIAM JAMES, 1907

Bookkeeping model information inconsistent with a stereotype that leads to a modification of the stereotype

Conversion model information inconsistent with a stereotype that leads to a radical change in the stereotype

Subtyping model information inconsistent with a stereotype that leads to the creation of a new sub-stereotype to accommodate the information without changing the initial stereotype

The "superior" blue-eyed kids made fun of the brown-eyed kids, refused to play with them, tattled on them to the teacher, thought up new restrictions and punishments for them, and even started a fistfight in the schoolyard. The "inferior" brown-eyed kids became self-conscious, depressed, and demoralized. They performed poorly on classroom tests that day.

The next day, Elliot switched the stereotypes about eye colour. She said she'd made a dreadful mistake—that brown-eyed people were really the superior ones. She told the brown-eyed kids to put their collars on the blue-eyed kids. They gleefully did so. The tables had turned—and the brown-eyed kids exacted their revenge.

On the morning of the third day, Elliot explained to her students that they had been learning about prejudice and discrimination, and how it feels to be a person of colour. The children discussed the two-day experience and clearly understood its message. In a follow-up, Elliot met with these students at a class reunion when they were in their mid-twenties. Their memories of the exercise were startlingly clear—they reported that the experience had a powerful and lasting impact on their lives. They felt that they were less prejudiced and more aware of discrimination against others because of this childhood experience.

Jane Elliot's eye-colour exercise has been used widely in classrooms and other settings (e.g., with prison staff) with the hope that experiencing discrimination firsthand will make people less likely to behave in discriminatory ways.

Revising Stereotypical Beliefs

Earlier, we mentioned that people tend to process information in ways that confirm their stereotypes—even if that information completely contradicts the stereotype. This may have left you feeling unconvinced that people can actually change. What sort of information would actually refute a stereotype? Let's say our next-door neighbour harbours two stereotypes that we find particularly annoying: He believes that professors are lazy and that immigrants are a drain on the welfare system. What would happen if we provided him with evidence that his stereotypes are incorrect? For example, what if we showed him data demonstrating that professors at the local university work a 50-hour week? What if we pointed out that unemployment rates are particularly low among immigrant groups? Would this information affect our neighbour's stereotypes?

Not necessarily. Renée Webber and Jennifer Crocker (1983) show that a great deal depends on how the disconfirming information is presented. According to these researchers, there are three possible models for revising stereotypical beliefs: (a) the **bookkeeping model**, wherein each piece of disconfirming information modifies the stereotype; (b) the **conversion model**, wherein the stereotype radically changes in response to a powerful salient piece of information; and (c) the **subtyping model**, wherein new subtype or subcategory stereotypes are created to accommodate the disconfirming information, unless one receives information that the disconfirming information applies to a large number of cases. Webber and Crocker conducted several experiments to see which model(s) might be right. They presented participants with information that disconfirmed their stereotypes about two occupational groups: librarians and corporate lawyers. In one condition, the participants received information in the bookkeeping style, one disconfirming fact after another. In another condition, the participants received conversion information, a single fact that strongly disconfirmed their stereotype. In the final condition, the participants received information that could lead them to create a subtype of their stereotype.

Did these three styles of disconfirming information change people's minds about their stereotypes?

Webber and Crocker found that the bookkeeping information and the subtyping information did weaken the participants' stereotypes, but that the conversion information did not. Why? When many members of the categorized group exhibited the disconfirming traits, participants employed a bookkeeping strategy and gradually modified their beliefs. In other words, to return to our example, if our neighbour found out, on many occasions, that numerous professors worked a 50-hour week, this would slowly but eventually lead him to abandon the notion that professors are lazy. When the disconfirming traits were concentrated among only a few individuals of the group, participants used a subtyping model. Thus, if our neighbour encountered a few hardworking professors, he might create a new subtype, but leave the original stereotype intact. However, if information was provided about many professors who contradicted the stereotype to at least some extent, the original stereotype did change. Finally, the conversion approach just didn't work: one fact about an out-group that was evidence against the stereotype just wasn't enough to change people's minds—even if it was a powerful piece of information.

Although laws prohibiting Asian immigrants from voting, running for office, or becoming lawyers were overturned in the 1960s, Herb Dhaliwal, former federal Fisheries Minister, had the rare distinction of being the first South Asian to hold a Ministerial position in Canada, or, indeed, anywhere in a Western democracy. Might a bigoted person have voted for him? Perhaps—if the bigot characterized him as "the exception that proves the rule."

The Contact Hypothesis

As you have perhaps experienced in your own life, repeated contact with members of an out-group can have a positive effect on stereotypes and prejudice. However, as we shall see, mere contact is not enough; it must be a special kind of contact. Let's take a look at what we mean by "a special kind of contact." In his strikingly prescient masterwork *The Nature of Prejudice*, Gordon Allport (1954) stated the contact hypothesis in this way:

> Prejudice may be reduced by equal status contact between majority and minority groups in the pursuit of common goals. The effect is greatly enhanced if this contact is sanctioned by institutional supports (i.e., by law, custom or local atmosphere), and provided it is of a sort that leads to the perception of common interests and common humanity between members of the two groups.

In other words, Allport is not talking about mere contact; he is clear that contact must be between people who are of equal status and in pursuit of common goals. Four decades of research have substantiated Allport's early claim that these conditions must be met before

> The mind of a bigot is like the pupil of the eye; the more light you pour upon it, the more it will contract.
> —OLIVER WENDELL HOLMES JR., 1901

> We must recognize that beneath the superficial classification of sex and race the same potentialities exist, recurring generation after generation only to perish because society has no place for them.
> —MARGARET MEAD, Male and Female, 1943

Mutual interdependence a situation in which two or more groups need each other and must depend on each other to accomplish a goal that is important to each group

contact will lead to a decrease in prejudice between groups (Cook, 1985). Let's now turn to a discussion of these conditions.

Two of the key factors in the success of contact are **mutual interdependence** and a *common goal* (Amir, 1969, 1976). In other words, it is important to create a situation in which the two groups have to cooperate to achieve something they both want. In a classic study, Sherif and colleagues (1961) created animosity and conflict between two groups of boys attending a camp. Later, they tried various ways of restoring harmony. The most successful approach was to stage situations in which both groups of boys had to work together toward the same goal. For example, on one occasion, the boys were promised an outing, but then the camp truck "broke down." The only way to get the truck going was for both groups of boys to work together and push the truck up a hill. These conditions of mutual interdependence and having a common goal ultimately fostered the creation of friendships between the two groups (see Figure 10.4).

The third condition is *equal status*. When status is unequal, interactions can easily follow stereotypical patterns—the bosses will act like stereotypical bosses, the employees will act like stereotypical subordinates—and no one will learn new, disconfirming information about the other group (Pettigrew, 1969; Wilder, 1984). The whole point of contact is to allow people to learn that their stereotypes are inaccurate; contact and interaction should lead to disconfirmation of negative stereotyped beliefs.

Fourth, contact must occur in a *friendly, informal setting*, where in-group members can interact with out-group members on a one-to-one basis (Brewer & Miller, 1984; Cook, 1984; Wilder, 1986). Simply placing two groups in contact in a room where they can remain segregated will do little to promote their understanding or knowledge of each other.

Fifth, through friendly, informal interactions *with multiple members* of the out-group, an individual will learn that his or her beliefs about the out-group are wrong. It is crucial for the individual to believe that the out-group members he or she comes to know

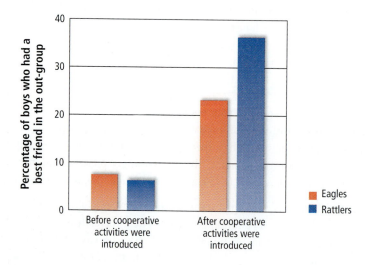

FIGURE 10.4 Intergroup Relations

Intergroup tensions were eased only after members engaged in cooperative activities.

(Adapted from Sherif et al., 1961)

"I wish we could have met under different circumstances . . . "
OLIPHANT ©. Reprinted with permission of UNIVERSAL PRESS SYNDICATE. All rights reserved.

are typical of their group; otherwise, the stereotype can be maintained by labelling one out-group member as the exception (Wilder, 1984).

Sixth and last, contact is most likely to lead to reduced prejudice when *social norms that promote and support equality* among groups are operating in the situation (Amir, 1969; Wilder, 1984). For example, if the boss in a work setting or the professor in a classroom creates and reinforces a norm of acceptance and tolerance, group members will modify their own behaviour to fit the norm.

To conclude, when these six conditions of contact—mutual interdependence; a common goal; equal status; informal interpersonal contact; multiple contacts; and social norms of equality—are met, suspicious or even hostile groups will reduce their stereotyping, prejudice, and discriminatory behaviour (Aronson & Bridgeman, 1979; Cook, 1984; Riordan, 1978).

Cooperation and Interdependence: The Jigsaw Classroom

Let's paint a scenario. Imagine a grade 6 student of Mexican origin, whom we will call Carlos. Carlos has been attending schools in an underprivileged neighbourhood his entire life. Because the schools in his neighbourhood were not well equipped or well staffed, his first five years of education were somewhat deficient. Suddenly, without much warning or preparation, he is bused to a school in a predominantly white, middle-class neighbourhood. Carlos must now compete against white middle-class students who have had better preparation than he has had, and who have been reared to hold white middle-class values, which include working hard in pursuit of good grades, raising one's hand enthusiastically whenever the teacher asks a question, and so on. In effect, Carlos has been thrust into a highly competitive situation for which he is unprepared and in which payoffs are made for abilities he has not yet developed. The white kids might quickly conclude that Carlos is stupid, unmotivated, and sullen—just as they had suspected (Wilder & Shapiro, 1989). Moreover, Carlos might conclude that the white kids are arrogant showoffs. This is an example of the self-fulfilling prophecy we discussed earlier.

Is it possible to get white students and minority students to have equal status, be mutually dependent, and pursue common goals? One of the authors of this textbook got to find out. In 1971, the school system of Austin, Texas, was desegregated. Within a few weeks, the schools were in turmoil. African-American, white, and Mexican-American children were in open conflict; fistfights broke out between the various racial groups in the corridors and schoolyards. The school superintendent invited Elliot Aronson, who was then a professor at the University of Texas, to enter the system with the mandate to do anything within reason to create a more harmonious environment. After spending a few days observing the dynamics of several classrooms, Aronson and his graduate students were strongly reminded of the situation that existed in the summer camp experiment described earlier (Sherif et al., 1961; see Figure 10.4). With the findings of that study in mind, they developed a technique that created an interdependent classroom atmosphere, designed to encourage the students of various racial and ethnic groups to pursue common goals. They called it the **jigsaw classroom**, because it resembled the assembling of a jigsaw puzzle (Aronson, 1992; Aronson et al., 1978; Aronson & Bridgeman, 1979; Aronson & Gonzalez, 1988; Aronson & Patnoe, 1997).

Here is how the jigsaw classroom works: Students are placed in diverse six-person learning groups. The day's lesson is divided into six paragraphs, so that each student has one segment of the written material. For example, if the students are to learn the life of Mother Teresa, her biography is arranged in six parts. Each student has possession of a unique and vital part of the information, which, like the pieces of a jigsaw puzzle, must be put together before anyone can learn the whole picture. The individual must learn his or her own section and teach it to the other members of the group—who do not have any other access to that material. Thus, if Debbie wants to do well on the ensuing exam about the life of Mother Teresa, she must pay close attention to Carlos (who is reciting on Mother Teresa's childhood), to Natalie (who is reciting on Mother Teresa's humanitarian actions), and so on.

Jigsaw classroom a classroom setting designed to reduce prejudice between children by placing them in small, desegregated groups and making each child dependent on the other children in the group to learn the course material and do well in the class

> Two are better than one because they have a good reward for their toil. For if they fail, one will lift up his fellow, but woe to him who is alone when he falls and has not another to lift him up. Again, if two lie together, they are warm; but how can one be warm alone?
>
> —ECCLESIASTES 4: 9–12

When the classroom is structured so students of various ethnic groups work together cooperatively, prejudice decreases.

Through the jigsaw process, the children begin to pay more attention to each other and to show respect for each other. As you might expect, a child like Carlos would respond to this treatment by simultaneously becoming more relaxed and more engaged; this would inevitably produce an improvement in his ability to communicate. And the other students would begin to realize that Carlos is a lot smarter than they had thought he was. They begin to like him. Carlos begins to enjoy school more, his academic performance begins to improve, and so does his self-esteem. The vicious circle has been broken.

The formal data that Aronson and his colleagues gathered from the jigsaw experiments were clear and striking. Compared to students in traditional classrooms, students in jigsaw groups showed a decrease in prejudice and stereotyping, as well as an increase in their liking for their group mates, both within and across ethnic boundaries. In addition, children in the jigsaw classrooms performed better on objective exams, liked school more, and showed a significantly greater increase in self-esteem than did children in traditional classrooms. Moreover, children in schools where the jigsaw technique was practised developed a greater ability to empathize with others and showed substantial evidence of true integration—that is, in the schoolyard there was far more intermingling among the various races and ethnic groups than in the yards of schools using more traditional classroom techniques (Aronson & Bridgeman, 1979). See Try It! below.

The jigsaw approach was first tested in 1971; since then, several similar cooperative techniques have been developed (Cook, 1985; Johnson & Johnson, 1987, 1989; Slavin & Cooper, 1999). The striking results described above have been successfully replicated in thousands of classrooms in all regions of the United States, and in other countries as well. Cooperative learning has become a major force within the field of public education and is generally accepted as one of the most effective ways of improving race relations, building empathy, and improving instruction in schools (Deutsch, 1997; Jürgen-Lohmann, Borsch, & Giesen, 2001; Slavin, 1996).

Thinking Critically
What are the underlying mechanisms that make the jigsaw classroom an effective means of reducing prejudice?

Jigsaw-Type Group Study

Try It!

The next time a quiz is coming up in one of your courses, try to organize a handful of your classmates into a jigsaw-type group for purposes of studying for the quiz.

Assign each person a segment of the reading. Each person is responsible for becoming the world's greatest expert on his or her material. Each person will organize the material into a report that she or he will present to the rest of the group. The rest of the group will feel free to ask questions to ensure that they fully understand the material. At the end of the session, ask the group members the following questions:

1. Compared to studying alone, was this more or less enjoyable?
2. Compared to studying alone, was this more or less efficient?
3. How do you feel about each person in the group—compared to how you felt about him or her prior to the session?
4. Would you like to do this again?

You should realize that this situation is probably a lot less powerful than the jigsaw groups described in this book. Why?

Summary

Prejudice is a widespread phenomenon, present in all walks of life, even though it has become less socially acceptable to express prejudice toward certain groups. People who are high in **modern prejudice** tend to be prejudiced, but aren't willing to admit it because current social norms prohibit them from doing so.

Social psychologists define **prejudice** as a hostile or negative attitude toward a distinguishable group of people based solely on their group membership. A **stereotype** is the cognitive component of the prejudiced attitude; it is defined as a generalization about a group whereby identical characteristics are assigned to virtually all members, regardless of actual variation among the members. **Discrimination**, the behavioural component of the prejudiced attitude, is defined as unjustified negative or harmful action toward members of a group based on their membership in that group.

Where does prejudice come from? We discussed prejudice as a by-product of our thoughts and feelings. First, social cognition processes (the way we think) are an important element in the creation and maintenance of stereotypes and prejudice. Categorization of people into groups leads to the formation of in-groups and out-groups. The in-group bias means that we will treat members of our own group more positively than we will members of the out-group, as demonstrated by the research on minimal groups. The perception of **out-group homogeneity** is another consequence of categorization: In-group members perceive out-group members as more similar to one another than the in-group members are to one another. Stereotypes—what we believe about different groups—are widely known in a culture; even if you do not endorse them, they can affect your cognitive processing of information about an out-group member. Recent research has shown that stereotypes can be selectively activated or inhibited, depending on motivational factors, most notably self-enhancement. The stereotypes that we believe out-groups hold of us, known as **meta-stereotypes**, also play a role in prejudice—we expect more negative interactions with and show more prejudice toward members of groups we believe hold negative stereotypes of us. Our emotions or moods also determine how prejudiced we are. When we are in a good mood (or have positive feelings toward a group), we are likely to evaluate members of out-groups more favourably than when we are in a bad mood (or have negative feelings toward that group).

Stereotyping, prejudice, and discrimination can have devastating effects on their targets. Research on **self-fulfilling prophecies** suggests that we may unknowingly create stereotypical behaviour in out-group members through our treatment of them. There is evidence that members of stigmatized groups may minimize the discrimination they experience and blame themselves for their poor performance. Other times, members of disadvantaged groups may be hypervigilant, readily attributing negative outcomes to discrimination, to preserve their self-esteem. Situational and motivation factors determine which process operates at any given time. Finally, members of an out-group also may experience **stereotype threat**—a fear that they might behave in a manner that confirms an existing stereotype about their group.

On a societal level, the most important question to be asked is this: How can prejudice be reduced? One approach is to "nip it in the bud" by teaching children not to be prejudiced. Social cognition research has indicated that stereotypes can be revised; the **bookkeeping model** and the **subtyping model** (but not the **conversion model**) describe processes through which negative stereotypes change. An especially effective way of reducing prejudice is through contact—bringing in-group and out-group members together. However, mere contact is not enough and can even exacerbate the existing negative attitudes. Instead, contact situations must include the following conditions: **mutual interdependence**; a common goal; equal status; informal, interpersonal contact; multiple contacts; and social norms of equality. The **jigsaw classroom**, a learning atmosphere in which children must depend on each other and work together to learn and to reach a common goal, has been found to be a powerful way to reduce stereotyping and prejudice among children of different ethnicities.

Key Terms

Bookkeeping model   (page 330)
Conversion model   (page 330)
Discrimination   (page 314)
Jigsaw classroom   (page 334)
Meta-stereotype   (page 322)
Modern prejudice   (page 311)
Mutual interdependence   (page 332)
Out-group homogeneity   (page 317)
Prejudice   (page 312)
Self-fulfilling prophecy   (page 325)
Stereotype   (page 312)
Stereotype threat   (page 327)
Subtyping model   (page 330)

Key Online Search Terms

Prejudice
Stereotypes
Discrimination
Modern racism/modern sexism
Stereotype threat
Contact hypothesis

If You Are Interested

Allport, G. (1954). *The nature of prejudice*. Reading, MA: Addison-Wesley. Written the same year as the landmark U.S. Supreme Court decision on desegregation, this classic work remains an exciting and penetrating analysis of the social psychology of prejudice.

Dion, K. L. (2002). The social psychology of perceived prejudice and discrimination. *Canadian Psychology, 43*, 1–10. Kenneth Dion, a social psychologist at the University of Toronto, was the 2001 recipient of the prestigious D. O. Hebb Award for Distinguished Contributions to Psychology as a Science. This article was written in recognition of this award. In it, Dion documents the many and varied effects of prejudice and discrimination on its victims. A thought-provoking look at the phenomenology of prejudice.

Wright, S. C., & Taylor, D. M. (2003). The social psychology of cultural diversity: Social stereotyping, prejudice, and discrimination. In M. A. Hogg & J. Cooper (Eds.), *Sage handbook of social psychology*. Thousand Oaks, CA: Sage. This chapter, written by two prominent Canadian social psychologists, provides a comprehensive, up-to-date review of the literature on stereotyping, prejudice, and discrimination. The chapter addresses issues such as stereotype threat, institutional discrimination, the effects of prejudice and stereotyping on its targets, and reducing prejudice. It highlights the contribution of social psychology to understanding and addressing societal problems stemming from prejudice and discrimination.

Weblinks

www.cpa.ca/cjbsnew/1996/vol28-3.html
Ethnic Relations in a Multicultural Society—Special Issue of the *Canadian Journal of Behavioural Science*
This site provides access to the full text of this issue, which contains articles dealing with ethnic attitudes, prejudice, and discrimination.

www.crr.ca/EN/Publications/ePubHome.htm
Canadian Race Relations Foundation
The Canadian Race Relations Foundation produces a variety of publications on racism and racial discrimination that can be accessed from this site.

www.adl.org
Anti-defamation League
Founded in 1913, this organization is the premier civil rights/human relations agency fighting anti-Semitism, prejudice, and bigotry.

www.beyondprejudice.com
Beyond Prejudice
This site discusses ways in which prejudice can be reduced, and myths about prejudicial behaviour.

Chapter 10 Practice Quiz

Check your knowledge of the concepts in this chapter by trying the following questions.

PREJUDICE, STEREOTYPING, AND DISCRIMINATION DEFINED

Multiple Choice

1. _____ is a generalization about a group of people for which identical characteristics are assigned to all group members.
   a. Stereotyping
   b. Discrimination
   c. Prejudice
   d. Racism

2. Allport described stereotypes as
   a. Murphy's law.
   b. the law of least effort.
   c. the law of cause and effect.
   d. the law of discrimination.

3. Stereotypes can be thought of as a particular kind of
   a. schema.
   b. defensive attribution.
   c. cognitive dissonance.
   d. availability heuristic.

True or False

4. Discrimination is a mostly Eastern phenomenon with little effect in Western cultures.
   ___ True
   ___ False

5. Stereotypes are not difficult to change when evidence presented challenges them.
   ___ True
   ___ False

Fill in the Blank

6. _____ is a hostile attitude toward a distinguishable group of people.
7. _____ is unjustified, harmful, and negative actions towards a member of a social group.

WHAT CAUSES PREJUDICE?

Multiple Choice

8. Which of the following is believed to cause prejudice?
   a. social cognition
   b. stereotypes
   c. mood
   d. all of the above

9. Stereotypes can be
   a. activated and inhibited.
   b. activated but not inhibited.
   c. inhibited but not activated.
   d. neither inhibited nor activated.

10. _____ is a person's belief regarding the stereotypes that out-group members hold about their own group.
    a. Media-stereotype
    b. Meta-stereotype
    c. Form-stereotype
    d. Outward-stereotype

11. Which of the following is the strongest predictor of prejudice?
    a. emotion
    b. symbolic beliefs
    c. behaviour
    d. stereotypes

True or False

12. Biological factors cause attitudes that reflect prejudice.
    ___ True
    ___ False

13. We tend to evaluate those that belong to our social group more positively than those that do not belong.
    ___ True
    ___ False

Fill in the Blank

14. The first step in prejudice is the creation of _____.
15. _____ is the perception that those in the out-group are more similar to one another.

EFFECTS OF STEREOTYPING, PREJUDICE, AND DISCRIMINATION

Multiple Choice

16. A self-fulfilling prophecy is when a person
    a. has an expectation about what another person is like.
    b. has an expectation that influences how he behaves towards another person.
    c. has an expectation that causes the other person to behave in a way consistent with those expectations.
    d. all of the above

17. When Corenblum and Annis (1993) presented white and Native children with drawings of white and Native boys and girls,
    a. the white children asked to play with the Native boys and girls.
    b. the Native children asked to play with the Native boys and girls.
    c. the Native and white children asked to play with the white boys and girls.
    d. the white girls, but not white boys, asked to play with the Native boys and girls.

18. Minority groups often
    a. are very sensitive to signs of discrimination.
    b. minimize discrimination.
    c. blame themselves for discrimination.
    d. all of the above

19. If you make the statement, "If I perform poorly on this test, it will reflect poorly on me and on my race," you are demonstrating a characteristic of
    a. jigsaw classroom.
    b. stereotype threat.
    c. contact hypothesis.
    d. self-blaming attribution.

True or False

20. Individual members of minority groups tend to minimize the discrimination they experience and blame themselves.
    ___ True
    ___ False

21. Despite past stereotypes, women are actually better at math than men.
    ___ True
    ___ False

Fill in the Blank

22. A _____ is the apprehension experienced by members of a minority group who fear they might behave in ways consistent with cultural stereotypes.

23. _____, self-blaming, and stereotype threat are examples of how discrimination affects target groups.

HOW CAN PREJUDICE AND DISCRIMINATION BE REDUCED?

Multiple Choice

24. In _____, information inconsistent with a stereotype modifies it.
    a. bookkeeping model
    b. conversion model
    c. subtyping model
    d. subtraction model

25. Which of the following is not a condition Allport outlined in his contact hypothesis?
    a. equal status
    b. informal setting
    c. multiple members of the out-group
    d. role playing

26. _____ is a classroom designed to reduce prejudice between children.
    a. Tension-reducing play area
    b. Anti-discrimination play structuring
    c. Anti-stereotyping teaching space
    d. Jigsaw classroom

True or False

27. The conversion model is successful in altering people's stereotypes.
    ___ True
    ___ False

28. Equal status between members of two groups is likely to facilitate stereotypes.
    ___ True
    ___ False

Fill in the Blank

29. The _____ classroom teaches children both interdependence and cooperation.
30. Two key factors for the contact hypothesis are mutual independence and _____.

PERSONALIZED STUDY PLAN

Want to check your answers and access more study resources? Visit the Companion Website for *Fundamentals of Social Psychology* at **www.pearsoned.ca/aronson**, where you'll find the above questions incorporated in a pre-test and post-test for each chapter. These tests will be automatically graded online, allowing you to check your answers. A Study Plan, like the one below, groups the questions by section within the chapter and shows you which sections you need to focus on for further study.

Your Results for "Chapter 10, Pretest"

OVERALL SCORE: 75% of 16 questions

Group	Score	Proficient
Prejudice, Stereotyping, and Discrimination Defined	2 of 4	No
What Causes Prejudice?	3 of 4	Yes
Effects of Stereotyping, Prejudice, and Discrimination	4 of 4	Yes
How Can Prejudice and Discrimination Be Reduced?	3 of 4	Yes

Glossary

Note: Chapter numbers are specified below in brackets.

Accessibility the extent to which schemas and concepts are at the forefront of people's minds and are therefore likely to be used when making judgments about the social world [3]

Actor/observer difference the tendency to see other people's behaviour as dispositionally caused, while focusing more on the role of situational factors when explaining one's own behaviour [3]

Affectively based attitude an attitude based primarily on people's feelings and emotions pertaining to the attitude object [5]

Aggression intentional behaviour aimed at causing either physical or psychological pain [9]

Aggressive stimulus an object that is associated with aggressive responses (e.g., a gun) and whose mere presence can increase the probability of aggression [9]

Altruism the desire to help another person even if involves a cost to the helper [9]

Anchoring and adjustment heuristic a mental shortcut that involves using a number or value as a starting point, and then adjusting one's answer away from this anchor; people often do not adjust their answers sufficiently [3]

Anxious/ambivalent attachment style an attachment style characterized by a concern that others will not reciprocate one's desire for intimacy, resulting in higher-than-average levels of anxiety [8]

Attachment styles the expectations people develop about relationships with others, based on the relationship they had with their primary caregiver when they were infants [8]

Attitude an evaluation of a person, object, or idea [5]

Attitude inoculation the process of making people immune to attempts to change their attitudes by initially exposing them to small doses of the arguments against their position [5]

Attribution theory a description of the way in which people explain the causes of their own and other people's behaviour [3]

Automatic processing thinking that is nonconscious, unintentional, involuntary, and effortless [3]

Availability heuristic a mental rule of thumb whereby people base a judgment on the ease with which they can bring something to mind [3]

Avoidant attachment style an attachment style characterized by a suppression of attachment needs, because attempts to be intimate have been rebuffed; people with this style find it difficult to develop intimate relationships [8]

Base rate information information about the frequency of members of different categories in the population [3]

Behaviourally based attitude an attitude based primarily on observations of how one behaves toward an attitude object [5]

Belief in a just world a form of defensive attribution wherein people assume that bad things happen to bad people and that good things happen to good people [3]

Bookkeeping model information inconsistent with a stereotype that leads to a modification of the stereotype [10]

Bystander effect the finding that the greater the number of bystanders who witness an emergency, the less likely it is that any one of them will help [9]

Catharsis the notion that "blowing off steam"—by performing an aggressive act, watching others engage in aggressive behaviour, or engaging in a fantasy of aggression—relieves built-up aggressive energies and hence reduces the likelihood of further aggressive behaviour [9]

Cognitive dissonance a feeling of discomfort caused by the realization that one's behaviour is inconsistent with one's attitudes or that one holds two conflicting attitudes [5]

Cognitively based attitude an attitude based primarily on a person's beliefs about the properties of an attitude object [5]

Communal relationships relationships in which people's primary concern is being responsive to the other person's needs [8]

Companionate love the feelings of intimacy and affection we feel for another person about whom we care deeply [8]

Comparison level people's expectations about the level of rewards and costs they deserve in a relationship [8]

Comparison level for alternatives people's expectations about the level of rewards and punishments they would receive in an alternative relationship [8]

Complementarity attraction to people who are opposite to us [8]

Compliance a change in behaviour due to a direct request from another person [6]

Conformity a change in behaviour due to the real or imagined influence of other people [6]

Construal the way in which people perceive, comprehend, and interpret the social world [1]

Contingency theory of leadership the theory that leadership effectiveness depends both on how task-oriented or relationship-oriented the leader is and on the amount of control and influence the leader has over the group [7]

Controlled processing thinking that is conscious, intentional, voluntary, and effortful [3]

Conversion model information inconsistent with a stereotype that leads to a radical change in the stereotype [10]

Correlation coefficient a statistical technique that assesses how well you can predict one variable based on another; for example, how well you can predict people's weight from their height [2]

Correlational method the technique whereby researchers systematically measure two or more variables, and assess the relation between them (i.e., how much one can be predicted from the other) [2]

Counter-attitudinal advocacy the process that occurs when a person states an opinion or attitude that runs counter to his or her private belief or attitude [5]

Cover story a description of the purpose of a study, given to participants, that is different from its true purpose; cover stories are used to maintain psychological realism [2]

Debriefing the process of explaining to the participants, at the end of the experiment, the purpose of the study and exactly what transpired [2]

Deception the procedure whereby participants are misled about the true purpose of a study or the events that will transpire [2]

Defensive attributions explanations for behaviour that avoid feelings of vulnerability and mortality [3]

Deindividuation the loosening of normal constraints on behaviour when people are in a group, leading to an increase in impulsive and deviant acts [7]

Dependent variable the variable a researcher measures to see if it is influenced by the independent variable; the researcher hypothesizes that the dependent variable will depend on the level of the independent variable [2]

Diffusion of responsibility each bystander's sense of responsibility to help decreases as the number of witnesses increases [9]

Discrimination unjustified negative or harmful action toward a member of a group, simply because of his or her membership in that group [10]

Dismissive avoidant style a type of avoidant attachment in which the person is self-sufficient and claims not to need close relationships [8]

Door-in-the-face technique a technique to get people to comply with a request, whereby people are presented first with a large request, which they are expected to refuse, and then with a smaller, more reasonable request, to which it is hoped they will acquiesce [6]

Downward social comparison the process whereby we compare ourselves to people who are worse than we are in a particular trait or ability [4]

Elaboration likelihood model the theory that there are two ways in which persuasive communications can cause attitude change; the *central route* occurs when people are motivated and have the ability to pay attention to the arguments in the communication, and the *peripheral route* occurs when people do not pay attention to the arguments but are instead swayed by surface characteristics (e.g., who gave the speech) [5]

Empathy the ability to experience events and emotions (e.g., joy and sadness) the way another person experiences them [9]

Empathy-altruism hypothesis the idea that when we feel empathy for a person, we will attempt to help him or her purely for altruistic reasons, regardless of what we have to gain [9]

Equity theory the theory holding that people are happiest with relationships in which the rewards and costs that a person experiences and the contributions that he or she makes to the relationship are roughly equal to the rewards, costs, and contributions of the other person [8]

Evolutionary approach an approach derived from evolutionary biology that states that men and women are attracted to different characteristics in each other (men are attracted by women's appearances; women are attracted by men's resources) because this maximizes their reproductive success [8]

Exchange relationships relationships governed by the need for equity (for a comparable ratio of rewards and costs) [8]

Experimental method the method by which the researcher randomly assigns participants to different conditions and ensures that these conditions are identical except for the independent variable (the one thought to have a causal effect on people's responses) [2]

External attribution the inference that a person is behaving a certain way because of something about the situation he or she is in; the assumption is that most people would respond the same way in that situation [3]

External justification a person's reason or explanation for dissonant behaviour that resides outside the individual (e.g., in order to receive a large reward or avoid a severe punishment) [5]

External validity the extent to which the results of a study can be generalized to other situations and to other people [2]

Fear-arousing communication a persuasive message that attempts to change people's attitudes by arousing their fears [5]

Fearful avoidant style a type of avoidant attachment in which close relationships are avoided due to mistrust and fears of being hurt [8]

Foot-in-the-door technique a technique to get people to comply with a request, whereby people are presented first with a small request, to which they are expected to acquiesce, followed by a larger request, to which it is hoped they will also acquiesce [6]

Frustration-aggression theory the theory that frustration—the perception that you are being prevented from obtaining a goal—will increase the probability of an aggressive response [9]

Fundamental attribution error the tendency to overestimate the extent to which people's behaviour is due to internal, dispositional factors and to underestimate the role of situational factors [1, 3]

Gestalt psychology a school of psychology stressing the importance of studying the subjective way in which an object appears in people's minds, rather than the objective, physical attributes of the object [1]

Great person theory the theory that certain key personality traits make a person a good leader, regardless of the nature of the situation facing the leader [7]

Group a collection of two or more people who interact with each other and are interdependent, in the sense that their needs and goals cause them to rely on each other [7]

Group cohesiveness qualities of a group that bind members together and promote liking between members [7]

Group polarization the tendency for groups to make decisions that are more extreme than the initial inclinations of their members [7]

Groupthink a kind of thinking in which maintaining group cohesiveness and solidarity is more important than considering the facts in a realistic manner [7]

Heuristic-systematic model of persuasion the theory that there are two ways that persuasive communications can cause attitude change; people either process the merits of the arguments, known as *systematic processing*, or use mental shortcuts (heuristics), such as "Experts are always right," known as *heuristic processing* [5]

Independent variable the variable a researcher changes or varies to see if it has an effect on some other variable [2]

Independent view of the self defining oneself in terms of one's own internal thoughts, feelings, and actions, and not in terms of the thoughts, feelings, and actions of other people [4]

Individual differences the aspects of people's personalities that make them different from other people [1]

Informational social influence conforming because we believe that others' interpretation of an ambiguous situation is more correct than ours and will help us choose an appropriate course of action [6]

Informed consent the procedure whereby researchers explain the nature of the experiment to participants before it begins and obtain their consent to participate [2]

Insufficient punishment the dissonance aroused when individuals lack sufficient external justification for having resisted a desired activity or object, usually resulting in individuals' devaluing the forbidden activity or object [5]

Integrative solution a solution to a conflict whereby the parties make trade-offs on issues according to their different interests; each side concedes the most on issues that are unimportant to it but that are important to the other side [7]

Interdependent view of the self defining oneself in terms of one's relationships to other people; recognizing that one's behaviour is often determined by the thoughts, feelings, and actions of others [4]

Internal attribution the inference that a person is behaving in a certain way because of something about him or her, such as his or her attitude, character, or personality [3]

Internal justification the reduction of dissonance by changing something about oneself (one's attitude or behaviour) [5]

Internal validity ensuring that nothing other than the independent variable can affect the dependent variable; this is accomplished by controlling all extraneous variables and by randomly assigning people to different experimental conditions [2]

Introspection the process whereby people look inward and examine their own thoughts, feelings, and motives [4]

Investment model the theory holding that people's commitment to a relationship depends on their satisfaction with the relationship in terms of rewards, costs, and comparison level; their comparison level for alternatives; and how much they have invested in the relationship that would be lost by leaving it [8]

Jigsaw classroom a classroom setting designed to reduce prejudice between children by placing them in small, desegregated groups and making each child dependent on the other children in the group to learn the course material and do well in the class [10]

Judgmental heuristics mental shortcuts people use to make judgments quickly and efficiently [3]

Justification of effort the tendency for individuals to increase their liking for something they have worked hard to attain [5]

Kin selection the idea that behaviour that helps a genetic relative is favoured by natural selection [9]

Looking-glass self the idea that we see ourselves through the eyes of other people and incorporate their views into our self-concept [4]

Lowballing an unscrupulous strategy whereby a salesperson induces a customer to agree to purchase a product at a very low cost, then subsequently raises the price; frequently, the customer will still make the purchase at the inflated price [6]

Mere exposure effect the finding that the more exposure we have to a stimulus, the more apt we are to like it [8]

Meta-stereotype a person's beliefs regarding the stereotype that out-group members hold about their own group [10]

Minority influence the case where a minority of group members influences the behaviour or beliefs of the majority [6]

Misattribution of arousal the process whereby people make mistaken inferences about what is causing them to feel the way they do [8]

Modern prejudice outwardly acting unprejudiced while inwardly maintaining prejudiced attitudes [10]

Mundane realism the extent to which an experiment is similar to real-life situations [2]

Mutual interdependence a situation in which two or more groups need each other and must depend on each other to accomplish a goal that is important to each group [10]

Negative-state relief hypothesis the idea that people help in order to alleviate their own sadness and distress [9]

Negotiation a form of communication between opposing sides in a conflict, in which offers and counteroffers are made and a solution occurs only when both parties agree [7]

Norm of reciprocity the expectation that helping others will increase the likelihood that they will help us in the future [9]

Normative social influence the influence of other people that leads us to conform in order to be liked and accepted by them; this type of conformity results in public compliance with the group's beliefs and behaviours, but not necessarily with private acceptance of the group's beliefs and behaviours [6]

Obedience conformity in response to the commands of an authority figure [6]

Observational method the technique whereby a researcher observes people and systematically records measurements of their behaviour [2]

Operational definition the precise specification of how variables are measured or manipulated [2]

Out-group homogeneity the perception that those in the out-group are more similar (homogeneous) to each other than they really are, as well as more similar than the members of the in-group [10]

Passionate love the feelings of intense longing, accompanied by physiological arousal, we feel for another person; when our love is reciprocated, we feel great fulfillment and ecstasy, but when it is not, we feel sadness and despair [8]

Perceptual salience information that is the focus of people's attention; people tend to overestimate the causal role of perceptually salient information [3]

Persuasive communication communication (e.g., a speech or television ad) advocating a particular side of an issue [5]

Pluralistic ignorance the phenomenon whereby bystanders assume that nothing is wrong in an emergency because no one else looks concerned [9]

Positive illusions idealization of our romantic relationships and partners in order to maintain the relationship [8]

Postdecision dissonance dissonance that is inevitably aroused after a person makes a decision; such dissonance is typically reduced by enhancing the attractiveness of the chosen alternative and devaluing the rejected alternative [5]

Prejudice a hostile or negative attitude toward a distinguishable group of people, based solely on their membership in that group [10]

Priming the process by which recent experiences increase a schema's or trait's accessibility [3]

Private acceptance conforming to other people's behaviour out of a genuine belief that what they are doing or saying is right [6]

Process loss any aspect of group interaction that inhibits good problem solving [7]

Propinquity effect the finding that the more we see and interact with people, the more likely they are to become our friends [8]

Prosocial behaviour any act performed with the goal of benefiting another person [9]

Psychological realism the extent to which the psychological processes triggered in an experiment are similar to psychological processes that occur in everyday life; psychological realism can be high in an experiment, even if mundane realism is low [2]

Public compliance conforming to other people's behaviour publicly, without necessarily believing in what they are doing or saying [6]

Random assignment to condition the process whereby all participants have an equal chance of taking part in any condition of an experiment; through random assignment, researchers can be relatively certain that differences in the participants' personalities or backgrounds are distributed evenly across conditions [2]

Random selection a way of ensuring that a sample of people is representative of a population, by giving everyone in the population an equal chance of being selected for the sample [2]

Rationalization trap the potential for dissonance reduction to produce a succession of self-justifications that ultimately results in a chain of stupid or immoral actions [5]

Reciprocal liking when you like someone and that person also likes you [8]

Reciprocity norm a social norm stating that receiving anything positive from another person requires you to reciprocate (or behave similarly) in response [6]

Relationship-oriented leader a leader who is concerned primarily with the feelings of and relationships between the workers [7]

Representativeness heuristic a mental shortcut whereby people classify something according to how similar it is to a typical case [3]

Reward/cost ratio in social exchange theory, the notion that there is a balance between the rewards that come from a relationship and the personal cost of maintaining the relationship. If the ratio is not favourable, the result is dissatisfaction with the relationship [8]

Schemas mental structures people use to organize their knowledge about the social world around themes or subjects; schemas affect what information we notice, think about, and remember [3]

Secure attachment style an attachment style characterized by trust, a lack of concern with being abandoned, and the view that one is worthy and well liked [8]

Self-affirmation theory a theory suggesting that people will reduce the impact of a dissonance-arousing threat to their self-concept by focusing on and affirming their competence in some dimension unrelated to the threat [4]

Self-awareness the act of thinking about ourselves [4]

Self-awareness theory the idea that when people focus their attention on themselves, they evaluate and compare their behaviour to their internal standards and values [4]

Self-concept the contents of the self; that is, our knowledge about who we are [4]

Self-discrepancy theory the theory that we become distressed when our sense of who we truly are—our actual self—is discrepant from our personal standards or desired self-conceptions [4]

Self-enhancement a tendency to hold unrealistically positive views about ourselves [4]

Self-evaluation maintenance theory the theory that one's self-concept can be threatened by another individual's behaviour and that the level of threat is determined by both the closeness of the other individual and the personal relevance of the behaviour [4]

Self-fulfilling prophecy the case whereby people (a) have an expectation about what another person is like, which (b) influences how they act toward that person, which (c) causes that person to behave consistently with people's original expectations [10]

Self-justification the tendency to justify one's actions in order to maintain one's self-esteem [5]

Self-perception theory the theory that when our attitudes and feelings are uncertain or ambiguous, we infer these states by observing our behaviour and the situation in which it occurs [4]

Self-schemas organized knowledge structures about ourselves, based on our past experiences, that help us understand, explain, and predict our own behaviour [4]

Self-serving attributions explanations for one's successes that credit internal, dispositional factors and explanations for one's failures that blame external, situational factors [3]

Self-verification theory a theory suggesting that people have a need to seek confirmation of their self-concept, whether the self-concept is positive or negative; in some circumstances, this tendency can conflict with the desire to uphold a favourable view of oneself [4]

Similarity attraction to people who are like us [8]

Social cognition how people think about themselves and the social world; more specifically, how people select, interpret, remember, and use social information [3]

Social comparison theory the idea that we learn about our own abilities and attitudes by comparing ourselves to other people [4]

Social exchange theory the theory holding that how people feel about a relationship depends on their perceptions of the rewards and costs of the relationship, the kind of relationship they deserve, and their chances of having a better relationship with someone else [8]

Social facilitation the tendency for people to do better on simple tasks and worse on complex tasks when they are in the presence of others and their individual performance can be evaluated [7]

Social impact theory the theory that conforming to social influence depends on the strength, immediacy, and number of other people in a group [6]

Social learning theory the theory that we learn social behaviour (e.g., aggression) by observing others and imitating them [9]

Social loafing the tendency for people to do worse on simple tasks but better on complex tasks when they are in the presence of others and their individual performance cannot be evaluated [7]

Social norms the implicit or explicit rules a group has for the acceptable behaviours, values, and beliefs of its members [6]

Social perception the study of how we form impressions of and make inferences about other people [3]

Social psychology the scientific study of the way in which people's thoughts, feelings, and behaviours are influenced by the real or imagined presence of other people [1]

Social roles shared expectations in a group about how particular people are supposed to behave [7]

Stereotype a generalization about a group of people in which identical characteristics are assigned to virtually all members of the group, regardless of actual variation among the members [10]

Stereotype threat the apprehension experienced by members of a minority group that they might behave in a manner that confirms an existing cultural stereotype [10]

Subjective norms people's beliefs about how those they care about will view the behaviour in question [5]

Subliminal messages words or pictures that are not consciously perceived but that supposedly influence people's judgments, attitudes, and behaviours [5]

Subtyping model information inconsistent with a stereotype that leads to the creation of a new sub-stereotype to accommodate the information without changing the initial stereotype [10]

Task-oriented leader a leader who is concerned more with getting the job done than with the feelings of and relationships between the workers [7]

Theory an organized set of principles that can be used to explain observed phenomena [2]

Theory of planned behaviour a theory that the best predictors of a person's planned, deliberate behaviours are the person's attitudes toward specific behaviours, subjective norms, and perceived behavioural control [5]

Triangular theory of love the idea that different kinds of love comprise varying degrees of three components: intimacy, passion, and commitment [8]

Unrealistic optimism a form of defensive attribution wherein people think that good things are more likely to happen to them than to their peers and that bad things are less likely to happen to them than to their peers [3]

Upward social comparison the process whereby we compare ourselves to people who are better than we are in a particular trait or ability [4]

Yale Attitude Change Approach the study of the conditions under which people are most likely to change their attitudes in response to persuasive messages; researchers in this tradition focus on "who said what to whom"—that is, on the source of the communication, the nature of the communication, and the nature of the audience [5]

References

Abelson, R. P., Kinder, D. R., Peters, M. D., & Fiske, S. T. (1982). Affective and semantic components in political person perception. *Journal of Personality and Social Psychology, 42,* 619–630.

Abrams, D., Wetherell, M., Cochrane, S., Hogg, M.A., & Turner, J. C. (1990). Knowing what to think by knowing who you are: Self-categorization and the nature of norm formation, conformity, and group polarization. *British Journal of Social Psychology, 29,* 97–119.

Adlag, R. J., & Fuller, S. R. (1993). Beyond fiasco: A reappraisal of the groupthink phenomenon and a new model of group decision processes. *Psychological Bulletin, 113,* 533–552.

Adler, J. (1997, Spring/Summer). It's a wise father who knows.... *Newsweek,* p. 73.

Ainsworth, M. D. S., Blehar, M. C., Waters, E., & Wall, S. (1978). *Patterns of attachment: A psychological study of the strange situation.* Hillsdale, NJ: Erlbaum.

Ajzen, I. (1985). From intentions to actions: A theory of planned behavior. In J. Kuhl & J. Beckmann (Eds.), *Action-control: From cognition to behavior* (pp. 11–39). Heidelberg, Germany: Springer.

Ajzen, I. (1996). The directive influence of attitudes on behavior. In P. M. Gollwitzer & J. A. Bargh (Eds.), *The psychology of action: Linking cognition and motivation to behavior* (pp. 385–403). New York: Guilford.

Ajzen, I., & Fishbein, M. (1980). *Understanding attitudes and predicting social behavior.* Englewood Cliffs, NJ: Prentice Hall.

Ajzen, I., & Sexton, J. (1999). Depth of processing, belief congruence, and attitude-behavior correspondence. In S. Chaiken & Y. Trope (Eds.), *Dual-process theories in social psychology* (pp. 117–138). New York: Guilford Press.

Akert, R. M. (1993). *The effect of autobiographical memories on the current definition of self.* Unpublished manuscript, Wellesley College.

Akert, R. M. (1998). *Terminating romantic relationships: The role of personal responsibility and gender.* Unpublished manuscript, Wellesley College.

Allen, M. (1991). Meta-analysis comparing the persuasiveness of one-sided and two-sided messages. *Western Journal of Speech Communication, 55,* 390–404.

Allen, M., Hale, J., Mongeau, P., Berkowits-Stafford, S., Stafford, S., Shanahan, W., Agee, P., Dillon, K., Jackson, R., & Ray, C. (1990). Testing a model of message sidedness: Three replications. *Communication Monographs, 57,* 274–291.

Allen, V. L., & Levine, J. M. (1969). Consensus and conformity. *Journal of Personality and Social Psychology, 5,* 389–399.

Allison, P. D. (1992). The cultural evolution of beneficient norms. *Social Forces, 71,* 279–301.

Allison, S. T., & Beggan, J. K. (1994). Estimating popular support for group decision outcomes: An anchoring and adjustment model. *Journal of Social Behavior and Personality, 9,* 617–638.

Allison, S. T., Beggan, J. K., & Midgley, E. H. (1996). The quest for "similar instances" and "simultaneous possibilities": Metaphors in social dilemma research. *Journal of Personality and Social Psychology, 71,* 479–497.

Allison, S. T., Mackie, D. M., Muller, M. M., & Worth, L. T. (1993). Sequential correspondence biases and perceptions of change: The Castro studies revisited. *Personality and Social Psychology Bulletin, 19,* 151–157.

Allport, G. (1954). *The nature of prejudice.* Reading, MA: Addison-Wesley.

Allport, G. W. (1985). The historical background of social psychology. In G. Lindzey & E. Aronson (Eds.), *The handbook of social psychology* (Vol. 1, pp. 1–46). Reading, MA: Addison-Wesley.

Amir, I. (1969). Contact hypothesis in ethnic relations. *Psychological Bulletin, 71,* 319–342.

Amir, Y. (1976). The role of intergroup contact in change of prejudice and ethnic relations. In P. Katz (Ed.), *Towards the elimination of racism.* New York: Pergamon Press.

Andersen, B. L., & Cyranowski, J. M. (1994). Women's sexual self-schema. *Journal of Personality and Social Psychology, 67,* 1079–1100.

Andersen, S. M. (1984). Self-knowledge and social inference: II. The diagnosticity of cognitive/affective and behavioral data. *Journal of Personality and Social Psychology, 46,* 294–307.

Andersen, S. M., & Bem, S. L. (1981). Sex typing and androgyny in dyadic interaction: Individual differences in responsiveness to physical attractiveness. *Journal of Personality and Social Psychology, 41,* 74–86.

Andersen, S. M., & Ross, L. D. (1984). Self-knowledge and social inference: I. The impact of cognitive/affective and behavioral data. *Journal of Personality and Social Psychology, 46,* 280–293.

Anderson, C. A. (1999). Attributional style, depression, and loneliness: A cross-cultural comparison of American and Chinese students. *Personality and Social Psychology Bulletin, 25,* 482–499.

Anderson, C. A., & Dill, K. E. (2000). Video games and aggressive thoughts, feelings, and behavior in the laboratory and in life. *Journal of Personality and Social Psychology, 78,* 772–790.

Archer, D., & Gartner, R. (1984). *Violence and crime in cross-national perspective.* New Haven, CT: Yale University Press.

Archer, D., & McDaniel, P. (1995). Violence and gender: Differences and similarities across societies. In R. B. Ruback & N. A. Weiner (Eds.), *Interpersonal violent behaviors: social and cultural aspects* (pp. 63–88). New York: Springer Publishing.

Archer, J. (2000). Sex differences in aggression between heterosexual partners: A meta-analytic review. *Psychological Bulletin, 126*, 651–680.

Arms, R. L., Russell, G. W., & Sandilands, M. L. (1979). Effects on the hostility of spectators of viewing aggressive sports. *Social Psychology Quarterly, 42*, 275–279.

Aron, A., & Aron, E. N. (1986). Falling in love: Prospective studies of self-concept change. *Journal of Personality and Social Psychology, 69*, 1102–1112.

Aron, A., & Westbay, L. (1996). Dimensions of the prototype of love. *Journal of Personality and Social Psychology, 70*, 535–551.

Aron, E. N., & Aron, A. (1997). Sensory processing sensitivity and its relation to introversion and emotionality. *Journal of Personality and Social Psychology, 73*, 345–368.

Aronson, E. (1968). Dissonance theory: Progress and problems. In R. P. Abelson, E. Aronson, W. J. McGuire, T. M. Newcomb, M. J. Rosenberg, and P. H. Tannenbaum (Eds.), *Theories of cognitive consistency: A Sourcebook* (pp. 5–27). Chicago: Rand McNally.

Aronson, E. (1969). The theory of cognitive dissonance: A current perspective. In L. Berkowitz (Ed.), *Advances in experimental social psychology* (Vol. 4, pp. 1–34). New York: Academic Press.

Aronson, E. (1992). Stateways can change folkways. In R. Baird & S. Rosenbaum (Eds.), *Bigotry, prejudice and hatred: Definitions, causes and solutions*. Buffalo, NY: Prometheus Books.

Aronson, E. (1997a). The giving away of psychology—and condoms. *APS Observer, 10*, 17–35.

Aronson, E. (1997b). The theory of cognitive dissonance: The evolution and vicissitudes of an idea. In C. McGarty & S. Alexander Haslam (Eds.), *The message of social psychology: Perspectives on mind in society* (pp. 20–35). Oxford, England: Blackwell Publishers, Inc.

Aronson, E. (1998). Dissonance, hypocrisy, and the self-concept. In E. Harmon-Jones & J. S. Mills, *Cognitive dissonance theory: Revival with revisions and controversies*. Washington, DC: American Psychological Association.

Aronson, E. (1999). *The social animal* (8th ed.). New York: Worth/Freeman.

Aronson, E., & Bridgeman, D. (1979). Jigsaw groups and the desegregated classroom: In pursuit of common goals. *Personality and Social Psychology Bulletin, 5*, 438–446.

Aronson, E., & Carlsmith, J. M. (1962). Performance expectancy as a determinant of actual performance. *Journal of Abnormal and Social Psychology, 65*, 178–182.

Aronson, E., & Carlsmith, J. M. (1963). Effect of severity of threat in the devaluation of forbidden behavior. *Journal of Abnormal and Social Psychology, 66*, 584–588.

Aronson, E., & Carlsmith, J. M. (1968). Experimentation in social psychology. In G. Lindzey & E. Aronson (Eds.), *The handbook of social psychology* (Vol. 2, pp. 1–79). Reading, MA: Addison-Wesley.

Aronson, E., Chase, T., Helmreich, R., & Ruhnke, R. (1974). A two-factor theory of dissonance reduction: The effect of feeling stupid or feeling awful on opinion change. *International Journal for Research and Communication, 3*, 59–74.

Aronson, E., Ellsworth, P. C., Carlsmith, J. M., & Gonzalez, M. H. (1990). *Methods of research in social psychology* (2nd ed.). New York: McGraw-Hill.

Aronson, E., Fried, C., & Stone, J. (1991). Overcoming denial and increasing the intention to use condoms through the induction of hypocrisy. *American Journal of Public Health, 81*, 1636–1638.

Aronson, E., & Gonzalez, A. (1988). Desegregation, jigsaw, and the Mexican-American experience. In P. A. Katz & D. Taylor (Eds.), *Towards the elimination of racism: Profiles in controversy* (pp. 310–330). New York: Plenum.

Aronson, E., & Mettee, D. (1968). Dishonest behavior as a function of differential levels of induced self-esteem. *Journal of Personality and Social Psychology, 9*, 121–127.

Aronson, E., & Mills, J. (1959). The effect of severity of initiation on liking for a group. *Journal of Abnormal and Social Psychology, 59*, 177–181.

Aronson, E., & Patnoe, S. (1997). *Cooperation in the classroom: The jigsaw method*. New York: Longman.

Aronson, E., Stephan, C., Sikes, J., Blaney, N., & Snapp, M. (1978). *The jigsaw classroom*. Beverly Hills, CA: Sage.

Aronson, E., Wilson, T. D., & Brewer, M. (1998). Experimental methods. In D. Gilbert, S. Fiske, & G. Lindzey (Eds.), *The handbook of social psychology* (4th ed., Vol. 1, pp. 99–142). New York: Random House.

Aronson, J., Cohen, J., & Nail, P. (1998). Self-affirmation theory: An update and appraisal. In E. Harmon-Jones & J. S. Mills, *Cognitive dissonance theory: Revival with revisions and controversies*. Washington, DC: American Psychological Association.

Aronson, J. M., Quinn, D., & Spencer, S. (1998). Stereotype threat and the academic underperformance of women and minorities. In J. K. Swim & C. Stangor (Eds.), *Stigma: The target's perspective* (pp. 83–103). San Diego, CA: Academic Press.

Asch, S. E. (1951). Effects of group pressure upon the modification and distortion of judgment. In H. Guetzkow (Ed.), *Groups, leadership, and men*. Pittsburgh, PA: Carnegie Press.

Asch, S. E. (1955). Opinions and social pressure. *Scientific American, 193*, 31–35.

Asch, S. E. (1956). Studies of independence and conformity: A minority of one against a unanimous majority. *Psychological Monographs, 70* (9, Whole No. 416).

Ashmore, R. D., Solomon, M. R., & Longo, L. C. (1996). Thinking about fashion models' looks: A multidimensional approach to the structure of perceived physical attractiveness. *Personality and Social Psychology Bulletin, 22*, 1083–1104.

Aspinwall, L. G., & Taylor, S. E. (1993). Effects of social comparison direction, threat, and self-esteem on affect, evaluation, and expected success. *Journal of Personality and Social Psychology, 64*, 708–722.

Atlas, R. S., & Pepler, D. J. (1998). Observations of bullying in the classroom. *Journal of Educational Research, 92*, 86–99.

Attridge, M., & Berscheid, E. (1994). Entitlement in romantic relationships in the United States: A social exchange perspective. In M. J. Lerner & G. Mikula (Eds.), *Entitlement and the affectional bond: Justice in close relationships* (pp. 117–148). New York: Plenum.

Badami, A. R. (1996). *Tamarind mem.* Toronto: Viking.

Bahrick, H. P., Hall, L. K., & Berger, S. A. (1996). Accuracy and distortion in memory for high school grades. *Psychological Science, 7*, 265–271.

Baize, H. R., & Schroeder, J. E. (1995). Personality and mate selection in personal ads: Evolutionary preferences in a public mate selection process. *Journal of Social Behavior and Personality, 10*, 517–536.

Baldwin, M. W. (1992). Relational schemas and the processing of social information. *Psychological Bulletin, 112*, 461–484.

Baldwin, M. W., Carrell, S. E., & Lopez, D. F. (1990). Priming relationship schemas: My advisor and the pope are watching me from the back of my mind. *Journal of Experimental Social Psychology, 26*, 435–454.

Baldwin, M. W., & Fehr, B. (1995). On the instability of attachment style ratings. *Personal Relationships, 2*, 247–261.

Baldwin, M. W., & Holmes, J. O. (1987). Salient private audiences and awareness of the self. *Journal of Personality and Social Psychology, 52*, 1087–1098.

Baldwin, M. W., Keelan, J. P. R., Fehr, B., Enns, V., & Koh-Rangarajoo, E. (1996). Social-cognitive conceptualizations of attachment working models: Availability and accessibility effects. *Journal of Personality and Social Psychology, 71*, 94–109.

Baldwin, M. W., & Meunier, J. (1999). The cued activation of attachment relational schemas. *Social Cognition, 17*, 209–227.

Baldwin, M. W., & Sinclair, L. (1996). Self-esteem and "if . . . then" contingencies of interpersonal acceptance. *Journal of Personality and Social Psychology, 71*, 1130–1141.

Bandura, A., Ross, D., & Ross, S. (1961). Transmission of aggression through imitation of aggressive models. *Journal of Abnormal and Social Psychology, 63*, 575–582.

Bandura, A., Ross, D., & Ross, S. (1963). Imitation of film-mediated aggressive models. *Journal of Abnormal and Social Psychology, 66*, 3–11.

Bargh, J. A. (1990). Auto-motives: Preconscious determinants of social interaction. In E. T. Higgins & R. M. Sorrentino (Eds.), *Handbook of motivation and cognition* (Vol. 2, pp. 93–130). New York: Guilford.

Bargh, J. A. (1994). The four horsemen of automaticity: Awareness, intention, efficiency, and control in social cognition. In R. S. Wyer Jr. & T. K. Srull (Eds.), *Handbook of Social Cognition* (Vol. 1, pp. 1–40). Hillsdale, NJ: Erlbaum.

Bargh, J. A. (1996). Automaticity in social psychology. In E. T. Higgins & A. W. Kruglanski (Eds.), *Social psychology: Handbook of basic principles* (pp. 169–183). New York: Guilford.

Bargh, J. A., & Ferguson, M. J. (2000). Beyond behaviorism: On the automaticity of higher mental processes. *Psychological Bulletin, 126*, 929-945.

Bargh, J. A., Gollwitzer, P.M., Lee-Chai, A., Barndollar, K., & Trotschel, R. (2001). The mated will: Nonconscious activation and pursuit of behavioral goals. *Journal of Personality and Social Psychology, 81*, 1014-1027.

Bargh, J. A., & McKenna, K. Y. A. (2004). The internet and social life. *Annual Review of Psychology, 55*, 573–590.

Bargh, J. A., McKenna, K. Y. A., & Fitzsimons, G. M. (2002). Can you see the real me? Activation and expression of the "true self" on the Internet. *Journal of Social Issues, 58*, 33–48.

Bargh, J. A., & Pietromonaco, P. (1982). Automatic information processing and social perception: The influence of trait information presented outside of conscious awareness on impression formation. *Journal of Personality and Social Psychology, 43*, 437–449.

Barker, R., Dembo, T., & Lewin, K. (1941). Frustration and aggression: An experiment with young children. *University of Iowa Studies in Child Welfare, 18*, 1–314.

Barley, S. R., & Bechky, B. A. (1994). In the backrooms of science: The work of technicians in science labs. *Work and Occupations, 21*, 85–126.

Baron, J. (1997). The illusion of morality as self-interest: A reason to cooperate in social dilemmas. *Psychological Science, 8*, 330–335.

Baron, R. A. (1972). Reducing the influence of an aggressive model: The restraining effects of peer censure. *Journal of Experimental Social Psychology, 8*, 266–275.

Baron, R. A. (1988). Negative effects of destructive criticism: Impact on conflict, self-efficacy, and task performance. *Journal of Applied Psychology, 73*, 199–207.

Baron, R. A. (1990). Countering the effects of destructive criticism: The relative efficacy of four interventions. *Journal of Applied Psychology, 75*, 235–245.

Baron, R. A., & Richardson, D. R. (1994). *Human aggression* (2nd ed.). New York: Plenum.

Baron, R. S. (1986). Distraction/conflict theory: Progress and problems. In L. Berkowitz (Ed.), *Advances in experimental social psychology* (Vol. 19, pp. 1–40). Orlando, FL: Academic Press.

Baron, R. S., Inman, M., Kao, C., & Logan, H. (1992). Emotion and superficial social processing. *Motivation and Emotion, 16*, 323–345.

Baron, R. S., Vandello, J. A., & Brunsman, B. (1996). The forgotten variable in conformity research: Impact of task importance on social influence. *Journal of Personality and Social Psychology, 71,* 915–927.

Bartholomew, B. D., & Anderson, C. A. (2002). Effects of violent video games on aggressive behavior: Potential sex differences. *Journal of Experimental Social Psychology, 38,* 283–290.

Bartholomew, K. (1990). Avoidance of intimacy: An attachment perspective. *Journal of Social and Personal Relationships, 7,* 147–178.

Bartholomew, K., & Horowitz, L. M. (1991). Attachment styles among young adults: A test of a four-category model. *Journal of Personality and Social Psychology, 61,* 226–244.

Bartlett, D. C. (1932). *Remembering.* Cambridge: Cambridge University Press.

Bass, B. M. (1990). *Bass and Stogdill's handbook of leadership: Theory, research, and managerial applications* (3rd ed.). New York: Free Press.

Bass, B. M. (1997). Does the transactional-transformational leadership paradigm transcend organizational and national boundaries? *American Psychologist, 52,* 130–139.

Bastien, D., & Hostager, T. (1988). Jazz as a process of organizational innovation. *Communication Research, 15,* 582–602.

Batson, C. D. (1991). *The altruism question: Toward a social-psychological answer.* Hillsdale, NJ: Erlbaum.

Batson, C. D. (1998). Altruism and prosocial behavior. In D. Gilbert, S. Fiske, & G. Lindzey (Eds.), *The handbook of social psychology* (4th ed., Vol. 2, pp. 282–316). New York: McGraw-Hill.

Batson, C. D. (2002). Addressing the altruism question experimentally. In S. G. Post & L. G. Underwood (Eds.), *Altruism and altruistic love: Science, philosophy, and religion in dialogue* (pp. 89–105). Oxford, England: Oxford University Press.

Batson, C. D., Ahmad, N., Lishner, D. A., & Tsang, J. (2002). Empathy and altruism. In C. R. Snyder & S. J. Lopez (Eds.), *Handbook of positive psychology* (pp. 485–498). New York: Oxford University Press.

Batson, C. D., Coke, J. S., Jasnoski, M. L., & Hanson, M. (1978). Buying kindness: Effect of an extrinsic incentive for helping on perceived altruism. *Personality and Social Psychology Bulletin, 4,* 86–91.

Batson, C. D., & Powell, A. A. (2003). Altruism and prosocial behavior. In T. Millon & M. J. Lerner (Eds.), *Handbook of psychology: Personality and social psychology* (Vol. 5, pp. 463–484). New York: Wiley.

Baumeister, R. F. (1991). *Escaping the self: Alcoholism, spirituality, masochism, and other flights from the burden of selfhood.* New York: Basic Books.

Baumeister, R. F., & Bratslavsky, E. (1999). Passion, intimacy, and time: Passionate love as a function of change in intimacy. *Personality and Social Psychology Review, 3,* 49–67.

Baumeister, R. F., & Leary, M. R. (1995). The need to belong: Desire for interpersonal attachment as a fundamental human motivation. *Psychological Bulletin, 117,* 497–529.

Baumeister, R. F., & Sommer, K. L. (1997). What do men want? Gender differences and two spheres of belongingness: Comment on Cross and Madson (1997). *Psychological Bulletin, 122,* 38–44.

Baumeister, R. F., Stillwell, A. M., & Heatherton, T. F. (1994). Guilt: An interpersonal approach. *Psychological Bulletin, 115,* 243–267.

Bazerman, M., & Neale, M. (1992). *Negotiating rationally.* New York: Free Press.

Beach, S., Tesser, A., Mendolia, M., & Anderson, P. (1996). Self-evaluation maintenance in marriage: Toward a performance ecology of the marital relationship. *Journal of Family Psychology, 10,* 379–396.

Beaman, A. L., Barnes, P. J., Klentz, B., & McQuirk, B. (1978). Increasing helping rates through informational dissemination: Teaching pays. *Personality and Social Psychology Bulletin, 4,* 406–411.

Beaman, A. L., Klentz, B., Diener, E., & Svanum, S. (1979). Objective self-awareness and transgression in children: A field study. *Journal of Personality and Social Psychology, 37,* 1835–1846.

Becker, M. H., & Josephs, J. G. (1988). AIDS and behavioral change to reduce risk: A review. *American Journal of Public Health, 78,* 394–410.

Behrman, M., Winocur, G., & Moscovitch, M. (1992). *Nature, 359,* 636–637.

Bell, S. T., Kuriloff, P. J., & Lottes, I. (1994). Understanding attributions of blame in stranger rape and date rape situations: An examination of gender, race, identification, and students' social perceptions of rape victims. *Journal of Applied Social Psychology, 24,* 1719–1734.

Bem, D. J. (1972). Self-perception theory. In L. Berkowitz (Ed.), *Advances in experimental social psychology* (Vol. 6, pp. 1–62). New York: Academic Press.

Bereczkei, T., Voros, S., Gal, A., & Bernath, L. (1997). Resources, attractiveness, and family commitment: Reproductive decisions in human mate choice. *Ethology, 103,* 681–699.

Berkow, J. H. (1989). *Darwin, sex, and status: Biological approaches to mind and culture.* Toronto: University of Toronto Press.

Berkowitz, L. (1978). Whatever happened to the frustration-aggression hypothesis? *American Behavioral Scientist, 21,* 691–708.

Berkowitz, L. (1987). Mood, self-awareness, and willingness to help. *Journal of Personality and Social Psychology, 52,* 721–729.

Berkowitz, L. (1988). Frustrations, appraisals, and aversively stimulated aggression. *Aggressive Behavior, 14,* 3–11.

Berkowitz, L. (1989). Frustration-aggression hypothesis: Examination and reformulation. *Psychological Bulletin, 106,* 59–73.

Berkowitz, L. (1993). *Aggression: Its causes, consequences, and control.* New York: McGraw-Hill.

Berkowitz, L., & LePage, A. (1967). Weapons as aggression-eliciting stimuli. *Journal of Personality and Social Psychology, 7,* 202–207.

Berscheid, E. (1985). Interpersonal attraction. In G. Lindzey & E. Aronson (Eds.), *The handbook of social psychology* (pp. 413–484). New York: McGraw-Hill.

Berscheid, E., & Hatfield, E. (1978). *Interpersonal attraction* (2nd ed.). Reading, MA: Addison-Wesley.

Berscheid, E., & Reis, H. T. (1998). Attraction and close relationships. In D. Gilbert, S. Fiske, & G. Lindzey (Eds.), *The handbook of social psychology* (4th ed., Vol. 2, pp. 193–281). New York: McGraw-Hill.

Berscheid, E., & Walster (Hatfield), E. (1974). A little bit about love. In T. L. Huston (Ed.), *Foundations of interpersonal attraction* (pp. 355-381). New York: Academic Press.

Berscheid, E., & Walster (Hatfield), E. (1978). *Interpersonal attraction*. Reading, MA: Addison-Wesley.

Bettencourt, B. A., & Miller, N. (1996). Gender differences in aggression as a function of provocation: A meta-analysis. *Psychological Bulletin, 119*, 422–447.

Bickman, L. (1974). The social power of a uniform. *Journal of Applied Social Psychology, 4*, 47–61.

Biernat, M., Crandall, C. S., Young, L. V., Kobrynowicz, D., & Halpin, S. M. (1998). All that you can be: Stereotyping of self and others in a military context. *Journal of Personality and Social Psychology, 75*, 301–317.

Billsberry, J. (Ed.) (1996*). The effective manager: Perspectives and illustrations.* London, England: Sage.

Bils, J., & Singer, S. (1996, August 16). Gorilla saves tot in Brookfield ape pit. *Chicago Tribune*, p. 1.

Bird, B. (2001, January 28). Love as fleeting as a bus ride. *Winnipeg Free Press*, p. B5.

Blanchfield, M. (2000, June 21). I will never be able to trust my leaders again. *Ottawa Citizen Online.* www.ottawacitizen.com/national/000227/3666380.html

Blascovich, J., Ginsburg, G. P., & Veach, T. L. (1975). A pluralistic explanation of choice shifts on the risk dimension. *Journal of Personality and Social Psychology, 31*, 422–429.

Blascovich, J., Mendes, W. B., Hunter, S. B., & Salomon, K. (1999). Social "facilitation" as challenge and threat. *Journal of Personality and Social Psychology, 77*, 68–77.

Blass, T. (1993). Psychological perspectives on the perpetrators of the Holocaust: The role of situational pressures, personal dispositions, and their interactions. *Holocaust and Genocide Studies, 7*, 30–50.

Blass, T. (1996). Attribution of responsibility and trust in the Milgram obedience experiment. *Journal of Applied Social Psychology, 26*, 1529–1535.

Blau, P. M. (1964). *Exchange and power in social life.* New York: Wiley.

Boadle, A. (1994, Nov. 8). Pictures of Somali beaten to death shock Canadians [Reuters]. http://burn.ucsd.edu/archives/riot-l/1994.Nov/0012.html

Bochner, S. (1994). Cross-cultural differences in the self-concept: A test of Hofstede's individualism/collectivism distinction. *Journal of Cross-Cultural Psychology, 25*, 273–283.

Bodenhausen, G. V. (1988). Stereotypic biases in social decision making and memory: Testing process models of stereotype use. *Journal of Personality and Social Psychology, 55*, 726–737.

Bodenhausen, G. V., & Lichtenstein, M. (1987). Social stereotypes and information-processing strategies. The impact of task complexity. *Journal of Personality and Social Psychology, 52*, 871–880.

Bond, C. F., Atoum, A. O., & VanLeeuwen, M. D. (1996). Social impairment of complex learning in the wake of public embarrassment. *Basic and Applied Social Psychology, 18*, 31–44.

Bond, C. F., & Titus, L. J. (1983). Social facilitation: A meta-analysis of 241 studies. *Psychological Bulletin, 94*, 264–292.

Bond, M. H. (1996). Chinese values. In M. H. Bond (Ed.), *The handbook of Chinese psychology* (pp. 208–226). Hong Kong: Oxford University Press.

Bond, R., & Smith, P. B. (1996). Culture and conformity: A meta-analysis of studies using Asch's (1952b, 1956) Line Judgment task. *Psychological Bulletin, 119*, 111–137.

Bornstein, R. F. (1989). Exposure and affect: Overview and meta-analysis of research, 1968–1987. *Psychological Bulletin, 106*, 265–289.

Bornstein, R. F., & D'Agostino, P. R. (1992). Stimulus recognition and the mere exposure effect. *Journal of Personality and Social Psychology, 63*, 545–552.

Bornstein, R. F., & Pittman, T. S. (Eds.). (1992). *Perception without awareness: Cognitive, clinical, and social perspectives.* New York: Guilford.

Bowlby, J. (1969). *Attachment and loss: Vol. 1. Attachment.* New York: Basic Books.

Bowlby, J. (1973). *Attachment and loss: Vol. 2. Separation: Anxiety and anger.* New York: Basic Books.

Bowlby, J. (1980). *Attachment and loss: Vol. 3. Loss.* New York: Basic Books.

Bradley, J. P., Nicol, A. A. M., Charbonneau, D., & Meyer, J. P. (2002). Personality correlates of leadership development in Canadian Forces officer candidates. *Canadian Journal of Behavioural Science, 34*, 92–103.

Bradshaw, R. H., Bubier, N. E., & Sullivan, M. (1994). The effects of age and gender on perceived facial attractiveness: A reply to McLellan and McKelvie. *Canadian Journal of Behavioral Science, 26*, 199–204.

Branscombe, N. R., & Wann, D. L. (1992). Role of identification with a group, arousal, categorization processes, and self-esteem in sports spectator aggression. *Human Relations, 45*, 1013–1033.

Breckler, S. J., & Wiggins, E. C. (1989). On defining attitude and attitude theory: Once more with feeling. In A. R. Pratkanis, S. J. Breckler, & A. G. Greenwald (Eds.), *Attitude structure and function* (pp. 407–427). Hillsdale, NJ: Erlbaum.

Brehm, J. W. (1956). Postdecision changes in the desirability of alternatives. *Journal of Abnormal and Social Psychology, 52,* 384–389.

Brewer, M. B. (1979). In-group bias in the minimal intergroup situation: A cognitive-motivational analysis. *Psychological Bulletin, 86,* 307–324.

Brewer, M. B., & Brown, R. J. (1998). Intergroup relations. In D. Gilbert, S. Fiske, & G. Lindzey (Eds.), *The handbook of social psychology* (4th ed., Vol. 2, pp. 554–594). New York: McGraw-Hill.

Brewer, M. B., & Gardner, W. L. (1996). Who is this "we"? Levels of collective identity and self representations. *Journal of Personality and Social Psychology, 71,* 83–93.

Brewer, M. B., & Miller, N. (1984). Beyond the contact hypothesis: Theoretical perspectives on desegregation. In N. Miller & M. B. Brewer (Eds.), *Groups in contact: The psychology of desegregation* (pp. 281–302). New York: Academic Press.

Brigham, J. C. (1980). Limiting conditions of the "physical attractiveness stereotype": Attributions about divorce. *Journal of Research in Personality, 14,* 365–375.

Brock, T. C., Edelman, S., Edwards, S., & Schuck, J. (1965). Seven studies of performance expectancy as a determinant of actual performance. *Journal of Experimental Social Psychology, 1,* 295–310.

Brown, J. D. (1990). Evaluating one's abilities: Shortcuts and stumbling blocks on the road to self-knowledge. *Journal of Experimental Social Psychology, 26,* 149–167.

Brown, R. (1965). *Social psychology.* New York: Free Press.

Brown, R. (1986). *Social psychology: The second edition.* New York: Free Press.

Bui, K-V. T., Peplau, L. A., & Hill, C. T. (1996). Testing the Rusbult Model of relationship commitment and stability in a 15-year study of hetereosexual couples. *Personality and Social Psychology Bulletin, 22,* 1244–1257.

Burger, J. M. (1981). Motivational biases in the attribution of responsibility for an accident: A meta-analysis of the defensive-attribution hypothesis. *Psychological Bulletin, 90,* 496–512.

Burger, J. M. (1999). The foot-in-the-door compliance procedure: A multiple-process analysis and review. *Personality and Social Psychology Review, 3,* 303–325.

Burgoon, M. (1993). Interpersonal expectations, expectancy violations, and emotional communication. *Journal of Language and Social Psychology, 12,* 30–48.

Burleson, B. R. (1994). Friendship and similarities in social-cognitive and communicative abilities: Social skill bases of interpersonal attraction in childhood. *Personal Relationships, 1,* 371–389.

Burleson, B. R., & Samter, W. (1996). Similarity in the communication skills of young adults: Foundations of attraction, friendship, and relationship satisfaction. *Communication Reports, 9,* 127–139.

Burns, J. M. (1978). *Leadership.* New York: Harper Torchbooks.

Burnstein, E., & Sentis, K. (1981). Attitude polarization in groups. In R. E. Petty, T. M. Ostrom, & T. C. Brock (Eds.), *Cognitive responses in persuasion* (pp. 197–216). Hillsdale, NJ: Erlbaum.

Burnstein, E., & Vinokur, A. (1977). Persuasive argumentation and social comparison as determinants of attitude polarization. *Journal of Experimental Social Psychology, 13,* 315–332.

Burt, M. R. (1980). Cultural myths and supports for rape. *Journal of Personality and Social Psychology, 38,* 217–230.

Bushman, B. J., Baumeister, R. F., & Stack, A. D. (1999). Catharsis, aggression, and persuasive influence: Self-fulfilling or self-defeating prophecies? *Journal of Personality and Social Psychology, 76,* 367–376.

Buss, D. (1996). The evolutionary psychology of human social strategies. In E. T. Higgins & A. W. Kruglanski (Eds.), *Social psychology: Handbook of basic principles* (pp. 3–38). New York: Guilford.

Buss, D. (1996). Sexual conflict: Evolutionary insights into feminism and the "battle of the sexes." In D. Buss & N. Malamuth (Eds.), *Sex, power, conflict: Evolutionary and feminist perspectives* (pp. 296–318). New York: Oxford University Press.

Buss, D. M. (1985). Human mate selection. *American Scientist, 73,* 47–51.

Buss, D. M. (1988a). The evolution of human intrasexual competition. *Journal of Personality and Social Psychology, 54,* 616–628.

Buss, D. M. (1988b). Love acts: The evolutionary biology of love. In R. J. Sternberg & M. L. Barnes (Eds.), *The psychology of love* (pp. 110–118). New Haven, CT: Yale University Press.

Buss, D. M. (1999). *Evolutionary psychology: The new science of the mind.* Needham Heights, MA: Allyn & Bacon.

Buss, D. M., Abbott, M., Angleitner, A., Biaggio, A., Blanco-Villasenor, A., Bruchon-Schweitzer, M., Ch'u, H., Czapinski, J., Deraad, B., Ekehammar, B., El Lohamy, N., Fioravanti, M., Georgas, J., Gjerde, P., Guttman, R., Hazan, F., Iwawaki, S., Janakiramaiah, N., Khosroshani, F., Kreitler, S., Lachenicht, L., Lee, M., Liik, K., Little, B., Mika, S., Moadel-Shahid, M., Moane, G., Montero, M., Mundy-Castle, A. C., Niit, T., Nsenduluka, E., Pienkowski, R., Pirttila-Backman, A., Ponce de Leon, J., Rousseau, J., Runco, M., Safir, M. P., Samuels, C., Sanitioso, R., Serpell, R., Smid, N., Spencer, C., Tadinac, M., Todorova, E. N., Troland, K., Van Den Brande, L., Van Heck, G., Van Langenhove, L., & Yang, K. (1990). International preferences in selecting mates: A study of 37 cultures. *Journal of Cross-Cultural Psychology, 21,* 5–47.

Buss, D. M., & Barnes, M. (1986). Preferences in human mate selection. *Journal of Personality and Social Psychology, 50,* 559–570.

Buss, D. M., & Kenrick, D. T. (1998). Evolutionary social psychology. In D. Gilbert, S. Fiske, & G. Lindzey (Eds.), *The* handbook of social psychology (4th ed., Vol. 2, pp. 982–1026). New York: Random House.

Buss, D. M., & Schmitt, D. P. (1993). Sexual strategies theory: An evolutionary perspective on human mating. *Psychological Bulletin, 100,* 204–232.

Butler, D., & Geis, F. L. (1990). Nonverbal affect responses to male and female leaders: Implications for leadership evaluations. *Journal of Personality and Social Psychology, 58,* 48–59.

Button, C. M., & Collier, D. R. (1991, June). A comparison of people's concepts of love and romantic love. Paper presented at the Canadian Psychological Association Conference, Calgary, Alberta.

Buunk, B. P., & Prins, K. S. (1998). Loneliness, exchange orientation, and reciprocity in friendships. *Personal Relationships, 5,* 1–14.

Byrne, D., & Clore, G. L. (1970). A reinforcement model of evaluative processes. *Personality: An International Journal, 1,* 103–128.

Byrne, D., Clore, G. L., & Smeaton, G. (1986). The attraction hypothesis: Do similar attitudes affect anything? *Journal of Personality and Social Psychology, 51,* 1167–1170.

Byrne, D., & Nelson, D. (1965). Attraction as a linear function of positive reinforcement. *Journal of Personality and Social Psychology, 1,* 659–663.

Cadinu, M. R., & Rothbart, M. (1996). Self-anchoring and differentiation processes in minimal group setting. *Journal of Personality and Social Psychology, 70,* 661–677.

Campbell, D. T., & Stanley, J. C. (1967). *Experimental and quasi-experimental designs for research.* Chicago: Rand McNally.

Campbell, J. D. (1986). Similarity and uniqueness: The effects of attribute type, relevance, and individual differences in self-esteem and depression. *Journal of Personality and Social Psychology, 50,* 281–294.

Campbell, J. D. (1990). Self-esteem and clarity of the self-concept. *Journal of Personality and Social Psychology, 59,* 538–549.

Campbell, J. D., Assanand, S., & DiPaula, A. (2000). Structural features of the self-concept and adjustment. In A. Tesser, R. B. Felson, & J. M. Suls (Eds.), *Psychological perspectives on self and identity* (pp. 67–87). Washington, DC: American Psychological Association.

Campbell, J. D., Fairey, P. J., & Fehr, B. (1986). Better than me or better than thee? Reactions to intrapersonal and interpersonal performance feedback. *Journal of Personality, 54,* 479–493.

Campbell, J. D., & Fehr, B. (1990). Self-esteem and perceptions of conveyed impressions: Is negative affectivity associated with greater realism? *Journal of Personality and Social Psychology, 58,* 122–133.

Campbell, J. D., Trapnell, P. D., Heine, S. J., Katz, I. M., Lavallee, L. F., & Lehman, D. R. (1996). "Self-concept clarity: Measurement, personality correlates, and cultural boundaries":

Correction. *Journal of Personality and Social Psychology, 70,* 141–156.

Cantor, J., Bushman, B. J., Huesmann, L. R., Groebel, J., Malamuth, N. M., Impett, E. A., Donnerstein, E., & Smith, S. (2001). Some hazards of television viewing: Fears, aggression, and sexual attitudes. In D. G. Singer & J. L. Singer (Eds.), *Handbook of children and the media* (pp. 207–307). Thousand Oaks, CA: Sage.

Cantor, N., & Kihlstrom, J. F. (1987). *Personality and social intelligence.* Englewood Cliffs, NJ: Prentice Hall.

Carli, L. L. (1999). Cognitive reconstruction, hindsight, and reactions to victims and perpetrators. *Personality and Social Psychology Bulletin, 25,* 966–979.

Carli, L. L., & Eagly, A. H. (1999). Gender effects on social influence and emergent leadership. In G. N. Powell (Ed.), *Handbook of gender and work* (pp. 203–222). Thousand Oaks, CA: Sage.

Carlson, M., Charlin, V., & Miller, N. (1988). Positive mood and helping behavior: A test of six hypotheses. *Journal of Personality and Social Psychology, 55,* 211–229.

Carlson, M., & Miller, N. (1987). Explanation of the relationship between negative mood and helping. *Psychological Bulletin, 102,* 91–108.

Carlston, D. E., & Skowronski, J. J. (1994). Savings in the relearning of trait information as evidence of spontaneous inference generation. *Journal of Personality and Social Psychology, 66,* 840–856.

Carnevale, P. J. (1986). Strategic choice in mediation. *Negotiation Journal, 2,* 41–56.

Cartwright, D., & Zander, A. (Eds.). (1968). *Group dynamics: Research and theory* (3rd ed.). New York: Harper & Row.

Carver, C. S. (2003). Self-awareness. In M. R. Leary & J. P. Tangney (Eds.), *Handbook of self and identity* (pp. 179–196). New York: Guilford Press.

Carver, C. S., & Scheier, M. F. (1981). *Attention and self-regulation: A control-theory approach to human behavior.* New York: Springer-Verlag.

Cate, R. M., & Lloyd, S. A. (1992). *Courtship.* Newbury Park, CA: Sage.

Chaiken, S. (1980). Heuristic versus systematic information processing and the use of source versus message cues in persuasion. *Journal of Personality and Social Psychology, 39,* 752–766.

Chaiken, S. (1987). The heuristic model of persuasion. In M. P. Zanna, J. M. Olson, & C. P. Herman (Eds.), *Social influence: The Ontario Symposium* (Vol. 5, pp. 3–39). Hillsdale, NJ: Erlbaum.

Chaiken, S., & Baldwin, M. W. (1981). Affective–cognitive consistency and the effect of salient behavioral information on the self perception of attitudes. *Journal of Personality and Social Psychology, 41,* 1–12.

Chaiken, S., Liberman, A., & Eagly, A. H. (1989). Heuristic and systematic information processing within and beyond the persuasion context. In J. S. Uleman & J. A. Bargh (Eds.), *Unintended thought* (pp. 212–252). New York: Guilford Press.

Chaiken, S., Wood, W., & Eagly, A. H. (1996). Principles of persuasion. In E. T. Higgins & A. W. Kruglanski (Eds.), *Social psychology: Handbook of basic principles* (pp. 702–742). New York: Guilford.

Chang, C., & Chen, J. (1995). Effects of different motivation strategies on reducing social loafing. *Chinese Journal of Psychology, 37,* 71–81.

Chapman, G. B., & Bornstein, B. H. (1996). The more you ask for, the more you get: Anchoring in personal injury verdicts. *Applied Cognitive Psychology, 10,* 519–540.

Chassin, L., Presson, C. G., & Sherman, S. J. (1990). Social psychological contributions to the understanding and prevention of adolescent cigarette smoking. *Personality and Social Psychology Bulletin, 16,* 133–151.

Cheadle, B. (2005, January 17). Volunteers recall grim work for Martin. *Winnipeg Free Press,* www.winnipegfreepress.com (accessed February 10, 2005).

Chemers, M. M. (2000). Leadership research and theory: A functional integration. *Group Dynamics: Theory, Research, and Practice, 4,* 27–43.

Chen, S., & Andersen, S. M. (1999). Relationships from the past in the present: Significant-other representations and transference in interpersonal life. In M. P. Zanna (Ed.), *Advances in experimental social psychology* (Vol. 31, pp. 123–190). San Diego, CA: Academic Press.

Chen, S., & Chaiken, S. (1999). The heuristic-systematic model in its broader context. In S. Chaiken & Y. Trope (Eds.), *Dual-process theories in social psychology* (pp. 73–96). New York: Guilford Press.

Chiu, C., Morris, M. W., Hong, Y., & Menon, T. (2000). Motivated cultural cognition: The impact of implicit cultural theories on dispositional attribution varies as a function of need for closure. *Journal of Personality and Social Psychology, 78,* 247–259.

Christensen, L. (1988). Deception in psychological research: When is its use justified? *Personality and Social Psychology Bulletin, 14,* 664–675.

Church, A. H. (1993). Estimating the effects of incentives on mail survey response rates: A meta-analysis. *Public Opinion Quarterly, 57,* 62–79.

Cialdini, R. B. (1993). *Influence: Science and practice* (3rd ed.). New York: HarperCollins.

Cialdini, R. B., Cacioppo, J., Basset, R., & Miller, J. (1978). Low-ball procedure for producing compliance: Commitment then cost. *Journal of Personality and Social Psychology, 36,* 463–476.

Cialdini, R. B., Darby, B. L., & Vincent, J. E. (1973). Transgression and altruism: A case for hedonism. *Journal of Experimental Social Psychology, 9,* 502–516.

Cialdini, R. B., & Fultz, J. (1990). Interpreting the negative mood-helping literature via "mega"-analysis: A contrary view. *Psychological Bulletin, 107,* 210–214.

Cialdini, R. B., Green, B. L., & Rusch, A. J. (1992). When tactical pronouncements of change become real change: The case of reciprocal persuasion. *Journal of Personality and Social Psychology, 63,* 30–40.

Cialdini, R. B., Kallgren, C. A., & Reno, R. R. (1991). A focus theory of normative conduct: A theoretical refinement and reevaluation of the role of norms in human behavior. In M. P. Zanna (Ed.), *Advances in experimental social psychology* (Vol. 24, pp. 201–234). San Diego, CA: Academic Press.

Cialdini, R. B., Reno, R. R., & Kallgren, C. A. (1990). A focus theory of normative conduct: Recycling the concept of norms to reduce littering in public places. *Journal of Personality and Social Psychology, 58,* 1015–1026.

Cialdini, R. B., Schaller, M., Houlihan, D., Arps, K., Fultz, J., & Beaman, A. L. (1987). Empathy-based helping: Is it selflessly or selfishly motivated? *Journal of Personality and Social Psychology, 52,* 749–758.

Cialdini, R. B., & Trost, M. R. (1998). Social influence: Social norms, conformity, and compliance. In D. Gilbert, S. Fiske, & G. Lindzey (Eds.), *The handbook of social psychology* (4th ed., Vol. 2, pp. 151–192). New York: McGraw-Hill.

Cialdini, R. B., Trost, M. R., & Newsom, J. T. (1995). Preference for consistency: The development of a valid measure and the discovery of surprising behavioral implications. *Journal of Personality and Social Psychology, 69,* 318–328.

Cialdini, R. B., Vincent, J. E., Lewis, S. K., Catalan, J., Wheeler, D., & Darby, B. L. (1975). Reciprocal concessions procedure for inducing compliance: The door-in-the-face technique. *Journal of Personality and Social Psychology, 31,* 206–215.

Clark, K., & Clark, M. (1947). Racial identification and preference in Negro children. In T. M. Newcomb & E. L. Hartley (Eds.), *Readings in social psychology* (pp. 169–178). New York: Holt.

Clark, M. S. (1984). Record keeping in two types of relationships. *Journal of Personality and Social Psychology, 47,* 549–577.

Clark, M. S. (1986). Evidence of the effectiveness of manipulations of communal and exchange relationships. *Personality and Social Psychology Bulletin, 12,* 414–425.

Clark, M. S., & Isen, A. M. (1982). Toward understanding the relationship between feeling states and social behavior. In A. H. Hastorf & A. M. Isen (Eds.), *Cognitive social psychology* (pp. 73–108). New York: Elsevier.

Clark, M. S., & Mills, J. (1979). Interpersonal attraction in exchange and communal relationships. *Journal of Personality and Social Psychology, 37,* 12–24.

Clark, M. S., & Mills, J. (1993). The difference between communal and exchange relationships: What it is and is not. *Personality and Social Psychology Bulletin, 19,* 684–691.

Clark, M. S., & Pataki, S. P. (1995). Interpersonal processes influencing attraction and relationships. In A. Tesser (Ed.), *Advanced Social Psychology* (pp. 282–331). New York: McGraw-Hill.

Clark, M. S., & Waddell, B. (1985). Perception of exploitation in communal and exchange relationships. *Journal of Social and Personal Relationships, 2,* 403–413.

Clark, R. D., III, & Maass, A. (1988). The role of social categorization and perceived source credibility in minority influence. *European Journal of Social Psychology, 18,* 347–364.

Clark, R. D., III, & Word, L. E. (1972). Why don't bystanders help? Because of ambiguity? *Journal of Personality and Social Psychology, 24,* 392–400.

Coats, E. (1998). www.stolaf.edu/cgi-bin/mailarchivesearch.pl?directory=/home/www/people/huff/SPSP&listname=archive98

Cohn, E. G. (1987). Changing the domestic violence policies of urban police departments: Impact of the Minneapolis experiment. *Responses to the Victimization of Women and Children, 10,* 22–24.

Collins, N. L., & Read, S. J. (1990). Adult attachment, working models, and relationship quality in dating couples. *Journal of Personality and Social Psychology, 58,* 644–663.

Collins, R. L. (1996). For better or worse: The impact of upward social comparison on self-evaluations. *Psychological Bulletin, 119,* 51–69.

Collins, W. A., & Sroufe, L. A. (1999). Capacity for intimate relationships: A developmental construction. In W. Furman, C. Feiring, & B. B. Brown (Eds.), *Contemporary perspectives on adolescent romantic relationships.* New York: Cambridge University Press.

Condon, J. W., & Crano, W. D. (1988). Inferred evaluation and the relation between attitude similarity and interpersonal attraction. *Journal of Personality and Social Psychology, 54,* 789–797.

Conway, M., & Dubé, L. (2002). Humor in persuasion on threatening topics: Effectiveness is a function of audience sex role orientation. *Personality and Social Psychology Bulletin, 28,* 863–873.

Cook, S. W. (1984). Cooperative interaction in multiethnic contexts. In N. Miller & M. Brewer (Eds.), *Groups in contact: The psychology of desegregation.* New York: Academic Press.

Cook, S. W. (1985). Experimenting on social issues: The case of school desegregation. *American Psychologist, 40,* 452–460.

Cooley, C. H. (1902). *Human nature and social order.* New York: Scribner's.

Corenblum, B., & Annis, R. (1993). Development of racial identity in minority and majority children: An affect discrepancy model. *Canadian Journal of Behavioral Science, 25,* 499–521.

Corenblum, B., & Stephan, W. G. (2001). White fears and Native apprehensions: An integrated threat theory approach to intergroup attitudes. *Canadian Journal of Behavioural Science, 33,* 251–268.

Correll, J., Park, P., Judd, C. M., & Wittenbrink, B. (2002). The police officer's dilemma: Using ethnicity to disambiguate potentially threatening individuals. *Journal of Personality and Social Psychology, 83,* 1314–1329.

Cosmides, L., & Tooby, J. (1992). Cognitive adaptations for social exchange. In J. H. Barkow, L. Cosmides, & J. Tooby (Eds.), *The adapted mind: Evolutionary psychology and the generation of culture* (pp. 163–228). New York: Oxford University Press.

Cottrell, N. B. (1968). Performance in the presence of other human beings: Mere presence, audience, and affiliation effects. In E. C. Simmel, R. A. Hoppe, & G. A. Milton (Eds.), *Social facilitation and imitative behavior* (pp. 91–110). Boston: Allyn & Bacon.

Cottrell, N. B., Wack, K. L., Sekerak, G. J., & Rittle, R. (1968). Social facilitation in dominant responses by the presence of an audience and the mere presence of others. *Journal of Personality and Social Psychology, 9,* 245–250.

Courneya, K. S., & Friedenreich, C. M. (1997). Determinants of exercise during colorectal cancer treatment: An application of the theory of planned behavior. *Oncology Nursing Forum, 24,* 1715–1723.

Courneya, K. S., & Friedenreich, C. M. (1999). Utility of the theory of planned behavior for understanding exercise during breast cancer treatment. *Psycho-Oncology, 8,* 112–122.

Craig, W. M., & Pepler, D. J. (1997). Observations of bullying and victimization in the school yard. *Canadian Journal of School Psychology, 13,* 41–60.

Crandall, C. S., D'Anello, S., Sakalli, N., Lazarus, E., Wieczorkowska, G., & Feather, N. T. (2001). An attribution-value model of prejudice: Anti-fat attitudes in six nations. *Personality and Social Psychology Bulletin, 27,* 30–37.

Crites, S. L., Jr., Fabrigar, L. R., & Petty, R. E. (1994). Measuring the affective and cognitive properties of attitudes: Conceptual and methodological issues. *Personality and Social Psychology Bulletin, 20,* 619–634.

Crocker, J., & Major, B. (1989). Social stigma and self-esteem: The self-protective properties of stigma. *Psychological Review, 96,* 608–630.

Cross, S. E., Bacon, P. L., & Morris, M. L. (2000). The relational-interdependent self-construal and relationships. *Journal of Personality and Social Psychology, 78,* 791–808.

Cross, S. E., & Gore, J. S. (2003). Cultural models of the self. In M. R. Leary & J. P. Tangney (Eds.), *Handbook of self and identity* (pp. 536–566). New York: Guilford Press.

Cross, S. E., & Madson, L. (1997). Elaboration of models of the self: Reply to Baumeister and Sommer (1997) and Martin and Rubble (1997). *Psychological Bulletin, 122,* 51–55.

Cross, S. E., & Madson, L. (1997). Models of the self: Self-construals and gender. *Psychological Bulletin, 122,* 5–37.

Crowley, A. E., & Hoyer, W. D. (1994). An integrative framework for understanding two-sided persuasion. *Journal of Consumer Research, 20,* 561–574.

Croyle, R. T., & Jemmott, J. B., III. (1990). Psychological reactions to risk factor testing. In J. A. Skelton & R. T. Croyle (Eds.), *The mental representation of health and illness (pp. 121–157). New York: Springer-Verlag.

Crutchfield, R. A. (1955). Conformity and character. *American Psychologist, 10,* 191–198.

Csikszentmihalyi, M., & Figurski, T. J. (1982). Self-awareness and aversive experience in everyday life. *Journal of Personality, 50,* 15–28.

Cunningham, M. R. (1986). Measuring the physical in physical attractiveness: Quasi-experiments on the sociobiology of female facial beauty. *Journal of Personality and Social Psychology, 50,* 925–935.

Cunningham, M. R., Barbee, A. R., & Pike, C. L. (1990). What do women want? Facialmetric assessment of multiple motives in the perception of male facial physical attractiveness. *Journal of Personality and Social Psychology, 59,* 61–72.

Cunningham, M. R., Roberts, A. R., Barbee, A. P., Druen, P. B., & Wu, C. (1995). "Their ideas of beauty are, on the whole, the same as ours": Consistency and variability in the cross-cultural perception of female physical attractiveness. *Journal of Personality and Social Psychology, 68,* 261–279.

Curtis, R. C., & Miller, K. (1986). Believing another likes or dislikes you: Behaviors making the beliefs come true. *Journal of Personality and Social Psychology, 51,* 284–290.

Czaczkes, B., & Ganzach, Y. (1996). The natural selection of prediction heuristics: Anchoring and adjustment versus representativeness. *Journal of Behavioral Decision Making, 9,* 125–139.

Dahl, D. W., Gorn, G. J., & Weinberg, C. B. (1998). Condom carrying behavior among college students. *Canadian Journal of Public Health, 89,* 368–370.

D'Angelo, A. M. (2000, February 14). No charges in bridge fall. *North Shore News.* www.nsnews.com/issues00/w021400/02110001.html

Darley, J. M. (1995). Constructive and destructive obedience: A taxonomy of principal-agent relationships. *Journal of Social Issues, 51,* 125–154.

Darley, J. M., & Akert, R. M. (1993). *Biographical interpretation: The influence of later events in life on the meaning of and memory for earlier events.* Unpublished manuscript, Princeton University.

Darley, J. M., & Batson, C. D. (1973). From Jerusalem to Jericho: A study of situational and dispositional variables in helping behavior. *Journal of Personality and Social Psychology, 27,* 100–108.

Darley, J. M., & Latané, B. (1968). Bystander intervention in emergencies: Diffusion of responsibility. *Journal of Personality and Social Psychology, 8,* 377–383.

Darwin, C. R. (1859). *The origin of species.* London: John Murray.

Dasgupta, N., & Greenwald, A. G. (2001). On the malleability of automatic attitudes: Combating automatic prejudice with images of admired and disliked individuals. *Journal of Personality and Social Psychology, 61,* 800–814.

Davidson, A. R., & Jaccard, J. J. (1979). Variables that moderate the attitude behavior relation: Results of a longitudinal survey. *Journal of Personality and Social Psychology, 37,* 1364–1376.

Davis, D. D., & Harless, D. W. (1996). Group versus individual performance in a price-searching experiment. *Organizational Behavior and Human Decision Processes, 66,* 215–227.

Davis, K. E., & Jones, E. E. (1960). Changes in interpersonal perception as a means of reducing cognitive dissonance. *Journal of Abnormal and Social Psychology, 61,* 402–410.

Davis, M. H., & Stephan, W. G. (1980). Attributions for exam performance. *Journal of Applied Social Psychology, 10,* 235–248.

Davison, K. P., Pennebaker, J. W., & Dickerson, S. S. (2000). Who talks? The social psychology of illness support groups. *American Psychologist, 55,* 205–217.

Davitz, J. (1952). The effects of previous training on post-frustration behavior. *Journal of Abnormal and Social Psychology, 47,* 309–315.

Dawes, R. M. (1998). Behavioral decision making and judgment. In D. Gilbert, S. Fiske, & G. Lindzey (Eds.), *The handbook of social psychology* (4th ed., Vol. 1, pp. 497–548). New York: McGraw Hill.

De Dreu, C. K. W., Harinck, F., & Van Vianen, A. E. M. (1999). Conflict and performance in groups and organizations. In C. L. Cooper & I. T. Robertson (Eds.), *International review of industrial and organizational psychology* (Vol. 14, pp. 369–414). Chichester, England: American Ethnological Press.

De Dreu, C. K. W., Weingart, L. R., & Kwon, S. (2000). Influence of social motives on integrative negotiation: A meta-analytic review and test of two theories. *Journal of Personality and Social Psychology, 78,* 889–905.

De Waal, F. (1996). *Good natured: The origins of right and wrong in humans and other animals.* Cambridge, MA: Harvard University Press.

Dean, K. E., & Malamuth N. M. (1997). Characteristics of men who aggress sexually and of men who imagine aggressing: Risk and moderating variables. *Journal of Personality and Social Psychology, 72,* 499–455.

Deaux, K. (1993). Reconstructing social identity. *Personality and Social Psychology Bulletin, 19,* 4–12.

Deaux, K., & Hanna, R. (1984). Courtship in the personals column: The influence of gender and sexual orientation. *Sex Roles, 11,* 363–375.

Deaux, K., & LaFrance, M. (1998). Gender. In D. T. Gilbert, S. T. Fiske, & G. Lindzey (Eds.), *The handbook of social psychology* (4th ed., Vol. 1, pp. 788–828). New York: McGraw-Hill.

DeBono, K. G., & Snyder, M. (1995). Acting on one's attitudes: The role of a history of choosing situations. *Personality and Social Psychology Bulletin, 21,* 629–636.

DeJong, W., & Winsten, J. A. (1989). *Recommendations for future mass media campaigns to prevent preteen and adolescent substance abuse.* Unpublished manuscript, Center for Health Communication, Harvard School of Public Health.

Desmond, E. W. (1987, November 30). Out in the open. *Time,* pp. 80–90.

Desportes, J. P., & Lemaine, J. M. (1988). The sizes of human groups: An analysis of their distributions. In D. Canter, J. C.

Jesuino, L. Soczka, & G. M. Stephenson (Eds.), *Environmental social psychology* (pp. 57–65). Dordrecht, Netherlands: Kluwer.

Deutsch, M. (1973). *The resolution of conflict: Constructive and destructive processes.* New Haven, CT: Yale University Press.

Deutsch, M. (1990). Cooperation, conflict, and justice. In S. A. Wheelan, E. A. Pepitone, & V. Abt (Eds.), *Advances in field theory* (pp. 149–164). Newbury Park, CA: Sage.

Deutsch, M. (1997). Comments on cooperation and prejudice reduction. At the symposium on Reflections on 100 Years of Social Psychology, April 1997, Yosemite National Park, CA.

Deutsch, M., & Gerard, H. G. (1955). A study of normative and informational social influence upon individual judgment. *Journal of Abnormal and Social Psychology, 51,* 629–636.

Deutsch, M., & Krauss, R. M. (1960). The effect of threat upon interpersonal bargaining. *Journal of Abnormal and Social Psychology, 61,* 181–189.

Deutsch, M., & Krauss, R. M. (1962). Studies of interpersonal bargaining. *Journal of Conflict Resolution, 6,* 52–76.

Devine, P. G. (1989a). Automatic and controlled processes in prejudice: The roles of stereotypes and personal beliefs. In A. R. Pratkanis, S. J. Breckler, & A. G. Greenwald (Eds.), *Attitude structure and function* (pp. 181–212). Hillsdale, NJ: Erlbaum.

Devine, P. G. (1989b). Stereotypes and prejudice: Their automatic and controlled components. *Journal of Personality and Social Psychology, 56,* 5–18.

Devine, P. G. (2003). A modern perspective on the classic American dilemma. *Psychological Inquiry, 14,* 244–250.

Dickerson, C., Thibodeau, R., Aronson, E., & Miller, D. (1992). Using cognitive dissonance to encourage water conservation. *Journal of Applied Social Psychology, 22,* 841–854.

Diener, E. (1980). Deindividuation: The absence of self-awareness and self-regulation in group members. In P. B. Paulus (Ed.), *Psychology of group influence* (pp. 209–242). Hillsdale, NJ: Erlbaum.

Diener, E., & Wallbom, M. (1976). Effects of self-awareness on antinormative behavior. *Journal of Research in Personality, 10,* 107–111.

Dienesch, R. M., & Liden, R. C. (1986). Leader-member exchange model of leadership: A critique and further development. *Academy of Management Review, 11,* 618–634.

Dijksterhuis, A., & van Knippenberg, A. (1996). The knife that cuts both ways: Facilitated and inhibited access to traits as a result of stereotype activation. *Journal of Experimental Social Psychology, 32,* 271–288.

Dillard, J. P. (1991). The current status of research on sequential-request compliance techniques. *Personality and Social Psychology Bulletin, 17,* 283–288.

Dion, C. (2000). *My story, my dream.* Toronto, ON: HarperCollins.

Dion, K., Berscheid, E., & Walster (Hatfield), E. (1972). What is beautiful is good. *Journal of Personality and Social Psychology, 24,* 285–290.

Dion, K. K. (2002). Cultural perspectives on facial attractiveness. In G. Rhodes (Ed.), *Facial attractiveness: Evolutionary, cognitive, and social perspectives* (pp. 239–259). Westport, CT: Ablex Publishing.

Dion, K. K., & Dion, K. L. (1996). Cultural perspectives on romantic love. *Personal Relationships, 3,* 5–17.

Dion, K. K., & Dion, K. L. (2001a). Gender and relationships. In R. K. Unger (Ed.), *Handbook of the psychology of women and gender* (pp. 256–271). New York: John Wiley & Sons.

Dion, K. K., & Dion, K. L. (2001b). Gender and cultural adaptation in immigrant families. *Journal of Social Issues, 57,* 511–521.

Dion, K. L. (2001). Immigrants' perceptions of discrimination in Toronto: The Housing New Canadians project. *Journal of Social Issues, 57,* 523–539.

Dion, K. L., & Dion, K. K. (1973). Correlates of romantic love. *Journal of Consulting and Clinical Psychology, 41,* 51–56.

Dion, K. L., & Dion, K. K. (1993). Gender and ethnocultural comparisons in styles of love. *Psychology of Women Quarterly, 17,* 463–473.

Dion, K. L., & Kawakami, K. (1996). Ethnicity and perceived discrimination in Toronto: Another look at the personal/group discrimination discrepancy. *Canadian Journal of Behavioural Science, 28,* 203–213.

Dittman, M. (2004, October). What makes good people do bad things? *Monitor on Psychology,* 68–69.

Dix, T. (1993). Attributing dispositions to children: An interactional analysis of attribution in socialization. *Personality and Social Psychology Bulletin, 19,* 633–643.

Dolin, D. J., & Booth-Butterfield, S. (1995). Foot-in-the-door and cancer prevention. *Health Communication, 7,* 55–66.

Dollard, J., Doob, L., Miller, N., Mowrer, O. H., & Sears, R. R. (1939). *Frustration and aggression.* New Haven, CT: Yale University Press.

Donnerstein, E. (1980). Aggressive erotica and violence against women. *Journal of Personality and Social Psychology, 39,* 269–272.

Donnerstein, E., & Berkowitz, L. (1981). Victim reactions in aggressive erotic films as a factor in violence against women. *Journal of Personality and Social Psychology, 41,* 710–724.

Donnerstein, E., & Donnerstein, M. (1976). Research in the control of interracial aggression. In R. G. Green & E. C. O'Neal (Eds.), *Perspectives on aggression* (pp. 133–168). New York: Academic Press.

Donnerstein, E., & Linz, D. (1994). Sexual violence in the mass media. In M. Costanzo, S. Oskamp et al. (Eds.), *Violence and the law: Claremont symposium on applied social psychology, Vol. 7* (pp. 9–36). Thousand Oaks, CA: Sage.

Double deception [Letter to the editor]. (2000, April 1). *Winnipeg Free Press.*

Dougherty, M. R. P., Gettys, C. F., & Ogden, E. E. (1999). MINERVA-DM: A memory process model of judgments of likelihood. *Psychological Review, 106,* 180–209.

Dovidio, J. F. (1984). Helping behavior and altruism: An empirical and conceptual overview. In L. Berkowitz (Ed.), *Advances in experimental social psychology* (Vol. 17, pp. 361–427). New York: Academic Press.

Dovidio, J. F., Evans, N., & Tyler, R. B. (1986). Racial stereotypes: The contents of their cognitive representations. *Journal of Experimental Social Psychology, 22,* 22–37.

Dovidio, J. F., & Gaertner, S. L. (1996). Affirmative action, unintentional racial biases, and intergroup relations. *Journal of Social Issues, 52,* 51–75.

Dovidio, J. F., Piliavin, J. A., Gaertner, S. I., Schroeder, D. A., & Clark, R. D. III. (1991). The arousal: cost-reward model and the process of intervention. In M. S. Clark (Ed.), *Review of personality and social psychology* (Vol. 12, pp. 86–118). Newbury Park, CA: Sage.

Drigotas, S. M., Safstrom, C. A., & Gentilia, T. (1999). An investment model of dating infidelity. *Journal of Personality and Social Psychology, 77,* 509–524.

Dryer, D. C., & Horowitz, L. M. (1997). When do opposites attract? Interpersonal complementarity versus similarity. *Journal of Personality and Social Psychology, 72,* 592–603.

Duck, J., Hogg, M., & Terry, D. (1995). Me, us and them: Political identification and the third-person effect in the 1993 Australian federal election. *European Journal of Social Psychology, 25,* 195–215.

Dugas, D. (2005, January 14). Canadians opened wallets in record numbers: Polls. *Winnipeg Free Press,* p. A14.

Dutton, D. G., & Aron, A. P. (1974). Some evidence for heightened sexual attraction under conditions of high anxiety. *Journal of Personality and Social Psychology, 30,* 510–517.

Duval, S., & Wicklund, R. A. (1972). *A theory of objective self-awareness.* New York: Academic Press.

Duval, T. S., & Silvia, P. J. (2002). Self-awareness, probability of improvement, and the self-serving bias. *Journal of Personality and Social Psychology, 82,* 49–61.

Eagly, A. H. (1987). *Sex differences in social behavior: A social-role interpretation.* Hillsdale, NJ: Erlbaum.

Eagly, A. H., Ashmore, R. D., Makhijani, M. G., & Longo, L. C. (1991). What is beautiful is good, but . . . : A meta-analytic review of research on the physical attractiveness stereotype. *Psychological Bulletin, 110,* 109–128.

Eagly, A. H., & Chaiken, S. (1975). An attribution analysis of communicator characteristics on opinion change: The case of communicator attractiveness. *Journal of Personality and Social Psychology, 32,* 136–244.

Eagly, A. H., & Chaiken, S. (1993). *The psychology of attitudes.* Fort Worth, TX: Harcourt Brace Jovanovich.

Eagly, A. H., & Chaiken, S. (1998). Attitude structure and function. In D. T. Gilbert, S. T. Fiske, & G. Lindzey (Eds.), *The handbook of social psychology* (4th ed., Vol. 1, pp. 269–322). New York: McGraw-Hill.

Eagly, A. H., & Crowley, M. (1986). Gender and helping behavior: A meta-analytic review of the social psychological literature. *Psychological Bulletin, 100,* 283–308.

Eagly, A. H., & Karau, S. J. (2002). Role congruity theory of prejudice toward female leaders. *Psychological Review, 109,* 573–598.

Eagly, A. H., Karau, S. J., & Makhijani, M. G. (1995). Gender and the effectiveness of leaders: A meta-analysis. *Psychological Bulletin, 117,* 125–145.

Eagly, A. H., Makhijani, M. G., & Klonsky, B. G. (1992). Gender and the evaluation of leaders: A meta-analysis. *Psychological Bulletin, 111,* 3–22.

Eargle, A., Guerra, N., & Tolan, P. (1994). Preventing aggression in inner-city children: Small group training to change cognitions, social skills, and behavior. *Journal of Child and Adolescent Group Therapy, 4,* 229–242.

Edmonds, S. (2000, May 5). Judge agrees anthrax vaccine unsafe. *The Canadian Press.* www.canoe.ca/Health0005/05_ anthrax.html (accessed July 26, 2000).

Educators for Social Responsibility. (2001). *About the Resolving Conflict Creatively Program.* www.esrnational.org/about-rccp.html.

Edwards, D. J. A. (1975). Returning a dropped object: Effect of response cost and number of potential helpers. *Journal of Social Psychology, 97,* 169–171.

Edwards, K. (1990). The interplay of affect and cognition in attitude formation and change. *Journal of Personality and Social Psychology, 59,* 202–216.

Edwards, K., & von Hippel, W. (1995). Hearts and minds: The priority of affective versus cognitive factors in person perception. *Personality and Social Psychology Bulletin, 21,* 996–1011.

Ekos Research Associates and Canadian Policy Research Networks. (1999, April). *Analysis of Volunteering: Results from the 1997 National Survey of Giving, Volunteering and Participating.* Applied Research Branch: Strategic Policy, Human Resources Canada.

Elig, T. W., & Frieze, I. H. (1979). Measuring causal attributions for success and failure. *Journal of Personality and Social Psychology, 38,* 270–277.

Elliot, J. (1977). The power and pathology of prejudice. In P. Zimbardo & F. Ruch (Eds.), *Psychology and life* (9th ed., diamond printing). Glenview, IL: Scott Foresman.

Ellsworth, P. C., & Mauro, R. (1998). Psychology and law. In D. Gilbert, S. Fiske, & G. Lindzey (Eds.), *The handbook of social psychology* (4th ed., Vol. 2, pp. 684–732). New York: McGraw Hill.

Emery, R. E., & Wyer, M. M. (1987). Divorce mediation. *American Psychologist, 42,* 472–480.

Endo, Y., Heine, S. J., & Lehman, D. R. (2000). Culture and positive illusions in close relationships: How my relationships are better than yours. *Personality and Social Psychology Bulletin, 26,* 1571–1586.

Eron, L. D. (1982). Parent-child interaction, television violence, and aggression of children. *American Psychologist, 37,* 197–211.

Eron, L. D. (1987). The development of aggressive behavior from the perspective of a developing behaviorism. *American Psychologist, 42,* 425–442.

Eron, L. D., Huesmann, L. R., Lefkowitz, M. M., & Walder, L. O. (1996). Does television violence cause aggression? In D. F. Greenberg (Ed.), *Criminal careers, 2*, 311–321. The International Library of Criminology, Criminal Justice, and Penology. Aldershot, England: Dartmouth Publishing Company Limited.

Esser, J. K. (1998). Alive and well after 25 years: A review of groupthink research. *Organizational Behavior and Human Decision Processes, 73*, 116–141.

Esses, V. M., & Gardner, R. C. (1996). Multiculturalism in Canada: Context and current status. *Canadian Journal of Behavioural Science, 28*, 145–152.

Esses, V. M., Haddock, G., & Zanna, M. P. (1993). Values, stereotypes, and emotions as determinants of intergroup attitudes. In D. M. Mackie & D. L. Hamilton (Eds.), *Affect, cognition, and stereotyping: Interactive processes in group perception*. San Diego, CA: Academic Press, Inc.

Esses, V. M., & Zanna, M. P. (1995). Mood and the expression of ethnic stereotypes. *Journal of Personality and Social Psychology, 69*, 1052–1068.

Estabrooks, P., & Carron, A. V. (1999). The influence of the group with elderly exercisers. *Small Group Research, 30*, 438–452.

Ester, C. (1995). Responding to school violence: Understanding today for tomorrow. *Canadian Journal of School Psychology, 11*, 108–116.

Estrada-Hollenbeck, M., & Heatherton, T. F. (1998). Avoiding and alleviating guilt through prosocial behavior. In J. Bybee (Ed.), *Guilt and children* (pp. 215–231). San Diego, CA: Academic Press.

Fabrigar, L. R., & Petty, R. E. (1999). The role of affective and cognitive bases of attitudes in susceptibility to affectively and cognitively based persuasion. *Personality and Social Psychology Bulletin, 25*, 363–381.

Fabrigar, L. R., Priester, J. R., Petty, R. E., & Wegener, D. T. (1998). The impact of attitude accessibility on elaboration of persuasive messages. *Personality and Social Psychology Bulletin, 24*, 339–352.

Falck, R., & Craig, R. (1988). Classroom-oriented, primary prevention programming for drug abuse. *Journal of Psychoactive Drugs, 20*, 403–408.

Fazio, R. H. (1990). Multiple processes by which attitudes guide behavior: The MODE model as an integrative framework. In M. P. Zanna (Ed.), *Advances in experimental social psychology* (Vol. 23, pp. 75–109). San Diego, CA: Academic Press.

Feeney, J. A., & Noller, P. (1990). Attachment style as a predictor of adult romantic relationships. *Journal of Personality and Social Psychology, 58*, 281–291.

Fehr, B. (1988). Prototype analysis of the concepts of love and commitment. *Journal of Personality and Social Psychology, 55*, 557–579.

Fehr, B. (1993). How do I love thee? Let me consult my prototype. In S. Duck (Ed.), *Individuals in relationships* (pp. 87–120). Newbury Park, CA: Sage.

Fehr, B. (1994). Prototype-based assessment of laypeople's views of love. *Personal Relationships, 1*, 309–331.

Fehr, B. (1996). *Friendship processes*. Thousand Oaks, CA: Sage Publications.

Fehr, B., & Broughton, R. (2001). Gender and personality differences in conceptions of love: An interpersonal theory analysis.

Fehr, B., & Russell, J. A. (1991). The concept of love viewed from a prototype perspective. *Journal of Personality and Social Psychology, 60*, 425–438.

Feingold, A. (1992a). Good-looking people are not what we think. *Psychological Bulletin, 111*, 304–341.

Felmlee, D. H. (1995). Fatal attractions: Affection and dissatisfaction in intimate relationships. *Journal of Social and Personal Relationships, 12*, 295–311.

Ferguson, M. J., & Bargh, J. A. (2004). How social perception can automatically influence behavior. *Trends in Cognitive Sciences, 8*, 33-39.

Festinger, L. (1954). A theory of social comparison processes. *Human Relations, 7*, 117–140.

Festinger, L. (1957). *A theory of cognitive dissonance*. Stanford, CA: Stanford University Press.

Festinger, L., & Carlsmith, J. M. (1959). Cognitive consequences of forced compliance. *Journal of Abnormal and Social Psychology, 58*, 203–211.

Festinger, L., & Maccoby, N. (1964). On resistance to persuasive communications. *Journal of Abnormal and Social Psychology, 68*, 359–366.

Festinger, L., Riecken, H. W., & Schachter, S. (1956). *When prophecy fails*. Minneapolis: University of Minnesota Press.

Festinger, L., Schachter, S., & Back, K. (1950). *Social pressures in informal groups: A study of human factors in housing*. New York: Harper & Bros.

Fiedler, F. (1967). *A theory of leadership effectiveness*. New York: McGraw-Hill.

Fiedler, F. (1978). The contingency model and the dynamics of the leadership process. In L. Berkowitz (Ed.), *Advances in experimental social psychology* (Vol. 11, pp. 59–112). Orlando, FL: Academic Press.

Fincham, F. D., & Bradbury, T. N. (1993). Marital satisfaction, depression, and attributions: A longitudinal analysis. *Journal of Personality and Social Psychology, 64*, 442–452.

Fink, B., & Penton-Voak, I. (2002). Evolutionary psychology of facial attractiveness. *Current Directions in Psychological Science, 11*, 154–158.

Finney, P. D. (1987). When consent information refers to risk and deception: Implications for social research. *Journal of Social Behavior and Personality, 2*, 37–48.

Fischer, W. F. (1963). Sharing in preschool children as a function of amount and type of reinforcement. *Genetic Psychology Monographs, 68*, 215–245.

Fischhoff, B. (1975). Hindsight foresight: The effect of outcome knowledge on judgment under uncertainty. *Journal of Experimental Psychology: Human Perception and Performance, 1*, 288–299.

Fishbein, M., & Ajzen, I. (1975). *Belief, attitude, intention, and behavior: An introduction to theory and research.* Reading, MA: Addison-Wesley.

Fiske, A. P., Kitayama, S., Markus, H. R., & Nisbett, R. E. (1998). The cultural matrix of social psychology. In D. Gilbert, S. Fiske, & G. Lindzey (Eds.), *The handbook of social psychology* (4th ed., Vol 2, pp. 915–981). New York: McGraw Hill.

Fiske, S., & Depret, E. (1996). Control, interdependence, and power: Understanding social cognition in its social context. In W. Stroebe & M. Hewstone (Eds.), *European Review of Social Psychology, 7*, 31–61. New York: Wiley.

Fiske, S. T. (1989a). Examining the role of intent: Toward understanding its role in stereotyping and prejudice. In J. S. Uleman & J. A. Bargh (Eds.), *Unintended thought* (pp. 253–283). New York: Guilford.

Fiske, S. T. (1989b). *Interdependence and stereotyping: From the laboratory to the Supreme Court (and back).* Invited address, American Psychological Association, New Orleans.

Fiske, S. T. (1993). Social cognition and social perception. *Annual Review of Psychology, 44*, 155–194.

Fitzsimons, G. M., & Bargh, J. A. (2004). Automatic self-regulation. In R. F. Baumeister & K. D. Vohs (Eds.). Handbook of self-regulation: Research, theory, and applications (pp. 151-170). New York: Guilford Press.

Fletcher, G. J. O., & Ward, C. (1988). Attribution theory and processes: A cross-cultural perspective. In M. H. Bond (Ed.), *The cross-cultural challenge to social psychology.* Newbury Park, CA: Sage.

Flowers, M. L. (1977). A lab test of some implications of Janis' groupthink hypothesis. *Journal of Personality and Social Psychology, 35*, 888–897.

Forgas, J. P., & Bower, G. H. (1987). Mood effects on person-perception judgments. *Journal of Personality and Social Psychology, 53*, 53–60.

Foster, M., & Matheson, K. (1999). Perceiving and responding to the personal/group discrimination discrepancy. *Personality and Social Psychology Bulletin, 25*, 1319–1329.

Frank, M. G., & Gilovich, T. (1988). The dark side of self and social perceptions: Black uniforms and aggression in professional sports. *Journal of Personality and Social Psychology, 54*, 74–85.

Frank, M. G., & Gilovich, T. (1989). Effect of memory perspective on retrospective causal attributions. *Journal of Personality and Social Psychology, 57*, 399–403.

Freedman, D., Pisani, R., Purves, R., & Adhikari, A. (1991). *Statistics* (2nd ed.). New York: Norton.

Freedman, J. (1965). Long-term behavioral effects of cognitive dissonance. *Journal of Experimental and Social Psychology, 1*, 145–155.

Freedman, J. L., & Fraser, S. C. (1966). Compliance without pressure: The foot-in-the-door technique. *Journal of Personality and Social Psychology, 4*, 195–202.

Freud, S. (1933). *New introductory lectures on psycho-analysis.* New York: Norton.

Fried, C., & Aronson, E. (1995). Hypocrisy, misattribution, and dissonance reduction: A demonstration of dissonance in the absence of aversive consequences. *Personality and Social Psychology Bulletin, 21*, 925–933.

Friedkin, N. E. (1999). Choice shift and group polarization. *American Sociological Review, 64*, 856–875.

Frodi, A. (1975). The effect of exposure to weapons on aggressive behavior from a cross-cultural perspective. *International Journal of Psychology, 10*, 283–292.

Fury, G., Carlson, E. A., & Sroufe, L. A. (1997). Children's representations of attachment relationships in family drawings. *Child Development, 68*, 1154–1164.

Gabriel, S., & Gardner, W. L. (1999). Are there "his" and "hers" types of interdependence? The implications of gender differences in collective versus relational interdependence for affect, behavior, and cognition. *Journal of Personality and Social Psychology, 77*, 642–655.

Gaertner, S. L., & Dovidio, J. F. (1986). The aversive form of racism. In J. F. Dovidio & S. L. Gaertner (Eds.), *Prejudice, discrimination, and racism: Theory and research* (pp. 61–89). New York: Academic Press.

Gagnon, A., & Bourhis, R. Y. (1996). Discrimination in the minimal group paradigm: Social identity or self-interest? *Personality and Social Psychology Bulletin, 22*, 1289–1301.

Gallup, G. G. (1977). Self-recognition in primates: A comparative approach to the bidirectional properties of consciousness. *American Psychologist, 32*, 329–338.

Gallup, G. G. (1993). Mirror, mirror on the wall, which is the most heuristic theory of them all? *New Ideas in Psychology, 11*, 327–335.

Gallup, G. G. (1994). Monkeys, mirrors, and minds. *Behavioral and Brain Sciences, 17*, 572–573.

Gallup, G. G. (1997). On the rise and fall of self-conception in primates. In J. G. Snodgrass & R. L. Thompson (Eds.), *The self across psychology: Self-recognition, self-awareness, and the self-concept.* New York: New York Academy of Sciences Press.

Gallup, G. G., & Suarez, S. D. (1986). Self-awareness and the emergence of mind in humans and other primates. In J. Suls & A. G. Greenwald (Eds.), *Psychological perspectives on the self* (Vol. 3, pp. 3–26). Hillsdale, NJ: Erlbaum.

Gangestad, S. W. (1989). Uncompelling theory, uncompelling data. *Behavioral and Brain Sciences, 12*, 525–526.

Gangestad, S. W. (1993). Sexual selection and physical attractiveness: Implications for mating dynamics. *Human Nature, 4*, 205–235.

Garb, H. N. (1996). The representativeness and past-behavior heuristics in clinical judgment. *Professional Psychology: Research and Practice, 27*, 272–277.

Gardner, W. L., Pickett, C. L., & Brewer, M. B. (2000). Social exclusion and selective memory: How the need to belong influences memory for social events. *Personality and Social Psychology Bulletin, 26*, 486–496.

Geen, R. (1994). Television and aggression: Recent developments in research and theory. In D. Zillmann, J. Bryant, & A. C. Huston (Eds.), *Media, children, and the family: Social scientific, psychodynamic, and clinical perspectives* (pp. 151–162). Hillsdale, NJ: Erlbaum.

Geen, R. (1998). Aggression and anti-social behavior. In D. Gilbert, S. Fiske, & G. Lindzey (Eds.), *The handbook of social psychology* (4th ed., Vol. 2, pp. 317–356). New York: McGraw Hill.

Geen, R. G. (1989). Alternative conceptions of social facilitation. In P. B. Paulus (Ed.), *Psychology of group influence* (2nd ed., pp. 15–51). Hillsdale, NJ: Erlbaum.

George, J. M. (1990). Personality, affect, and behavior in groups. *Journal of Applied Psychology, 75*, 107–116.

George, J. M., & Brief, A. P. (1992). Feeling good–doing good: A conceptual analysis of the mood at work–organizational spontaneity relationship. *Psychological Bulletin, 112*, 310–329.

Gerard, H. B., Wilhelmy, R. A., & Conolley, E. S. (1968). Conformity and group size. *Journal of Personality and Social Psychology, 8*, 79–82.

Gerdes, E. P. (1979). College students' reactions to social psychological experiments involving deception. *Journal of Social Psychology, 107*, 99–110.

Gibbons, F. X. (1978). Sexual standards and reactions to pornography: Enhancing behavioral consistency through self-focused attention. *Journal of Personality and Social Psychology, 36*, 976–987.

Giesler, R., Josephs, R., & Swann, W. (1996). Self-verification in clinical depression: The desire for negative evaluation. *Journal of Abnormal Psychology, 105*, 358–368.

Gigerenzer, G., & Goldstein, D. G. (1996). Reasoning the fast and frugal way: Models of bounded rationality. *Psychological Review, 103*, 650–669.

Gilbert, D. T. (1991). How mental systems believe. *American Psychologist, 46*, 107–119.

Gilbert, D. T. (1993). The assent of man: Mental representation and the control of belief. In D. M. Wegner & J. W. Pennebaker (Eds.), *The handbook of mental control* (pp. 57–87). Englewood Cliffs, NJ: Prentice Hall.

Gilbert, D. T. (1998a). Ordinary personology. In D. T. Gilbert, S. T. Fiske, & G. Lindzey (Eds.), *The handbook of social psychology* (4th ed., Vol. 2, pp. 89–150). New York: McGraw-Hill.

Gilbert, D. T. (1998b). Speeding with Ned: A personal view of the correspondence bias. In J. M. Darley & J. Cooper (Eds.), *Attribution and social interaction* (pp. 5–36). Washington, DC: American Psychological Association.

Gilbert, D. T., & Malone, P. S. (1995). The correspondence bias. *Psychological Bulletin, 117*, 21–38.

Gilovich, T., Medvec, V. H., & Savitsky, K. (2000). The spotlight effect in social judgment: An egocentric bias in estimates of the salience of one's own actions and appearance. *Journal of Personality and Social Psychology, 78*, 211–222.

Gimlin, D. (1994). The anorexic as overconformist: Toward a reinterpretation of eating disorders. In K. A. Callaghan (Ed.), *Ideals of feminine beauty: Philosophical, social, and cultural dimensions* (pp. 99–111). Westport, CT: Greenwood.

Goethals, G. R., & Darley, J. M. (1977). Social comparison theory: An attributional approach. In J. M. Suls & R. L. Miller (Eds.), *Social comparison processes: Theoretical and empirical perspectives* (pp. 259–278). Washington, DC: Hemisphere/Halsted.

Gold, J. A., Ryckman, R. M., & Mosley, N. R. (1984). Romantic mood induction and attraction to a dissimilar other: Is love blind? *Personality and Social Psychology Bulletin, 10*, 358–368.

Goldstein, J. H., & Arms, R. L. (1971). Effect of observing athletic contests on hostility. *Sociometry, 34*, 83–90.

Goleman, D. (1982, January). Make-or-break resolutions. *Psychology Today*, p. 19.

Goodman, N. G. (Ed.). (1945). *A Benjamin Franklin reader*. New York: Crowell.

Gorassini, D. R., & Olson, J. M. (1995). Does self-perception change explain the foot-in-the-door effect? *Journal of Personality and Social Psychology, 69*, 91–105.

Graham, K., & Wells, S. (2001a). The two worlds of aggression for men and men. *Sex Roles, 45*, 595–622.

Graham, K., & Wells, S. (2001b). Aggression among young adults in the social context of the bar. *Addiction Research & Theory, 9*, 193–219.

Graham, K., West, P., & Wells, S. (2000). Evaluating theories of alcohol-related aggression using observations of young adults in bars. *Addiction, 95*, 847–863.

Granberg, D., & Brown, T. (1989). On affect and cognition in politics. *Social Psychology Quarterly, 52*, 171–182.

Grant, P. R. (1992). Ethnocentrism between groups of unequal power in response to perceived threat to social identity and valued resources. *Canadian Journal of Behavioural Science, 24*, 348–370.

Grant, P. R. (1993). Reactions to intergroup similarity: Examination of the similarity-differentiation and the similarity-attraction hypothesis. *Canadian Journal of Behavioral Science, 25*, 28–44.

Greenberg, J., & Pyszczynski, T. (1985). The effect of an overheard slur on evaluations of the target: How to spread a social disease. *Journal of Experimental Social Psychology, 21*, 61–72.

Greenberg, J., Pyszczynski, T., & Solomon, S. (1986). The causes and consequences of the need for self-esteem: A terror management theory. In R. F. Baumeister (Ed.), *Public self and private self* (pp. 189–212). New York: Springer-Verlag.

Greening, L., & Chandler, C. C. (1997). Why it can't happen to me: The base rate matters, but overestimating skill leads to underestimating risk. *Journal of Applied Social Psychology, 27,* 760–780.

Greenwald, A. G., & Banaji, M. R. (1989). The self as a memory system: Powerful, but ordinary. *Journal of Personality and Social Psychology, 57,* 41–54.

Greenwald, A. G., McGhee, D. E. & Schwartz, J. L. K. (1998). Measuring individual differences in implicit cognition: The Implicit Association Test. *Journal of Personality and Social Psychology, 74,* 1464–1480.

Greenwald, A. G., Nosek, B. A, & Banaji, M. R. (2003). Understanding and using the Implicit Association Test: I. An improved scoring algorithm. *Journal of Personality and Social Psychology, 85,* 197–216.

Greenwald, A. G., Spangenberg, E. R., Pratkanis, A. R., & Eskenazi, J. (1991). Double-blind tests of subliminal self-help audiotapes. *Psychological Science, 2,* 119–122.

Griffin, D., & Buehler, R. (1999). Frequency, probability, and prediction: Easy solutions to cognitive illusions. *Cognitive Psychology, 38,* 48–78.

Griffin, D., Gonzalez, R., & Varey, C. (2001). The heuristics and biases approach to judgment under uncertainty. In A. Tesser (Ed.), *Blackwell handbook of social psychology* (Vol. 1, pp. 207–235). Oxford, UK: Blackwell Publishers.

Griffin, E., & Sparks, G. G. (1990). Friends forever: A longitudinal exploration of intimacy in same-sex pairs and platonic pairs. *Journal of Social and Personal Relationships, 7,* 29–46.

Grusec, J. E. (1991). The socialization of altruism. In M. S. Clark (Ed.), *Review of personality and social psychology* (Vol. 12, pp. 9–33). Newbury Park, CA: Sage.

Grusec, J. E., Kuczynski, L., Rushton, J. P., & Simutis, Z. M. (1979). Modeling, direct instruction, and attributions: Effects on altruism. *Developmental Psychology, 14,* 51–57.

Guerin, B. (1986). Mere presence effects in humans: A review. *Journal of Experimental Social Psychology, 22,* 38–77.

Guerin, B. (1993). *Social facilitation.* Cambridge, England: Cambridge University Press.

Guimond, S. (1999). Attitude change during college: Normative or informational social influence? *Social Psychology of Education, 2,* 237–261.

Guimond, S. (2000). Group socialization and prejudice: The social transmission of intergroup attitudes and beliefs. *European Journal of Social Psychology, 30,* 335–354.

Guimond, S., & Palmer, D. L. (1996). The political socialization of commerce and social science students: Epistemic authority and attitude change. *Journal of Applied Social Psychology, 26,* 1985-2013.

Guisinger, S., & Blatt, S. J. (1994). Individuality and relatedness: Evolution of a fundamental dialect. *American Psychologist, 49,* 104–111.

Gustafson, R. (1989). Frustration and successful vs. unsuccessful aggression: A test of Berkowitz' completion hypothesis. *Aggressive Behavior, 15,* 5–12.

Haddock, G., & Zanna, M. P. (1994). Preferring "housewives" to "feminists": Categorization and the favorability of attitudes toward women. *Psychology of Women Quarterly, 18,* 25–52.

Haddock, G., & Zanna, M. P. (1998). Assessing the impact of affective and cognitive information in predicting attitudes toward capital punishment. *Law and Human Behavior, 22,* 325–339.

Haddock, G., Zanna, M. P., & Esses, V. M. (1993). Assessing the structure of prejudicial attitudes: The case of attitudes toward homosexuals. *Journal of Personality and Social Psychology, 65,* 1105–1118.

Haddock, G., Zanna, M. P., & Esses, V. M. (1994). The (limited) role of trait-laden stereotypes in predicting attitudes toward Native peoples. *British Journal of Social Psychology, 33,* 83–106.

Hadjistavropoulos, T., & Genest, M. (1994). The understanding of the role of physical attractiveness in dating preferences: Ignorance or taboo? *Canadian Journal of Behavioral Science, 26,* 298–318.

Hafer, C. L. (2000a). Do innocent victims threaten the belief in a just world? Evidence from a modified Stroop task. *Journal of Personality and Social Psychology, 79,* 165–173.

Hafer, C. L. (2000b). Investment in long-term goals and commitment to just means drive the need to believe in a just world. *Personality and Social Psychology Bulletin, 26,* 1059–1073.

Hamilton, V. L., Sanders, J., & McKearney, S. J. (1995). Orientations toward authority in an authoritarian state: Moscow in 1990. *Personality and Social Psychology Bulletin, 21,* 356–365.

Hamilton, W. D. (1964). The genetical evolution of social behavior. *Journal of Theoretical Biology, 7,* 1–52.

Haney, C., Banks, C., & Zimbardo, P. (1973). Interpersonal dynamics in a simulated prison. *International Journal of Criminology and Penology, 1,* 69–97.

Harmon-Jones, E., & Mills, J.S. (1998). *Cognitive dissonance theory: Revival with revisions and controversies.* Washington, DC: American Psychological Association.

Harris, B. (1986). Reviewing 50 years of the psychology of social issues. *Journal of Social Issues, 42,* 1–20.

Harris, M. B., Benson, S. M., & Hall, C. (1975). The effects of confession on altruism. *Journal of Social Psychology, 96,* 187–192.

Harris, P. (1996). Sufficient grounds for optimism? The relationship between perceived controllability and optimistic bias. *Journal of Social and Clinical Psychology, 15,* 9–52.

Hart, D., & Damon, W. (1986). Developmental trends in self-understanding. *Social Cognition, 4,* 388–407.

Hartstone, M., & Augoustinos, M. (1995). The minimal group paradigm: Categorization into two versus three groups. *European Journal of Social Psychology, 25,* 179–193.

Hartup, W. W., & Laursen, B. (1999). Relationships as developmental contexts: Retrospective themes and contemporary issues. In W. A. Collins & B. Laursen (Eds.), *Relationships as developmental contexts: Minnesota Symposia on Child Psychology* (Vol. 30, pp. 13–35). Mahwah, NJ: Erlbaum.

Hassebrauck, M., & Buhl, T. (1996). Three-dimensional love. *Journal of Social Psychology, 136*, 121–122.

Hastie, R. (1980). Memory for behavioral information that confirms or contradicts a personality impression. In R. Hastie, T. M. Ostrom, E. B. Ebbesen, R. S. Wyer, D. L. Hamilton, & D. E. Carlston (Eds.), *Person memory: The cognitive basis of social perception* (pp. 141–172). Hillsdale, NJ: Erlbaum.

Hastie, R., & Pennington, N. (1991). Cognitive and social processes in decision making. In L. B. Resnick, J. M. Levine, & S. D. Teasley (Eds.), *Perspectives on socially shared cognition* (pp. 308–327). Washington, DC: American Psychological Association.

Hastie, R., & Pennington, N. (1995). The big story: Is it a story? In R. S. Wyer Jr. (Ed.), *Knowledge and memory: The real story. Advances in social cognition* (Vol. 8, pp. 133–138). Hillsdale, NJ: Erlbaum.

Hastie, R., & Pennington, N. (2000). Explanation-based decision making. In T. Connolly & H. R. Arkes (Eds.), *Judgment and decision making: An interdisciplinary reader* (2nd ed., pp. 212–228). New York: Cambridge University Press.

Hastie, R., Penrod, S. D., & Pennington, N. (1983). *Inside the jury*. Cambridge MA: Harvard University Press.

Hatfield, E., Greenberger, E., Traupmann, J., & Lambert, P. (1982). Equity and sexual satisfaction in recently married couples. *Journal of Sex Research, 18*, 18–32.

Hatfield, E., & Rapson, R. L. (1993). *Love, sex, and intimacy: Their psychology, biology, and history.* New York: HarperCollins.

Hatfield, E., & Sprecher, S. (1986a). *Mirror, mirror: The importance of looks in everyday life.* Albany: State University of New York Press.

Hatfield, E., & Sprecher, S. (1986b). Measuring passionate love in intimate relationships. *Journal of Adolescence, 9,* 383–410.

Hatfield, E., & Sprecher, S. (1995). Men's and women's preferences in marital partners in the United States, Russia, and Japan. *Journal of Cross-Cultural Psychology, 26*, 728–750.

Hatfield, E., & Walster, G. W. (1978). *A new look at love.* Reading, MA: Addison-Wesley.

Haugtvedt, C. P., & Wegener, D. T. (1994). Message order effects in persuasion: An attitude strength perspective. *Journal of Consumer Research, 21,* 205–218.

Hazan, C., & Shaver, P. (1987). Romantic love conceptualized as an attachment process. *Journal of Personality and Social Psychology, 52,* 511–524.

Hazan, C., & Shaver, P. (1994a). Attachment as an organizational framework for research on close relationships. *Psychological Inquiry, 5,* 1–22.

Hazan, C., & Shaver, P. (1994b). Deeper into attachment theory. *Psychological Inquiry, 5,* 68–79.

Hébert, Y., Bernard, J., deMan, A. F., & Farrar, D. (1989). Factors related to the use of condoms among French-Canadian university students. *The Journal of Social Psychology, 129,* 707–709.

Heider, F. (1958). *The psychology of interpersonal relations.* New York: Wiley.

Heine, S. J. (2001). Self as cultural product: An examination of East Asian and North American selves. *Journal of Personality, 69,* 881–906.

Heine, S. J., & Lehman, D. R. (1995). Cultural variation in unrealistic optimism: Does the West feel more vulnerable than the East? *Journal of Personality and Social Psychology, 68,* 595–607.

Heine, S. J., & Lehman, D. R. (1997a). Culture, dissonance, and self-affirmation. *Personality and Social Psychology Bulletin, 23,* 389–400.

Heine, S. J., & Lehman, D. R. (1997b). The cultural construction of self-enhancement: An examination of group serving biases. *Journal of Personality and Social Psychology, 72,* 1268–1283.

Heine, S. J., & Lehman, D. R. (1999). Culture, self-discrepancies, and self-satisfaction. *Personality and Social Psychology Bulletin, 25,* 915–925.

Heine, S. J., Lehman, D. R., Markus, H. R., & Kitayama, S. (1999). Is there a universal need for positive self-regard? *Psychological Review, 106,* 766–794.

Heine, S. J., & Renshaw, K. (2002). Interjudge agreement, self-enhancement, and liking: Cross-cultural perspectives. *Personality and Social Psychology Bulletin, 28,* 578–587.

Heine, S. J., Takata, T., & Lehman, D. R. (2000). Beyond self-presentation: Evidence for self-criticism among Japanese. *Personality and Social Psychology Bulletin, 26,* 71–78.

Helgeson, V. S. (1994). The effects of self-beliefs and relationship beliefs on adjustment to a relationship stressor. *Personal Relationships, 1,* 241–258.

Henderson-King, E., & Nisbett, R. E. (1996). Anti-black prejudice as a function of exposure to the negative behavior of a single black person. *Journal of Personality and Social Psychology, 71,* 654–664.

Henry, R. A. (1995). Using relative confidence judgments to evaluate group effectiveness. *Basic and Applied Social Psychology, 16,* 333–350.

Her Majesty the Queen v. Warren Paul Glowatski. (1999, June 2). *British Columbia Superior Courts Reasons for Judgements Database.* (Docket No. 95773). www.courts.gov.bc.ca/jdb%2Dtxt/sc/99/08/s99%2D0836.txt (accessed June 29, 2000).

Herold, E. S., & Mewhinney, D. (1993). Gender differences in casual sex and AIDS prevention: A survey of dating bars. *The Journal of Sex Research, 30,* 36–42.

Hersh, S. M. (1970). *My Lai 4: A report on the massacre and its aftermath.* New York: Vintage Books.

Hertwig, R., Gigerenzer, G., & Hoffrage, U. (1997). The reiteration effect in hindsight bias. *Psychological Review, 104,* 194–202.

Herzog, T. A. (1994). Automobile driving as seen by the actor, the active observer, and the passive observer. *Journal of Applied Social Psychology, 24*, 2057–2074.

Higgins, E. T. (1987). Self-discrepancy: A theory relating self and affect. *Psychological Review, 94*, 319–340.

Higgins, E. T. (1989). Knowledge accessibility and activation: Subjectivity and suffering from unconscious sources. In J. S. Uleman & J. A. Bargh (Eds.), *Unintended thought* (pp. 75–123). New York: Guilford Press.

Higgins, E. T. (1989). Self-discrepancy theory: What patterns of self-beliefs cause people to suffer? In L. Berkowitz (Ed.), *Advances in experimental social psychology* (Vol. 22, pp. 93–136). New York: Academic Press.

Higgins, E. T. (1996). Knowledge application: Accessibility, applicability, and salience. In E. T. Higgins and A. R. Kruglanski (Eds.), *Social psychology: Handbook of basic principles* (pp. 133–168). New York: Guilford.

Higgins, E. T. (1999). Self-discrepancy: A theory relating self and affect. In R. F. Baumeister (Ed.), *The self in social psychology* (pp. 150–181). Philadelphia: Psychology Press.

Higgins, E. T., & Bargh, J. A. (1987). Social cognition and social perception. *Annual Review of Psychology, 38*, 369–425.

Higgins, E. T., Bond, R. N., Klein, R., & Strauman, T. (1986). Self-discrepancies and emotional vulnerability: How magnitude, accessibility, and type of discrepancy influence affect. *Journal of Personality and Social Psychology, 51*, 5–15.

Higgins, E. T., & Brendl, C. M. (1995). Accessibility and applicability: Some "activation rules" influencing judgment. *Journal of Experimental Social Psychology, 31*, 218–243.

Higgins, E. T., Klein, R., & Strauman, T. (1987). Self-discrepancies: Distinguishing among self-states, self-state conflicts, and emotional vulnerabilities. In K. M. Yardley & T. M. Honess (Eds.), *Self and identity: Psychosocial perspectives* (pp. 173–186). New York: Wiley.

Higgins, E. T., Rholes, W. S., & Jones, C. R. (1977). Category accessibility and impression formation. *Journal of Experimental Social Psychology, 13*, 141–154.

Hill, A. J., Boudreau, F., Amyot, E., Dery, D., & Godin, G. (1997). Predicting the stages of smoking acquisition according to the theory of planned behavior. *Journal of Adolescent Health, 21*, 107–115.

Hilton, A., Potvin, L., & Sachdev, I. (1989). Ethnic relations in rental housing: A social psychological approach. *Canadian Journal of Behavioural Science, 21*, 121–131.

Hoaken, P. N. S., & Pihl, R. O. (2000). The effects of alcohol intoxication on aggressive responses in men and women. *Alcohol and Alcoholism, 35*, 471–477.

Hoeksema–van Orden, C. Y. D., Gaillard, A. W. K., & Buunk, B. P. (1998). Social loafing under fatigue. *Journal of Personality and Social Psychology, 75*, 1179–1190.

Hoffman, A. J., Gillespie, J. J., Moore, D. A., Wade-Benzoni, K. A., Thompson, L. L., & Bazerman, M. H. (1999). A mixed-motive perspective on the economics versus environmental debate. *American Behavioral Scientist, 42*, 1254–1276.

Hofstede, G. (1984). *Culture's consequences: International differences in work-related values*. Newbury Park, CA: Sage.

Hofstede, G. (1986). Cultural differences in teaching and learning. *International Journal of Intercultural Relations, 10*, 301–320.

Hogg, M. A. (1992). *The social psychology of group cohesiveness: From attraction to social identity*. London, England: Harvester-Wheatsheaf.

Hogg, M. A. (1993). Group cohesiveness: A critical review and some new directions. In W. Stroebe & M. Hewstone (Eds.), *European review of social psychology* (Vol. 4, pp. 85–111). Chichester, England: Wiley.

Hogg, M. A., & Abrams, D. (1988). *Social identifications*. London: Routledge. (cf. Chapter 3)

Hogg, M. A., & Hains, S. C. (1998). Friendship and group identification: A new look at the role of cohesiveness in groupthink. *European Journal of Social Psychology, 28*, 323–341.

Hollander, E. P. (1958). Conformity, status, and idiosyncrasy credit. *Psychological Review, 65*, 117–127.

Hollander, E. P. (1985). Leadership and power. In G. Lindzey & E. Aronson (Eds.), *Handbook of social psychology* (3rd ed., Vol. 2, pp. 485–537). New York: McGraw-Hill.

Holtz, R. (1997). Length of group membership, assumed similarity, and opinion certainty: The dividend for veteran members. *Journal of Applied Social Psychology, 27*, 539–555.

Holtzworth-Munroe, A., Bates, L., Smutzer, N., & Sandin, E. (1997). A brief review of the research on husband violence. *Aggression and Violent Behavior, 2*, 65–99.

Homans, G. C. (1961). *Social behavior: Its elementary forms*. New York: Harcourt Brace & World.

House, R. J. (1971). A path-goal theory of leadership effectiveness. *Administrative Science Quarterly, 16*, 321–338.

Hovland, C. I., Janis, I. L., & Kelley, H. H. (1953). *Communication and persuasion: Psychological studies of opinion change*. New Haven, CT: Yale University Press.

Hovland, C. I., & Weiss, W. (1951). The influence of source credibility on communication effectiveness. *Public Opinion Quarterly, 15*, 635–650.

Hsu, S. S. (1995, April 8). Fredericksburg searches its soul after clerk is beaten as 6 watch. *Washington Post*, pp. A1, A13.

Huesmann, L. R. (1982). Television violence and aggressive behavior. In D. Pearly, L. Bouthilet, & J. Lazar (Eds.), *Television and behavior: Vol. 2. Technical reviews* (pp. 220–256). Washington, DC: National Institute of Mental Health.

Huesmann, L. R., & Miller, L. S. (1994). Long-term effects of repeated exposure to media violence in childhood. In L. R. Huesmann (Ed.), *Aggressive behavior: Current perspectives* (pp. 153–186). New York: Plenum.

Hughes, J. N., & Hasbrouck, J. E. (1996). Television violence: Implications for violence prevention. *School Psychology Review, 25,* 134–151.

Huguet, P., Galvaing, M. P., Monteil, J. M., & Dumas, F. (1999). Social presence effects in the Stroop task: Further evidence for an attentional view of social facilitation. *Journal of Personality and Social Psychology, 77,* 1011–1025.

Hui, C. H., & Triandis, H. C. (1986). Individualism-collectivism: A study of cross-cultural researchers. *Journal of Cross-Cultural Psychology, 17,* 225–248.

Hull, J. G. (1981). A self-awareness model of the causes and effects of alcohol consumption. *Journal of Personality and Social Psychology, 90,* 586–600.

Hull, J. G., & Young, R. D. (1983). Self-consciousness, self-esteem, and success-failure as determinants of alcohol consumption in male social drinkers. *Journal of Personality and Social Psychology, 44,* 1097–1109.

Hull, J. G., Young, R. D., & Jouriles, E. (1986). Applications of the self-awareness model of alcohol consumption: Predicting patterns of use and abuse. *Journal of Personality and Social Psychology, 51,* 790–796.

Hynie, M., & Lydon, J. E. (1995). Women's perceptions of female contraceptive behavior: Experimental evidence of the sexual double standard. *Psychology of Women Quarterly, 19,* 563–581.

Hynie, M., & Lydon, J. E. (1996). Sexual attitudes and contraceptive behavior revisited: Can there be too much of a good thing? *Journal of Sex Research, 33,* 127–134.

Hynie, M., Lydon, J. E., Cote, S., & Wiener, S. (1998). Relational sexual scripts and women's condom use: The importance of internalized norms. *Journal of Sex Research, 35,* 370–380.

Ickes, W., Patterson, M. L., Rajecki, D. W., & Tanford, S. (1982). Behavioral and cognitive consequences of reciprocal versus compensatory responses to preinteraction expectancies. *Social Cognition, 1,* 160–190.

Isen, A. M. (1987). Positive affect, cognitive processes, and social behavior. In L. Berkowitz (Ed.), *Advances in experimental social psychology* (Vol. 20, pp. 203–253). San Diego, CA: Academic Press.

Isen, A. M. (1999). Positive affect. In T. Dalgleish & M. J. Power (Eds.), *Handbook of cognition and emotion* (pp. 521–539). Chichester, England: Wiley.

Isen, A. M., & Levin, P. A. (1972). Effect of feeling good on helping: Cookies and kindness. *Journal of Personality and Social Psychology, 21,* 384–388.

Isenberg, D. J. (1986). Group polarization: A critical review and meta-analysis. *Journal of Personality and Social Psychology, 50,* 1141–1151.

Jackson, J. M., & Williams, K. D. (1985). Social loafing on difficult tasks: Working collectively can improve performance. *Journal of Personality and Social Psychology, 49,* 937–942.

Jackson, J. W. (1993). Realistic group conflict theory: A review and evaluation of the theoretical and empirical literature. *Psychological Record, 43,* 395–413.

Jacowitz, K. E., & Kahneman, D. (1995). Measures of anchoring in estimation tasks. *Personality and Social Psychology Bulletin, 21,* 1161–1166.

James, J. M., & Bolstein, R. (1992). Large monetary incentives and their effect on mail survey response rates. *Public Opinion Quarterly, 56,* 442–453.

James, W. (1890). *The principles of psychology.* New York: Holt.

Jamieson, D. W., Lydon, J. E., & Zanna, M. P. (1987). Attitude and activity preference similarity: Differential bases of interpersonal attraction for low and high self-monitors. *Journal of Personality and Social Psychology, 53,* 1052–1060.

Janis, I. L. (1972). *Victims of groupthink.* Boston: Houghton Mifflin.

Janis, I. L. (1982). *Groupthink* (2nd ed.). Boston: Houghton Mifflin.

Janis, I. L., & Feshbach, S. (1953). Effects of fear-arousing communications. *Journal of Abnormal and Social Psychology, 49,* 78–92.

Jepson, C., & Chaiken, S. (1990). Chronic issue-specific fear inhibits systematic processing of persuasive communications. *Journal of Social Behavior and Personality, 5,* 61–84.

Job, R. F. S. (1988). Effective and ineffective use of fear in health promotion campaigns. *American Journal of Public Health, 78,* 163–167.

Johnson, D. W., & Johnson, R. T. (1987). *Learning together and alone: Cooperative, competitive, and individualistic learning* (2nd ed.). Englewood Cliffs, NJ: Prentice Hall.

Johnson, D. W., & Johnson, R. T. (1989). *A meta-analysis of cooperative, competitive, and individualistic goal structures.* Hillsdale, NJ: Erlbaum.

Johnson, H. (2001). Contrasting views of the role of alcohol in cases of wife assault. *Journal of Interpersonal Violence, 16,* 54–72.

Johnson, J. T., & Boyd, K. R. (1995). Dispositional traits versus the content of experience: Actor/observer differences in judgments of the "authentic self." *Personality and Social Psychology Bulletin, 21,* 375–383.

Johnson, T. E., & Rule, B. G. (1986). Mitigating circumstance information, censure, and aggression. *Journal of Personality and Social Psychology, 50,* 537–542.

Jones, D., & Hill, K. (1993). Criteria of facial attractiveness in five populations. *Human Nature, 4,* 271–296.

Jones, E. E. (1990). *Interpersonal perception.* New York: Freeman.

Jones, E. E., & Harris, V. A. (1967). The attribution of attitudes. *Journal of Experimental Social Psychology, 3,* 1–24.

Jones, E. E., & Nisbett, R. E. (1972). The actor and the observer: Divergent perceptions of the causes of behavior. In E. E. Jones, D. E. Kanouse, H. H. Kelley, R. E. Nisbett, S. Valins, & B. Weiner (Eds.), *Attribution: Perceiving the causes of behavior* (pp. 79–94). Morristown, NJ: General Learning Press.

Josephson, W. (1987). Television violence and children's aggression: Testing the priming, social script, and disinhibition prediction. *Journal of Personality and Social Psychology, 53,* 882–890.

Judd, C., & McClelland, G. (1998). Measurement. In D. Gilbert, S. Fiske, & G. Lindzey (Eds.), *The handbook of social psychology* (4th ed., Vol. 1, pp. 180–232). New York: Random House.

Judd, C. M., & Park, B. (1988). Out-group homogeneity: Judgments of variability at the individual and group levels. *Journal of Personality and Social Psychology, 54*, 778–788.

Jürgen-Lohmann, J., Borsch, F., & Giesen, H. (2001). Kooperatives Lernen an der Hochschule: Evaluation des Gruppenpuzzles in Seminaren der Pädagogischen Psychologie. *Zeitschrift für Pädagogische Psychologie, 15*, 74–84.

Kahneman, D., & Tversky, A. (1973). On the psychology of prediction. *Psychological Review, 80*, 237–251.

Kalin, R., & Berry, J. W. (1996). Interethnic attitudes in Canada: Ethnocentrism, consensual hierarchy and reciprocity. *Canadian Journal of Behavioural Sciences, 28*, 253–261.

Kalven, H., Jr., & Zeisel, H. (1966). *The American jury.* Boston: Little, Brown.

Karau, S. J., & Williams, K. D. (1993). Social loafing: A meta-analytic review and theoretical integration. *Journal of Personality and Social Psychology, 65*, 681–706.

Karau, S. J., & Williams, K. D. (1995). Social loafing: Research findings, implications, and future directions. *Current Directions in Psychological Science, 5*, 134–140.

Kassarjian, H., & Cohen, J. (1965). Cognitive dissonance and consumer behavior. *California Management Review, 8*, 55–64.

Katz, D. (1960). The functional approach to the study of attitudes. *Public Opinion Quarterly, 24*, 163–204.

Kawakami, K., Dion, K. L., & Dovidio, J. F. (1998). Racial prejudice and stereotype activation. *Personality and Social Psychology Bulletin, 24*, 407–416.

Keelan, J. P. R., Dion, K. L., & Dion, K. K. (1994). Attachment style and heterosexual relationships among young adults: A short-term panel study. *Journal of Social and Personal Relationships, 11*, 201–214.

Kelley, H. H. (1955). The two functions of reference groups. In G. E. Swanson, T. M. Newcomb, & E. L. Hartley (Eds.), *Readings in social psychology* (2nd ed., pp. 410–414). New York: Holt.

Kelley, H. H. (1983). Love and commitment. In H. H. Kelley, E. Berscheid, A. Christensen, J. H. Harvey, T. L. Huston, G. Levinger, E. McClintock, L. A. Peplau, & D. R. Peterson (Eds.), *Close relationships* (pp. 265–314). New York: Freeman.

Kelley, H. H., & Thibaut, J. (1978). *Interpersonal relations: A theory of interdependence.* New York: Wiley.

Kelman, H. C. (1997). Group processes in the resolution of international conflicts: Experiences from the Israeli–Palestinian case. *American Psychologist, 52*, 212–220.

Kenny, D., Kashy, D., & Bolger, N. (1998). Data analysis in social psychology. In D. Gilbert, S. Fiske, & G. Lindzey (Eds.), *The handbook of social psychology* (4th ed., Vol. 1, pp. 233–268). New York: McGraw-Hill.

Kenny, D. A. (1994). Using the social relations model to understand relationships. In R. Erber & R. Gilmour (Eds.), *Theoretical Frameworks for Personal Relationships* (pp. 111–127). Hillsdale, NJ: Erlbaum.

Kent, M. V. (1994). The presence of others. In A. P. Hare, H. H. Blumberg, M. F. Davies, & M. V. Kent (Eds.), *Small group research: A handbook* (pp. 81–105). Norwood, NJ: Ablex.

Kerr, N. L., & Stanfel, J. A. (1993). Role schemata and member motivation in task groups. *Personality and Social Psychology Bulletin, 19*, 432–442.

Ketelaar, T., & Ellis, B. J. (2000). Are evolutionary explanations unfalsifiable? Evolutionary psychology and the Lakatosian philosophy of science. *Psychological Inquiry, 11*, 1–21.

Key, W. B. (1973). *Subliminal seduction.* Englewood Cliffs, NJ: Signet.

Key, W. B. (1989). *Age of manipulation: The con in confidence and the sin in sincere.* New York: Holt.

Kiesler, C. A., & Kiesler, S. B. (1969). *Conformity.* Reading, MA: Addison-Wesley.

Killen, J. D. (1985). Prevention of adolescent tobacco smoking: The social pressure resistance training approach. *Journal of Child Psychology and Psychiatry, 26*, 7–15.

Kim, U., Triandis, H. C., Kagitcibasi, C., Choi, S. C., & Yoon, G. (Eds.) (1994). *Individualism and collectivism: Theory, method and applications.* Thousand Oaks, CA: Sage.

Kirkpatrick, L. A., & Davis, K. E. (1994). Attachment style, gender, and relationship stability: A longitudinal analysis. *Journal of Personality and Social Psychology, 66*, 502–512.

Kirkpatrick, L. A., & Hazan, C. (1994). Attachment styles and close relationships: A four-year prospective study. *Personal Relationships, 1*, 123–142.

Kitayama, S., & Markus, H. R. (1994). Culture and the self: How cultures influence the way we view ourselves. In D. Matsumoto (Ed.), *People: Psychology from a cultural perspective* (pp. 17–37). Pacific Grove, CA: Brooks/Cole.

Klein, W. M. (1996). Maintaining self-serving social comparisons: Attenuating the perceived significance of risk-increasing behaviors. *Journal of Social and Clinical Psychology, 15*, 120–142.

Klenke, K. (1996). *Women and leadership: A contextual perspective.* New York: Springer.

Knox, R. E., & Inkster, J. A. (1968). Postdecision dissonance at post time. *Journal of Personality and Social Psychology, 8*, 319–323.

Koestner, R., & Wheeler, L. (1988). Self-presentation in personal advertisements: The influence of implicit notions of attraction and role expectations. *Journal of Social and Personal Relationships, 5*, 149–160.

Kogan, N., & Wallach, M. A. (1964). *Risk-taking: A study in cognition and personality.* New York: Holt.

Kojetin, B. A. (1993). Adult attachment styles with romantic partners, friends, and parents. Unpublished doctoral dissertation, University of Minnesota, Minneapolis.

Krajick, K. (1990, July 30). Sound too good to be true? Behind the boom in subliminal tapes. *Newsweek, 116*, 60–61.

Krakow, A., & Blass, T. (1995). When nurses obey or defy inappropriate physician orders: Attributional differences. *Journal of Social Behavior and Personality, 10,* 585–594.

Krauss, R. M., & Deutsch, M. (1966). Communication in interpersonal bargaining. *Journal of Personality and Social Psychology, 4,* 572–577.

Kremer, J. F., & Stephens, L. (1983). Attributions and arousal as mediators of mitigation's effects on retaliation. *Journal of Personality and Social Psychology, 45,* 335–343.

Kressel, K., & Pruitt, D. G. (1989). A research perspective on the mediation of social conflict. In K. Kressel & D. G. Pruitt (Eds.), *Mediation research: The process and effectiveness of third party intervention* (pp. 394–435). San Francisco: Jossey-Bass.

Kristiansen, C. M., & Giulietti, R. (1990). Perceptions of wife abuse: Effects of gender, attitudes toward women, and just-world beliefs among college students. *Psychology of Women Quarterly, 14,* 177–189.

Krosnick, J. A., & Alwin, D. F. (1989). Aging and susceptibility to attitude change. *Journal of Personality and Social Psychology, 57,* 416–425.

Krueger, J., Ham, J. J., & Linford, K. (1996). Perceptions of behavioral consistency: Are people aware of the actor-observer effect? *Psychological Science, 7,* 259–264.

Kruglanski, A. W., & Mayseless, O. (1990). Classic and current social comparison research: Expanding the perspective. *Psychological Bulletin, 108,* 195–208.

Kruglanski, A. W., & Webster, D. M. (1991). Group members' reactions to opinion deviates and conformists at varying degrees of proximity to decision deadline and of environmental noise. *Journal of Personality and Social Psychology, 61,* 212–225.

Krull, D. (1993). Does the grist change the mill? The effect of the perceiver's inferential goal on the process of social inference. *Personality and Social Psychology Bulletin, 19,* 340–348.

Kubitschek, W. N., & Hallinan, M. T. (1998). Tracking and students' friendships. *Social Psychology Quarterly, 61,* 1–15.

Kunda, Z. (1999). *Social cognition: Making sense of people.* Cambridge, MA: The MIT Press.

Kunda, Z., Sinclair, L., & Griffin, D. (1997). Equal ratings but separate meanings: Stereotypes and the construal of traits. *Journal of Personality and Social Psychology, 72,* 720–734.

Kunz, P. R., & Woolcott, M. (1976). Season's greetings: From my status to yours. *Social Science Research, 5,* 269–278.

Kurdek, L. A. (1992). Assumptions versus standards: The validity of two relationship cognitions in heterosexual and homosexual couples. *Journal of Family Psychology, 16,* 164–170.

Kwok, D. C. (1995). The self-perception of competence by Canadian and Chinese children. *Psychologia: An International Journal of Psychology in the Orient, 38,* 9–16.

Kwong, M. J., Bartholomew, K., & Dutton, D. G. (1999). Gender differences in patterns of relationship violence in Alberta. *Canadian Journal of Behavioural Science, 31,* 150–160.

La Gaipa, J. J. (1982). Rules and rituals in disengaging from relationships. In S. Duck (Ed.), *Personal relationships: Vol. 4. Dissolving personal relationships* (pp. 189–210). London: Academic Press.

Lalancette, M. F., & Standing, L. (1990). Asch fails again. *Social Behavior and Personality, 18,* 7–12.

Lalonde, R. N., Moghaddam, F. M., & Taylor, D. M. (1987). The process of group differentiation in a dynamic intergroup setting. *Journal of Social Psychology, 127,* 273–287.

Lambert, A. J., & Raichle, K. (2000). The role of political ideology in mediating judgments of blame in rape victims and their assailants: A test of the just world, personal responsibility, and legitimization hypotheses. *Personality and Social Psychology Bulletin, 26,* 853–863.

Langlois, J. H., Kalakanis, L., Rubenstein, A. J., Larson, A., Hallam, M., & Smoot, M. (2000). Maxims or myths of beauty? A meta-analytic and theoretical review. *Psychological Bulletin, 126,* 390–423.

LaPiere, R. T. (1934). Attitudes vs. actions. *Social Forces, 13,* 230–237.

Latané, B. (1981). The psychology of social impact. *American Psychologist, 36,* 343–356.

Latané, B. (1987). From student to colleague: Retracing a decade. In N. E. Grunberg, R. E. Nisbett, J. Rodin, & J. E. Singer (Eds.), *A distinctive approach to psychological research: The influence of Stanley Schachter* (pp. 66–86). Hillsdale, NJ: Erlbaum.

Latané, B., & Darley, J. M. (1968). Group inhibition of bystander intervention. *Journal of Personality and Social Psychology, 10,* 215–221.

Latané, B., & Darley, J. M. (1970). *The unresponsive bystander: Why doesn't he help?* Englewood Cliffs, NJ: Prentice Hall.

Latané, B., Williams, K., & Harkins, S. (1979). Many hands make light work: The causes and consequences of social loafing. *Journal of Personality and Social Psychology, 37,* 822–832.

Lau, R. R., & Russell, D. (1980). Attributions in the sports pages: A field test of some current hypotheses about attribution research. *Journal of Personality and Social Psychology, 39,* 29–38.

Laughlin, P. R. (1980). Social combination processes of cooperative problem-solving groups as verbal intellective tasks. In M. Fishbein (Ed.), *Progress in social psychology* (Vol. 1, pp. 127–155). Hillsdale, NJ: Erlbaum.

Laver, R. (1994, October 17). Apocolypse now. *Maclean's,* p. 14.

Lavoie, F., Robitaille, L., & Hébert, M. (2000). Teen dating relationships and aggression. *Violence against Women, 6,* 6–36.

Lawler, E. J., & Thye, S. R. (1999). Bringing emotions into social exchange theory. *Annual Review of Sociology, 25,* 217–244.

Lea, M., & Spears, R. (1995). Love at first byte: Building personal relationships over computer networks. In J. T. Wood & S. W. Duck (Eds.), *Understudied relationships: Off the beaten track* (pp. 197–233). Thousand Oaks, CA: Sage.

Lea, M., Spears, R., & de Groot, D. (2001). Knowing me, knowing you: Anonymity effects on social identity processes within groups. *Personality and Social Psychology Bulletin, 27,* 526–537.

Lee, F., Hallahan, M., & Herzog, T. (1996). Explaining real-life events: How culture and domain shape attributions. *Personality and Social Psychology Bulletin, 22,* 732–741.

Lee, Y., & Seligman, M. E. P. (1997). Are Americans more optimistic than the Chinese? *Personality and Social Psychology Bulletin, 23,* 32–40.

Leippe, M., & Eisenstadt, D. (1998). A self-accountability model of dissonance reduction: Multiple modes on a continuum of elaboration. In E. Harmon-Jones & J. S. Mills, *Cognitive dissonance theory: Revival with revisions and controversies.* Washington, DC: American Psychological Association.

Leippe, M. R., & Eisenstadt, D. (1994). Generalization of dissonance reduction: Decreasing prejudice through induced compliance. *Journal of Personality and Social Psychology, 67,* 395–413.

Leishman, K. (1988, February). Heterosexuals and AIDS. *Atlantic Monthly.*

Lemieux, R., & Hale, J. L. (1999). Intimacy, passion, and commitment in young romantic relationships: Successfully measuring the triangular theory of love. *Psychological Reports, 85,* 497–503.

Lemyre, L., & Smith, P. M. (1985). Intergroup discrimination and self-esteem in the minimal group paradigm. *Journal of Personality and Social Psychology, 49,* 660–670.

Lepore, L., & Brown, R. (1997). Category and stereotype activation: Is prejudice inevitable? *Journal of Personality and Social Psychology, 72,* 275–287.

Lepper, M. (1995). Theory by numbers? Some concerns about meta-analysis as a theoretical tool. *Applied Cognitive Psychology, 9,* 411–422.

Lepper, M. (1996). Intrinsic motivation and extrinsic rewards: A commentary on Cameron and Pierce's meta-analysis. *Review of Educational Research, 66,* 5–32.

Lepper, M. R., Greene, D., & Nisbett, R. E. (1973). Undermining children's intrinsic interest with extrinsic reward: A test of the overjustification hypothesis. *Journal of Personality and Social Psychology, 28,* 129–137.

Lerner, M. J. (1980). *The belief in a just world: A fundamental decision.* New York: Plenum.

Lerner, M. J., & Miller, D. T. (1978). Just world research and the attribution process: Looking back and ahead. *Psychological Bulletin, 85,* 1030–1051.

Leung, K. (1996). Beliefs in Chinese culture. In M. H. Bond (Ed.), *The handbook of Chinese psychology* (pp. 247–262). Hong Kong: Oxford University Press.

Leventhal, H., Watts, J. C., & Pagano, F. (1967). Effects of fear and instructions on how to cope with danger. *Journal of Personality and Social Psychology, 6,* 313–321.

Levine, J. M. (1989). Reaction to opinion deviance in small groups. In P. B. Paulus (Ed.), *Psychology of group influence* (2nd ed., pp. 187–231). Hillsdale, NJ: Erlbaum.

Levine, J. M., & Moreland, R. L. (1998). Small groups. In D. Gilbert, S. Fiske, & G. Lindzey (Eds.), *The handbook of social psychology* (4th ed., Vol. 2, pp. 415–469). New York: McGraw Hill.

Levine, J. M., & Thompson, L. (1996). Conflict in groups. In E. T. Higgins & A. W. Kruglanski (Eds.), *Social psychology: Handbook of basic principles* (pp. 745–776). New York: Guilford.

Levine, R., Sato, S., Hashimoto, T., & Verma, J. (1995). Love and marriage in eleven cultures. *Journal of Cross Cultural Psychology, 26,* 554–571.

Lewin, K. (1943). Defining the "field at a given time." *Psychological Review, 50,* 292–310.

Lewin, K. (1948). *Resolving social conflicts: Selected papers in group dynamics.* New York: Harper.

Lewis, M., & Brooks, J. (1978). Self-knowledge and emotional development. In M. Lewis & L. Rosenblum (Eds.), *The development of affect* (pp. 205–226). New York: Plenum.

L'Heureux-Dubé, C. (2001). Beyond the myths: Equality, impartiality, and justice. *Journal of Social Distress and the Homeless, 10,* 87–104.

Liberman, A., & Chaiken, S. (1992). Defensive processing of personally relevant health messages. *Personality and Social Psychology Bulletin, 18,* 669–679.

Lin, Y. H. W., & Rusbult, C. E. (1995). Commitment to dating relationships and cross-sex friendships in America and China. *Journal of Social and Personal Relationships, 12,* 7–26.

Linville, P. W., Fischer, G. W., & Salovey, P. (1989). Perceived distributions of characteristics of in-group and out-group members: Empirical evidence and a computer simulation. *Journal of Personality and Social Psychology, 57,* 165–188.

Linz, D. G., Donnerstein, E., & Penrod, S. (1984). The effects of multiple exposures to filmed violence against women. *Journal of Communication, 34,* 130-147.

Linz, D. G., Donnerstein, E., & Penrod, S. D. (1988). Effects of long-term exposure to violent and sexually degrading depictions of women. *Journal of Personality and Social Psychology, 55,* 758–768.

Lippmann, W. (1922). *Public opinion.* New York: Free Press.

Lloyd, S. A., & Cate, R. M. (1985). The developmental course of conflict in dissolution of premarital relationships. *Journal of Social and Personal Relationships, 2,* 179–194.

Lockwood, P., & Kunda, Z. (1997). Superstars and me: Predicting the impact of role models on the self. *Journal of Personality and Social Psychology, 73,* 91–103.

Lockwood, P., & Kunda, Z. (1999). Increasing salience of one's best selves can undermine inspiration by outstanding role models. *Journal of Personality and Social Psychology, 76,* 214–228.

Lockwood, P., & Kunda, Z. (2000). Outstanding role models: Do they inspire or demoralize us? In A. Tesser, R. B. Felson, & J. M. Suls (Eds.), *Psychological perspectives on self and identity* (pp. 147–170). Washington, DC: American Psychological Association.

London, P. (1970). The rescuers: Motivational hypotheses about Christians who saved Jews from the Nazis. In J. R. Macaulay & L.

Berkowitz (Eds.), *Altruism and helping behavior* (pp. 241–250). New York: Academic Press.

Lord, C. G., Scott, K. O., Pugh, M. A., & Desforges, D. M. (1997). Leakage beliefs and the correspondence bias. *Personality and Social Psychology Bulletin, 23,* 824–836.

Lore, R. K., & Schultz, L. A. (1993). Control of human aggression. *American Psychologist, 48,* 16–25.

Lott, A. J., & Lott, B. E. (1974). The role of reward in the formation of positive interpersonal attitudes. In T. Huston (Ed.), *Foundations of interpersonal attraction.* New York: Academic Press.

Luby, V., & Aron, A. (1990, July). A prototype structuring of love, like, and being in love. Paper presented at the Fifth International Conference on Personal Relationships, Oxford, UK.

Lumsdaine, A. A., & Janis, I. L. (1953). Resistance to "counterpropaganda"; produced by one-sided and two-sided "propaganda" presentations. *Public Opinion Quarterly, 17,* 311–318.

Lundy, D. E., Tan, J., & Cunningham, M. R. (1998). Heterosexual romantic preferences: The importance of humor and physical attractiveness for different types of relationships. *Personal Relationships, 5,* 311–325.

Lupfer, M. B., & Layman, E. (1996). Invoking naturalistic and religious attributions: A case of applying the availability heuristic? The representativeness heuristic? *Social Cognition, 14,* 55–76.

Maccoby, E. E. (1990). Gender and relationships: A developmental account. *American Psychologist, 45,* 513–520.

MacCoun, R. J. (1989). Experimental research on jury decision-making. *Science, 244,* 1046–1050.

MacDonald, G., Zanna, M. P., & Holmes, J. G. (2000). An experimental test of the role of alcohol in relationship conflict. *Journal of Experimental Social Psychology, 36,* 182–193.

MacDonald, T., Zanna, M., & Fong, G. (1996). Why common sense goes out the window: Effects of alcohol on intentions to use condoms. *Personality and Social Psychology Bulletin, 22,* 763–775.

MacDonald, T. K., Fong, G. T., Zanna, M. P., & Martineau A. M. (2000). Alcohol myopia and condom use: Can alcohol intoxication be associated with more prudent behaviour? *Journal of Personality and Social Psychology, 78,* 605–619.

Mackie, D. M. (1987). Systematic and nonsystematic processing of majority and minority persuasive communications. *Journal of Personality and Social Psychology, 53,* 41–52.

Maclean, N. (1983). *A river runs through it.* Chicago: University of Chicago Press.

Magaro, P. A., & Ashbrook, R. M. (1985). The personality of societal groups. *Journal of Personality and Social Psychology, 48,* 1479–1489.

Magoo, G., & Khanna, R. (1991). Altruism and willingness to donate blood. *Journal of Personality and Clinical Studies, 7,* 21–24.

Maier, N. R. F., & Solem, A. R. (1952). The contribution of a discussion leader to the quality of group thinking: The effective use of minority opinions. *Human Relations, 5,* 277–288.

Maio, G. R., Esses, V. M., & Bell, D. W. (1994). The formation of attitudes toward new immigrant groups. *Journal of Applied Social Psychology, 24,* 1762–1776.

Major, B., Quinton, W. J., & McCoy, S. K. (2002). Antecedents and consequences of attribution to discrimination: Theoretical and empirical advances. In M. P. Zanna (Ed.), *Advances in experimental psychology* (Vol. 34). San Diego, CA: Academic Press.

Malamuth, N. M. (1981). Rape fantasies as a function of exposure to violent sexual stimuli. *Archives of Sexual Behavior, 10,* 33–47.

Malamuth, N. M. (1986). Predictors of naturalistic sexual aggression. *Journal of Personality and Social Psychology, 50,* 953–962.

Malamuth, N. M., & Briere, J. (1986). Sexual violence in the media: Indirect effects on aggression against women. *Journal of Social Issues, 42,* 75–92.

Malamuth, N. M., & Check, J. U. (1981). The effects of mass media exposure on acceptance of violence against women: A field experiment. *Journal of Sex Research, 15,* 436–446.

Malamuth, N. M., Linz, D., Heavey, C. L., Barnes, G., & Acker, M. (1995). Using the confluence model of sexual aggression to predict men's conflict with women: A 10-year follow-up study. *Journal of Personality and Social Psychology, 69,* 353–369.

Malle, B. F., & Horowitz, L. M. (1995). The puzzle of negative self-views: An exploration using the schema concept. *Journal of Personality and Social Psychology, 68,* 470–484.

Malle, B. F., & Knobe, J. (1997). Which behaviors do people explain? A basic actor-observer asymmetry. *Journal of Personality and Social Psychology, 72,* 288–304.

Manis, M., Shedler, J., Jonides, J., & Nelson, T. E. (1993). Availability heuristic in judgments of set size and frequency of occurrence. *Journal of Personality and Social Psychology, 65,* 448–457.

Manstead, A. S. R. (1997). Situations, belongingness, attitudes, and culture: Four lessons learned from social psychology. In G. McGarty & H. S. Haslam (Eds.), *The message of social psychology: Perspectives on mind and society* (pp. 238–251). Oxford: Blackwell.

Maracek, J., & Mettee, D. R. (1972). Avoidance of continued success as a function of self-esteem, level of esteem certainty, and responsibility for success. *Journal of Personality and Social Psychology, 22,* 90–107.

Markus, H. (1977). Self-schemata and processing information about the self. *Journal of Personality and Social Psychology, 35,* 63–78.

Markus, H., & Kitayama, S. (1991). Culture and the self: Implications for cognition, emotion, and motivation. *Psychological Review, 98,* 224–253.

Markus, H. R., & Kitayama, S. (2001). The cultural construction of self and emotion: Implications for social behavior. In W. G. Parrott (Ed.), *Emotions in social psychology: Essential readings* (pp. 119–137). Philadelphia: Psychology Press.

Markus, H. R., Kitayama, S., & Heiman, R. J. (1996). Culture and "basic" psychological principles. In E. T. Higgins & A. W.

Kruglanski (Eds.), *Social psychology: Handbook of basic principles* (pp. 857–913). New York: Guilford.

Markus, H. R., & Nurius, P. (1986). Possible selves. *American Psychologist, 41,* 954–969.

Markus, H. R., & Zajonc, R. B. (1985). The cognitive perspective in social psychology. In G. Lindzey & E. Aronson (Eds.), *Handbook of social psychology* (3rd ed., Vol. 1, pp. 137–230). New York: McGraw-Hill.

Maticka-Tyndale, E. (1992). Social construction of HIV transmission and prevention among heterosexual young adults. *Social Problems, 39,* 238–252.

Maticka-Tyndale, E., Herold, E. S., & Mewhinney, D. (1998). Casual sex on spring break: Intentions and behaviors of Canadian students. *Journal of Sex Research, 35,* 254–264.

Maticka-Tyndale, E., Herold, E. S., & Mewhinney, D. (2001). Casual sex on spring break: Intentions and behaviors of Canadian students. In R. F. Baumeister (Ed.), *Social psychology and human sexuality: Key readings in social psychology* (pp. 173–186). Philadelphia, PA: Psychology Press.

McAlister, A., Perry, C., Killen, J., Slinkard, L. A., & Maccoby, N. (1980). Pilot study of smoking, alcohol, and drug abuse prevention. *American Journal of Public Health, 70,* 719–721.

McAllister, H. A. (1996). Self-serving bias in the classroom: Who shows it? Who knows it? *Journal of Educational Psychology, 88,* 123–131.

McArthur, L. Z., & Berry, D. S. (1987). Cross cultural agreement in perceptions of babyfaced adults. *Journal of Cross-Cultural Psychology, 18,* 165–192.

McCarthy, J. F., & Kelly, B. R. (1978). Aggressive behavior and its effect on performance over time in ice hockey athletes: An archival study. *International Journal of Sport Psychology, 9,* 90–96.

McCauley, C. (1989). The nature of social influence in groupthink: Compliance and internalization. *Journal of Personality and Social Psychology, 57,* 250–260.

McConahay, J. B. (1986). Modern racism, ambivalence, and the Modern Racism Scale. In J. F. Dovidio & S. L. Gaertner (Eds.), *Prejudice, discrimination, and racism: Theory and Research* (pp. 91–125). New York: Academic Press.

McDonald, J., & McKelvie, S. J. (1992). Playing safe: Helping rates for a dropped mitten and a box of condoms. *Psychological Reports, 71,* 113–114.

McFarland, C., & Miller, D. (1990). Judgments of self-other similarity. *Personality and Social Psychology Bulletin, 16,* 475–484.

McFarland, C., & Miller, D. T. (1994). The framing of relative performance feedback: Seeing the glass as half empty or half full. *Journal of Personality and Social Psychology, 66,* 1061–1073.

McGuire, W. J. (1964). Inducing resistance to persuasion. In L. Berkowitz (Ed.), *Advances in experimental social psychology* (Vol. 1, pp. 192–229). New York: Academic Press.

McGuire, W. J. (1968). Personality and susceptibility to social influence. In E. F. Borgatta & W. W. Lambert (Eds.), *Handbook of personality theory and research* (pp. 1130–1187). Chicago: Rand McNally.

McKelvie, S. J. (1995). Biases in the estimated frequency of names. *Perceptual and Motor Skills, 81,* 1331–1338.

McKelvie, S. J. (1997). The availability heuristic: Effects of fame and gender on the estimated frequency of male and female names. *Journal of Social Psychology, 137,* 63–78.

McKelvie, S. J., & McLellan, B. (1993). Effects of age and gender on perceived facial attractiveness. Reply. *Canadian Journal of Behavioral Science, 26,* 205–209.

McKenna, K. Y. A., Green, A. S., & Gleason, M. J. (2002). Relationship formation on the Internet: What's the big attraction? *Journal of Social Issues, 58,* 9–31.

Mead, G. H. (1934). *Mind, self, and society.* Chicago: University of Chicago Press.

Meeus, W. H. J., & Raaijmakers, Q. A. W. (1995). Obedience in modern society: The Utrecht Studies. *Journal of Social Issues, 51,* 155–175.

Meindl, J. R., & Lerner, M. J. (1984). Exacerbation of extreme response to an out-group. *Journal of Personality and Social Psychology, 47,* 71–83.

Menec, V. H., & Perry, R. P. (1998). Reactions to stigmas among Canadian students: Testing attribution-affect-help judgment model. *Journal of Social Psychology, 138,* 443–453.

Menec, V. H., Perry, R. P., Struthers, C. W., Schonwetter, D. J., Hechter, F. J., & Eichholz, B. L. (1994). Assisting at-risk college students with attributional retraining and effective teaching. *Journal of Applied Social Psychology, 24,* 675–701.

Merikle, P. M. (1988). Subliminal auditory messages: An evaluation. *Psychology and Marketing, 5,* 355–372.

Meyer, P. (1999). The sociobiology of human cooperation: The interplay of ultimate and proximate causes. In J. M. G. van der Dennen & D. Smillie (Eds.), *The Darwinian heritage and sociobiology: Human evolution, behavior, and intelligence* (pp. 49–65). Westport, CT: Praeger.

Michaels, J. W., Blommel, J. M., Brocato, R. M., Linkous, R. A., & Rowe, J. S. (1982). Social facilitation and inhibition in a natural setting. *Replications in Social Psychology, 2,* 21–24.

Milgram, S. (1963). Behavioral study of obedience. *Journal of Abnormal and Social Psychology, 67,* 371–378.

Milgram, S. (1974). *Obedience to authority: An experimental view.* New York: Harper & Row.

Milgram, S. (1976). Obedience to criminal orders: The compulsion to do evil. In T. Blass (Ed.), *Contemporary social psychology: Representative readings* (pp. 175–184). Itasca, IL: F. E. Peacock.

Miller, A. G. (1986). *The obedience experiments: A case study of controversy in social science.* New York: Praeger.

Miller, A. G., Ashton, W., & Mishal, M. (1990). Beliefs concerning the features of constrained behavior: A basis for the fundamental attribution error. *Journal of Personality and Social Psychology, 59,* 635–650.

Miller, C. E., & Anderson, P. D. (1979). Group decision rules and the rejection of deviates. *Social Psychology Quarterly, 42,* 354–363.

Miller, C. T. (1982). The role of performance-related similarity in social comparison of abilities: A test of the related attributes hypothesis. *Journal of Experimental Social Psychology, 18,* 513–523.

Miller, D. T., & McFarland, C. (1987). Pluralistic ignorance: When similarity is interpreted as dissimilarity. *Journal of Personality and Social Psychology, 53,* 298–305.

Miller, D. T., & Ross, M. (1975). Self-serving biases in the attribution of causality: Fact or fiction? *Psychological Bulletin, 82,* 213–225.

Miller, J. G. (1984). Culture and the development of everyday social explanation. *Journal of Personality and Social Psychology, 46,* 961–978.

Miller, N., & Campbell, D. T. (1959). Recency and primacy in persuasion as a function of the timing of speeches and measurements. *Journal of Abnormal and Social Psychology, 59,* 1–9.

Mills, J. (1958). Changes in moral attitudes following temptation. *Journal of Personality, 26,* 517–531.

Mills, J., & Clark, M. S. (1982). Communal and exchange relationships. In L. Wheeler (Ed.), *Review of personality and social psychology* (Vol. 2, pp. 121–144). Beverly Hills, CA: Sage.

Mills, J., & Clark, M. S. (1994). Communal and exchange relationships: Controversies and research. In R. Erber & R. Gilmour (Eds.), *Theoretical frameworks for personal relationships* (pp. 29–42). Hillsdale, NJ: Erlbaum.

Mohamed, A. A., & Wiebe, F. A. (1996). Toward a process theory of groupthink. *Small Group Research, 27,* 416–430.

Montemayor, R., & Eisen, M. (1977). The development of self-conceptions from childhood to adolescence. *Developmental Psychology, 13,* 314–319.

Moore, T. E. (1995). Subliminal self-help tapes: An empirical test of perceptual consequences. *Canadian Journal of Behavioural Science, 27,* 9–20.

Moreland, R. L. (1987). The formation of small groups. In C. Hendrick (Ed.), *Review of personality and social psychology* (Vol. 8, pp. 80–110). Newbury Park, CA: Sage.

Moreland, R. L., & Beach, R. (1992). Exposure effects in the classroom: The development of affinity among students. *Journal of Experimental Social Psychology, 28,* 255–276.

Moreland, R. L., & Zajonc, R. B. (1982). Exposure effects in person perception: Familiarity, similarity, and attraction. *Journal of Experimental Social Psychology, 18,* 395–415.

Morgan, H. J., & Shaver, P. R. (1999). Attachment processes and commitment to romantic relationships. In J. M. Adams & W. H. Jones, *Handbook of interpersonal commitment and relationship stability* (pp. 109–124). New York: Klewer.

Morris, M. W., & Peng, K. (1994). Culture and cause: American and Chinese attributions for social and physical events. *Journal of Personality and Social Psychology, 67,* 949–971.

Morris, W. N., & Miller, R. S. (1975). The effects of consensus-breaking and consensus-preempting partners on reduction of conformity. *Journal of Experimental Social Psychology, 11,* 215–223.

Morry, M. M., & Staska, S. L. (2001). Magazine exposure: Internalization, self-objectification, eating attitudes, and body satisfaction in male and female university students. *Canadian Journal of Behavioural Science, 33,* 269–279.

Morry, M. M., & Winkler, E. (2001). Student acceptance and expectation of sexual assault. *Canadian Journal of Behavioural Science, 33,* 188–192.

Moscovici, S. (1985). Social influence and conformity. In G. Lindzey & E. Aronson (Eds.), *Handbook of social psychology* (Vol. 2, pp. 347–412). New York: McGraw Hill.

Moscovici, S. (1994). Three concepts: Minority, conflict, and behavioral style. In S. Moscovici, A. Mucchi-Faina, & A. Maass (Eds.), *Minority influence* (pp. 233–251). Chicago: Nelson-Hall.

Moscovici, S., & Nemeth, C. (1974). Minority influence. In C. Nemeth (Ed.), *Social psychology: Classic and contemporary integrations* (pp. 217–249). Chicago: Rand McNally.

Moskalenko, S., & Heine, S. J. (2002). Watching your troubles away: Television viewing as a stimulus for subjective self-awareness. *Personality and Social Psychology Bulletin, 29,* 76–85.

Mullen, B. (1986). Atrocity as a function of lynch mob composition: A self-attention perspective. *Personality and Social Psychology Bulletin, 12,* 187–197.

Mullen, B., Anthony, T., Salas, E., & Driskell, J. E. (1994). Group cohesiveness and quality of decision making: An integration of tests of the groupthink hypothesis. *Small Group Research, 25,* 189–204.

Mullen, B., Brown, R., & Smith, C. (1992). Ingroup bias as a function of salience, relevance, and status: An integration. *European Journal of Social Psychology, 22,* 103–122.

Mummery, W. K., & Wankel, L. M. (1999). Training adherence in adolescent competitive swimmers: An application of the theory of planned behavior. *Journal of Sport and Exercise Psychology, 21,* 313–328.

Murdoch, D., Pihl, R. O., & Ross, D. (1990). Alcohol and crimes of violence: Present issues. *The International Journal of Addictions, 25,* 1065–1081.

Murray, S. L., Bellavia, G., Feeney, B., Holmes, J. G., & Rose, P. (2001). The contingencies of interpersonal acceptance: When romantic relationships function as a self-affirmational resource. *Motivation and Emotion, 25,* 163–189.

Murray, S. L., Haddock, G., & Zanna, M. P. (1996). On creating value-expressive attitudes: An experimental approach. In Seligman, C., Olson, J. M., & Zanna, M. P. (Eds.), *The psychology of values: The Ontario Symposium* (Vol. 8). Mahwah, NJ: Lawrence, Erlbaum.

Murray, S. L., & Holmes, J. G. (1997). A leap of faith? Positive illusions in romantic relationships. *Personality and Social Psychology Bulletin, 23,* 586–604.

Murray, S. L., & Holmes, J. G. (1999). The (mental) ties that bind: Cognitive structures that predict relationship resilience. *Journal of Personality and Social Psychology, 77,* 1228–1244.

Murray, S. L., Holmes, J. G., Dolderman, D., & Griffin, D. W. (2000). What the motivated mind sees: Comparing friends' perspectives to married partners' views of each other. *Journal of Experimental Social Psychology, 36,* 600–620.

Murray, S. L., Holmes, J. G., & Griffin, D. W. (1996a). The benefits of positive illusions: Idealization and the construction of satisfaction in close relationships. *Journal of Personality and Social Psychology, 70,* 79–98.

Murray, S. L., Holmes, J. G., & Griffin, D. W. (1996b). The self-fulfilling nature of positive illusions in romantic relationships: Love is not blind, but prescient. *Journal of Personality and Social Psychology, 71,* 1155–1180.

Murray, S. L., Holmes, J. G., MacDonald, G., & Ellsworth, P. C. (1998). Through the looking glass darkly? When self-doubts turn into relationship insecurities. *Journal of Personality and Social Psychology, 75,* 1459–1480.

Myers, D. G., & Arenson, S. J. (1972). Enhancement of dominant risk tendencies in group discussion. *Psychological Reports, 30,* 615–623.

Nario, M. R., & Branscombe, N. R. (1995). Comparison processes in hindsight and causal attribution. *Personality and Social Psychology Bulletin, 21,* 1244–1255.

Nemeth, C. J., & Chiles, C. (1988). Modeling courage: The role of dissent in fostering independence. *European Journal of Social Psychology, 18,* 275–280.

Neuberg, S. L. (1988). Behavioral implications of information presented outside of awareness: The effect of subliminal presentation of trait information on behavior in the Prisoner's Dilemma game. *Social Cognition, 6,* 207–230.

Newcomb, T. M. (1961). *The acquaintance process.* New York: Holt, Rinehart & Winston.

Newman, L. S. (1991). Why are traits inferred spontaneously? A developmental approach. *Social Cognition, 9,* 221–253.

Newman, L. S. (1996). Trait impressions as heuristics for predicting future behavior. *Personality and Social Psychology Bulletin, 22,* 395–411.

Newman, L. S., & Uleman, J. S. (1993). When are you what you did? Behavior identification and dispositional inference in person memory, attribution, and social judgment. *Personality and Social Psychology Bulletin, 19,* 513–525.

Nguyen, M., Beland, F., Otis, J., & Potvin, L. (1996). Diet and exercise profiles of 30- to 60-year-old male smokers: Implications for community heart health programs. *Journal of Adolescent Health, 21,* 107–115.

Niedenthal, P. M., & Beike, D. R. (1997). Interrelated and isolated self-concepts. *Personality and Social Psychology Review, 1,* 106–128.

Nisbett, R. E., & Ross, L. (1980). *Human inference: Strategies and shortcomings of human judgment.* Englewood Cliffs, NJ: Prentice Hall.

Nowak, A., Szamrej, J., & Latané, B. (1990). From private attitude to public opinion: A dynamic theory of social impact. *Psychological Review, 97,* 362–376.

Oakes, P. J., & Turner, J. C. (1980). Social categorization and intergroup behavior: Does minimal intergroup discrimination make social identity more positive? *European Journal of Social Psychology, 10,* 295–301.

O'Connor, K. M., & Carnevale, P. J. (1997). A nasty but effective negotiation strategy: Misrepresentation of a common-value issue. *Personality and Social Psychology Bulletin, 23,* 504–515.

O'Hara, J. (2000, March 6). The hell of hazing. *Maclean's,* pp. 50–52.

Ohbuchi, K., Kameda, M., & Agarie, N. (1989). Apology as aggression control: Its role in mediating appraisal of and response to harm. *Journal of Personality and Social Psychology, 56,* 219–227.

Ohbuchi, K., & Sato, K. (1994). Children's reactions to mitigating accounts: Apologies, excuses, and intentionality of harm. *Journal of Social Psychology, 134,* 5–17.

Olson, J. M., Roese, N. J., & Zanna, M. P. (1996). Expectancies. In E. T. Higgins & A. W. Kruglanski (Eds.), *Social psychology: Handbook of basic principles* (pp. 211–238). New York: Guilford.

Olson, J. M., & Zanna, M. P. (1993). Attitudes and attitude change. *Annual Review of Psychology, 44,* 117–154.

Olweus, D. (1994). *Bullying at school: What we know and what we can do.* London: Blackwell Publishers.

Olweus, D. (1995a). Annotation: Bullying at school: Basic facts and effects of a school-based intervention program. *Journal of Child Psychology and Psychiatry, 35,* 1171–1190.

Olweus, D. (1995b). Bullying or peer abuse at school: Facts and interventions. *Current Directions in Psychological Science, 4,* 196–200.

Olweus, D. (1995c). Bullying or peer abuse in school: Intervention and prevention. In G. Davies, S. Lloyd-Bostock, M. McMurran, & C. Wilson (Eds.), *Psychology, law, and criminal justice: International developments in research and practice* (pp. 248–263). Berlin, Germany: Walter de Gruyter.

Olweus, D. (1996). Bullying at school: Knowledge base and an effective intervention program. In C. Ferris & T. Grisso (Eds.), *Understanding aggressive behavior in children.* New York Academy of Sciences, Annals of the New York Academy of Sciences, Vol. 794 (pp. 265–276). New York: Academy of Sciences.

Olweus, D. (1997). Tackling peer victimization with a school-based intervention program. In D. Fry & K. Bjorkqvist (Eds.), *Cultural variation in conflict resolution: Alternatives to violence* (pp. 215–231). Mahwah, NJ: Erlbaum.

Osbeck, L. M., Moghaddam, F. M., & Perrault, S. (1997). Similarity and attraction among majority and minority groups in a multicultural context. *International Journal of Intercultural Relations, 21,* 113–123.

Ostrom, T., & Sedikides, C. (1992). Out-group homogeneity effects in natural and minimal groups. *Psychological Bulletin, 112,* 536–552.

Page, S. (1998). Accepting the gay person: Rental accommodation in the community. *Journal of Homosexuality, 36,* 31–39.

Page, S. (1999). Accommodating persons with AIDS: Acceptance and rejection in rental situations. *Journal of Applied Social Psychology, 29,* 261–270.

Paolucci-Oddone, E., Genius, M., & Violato, C. (2000). A meta-analysis of the published research on the effects of pornography. In C. Violato (Ed.), *The changing family and child development* (pp. 48–59). Burlington, VT: Ashgate Publishing.

Patch, M. E., Hoang, V. R., & Stahelski, A. J. (1997). The use of metacommunication in compliance: Door-in-the-face and single-request strategies. *Journal of Social Psychology, 137,* 88–94.

Patterson, A. (1974, September). *Hostility catharsis: A naturalistic quasi-experiment.* Paper presented at the meeting of the American Psychological Association, New Orleans.

Patterson, L. A., Cameron, J. E., & Lalonde, R. N. (1996). The intersection of race and gender: Examining the politics of identity in women's studies. *Canadian Journal of Behavioural Science, 28,* 229–239.

Paulhus, D. L. (1998). Interpersonal and intrapsychic adaptiveness of trait self-enhancement: A mixed blessing? *Journal of Personality and Social Psychology, 74,* 1197–1208.

Pennebaker, J. W. (1990). *Opening up: The healing powers of confiding in others.* New York: William Morrow.

Pennington, N., & Hastie, R. (1988). Explanation-based decision making: Effects of memory structure on judgment. *Journal of Experimental Psychology: Learning, Memory, and Cognition, 14,* 521–533.

Pennington, N., & Hastie, R. (1990). Practical implications of psychological research on juror and jury decision making. *Personality and Social Psychology Bulletin, 16,* 90–105.

Pennington, N., & Hastie, R. (1992). Explaining the evidence: Tests of the story model for juror decision making. *Journal of Personality and Social Psychology, 62,* 189–206.

Pennington, N., & Hastie, R. (1993). Reasoning in explanation-based decision making. *Cognition, 49,* 123–163.

Pepler, D. J., & Craig, W. M. (1995). A peek behind the fence: Naturalistic observations of aggressive children with remote audiovisual recording. *Developmental Psychology, 31,* 548–553.

Pepler, D. J., & Craig, W. M. (2005). Aggressive girls on troubled trajectories: A developmental perspective. In D. J. Pepler, K. C. Madsen, C. Webster, & K. S. Levene (Eds.), *The development and treatment of girlhood aggression* (pp. 3–28) Mahwah, NJ: Lawrence Erlbaum.

Pepler, D. J., Craig, W. M., Ziegler, S., & Charach, A. (1994). An evaluation of anti-bullying intervention in Toronto schools. *Canadian Journal of Community Mental Health, 13,* 95–110.

Perlini, A. H., Bertolissi, S., & Lind, D. L. (1999). The effect of women's age and physical appearance on evaluations of attractiveness and social desirability. *Journal of Social Psychology, 139,* 343–351.

Perlini, A. H., & Ward, C. (2000). HIV prevention intentions: The effects of role-play and behavioural commitment on knowledge and attitudes. *Canadian Journal of Behavioural Science, 32,* 133–143.

Perrott, S. B., Miller, Y. M., & Delaney, M. E. (1997). Attitudes toward the mandatory arrest response to domestic battering: Gender and institutional differences from a traditional and a women's university. *Legal and Criminological Psychology, 2,* 35–49.

Peters, L. H., Hartke, D. D., & Pohlmann, J. T. (1985). Fiedler's contingency theory of leadership: An application of the meta-analysis procedures of Schmidt and Hunter. *Psychological Bulletin, 97,* 274–285.

Petrie, T. A., Austin, L. J., Crowley, B. J., Helmcamp, A., Johnson, C. E., Lester, R., Rogers, R., Turner, J., & Walbrick, K. (1996). Sociocultural expectations for attractiveness for males. *Sex Roles, 35,* 581–602.

Pettigrew, T. F. (1969). Racially separate or together? *Journal of Social Issues, 25,* 43–69.

Pettigrew, T. F. (1998). Reactions toward the new minorities of Western Europe. *Annual Review of Sociology, 24,* 77–103.

Petty, R. E. (1995). Attitude change. In A. Tesser (Ed.), *Advanced social psychology* (pp. 195–255). New York: McGraw-Hill.

Petty, R. E., & Cacioppo, J. T. (1986). *Communication and persuasion: Central and peripheral routes to attitude change.* New York: Springer-Verlag.

Petty, R. E., Haugtvedt, C. P., & Smith, S. M. (1995). Elaboration as a determinant of attitude strength. In R. E. Petty & J. A. Krosnick (Eds.), *Attitude strength: Antecedents and consequences* (pp. 93–130). Mahway, NJ: Erlbaum.

Petty, R. E., & Wegener, D. T. (1998). Attitude change: Multiple roles for persuasion variables. In D. T. Gilbert, S. T. Fiske, & G. Lindzey (Eds.), *The handbook of social psychology* (4th ed., Vol. 1, pp. 323–390). New York: McGraw-Hill.

Petty, R. E., & Wegener, D. T. (1999). The elaboration likelihood model: Current status and controversies. In S. Chaiken & Y. Trope (Eds.), *Dual-process theories in social psychology* (pp. 41–72). New York: Guilford Press.

Petty, R. E., Wegener, D. T., & Fabrigar, L. R. (1997). Attitudes and attitude change. *Annual Review of Psychology, 48,* 609–647.

Pierce, T., & Lydon, J. E. (2001). Global and specific relational models in the experience of social interactions. *Journal of Personality and Social Psychology, 80,* 613–631.

Pihl, R. O., & Peterson, J. (1995). Drugs and aggression: Correlations, crime and human manipulative studies and some proposed mechanisms. *Journal of Psychiatric Neuroscience, 20,* 141–149.

Pihl, R. O., Young, S. N., Harden, P., Plotnick, S., Chamberlain, B., & Ervin, F. R. (1995). Acute effect of altered tryptophan levels and alcohol on aggression in normal human males. *Psychopharmacology, 119,* 353–360.

Piliavin, J. A., & Charng, H. (1990). Altruism: A review of recent theory and research. *Annual Review of Sociology, 16,* 27–65.

Pittman, T. S., & D'Agostino, P. R. (1985). Motivation and attribution: The effects of control deprivation on subsequent information processing. In J. Harvey & G. Weary (Eds.), *Attribution: Basic issues and applications.* New York: Academic Press.

Pleban, R., & Tesser, A. (1981). The effects of relevance and quality of another's performance on interpersonal closeness. *Social Psychology Quarterly, 44,* 278–285.

Pope, H. G., Jr., Olivardia, R., Gruber, A. J., & Borowiecki, J. (1999). Evolving ideals of male body image as seen through action toys. *International Journal of Eating Disorders, 26,* 65–72.

Povinelli, D. J. (1993). Reconstructing the evolution of mind. *American Psychologist, 48,* 493–509.

Povinelli, D. J. (1994). A theory of mind is in the head, not the heart. *Behavioral and Brain Sciences, 17,* 573–574.

Povinelli, D. J., Landau, K. R., & Perilloux, H. K. (1996). Self-recognition in young children using delayed versus live feedback: Evidence of a developmental asynchrony. *Child Development, 67,* 1540–1554.

Pratkanis, A. R. (1992). The cargo-cult science of subliminal persuasion. *Skeptical Inquirer, 16,* 260–272.

Prentice, D. A., Miller, D. T., & Lightdale, J. R. (1994). Asymmetries in attachments to groups and to their members: Distinguishing between common-identity and common-bond groups. *Personality and Social Psychology Bulletin, 20,* 484–493.

Prentice-Dunn, S., & Rogers, R. W. (1989). Deindividuation and the self-regulation of behavior. In P. B. Paulus (Ed.), *Psychology of group influence* (2nd ed., pp. 87–109). Hillsdale, NJ: Erlbaum.

Pruegger, V. J., & Rogers, T. B. (1993). Development of a scale to measure cross-cultural sensitivity in the Canadian context. *Canadian Journal of Behavioural Science, 25,* 615–621.

Pruitt, D. G. (1998). Social conflict. In D. Gilbert, S. Fiske, & G. Lindzey (Eds.), *The handbook of social psychology* (4th ed., Vol. 2, pp. 470–503). New York: McGraw Hill.

Pyszczynski, T. A., Greenberg, J., & LaPrelle, J. (1985). Social comparison after success and failure: Biased search for information consistent with a self-serving conclusion. *Journal of Experimental Social Psychology, 21,* 195–211.

Quattrone, G. A. (1986). On the perception of a group's variability. In S. Worchel & W. G. Austin (Eds.), *Psychology of intergroup relations* (2nd ed.). Chicago: Nelson-Hall.

Quattrone, G. A., & Jones, E. E. (1980). The perception of variability within ingroups and outgroups: Implications for the law of small numbers. *Journal of Personality and Social Psychology, 38,* 141–152.

Quinn, K. A., Macrae, C. N., & Bodenhausen, G. V. (2003). Stereotyping and impression formation: How categorical thinking shapes person perception. In M. A. Hogg & J. Cooper (Eds.), *Sage handbook of social psychology* (pp. 87–109). Thousand Oaks, CA: Sage.

Quinn, K. A., Roese, N. J., Pennington, G. L., & Olson, J. M. (1999). The personal/group discrimination discrepancy: The role of informational complexity. *Personality and Social Psychology Bulletin, 25,* 1430–1440.

R. v. Ewanchuk. (1998). Alberta Court of Appeal, 52. Database available at www.albertacourts.ab.ca/webpage/jdb/ current_judgments-ca.htm.

Rajecki, D. W., Bledsoe, S. B., & Rasmussen, J. L. (1991). Successful personal ads: Gender differences and similarities in offers, stipulations, and outcomes. *Basic and Applied Social Psychology, 12,* 457–469.

Rajecki, D. W., Kidd, R. F., & Ivins, B. (1976). Social facilitation in chickens: A different level of analysis. *Journal of Experimental Social Psychology, 12,* 233–246.

Reeves, R. A., Baker, G. A., Boyd, J. G., & Cialdini, R. B. (1991). The door-in-the-face technique: Reciprocal concessions vs. self-presentational explanations. *Journal of Social Behavior and Personality, 6,* 545–558.

Regan, P. C. (1998). Of lust and love: Beliefs about the role of sexual desire in romantic relationships. *Personal Relationships, 5,* 139–157.

Regan, P. C., & Berscheid, E. (1997). Gender differences in characteristics desired in a potential sexual and marriage partner. *Journal of Psychology and Human Sexuality, 9,* 25–37.

Regan, P. C., & Berscheid, E. (1999). *Lust: What we know about human sexual desire.* Thousand Oaks, CA: Sage.

Regan, P. C., Snyder, M., & Kassin, S. M. (1995). Unrealistic optimism: Self-enhancement or person positivity? *Personality and Social Psychology Bulletin, 21,* 1073–1082.

Rehm, J., Steinleitner, M., & Lilli, W. (1987). Wearing uniforms and aggression: A field experiment. *European Journal of Social Psychology, 17,* 357–360.

Reichl, A. J. (1997). Ingroup favouritism and outgroup favouritism in low status minimal groups: Differential responses to status-related and status-unrelated measures. *European Journal of Social Psychology, 27,* 617–633.

Reis, H. T., & Patrick, B. C. (1996). Attachment and intimacy: Component processes. In E. T. Higgins & A. W. Kruglanski (Eds.), *Social psychology: Handbook of basic principles* (pp. 523–563). New York: Guilford Press.

Reis, T. J., Gerrard, M., & Gibbons, F. X. (1993). Social comparison and the pill: Reactions to upward and downward comparison of contraceptive behavior. *Personality and Social Psychology Bulletin, 19,* 13–20.

Reno, R., Cialdini, R., & Kallgren, C. A. (1993). The transsituational influence of social norms. *Journal of Personality and Social Psychology, 64,* 104–112.

Reynolds, L. (2000, March 22). Some folks call Tillie "a miracle worker." *Winnipeg Free Press,* p. D3.

Rhodes, G., Yoshikawa, S., Clark, A., Lee, K., McKay, R., & Akamatsu, S. (2001). Attractiveness of facial averageness and symmetry in non-Western cultures: In search of biologically based standards of beauty. *Perception, 30,* 611–625.

Rhodes, N., & Wood, W. (1992). Self-esteem and intelligence affect influenceability: The mediating role of message reception. *Psychological Bulletin, 111,* 156–171.

Rholes, W. S., Newman, L. S., & Ruble, D. N. (1990). Understanding self and other: Developmental and motivational aspects of perceiving persons in terms of invariant dispositions. In E. T. Higgins & R. M. Sorrentino (Eds.), *Handbook of motivation and cognition: Foundations of social behavior* (Vol. 2). New York: Guilford.

Ringelmann, M. (1913). Recherches sur les moteurs animés: Travail de l'homme. *Annales de l'Institut National Argonomique,* 2e srie, tom 12, 1–40.

Riordan, C. A. (1978). Equal-status interracial contact: A review and revision of a concept. *International Journal of Intercultural Relations, 2,* 161–185.

Robins, R. W., Spranca, M. D., & Mendelsohn, G. A. (1996). The actor-observer effect revisited: Effects of individual differences and repeated social interactions on actor and observer attributions. *Journal of Personality and Social Psychology, 71,* 375–389.

Roesch, S. C., & Amirkhan, J. H. (1997). Boundary conditions for self-serving attributions: Another look at the sports pages. *Journal of Applied Social Psychology, 27,* 245–261.

Roese, N. J., & Olson, J. M. (1996). Counterfactuals, causal attributions, and the hindsight bias: A conceptual integration. *Journal of Experimental Social Psychology, 32,* 197–227.

Rogers, R. (1983). Cognitive and physiological processes in fear appeals and attitude change: A revised theory of protection motivation. In J. T. Cacioppo & R. E. Petty (Eds.), *Social psychophysiology: A sourcebook* (pp. 153–176). New York: Guilford Press.

Rosch, E., & Lloyd, B. (Eds.). (1978). *Cognition and categorization.* Hillsdale, NJ: Erlbaum.

Rosenberg, L. A. (1961). Group size, prior experience, and conformity. *Journal of Abnormal and Social Psychology, 63,* 436–437.

Rosenberg, M. J., Davidson, A. J., Chen, J., Judson, F. N., & Douglas, J. M. (1992). Barrier contraceptives and sexually transmitted diseases in women: A comparison of female-dependent methods and condoms. *American Journal of Public Health, 82,* 669–674.

Rosenblatt, P. C. (1974). Cross-cultural perspectives on attraction. In T. L. Huston (Ed.), *Foundations of interpersonal attraction* (pp. 79–99). New York: Academic Press.

Rosenhan, D. L. (1970). The natural socialization of altruistic autonomy. In J. R. Macaulay & L. Berkowitz (Eds.), *Altruism and helping behavior* (pp. 251–268). New York: Academic Press.

Rosenthal, A. M. (1964). *Thirty-eight witnesses.* New York: McGraw-Hill.

Ross, L. (1977). The intuitive psychologist and his shortcomings: Distortions in the attribution process. In L. Berkowitz (Ed.), *Advances in experimental social psychology* (Vol. 10, pp. 173–220). Orlando, FL: Academic Press.

Ross, L. (1998). Comment on Gilbert. In J. M. Darley & J. Cooper (Eds.), *Attribution and social interaction* (pp. 53–66). Washington, DC: American Psychological Association.

Ross, L., Amabile, T. M., & Steinmetz, J. L. (1977). Social roles, social control, and biases in social perception. *Journal of Personality and Social Psychology, 35,* 485–494.

Ross, L., & Nisbett, R. E. (1991). *The person and the situation: Perspectives of social psychology.* New York: McGraw-Hill.

Ross, L., & Samuels, S. M. (1993). *The predictive power of personal reputation versus labels and construal in the Prisoner's Dilemma game.* Unpublished manuscript, Stanford University.

Ross, L., & Ward, A. (1995). Psychological barriers to dispute resolution. In M. P. Zanna (Ed.), *Advances in experimental social psychology* (Vol. 27, pp. 255–304). San Diego, CA: Academic Press.

Ross, L., & Ward, A. (1996). Naive realism: Implications for social conflict and misunderstanding. In T. Brown, E. Reed, & E. Turiel (Eds.), *Values and knowledge.* Hillsdale, NJ: Erlbaum.

Ross, L. R., & Spinner, B. (2001). General and specific attachment representations in adulthood: Is there a relationship? *Journal of Social and Personal Relationships, 18,* 747–766.

Ross, M., & Olson, J. M. (1981). An expectancy-attribution model of the effects of placebos. *Psychological Review, 88,* 408–437.

Ross, M., & Sicoly, F. (1979). Egocentric biases in availability and attribution. *Journal of Personality and Social Psychology, 45,* 257–267.

Ross, W., & La Croix, J. (1996). Multiple meanings of trust in negotiation theory and research: A literature review and integrative model. *International Journal of Conflict Management, 7,* 314–360.

Rotenberg, K. J. (1998). Stigmatizations of transitions in loneliness. *Journal of Social and Personal Relationships, 15,* 565–576.

Rothman, A. J., & Hardin, C. D. (1997). Differential use of the availability heuristic in social judgment. *Personality and Social Psychology Bulletin, 23,* 123–138.

Rubin, Z. (1970). Measurement of romantic love. *Journal of Personality and Social Psychology, 16,* 265–273.

Rubin, Z., Peplau, L. A., & Hill, C. T. (1981). Loving and leaving: Sex differences in romantic attachments. *Sex Roles, 7,* 821–835.

Rudman, L. A., & Borgida, E. (1995). The afterglow of construct accessibility: The behavioral consequences of priming men to view women as sexual objects. *Journal of Experimental Social Psychology, 31,* 493–517.

Ruggiero, K., & Taylor, D. (1997). Why minority group members perceive or do not perceive the discrimination that confronts them: The role of self-esteem and perceived control. *Journal of Personality and Social Psychology, 72,* 373–389.

Rusbult, C. E. (1980). Commitment and satisfaction in romantic associations: A test of the investment model. *Journal of Experimental Social Psychology, 16,* 172–186.

Rusbult, C. E. (1983). A longitudinal test of the investment model: The development (and deterioration) of satisfaction and commitment in heterosexual involvements. *Journal of Personality and Social Psychology, 45,* 101–117.

Rusbult, C. E. (1991). *Commitment processes in close relationships: The investment model.* Paper presented at the meeting of the American Psychological Association, San Francisco.

Rusbult, C. E., & Buunk, A. P. (1993). Commitment processes in close relationships: An interdependence analysis. *Journal of Social and Personal Relationships, 10,* 175–204.

Rusbult, C. E., & Martz, J. M. (1995). Remaining in an abusive relationship: An investment model analysis of nonvoluntary dependence. *Personality and Social Psychology Bulletin, 21,* 558–571.

Rusbult, C. E., Martz, J. M., & Agnew, C. R. (1998). The investment model scale: Measuring commitment level, satisfaction level, quality of alternatives, and investment size. *Personal Relationships, 5,* 357–391.

Rusbult, C. E., & Van Lange, P. A. M. (1996). Interdependence processes. In E. T. Higgins & A. W. Kruglanski (Eds.), *Social psychology: Handbook of basic principles* (pp. 564–596). New York: Guilford.

Rushton, J. P. (1975). Generosity in children: Immediate and long-term effects of modeling, preaching, and moral judgment. *Journal of Personality and Social Psychology, 31,* 459–466.

Rushton, J. P. (1989). Genetic similarity, human altruism, and group selection. *Behavioral and Brain Sciences, 12,* 503–559.

Russell, G. W. (1983). Psychological issues in sports aggression. In J. H. Goldstein (Ed.), *Sports violence.* New York: Springer-Verlag.

Ryan, B., Jr. (1991). *It works! How investment spending in advertising pays off.* New York: American Association of Advertising Agencies.

Salovey, P., Mayer, J. D., & Rosenhan, D. L. (1991). Mood and helping: Mood as a motivator of helping and helping as a regulator of mood. In M. S. Clark (Ed.), *Prosocial behavior: Review of personality and social psychology* (Vol. 12, pp. 215–237). Newbury Park, CA: Sage.

Salovey, P., & Rodin, J. (1985). Cognitions about the self: Connecting feeling states and social behavior. In P. Shaver (Ed.), *Self, situations, and social behavior: Review of personality and social psychology* (Vol. 6, pp. 143–166). Beverly Hills, CA: Sage.

Sande, G., Goethals, G., Ferrari, L., & Worth, L. (1989). Value guided attributions: Maintaining the moral self-image and the diabolical enemy-image. *Journal of Social Issues, 45,* 91–118.

Sande, G. H., Goethals, G. R., & Radloff, C. E. (1988). Perceiving one's own traits and others': The multifaceted self. *Journal of Personality and Social Psychology, 54,* 13–20.

Sande, G. N., Ellard, J. H., & Ross, M. (1986). Effect of arbitrarily assigned status labels on self-perceptions and social perceptions: The mere position effect. *Journal of Psychology and Social Psychology, 50,* 684–689.

Sanders, G. S. (1983). An attentional process model of social facilitation. In A. Hare, H. Bumberg, V. Kent, & M. Davies (Eds.), *Small groups.* London: Wiley.

Sanger, D. E. (1993, May 30). The career and the kimono. *New York Times Magazine,* pp. 18–19.

Sanna, L. J. (1992). Self-efficacy theory: Implications for social facilitation and social loafing. *Journal of Personality and Social Psychology, 62,* 774–786.

Sato, T., & Cameron, J. E. (1999). The relationship between collective self-esteem and self construal in Japan and Canada. *Journal of Social Psychology, 139,* 426–435.

Savitsky, K. (1998). SPSP Email List Archive. www.stolaf.edu/cgi-bin

Savitsky, K., Medvec, V. H., Charlton, A. E., & Gilovich, T. (1998). "What, me worry?" Arousal, misattribution, and the effect of temporal distance on confidence. *Personality and Social Psychology Bulletin, 24,* 529–536.

Schachter, S. (1951). Deviation, rejection, and communication. *Journal of Abnormal and Social Psychology, 46,* 190–207.

Schachter, S. (1977). Nicotine regulation in heavy and light smokers. *Journal of Experimental Psychology: General, 106,* 5–12.

Schafer, M., & Crichlow, S. (1996). Antecedents of groupthink: A quantitative study. *Journal of Conflict Resolution, 40,* 415–435.

Schaller, M., & Conway, L. G., III. (1999). Influence of impression-management goals on the emerging contents of group stereotypes: Support for social-evolutionary process. *Personality and Social Psychology Bulletin, 25,* 819–833.

Schaller, M., & Conway, L. G., III. (2001). From cognition to culture: The origins of stereotypes that really matter. In G. B. Moskowitz (Ed.), *Cognitive social psychology: The Princeton symposium on the legacy and future of social cognition* (pp. 163–176). Mahwah, NJ: Lawrence Erlbaum.

Schaller, M., & Conway, L. G., III, & Tanchuk, T. L. (2002). Selective pressures on the once and future contents of ethnic stereotypes: Effects of the communicability of traits. *Journal of Personality and Social Psychology, 82,* 861–877.

Schaller, M., & O'Brien, M. (1992). "Intuitive analysis of covariance" and group stereotype formation. *Personality and Social Psychology Bulletin, 18,* 776–785.

Schriesheim, C. A., Tepper, B. J., & Tetrault, L. A. (1994). Least preferred co-worker score, situational control, and leadership effectiveness: A meta-analysis of contingency model performance predictions. *Journal of Applied Psychology, 79,* 561–573.

Schwarz, N. (1998). Accessible content and accessibility experiences: The interplay of declarative and experiential information in judgment. *Personality and Social Psychology Review, 2,* 87–99.

Scott, S. (2002, October). The man who reads faces. *Elm Street,* pp. 78–91.

Sears, D. O. (1981). Life stage effects on attitude change, especially among the elderly. In S. B. Kiesler, J. N. Morgan, & V. K. Oppenheimer (Eds.), *Aging: Social change* (pp. 183–204). New York: Academic Press.

Secord, P. F., & Backman, C. W. (1964). *Social psychology.* New York: McGraw-Hill.

Sedikides, C., Campbell, W. K., Reeder, G. D., & Elliot, A. J. (1998). The self-serving bias in relational context. *Journal of Personality and Social Psychology, 74,* 378–386.

Sedikides, C., & Skowronski, J. J. (1997). The symbolic self in evolutionary context. *Personality and Social Psychology Review, 1,* 80–102.

Segal, M. W. (1974). Alphabet and attraction: An unobtrusive measure of the effect of propinquity in a field setting. *Journal of Personality and Social Psychology, 30,* 654–657.

Seppa, N. (1997). Children's TV remains steeped in violence. *APA Monitor, 28,* 36.

Sergios, P. A., & Cody, J. (1985). Physical attractiveness and social assertiveness skills in male homosexual dating behavior and partner selection. *Journal of Social Psychology, 125,* 505–514.

Shackelford, T. K., & Buss, D. M. (1996). Betrayal in mateships, friendships, and coalitions. *Personality and Social Psychology Bulletin, 22,* 1151–1164.

Sharpe, D., Adair, J. G., & Roese, N. J. (1992). Twenty years of deception research: A decline in subjects' trust? *Personality and Social Psychology Bulletin, 18,* 585–590.

Sharpe, D., & Taylor, J. K. (1999). An examination of variables from a social-developmental model to explain physical and psychological dating violence. *Canadian Journal of Behavioural Science, 31,* 165–175.

Shavitt, S. (1989). Operationalizing functional theories of attitude. In A. R. Pratkanis, S. J. Breckler, & A. G. Greenwald (Eds.), *Attitude structure and function* (pp. 311–337). Hillsdale, NJ: Erlbaum.

Shavitt, S. (1990). The role of attitude objects in attitude function. *Journal of Experimental Social Psychology, 26,* 124–148.

Shepperd, J. A. (1995). Remedying motivation and productivity loss in collective settings. *Current Directions in Psychological Science, 4,* 131–134.

Sherif, M. (1936). *The psychology of social norms.* New York: Harper.

Sherif, M., Harvey, O. J., White, J., Hood, W., & Sherif, C. (1961). *Intergroup conflict and cooperation: The robber's cave experiment.* Norman: University of Oklahoma, Institute of Intergroup Relations.

Sherman, I. W., & Berk, R. A. (1984). The specific deterrent effects of arrest for domestic assault. *American Sociological Review, 49,* 261–272.

Shestowsky, D., Wegener, D. T., & Fabrigar, L. R. (1998). Need for cognition and interpersonal influence: Individual differences in impact on dyadic decisions. *Journal of Personality and Social Psychology, 74,* 1317–1328.

Siero, F. W., Bakker, A. B., Dekker, G. B., & van den Burg, M. T. C. (1996). Changing organizational energy consumption behavior through comparative feedback. *Journal of Environmental Psychology, 16,* 235–246.

Signorielli, N., Gerbner, G., & Morgan, M. (1995). Violence on television: The cultural indicators test. *Journal of Broadcasting and Electronic Media, 39,* 278–283.

Simmie, S. (1999, November 20). Pumping up the "level of cruelty." *Toronto Star,* p. A3.

Simon, H. A. (1990). A mechanism for social selection and successful altruism. *Science, 250,* 1665–1668.

Simonton, D. K. (1987). *Why presidents succeed: A political psychology of leadership.* New Haven, CT: Yale University Press.

Simpson, J. A. (1990). Influence of attachment styles on romantic relationships. *Journal of Personality and Social Psychology, 59,* 971–980.

Simpson, J. A., & Kenrick, D. T. (Eds.). (1997). *Evolutionary social psychology.* Mahwah, NJ: Erlbaum.

Simpson, J. A., Rholes, W. S., & Philips, D. (1996). Conflict in close relationships: An attachment perspective. *Journal of Personality and Social Psychology, 71,* 899–914.

Sinclair, G. (2000, June 30). Home-grown heroes. *Winnipeg Free Press,* pp. A1, A4.

Sinclair, L., & Kunda, Z. (1999). Reactions to a black professional: Motivated inhibition and activation of conflicting stereotypes. *Journal of Personality and Social Psychology, 77,* 885–904.

Sinclair, L., & Kunda, Z. (2000). Motivated stereotyping of women: She's fine if she praised me but incompetent if she criticized me. *Personality and Social Psychology Bulletin, 26*(11), 1329–1342.

Slavin, R. (1996). Cooperative learning in middle and secondary schools. (Special section: Young adolescents at risk) *Clearing House, 69,* 200–205.

Slavin, R. E., & Cooper, R. (1999). Improving intergroup relations: Lessons learned from cooperative learning programs. *Journal of Social Issues, 55,* 647–663.

Sloan, J. H., Kellerman, A. L., Reay, D. T., Ferris, J. A., Koepsell, T., Rivara, F. P., Rice, C., Gray, L., & LoGerfo, J. (1988). Handgun regulations, crime, assaults, and homicide: A tale of two cities. *New England Journal of Medicine, 319,* 1256–1261.

Slovic, P., Fischhoff, B., & Lichtenstein, S. (1976). Cognitive processes and societal risk taking. In J. S. Carroll & J. W. Payne (Eds.), *Cognition and social behaviour* (pp. 165–184). New York: John Wiley & Sons.

Slovic, P., & Lichtenstein, S. (1971). Comparison of Bayesian and regression approaches to the study of information processing in judgment. *Organizational Behavior and Human Performance, 6,* 649–744.

Smith, D. D. (1976). The social content of pornography. *Journal of Communication, 26,* 16–24.

Smith, M. B., Bruner, J., & White, R. W. (1956). *Opinions and personality.* New York: Wiley.

Smith, S. S., & Richardson, D. (1983). Amelioration of deception and harm in psychological research: The important role of debriefing. *Journal of Personality and Social Psychology, 44,* 1075–1082.

Snyder, M., & DeBono, K. G. (1989). Understanding the functions of attitudes: Lessons for personality and social behavior. In A. R. Pratkanis, S. J. Breckler, & A. G. Greenwald (Eds.), *Attitude structure and function* (pp. 339–359). Hillsdale, NJ: Erlbaum.

Snyder, M., Tanke, E. D., & Berscheid, E. (1977). Social perception and interpersonal behavior: On the self-fulfilling nature of social stereotypes. *Journal of Personality and Social Psychology, 35,* 656–666.

Soames, R. F. (1988). Effective and ineffective use of fear in health promotion campaigns. *American Journal of Public Health, 78,* 163–167.

Solomon, L. Z., Solomon, H., & Stone, R. (1978). Helping as a function of number of bystanders and ambiguity of emergency. *Personality and Social Psychology Bulletin, 4,* 318–321.

Sommers, E. K., & Check, J. V. (1987). An empirical investigation of the role of pornography in the verbal and physical abuse of women. *Violence and Victims, 2,* 189–209.

Sorrels, J. P., & Kelley, J. (1984). Conformity by omission. *Personality and Social Psychology Bulletin, 10,* 302–305.

South, S. J., & Lloyd, K. M. (1995). Spousal alternatives and marital dissolution. *American Sociological Review, 60,* 21–35.

Spencer, S. J., Josephs, R. A., & Steele, C. M. (1993). Low self-esteem: The uphill battle for self-integrity. In R. F. Baumeister (Ed.), *Self-esteem and the puzzle of low self-regard* (pp. 21–36). New York: Wiley.

Spencer, S. J., Steele, C. M., & Quinn, D. M. (1999). Stereotype threat and women's math performance. *Journal of Experimental Social Psychology, 35,* 4–28.

Spitzberg, B. H., & Rhea, J. (1999). Obsessive relational intrusion and sexual coercion victimization. *Journal of Interpersonal Violence, 14,* 3–20.

Spitzer, B. L., Henderson, K. A., & Zivian, M. T. (1999). Gender differences in population versus media body sizes: A comparison over four decades. *Sex Roles, 40,* 545–565.

Sprecher, S. (1994). Two sides to the breakup of dating relationships. *Personal Relationships, 1,* 199–222.

Sprecher, S. (1998). The effect of exchange orientation on close relationships. *Social Psychology Quarterly, 61,* 230–231.

Sprecher, S., & Fehr, B. (1998). The dissolution of close relationships. In J.H. Harvey (Ed.), *Perspectives of loss: A sourcebook* (pp. 99–112). Philadelphia, PA: Taylor & Francis.

Sprecher, S., Felmlee, D., Metts, S., Fehr, B., & Vanni, D. (1998). Factors associated with distress following the breakup of a close relationship. *Journal of Social and Personal Relationships, 15,* 791–809.

Sprecher, S., & Metts, S. (1989). Development of the "Romantic Beliefs Scale" and examination of the effects of gender and gender-role orientation. *Journal of Social and Personal Relationships, 6,* 387–411.

Sprecher, S., & Schwartz, P. (1994). Equity and balance in the exchange of contributions in close relationships. In M. J. Lerner & G. Mikula (Eds.), *Entitlement and the affectional bond: Justice in close relationships* (pp. 11–42). New York: Plenum.

Sprink, K. S., & Carron, A. V. (1994). Group cohesion effects in exercise classes. *Small Group Research, 25,* 26–42.

Stangor, C., & McMillan, D. (1992). Memory for expectancy-congruent and expectancy-incongruent information: A review of the social and social developmental literatures. *Psychological Bulletin, 111,* 42–61.

Stasser, G. (2000). Information distribution, participation, and group decision: Explorations with the DISCUSS and SPEAK models. In D. R. Ilgen & C. L. Hulin (Eds.), *Computational modeling of behavior in organizations: The third scientific discipline* (pp. 135–161). Washington, DC: American Psychological Association.

Stasser, G., & Titus, W. (1985). Pooling of unshared information in group decision making: Biased information sampling during discussion. *Journal of Personality and Social Psychology, 48,* 1467–1478.

Statistics Canada. (1997). Causes of death—Shelf tables. Ottawa, ON: Ministry of Industry. No. 84F0208XPB.

Statistics Canada. (1999a, January 29). *The Daily.*

Statistics Canada. (1999b, July 18). Crime statistics. *The Daily.* www. statcan.ca/Daily/English/000718/d000718a.htm (accessed July 25, 2000).

Statistics Canada. (2000). *Family violence in Canada: A statistical profile.* Ottawa, ON: Ministry of Industry. No. 85-224-XIE.

Steele, C. (1997). A threat in the air: How stereotypes shape intellectual identity and performance. *American Psychologist, 52,* 613–629.

Steele, C. M. (1988). The psychology of self-affirmation: Sustaining the integrity of the self. In L. Berkowitz (Ed.), *Advances in experimental social psychology* (Vol. 21, pp. 261–302). New York: Academic Press.

Steele, C. M., & Aronson, J. (1995a). Stereotype vulnerability and intellectual performance. In E. Aronson (Ed.), *Readings about the social animal* (7th ed.). New York: Freeman.

Steele, C. M., & Aronson, J. (1995b). Stereotype-threat and the intellectual test performance of African-Americans. *Journal of Personality and Social Psychology, 69,* 797–811.

Steele, C. M., Hoppe, H., & Gonzales, J. (1986). *Dissonance and the lab coat: Self-affirmation and the free choice paradigm.* Unpublished manuscript, University of Washington.

Steele, C. M., & Liu, T. J. (1981). Making the dissonance act unreflective of the self: Dissonance avoidance and the expectancy of a value-affirming response. *Personality and Social Psychology Bulletin, 7,* 383–387.

Steele, C. M., Spencer, S. J., & Josephs, R. (1992). *Seeking self-relevant information: The effects of self-esteem and stability of the information.* Unpublished manuscript, University of Michigan.

Steele, C. M., Spencer, S. J., & Lynch, M. (1993). Self-image resilience and dissonance: The role of affirmational resources. *Journal of Personality and Social Psychology, 64,* 885–896.

Steiner, I. D. (1972). *Group process and productivity.* New York: Academic Press.

Sternberg, R. J. (1986). A triangular theory of love. *Psychological Review, 93,* 119–135.

Sternberg, R. J. (1988). *The triangle of love.* New York: Basic Books.

Sternberg, R. J. (1997). Construct validation of a triangular love scale. *European Journal of Social Psychology, 27*, 313–335.

Sternberg, R. J., & Beall, A. E. (1991). How can we know what love is? An epistemological analysis. In G. J. O. Fletcher & F. D. Fincham (Eds.), *Cognition in close relationships* (pp. 257–278). Hillsdale, NJ: Erlbaum.

Stewart, D. D., & Stasser, G. (1995). Expert role assignment and information sampling during collective recall and decision making. *Journal of Personality and Social Psychology, 69*, 619–628.

Stone, J., Aronson, E., Crain, A. L., Winslow, M. P., & Fried, C. (1994). Inducing hypocrisy as a means of encouraging young adults to use condoms. *Personality and Social Psychology Bulletin, 20*, 116–128.

Stormo, K. J., Lang, A. R., & Stritzke, W. G. K. (1997). Attributions about acquaintance rape: The role of alcohol and individual differences. *Journal of Applied Social Psychology, 27*, 279–305.

Storms, M. D., & Nisbett, R. E. (1970). Insomnia and the attribution process. *Journal of Personality and Social Psychology, 16*, 319–328.

Strack, F., & Mussweiler, T. (1997). Explaining the enigmatic anchoring effect. *Journal of Personality and Social Psychology, 73*(3), 437-446.

Strube, M., & Garcia, J. (1981). A meta-analysis investigation of Fiedler's contingency model of leadership effectiveness. *Psychological Bulletin, 90*, 307–321.

Suls, J. M., Martin, R., & Wheeler, L. (2000). Three kinds of opinion comparison: The triadic model. *Personality and Social Psychology Review, 4*, 219–237.

Summers, G., & Feldman, N. S. (1984). Blaming the victim versus blaming the perpetrator: An attributional analysis of spouse abuse. *Journal of Social and Clinical Psychology, 2*, 339–347.

Support, Concern and Resources for Eating Disorders. (2002). Eating disorder: Statistics and facts. www.eating-disorder.org/facts.html (accessed December 17, 2002).

Swann, W. (1996). *Self-traps: The elusive quest for higher self-esteem*. New York: W. H. Freeman & Co.

Swann, W. B., Bosson, J. K., & Pelham, B. W. (2002). Different partners, different selves: Strategic self-verification of circumscribed identities. *Personality and Social Psychology Bulletin, 28*, 1215–1228.

Swann, W. B., Jr. (1990). To be adored or to be known? The interplay of self-enhancement and self-verification. In E. T. Higgins & R. M. Sorrentino (Eds.), *Handbook of motivation and cognition* (Vol. 2, pp. 404–448). New York: Guilford Press.

Swann, W. B., Jr., & Ely, R. J. (1984). A battle of the wills: Self-verification versus behavioral confirmation. *Journal of Personality and Social Psychology, 46*, 1287–1302.

Swann, W. B., Jr., & Hill, C. A. (1982). When our identities are mistaken: Reaffirming self-conceptions through social interaction. *Journal of Personality and Social Psychology, 43*, 59–66.

Swann, W. B., Jr., Hixon, G., & De La Ronde, C. (1992). Embracing the bitter "truth": Negative self-concepts and marital commitment. *Psychological Science, 3*, 118–121.

Swann, W. B., Jr., & Pelham, B. W. (1988). *The social construction of identity: Self-verification through friend and intimate selection.* Unpublished manuscript, University of Texas–Austin.

Swann, W. B., Jr., & Schroeder, D. B. (1995). The search for beauty and truth: A framework for understanding reactions to evaluations. *Personality and Social Psychology Bulletin, 21*, 1307–1318.

Swann, W. B., Jr., Stein-Seroussi, A., & McNulty, S. E. (1992). Outcasts in a white-lie society: The enigmatic worlds of people with negative self-concepts. *Journal of Personality and Social Psychology, 62*, 618–624.

Swap, W. C. (1977). Interpersonal attraction and repeated exposure to rewarders and punishers. *Personality and Social Psychology Bulletin, 3*, 248–251.

Symons, D. (1979). *The evolution of human sexuality*. New York: Oxford University Press.

Tafarodi, R. W., Kang, S., & Milne, A. B. (2002). When different becomes similar: Compensatory conformity in bicultural visible minorities. *Personality and Social Psychology Bulletin, 28*, 1131–1142.

Tait, E. (2002, November 18). Bombers' defence "blew it." *Winnipeg Free Press*, p. C4.

Tajfel, H. (1982a). *Social identity and intergroup relations.* Cambridge, England: Cambridge University Press.

Tajfel, H. (1982b). Social psychology of intergroup relations. *Annual Review of Psychology, 33*, 1–39.

Tajfel, H., & Billig, M. (1974). Familiarity and categorization in intergroup behavior. *Journal of Experimental Social Psychology, 10*, 159–170.

Tajfel, H., & Turner, J. C. (1979). An integrative theory of social contact. In W. Austin & S. Worchel (Eds.), *The social psychology of intergroup relations.* Monterey, CA: Brooks/Cole.

Tanford, S., & Penrod, S. (1984). Social influence model: A formal integration of research on majority and minority influence processes. *Psychological Bulletin, 95*, 189–225.

Tang, K. (2000). Cultural stereotypes and the justice system: The Canadian case of R. v. Ewanchuk. *International Journal of Offender Therapy and Comparative Criminology, 44*, 681–691.

Taylor, D., Ruggiero, K. M., & Louis, W. R. (1996). Personal/group discrimination discrepancy: Towards a two-factor explanation. *Canadian Journal of Behavioural Science, 28*, 193–202.

Taylor, D. M., Wright, S. C., Moghaddam, F. M., & Lalonde, R. M. (1990). The personal/group discrimination discrepancy: Perceiving my group, but not myself, to be a target of discrimination. *Personality and Social Psychology Bulletin, 16*, 254–262.

Taylor, S. E. (1981). A categorization approach to stereotyping. In D. L. Hamilton (Ed.), *Cognitive processes in stereotyping and intergroup relations* (pp. 418–429). Hillsdale, NJ: Erlbaum.

Taylor, S. E., & Crocker, J. (1981) Schematic bases of social information processing. In E. T. Higgins, C. P. Herman, & M. P.

Zanna (Eds.), *Social cognition: The Ontario Symposium* (Vol. 1, pp. 89–134). Hillsdale, NJ: Erlbaum.

Taylor, S. E., & Falcone, H. (1982). Cognitive bases of stereotyping: The relationship between categorization and prejudice. *Personality and Social Psychology Bulletin, 8,* 426–432.

Taylor, S. E., & Fiske, S. T. (1975). Point of view and perceptions of causality. *Journal of Personality and Social Psychology, 32,* 439–445.

Taylor, S. P., & Leonard, K. E. (1983). Alcohol and human physical aggression. In R. Geen & E. Donnerstein (Eds.), *Aggression: Theoretical and empirical reviews.* New York: Academic Press.

Teger, A. L., & Pruitt, D. G. (1967). Components of group risk taking. *Journal of Experimental Social Psychology, 3,* 189–205.

Tesser, A. (1980). Self-esteem maintenance in family dynamics. *Journal of Personality and Social Psychology, 39,* 77–91.

Tesser, A. (1988). Toward a self-evaluation maintenance model of social behavior. In L. Berkowitz (Ed.), *Advances in experimental social psychology* (Vol. 21, pp. 181–227). Orlando, FL: Academic Press.

Tesser, A., Campbell, J., & Mickler, S. (1983). The role of social pressure, attention to the stimulus, and self-doubt in conformity. *European Journal of Social Psychology, 13,* 217–233.

Tesser, A., Martin, L., & Mendolia, M. (1995). The impact of thought on attitude extremity and attitude-behavior consistency. In R. Petty & J. Krosnick (Eds.), *Attitude strength: Antecedents and consequences* (pp. 73–92). Ohio State University series on attitudes and persuasion, Vol. 4. Mahwah, NJ: Lawrence Erlbaum Associates.

Tesser, A., & Paulus, D. (1983). The definition of self: Private and public self-evaluation management strategies. *Journal of Personality and Social Psychology, 44,* 672–682.

Tesser, A., & Smith, J. (1980). Some effects of friendship and task relevance on helping: You don't always help the one you like. *Journal of Experimental Social Psychology, 16,* 582–590.

Tetlock, P. E., Peterson, R. S., McGuire, C., Chang, S., & Field, P. (1992). Assessing political group dynamics: A test of the groupthink model. *Journal of Personality and Social Psychology, 63,* 403–425.

Thibaut, J. W., & Kelley, H. H. (1959). *The social psychology of groups.* New York: Wiley.

Thibodeau, R., & Aronson, E. (1992). Taking a closer look: Reasserting the role of the self-concept in dissonance theory. *Personality and Social Psychology Bulletin, 18,* 591–602.

Thomas, W. I. (1928). *The child in America.* New York: Alfred A. Knopf.

Thompson, C. P., Skowronski, J. J., Larsen, S. F., & Betz, A. (1996). *Autobiographical memory: Remembering what and remembering when.* Mahwah, NJ: Erlbaum.

Thompson, L. (1995). They saw a negotiation: Partisanship and involvement. *Journal of Personality and Social Psychology, 68,* 839–853.

Thompson, L. (1997). *The mind and heart of the negotiator.* Englewood Cliffs, NJ: Prentice-Hall.

Thompson, L., & Hrebec, D. (1996). Lose-lose agreements in interdependent decision making. *Psychological Bulletin, 120,* 396–409.

Thomsen, C. T., & Borgida, E. (1996). Throwing out the baby with the bathwater? Let's not overstate the overselling of the base rate fallacy. *Behavioral and Brain Sciences, 19,* 39–40.

Toi, M., & Batson, C. D. (1982). More evidence that empathy is a source of altruistic motivation. *Journal of Personality and Social Psychology, 43,* 281–292.

Tougas, F., Brown, R., Beaton, A. M., & Joly, S. (1995). Neosexism: Plus ça change, plus c'est pareil. *Personality and Social Psychology Bulletin, 21,* 842–849.

Trafimow, D., & Schneider, D. J. (1994). The effects of behavioral, situational, and person information on different attribution judgments. *Journal of Experimental Social Psychology, 30,* 351–369.

Trafimow, D., & Wyer, R. S. (1993). Cognitive representation of mundane social events. *Journal of Personality and Social Psychology, 64,* 365–376.

Trapnell, P. D., & Campbell, J. D. (1999). Private self-consciousness and the five-factor model of personality: Distinguishing rumination from reflection. *Journal of Personality and Social Psychology, 76,* 284–304.

Trappey, C. (1996). A meta-analysis of consumer choice and subliminal advertising. *Psychology and Marketing, 13,* 517–530.

Traupmann, J., Petersen, R., Utne, M., & Hatfield, E. (1981). Measuring equity in intimate relations. *Applied Psychology Measurement, 5,* 467–480.

Triandis, H. C. (1989). The self and social behavior in differing cultural contexts. *Psychological Review, 96,* 506–520.

Triandis, H. C. (1990). Cross-cultural studies of individualism and collectivism. In J. J. Berman (Ed.), *Nebraska Symposium on Motivation, 1989* (pp. 41–133). Lincoln: University of Nebraska Press.

Triandis, H. C. (1995). *Individualism and Collectivism.* Boulder, CO: Westview Press.

Triplett, N. (1898). The dynamogenic factors in pace making and competition. *American Journal of Psychology, 9,* 507–533.

Trivers, R. (1985). *Social evolution.* Menlo Park, CA: Benjamin-Cummings.

Trivers, R. L. (1971). The evolution of reciprocal altruism. *Quarterly Review of Biology, 46,* 35–57.

Tseëlon, E. (1995). *The presentation of woman in everyday life.* Thousand Oaks, CA: Sage.

Turner, C., & Simons, L. (1974). Effects of subject sophistication and evaluation apprehension on aggressive responses to weapons. *Journal of Personality and Social Psychology, 30,* 341–348.

Turner, C., Simons, L., Berkowitz, L., & Frodi, A. (1977). The stimulating and inhibiting effects of weapons on aggressive behavior. *Aggressive Behavior, 3,* 355–378.

Turner, J. C., Hogg, M. A., Oakes, P. J., Reicher, S. D., & Wetherell, M. S. (1987). *Rediscovering the social group: A self-categorization theory.* Oxford, UK: Blackwell Publishers.

Turner, M. E., Pratkanis, A. R., Probasco, P., & Leve, C. (1992). Threat, cohesion, and group effectiveness: Testing a social identity maintenance perspective on groupthink. *Journal of Personality and Social Psychology, 63,* 781–796.

Tversky, A., & Kahneman, D. (1973). Availability: A heuristic for judging frequency and probability. *Cognitive Psychology, 5,* 207–232.

Tversky, A., & Kahneman, D. (1974). Judgment under uncertainty: Heuristics and biases. *Science, 185,* 1124–1131.

Twenge, J. M., Baumeister, R. F., Tice, D. M., & Stucke, T. S. (2001). If you can't join them, beat them: Effects of social exclusion on aggressive behavior. *Journal of Personality and Social Psychology, 81,* 1058–1069.

Uehara, E. S. (1995). Reciprocity reconsidered: Gouldner's "moral norm of reciprocity" and social support. *Journal of Social and Personal Relationships, 12,* 483–502.

Uleman, J. S., & Moskowitz, G. B. (1994). Unintended effects of goals on unintended inferences. *Journal of Personality and Social Psychology, 66,* 490–501.

Uranowitz, S. W. (1975). Helping and self-attributions: A field experiment. *Journal of Personality and Social Psychology, 32,* 852–854.

Valins, S. (1966). Cognitive effects of false heart-rate feedback. *Journal of Personality and Social Psychology, 4,* 400–408.

VanOostrum, N., & Horvath, P. (1997). The effects of hostile attribution on adolescents' aggressive responses to social situations. *Canadian Journal of School Psychology, 13,* 729–738.

Van Overwalle, F., & De Metsenaere, M. (1990). The effects of attribution-based intervention and study strategy training on academic achievement in college freshmen. *British Journal of Educational Psychology, 60,* 299–311.

Vargas Llosa, M. (1986, February 16). My son the Rastafarian. *New York Times Magazine,* pp. 20–30, 41–43, 67.

Vidyasgar, P., & Mishra, H. (1993). Effect of modelling on aggression. *Indian Journal of Clinical Psychology, 20,* 50–52.

Voissem, N. H., & Sistrunk, F. (1971). Communication schedules and cooperative game behavior. *Journal of Personality and Social Psychology, 19,* 160–167.

Von Hippel, W., Jonides, J., Hilton, J. L., & Narayan, S. (1993). Inhibitory effect of schematic processing on perceptual encoding. *Journal of Personality and Social Psychology, 64,* 921–935.

Vorauer, J. D. (2003). Dominant group members in intergroup interaction: Safety or vulnerability in numbers? *Personality and Social Psychology Bulletin, 29,* 498–511.

Vorauer, J. D., & Claude, S. D. (1998). Perceived versus actual transparency of goals in negotiation. *Personality and Social Psychology Bulletin, 24,* 371–385.

Vorauer, J. D., Hunter, A. J., Main, K., & Roy, S. (2000). Meta-stereotype activation: Evidence from indirect measures for specific evaluative concerns experienced by members of dominant groups in intergroup interaction. *Journal of Personality and Social Psychology, 78,* 690–707.

Vorauer, J. D., & Kumhyr, S. M. (2001). Is this about you or me? Self- versus other-directed judgments and feelings in response to intergroup interaction. *Personality and Social Psychology Bulletin, 27,* 706–719.

Vorauer, J. D., Main, K., & O'Connell, G. B. (1998). How do individuals expect to be viewed by members of lower status groups? Content and implications of meta stereotypes. *Journal of Personality and Social Psychology, 75,* 917–937.

Wallach, M. A., Kogan, N., & Bem, D. J. (1962). Group influences on individual risk taking. *Journal of Abnormal and Social Psychology, 65,* 75–86.

Walsh, M., Hickey, C., & Duffy, J. (1999). Influence of item content and stereotype situation on gender differences in mathematical problem solving. *Sex Roles, 41,* 219–240.

Walster, E. (1966). Assignment of responsibility for an accident. *Journal of Personality and Social Psychology, 3,* 73–79.

Walster (Hatfield), E., Aronson, V., Abrahams, D., & Rottman, L. (1966). Importance of physical attractiveness in dating behavior. *Journal of Personality and Social Psychology, 5,* 508–516.

Walster, E., & Festinger, L. (1962). The effectiveness of "overheard" persuasive communication. *Journal of Abnormal and Social Psychology, 65,* 395–402.

Walster, E., Walster, G. W., & Berscheid, E. (1978). *Equity: Theory and research.* Boston: Allyn & Bacon.

Walther, J., Anderson, J. F., & Park, D. W. (1994). Interpersonal effects in computer mediated interaction: A meta-analysis of social and antisocial communication. *Communication Research, 21,* 460–487.

Wang, T., Brownstein, R., & Katzev, R. (1989). Promoting charitable behavior with compliance techniques. *Applied Psychology: An International Review, 38,* 165–184.

Wänke, M., Schwarz, N., Bless, H. (1995). The availability heuristic revisited: Experienced ease of retrieval in mundane frequency estimates. *Acta Psychologica, 89,* 83–90.

Watkins, D., Adair, J., Akande, A., Gerong, A., McInerney, D., Sunar, D., Watson, S., Wen, Q., & Wondimu, H. (1998). Individualism-collectivism, gender and the self-concept: A nine-culture investigation. *Psychologia: An International Journal of Psychology in the Orient, 41,* 259–271.

Watkins, D., Akande, A., Fleming, J., Ismail, M., Lefner, K., Regmi, M., Watson, S., Yu, J., Adair, J., Cheng, C., Gerong, A., McInerney, D., Mpofu, E., Singh-Sengupta, S., & Wondimu, H. (1998). Cultural dimensions, gender, and the nature of self-concept: A fourteen-country study. *International Journal of Psychology, 33,* 17–31.

Watson, R. I. (1973). Investigation into deindividuation using a cross-cultural survey technique. *Journal of Personality and Social Psychology, 25,* 342–345.

Watson, W. E., Johnson, L., Kumar, K., & Critelli, J. (1998). Process gain and process loss: Comparing interpersonal processes and performance of culturally diverse and non-diverse teams across time. *International Journal of Intercultural Relations, 22*, 409–430.

Webber, R., & Crocker, J. (1983). Cognitive processes in the revision of stereotypic beliefs. *Journal of Personality and Social Psychology, 45*, 961–977.

Webster, D. M. (1993). Motivated augmentation and reduction of the overattributional bias. *Journal of Personality and Social Psychology, 65*, 261–271.

Wegener, D. T., & Petty, R. E. (1994). Mood management across affective states: The hedonic contingency hypothesis. *Journal of Personality and Social Psychology, 66*, 1034–1048.

Wegner, D. M., & Bargh, J. A. (1998). Control and automaticity in social life. In D. Gilbert, S. Fiske, & G. Lindzey (Eds.), *The handbook of social psychology* (4th ed., Vol. 1, pp. 446–498). New York: McGraw Hill.

Weiner, B., Amirkhan, J., Folkes, V. S., & Verette, J. A. (1987). An attributional analysis of excuse giving: Studies of a naive theory of emotion. *Journal of Personality and Social Psychology, 52*, 316–324.

Weinstein, N. D. (1980). Unrealistic optimism about future life events. *Journal of Personality and Social Psychology, 39*, 806–820.

Weinstein, N. D., & Klein, W. M. (1996). Unrealistic optimism: Present and future. *Journal of Social and Clinical Psychology, 15*, 1–8.

Weir, W. (1984, October 15). Another look at subliminal "facts." *Advertising Age,* p. 46.

Wekerle, C., & Wall, A. (2002). Introduction: The overlap between relationship violence and substance abuse. In C. Wekerle & A. Wall (Eds.), *The violence and addiction equation* (pp. 1–21). New York: Taylor & Francis.

Wells, S., Graham, K., & West, P. (2000). Alcohol-related aggression in the general population. *Journal of Studies on Alcohol, 61*, 626–632.

Wells, W. D. (Ed.), (1997). *Measuring advertising effectiveness.* Mahwah, NJ: Erlbaum.

Werner, C., & Parmelee, P. (1979). Similarity of activity preferences among friends: Those who play together stay together. *Social Psychology Quarterly, 42*, 62–66.

Weyant, J. M. (1996). Application of compliance techniques to direct-mail requests for charitable donations. *Psychology and Marketing, 13*, 157–170.

Whatley, M. A., Webster, J. M., Smith, R. H., & Rhodes, A. (1999). The effect of a favor on public and private compliance: How internalized is the norm of reciprocity? *Basic and Applied Social Psychology, 21*, 251–259.

Wheeler, L., Koestner, R., & Driver, R. (1982). Related attributes in the choice of comparison others: It's there, but it isn't all there is. *Journal of Experimental Social Psychology, 18*, 489–500.

Wheeler, L., & Kunitate, M. (1992). Social comparison in everyday life. *Journal of Personality and Social Psychology, 62*, 760–773.

Wheeler, L., Martin, R., & Suls, J. (1997). The proxy model of social comparison for self-assessment of ability. *Personality and Social Psychology Review, 1*, 54–61.

White, H. (1997). Longitudinal perspective on alcohol and aggression during adolescence. In M. Galanter (Ed.), *Recent developments in alcoholism, Vol. 13: Alcohol and violence: Epidemiology, neurobiology, psychology, family issues* (pp. 81–103). New York: Plenum.

White, L. K. (1990). Determinants of divorce: A review of research in the eighties. *Journal of Marriage and the Family, 52*, 904–912.

Whitley, B. E., & Frieze, I. H. (1985). Children's causal attributions for success and failure in achievement settings: A meta-analysis. *Journal of Educational Psychology, 77*, 608–616.

Wicker, A. W. (1969). Attitudes versus actions: The relationship between verbal and overt behavioral responses to attitude objects. *Journal of Social Issues, 25*, 41–78.

Wilder, D. A. (1984). Intergroup contact: The typical member and the exception to the rule. *Journal of Experimental Psychology, 20*, 177–194.

Wilder, D. A. (1986). Social categorization: Implications for creation and reduction of intergroup bias. In L. Berkowitz (Ed.), *Advances in experimental social psychology* (Vol. 19, pp. 291–355). New York: Academic Press.

Wilder, D. A., & Shapiro, P. N. (1989). Role of competition-induced anxiety in limiting the beneficial impact of positive behavior by an out-group member. *Journal of Personality and Social Psychology, 56*, 60–69.

Williams, K., Harkins, S., & Latané, B. (1981). Identifiability as a deterrent to social loafing: Two cheering experiments. *Journal of Personality and Social Psychology, 40*, 303–311.

Williamson, G. M., & Clark, M. S. (1989). Providing help and desired relationship type as determinants of changes in moods and self-evaluations. *Journal of Personality and Social Psychology, 56*, 722–734.

Williamson, G. M., & Clark, M. S. (1992). Impact of desired relationship type on affective reactions to choosing and being required to help. *Personality and Social Psychology Bulletin, 18*, 10–18.

Wilson, T. D. (2002). *Strangers to ourselves: Discovering the adaptive unconscious.* Cambridge, MA: Harvard University Press.

Wilson, T. D., & Brekke, N. C. (1994). Mental contamination and mental correction: Unwanted influences on judgments and evaluations. *Psychological Bulletin, 116*, 117–142.

Wilson, T. D., Houston, C. E., Etling, K. M., & Brekke, N. (1996). A new look at anchoring effects: Basic anchoring and its antecedents. *Journal of Experimental Psychology: General, 125*, 387–402.

Wilson, T. D., Houston, C. E., & Meyers, J. M. (1998). Choose your poison: Effects of lay beliefs about mental processes on attitude change. *Social Cognition, 16*(1), 114–132.

Wilson, T. D., & Linville, P. W. (1982). Improving the academic performance of college freshmen: Attribution therapy revisited. *Journal of Personality and Social Psychology, 42*, 367–376.

Wilson, T. D., & Linville, P. W. (1985). Improving the performance of college freshmen using attributional techniques. *Journal of Personality and Social Psychology, 49*, 287–293.

Winslow, R. W., Franzini, L. R., & Hwang, J. (1992). Perceived peer norms, casual sex, and AIDS risk prevention. *Journal of Applied Social Psychology, 22,* 1809–1827.

Wood, J. V. (1989). Theory and research concerning social comparisons of personal attributes. *Psychological Bulletin, 106,* 231–248.

Wood, J. V. (1996). What is social comparison and how should we study it? *Personality and Social Psychology Bulletin, 22,* 520–537.

Wood, J. V., Michela, J. L., & Giordano, C. (2000). Downward comparison in everyday life: Reconciling self-enhancement models with the mood-cognition priming model. *Journal of Personality and Social Psychology, 79,* 563–579.

Wood, J. V., Taylor, S. E., & Lichtman, R. R. (1985). Social comparison in adjustment to breast cancer. *Journal of Personality and Social Psychology, 49,* 1169–1183.

Wood, J. V., & VanderZee, K. (1997). Social comparisons among cancer patients: Under what conditions are comparisons upward and downward? In B. P. Buunk and F. X. Gibbons (Eds.), *Health, coping, and well-being: Perspectives from social comparison theory.* Mahwah, NJ: Lawrence Erlbaum Associates, Publishers.

Wood, W. (1987). Meta-analytic review of sex differences in group performance. *Psychological Bulletin, 102,* 53–71.

Wood, W., Lundgren, S., Ouelette, J. A., Busceme, S., & Blackstone, J. (1994). Minority influence: A meta-analytic review of social influence processes. *Psychological Bulletin, 115,* 323–345.

Wood, W., Wong, F. Y., & Chachere, G. (1991). Effects of media violence on viewers' aggression in unconstrained social interaction. *Psychological Bulletin, 109,* 371–383.

Word, C. O., Zanna, M. P., & Cooper, J. (1974). The nonverbal mediation of self-fulfilling prophecies in interracial interaction. *Journal of Experimental Social Psychology, 10,* 109–120.

Wright, R. (1994). *The moral animal: Why we are the way we are: The new science of evolutionary psychology.* New York: Random House.

Wright, S. C., & Taylor, D. M. (2003). The social psychology of cultural diversity: Social stereotyping, prejudice, and discrimination. In M. A. Hogg & J. Cooper (Eds.), *Sage handbook of social psychology.* Thousand Oaks, CA: Sage.

Wyer, R. S., & Srull, T. K. (1989). *Memory and cognition in its social context.* Hillsdale, NJ: Erlbaum.

Wyer, R. S., Jr. (1988). Social memory and social judgment. In P. R. Solomon, G. R. Goethals, C. M. Kelley, & B. R. Stephens (Eds.), *Perspectives on memory research.* New York: Springer-Verlag.

Yik, M. S., Bond, M. H., & Paulhus, D. L. (1998). Do Chinese self-enhance or self-efface? It's a matter of domain. *Personality and Social Psychology Bulletin, 24,* 399–406.

Yudko, E., Blanchard, D., Henne, J., & Blanchard, R. (1997). Emerging themes in preclinical research on alcohol and aggression. In M. Galanter (Ed.), *Recent developments in alcoholism, Vol. 13: Alcohol and violence: Epidemiology, neurobiology, psychology, family issues* (pp. 123–138). New York: Plenum.

Zajonc, R. B. (1965). Social facilitation. *Science, 149,* 269–274.

Zajonc, R. B. (1968). Attitudinal effects of mere exposure. *Journal of Personality and Social Psychology, 9,* Monograph Suppl. No. 2, Pt. 2.

Zajonc, R. B. (1980). Compresence. In P. B. Paulus (Ed.), *Psychology of group influence* (pp. 35–60). Hillsdale, NJ: Erlbaum.

Zajonc, R. B., Heingartner, A., & Herman, E. M. (1969). Social enhancement and impairment of performance in the cockroach. *Journal of Personality and Social Psychology, 13,* 83–92.

Zajonc, R. B., & Sales, S. M. (1966). Social facilitation of dominant and subordinate responses. *Journal of Experimental Social Psychology, 2,* 160–168.

Zanna, M., Goethals, G. R., & Hill, J. (1975). Evaluating a sex-related ability: Social comparison with similar others and standard setters. *Journal of Experimental Social Psychology, 11,* 86–93.

Zanna, M., & Rempel, J. K. (1988). Attitudes: A new look at an old concept. In D. Bar-Tal & A. W. Kruglanski (Eds.), *The social psychology of attitudes* (pp. 315–334). New York: Cambridge University Press.

Zanna, M. P., & Fazio, R. H. (1982). The attitude-behavior relation: Moving toward a third generation of research. In M. P. Zanna, E. T. Higgins, & C. P. Herman (Eds.), *Consistency in social behavior: The Ontario Symposium* (Vol. 2, pp. 283–301). Hillsdale, NJ: Erlbaum.

Zanna, M. P., & Sande, G. N. (1987). The effects of collective actions on the attitudes of individual group members: A dissonance analysis. In M. P. Zanna, J. M. Olson, C. P. Herman (Eds.), *The Ontario Symposium* (Vol. 5: Social Influence).

Zanot, E. J., Pincus, J. D., & Lamp, E. J. (1983). Public perceptions of subliminal advertising. *Journal of Advertising, 12,* 39–45.

Zebrowitz-McArthur, L. (1988). Person perception in cross-cultural perspective. In M. H. Bond (Ed.), *The cross-cultural challenge to social psychology* (pp. 245–265). Newbury Park, CA: Sage.

Zillman, D., & Bryant, J. (1984). Effects of massive exposure to pornography. In N. M. Malamuth & E. Donnerstein (Eds.), *Pornography and sexual aggression* (pp. 115–138). Orlando, FL: Academic Press.

Zillmann, D. (1978). Attribution and misattribution of excitatory reactions. In J. H. Harvey, W. J. Ickes, & R. F. Kidd (Eds.), *New directions in attribution research* (Vol. 2, pp. 335–370). Hillsdale, NJ: Erlbaum.

Zimbardo, P., & Andersen, S. (1993). Understanding mind control: Exotic and mundane mental manipulations. In M. D. Langone (Ed.), *Recovery from cults* (pp. 104–125). New York: Norton.

Zimbardo, P. G. (1970). The human choice: Individuation, reason, and order versus deindividuation, impulse, and chaos. In W. J. Arnold & D. Levine (Eds.), *Nebraska Symposium on Motivation: 1969* (Vol. 17, pp. 237–307). Lincoln: University of Nebraska Press.

Zuber, J. A., Crott, H. W., & Werner, J. (1992). Choice shift and group polarization: An analysis of the status of arguments and social decision schemes. *Journal of Personality and Social Psychology, 62*, 50–61.

Zuwerink, J., Monteith, M., Devine, P., & Cook, D. (1996). Prejudice toward Blacks: With and without compunction? *Basic and Applied Social Psychology, 18*, 131–150.

Credits

Chapter 1

Text and Art: p. 12: Figure 1.1 adapted from L. Ross and S. M. Samuels, *The Predictive Power of Personal Reputation versus Labels and Construal in the Prisoner's Dilemma Game.* Unpublished manuscript, Stanford University, © 1993. Reprinted by permission of Lee Ross.

Photos and Cartoons: p. 2: © James Robert Fuller/CORBIS; **p. 3:** Adrian Wyld/CP Photo Archive; **p. 8:** Sayyid Azim/CP Photo Archive; **p. 10:** © B. Seitz/Photo Researchers; **p.13:** Rick Kopstein.

Chapter 2

Text and Art: p. 39: Figure 2.2 from "Canadian code of ethics for psychologists," Canadian Psychological Association, 1991, and "Ethical principles of psychologists and code of conduct," *American Psychologist*, 47, pp. 1597–1611, Copyright 1992 by the American Psychological Association. Adapted with permission.

Photos and Cartoons: p. 20: Melissa Farlow/Aurora Photos; **p. 21:** AP/Wide World Photos; **p. 28:** Joe Bryska/Winnipeg Free Press; **p. 38:** © 1993 FarWorks, Inc./Distributed by Universal Press Syndicate. All rights reserved.

Chapter 3

Text and Art: p. 53: Figure 3.2 from "Category accessibility and impression formation," by E. T. Higgins, W. S. Rholes, and C. R. Jones, in *Journal of Experimental Social Psychology*, 13, pp. 141–154. © 1977 by Academic Press. Reproduced by permission of the publisher. **p. 60:** Figure 3.3 from Gilbert, D. T. (1991). How mental systems believe. *American Psychologist*, 46, 107–119. Adapted by permission. **p. 65:** Figure 3.4 adapted from Jones and Harris, "Attribution of attitudes," *Journal of Experimental Psychology*, 3. Copyright 1967. Reprinted by permission of Academic Press. **p. 68:** Figure 3.5 from Taylor, et al., "Point of view and perception of causality," *Journal of Personality and Social Psychology*, 32. Copyright 1975 by the American Psychological Association. Adapted by permission. **p. 69:** Morris, M.W., & Peng, K. (1994). Culture and Cause: American and Chinese attribution for social and physical events. *Journal of Personality and Social Psychology*, 67, pages 949-971. Copyright © 1994 by the American Psychological Association; **p. 71:** With permission from Rhona Raskin, Clinical Counsellor and Advice Columnist.

Photos and Cartoons: p. 46: Rainer Grosskopf/Getty Images Inc.–Stone Allstock; **p. 47:** Photograph by KC Armstrong; **p. 61:** Joshua Correll/Courtesy Charles Judd, University of Colorado at Boulder; **p. 63:** Hartmut Schwarzbach/Peter Arnold, Inc.; **p. 72:** Rusty Barton.

Chapter 4

Text and Art: p. 86: Adapted from Campbell, J.D., Trapnell, P.S., Heine, S.J., Katz, I.M., Lavallee, L.F., & Lehman, D.R. (1996). Self-Concept Clarity: Measurement, Personality Correlates, and Cultural Boundaries. *Journal of Personality and Social Psychology*, 70, pages 141-156. Copyright © 1996 by the American Psychological Association. Adapted and Reprinted with permission. **p. 89:** Excerpt from S. E. Cross, P. L. Bacon, and M. L. Morris, "The relational-interdependent self-construal and relationships," *Journal of Personality and Social Psychology, 78*, pp. 791–808. © 2000 by the American Psychological Association. Reprinted with permission. **p. 92:** Figure 4.1 from Carver and Scheier, *Attention and Self-Regulation: A Control Theory Approach to Human Behavior.* Copyright 1981. Reprinted by permission of Springer-Verlag. **p. 99:** Lockwood, P. & Kunda, Z. Increasing salience of one's best selves can undermine inspiration by outstanding role models. *The Journal of Personality and Social Psychology*, 76, p. 217. Copyright © 1999 by the American Psychological Association. Reprinted with permission. **p. 107:** Steele, C.M., Hoppe H., & Gonzales, J. (1986). Dissonance and the lab coat:Self-Affirmation and the Free Choice Paradigm. Unpublished manuscript, University of Washington.

Photos and Cartoons: p. 82: Getty Images, Inc; **p. 85:** PT Santana/Getty Images Inc. - Stone Allstock; **p. 88:** AP/Wide World Photos; **p. 93:** Frascino © 1977 The New Yorker Collection. All rights reserved. **p. 96L:** © Eric Berndt/Unicorn Photos; **p. 96M:** © Mark Baldwin; **p. 96R:** © Mark Baldwin; **p. 100:** Hamilton from The New Yorker Collection. All rights reserved. **p. 101:** © Richard Lord/The Image Works; **p. 102:** © David Young-Wolff/PhotoEdit Inc.

Chapter 5

Text and Art: p. 124: Figure 5.1 adapted from Ajzen/Fishbein, *Understanding Attitudes and Predicting Social Behavior*. Copyright 1980. Reprinted by permission of Pearson Education, Upper Saddle River, NJ; **p. 135:** Figure 5.4 adapted from Shavitt, "The role of attitude objects in attitude function," *Journal of Social Psychology*, 26, pp. 124–148. Copyright 1990. Reprinted by permission. **p. 144:** Figure 5.6 from Aronson and Mills, "The effect of severity of initiation on liking for a group," *Journal of Abnormal and Social Psychology*, 1959.

Photos and Cartoons: p. 118: © Ribeiro Antonio/Ponopresse; **p. 119:** © Michael Ponomareff/Ponopresse; **p. 121:** Robert Kusel Photography, Inc.; **p. 126:** © Sexuality Education Resource Centre, Winnipeg; **p. 128:** Courtesy of Ford Motor Company of Canada, Ltd.; **p. 132:** Canadian Public Health Association; **p. 134:** Pepsi-Cola North America/Pepsi-Cola Company; **p. 136:** American Association of Advertising Agencies; **p. 140:** Dennis MacDonald/PhotoEdit Inc.; **p. 142:** Dennis MacDonald/PhotoEdit Inc; **p. 143:** © DND Photo/Sgt. Matheson (Neg # IHC88-12-2); **p. 145:** Courtesy of the University of Vermont; **p. 149:** Will Faller; **p. 150:** AFP/Getty Images.

Chapter 6

Text and Art: p. 164: Figure 6.1 adapted from Sherif, *The Psychology of Social Norms*. Copyright 1936 by HarperCollins Publishers. Reprinted by permission. **p. 171:** Figure 6.2 from Asch, "Studies of independence and conformity: A minority of one against a unanimous majority," *Psychological Monographs*, 70 (9, Whole No. 416); **p. 178:** Figure 6.3 adapted from Ciardini, R.B., Vincent, J.E., Lewis, S.K., Catalan, J., Wheeler, D., & Darby, B.L. (1975). Reciprocal concessions procedure for inducing compliance: The Door-in the face-technique. *Journal of Personality and Social Psychology*, 31. Pages 206-215. Copyright © 1975 by the American Psychological Association; and Freedman, J.L. & Fraser, S.C. (1966). Compliance without Pressure: the foot-in the door technique. *Journal of Personality and Social Psychology*, 4, pages 195-202. Copyright © 1966 by the American Psychological Association; **p. 185:** Figure 6.4 from S. Milgram, *From Obedience to Authority*. Copyright 1974. Reprinted by permission of HarperCollins Publishers, Inc.

Photos and Cartoons: p. 160: Imagestate/Firstlight.ca; **p. 161:** Peter Blashill/The Province; **p. 168:** Keith Morison/PDI; **p. 172:** Copyright © William Vandivert; **p. 173:** Picture Desk Inc./Kobal Collection; **p. 175:** Bill Becker/CP Photo Archive; **p. 181:** AFP/Getty Images; **p. 183:** Copyright © 1965 by Stanley Milgram. From "Obedience" (film) distributed by the Pennsylvania State University PCR. Courtesy of Alexandra Milgram.

Chapter 7

Text and Art: p. 203: Figure 7.1 from Cotrell, et al., "Social facilitation in dominant responses by the presence of an audience and the mere presence of others," *Journal of Personality and Social Psychology*, 9. Copyright 1968 by the American Psychological Association. Adapted by permission. **p. 204:** Figure 7.2 from Jackson, et al., "Social Loafing on difficult tasks," *Journal of Personality and Social Psychology*, 49. Copyright 1985 by the American Psychological Association. Adapted by permission. **p. 210:** Figure 7.3 adapted from Janis, *Victims of Groupthink*. Copyright 1982 by Houghton Mifflin and Company. Reprinted by permission. **p. 214:** Figure 7.4 from Jackson, "Deindividuation and valence of cues," *Journal of Personality and Social Psychology*, 49. Copyright 1985 by the American Psychological Association. Adapted by permission. **p. 217:** Figure 7.5 from Deutsch and Krauss, "The effect of threat upon interpersonal bargaining," *Journal of Abnormal and Social Psychology*, 1960, pp. 181–189; **p. 218:** Figure 7.6 from Deutsch & Krauss, "Studies of interpersonal bargaining," *Journal of Conflict Resolution*, 6, pp. 52–76. Copyright 1962. Reprinted by permission of Sage Publications.

Photos and Cartoons: p. 194: Stephen Thorne/CP Photo Archive; **p. 195L:** © Louise Richard; **p. 195R:** Mike Pinder/CP Photo Archive **p. 198:** Philip G. Zimbardo, Inc.;

p. 201: Getty Images Inc.–Hulton Archive Photos Copyright © Reuters/Russell Boyce/Archive Photos; **p. 206:** Rick Madonik/CP Photo Archive; **p. 211:** Bruce Weaver/AP/Wide World Photos; **p. 216:** Joe Raedle/Getty Images, Inc.; **p. 219:** Joe Gibbons/CP Photo Archive.

Chapter 8

Text and Art: p. 235: Figure 8.1 from Curtis, R.C. & Miller, K. (1986) Believing another likes or dislikes you: Behaviors making beliefs come true. *Journal of Personality and Social Psychology*, 51, pages 284-290. Copyright©1986 by the American Psychology Association; **p. 242:** Figure 10.4 adapted from Sternberg, *The Triangle of Love*. Copyright 1988. Reprinted by permission of HarperCollins Publishers, Inc.; **p. 243:** Fehr, B.(1988). Prototype Analysis of the Concepts of Love and Commitment. *Journal of Personality and Social Psychology*, 55, pages 557-579. Copyright©1988 by the American Psychological association. Reprinted with permission. **p. 249:** Adapted from Bartholomew, K. & Horowitz, L.M. (1991). Attachment Styles Among Young Adults: A test of a four-category model. *Journal of Personality and Social Psychology*, 61, p.226-244. Copyright © 1991 by the American Psychological Association. Reprinted with permission. **p. 252:** Figure 8.3 adapted from Rusbult, "A longitudinal test of the investment model," *Journal of Personality and Social Psychology*, 45. Copyright 1983 by the Amerian Psychological Association. Adapted by permission.

Photos and Cartoons: p. 233: Copyright © The New Yorker Collection 1998 Sam Gross from cartoonbank.com. All rights reserved. **p. 228:** Jonathan Player/The New York Times; **p. 229:** Ted Kawalerski Photography Inc./The Image Bank/Getty Images; **p. 232:** Michael Newman/PhotoEdit, Inc.; **p. 237TL:** Evan Agostini/Getty Images, Inc. – Liaison; p. **237TC:** Getty Images Inc. - Hulton Archive Photos; **p. 237TR:** Mike Grey/Getty Images, Inc. – Hulton Archive Photos; **p. 237BL:** Jeff Manzetti/AP/Wide World Photos; **p. 237 BC:** AP/Wide World Photos; **p. 237BR:** Aaron Rapoport/Fox/Picture Desk, Inc./Kobal Collection; **p. 239:** © Capilano Suspension Bridge and Park; **p. 240:** Anita Weber/SIPA Press; **p. 244:** Bruce Dale/National Geographic Image Collection; **p. 248:** Copyright © Elizabeth Crew/The Image Works; **p. 253L:** David Hanover/Getty Images, Inc. – Stone Allstock; **p. 253R:** Gary Buss/Getty Images, Inc. – Taxi; **p. 255:** Copyright © Jeff Greenberg/The Image Works.

Chapter 9

Text and Art: p. 270: Figure 9.1 from Batson, *The Altrusim Question: Toward a Social Psychological Answer*. 1991 Lawrence Erlbaum Associates; **p. 272:** Figure 9.2 from M. Toi and C. D. Batson, "More evidence that empathy is a source of altruistic motivation," *Journal of Personality and Social Psychology*, 43, pp. 281–292. Copyright 1982. Reprinted by permission. **p. 276:** Figure 9.3 adapted from Latané & Darley, *The Unresponsive Bystander: Why Doesn't He Help?* Copyright 1970. Reprinted by permission of Simon & Schuster. **p. 280:** Figure 9.4 from Darley, et al., "Bystander intervention in emergencies: Diffusion and responsibility," *Journal of Personality and Social Psychology*, 8. Copyright 1968 by the American Psychological Association. Adapted by permission.

Photos and Cartoons: p. 264: Koji Sasahara/CP Photo Archive; **p. 266L:** Joe Byrska/Winnipeg Free Press; **p. 266R:** Winnipeg Free Press; **p. 268:** Steve Mason/Getty Images, Inc. – Photodisc; **p. 269:** Robert Allison/Contact Press Images Inc.; **p. 271:** © 1995 Watterson/Distributed by Universal Press Syndicate; **p. 273:** Elena Rooraid//PhotoEdit, Inc.; **p. 278:** Steve McCurry/Magnum Photos; **p. 279:** New York Times Pictures; **p. 282:** Erlanson Productions/The Image Bank/Getty Images; **p. 283:** Aneal Vohra/MaXx Images; **p. 285:** Catherine Ursillo/Photo Researchers, Inc.; **p. 286:** Albert Bandura, Stanford University/Albert Bandura, D. Ross & S.A. Ross, Imitation of film-mediated aggressive models. *Journal of Abnormal and Social Psychology*, 1963, 66. P.8; **p. 288:** Sidney Baldwin/Warner Bros. Productions Ltd./ Regency Enterprises/Picture Desk, Inc./Kobal Collection; **p. 291:** Yellow Dog Productions/Getty Images, Inc. – Image Bank; **p. 293T:** Dana Fradon © 1985 from the New Yorker Collection. All rights reserved. **p. 293B:** Adrian Wyld/CP Photo Archive; **p. 295:** Copyright © Eastcott/Momatiuk/The Image Works; **p. 297:** Copyright © Jennie Woodcock/CORBIS; **p. 299:** Photo Researchers, Inc.; **p. 301:** CP Photo Archive.

Chapter 10

Text and Art: p. 308: © Mary Young; **p. 318:** Figure 10.1 from Quattrone, et al., "The perception of variability within ingroups and outgroups: Implications for the law of small numbers," *Journal of Personality and Social Psychology, 38*. Copyright 1980 by the American Psychological Association.

Adapted by permission. **p. 321:** Sinclair, L. & Kunda, Z. (1999). Relations to black Professional: Motivated inhibition and activation of conflicting stereotypes. *Journal of Personality and Social Psychology*, 77 pages. 885-904. Copyright © 1999 by the American Psychology Association. Reprinted with permission. **p. 332:** Figure 13.8 adapted from Sherif, "Intergroup conflict and cooperation: The Robber's Cave Experiment." Copyright 1961. Reprinted by permission of O.J. Harvey.

Photos and Cartoons: p. 309: © Mary Young; **p. 314:** Christoph Wilhelm/Getty Images, Inc. – Taxi: **p. 317:** © Gary Rush (McGill Sports Info); **p. 316:** Alain ® 1951 The New Yorker: 25th Annual Album, Harper & Bros; **p. 317:** © Gary Rush (McGill Sports Info); **p. 319:** Photograph courtesy of Ron Baxter Smith; **p. 323:** Michael Newman/PhotoEdit, Inc.; **p. 325:** Laura Dwight/PhotoEdit, Inc; **p. 328:** © 1992 Gary Hallgren; **p. 331:** Fred Chartrand/CP Photo Archive; p. 333: OLIPHANT ©. Reprinted with permission of Universal Press Syndicate. All rights reserved. **p. 334:** Tom Watson/Merrill Education.

Name Index

Abelson, R.P., 121
Abrams, D., 317
Adair, J., 88
Adair, J.G., 39
Adlag, R.J., 211
Adler, J., 29
Agarie, N., 300
Agnew, C.R., 251, 255
Ainsworth, A., 247–248
Ajzen, I., 124, 124n
Akande, A., 88
Akert, R.M., 50, 94, 95, 166, 256
Allen, M., 129
Allen, V.L., 175
Allison, P.D., 165
Allison, S.T., 57, 65, 216
Allport, G., 312, 331
Alwin, D.F., 129
Amabile, T.M., 66
Amir, I., 332, 333
Amirkhan, J.H., 73
Andersen, B.L., 94
Andersen, S., 211
Andersen, S.M., 93
Anderson, C.A., 74, 288
Anderson, J.F., 232
Anderson, P.D., 167
Anderson, S.M., 51
Annis, R., 324
Archer, D., 285, 294
Archer, J., 295
Arenson, S.J., 213
Arins, R.L., 299
Aron, A., 239, 242, 243, 255
Aron, E.N., 255
Arone, S., 150
Aronson, E., 14, 22, 34, 38, 110, 111, 138–140, 142, 144n, 147, 148, 151, 297, 299, 333, 334, 335
Aronson, J., 105
Aronson, J.M., 328
Asch, S.E., 170–172, 175, 184
Ashbrook, R.M., 197
Ashmore, R.D., 237
Ashton, W., 65
Aspinwall, L.G., 98
Assanand, S., 85

Atlas, R.S., 25
Atoum, A.O., 202
Attridge, M., 251
Augoustinos, M., 318

Back, K., 231
Backman, C.W., 234
Bacon, P.L., 88, 89, 89n
Bahrick, H.P., 94
Baize, H.R., 247
Baldwin, M.W., 94, 95, 96, 136, 249, 250
Banaji, M.R., 71
Bandura, A., 286
Banks, C., 198
Baranovski, M., 206
Barbee, A.R., 236
Bargh, J.A., 49, 51, 59, 65, 136, 232–233
Barker, R., 290
Barley, S.R., 197
Barnes, M., 236, 246
Baron, J., 268
Baron, R.A., 284–285, 291, 300, 301
Baron, R.S., 133, 165, 202
Bartholomew, B.D., 288
Bartholomew, K., 249, 295
Bartlett, D.C., 49
Bass, B.M., 213
Bastien, D., 197
Batson, C.D., 269–272, 272f, 273, 277, 282
Baumeister, R.F., 88, 91, 197, 255, 275, 298
Baytalan, G., 4
Bazerman, M., 218
Beach, S., 102, 231
Beall, A.E., 242
Beaman, A.L., 91, 284
Bechky, B.A., 197
Becker, M.H., 132
Beggan, J.K., 57, 216
Behrman, M., 47–48
Beike, D.R., 97
Bell, D.W., 322
Bem, D.J., 93, 123, 212, 212n
Bereczkei, T., 247
Berger, S.A., 94
Berk, R.A., 298
Berkow, J.H., 246
Berkowitz, L., 274, 284, 289, 290, 294, 297–298

Berry, D.S., 236
Berry, J.W., 316
Berscheid, E., 231, 233, 234, 236, 237, 238, 241, 246, 251, 252
Bertolissi, S., 237
Bettencourt, B.A., 295
Bickman, L., 165
Biernat, M., 215
Billig, M., 317
Billsberry, J., 213
Bils, J., 269
Bird, B., 229–230
Blanchfield, M., 168
Blascovich, J., 202, 213
Blass, T., 183, 184
Blatt, J.J., 174
Blau, P.M., 250
Bledsoe, S.B., 247
Bless, H., 55
Boadle, A., 150
Bochner, S., 87
Bodenhausen, G.V., 315, 320
Bolger, N., 22
Bolstein, R., 178
Bond, C.F., 200, 202
Bond, M.H., 74, 109
Bond, R., 174
Booth-Butterfield, S., 179
Borgida, E., 51, 55
Bornstein, B.H., 57, 231
Bornstein, R.F., 136
Borsch, F., 335
Bourhis, R.Y., 317
Bower, G.H., 274
Bowlby, J., 247
Boyd, K.R., 70
Bradbury, T.N., 255
Bradley, J.P., 213
Bradshaw, R.H., 247
Branscombe, N.R., 22, 299
Bratslavsky, E., 255
Breckler, S.J., 121
Brehm, J., 140
Brekke, N.C., 133
Brendl, C.M., 51
Brewer, M., 22, 34
Brewer, M.B., 88, 197, 316, 317, 332
Bridgeman, D., 333, 334, 335
Brief, A.P., 274
Brière, J., 289
Brigham, J.C., 237
Brooks, J., 84

Broughton, R., 90
Brown, J.D., 97
Brown, R., 213, 311, 317
Brown, R.J., 316
Brown, T., 121
Brownstein, R., 178
Brunel, J., 121
Brunsman, B., 165
Bryant, J., 289
Bubier, N.E., 247
Buehler, R., 56
Buhl, T., 242
Bui, K-V. T., 251
Burger, J.M., 66, 179
Burgoon, M., 49
Burleson, B.R., 234
Burns, J.M., 213
Burnstein, E., 213
Burt, M.R., 66
Bushman, B.J., 298
Buss, D.M., 236, 246, 267, 268, 315
Butler, D., 215
Button, C.M., 243
Buunk, A.P., 251
Buunk, B.P., 203, 253
Byrne, D., 233, 234

Cacioppo, J.T., 129, 130
Cadinu, M.R., 57
Cameron, J.E., 109, 310
Campbell, D.T., 34, 129
Campbell, J., 165
Campbell, J.D., 85, 86n, 87–88, 103, 109
Cantor, J., 287
Cantor, N., 94
Carli, L., 49, 215
Carlsmith, J.M., 38, 110, 146, 148, 297
Carlson, E.A., 248, 274
Carlson, M., 274
Carlston, D.E., 65
Carnevale, P.J., 220
Carrell, S.E., 96, 136
Carron, A.V., 125, 210
Cartwright, D., 196
Carver, C.S., 92n, 207
Cate, R.M., 234, 256
Chachere, G., 287
Chaiken, S., 93, 120, 129, 130, 133
Chandler, C.C., 75
Chang, C., 205
Chapman, G.B., 57
Chappell, K., 47–48

Charlin, V., 274
Charng, H., 273
Chassin, L., 138
Check, J.V., 289
Chemers, M.M., 213, 215
Chen, J., 205
Chen, S., 51
Chiles, C., 175
Chiu, C., 69
Christensen, L., 39
Church, A.H., 178
Cialdini, R.B., 163, 165, 170, 171, 178, 178n, 179, 180, 274–275
Clark, K., 324
Clark, M., 324
Clark, M.S., 253, 274
Clark, R.D., 174
Clark, R.D. III, 279
Claude, S.D., 219
Clore, G.L., 234
Coats, E., 283
Cody, J., 236
Cohen, J., 105, 140
Cohn, E.G., 298
Collier, D.R., 243
Collins, N.L., 248
Collins, R.L., 97
Collins, W.A., 248
Condon, J.W., 234
Conolley, E.S., 174
Conway, L.G. III, 313
Conway, M., 133
Cook, S.W., 332, 333, 335
Cooley, C.M., 95
Cooper, J., 325
Cooper, R., 335
Corenblum, B., 317, 323, 324
Correll, J., 61, 62
Cosmides, L., 268
Cottrell, N.B., 202
Courneya K.S., 125
Craig, R., 138
Craig, W., 25, 26
Craig, W.M., 295
Crandall, C.S., 67
Crano, W.D., 234
Crichlow, S., 211
Crites, S.L. Jr., 122
Crocker, J., 49, 327, 330, 331
Croft, H.W., 213
Cross, S.E., 87, 88, 89, 89n, 90, 205
Crowley, A.E., 129

Crowley, M., 273
Croyle, R.T., 140
Crutchfield, R.A., 172
Csikszentmihalyi, M., 90
Cunningham, M.R., 236, 246
Curtis, R., 234, 235n
Cyranowski, J.M., 94
Czaczkes, B., 57

D'Agostino, P.R., 65, 231
Dahl, D.W., 127
Damon, W., 84
D'Angelo, A.M., 64
Darby, B.L., 274–275
Darley, J.M., 24, 30, 31, 32, 33, 34, 36
Darwin, C., 267
Davidson, A., 124, 125n
Davis, D.D., 208
Davis, K., 149
Davis, K.E., 248
Davis, M.H., 72
Davison, K.P., 98
Davitz, J., 300
Dawes, R.M., 55
De Dreu, C.K.W., 216, 218
de Groot, D., 205
De La Ronde, C., 110
De Metsenaere, M., 64
de Waal, F., 268
Dean, K.E., 289
Deaux, K., 90, 94, 215, 247
DeBono, K.G., 124, 133
DeJong, W., 132
Delaney, M.E., 9, 67
Dembo, T., 290
Depret, E., 313
Desmond, E.W., 292
Desportes, J.P., 197
Deutsch, M., 163, 171, 216, 217n, 218, 218n, 335
Devine, P.G., 59, 319, 320
Di Paula, A., 85
Dickerson, C., 14, 148
Dickerson, S.S., 98
Diener, E., 91, 206
Dienesch, R.M., 214
Dijksterhuis, A., 51
Dill, K.E., 288
Dillard, J.P., 179
Dion, C., 210
Dion, K.K., 236, 237, 244, 248, 310
Dion, K.L., 244, 248, 310, 311, 326
Dittman, M., 185, 198

Dix, T., 68
Dolin, D.J., 179
Dollard, J., 290, 298
Donnerstein, E., 289, 290, 301
Donnerstein, M., 301
Dougherty, M.R.P., 55
Dovidio, J.F., 268, 311, 315
Drigotas, S.M., 251
Driver, R., 97
Dryer, D.C., 234
Dubé, L., 133
Duck, J., 318
Duffy, J., 328
Dutton, D., 239
Dutton, D.G., 295
Duval, S., 91, 207
Duval, T.S., 91

Eagly, A.H., 120, 129, 205, 215, 237, 273
Eargle, A., 300
Edwards, D.J.A., 281
Edwards, K., 133
Eisen, M., 84
Eisenstadt, D., 146
Elig, T.W., 72
Ellard, J.H., 74
Elliot, J., 329–330
Ellis, B.J., 267
Ellsworth, P.C., 38, 176
Ely, R.J., 111
Emery, R.E., 220
Endo, Y., 109
Eron, L.D., 14, 27, 287
Esser, J.K., 211
Esses, V.M., 123, 311, 322, 323
Estabrooks, P., 125
Ester, C., 300
Estrada-Hollenbeck, M., 275
Evans, N., 315

Fabrigar, C.R., 133
Fabrigar, L.R., 74, 122, 129, 130
Fairey, P.J., 103
Falck, R., 138
Falcone, H., 313
Fazio, R.H., 124
Feeney, J.A., 248
Fehr, B., 49, 85, 88, 90, 103, 231, 232, 234, 242, 243, 250, 254
Feingold, A., 237, 238
Feldman, N.S., 9, 67
Felmlee, D., 254

Feshbach, S., 133
Festinger, L., 25, 97, 129, 146, 231
Fiedler, F., 213, 214, 214f
Figurski, T.H., 90
Fincham, F.D., 255
Fink, B., 236
Finney, P.D., 39
Fischer, G.W., 317
Fischer, W.F., 282
Fischhoff, B., 22, 58
Fishbein, M., 124
Fiske, A.P., 244
Fiske, S., 313
Fiske, S.T., 49, 59, 67–68, 68n
Fitzsimons, G.M., 232
Fletcher, G.J.O., 68
Flowers, M.L., 211
Fong, G., 127
Forgas, J.P., 274
Foster, M., 326
Frank, M.G., 70, 207
Franzini, L.R., 126
Fraser, S.C., 178n, 179
Freedman, D., 27
Freedman, J., 142, 297
Freedman, J.L., 178n, 179
Freud, S., 299
Fried, C., 147, 148
Friedenreich, C.M., 125
Friedkin, N.E., 213
Frieze, I.H., 72
Frodi, A., 294
Frost, M.R., 177\178
Fuller, S.R., 211
Fultz, J., 274
Fury, G., 248

Gabriel, S., 88, 89–90
Gaertner, S.L., 311
Gagnon, A., 317
Gaillard, A.W.K., 203
Gallup, G.G., 84
Gangestad, S.W., 247
Ganzach, Y., 57
Garb, H.N., 55
Garcia, J., 215
Gardner, R.C., 311
Gardner, W.L., 88, 89–90, 197
Gartner, R., 294
Geen, R.G., 199, 200, 284, 287
Geis, F.L., 215
Genest, M., 236

Genius, M., 290
Genovese, K., 21, 24, 276
Gentilia, T., 251
George, J.M., 197, 274
Gerard, H.B., 174
Gerard, H.G., 163, 171
Gerbner, G., 287
Gerdes, E.P., 39
Gerrard, M., 98
Gettys, C.F., 55
Gibbons, F.X., 91, 98
Giesen, H., 335
Giesler, R., 110
Gigerenzer, G., 22, 54
Gilbert, D.T., 60, 60f, 60n, 62, 65, 67
Gilovich, T., 57, 70, 207
Gimlin, D., 172
Ginsburg, G.P., 213
Giordano, C., 98
Giulietti, R., 9, 67
Gleason, M.J., 232–233
Goethals, G.R., 84, 97
Gold, J.A., 234
Goldstein, D.G., 54
Goldstein, J.H., 299
Goleman, D., 140
Gonzales, J., 106, 107, 107n
Gonzalez, A., 334
Gonzalez, M.H., 38
Gonzalez, R., 54
Goodman, N.G., 83
Gorassini, D.R., 179
Gore, J.S., 87
Gorn, G.J., 127
Graham, K., 292, 295
Granberg, D., 121
Grant, P.R., 317
Green, A.S., 232
Green, B.C., 178
Greenberg, J., 75, 98, 319
Greene, D., 23
Greening, L., 75
Greenwald, A.G., 71, 135–136
Griffin, D., 54, 56, 315
Griffin, D.W., 245
Griffin, E., 231
Grusec, J.E., 282
Guerin, B., 199, 200
Guerra, N., 300
Guimond, S., 67, 317
Guisinger, S., 174
Gustafson, R., 290

Haddock, G., 121, 123, 322
Hadjistavropoulos, T., 236
Hafer, C., 75
Hains, S.C., 211
Hale, J.L., 242
Hall, L.K., 94
Hallahan, M., 70
Hallinan, M.T., 234
Ham, J.J., 71
Hama, N., 62–64
Hamilton, V.L., 183
Hamilton, W.D., 267
Haney, C., 198
Hanna, R., 247
Hardin, C.D., 55
Harinck, F., 216
Harkins, S., 203
Harless, D.W., 208
Harmon-Jones, E., 138
Harris, B., 14
Harris, P., 75
Harris, V.A., 65, 65n, 66
Hart, D., 84
Hartke, D.D., 215
Hartstone, M., 318
Hartup, W.W., 248
Hasbrouck, J.E., 287
Hassebrauck, M., 242
Hastie, R., 49, 50–51, 177
Hatfield, E., 234, 237, 241, 241n, 246, 247, 252–253
   see also Walster, E.
Haugtvedt, C.P., 129, 130
Hazen, C., 248, 250
Heatherton, T.F., 275
Hébert, M., 288
Hébert, Y., 23
Heider, F., 62, 65, 67
Heiman, R.J., 162, 174, 244
Heine, S.J., 74, 75, 86n, 87, 91, 102, 107, 109, 244
Heingartner, A., 199
Helgeson, V.S., 256
Henderson, K.A., 172
Henderson-King, E., 319
Henry, R.A., 208
Herman, E.M., 199
Herold, E.S., 126, 127
Hertwig, R., 22
Herzog, T., 70
Herzog, T.A., 70
Hickey, C., 328
Higgins, E.T., 49, 51, 52, 53n, 100, 101

Hill, A.J., 125
Hill, C.A., 110
Hill, C.T., 243, 251
Hill, J., 97
Hill, K., 236
Hilton, A., 318
Hixon, G., 110
Hoaken, P.N.S., 292, 295
Hoang, V.R., 178
Hoeksema-van Orden, C.Y.D., 203
Hoffman, A.J., 219
Hoffrage, U., 22
Hofstede, G., 162, 244
Hogg, M., 318
Hogg, M.A., 174, 210, 211, 317
Hollander, E.P., 213, 214
Holmes, J.G., 245, 292
Holmes, J.O., 95, 106
Holtz, R., 234
Holtzworth-Munroe, A., 292
Homans, G.C., 250, 252, 268
Hong, Y., 69
Hoppe, H., 106, 107, 107n
Horowitz, L.M., 94, 234, 249
Horvarth, P., 291
Hostager, T., 197
House, R.J., 214
Houston, C.E., 137
Hovland, C.I., 128, 129
Hoyer, W.D., 129
Hrebec, D., 219
Hsu, S.S., 276
Huesmann, L.R., 287
Hughes, J.N., 287
Huguet, P., 202
Hui, C.H., 244
Hull, J.G., 91
Hwang, J., 126
Hynie, M., 126, 127

Ickes, W., 316
Inkster, J.A., 141
Isen, A.M., 274
Isenberg, D.J., 213
Ivins, B., 200

Jaccard, J., 124, 125n
Jackson, J.M., 204, 204n
Jackson, J.W., 172
Jacowitz, K.E., 57
James, J.M., 178
James, W., 53, 84, 95

Jamieson, D.W., 234
Janis, I.L., 128, 129, 133, 210, 210n, 211
Jemmott, J.R. III, 140
Jepson, C., 133
Job, R.F.S., 132
Johnson, D.W., 335
Johnson, H., 292
Johnson, J.T., 70
Johnson, R.T., 335
Johnson, T.E., 291
Jones, C., 52, 53n
Jones, D., 236
Jones, E.E., 65, 65n, 66, 67, 70, 71, 149, 317, 318n
Josephs, J.G., 132
Josephs, R., 110, 111
Josephs, R.A., 152
Josephson, W., 14, 35, 59, 287
Jouret, L., 5, 8, 10, 119–120, 152, 162, 165
Jouriles, E., 91
Judd, C., 22
Judd, C.M., 318
Jürgen-Lohmann, J., 335

Kahneman, D., 55, 56, 57, 58
Kalin, R., 316
Kallgren, C.A., 163, 170, 171
Kalven, H. Jr., 176
Kameda, M., 300
Kang, S., 174
Karau, S.J., 203, 205, 215
Kashy, D., 22
Kassarjian, H., 140
Kassin, S.M., 75
Katz, D., 121
Katz, I.M., 86n
Katzev, R., 178
Kawakami, K., 311, 326
Keelan, J.P.R., 248
Kelley, H.H., 128, 163, 216, 250, 251, 268
Kelley, J., 171
Kelly, B.R., 286
Kelman, H.C., 14
Kenny, D., 22
Kenny, D.A., 234
Kenrick, D.T., 267, 315
Kent, M.V., 199
Kerr, N.L., 49
Kesey, Ken, 51
Ketelaar, T., 267
Key, W.B., 135
Khanna, R., 273

Kidd, R.F., 200
Kiesler, C.A., 162
Kiesler, S.B., 162
Kihlstrom, J.F., 94
Killen, J.D., 138
Kim, U., 174
Kirkpatrick, L.A., 248, 250
Kitayama, S., 68, 87, 162, 174, 244
Klein, R., 100
Klein, W.M., 75
Klenke, K., 213, 215
Klonsky, B.G., 215
Knobe, J., 71
Knox, R.E., 141
Koestner, R., 97, 247
Kogan, N., 212, 212n
Kojetin, B.A., 250
Krajick, K., 135
Krakow, A., 184
Krauss, R.M., 216, 217n, 218, 218n
Kremer, J.F., 291
Kressel, K., 220
Kristiansen, C.M., 9, 67
Krosnick, J.A., 129
Krueger, J., 71
Kruglanski, A.W., 97, 167
Krull, D., 70
Kubitschek, W.N., 234
Kumhyr, S.M., 321
Kunda, Z., 49, 98, 99n, 104, 315, 320, 321, 321n
Kunitate, M., 98
Kunz, P.R., 179
Kurdek, L.A., 251
Kuriloff, P.J., 66
Kwok, D.C., 109
Kwon, S., 218
Kwong, M.J., 295

La Gaipa, J., 255
LaCroix, J., 220
LaFrance, M., 90, 215
Lalancettte, M.F., 174
Lalonde, R.N., 310, 316
Lambert, A.J., 66
Lamp, E.J., 134
Landau, K.R., 84
Lang, L.R., 66
Langlois, J.H., 236
LaPiere, R.T., 123, 124
Laplante, G., 265
LaPrelle, J., 98
Latané, B., 24, 30, 31, 32, 33, 34, 36

Lau, R., 73
Laughlin, P.R., 208
Laursen, B., 248
Lavalle, L.F., 86n
Laver, R., 119
Lavoie, F., 288
Lawler, E.S., 268
Layman, E., 55
Lea, M., 205, 232
Leary, M.R., 197
Lee, F., 70
Lee, Y., 74
Lehman, D.R., 74, 75, 86n, 102, 107, 109
Leippe, M., 146
Leishman, K., 140
Lemaine, J.M., 197
Lemieux, R., 242
Lemyre, L., 317
Leonard, K.E., 292
LePage, A., 294
Lepore, L., 311
Lepper, M.R., 23
Lerner, M.J., 66, 75, 317
Leung, K., 74
Leventhal, H., 132
Levine, J.M., 167, 175, 197, 210, 216
Levine, R., 244
Lewin, K., 196, 290
Lewis, M., 84
L'Heureux-Dubé, C., 66–67
Liberman, A., 129, 133
Lichtenstein, M., 315
Lichtenstein, S., 57, 58
Lichtman, R.R., 98
Liden, R.C., 214
Lightdale, J.R., 210
Lilli, W., 207
Lin, Y.H.W., 251
Lind, D.L., 237
Linford, K., 71
Linville, P.W., 64, 317
Linz, D., 289
Lippmann, W., 312
Liu, T.J., 106
Lloyd, B., 316
Lloyd, K.M., 251
Lloyd, S.A., 234, 256
Lockwood, P., 98, 99n, 104
London, P., 282
Longo, L.C., 237
Lopez, D.F., 96, 136
Lord, C.G., 66

Lore, R.K., 284
Lott, A.J., 250
Lott, B.E., 250
Lottes, I., 66
Louis, W.R., 326
Luby, V., 243
Lumsdaine, A.A., 129
Lundy, D.E., 246
Lupfer, M.B., 55
Lydon, J.E., 126, 127, 234, 250
Lynch, M., 152

Maass, A., 174
Maccoby, E.E., 88
Maccoby, N., 129
MacCoun, R.J., 176
MacDonald, G., 292
MacDonald, T., 127
Maclean, N., 104
Macrae, C.N., 320
Madson, L., 88, 89, 90, 205
Magaro, P.A., 197
Magoo, G., 273
Maier, N.R.F., 208
Main, K., 322
Maio, G.R., 322
Major, B., 327
Makhijani, M.G., 215
Malamuth, N.M., 289
Malle, B.F., 71, 94
Malone, P.S., 67
Manis, M., 55
Manstead, A.S.R., 197
Maracek, J., 110, 111
Markus, H., 49, 68, 174
Markus, H.R., 50, 87, 94, 162, 244
Martin, L., 102
Martin, R., 97
Martz, J.M., 251, 255
Matheson, K., 326
Maticka-Tyndale, E., 126, 127
Mauro, R., 176
Mayer, J.D., 274
Mayseless, O., 97
McAlister, A., 138
McAllister, H.A., 72
McArthur, L.L., 236
McCarthy, J.F., 286
McCauley, C., 211
McClelland, G., 22
McConahay, J.B., 311
McCoy, S.K., 327

McDaniel, P., 285
McDonald, J., 281
McFarland, C., 97, 109
McGuire, W., 137, 138
McGuire, W.J., 174
McKearney, S.J., 183
McKelvie, S.J., 55, 247, 281
McKenna, K.Y.A., 232–233
McLellan, B., 247
McMillan, D., 49
McNulty, S.E., 235
Mead, G.H., 95
Medvec, V.H., 57
Meeus, W.H.J., 184
Meindl, J.R., 317
Mendelsohn, G.A., 70
Mendolia, M., 102
Menec, V.H., 64, 67
Menon, T., 69
Merikle, P.M., 135
Mettee, D., 151
Mettee, D.R., 110, 111
Metts, S., 243
Meunier, J., 95
Mewhinney, D., 126, 127
Meyer, P., 267
Meyers, J.M., 137
Michaels, J.W., 200
Michela, J.L., 98
Mickler, S., 165
Midgley, E.H., 216
Milgram, S., 182–184, 183n, 185n, 186, 198
Miller, A.G., 65, 183
Miller, C.E., 167
Miller, C.T., 97
Miller, D., 109
Miller, D.T., 66, 72, 97, 210
Miller, J., 69
Miller, K., 234, 235n
Miller, L.S., 287
Miller, N., 129, 274, 295, 332
Miller, R.S., 175
Miller, Y.M., 9, 67
Mills, J., 138, 141, 142, 144n, 253
Milne, A.B., 174
Mishal, M., 65
Mishra, H., 301
Moghaddam, F.M., 316
Mohamed, A.A., 211
Montemayor, R., 84
Moore, T.E., 135
Moreland, R.L., 197, 210, 231

Morgan, H.J., 248
Morgan, M., 287
Morris, M., 69
Morris, M.L., 88, 89, 89n
Morris, M.W., 69n, 69
Morris, W.N., 175
Morry, M.M., 9, 173
Moscovici, S., 172, 176
Moscovitch, M., 48
Moskalenko, S., 91
Mosley, N.R., 234
Mullen, B., 205, 211, 317
Mummery, W.K., 125
Murdoch, D., 292
Murray, S., 106
Murray, S.L., 121, 235, 245
Mussweiler, T., 57
Myers, D.G., 213

Nail, P., 105
Nario, M.R., 22
Neale, M., 218
Nelson, D., 233
Nemeth, C.J., 175, 176
Neuberg, S.L., 137
Newcomb, T.M., 231, 233
Newman, L.S., 65, 66, 68
Newsom, J.T., 179
Nguyen, M., 125
Nisbett, R.E., 23, 54, 65, 66, 67, 70, 71, 238, 319
Noller, P., 248
Nowak, A., 174
Nurius, P., 94

Oakes, P.J., 317
O'Brien, M., 313
O'Connell, G.B., 322
O'Connor, K.M., 220
Ogden, E.E., 55
O'Hara, J., 144
Ohbuchi, K., 300
Olson, J.M., 22, 49, 120, 179, 238
Olweus, D., 26, 297
Ostrom, T., 318
Owada, M., 85–87

Pagano, F., 132
Page, S., 314
Palmer, D.L., 67
Paolucci-Oddone, E., 290
Park, B., 318
Park, D.W., 232

Parmelee, P., 234
Pataki, S.P., 253
Patch, M.E., 177–178
Patnoe, S., 334
Patrick, B.C., 248
Patterson, A., 299
Patterson, L.A., 310
Paulhus, D.L., 105, 109
Pelham, B.W., 110, 111
Peng, K., 69, 69n
Pennebaker, J.W., 98, 299
Pennington, N., 50–51, 177
Penrod, S., 172, 289
Penrod, S.D., 177
Penton-Voak, I., 236
Peplau, L.A., 243, 251
Pepler, D.J., 25, 295, 297
Perilloux, H.K., 84
Perlini, A.H., 130, 237
Perrott, S.B., 9, 67
Perry, R.P., 67
Peters, L., 215
Peterson, J., 292
Petrie, T.A., 173
Pettigrew, T.F., 311, 332
Petty, R.E., 122, 129, 130, 132, 133, 274
Phillipos, D., 248
Pickett, C.L., 197
Pierce, T., 250
Pietromonaco, P., 136
Pihl, R.O., 292, 295
Pike, C.L., 236
Piliavin, J.A., 273
Pincus, J.D., 134
Pittman, T.S., 65, 136
Pleban, R., 104
Pohlmann, J.J., 215
Potvin, L., 318
Povinelli, D.J., 84
Powell, A.A., 271
Pratkanis, A.R., 135
Prentice, D.A., 210
Prentice-Dunn, S., 206
Presson, C.G., 138
Prins, K.S., 253
Pruegger, V.J., 311
Pruitt, D.G., 213, 216, 218, 220
Pyszczynski, T., 75, 319
Pyszczynski, T.A., 98

Quattrone, G.A., 317, 318n
Quinn, D., 328

Quinn, K.A., 320, 326
Quinton, W.J., 327

Raaijmakers, Q.A.W., 184
Radloff, C.E., 84–85
Raichle, K., 66
Rajecki, D.W., 200, 247
Rapson, R.L., 247
Rasmussen, J.L., 247
Read, S.J., 248
Reeves, R.A., 178
Regan, P.C., 75, 241, 246
Rehm, J., 207
Reichl, A.J., 317
Reis, H.T., 231, 233, 236, 238, 248
Reis, T.J., 98
Rempel, J.K., 120, 121
Reno, R.R., 163, 170, 171
Renshaw, K., 109
Reynolds, L., 28
Rhea, J., 173
Rhodes, G., 236
Rhodes, N., 129
Rholes, S., 52, 53n
Rholes, W.S., 68, 248
Richardson, D., 39
Richardson, D.R., 284–285
Riecken, H.W., 25
Ringelmann, M., 203
Riordan, C.A., 333
Robins, R.W., 70
Robitaille, L., 288
Rodin, J., 274
Roesch, S.C., 73
Roese, N.J., 22, 39, 49
Rogers, R., 132, 206
Rogers, T.B., 311
Rokosh, J., 265
Rosch, E., 316
Rosenberg, L.A., 174
Rosenberg, M.J., 28
Rosenblatt, P.C., 247
Rosenham, D.L., 274
Rosenhan, D.L., 274, 282
Ross, D., 286, 292
Ross, L., 11, 12, 12n, 54, 62, 65, 66, 71, 220
Ross, L.D., 93
Ross, L.R., 249–250
Ross, M., 72, 74, 238
Ross, S., 286

Ross, W., 220
Rotenberg, K.J., 67
Rothbart, M., 57
Rothman, A.J., 55
Rubin, Z., 243
Ruble, D.N., 68
Rudman, L.A., 51
Ruggiero, K.M., 326, 327
Rule, B.G., 291
Rupert, J., 265
Rusbult, C.E., 251, 252n, 255
Rusch, A.J., 178
Rushton, J.P., 282, 315
Russell, D., 73
Russell, G.W., 299
Russell, J.A., 242
Ryan, B. Jr., 133
Ryckman, R.M., 234

Sachdev, I., 318
Sales, S.M., 200
Salovey, P., 274, 317
Samter, W., 234
Samuels, S., 11, 12, 12n
Sande, G.H., 84
Sande, G.N., 73, 74
Sanders, G.S., 202
Sanders, J., 183
Sandilands, M.L., 299
Sanger, D.E., 87
Sanna, L.J., 199
Sato, K., 300
Sato, T., 109
Satstrom, C.A., 251
Savilsky, K., 57
Savistky, 283
Savitsky, K., 238
Schachter, S., 25, 167, 168, 176, 231, 238
Schafer, M., 211
Schaller, M., 313
Scheier, M.R., 91, 207
Scheler, M.F., 92n
Schmitt, D.P., 246
Schneider, D.J., 49
Schriesheim, C.A., 215
Schroeder, J.E., 247
Schultz, L.A., 284
Schwartz, P., 252–253
Schwarz, N., 55
Scott, S., 48
Sears, D.O., 129

Secord, P.F., 234
Sedikides, C., 72, 84, 318
Segal, M.W., 231
Seligman, M.E.P., 74
Sentis, K., 213
Seppa, N., 286–287
Sergios, P.A., 236
Sexton, J., 124
Shackelford, T.K., 268
Shapiro, P.N., 333
Sharpe, D., 39, 295
Shaver, P., 248
Shavitt, S., 133–134, 135n
Shepperd, J.A., 203
Sherif, M., 163, 164, 164n, 165, 332, 332n, 334
Sherman, I.W., 298
Sherman, S.J., 138
Sheslowsky, D., 74
Sicoly, F., 74
Siero, F., 99
Signorielli, N., 287
Silvia, P.J., 91
Simmie, S., 206
Simon, H.A., 268
Simons, L., 294
Simonton, D.K., 213
Simpson, J.A., 248, 267
Sinclair, L., 95, 315, 320, 321, 321n
Singer, S., 269
Sistrunk, F., 218
Skowronski, J.J., 65, 84
Slavin, R.E., 335
Sloan, J.H., 294
Slovic, P., 57, 58
Smeaton, G., 234
Smith, C., 317
Smith, D.D., 290
Smith, J., 105
Smith, M.B., 121
Smith, P.B., 174
Smith, P.M., 317
Smith, S.M., 130
Smith, S.S., 39
Snyder, M., 75, 124, 133, 238
Soames, R.F., 132
Solem, A.R., 208
Solomon, H., 279
Solomon, L.Z., 279
Solomon, M.R., 237
Solomon, S., 75
Sommer, K.L., 88

Sommers, E.K., 289
Sorrels, J.P., 171
South, S.J., 251
Sparks, G.G., 231
Spears, R., 205, 232
Spencer, S., 328
Spencer, S.J., 111, 152
Spinner, B., 249–250
Spitzberg, R.M., 173
Spitzer, B.L., 172
Spranca, M.D., 70
Sprecher, S., 237, 241, 241n, 243, 246, 249, 253, 254, 256
Sprink, K.S., 210
Sroule, L.A., 248
Srull, T.K., 51
Stack, A.D., 298
Stahelski, A.J., 178
Standing, L., 174
Stanfel, J.A., 49
Stangor, C., 49
Stanley, J.C., 34
Staska, S.L., 173
Stasser, G., 209
Steele, C., 328
Steele, C.M., 105, 106, 107, 107n, 111, 151–152
Stein-Seroussi, A., 235
Steiner, I., 208
Steinleitner, M., 207
Steinmetz, J.L., 66
Stephan, W.G., 72, 317, 323
Stephens, L., 291
Sternberg, R.J., 242, 242n
Stewart, D.D., 209
Stillwell, A.M., 275
Stone, J., 14, 147, 148
Stone, R., 279
Stormo, K.J., 66
Storms, M.D., 238
Strack, F., 57
Strauman, T., 100
Stritzke, W.G.K., 66
Strube, M., 215
Suarez, S.D., 84
Sullivan, M., 247
Suls, J.M., 97
Summers, G., 9, 67
Swann, W.B. Jr., 110–111, 235
Swap, W.C., 231
Symons, D., 246
Szamrej, J., 174

Tafarodi, R.W., 174
Tait, E., 73
Tajfel, H., 316, 317
Takata, T., 74
Tan, J., 246
Tanchuk, T.L., 313
Tanford, S., 172
Tang, K., 67
Tanke, E.D., 238
Taylor, D., 326, 327
Taylor, D.M., 312, 316, 327, 329
Taylor, J.K., 295
Taylor, S.E., 49, 67–68, 68n, 98, 312–313, 316
Taylor, S.P., 292
Teger, A.L., 213
Tepper, B.J., 215
Terry, D., 318
Tesser, A., 102, 103, 104, 105, 165
Tetlock, P.E., 211
Tetrault, L.A., 215
Thibaut, J., 250, 251
Thibaut, J.W., 216, 268
Thibodeau, R., 138
Thomas, W.I., 163
Thompson, 94
Thompson, L., 216, 219, 220
Thomsen, C.T., 55
Thye, S.R., 268
Titus, L.J., 200
Titus, W., 209
Toi, M., 271–272, 272f
Tolan, P., 300
Tooby, J., 268
Tougas, Francine, 311
Trafimow, D., 49
Trapnell, P.D., 85, 86n
Trappey, C., 135
Traupmann, J., 253
Triandis, H.C., 69, 87, 244
Triplett, N., 200
Trivers, R.L., 268, 315
Trost, M.R., 163, 165, 171, 178, 179
Tseëlon, E., 236
Turner, 294
Turner, C., 294
Turner, J.C., 316, 317
Turner, M.E., 211
Tversky, A., 55, 56, 57, 58
Twenge, J., 293, 294
Tyler, R.B., 315

Uchara, E.S., 178
Uleman, J.S., 65
Uranowitz, S.W., 282

Valins, S., 238
van Knippengerg, A., 51
Van Lange, P.A.M., 251
Van Overwalle, F., 64
Van Vianen, A.E.M., 216
Vandello, J.A., 165
VanderZee, K., 98
VanLeeuwen, M.D., 202
VanOostum, N., 291
Varey, C., 54
Vargas Llosa, M., 83
Veach, T.L., 213
Vidyasgar, P., 301
Vincent, J.E., 274–275
Vinokur, A., 213
Violato, C., 290
Virk, R., 161–162
Voissem, N.H., 218
von Hippel, W., 49, 133
Vorauer, J.D., 219, 321, 322

Waddell, B., 253
Wall, A., 292
Wallach, M.A., 212, 212n
Wallbom, M., 91
Walsh, M., 328
Walster, E., 66, 129, 234, 252
see also Hatfield, E.
Walster, G.W., 252
Walster (Hatfield), E., 235–236, 237, 240
see also Hatfield, E.; Walster, E.
Walther, J., 232
Wang, T., 178
Wänke, M., 55
Wankel, L.M., 125
Wann, D.L., 299
Ward, A., 220
Ward, C., 68, 130
Watkins, D., 88
Watson, R., 206
Watson, W.E., 208
Watts, J.C., 132
Webber, R., 330, 331
Webster, D.M., 70, 167
Wegener, D.T., 74, 129, 130, 274
Wegner, D.M., 59

Weinberg, C.B., 127
Weiner, B., 300
Weingart, L.R., 218
Weinstein, N.D., 75
Weir, W., 134
Weiss, W., 129
Wekerle, C., 292
Wells, S., 292, 295
Wells, W.D., 133
Werner, C., 234
Werner, J., 213
West, P., 292
Westbay, L., 242, 243
Weyant, J.M., 180
Whatley, M.A., 178
Wheeler, L., 97, 98, 247
White, H., 292
White, L.K., 254
White, R.W., 121
Whitley, B.E., 72
Wicker, A., 124
Wicklund, R.A., 91, 207
Wiebe, F.A., 211
Wiggins, E.C., 121
Wilder, D.A., 332, 333
Wilhelmy, R.A., 174
Williams, K., 203
Williams, K.D., 203, 204, 204n, 205
Williams, K.R., 203
Williamson, G.M., 253, 274
Wilson, T.D., 22, 34, 57, 64, 90, 133, 137
Winkler, E., 9

Winocur, G., 47
Winslow, R.W., 126
Winsten, J.A., 132
Wong, F.Y., 287
Wood, J.V., 97, 98
Wood, W., 129, 176, 205, 287
Woolcott, M., 179
Word, C., 325
Word, L.E., 279
Wright, R., 267
Wright, S.C., 312, 327, 329
Wyer, M.M., 220
Wyer, R.S., 49, 51
Wyer, R.S. Jr., 315

Yik, M.S., 109
Young, R.D., 91
Yudko, E., 292

Zajonc, R.B., 50, 199, 200, 201, 202, 231
Zander, A., 196
Zanna, M.P., 49, 74, 97, 120, 121, 123, 124, 127, 234, 292, 322, 323, 325
Zanot, E.J., 134
Zebrowitz-McArthur, L., 69
Zeisel, H., 176
Zillmann, D., 238, 289
Zimbardo, P., 181, 185, 198, 206, 211
Zivian, M.T., 172
Zuber, J.A., 213
Zuwerink, J., 319

Subject Index

accessibility, 51, 52f, 53f
activation of stereotypes, 319–321
actor/observer difference, 70–71
advertising
    and attitude change, 133–137
        subliminal advertising, 134–137
        tailoring to attitudes, 133–134
affective information, 135f
affectively based attitude, 121, 122, 135f
aftermath of bad deeds, 149–151
aggression
    aggressive stimulus, presence of, 294
    alcohol, 292–293
    anger management, 299–301
    apology and, 300
    catharsis, 298–299
    cross-cultural variability in violence, 285
    defined, 284
    direct provocation, 291
    frustration-aggression theory, 290
    gender differences, 294–295
    imitation and, 286–287
    and insults, 292
    modelling nonaggressive behaviour, 300–301
    nature of, 284–285
    pornography, violence in, 288–290
    problem-solving skills and, 300
    punishment and, 297–298
    reciprocation, 291
    reducing aggressive behaviour, 297–301
    sexual aggression, 288–290
    situational causes, 285–295
    and social exclusion, 293–294
    social learning theory, 286–287
    and sports, 207
    television violence, 35, 287
    and television violence, 35
    universaility of, 284–285
    video game violence, 288
    wars, 285
aggressive behaviour. *See* aggression
aggressive stimulus, 294
alcohol, and aggression, 292–293
allies, 175
altruism
    see also prosocial behaviour
    costs and rewards of, 268–269
    defined, 267
    and empathy, 269–272, 270f
    kin selection, 267
    norm of reciprocity, 268
    vs. self-interest, 272f
ambiguous situations, 52f, 165, 166
American Psychological Association, 15, 113
American Sociological Association, 222
anchoring and adjustment heuristic, 56–59
anger management
    apology, 300
    communication training, 299
    modelling nonaggressive behaviour, 300–301
    problem-solving skills, 299
anthrax vaccine, 168, 195–196
Anti-defamation League, 337
anxious/ambivalent attachment style, 248
apology, 300
Arone, Shidane, 150
arousal
    and the dominant response, 201
    misattribution of arousal, 238–239
    presence of others and, 201–202
Asch line judgment studies, 170–172, 171f
Asian cultures, 87
assumption of responsibility, 279–281
Athena Educational Partners, 133
atrocities, 182
attachment styles
    anxious/ambivalent attachment style, 248
    avoidant attachment style, 248–249
    defined, 247
    dismissive avoidant style, 249
    fearful avoidant style, 248–249
    multiple attachment representations, 249–250
    secure attachment style, 247
attachment theory
    attachment styles, types of, 247–249
    key assumption of, 248
    website, 258
attitude change
    advertising and, 133–137
    aftermath of bad deeds, 149–151
    attitude inoculation, 137–138
    and behavioural changes, 138–140
    fear and, 131–133
    insufficient justification, psychology of, 145–149

justification of effort, 142–144
learning from mistakes, 151
peer pressure, resisting, 138
persuasion, 127–131
postdecision dissonance, 140–141
rationalization trap, 151
resistance to, 137–151, 152
Yale Attitude Change Approach, 128, 129*f*
attitude inoculation, 137–138
attitudes
	affectively based attitude, 121, 122, 135*f*
	behaviourally based attitudes, 122–123
	changes in. *See* attitude change
	cognitively based attitudes, 121, 122, 135*f*
	components of, 312
	defined, 120
	described, 120
	intentions, 125
	prediction of behaviour, 123–127
	prejudice. *See* prejudice
	sources of, 120–123
	specific attitudes, 125*t*
	and theory of planned behaviour, 123–127, 124*f*
attraction
	complementarity, 233–234
	major antecedents of, 231–240
	mere exposure effect, 231
	and misattribution of arousal, 238–239
	physical attractiveness, 235–238
	propinquity effect, 231–232
	reciprocal liking, 234
	similarity, 233–234
attribution theory
	actor/observer difference, 70–71
	attributional process, 62–64
	belief in a just world, 75
	defensive attributions, 75
	defined, 62
	external attribution, 62–63
	fundamental attribution error, 65–70
	internal attribution, 62
	misattribution of arousal, 238–239
	self-serving attributions, 72–74
	unrealistic optimism, 75
	website, 77
attributional process, 62–64
authority, obedience to, 181–183
automatic processing, 59–60, 60*f*, 61–62
availability, 55
availability heuristic, 54–55
avoidant attachment style, 248–249
Baranovski, Matti, 206

bargaining, 218–220
base rate information, 56
battered wives, 67
Baytalan, Greg, 4
beauty standards, 236–238
behaviour, prediction of, 123–127
behavioural changes, 138–140
behavioural intentions, 124–127
behaviourally based attitudes, 122–123
belief in a just world, 75
Bird, Bradley, 229–230
blaming the victim. *See* victims
body image, 172–173
bookkeeping model, 330
breaking the rules, 169
breaking-up experience, 256
bullying, 25, 26, 297
bystander effect, 280
bystander intervention, 280*f*
	see also Genovese, Kitty
	assumption of responsibility, 279–281
	bystander effect, 280
	deciding to implement the help, 281
	decision tree, 276*f*
	diffusion of responsibility, 280
	emergency, interpretation of, 277–279
	knowing how to help, 281
	noticing an event, 277
	pluralistic ignorance, 278–279

Canadian Airborne Regiment, 150
Canadian Code of Ethics for Psychologists, 39*f*, 41
Canadian Journal of Behavioural Science, 337
Canadian Psychological Association, 15, 37
Canadian Race Relations Foundation, 337
catharsis, 298–299
causal attribution. *See* attribution theory
causation, 27–30, 29
central route to persuasion, 129–130
Chappell, Kevin, 47–48
children
	attachment, 247–249
	bullying, 297
	internalization of cultural norms, 109
	jigsaw classroom, 333–335
	learning not to hate, 329–330
	prosocial behaviour, learning, 282
Choice Dilemmas Questionnaire (CDQ), 212
classic research
	Aronson and Carlsmith (insufficient punishment), 148–149

Aronson and Mettee (self-affirmation and cheating), 151
Aronson and Mills (dissonance reduction and effort), 142–143
Asch (conformity and allies), 175
Asch (line judgment studies), 170–171
Bandura and colleagues (social learning theory), 286
Barker, Dembo and Lewin (frustration-aggression theory), 290
Berkowitz and LePage (aggressive stimulus), 294
Brehm (postdecision dissonance), 140–141
Campbell (false uniqueness effect), 109
Chaiken and Baldwin (self-perception theory), 93–94
Clark and Clark (black doll experiment), 324
Darley and Batson (Good Samaritan), 277
Davis and Jones (hating our victims), 149
Davitz (anger management), 300
Deutsch and Krauss (threats and conflict resolution), 216
Festinger, Riecken and Schacter (doomsday cult), 25
Festinger, Schachter and Back (propinquity effect), 231
Festinger and Carlsmith (counter-attitudinal advocacy), 146
Freedman and Fraser (foot-in-the-door technique), 179
Greenberg and Pyszczynski (activation of stereotypes), 319
Haney, Banks and Zimbardo (mock prison experiment), 198
Hazan and Shaver (attachment style), 248
Higgins, Rholes and Jones (priming effect), 52–53
Jones and Harris (fundamental attribution error), 65–66
Kahenman and Tversky (engineer-and-lawyer problem), 56
Knox and Inkster (postdecision dissonance), 141
Latané and Darley (bystander effect), 279–280
Latané and Darley (pluralistic ignorance), 278
Milgram (obedience), 182–183
Mills (dissonance reduction and moral standards), 141
Newcomb (similarity and friendship), 233
Quattrone and Jones (out-group homogeneity), 317–318
Ross and Samuels (Wall Street Game/Community Game), 11
Ross and Sicoly (self-serving biases), 74
Sherif and colleagues (mutual interdependence), 332
Sherif (informational social influence), 163–164
Snyder, Tanke and Berscheid (self-fulfilling prophecy and beauty), 238
Steele, Hoppe and Gonzales (self-affirmation), 106
Toi and Batson (empathy *vs.* self-interest), 271–272
Tversky and Kahneman (availability heuristic), 55
Wallach, Kogan and Bem (group decision and risk), 212
Walster (Hatfield) and colleagues (physical appearance and first impresions), 235
Word, Zanna and Cooper (self-fulfilling prophecy and stereotypes/discrimination), 325
Zajonc, Heingartner and Herman (cockroaches' behaviour), 199
Zajonc (arousal and the dominant response), 201
close relationships. *See* relationships
cockroaches, 199–200
cognition. *See* social cognition
cognitive dissonance
    see also dissonance reduction
    and attitude change, 138–140
    defined, 138
    insufficient punishment, 148–149
    justification of effort, 142–144
    postdecision dissonance, 140–141
    reducing, 139f
    and self-affirmation, 105, 107f
    and threat to self-esteem, 105
cognitive information, 135f
cognitively based attitudes, 121, 122, 135f
college, adjustment to, 64
commitment, 242, 252
common goal, 332
communal relationships, 253–254
communication
    fear-arousing communication, 131–133
    persuasive communication, 127–131
    training, and anger management, 299
companionate love, 241, 242
comparison level, 251
comparison level for alternatives, 251
complementarity, 233–234
compliance
    defined, 177
    door-in-the-face technique, 177–179
    foot-in-the-door technique, 179–180
    increasing, with a request, 178f
    lowballing, 180
    obedience, 181–183
    reciprocity norm, 178

condom use, 126–127
conflict. *See* group conflict and cooperation
conflicting motives, 110
conformity
    compliance, 177–180
    and culture, 174
    defined, 162
    informational social influence, 163–166
    minority influence, 176, 177
    normative social influence, 167–175, 183–184
    reasons for, 162–163
    and social good, 169–170
    social impact theory, 173–174
    when it happens, 162–163
conservation of water, 147–148
construal, 12
contact hypothesis, 331–333
contingency theory of leadership, 214–215, 214*f*
controlled processing, 59–60
conversion model, 330
cooperation, 12*f*, 333–335
    see also group conflict and cooperation
correlation coefficient, 27
correlational method
    vs. causation, 27–30, 29
    correlation coefficient, 27
    defined, 27
    limits of, 27–30
counter-attitudinal advocacy, 145–147
courtrooms
    jury deliberation, 176–177
    minority influence in, 176–177
    rape myth, 66–67
    and schemas, 50–51
cover story, 35
crisis situations, 165, 166
culture
    Asian cultures, 87
    and beauty, 236–238
    children's internalization of cultural norms, 109
    and conformity, 174
    and fundamental attribution error, 69–70, 69*f*
    individualist cultures, 88–89
    and love, 244–245
    the self, definition of, 85–88
    and self-affirmation, 107–108
    and self-discrepancies, 101–102
    and self-enhancement, 109
    and self-serving bias, 74
    and social loafing, 205
    and violence, 285
    Western cultures, 87

debriefing, 38–39
deception, 37–38
decisions
    and dissonance reduction, 141–142
    group decisions. *See* group decisions
    justifying decisions, 141
    postdecision dissonance, 140–141
defensive attributions, 75
deindividuation, 205–208
dependent variables, 32, 33*f*
descriptive methods of research
    correlational method, 26–30
    observational method, 25–26, 30
Di Mambro, Joseph. *See* Solar Temple cult
difficult tasks, 200
diffusion of responsibility, 24, 280–281
direct provocation, 291
discrimination
    see also prejudice
    contact hypothesis, 331–333
    defined, 314
    effects of, 324–329
    against gays and lesbians, 314
    in housing market, 314
    jigsaw classroom, 333–335
    learning not to hate, 329–330
    reducing discrimination, 329–335
    self-blaming attributions, 326–327
    and self-fulfilling prophecy, 325
dismissive avoidant style, 249
dissonance reduction, 105, 108
    see also cognitive dissonance
    hating our victims, 149–151
    insufficient justification, 145–149
    insufficient punishment, 148–149
    and justification of effort, 142–144
    moral standards and, 141–142
    post-decision, 140–141
    rationalization trap, 151
    and self-justification, 149
distancing in the family, 104
door-in-the-face technique, 177–179
downward social comparison, 98

effort, justification of, 142–144
elaboration likelihood model, 130–131, 131*f*
emergencies, 166, 277–279
empathy, 269–272, 270*f*
empathy-altruism hypothesis, 269–272, 270*f*
empirical science, 22–23
ending close relationships, 254–256
equal status, 332

equity theory, 252
ethical issues, 37–39, 41
evaluation apprehension, 202
evidence, in court, 50–51
evolutionary approach, 246–247, 267–268
Ewanchuk, Steve, 66
exchange relationships, 253–254
experimental method
    cover story, 35
    defined, 30
    dependent variables, 32, 33f
    described, 31–32
    external validity, 34–36
    generalizability across people, 36
    generalizability across situations, 34–36
    independent variables, 32, 33f
    internal validity, 32–34
    mundane realism, 34
    psychological realism, 34–36
    random assignment to condition, 33
    random selection, 36
experts, 166
external attribution, 62–63
external justification, 145
external validity
    defined, 34
    generalizability across situations, 34–36

familiarity, 231
fear-arousing communication, 131–133
fearful avoidant style, 248–249
Flett, Rocky, 265–266
foot-in-the-door technique, 179–180
Friends, 83
frustration-aggression theory, 290
fundamental attribution error, 65f
    cultural explanation of, 69–70, 69f
    defined, 8, 65
    empirical demonstrations, 65–66
    explanations for, 67–70
    information availability, 70–71
    perceptual salience, 68, 70–71
    point of, 66
    victim blaming, 9–10, 66–67

gays and lesbians, 314
gender differences
    aggression, 294–295
    leadership, 215
    love and romantic beliefs, 243–244
    in personal ads, 246–247
    in prosocial behaviour, 273–274
    the self, definition of, 88–90
    social loafing, 205
generalizability across people, 36
generalizability across situations, 34–36
genes, 267–268
genocides, 182
Genovese, Kitty, 21, 24, 276
    see also bystander intervention
Gestalt psychology, 13
Golden Rule, 282
great person theory, 213–214
group cohesiveness, 210–211
group conflict and cooperation
    bargaining, 218–220
    integrative solution, 219
    negotiation, 218–220
    threats, as conflict resolution method, 216–218
    tracking game, 216, 217f, 218f
group decisions
    group cohesiveness, 210–211
    group polarization, 211–213
    groupthink, 210, 210f, 211, 222
    leadership, 213–215
    process loss, 208–211
group influence
    arousal, 201–202
    deindividuation, 205–208
    dominant response, 201
    evaluation apprehension, 202
    pool hall performance, 200
    social facilitation, 199–200, 203f
    social loafing, 202–205, 203f, 204f
group polarization, 211–213
groups
    composition of, 197–199
    conflict. *See* group conflict and cooperation
    cooperation. *See* group conflict and cooperation
    defined, 196
    function of, 197–199
    in-group, 316
    influence of, 199–208
    leadership, 213–215
    out-group, 316
    simple *vs.* difficult tasks, 200
    social roles, 197–199
    why people join, 197
groupthink, 210, 210f, 211, 222
Hama, Nadia, 62–64
hating our victims, 149–151
hazing, 4–5, 144–145
helping behaviour. *See* altruism; prosocial behaviour
heuristic processing, 130

heuristic-systematic model of persuasion, 129–130
heuristics
    anchoring and adjustment heuristic, 56–59
    availability heuristic, 54–55
    base rate information, 56
    described, 54
    judgmental heuristics, 54
    representative heuristic, 55–56
hidden persuasion techniques, 135
hurry, 277
hypotheses, 23–24

imitation, 286–287
in-group, 316
independent variables, 32, 33f
independent view of the self, 87
individual differences, 7
individualist cultures, 88–89
informal settings, 332
information availability, 70–71
informational social influence
    ambiguous situations, 165
    crisis situations, 165
    defined, 163
    in emergencies, 166
    experts, 166
    illustration of, 163–164, 164f
    and minority influence, 176
    private acceptance, 164
    public compliance, 164
    role of, 184–186
informed consent, 37
initiation, 143
instincts, 267–268
insufficient justification
    conservation of water, 147–148
    counter-attitudinal advocacy, 145–147
    insufficient punishment, 148–149
    self-justification, 149
insufficient punishment, 148–149
insults, 292
integrative solution, 219
interdependence, 333–335
interdependent view of the self, 87
internal attribution, 62
internal justification, 145
internal validity, 32–34
International Association for Relationship Research, 258
Internet. *See* weblinks
Internet relationships, 232–233
interpersonal attraction. *See* attraction
intimacy, 242

intimate relationships. *See* relationships
introspection, 90–92
investment model of commitment, 251, 252f
Iraqi prisoners, 150, 182, 185–186

jigsaw classroom, 333–335
Jonestown cult, 8
Jouret, Luc. *See* Solar Temple cult
Journal of Personality and Social Psychology, 15
judgmental heuristics, 54
    see also heuristics
jury deliberation, 176–177
justification
    decisions, 141
    of effort, 142–144
    external justification, 145
    internal justification, 145
    rationalization trap, 151
    self-justification, 149

kin selection, 267
knowing how to help, 281
knowing ourselves. *See* self-awareness

Laplante, Gino, 265
lawyers, and evidence, 50–51
leadership in groups
    contingency theory of leadership, 214–215, 214f
    gender and leadership, 215
    great person theory, 213–214
    relationship-oriented leader, 214
    task-oriented leader, 214
learning from mistakes, 151
learning not to hate, 329–330
lesbians and gays, 314
liking. *See* attraction
littering, 169–170
long-distance propinquity, 232
looking-glass self, 95–97
love
    see also relationships
    companionate love, 241, 242
    and culture, 244–245
    evolutionary approach, 246–247
    and gender, 243–244
    ordinary people's definition of, 242–243
    passionate love, 241
    ratings of features of love, 243t
    romantic love, 244
    triangular theory of love, 242, 242f
lowballing, 180

media violence, 35, 287, 303
mental strategies and shortcuts. *See* heuristics
mere exposure effect, 231
meta-stereotypes, 321–322
minority influence
    in the courtroom, 176–177
    defined, 176
    and informative social influence, 176
    jury deliberation, 176–177
misattribution of arousal, 238–239
modelling
    nonaggressive behaviour, 300–301
    prosocial behaviour, 282
modern prejudice, 311
mood
    and prejudice, 322–324
    and prosocial behaviour, 274–275
moral standards, and dissonance reduction, 141–142
Movement for the Restoration of the Ten Commandments of God, 8–9
multiculturalism, 310, 311
multiple attachment representations, 249–250
mundane realism, 34
mutual interdependence, 332
My Lai massacre, 181–182

negative correlation, 54
negative-state relief hypothesis, 274
negotiation, 218–220
Neosexism Scale, 311
nonaggressive behaviour, 300–301
norm of reciprocity, 268
normative social influence
    an ally, importance of, 175
    Asch line judgment studies, 170–172, 171*f*
    body image, 172–173
    breaking the rules, 169
    defined, 167
    resisting, 175
    role of, 183–184
    social impact theory, 173–174
    social norms, 167
    stop and think, as resistance, 175
    when people conform, 173–174
norms
    children's internalization of cultural norms, 109
    vs. roles, 197
    and sexual behaviour, 126
    social norms, 167
    subjective norms, 125, 126

obedience, 181–183
observational method, 25–26, 30
operational definition, 26
out-group, 316
out-group homogeneity, 317–318
Owada, Masako, 85–87

passion, 242
passionate love, 241
passionate love scale, 241
peer pressure, resisting, 138
perceived behaviour control, 125, 127
perception. *See* social perception
perceptual salience, 68, 70–71
peripheral route to persuasion, 129–130
person next door, 231–232
personal ads, 246–247
personality psychology, 15
persuasive communication
    central route to persuasion, 129–130
    defined, 128
    elaboration likelihood model, 130–131, 131*f*
    and group polarization, 213
    heuristic-systematic model of persuasion, 129–130
    hidden persuasion techniques, 135
    peripheral route to persuasion, 129–130
    website, 155
    Yale Attitude Change Approach, 128, 129*f*
physical attractiveness, 235–238
pluralistic ignorance, 278–279
pool hall performance, 200
pornography, violent, 288–290
positive correlation, 27
positive illusions, 108, 245
postdecision dissonance, 140–141
prejudice
    affect, 322–324
    causes of, 314–324
    contact hypothesis, 331–333
    defined, 312
    despising your own group, 324
    effects of, 324–329
    internalizing, 324
    jigsaw classroom, 333–335
    learning not to hate, 329–330
    modern prejudice, 311
    mood and, 322–324
    out-group homogeneity, 317–318
    prediction of, 322\323
    reducing prejudice, 329–335
    and self-fulfilling prophecy, 325
    and social categorization, 316–317

and social cognition, 315–318
stereotype threat, 327–329
stereotypes, 312–313, 318–322, 330–331
primacy effect, 129
priming, 51–53, 52*f*, 53*f*
private acceptance, 164
problem-solving skills, 299
process loss
    defined, 208
    examples of, 208–211
    failure to share unique information, 209–211
    group cohesiveness, 210–211
    groupthink, 210, 210*f*, 211
propaganda, 155
propinquity effect, 231–232
prosocial behaviour
    see also altruism
    assumption of responsibility, 279–281
    bystander effect, 280
    bystander intervention, 276–281
    deciding to implement the help, 281
    defined, 267
    diffusion of responsibility, 280–281
    evolutionary psychology, 267–268
    gender differences, 273
    instincts, 267–268
    kin selection, 267
    knowing how to help, 281
    modelling, 282
    mood, effects of, 274–275
    motives underlying, 267–272
    negative-state relief hypothesis, 274
    noticing an event, 277–279
    personal determinants of, 273–275
    pluralistic ignorance, 278–279
    promoting helping behaviour, 282
    rewards, 282
    and self-interest, 268–269
    situational determinants, 276–281
    social exchange theory, 268–269
provocation, 291
psychological realism, 34–36
psychologist, 3
public compliance, 164
punishment, and aggression, 297–298

qualitative research web sites, 41

R. v. Ewanchuk, 66
race
    and stereotype threat, 327–328
    and stereotyping, 319–321

random assignment to condition, 33
random selection, 36
rape myth, 66–67
rationalization trap, 151, 152
raves, 167
realism
    mundane realism, 34
    psychological realism, 34–36
reasoning quiz, 58
recency effect, 129
reciprocal liking, 234
reciprocation, 291
reciprocity norm, 178
relational interdependence, 89
relationship-oriented leader, 214
relationships
    attachment styles, 247–250
    breaking-up experience, 256
    communal relationships, 253–254
    comparison level, 251
    comparison level for alternatives, 251
    ending close relationships, 254–256
    equity theory, 252
    evolutionary explanations, 246–247
    exchange relationships, 253–254
    Internet relationships, 232–233
    investment model of commitment, 251, 252*f*
    love, 240–245
    multiple attachment representations, 249–250
    personal ads, gender differences in, 246, 247
    positive illusions, role of, 245
    reasons for, 245–254
    reward/cost ratio, 250
    social exchange theory, 250–252
    violence in, 296
    why relationships end, 254–255
representative heuristic, 55–56
research
    see also classic research
    correlational method, 26–30
    debriefing, 38–39
    deception, 37–38
    descriptive methods, 25–30
    ethical issues, 37–39
    experimental method, 30–36
    hypotheses, 23–24
    informed consent, 37
    observational method, 25–26, 30
    summary of research methods, 24*t*
    theory, 23–24
Research Ethics Board, 38
Research Methods Knowledge Base, 41

responsibility, assumption of, 279–281
reward/cost ratio, 250
risky shift, 212
risky situations, 167
Rokosh, John, 265
roles, 197–199
Rupert, Jake, 265

schemas
    accessibility, 51, 52*f*, 53*f*
    ambiguous situations, 52*f*
    applying schemas, 51–53
    in the courtroom, 50–51
    defined, 49
    described, 49–53
    influences of, 94
    priming, 51–53, 52*f*, 53*f*
    self-schemas, 94–95
    and stereotypes, 315
secure attachment style, 247
the self
    see also self-concept
    cultural differences in definition of, 85–88
    dissatisfaction with, 91
    escaping the self, 91
    gender differences in definition of, 88–90
    independent view of the self, 87
    interdependent view of the self, 87
    looking-glass self, 95–97
    nature of, 84–90
self-affirmation theory, 105–108, 151
self-awareness
    defined, 84
    internal audience, effects of, 96
    introspection, 90–92
    looking-glass self, 95–97
    negative effects, 91
    observations of our own behaviour, 93–94
    positive effects, 91–92
    and the presence of others, 207–208
    self-perception theory, 93–94
    self-schemas, 94–95
    social comparison theory, 97
    social interaction and, 95–97
self-awareness theory, 91–92, 92*f*
self-concept
    see also the self; self-esteem
    clarity, 85, 87–88
    and conflicting motives, 110
    defined, 84
    and gender stereotypes, 88
    nature of, 84–90

    relational interdependence, 88, 89
    sentence completion test, 88
    threats to, 101, 103, 105
self-discrepancy theory, 100–102
self-enhancement, 108–109
self-esteem
    see also self-concept
    close relationships, and boosts to self-esteem, 106
    distancing in the family, 104
    positive illusions, 108
    restoring our self-esteem, 104–105
self-evaluation
    accuracy of, 108–111
    downward social comparison, 98
    focus on usual self, 98–100
    need for positive self-evaluation, 97
    self-affirmation theory, 105–108
    self-discrepancy theory, 100–102
    self-enhancement, 108–109
    self-evaluation maintenance theory, 102–105, 103*f*
    self-verification, 109–111
    upward social comparison, 98, 99
self-evaluation maintenance theory, 102–105, 103*f*
self-fulfilling prophecy
    and beauty, perception of, 238
    defined, 325
    demonstration of, 326*f*
    and discrimination, 325
    and prejudice, 325
    and reciprocal liking, 234
    and stereotypes, 325
    self-interest, 268–269, 272*f*
self-justification, 149
self-perception theory, 93–94, 122
self-schemas, 94–95
self-serving attributions, 72–74
self-verification theory, 109–111
sexual behaviour
    behavioural intentions, 127
    condom use, 126–127
    perceived behaviour control, 127
    and subjective norms, 126
    and theory of planned behaviour, 126–127
similarity, 233–234
simple tasks, 200
smoking, 139–140
social categorization, 316–317
social cognition
    ambiguous situations, 52*f*
    automatic processing, 59–60, 60*f*, 61–62
    causal attribution, 62–75
    controlled processing, 59–60

defined, 48
heuristics, 54–59
out-group homogeneity, 317–318
and prejudice, 315–318
schemas, 49–53
social categorization, 316–317
social comparison
    downward social comparison, 98
    and group polarization, 213
    social good, promotion of, 99
    upward social comparison, 98, 99
social comparison theory, 97
social exchange theory
    comparison level, 251
    comparison level for alternatives, 251
    defined, 250
    empirical support, 251
    investment model of commitment, 251, 252*f*
    negative-state relief hypothesis, 274
    prosocial behaviour, 268–269
    reward/cost ratio, 250
social exclusion, 293–294
social facilitation, 203*f*
    arousal, 201–202
    defined, 201
    described, 199–200
    dominant response, 201
    evaluation apprehension, 202
    pool hall performance, 200
    simple *vs.* difficult tasks, 200
social good
    and conformity, 169–170
    and counter-attitudinal advocacy, 146–147
    promotion of, 99
social identity products, 134
social impact theory, 173–174
social influence
    and cooperation, 12*f*
    described, 6
    groups, 199–208
    informational social influence, 163–166, 184–186
    minority influence, 176, 177
    normative social influence, 167–175, 183–184
    power of, 8–11
    subjectivity of the social situation, 12–13
    underestimating the power of, 10–11
social interaction
    looking-glass self, 95–97
    self-awareness through, 95–97
    social comparison theory, 97
social learning theory, 286–287
social loafing, 202–205, 203*f*, 204*f*

social norms, 167
social perception
    ambiguous situations, 52*f*
    automatic processing, 59–60, 60*f*, 61–62
    causal attribution, 62–75
    controlled processing, 59–60
    defined, 48
    heuristics, 54–59
    schemas, 49–53
social problems, 13–14
social psychology
    in the courtroom, 50–51
    defined, 6
    described, 6–7
    as empirical science, 22–23
    ethical issues, 37–39
    vs. personality psychology, 15
    related disciplines, comparisons with, 7*t*
    and social problems, 13–14
    vs. sociology, 6–7
social roles, 197–199
social situation, subjectivity of, 12–13
Society for Consumer Psychology, 155
sociology, 6–7
Solar Temple cult, 5, 8, 10, 119–120, 152, 162, 165
solutions to social problems, 14
specific attitudes, 125*t*
sports
    and aggression, 207
    and self-serving attributions, 72–74
stereotype threat, 327–329
stereotypes
    activation of, 319–321
    bookkeeping model, 330
    conversion model, 330
    defined, 312
    described, 312–313
    effects of, 324–329
    meta-stereotypes, 321–322
    and race, 319–321
    revising stereotypical beliefs, 330–331
    and schemas, 315
    and self-fulfilling prophecy, 325
    sources of, 313
    subtyping model, 330
subjective norms, 125, 126
subliminal messages
    claims of, 134–135
    debunking claims about, 135–136
    defined, 134
    evidence for, 136–137
subtyping model, 330

suicide, 91
systematic processing, 130

task-oriented leader, 214
team uniforms, 207
television violence, 35, 287
theory, 23–24
theory of planned behaviour, 124f
    defined, 124
    intentions, 125
    and safer sex, 126–127
    specific attitudes, 125t
threats, 216–218
tracking game, 216, 217f, 218f
Tri-Council Policy Statement, 38
triangular theory of love, 242, 242f
tsunami disaster, 3–4

Uganda cult, 8–9
university, adjustment to, 64
unrealistic optimism, 75
unshared information condition, 209–211
upward social comparison, 98, 99
utilitarian products, 134

validity
    external validity, 34–36
    internal validity, 32–34
variables, 32, 33f
victims
    blaming, 9–10, 66–67
    hating our victims, 149–151
video game violence, 288
violence
    cross-cultural variability in, 285
    in intimate relationships, 296
    pornography, 288–290
    television violence, 35, 287
    in video games, 288
Virk, 166
Virk, Reena, 161–162
visual agnosia, 47

wars, 285
weblinks
    Adbusters, 155
    American Psychological Association, 15
    Anti-defamation League, 337
    Attachment Theory and Research, 258
    Attribution Theory, 77
    Being Human and the Illusory Correlation, 77
    Beyond Prejudice, 337
    Canadian Code of Ethics for Psychologists, 41
    Canadian Journal of Behavioural Science, 337
    Canadian Psychological Association, 15
    Canadian Race Relations Foundation, 337
    Collective Behavior and the Social Psychologies of Social Institutions, 222
    Collective Behaviour and Social Movements, 222
    Current Research in Social Psychology, 15
    Dr. Driving's Road Rage and Aggressive Driving Prevention, 303
    Ethnic Relations in a Multicultural Society, 337
    Giraffe Heros Project, 303
    Group Dynamics, 222
    Groupthink, 222
    International Association for Relationship Research, 258
    Journal of Personality and Social Psychology, 15
    Media Violence, 303
    National Clearinghouse on Family Violence, 303
    Primer of Practical Persuasion and Influence, 155
    Propaganda, 155
    psychological research on the Net, 41
    qualitative research web sites, 41
    Research Methods Knowledge Base, 41
    Social Cognition Paper Archive and Information Center, 77
    Social Psychology Network, 15
    Society for Consumer Psychology, 155
    Society for Personality and Social Psychology, 113
    Society for the Psychological Study of Social Issues, 15
    Volunteerism Canada, 303
    What Makes Kids Care, 303
Western cultures, 87
women
    see also gender differences
    and beauty standards, 236–238
    leadership styles, 215
    and stereotype threat, 328–329
    and their bodies, 172–173
    and violent pornography, 288–290

Yale Attitude Change Approach, 128